Study Guide
for use with

Understanding Psychology
Eighth Edition

Robert S. Feldman
University of Massachusetts—Amherst

Prepared by
Rachel August
California State University, Sacramento

With ESL Sections Prepared by
Lisa Valentino
Seminole Community College

D0144337

McGraw Hill

Boston   Burr Ridge, IL   Dubuque, IA   Madison, WI   New York   San Francisco   St. Louis
Bangkok   Bogotá   Caracas   Kuala Lumpur   Lisbon   London   Madrid   Mexico City
Milan   Montreal   New Delhi   Santiago   Seoul   Singapore   Sydney   Taipei   Toronto

The **McGraw·Hill** Companies

McGraw-Hill Higher Education

Study Guide for use with
Understanding Psychology
Robert S. Feldman

Published by McGraw-Hill Higher Education, an imprint of The McGraw-Hill Companies, Inc.,
1221 Avenue of the Americas, New York, NY 10020. Copyright © 2008, 2005, by The McGraw-Hill
Companies, Inc. All rights reserved. Printed in the United States of America. No part of this publication may be
reproduced or distributed in any form or by any means, or stored in a database or retrieval system, without prior
written consent of The McGraw-Hill Companies, Inc., including, but not limited to, in any network or other
electronic storage or transmission, or broadcast for distance learning.

1 2 3 4 5 6 7 8 9 0 QPD/QPD 0 9 8 7 6

ISBN 978-0-07-330723-7
MHID 0-07-330723-8

www.mhhe.com

Contents

Introduction

Using *Understanding Psychology*: Strategies for Effective Study

Understanding Psychology has been written with the reader in mind, and it therefore includes several unique features that will help you maximize your learning of the concepts, theories, facts, and other kinds of information that make up the field of psychology. To take advantage of these features, you should take several steps when reading and studying the book. The *Student Study Guide* was designed to help the student take full advantage of the features in the textbook, and the steps recommended for the text have been incorporated into this *Study Guide*. By following these steps, you will not only get the most from reading and studying *Understanding Psychology*, but you will also develop habits that will help you study other texts more effectively and think critically about material you are learning. Among the most important steps are the following:

Familiarize yourself with the logic of the book's structure. Begin by reading the Table of Contents. It provides an overview of the topics that will be covered and gives a sense of the way the various topics are interrelated. Next, review the Preface, which describes the book's major features. Note how each module is a self-contained unit; that provides logical starting and stopping points for reading and studying. Also note the major highlights of each set of modules: a topic-opening outline, a Prologue, a Looking Ahead section that includes module objectives, and a P.O.W.E.R. learning system, which will include module goals, the organizational format, a Work section, an Evaluate section, and a Rethink section to help you increase your ability to learn and retain information and to think critically. At the end of each set of modules, three tests are provided so you can review and evaluate the skills you have acquired while studying each set of modules. Answers to all of the work and evaluation sections are located at the end of each set of modules, along with answers to the practice tests. Because every module is structured in the same way, you are provided with a set of familiar landmarks as you chart your way through new material, allowing you to organize the module's content more readily. This study guide is designed to lead you through each of these steps.

Title Bars. Each module is divided by title bars like the one shown below, and each title bar provides recommendations for what can be done with the material provided.

Test your knowledge of the material in each set of modules by answering the **Multiple-Choice Questions**. These questions have been placed in three Practice Tests. The first two tests consist of questions that will test your recall of factual knowledge. The third test contains questions that are challenging and primarily test for conceptual knowledge and your ability to apply that knowledge. Check your answers and review the feedback using the Answer Key at the end of each chapter of the *Study Guide*.

The ***Keys to Excellence: Study Skills* and *Spotlight on Terminology and Language—ESL Pointers*** sections are intended to facilitate the comprehension and retention of the text material by non-native speakers of English, focusing on 490-plus key terms and concepts in ***Understanding Psychology, Eighth Edition***. The *Keys to Excellence: Study Skills* section in the front of the Study Guide provides tips to identifying in-text language cues and organizing study materials accordingly. The *Spotlight on Terminology and Language—ESL Pointers* sections in each set of modules provide clarification of many content-specific idiomatic phrases by defining them in context.

The new edition of the ***Understanding Psychology Student Study Guide*** provides students with the option of using *P.O.W.E.R. Learning*, a systematic approach to learning and studying based on five key steps (*P*repare, *O*rganize, *W*ork, *E*valuate, and *R*ethink). Based on empirical research, *P.O.W.E.R. Learning* systematizes the acquisition of new material by providing a learning framework. The system stresses the importance of learning objectives, self-evaluation, and critical thinking. The elements of the *P.O.W.E.R. Learning* system can also be used in conjunction with other learning systems, such as *SQ3R*. Specifically, use of the *P.O.W.E.R. Learning* system entails the following steps:

- ***Prepare.*** Before starting any journey, we need to know where we are headed. Academic journeys are no different; we need to know what our goals are. The *Prepare* stage consists of thinking about what we hope to attain from reading a particular section of the text by identifying specific goals we seek to accomplish. In your ***Understanding Psychology Student Study Guide,*** these goals are presented in the form of broad questions that start each major section.

- ***Organize.*** Once we know what our goals are, we need to develop a route to accomplish those goals. The *Organize* stage involves developing a mental roadmap of where we are headed. The ***Understanding Psychology Student Study Guide*** highlights the organization of each upcoming section. Read the outline to get an idea of what topics are covered and how they are organized.

- ***Work.*** The heart of the *P.O.W.E.R. Learning* system entails actually reading and studying the material presented in the book. In some ways, *Work* is the easy part, because if you have carried out the steps in the preparation and organization stages, you'll know where you're headed and how to get there. Of course, it's not so simple—you'll need the motivation to conscientiously read and think about the material presented in the chapter. And remember, the main text isn't the only material you need to read and think about. It's also important to read the boxes, the marginal glossary terms, and the special sections in order to gain a full understanding of the material, so be sure to include them as part of the *Work* of reading the module and then use the *Work* section of your study guide to support your text reading.

- *Evaluate.* The fourth step, *Evaluate*, provides you with the opportunity to determine how effectively you have mastered the material. The **Understanding Psychology Student Study Guide** has matching tests following each *Work* section that permits a rapid check of your understanding of the material. Evaluating your progress is essential to assessing your degree of mastery of the material.

- *Rethink.* The final step in *P.O.W.E.R. Learning* involves critical thinking, which entails reanalyzing, reviewing, questioning, and challenging assumptions. It provides the opportunity to look at the big picture by thinking about how material fits with other information you have already learned. Every major section of **Understanding Psychology, 8/e,** ends with a *Rethink* section that contains thought-provoking questions. Answering them will help you understand the material more fully and at a deeper level.

If you want to maximize your potential to master the material in **Understanding Psychology, 8/e**, use *P.O.W.E.R. Learning*. Taking the time and effort to work through the steps of the system is a proven technique for understanding and learning the material.

Supplementing *P.O.W.E.R. Learning* with *SQ3R*

Although *P.O.W.E.R. Learning* is the learning strategy that is built into the book and consequently easiest to use, it is not the only system compatible with the book. For example, some readers may wish to supplement the *P.O.W.E.R. Learning* system with the *SQ3R* method, which includes a series of five steps, designated by the initials *S-Q-R-R-R*. The first step is to *survey* the material by reading the module outlines, module headings, figure captions, recaps, and Looking Ahead and Looking Back sections, providing yourself with an overview of the major points of the module. The next step is to *question*. Formulate questions about the material, either aloud or in writing, before actually reading a section. The queries posed in the *Prepare* sections and the *Evaluate* and *Rethink* questions are also good sources of questions.

The next three steps in *SQ3R* ask you to *read, recite,* and *review* the material. *Read* carefully and, even more important, read actively and critically. While you are reading, answer the questions you have asked yourself. Critically evaluate material by considering the implications of what you are reading, thinking about possible exceptions and contradictions, and examining underlying assumptions. The *recite* step involves describing and explaining to yourself (or a friend) the material you have just read and answering the questions you have posed earlier. Recite aloud; the recitation process helps identify your degree of understanding of the material you have just read. Finally, *review* the material, looking it over, reading the Looking Back summaries, and answering the in-text review questions.

Final Comments

Find a location and time. The last aspect of studying that warrants mention is that *when* and *where* you study are in some ways as important as *how* you study. One of the truisms of the psychological literature is that we learn things better, and are able to recall them longer, when we study material in small chunks over several study sessions, rather than massing our study into one lengthy period. This implies that all-night studying just before a test is going to be less effective—and a lot more tiring—than employing a series of steady, regular study sessions.

In addition to carefully timing your studying, you should seek out a special location to study. It doesn't really matter where it is, as long as it has minimal distractions and is a place that you use *only* for studying. Identifying a special "territory" allows you to get in the right mood for study as soon as you begin.

Use a study strategy. Although we are expected to study and ultimately to learn a wide array of material throughout our schooling, we are rarely taught any systematic strategies that permit us to study more effectively. Yet, just as we wouldn't expect a physician to learn human anatomy by trial and error, it is the unusual student who is able to stumble on a truly effective studying strategy.

The *P.O.W.E.R. Learning* system (as well as *SQ3R*) provides a proven means of increasing your study effectiveness. Yet you need not feel tied to a particular strategy. You might want to combine other elements into your own study system. For example, learning tips and strategies for critical thinking will be presented throughout ***Understanding Psychology***, such as in Module 20 when the use of mnemonics (memory techniques for organizing material to help its recall) are discussed. If these tactics help you successfully master new material, stick with them.

By using the proven *P.O.W.E.R. Learning* system, you will maximize your understanding of the material in this book and will master techniques that will help you learn and think critically in all of your academic endeavors. More important, you will optimize your understanding of the field of psychology. It is worth the effort. The excitement, challenge, and promise that psychology holds for you is immense.

Robert Feldman

Keys To Excellence: Study Skills

The following study strategies will help you think deeply and critically about what you read. Non-native speakers of English should find this section especially helpful.

Words are the instruments of communication, learning, and thinking. Use keywords to trigger your consolidation of material. One keyword can initiate the recall of a whole cluster of ideas. A few keywords can form a chain from which you can reconstruct an entire lecture.

Learning involves digesting what you read and actively using the information, as follows:

- *Digesting*: Give yourself time for a thinking pause after you finish a paragraph and summarize it. The thinking pause will provide time for the main idea to sink in and connect with information you already know.

- *Using New Information*: Consciously rehearse what you've learned. Repetition can often be the key to remembering. Always strive to link what you learn to what you already know. Reinforce new ideas by associating them with the things close to you in your own life.

Recognizing Patterns of Organization

Organizational patterns help organize a reader's thoughts and help you better comprehend key concepts. As your brain works to make sense of the world around you, it tries to fit everything into a recognizable shape and pattern that has meaning for you. Placing work into reasonable blocks of information makes it easier for your brain to understand and remember information.

There are four basic approaches, or *patterns*, that writers use in presenting concepts:

- Describing the concept in the form of a generalization
- Explaining the similarities and/or differences of the concept as compared to other concepts
- Using cause and effect to show the active relationship of the concept to other concepts and to a bigger picture (e.g., a theory)
- Including a series of events or steps, breaking the concept down into digestible pieces

Familiarize yourself with the organizational pattern the text author is using. By recognizing the structure of the author's writing style, you will be better prepared to organize your studying and note-taking strategy. Recognizing patterns helps you anticipate information that is coming and incorporate and assimilate it within your existing knowledge base. You become more involved in your own learning process by focusing on the presentation of the material. You can think of yourself as a partner with the author as you learn this new information.

Use Signal Words to Organize Reading

Words can be used as obvious indicators of the direction of a writer's thoughts. These signal words for patterns can also be referred to as *transitional words*. Writers use these words to mark the shifts and turns in their thinking. Following these signal words, readers can identify when the writer is moving from one idea to the next. Using signal words and phrases imposes a recognizable order on ideas, facts, and details.

Different kinds of signal words can alert you to what type of material is to follow. For example, the following *comparison and contrast* signal words and phrases can be used to explain similarities and/or differences:

- However
- Although
- Rather
- Conversely
- Different from
- In contrast
- Instead
- More than

- But
- While
- Yet
- Less than
- On the other hand
- One difference
- Unlike
- Another major difference

When you read sentences, use signal words and organizational clues. If you see "on the one hand," watch for the words "on the other hand," which introduces the other side of the argument.

The following are *cause and effect* signal words and phrases that call attention to a concept's connection to other concepts and its role in an overriding theme:

- Therefore
- As a result
- Accordingly

- Consequently
- Because

Sequencing signal words help you notice important events and the logical progression of material. Sequence word and phrase examples are:

- Near
- Until
- First
- For the next
- Then
- Finally

- After
- Last
- While
- Later
- Before
- The following

Signal words that are used to add *emphasis*, and in doing so distinguish important points to take note of, are:

- Most important
- Remember that
- Pay attention to
- Above all
- In conclusion

- A key (component, feature, etc.)
- The main idea
- Of primary concern
- Most significant

Creating Study Cards

Use three-by-five-inch notecards to learn your vocabulary words by recitation and repetition. Select a word you want to remember and write the word on the front of a card. On the back of the card, write the complete sentence in which the word occurs in the text. Then, write the same word in a meaningful context that is familiar to you. This process will reinforce your use of the term and help you incorporate it more fully into your current vocabulary base.

To study the word, always look first at the front of the card. Pronounce the word. Think about the word and how you would define it. Put the word in a new sentence, and then check the use and definition of the word on the back of the card. The best part about using these study cards is that you can take them just about anywhere and use them for review in your spare time.

Understanding and Applying the Steps of Marking a Text

The purpose of making marks in a text is to create your own personal roadmap to make navigating through the material easier. Marking a textbook will help you accumulate information in an orderly and systematic way. You can underline important words and sentences and make notes in the margins about them. Paraphrase important statements in the top and bottom margins of your text to simplify concepts into kernels of important information. Circle words, phrases, and theorists' names where they appear, or rewrite them in the margin if they seem meaningful or are difficult to grasp. Seeing these words stand out on the page will draw you back to review them. Use memory-jogging abbreviations to stimulate your recall of information. Circle numbers that indicate a series of arguments, facts, or ideas—either main or supporting. Develop visual diagrams of the concepts when you can. Consider all blank spaces as flexible note-taking areas. By marking your book, you are turning your textbook into your own custom-made study guide. Referring back to your marginal notes, you will be able to review the essential material at a glance just by flipping back through the pages.

Using special marks and colors, you can highlight and differentiate between different types of material. By creating a key of marks and colors, you can easily identify where certain types of information can be found. You might choose to highlight key terms in yellow marker or draw squares around theorists' names. One successful method of marking is to star (*) the beginning of a sentence, paragraph, questions, and so on that you believe your instructor may quiz you on. Instructors may suggest, through their emphasis in class, that certain information is likely to appear on an exam. Finding the coverage of this material in your text and starring it will distinguish it as a potential test question. Then, when you revisit your text, you can better focus your studying time.

Vocabulary

Knowing the meaning of prefixes, roots, and suffixes can unlock the meaning of unfamiliar words. Common word parts are building blocks used in forming many English words. Increasing your awareness of these basic word parts helps unlock the meaning of unfamiliar words.

- **Root.** A root is a basic word part to which prefixes, suffixes, or both are added.
- **Prefix.** A prefix is a word part added to the beginning of a word. Following is a list of some common prefixes with their meanings.
- **Suffix.** A suffix is a word part added to the end of a word. Although a suffix may affect a word's meaning slightly, it is more likely to affect how the word is used in a sentence.

PREFIX	MEANING
• A-	in, on, at
• Ab-	from, away
• Ad-, a-	to, toward
• An-, a-	not, without
• Ambi-, amphi-	around, both
• Ana-	back, opposite
• Ante-	before
• Anti-	against, opposite
• Cata-	break down
• Circum-	around
• Con-	with, together
• Contra-	against
• Dia-	through
• Dis-	apart
• Dys-	ill
• Extra-	beyond
• Fore-	before
• Hyper-	over, beyond
• Hypo-	under
• Inter-	between
• Intra	within
• Para-	beside
• Post-	after
• Re-	before
• Retro-	backward
• Sub-	under
• Super-	over
• Trans-	across
• Ultra-	beyond
• Un-	not

*For an online glossary, go to www.mhhe.com/feldmanup8.

Chapter 1: Introduction to Psychology

Overview

Module 1 defines psychology as the scientific study of behavior and mental processes. The diversity of the field of psychology is illustrated by listing several of the subfields of psychology. This is followed by samples of questions that each psychological subfield attempts to answer. A portrait of psychologists illustrates both the types of psychologists and the educational requirements necessary for those who choose careers in the field of psychology. The module goes on to examine the different careers that are available to psychologists in today's workplace.

Module 2 presents the historical roots of psychology with attention to the roles that women have played in the development of the discipline. The module then goes on to trace the events that led to the five basic perspectives in psychology today: neuroscience, psychodynamic, cognitive, behavioral, and humanistic. This is followed by a discussion on the role that psychology plays in the study of violence.

Module 3 presents the five key issues in psychology today: nature versus nurture, conscious versus unconscious causes of behavior, observable behavior versus internal mental processes, free will versus determinism, and individual differences versus universal principles. These key issues are used to understand how culture, ethnicity, and race influence behavior.

To further investigate the topics covered in this chapter, you can visit the related Web sites by visiting the following link: www.mhhe.com/feldmanup8.

Prologue: A Calamity Called Katrina
Looking Ahead

Module 1:
Psychologists at Work

The Subfields of Psychology: Psychology's Family Tree
Working at Psychology

- ***What is the science of psychology?***
- ***What are the major specialties in the field of psychology?***
- ***Where do psychologists work?***

Psychologists at Work

[a] _____ is defined as the scientific study of behavior and mental processes. Psychologists investigate what people do as well as their thoughts, feelings, perceptions, reasoning processes, and memories. They also investigate the biological foundations of these processes. Psychology relies on the scientific method to discover ways of explaining, predicting, modifying, and improving behavior. The study of behavior and mental processes involves examining animals as well as humans to find the general laws that govern the behavior of all organisms.

Contrary to the mistaken view held by many people that psychology is interested only in abnormal behavior, psychologists examine a wide array of behaviors and mental processes. The specialty areas, or subfields, are described in the order in which they appear throughout the text.

[b] _____ examine how the brain and nervous system, as well as other biological processes, impact behavior. More generally, they are concerned with how our bodies influence our behavior.

[c] _____ *psychology* is both a specialty and a task undertaken by most psychologists. The scientific work of psychology requires experimental methods to be applied wherever possible. **[d]** _____ *psychology* is a specialty within experimental psychology that focuses on higher mental functions such as thinking, language, memory, problem solving, reasoning, and decision making, among other processes.

Emerging areas of psychology include: **[e]** _____, a subfield that seeks to identify behavior patterns that are a result of our genetic inheritance; **[f]** _____, which unites the areas of neuroscience and clinical psychology. The latter subfield examines how psychological disorders originate in biological factors. This specialty area has led to promising new medications to treat psychological disorders.

In contrast to the more emergent forms of psychology, there are several subfields of psychology with somewhat longer histories. Among those is **[g]** _____ psychology, which deals with studying, diagnosing, and treating psychological disorders. **[h]** _____ psychology focuses mostly on helping people adjust to challenges and changes in their education, social world, and career. **[i]** _____ psychology examines how other people affect individuals' thoughts, feelings, and behavior. [j] _____ psychology explores psychological similarities and differences across various culture and ethnic groups.

Psychologists are employed in a variety of settings. Most doctoral-level psychologists are employed by [k] _____ or are self-employed. Others work in hospitals, mental health clinics, schools, etc. About [l]_____ of all psychologists are found in the United States and about half of all psychologists are women. [m]_____ is one of the great concerns among today's psychologists. Racial and ethnic minorities are underrepresented in the field, and only 6 percent of all psychologists are members of a racial minority group.

Most psychologists have a(n) [n]_____, which requires four or five years of work after a bachelor's degree. About one-third of those in the field have two to three years of schooling after their bachelor's degree and have [o]_____ degrees. Both students and current members of the field share a common desire to improve the human condition.

The most common area of employment for students who receive a bachelor's degree in psychology is in the [p] _____ field, including working in an administrative capacity, as a counselor, or providing direct care.

Evaluate

PART A

_____ 1. health psychology

_____ 2. clinical psychology

_____ 3. personality psychology

_____ 4. behavioral genetics

_____ 5. social psychology

a. The branch of psychology that explores the relationship of psychological factors and physical ailments or disease.

b. The branch of psychology that examines how people's thoughts, feelings, and actions are affected by others.

c. The branch of psychology that focuses on how biological mechanisms allow inherited behavior to be displayed.

d. The branch of psychology that deals with the study, diagnosis, and treatment of psychological disorders.

e. The branch of psychology that focuses on the extent to which behavior is the same over time, and on traits that make each of us unique.

3

PART B

_____ 6. behavioral neuroscience

_____ 7. experimental psychology

_____ 8. cognitive psychology

_____ 9. developmental psychology

_____ 10. counseling psychology

a. The branch that studies the processes of sensing, perceiving, learning, and thinking about the world.

b. The branch that focuses on helping people adjust to educational, social, and career challenges.

c. The branch that specializes in how the brain and nervous system connect to behavior.

d. The branch that studies how people grow and change throughout the course of their lives.

e. The branch that focuses on the study of higher mental processes, including thinking, language, memory, problem solving, knowing, reasoning, judging, and decision making.

Rethink

1-1   Do you think intuition and common sense are sufficient for understanding why people act the way they do? In what ways is a scientific approach appropriate for studying human behavior?

1-2   _From an educator's perspective:_ Suppose you are a teacher who has a 7-year-old child in your class who is having unusual difficulties learning to read. Imagine that you can consult as many psychologists with different specialties as you want. What are the different types of psychologists that you might approach to address the problem?

Spotlight on Terminology and Language—ESL Pointers

Page 4"Prologue: A **Calamity** called Katrina"

A **Calamity** is a disaster.

Page 4 "At first it caused barely **a ripple in the air,** but the eventual result, a monster hurricane named Katrina, bore down on New Orleans, bombarding the city and surrounding coastline with winds of over 150 miles per hour and waves higher than 20 feet.

A ripple in the air suggests that the wind was blowing gently. A small pebble dropped into a pond would cause a **ripple** on the surface, not a big wave.

Page 4 "The **torrents** of water that lashed New Orleans in August 2005 caused levees built to keep Lake Pontchartrain from overflowing into the city's low-lying neighborhoods to give way, flooding much of the area."

Torrents are fast moving water. In this case the author is trying to show that the heavy amount of rain from the hurricane caused waves of fast moving water to flow through the city.

Page 4 "People thousands of miles away rushed to the **afflicted** areas to help search victims, evacuate stranded residents and rebuild the Big Easy."

Afflicted means troubled or badly affected. New Orleans or the "Big Easy" was in trouble after the hurricane hit.

Page 4 Although it originated as a geological event, Hurricane Katrina and its **aftermath gave rise to** a host of intriguing questions.

Aftermath means outcome or the result of an event. **Gave rise to** means to create something.

Page 4 "Social psychologists would examine the reasons for the **outpouring** of support for the astronauts' families after their deaths."
    Outpouring of support suggests strong positive emotions of support. There was an **outpouring** of support for Private First Class Jessica Lynch after she was rescued from being a POW in 2003. Her community worked together to build her a house she could navigate with her injuries, and her town welcomed her return with parades and well wishes. The community worked together to try to take care of her financially, psychologically, and physically.

Page 4 "Can people change their **dysfunctional** behavior?"
    Dysfunctional behavior is not performing in a way that is normally expected. When you counsel a **dysfunctional** family, perhaps the siblings and the parents are not communicating at all, or behaviors of a family member are very different than would be expected for their age and culture.

Page 5 "Should the field **encompass** the study of such a diverse topics as physical and mental health, perception, dreaming and motivation?"

To **encompass** is to include. What are some of the diverse topics you expect to find the field of psychology including?

Page 5 "Most psychologists have answered these questions with the argument that the field should be **receptive** to a variety of viewpoints and approaches."

Receptive means interested in the ideas and theoretical approaches

Page 5 "A month after losing his arm in an industrial accident, Henry Washington sits with his eyes closed as Hector Valdez, a research psychologist who studies the **perception** of touch, dribbles warm water on his cheek."
    Perception involves using your senses to acquire information about your environment. In psychology, **perception** involves any of the neurological processes of acquiring and mentally interpreting information from the senses. A **perception** can be an idea, a feeling, an impression, or a thought.

Page 5 "The **sensation** is so strong that he checks to be sure that the arm is still missing."

Sensation is a physical feeling. Sometimes it can be a vague or general feeling not attributable to an obvious cause. You have a **sensation** when one or more of your sense organs is stimulated.

Page 5 "By comparing twins who have lived together **virtually** all their lives with those who have been separated from birth, Poirier is seeking to determine the relative influence of heredity and experience on human behavior."

Virtually means that for all practical purposes, these twins have lived together. If there is a time when they haven't lived together, it's a very brief period.

Page 5 "**Methodically**—and painfully— **recounting** events that occurred in his youth, the college student **discloses** a childhood secret that he has revealed previously to no one."

Methodical means in a systematic, organized manner. The college student arranged the way he told his story, so that he told it in a systematic and orderly method. He told it **methodically**.

To **recount** is to review, call to mind, and tell the particular details of this secret. **Recounting** is to tell about an event, to report, or describe the event. When you **recount** and narrate an event, people now know about it.

Disclose is to reveal or confess. As it is **disclosed**, he has revealed his secret. Are there some events in your life that you have **recounted methodically** as you have **disclosed** them?

Page 5 "Although the last scene might be the only one that fits your image of the practice of psychology, each of these episodes describes work carried out by **contemporary** psychologists."

To be **contemporary** is to be modern; to be up-to-date. Health psychologists, developmental psychologists, cognitive psychologists, clinical neuropsychologists, evolutionary psychologists, and clinical psychologists are just a few of the major subfields of psychology of a **contemporary** psychologist.

Page 5 "This **breadth** is reflected in the definition of the field: Psychology is the scientific study of behavior and mental processes."

Breadth has to do with the comprehensive quality of definition of the science of psychology.

Page 5 "Should the field **encompass** the study of such diverse topics as physical and mental health, perception, dreaming, and motivation?"

To **encompass** is to include. What are some of the diverse topics you expect to find the field of psychology including?

Page 5 "Most psychologists have answered these questions with the argument that the field should be **receptive** to a variety of viewpoints and approaches."

Receptive means interested in the ideas and theoretical approaches.

Page 6 "As the study of psychology has grown, it has given rise to a number of **subfields** (described in Figure 2 and illustrated in Interactivity 1-1)."

Subfields are smaller parts within a larger field.

Page 6 "The subfields of psychology **can be likened to** an extended family, with assorted nieces and nephews, aunts and uncles and cousins who, although they may not interact on a day-to-day basis, are related to one another because they share a common goal: understanding behavior."

Can be likened to means to be compared to. In the example the author is comparing the parts of the field of psychology to the parts of a family.

Page 6 "In the most fundamental sense, people are **biological organisms.**"

The term **biological organism** refers to a living being.

Page 6 "For example, they may examine the link between specific sites in the brain and the muscular **tremors** of people affected by Parkinson's disease or attempt to determine how emotions are are related to physical sensations."

When you body shakes as a result of physical weakness or emotional stress, this is an involuntary **trembling**, or quivering of voluntary muscle. These **tremors** vary in intensity and duration.

Page 6 "Behavioral neuroscientists might want to know what physiological changes occurred in people who fled New Orleans as Hurricane Katrina was **bearing down** on the city."

In this sentence the term **bearing down means** approaching.

Page 6 "These universal **milestones** in development are also singularly special and unique for each person."

Milestones are important events in a person's life.

Page 8 "Almost every college has a **center** staffed with counseling psychologists."

In this sentence the term **center** refers to a clinic or office where students come to get advice.

Page 8 "Our complex networks of social **interrelationships** are the focus of study for a number of subfields of psychology."

The prefix **inter** means between, among, in the midst of something. When we talk about **interrelationships**, we mean carried on between groups, occurring between and shared by the groups. What are some of the social **interrelationships** you have as part of your lifestyle?

Page 8 "Cross-cultural psychology investigates the similarities and **differences** in **psychological functioning** in and across various cultures and ethnic groups."

Psychological functioning refers the workings of the brain and mental processes including thinking, memory, intelligence and learning.

Page 8 "For example, they may examine the link between specific sites in the brain and the muscular **tremors** of people affected by Parkinson's disease or attempt to determine how our emotions are related to physical sensations."
When your body shakes as a result of physical weakness or emotional stress, this is an involuntary **trembling**, or quivering, of muscle. These **tremors** vary in intensity and duration.

Page 8 "If you have ever wondered why you are susceptible to **optical** illusions, how your body registers pain, or how you can study with the greatest effectiveness, an experimental psychologist can answer your questions."
Anything **optic** pertains to the eye or vision. An **optical** illusion is a misleading image presented to

the vision.

Page 8 "Our complex networks of social **interrelationships** are the focus of study for a number of subfields of psychology."

The prefix **inter-** means between, among, in the midst of something. When we talk about **interrelationships**, we mean carried on between groups, occurring between and shared by the groups. What are some of the social **interrelationships** you have as part of your lifestyle?

Page 9 **"Although they are increasingly popular, evolutionary explanations of behavior have stirred** controversy."

In this sentence the word **stirred** means that the explanations created controversy, like when you stir pancake batter and mix it up.

Page 9 "By suggesting that many significant behaviors unfold automatically because they are **wired** into the human species, evolutionary approaches minimize the role of the environmental and social forces."

Wired, in this context means to be genetically determined or inborn. Evolutionary psychologists suggest that behavior is determined by people's genetic make-up.

Page 9 **"Building on** advances in our understanding of the structure and chemistry of the brain, this specialty has already led to promising new treatments for psychological disorders as well as debates over the use of medication to control behavior."

To **build on** means that events and decisions are based on information that was known previously. In this sentence the author is saying that the new treatments that were developed were based on earlier research.

Page 9 "Candidates must have the ability to establish a **rapport** with senior business executives and help them find innovative, practical, and psychologically sound solutions to problems concerning people and organizations."

When you establish **rapport** with someone, it means you develop a relationship with that person. Psychologists need to be able to establish **rapport** with a patient so that the patient has confidence in the psychologist. The establishment of **rapport** is an important initial component of successful psychotherapy.

Page 9 "Candidates must have the ability to establish a **rapport** with senior business executives and help them find innovative, practical, and psychologically sound solutions to problems concerning people and organizations."

When you establish **rapport** with someone, you develop a relationship with that person. Psychologists need to be able to establish **rapport** with a patient so the patient has confidence in the psychologist. Establishing **rapport** is an important initial component of successful psychotherapy.

Page 10 "First, the field of psychology is **diminished** by a lack of the diverse perspectives and talents that minority-group members can provide. Furthermore, minority-group psychologists serve as role models for members of minority communities, and their lack of representation in the profession might **deter** other minority-group members from entering the field."

To **diminish** is to make less of or decrease. The lack of representation of minority psychologists in the field of psychology subtracts from the authority of the field. It also **deters**, and may discourage or inhibit, minority group members from entering the field of psychology. Have there been activities you have felt **deterred** from because you have not observed people like you?

Page 10 "First, the field of psychology is **diminished** by a lack of the diverse perspectives and talents that minority-group members can provide. Furthermore, minority-group psychologists serve as role models for members of minority communities, and their lack of representation in the profession might **deter** other minority-group members from entering the field."

To **diminish** is to decrease. The lack of representation of minority psychologists in the field of psychology subtracts from the authority of the field. It also **deters**, and may discourage or inhibit, minority-group members from entering the field of psychology. Have you have felt **deterred** from certain activities because you have not observed people like you doing them?

Page 12 "Because undergraduates who specialize in psychology develop good **analytical** skill, are trained to **think critically** and are able to **synthesize** and evaluate information well, employers in business, industry and the government value their preparation."

A student who has good **analytical** skills is able to separate and break up an event into its component parts or ingredients. Can you analyze, or carefully determine the procedures you use to check you competence in learning the psychology text material?

Critical Thinking refers to a deliberate from of thinking in which the person questions the assumptions and conclusions being presented.

You are **synthesizing** the material learned from your psychology textbook as you use your skills of reasoning to learn the general principles and apply them to your understanding of particular situations. You **synthesize** the information as you combine it and put it together and use it to understand psychological circumstances.

Page 12 "The most common areas of employment for psychology majors are in the **social services**, including working as an administrator, serving as a counselor and providing direct care."

Social Services are government organizations that provide monetary help and social support for people who need it.

Page 12 "Because undergraduates who specialize in psychology develop good **analytical** skills, are trained to think critically, and are able to **synthesize** and evaluate information well, employers in business, industry, and the government value their preparation.

A student who has good **analytical** skills is able to separate an event into its component parts or ingredients. Can you analyze, or carefully determine, the procedures you use to check your competence in learning the psychology text material?

You are **synthesizing** the material learned from your psychology textbook as you use your skills of reasoning to learn the general principles and apply them to your understanding of particular situations. You **synthesize** the information as you combine it and use it to understand psychological circumstances.

Page 13 "Luis is unique in his manner of responding to crisis situation, with an **even temperament** and a positive outlook."

Individuals with an **even temperament** are those who do not show a high degree of emotional change.

Module 2: A Science Evolves: Past, Present, and Future

The Roots of Psychology
Today's Perspectives

Applying Psychology in the 21st Century:
Psychology Matters

- *What are the historical roots of the field of psychology?*
- *What are the major approaches used by contemporary psychologists?*

A Science Evolves: Past, Present, and Future

The era of scientific psychology is usually dated from the establishment of an experimental psychology laboratory by Wilhelm Wundt in 1879.

The perspective associated with Wundt's laboratory is called [a] _____. It focused on the elements, or building blocks, that constitute the foundation of perception,

thinking, and emotions. Structuralism utilized a technique called [b] _____ to examine these elements. Introspection required the subject to report how a stimulus was

experienced. A perspective called [c] _____ replaced structuralism, and instead of focusing on the structure of mental elements, it focused on how the mind works and how people adapt to environments. William James was the leading functionalist in the early 1900s, and one of the leading educators, John Dewey, took a functionalist approach in his

development of school psychology. [d] _____ was another reaction to structuralism that developed in the early 1900s. The gestalt approach examines phenomena in terms of the whole experience rather than the individual elements, and gestalt psychologists are identified with the maxim "the whole is greater than the sum of the parts."

Several early female contributors to the field of psychology were Leta Stetter Hollingworth,

known for her focus on [e] _____ and for an early focus on women's issues, and June Etta Downey, who studied personality traits in the 1920s. Also among the early contributors were Karen Horney, who focused on the social and cultural factors behind the

development of [f] _____, and Anna Freud, whose contributions were in the field of abnormal behavior.

Contemporary psychology is now dominated by five major conceptual perspectives. The **[g]** _____ perspective is focused on the study of how the inheritance of certain characteristics influences behavior, as well as how the brain and nervous system affect behavior. The **[h]** _____ perspective views behavior as motivated by inner and unconscious forces over which the individual can exert little control. The psychodynamic perspective, developed by Sigmund Freud in the early 1900s, has been a major influence in twentieth-century thinking and continues to have an influence in the treatment of mental disorders. The **[i]** _____ perspective evolved from the structuralists' concern with trying to understand the mind, to a study of how we internally represent the outside world and how this representation influences behavior. This includes how we think and how we understand. The **[j]** _____ perspective began as a reaction to the failure of other early perspectives to base the science of psychology on observable phenomena. John B. Watson developed behaviorism as a study of how environmental forces influence behavior. He suggested that observable behavior, measured objectively, should be the focus of the field. His views were shared by B. F. Skinner, probably the best-known psychologist. The **[k]** _____ perspective rejects the deterministic views of the other perspectives and instead focuses on the unique ability of humans to seek higher levels of maturity and fulfillment and to express **[l]** _____. All of the major perspectives have active practitioners and continuing research programs.

Evaluate

_____ 1. neuroscience perspective

a. The psychological perspective that suggests that observable behavior should be the focus of study.

_____ 2. psychodynamic perspective

b. The psychological perspective that views behavior from the perspective of biological functioning.

_____ 3. cognitive perspective

_____ 4. behavioral perspective

c. The psychological perspective based on the belief that behavior is motivated by inner forces over which the individual has little control.

_____ 5. humanistic perspective

d. The psychological perspective that suggests that people are in control of their lives.

e. The psychological perspective that focuses on how people think, understand, and know the world.

Rethink

2-1   Focusing on one of the five major perspectives in use today (i.e., neuroscience, psychodynamic, cognitive, behavioral, or humanistic), can you describe the sorts of research questions and studies that researchers using that perspective might pursue?

2-2   *From a journalist's perspective:* Choose a current major political controversy. What psychological approaches or perspectives can be applied to that issue?

Spotlight on Terminology and Language—ESL Pointers

Page 15 "Trephining consisted of chipping a hole in a patient's skull with **crude** stone instruments."

Crude instruments are tools that are simple and unrefined. The tools used by the ancient healers were very basic and did not allow for any precision.

Page 15 "Franz Josef Gall, an eighteenth-century physician, argued that a trained observer could **discern** intelligence, moral character, and other basic personality characteristics from the shape and number of bumps on a person's skull."

To **discern** means to be able to detect, usually with senses other than vision. Can you discern an unfamiliar odor in a room? Are you capable of **discerning**, revealing insight and understanding, when you are in an uncomfortable situation?

Page 15 "Although these explanations might sound **far-fetched**, in their own times they represented the most advanced thinking about what might be called the psychology of the era."

Far-fetched explanations are those that are exaggerated and hard to believe.

Page 15 "As sciences go, psychology is one of the **"new kids on the block."**"

The term "new kids on the block" is a slang term used to suggest that something or someone is young and inexperienced. In this case the author is pointing out that the discipline of psychology is a very new discipline.

Page 15 "Psychology's roots can be traced back to the ancient Greeks and Romans, and philosophers argued for hundreds of years about some of the questions psychologists **grapple** with today."

To **grapple** is to struggle and to work to come to grips with. As we **grapple** to understand what we are reading, we cope with the new knowledge and deal with needing to understand it by working to make sense of it – by synthesizing and analyzing the new information.

Page 15 "For example, the 17th century British philosopher John Locke (1632-1704) believed that children were born into the world with minds like **"blank slates"** (*tabula rasa* in Latin) and that their experiences determined what kind of adults they would become."

Blank slates" (*tabula rasa*) are tablets that are not written on. John Locke argued that children were born into the world empty so that their life experiences

Page 16 "These drawbacks led to the evolution of new approaches, which largely **supplanted** structuralism."

To **supplant** is to replace. Structuralism was **supplanted** with the **evolution** of new approaches to understand the fundamental elements of the mind.

Page 17 "Led by the American psychologist William James, the functionalists examined how behavior allows people to satisfy their needs and how our "**stream of consciousness**" permits us to adapt to our environment."

William James and the functionalists used the term "**stream of consciousness**" to describe human awareness. These theorists propose that human consciousness or awareness is constantly moving much like water in a stream.

Page 17 " Instead of considering the individual parts that make up thinking, gestalt psychologists took the **opposite tack**, concentrating on how people consider individual elements together as units or wholes."

When you take the **opposite tack**, you move in a different direction, or shift your focus. Generally when you are experimenting with a new method of action, you are trying a new **tack**.

Page 18 "She collected date to **refute** the view, popular in the early 1900s, that women's abilities periodically declined during parts of the menstrual cycle.

Refute is to disprove – to prove false. Who is the psychologist that collected this data?

Page 18 "Karen Horney focused on the social and cultural factors behind personality, and June Etta Downey **spearheaded** the study of personality traits and became the first woman to head a psychology department at a state university."

To **spearhead** means to be the leading element, to take a leading role. Often, the person who **spearheads** an activity is the leader and the leading force. Have you **spearheaded** any efforts to improve your community or your academic institution?

Page 18 "Because every behavior can be broken down to some extent into its biological components, the neuroscience perspective has **broad appeal**."

When something has **broad appeal** it is attractive to a large number of people.

Page 19 "**Proponents** of the psychodynamic perspective believe that behavior is motivated by inner forces and conflicts about which we have little awareness or control."

A **proponent** is an advocate, someone who argues in favor of something such as a legislative measure or a doctrine. Are you a **proponent** of one specific psychological perspective?

Page 19 "Dreams and **slips of the tongue** are viewed as indications of what a person is truly feeling within a **seething cauldron of unconscious psychic activity**."

Slips of the tongue are words that people say accidentally. According to the psychodynamic perspective, these statements indicate a pot of angry conflicts and tensions (**seething cauldron**) that are located beneath the awareness (**unconscious psychic activity**).

Page 19 "In fact, Watson believed rather optimistically that it was possible to **elicit** any desired type of behavior by controlling a person's environment.

Elicit means to bring out, to draw forth a behavior. Do some learning environments **elicit** different behaviors from you as a student?

Page 20 "Give me a dozen healthy infants, well-formed, and my own specified world to bring them up in and I'll guarantee to take any one at random and train him to become any type of specialist I might select—doctor, lawyer, artist, merchant-chief, and yes, even beggar-man and thief, regardless of his talents, **penchants**, tendencies, abilities, vocations and race of his ancestors" (Watson, 1924)

Penchants are a strong tendency or liking for something.

Page 20 "As we will see, the behavioral perspective **crops up** along every **byway** of psychology;"

When something **crops up** it occurs. In this sentence the author is telling us that the behavioral perspective will be discussed repeatedly throughout the text.

A **byway** is generally a secondary aspect. The behavioral perspective is used to explain much of how people learn behaviors, and in designing programs to implement change.

Page 20 "It is important not to let the abstract qualities of the broad approaches we have discussed **lull** you into thinking that they are purely theoretical: These perspectives underlie ongoing work of a practical nature, as we will discuss throughout this book."

Lull as it is used here suggests that you might want to relax your vigilance on understanding the various psychological perspectives helping to explain different aspects of behavior and mental processes. You want to take care not to be **lulled** into a false sense of security about your psychological knowledge.

Page 21 "As we'll see in Module 48 when we discuss abnormal behavior, psychologists are gaining an understanding of the factors that lead people to **embrace suicide** and to engage in terrorism to further a cause in which they deeply believe."

Suicide is the act of killing one self. When someone **embrace(s) suicide** they accept the idea that killing oneself is acceptable.

Page 21 "Memories of crimes are often **clouded** by emotion, and the questions asked by police investigators often elicit inaccurate responses."

When memories are **clouded** they are hard to remember or understand with a lot of details.

Module 3: Psychology's Key Issues and Controversies

Exploring Diversity: Understanding How Culture, Ethnicity, and Race Influence Behavior

Psychology's Future

Becoming an Informed Consumer of Psychology: Thinking Critically About Psychology: Distinguishing Legitimate Psychology from Pseudo-Psychology

- *What are psychology's key issues and controversies?*
- *What is the future of psychology likely to hold?*

Psychology's Key Issues and Controversies

The field of psychology is more unified than one might expect. Psychologists agree on the key issues of psychology, and psychologists, no matter what their area of specialization, rely on one of the five major perspectives.

Few psychologists identify exclusively with one perspective. However, not every branch can utilize any perspective equally well. Neuroscience is far more focused on the biological perspective than on others. Social psychologists are more likely to find the cognitive perspective to be more useful than the biological perspective.

Major issues and questions form a common ground for psychology. The question of [a]

_____ places perspectives that focus on the environmental influences on behavior against the perspectives that focus on inheritable traits. The perspective to which a psychologist subscribes determines the view taken concerning this issue. The question of

whether behavior is determined by [b] _____ forces also separates psychological perspectives. The psychodynamic perspective interprets behavior as influenced by unconscious forces, whereas the cognitive perspective may attribute abnormal behavior to faulty (conscious) reasoning. The issue of observable behavior versus internal mental processes places the behavioral perspective against the cognitive perspective. Some psychologists rely on the behavioral perspective. Their contention is that only [c] _____ is a legitimate source

of information. The controversial question of free will versus [d] _____ raises such issues as whether abnormal behavior is a result of intentional choice. The focus of the final issue is to determine how much of our behavior is a consequence of our unique and special qualities and how much is [e] _____. Interests in individual differences conflict with the desire to find universal principles. These five key issues should not be viewed in an either-or manner, but instead they should be understood as creating a continuum along which psychologists would place themselves.

Psychology will become increasingly specialized as the knowledge base grows. As our understanding grows, more psychologists will focus on **[f]** _____ of psychological disorders rather than treatment. The study of issues of **[g]** _____, such as violence, prejudice, poverty, and technological disasters, will allow psychologists to make important contributions toward their resolution.

Racial, ethnic, and **[h]** _____ issues will also become more critical to psychologists as the population becomes more diverse and as the socioeconomic decisions we anticipate making become more universal.

Evaluate

_____ 1. nature versus nurture

_____ 2. free will versus determinism

_____ 3. observable behavior versus internal mental process

_____ 4. conscious versus unconscious behavior

_____ 5. individual differences versus universal principles

a. How much of our behavior is produced by forces we are aware of and how much is caused by unconscious activity?

b. Should psychology focus on behavior that can be observed or on unseen thinking processes?

c. How much of our behavior is unique and how much reflects the culture and society in which we live?

d. How much behavior is individual choice and how much is produced by factors beyond our control?

e. How much behavior results from heredity and how much from environment?

Rethink

3-1   "The fact that some businesses now promote their ability to help people 'expand their minds beyond virtual reality' shows the great progress psychology has made lately." Criticize this statement in light of what you know about professional psychology and pseudo-psychology.

3-2   *From a social worker's perspective:* Imagine that you have a caseload of clients who come from diverse cultures, ethnicities, and races. How might you consider their diverse backgrounds when interacting with them and when assisting them with identifying and obtaining social services?

Spotlight on Terminology and Language—ESL Pointers

Page 23 "As you consider the many topics and perspectives that make up psychology, ranging from a narrow focus on minute biochemical influences on behavior to a broad focus on social behaviors, you might find yourself thinking that the discipline lacks **cohesion**."

Cohesion involves seeing how something sticks together. The field of psychology has **cohesion** because the five theoretical perspectives, cognitive, psychodynamic, humanistic, biological and behavioral, are consistently used to explain and predict behavior.

Page 24 "How much of our behavior is due to heredity (or 'nature') and how much is due to environment ('nurture'), and what is the **interplay** between the two forces?"

Interplay is the relationship. How do nature and nurture act on and react to each other?

Page 24 "A psychologists' take on this issue depends partly on which major perspective she or he **subscribes to**."

Subscribe to means aligning oneself with – supporting a theory or view. Can you identify the psychological theory you **subscribe to**?

Page 24 "For example, clinical psychologists adopting a psychodynamic perspective argue that psychological disorders are brought about by unconscious factors, whereas psychologists employing the cognitive perspective suggest that psychological disorders largely are the result of **faulty** thinking processes."

Faulty thinking is thinking that is flawed or inaccurate.

Page 24 "How much of our behavior is a matter of free will (choices made freely by an individual), and how much is subject to determinism, the notion that behavior is largely produced by factors beyond people's **willful** control?"

Willful is voluntary control. You make a choice or a decision without the undue influence of others.

Page 24 "Other psychologists disagree and **contend** that such individuals are the victims of forces beyond their control."

To **contend** is to assert or state this point of view.

Page 24 "Psychologists who rely on the neuroscience perspective tend to look for universal principles of behavior, such as how the nervous system operates or the way certain hormones automatically **prime** us for sexual activity."

Prime is to prepare. Our hormones **prime** us, or prepare us, for many activities.

Page 25 "**Subcultural**, ethnic, racial, and socioeconomic differences are increasingly important targets of study by psychologists (Tucker & Herman, 2002)."

A **subcultural** group is a group within a culture, but with ethnic, regional, social or economic characteristic patterns or behaviors that serve to distinguish it from that general cultural identity.

Page 26 "For example, the amount of research conducted in the United States on groups other than white middle-class college students is **woefully** small."

17

Woefully means sadly or unhappily. The amount of research done on groups other than white middle class college students is **woefully,** or unhappily, a very small amount.

Page 27 "Something so profound it will **launch** your brain beyond **Virtual Reality**...and transform your mind and soul forever."

To **launch** something is to send it off. Here the quote is telling us that a technology will send a person's brain to a place even more unusual then an artificial reality (**Virtual reality**)

Page 27 "From advertisements to television and radio talk shows to the Internet, we are **subjected to a barrage of information** about psychology."

When we are **subjected to a barrage of information** we are presented with information rapidly and continuously.

Page 27 "How can we separate accurate information, which is backed by science and objective research, from pseudo-psychology based on **anecdotes**, opinions, and even outright fraud?"

An **anecdote** is a short personal account of an event.

Page 27 "Keep in mind that there is no **free ride**."

A **free ride** is a slang term for getting something for nothing.

Page 27 "Be wary of simple, **glib** responses to major difficulties."

Glib responses are comments that lack thought and are insincere and shallow and should not be taken seriously.

Page 28 "The **notion of infallibility** is best left to the **realm of religion**, and you should approach psychological information and advice from a critical and thoughtful perspective."

A **notion** is an idea. The **notion of infallibility** refers to the idea that a person is unable to make a mistake.

A **realm** is defined area of study or interest. The **realm of religion** is the area of interest surrounding people's personal beliefs, values and attitudes concerning a god or gods.

Page 28 "Despite these cautions, you should remember that the field of psychology has provided a wealth of information that people can **draw upon** for suggestions about every phase of life."

To **draw upon** suggestions means to use them to make conclusions. People use (**draw upon**) all of the information provided by psychology for ideas about what to do in each period of life.

Test your knowledge of modules 1, 2, and 3 by answering these questions. These questions have been placed in three Practice Tests. The first two tests consist of questions that will test your recall of factual knowledge. The third test contains questions that are challenging and primarily test for conceptual knowledge and your ability to apply that knowledge. Check your answers and review the feedback using the Answer Key on the following pages of the *Study Guide*.

PRACTICE TEST 1:

1. Observing future trends in the field of psychology,
    a.   the future trend will be to encourage psychologists to be generalists rather than specialists.
    b.   new theoretical models are unlikely to develop.
    c.   psychologists will likely become less involved in broad public issues.
    d.   psychological treatment will continue to become more accessible.

2. The behavioral perspective places a major emphasis on:
    a.   observable behavior.
    b.   inner forces.
    c.   free will.
    d.   understanding concepts.

3. A cognitive psychologist would be most interested in:
    a.   the learning process.
    b.   our perceptions of the world around us.
    c.   dreams.
    d.   the functioning of the brain.

4. Which of the following sources of evidence would be the least acceptable to behaviorists like John B. Watson?
    a.   Evidence gathered using introspection
    b.   Evidence from intelligence tests
    c.   Evidence regarding emotional growth and development
    d.   Evidence from perception and sensation experiments

5. Dr. Gaipo is investigating the influence of inherited characteristics on behavior. This would be a focus on the:
    a.   cognitive perspective.
    b.   psychodynamic perspective.
    c.   behavioral perspective.
    d.   neuroscience perspective.

6. Leta Stetter Hollingworth is known for her contributions in:
    a.   the concept of a kindergarten.
    b.   the area of child and adolescent development.
    c.   the idea that males and females are psychologically different.
    d.   the study of personality traits.

7. "The whole is greater than the sum of the parts" is a postulate of:
    a.   structuralism.
    b.   functionalism.
    c.   gestalt psychology.
    d.   behaviorism.

8. One difficulty psychologists have had in making progress on research which includes cross-cultural perspectives is that
    a. most psychologists are uninterested in addressing issues of race as they relate to psychology.
    b. there is no universal agreement about the meanings of the terms "race" and "ethnic groups."
    c. there are few truly different cultures to examine.
    d. most psychologists believe that biological explanations of behavior are more important than environmental or cultural explanations.

9. Developmental psychology is the study of:
    a. the biological basis of behavior.
    b. how people grow and change both physically and socially throughout their lives.
    c. how people's thoughts, feelings, and actions are affected by others.
    d. the study, diagnosis, and treatment of abnormal behavior.

10. Which of the following would be considered a "perspective" in psychology?
    a. Psychodynamic psychology
    b. Cross-cultural psychology
    c. Experimental psychology
    d. Counseling psychology

11. Which of the following psychologists would most likely be involved primarily in administering tests and utilizing evaluative instruments to assess abnormal behavior?
    a. Counseling psychologist
    b. Health psychologist
    c. Personality psychologist
    d. Clinical psychologist

12. The focus of developmental psychology is on:
    a. applications such as improving the parenting skills of adults.
    b. understanding growth and changes occurring throughout life.
    c. development and maintenance of healthy interpersonal relationships as in friendships, co-worker relationships, and marriages.
    d. identifying behavioral consistencies throughout life.

13. Which type of psychologists might be called into New Orleans in the aftermath of Hurricane Katrina to identify ways in which people could be coping with the stress of rebuilding their homes and lives?
    a. Experimental
    b. Health
    c. Developmental
    d. Cognitive

14. Psychology was established formally in 1879 when:
    a. Sigmund Freud began psychoanalysis.
    b. the American Psychological Association was founded.
    c. William James, an American, published his first major book.
    d. Wilhelm Wundt founded his psychology laboratory in Germany.

15. The problem that psychology faces of losing its diversity as a discipline can best be corrected by:
    a. social psychologists becoming more active trainers of psychologists.
    b. more studies in cultural psychology based on demonstrating the importance of diversity.
    c. increasing the ethnic sensitivity of counseling and clinical psychologists.
    d. increasing the number of minorities in the profession.

_____ 16. gestalt psychology

_____ 17. pseudo-psychology

_____ 18. introspection

_____ 19. functionalism

_____ 20. structuralism

a. The ability to describe one's own mental images and emotional reactions.

b. Emphasized the function or purpose of behavior.

c. Early approach Wundt hoped would help clients analyze images and sensations as basic elements of perception.

d. Pseudoscience based on anecdotes, opinions, and even fraud.

e. Focus on perception and thinking as a "whole rather than individual elements."

21. Psychologists play many roles in society, including teacher, _____, and clinical practitioner.

22. Studies show that watching violence in the media has led to a(n) _____ in subsequent aggression.

23. Psychologists who focus on the consistency of people's behavior over time are _____psychologists.

24. Research in psychology demonstrates that eyewitness testimony in criminal cases if often _____.

25. To suggest that a person has developed a mental illness, such as depression, because of their genetic makeup is to suggest that the illness was cause by _____ rather than _____.

26. Describe the perspective that best fits your current understanding of why people behave the way they do. Be sure to explain why you selected this particular perspective. Which perspectives do you reject? Why?

PRACTICE TEST 2:

1. The relationship of experimental psychology and cognitive psychology might best be described as:
   a. only experimental psychology conducts experiments.
   b. cognitive psychology is not interested in studying learning.
   c. cognitive psychology is a specialty area of experimental psychology.
   d. experimental psychology is a specialty of cognitive psychology.

2. Although their interests are diverse, psychologists share a common:
   a. concern for applying their knowledge to social situations.
   b. interest in mental processes or behavior.
   c. respect for the ideas of psychoanalyst Sigmund Freud.
   d. interest in the study of animals' behavior.

3. Dr. Phil's new TV show will include a panel of obese women whose average weight is 450 pounds. This program may be especially interesting to:
   a. school psychologists.
   b. social psychologists.
   c. cognitive psychologists.
   d. health psychologists.

4. Questions concerning such topics as how we are influenced by others and why we form relationships with each other are studied by:
   a. counseling psychologists.
   b. social psychologists.
   c. clinical psychologists.
   d. health psychologists.

5. A health psychologist would be most likely to study:
   a. the impact of smoking on health.
   b. experimental ethics.
   c. the effects of crowding on behavior.
   d. program effectiveness.

6. If executives of a company believe their employees are suffering from low morale, they are likely to seek the advice of:
   a. social psychologists.
   b. counseling psychologists.
   c. clinical psychologists.
   d. industrial-organizational psychologists.

7. While psychologists are employed in all of the following areas, the largest proportion of psychologists are employed:
   a. privately at their own independent practices.
   b. in hospitals or mental institutions.
   c. at colleges or universities.
   d. in private businesses or industries.

8. Which of these questions would most interest a functionalist?
   a. What are the best human values?
   b. What are the contents of the mind?
   c. How do nerves work?
   d. How do the person's thoughts help her to get along in daily life?

9. The representation of women in psychology, as compared to the number of men in psychology, is expected to _____ by the year 2010.
   a. decrease
   b. remain about the same
   c. increase, with the number of women still trailing the number of men
   d. increase, with women eventually outnumbering men

10. Gestalt psychology was developed:
    a. around 1850.
    b. in 1879.
    c. during the early 1900s.
    d. in the 1950s.

11. John B. Watson was the first American psychologist to follow the:
    a. behavioral perspective.
    b. humanistic perspective.
    c. cognitive perspective.
    d. psychodynamic perspective.

12. "Slips of the tongue" are seen by _____ psychologists as revealing the unconscious mind's true beliefs or wishes.
    a. cognitive
    b. psychodynamic
    c. biological
    d. humanistic

13. Which of the following types of psychologists would be most interested in the "unconscious" side of the conscious versus unconscious determinants of behavior issue?
    a. A behavioral experimental psychologist
    b. A humanistic psychologist
    c. A psychodynamic clinical psychologist
    d. A sports psychologist

14. Sigmund Freud believed that behavior is motivated by:
    a. subconscious inner forces.
    b. a desire to achieve personal fulfillment.
    c. the natural tendency to organize data through perception.
    d. inherited characteristics.

15. Authors who write self-help books that promote quick cures for psychological problems should be doubted because:
    a. if the procedures worked as stated, they would already be applied widely.
    b. only medically based therapies are fast.
    c. the American Psychological Association would suppress any procedures that would cut back on the income earned by therapists.
    d. the books' authors are overqualified to write on those topics.

_____ 16. Sigmund Freud   a. The first laboratory

_____ 17. John Locke   b. Functionalism

_____ 18. Mary Calkins   c. Tabula rasa

_____ 19. Wilhelm Wundt   d. Psychoanalysis

_____ 20. William James   e. An American Psychological Association president

21. The _____ perspective of psychology states that actions, feelings, and thoughts are associated with bodily events.

22. Marcus is having difficulty in school and needs to engage help from a professional. If he wants to improve his academic performance, he should seek the assistance of a(n) _____ psychologist.

23. The famous psychologist _____ is credited with the development of psychoanalysis.

24. The father of modern psychology is _____.

25. A perspective in psychology that was developed to enhance human potential is the _____ perspective.

26.   Select two of the key issues for psychology and describe how the resolution of these issues one way or the other would change the way you view yourself and others, your goals, and your immediate responsibility for your own success.

PRACTICE TEST 3: Conceptual, Applied, and Challenging Questions

1.   What kind of psychologist would have a special interest in studying the aspects of an earthquake that people are most likely to recall?
      a.   Social psychologist
      b.   Industrial-organizational psychologist
      c.   Educational psychologist
      d.   Cognitive psychologist

2.   Professor Bianchi has identified a trait he calls persistence, and he has begun to conduct research on the consistency of this trait in various situations. Professor Bianchi is most likely:
      a.   a social psychologist.
      b.   a cross-cultural psychologist.
      c.   an educational psychologist.
      d.   a personality psychologist.

3.   Aaron falls when coming down the escalator and drops his packages and injures his leg. Which type of psychologist would be most interested in whether other shoppers offered assistance?
      a.   A social psychologist
      b.   A behavioral neuroscience psychologist
      c.   A clinical psychologist
      d.   An industrial-organizational psychologist

4.   Ed Smith, an architect interested in designing kindergarten classrooms that would offer an environment that promotes learning might consult with:
      a.   a clinical psychologist.
      b.   a school psychologist.
      c.   a personality psychologist.
      d.   a counseling psychologist.

5.   The procedure for studying the mind, in which structuralists train people to describe carefully, in their own words, what they experienced upon being exposed to various stimuli, is called:
      a.   cognition.
      b.   mind expansion.
      c.   perception.
      d.   introspection.

6.   Most psychologists today believe that understanding human behavior requires:
      a.   anecdotal evidence combined with systematic research.
      b.   the application of a wide variety of approaches, or perspectives, in psychology.
      c.   that all psychologists are trained in clinical psychology.
      d.   the application of functionalism, as opposed to structuralism.

7.   The major distinction between educational and school psychology is that:
      a.   educational psychology is devoted to improving the education of students who have special needs, and school psychology is devoted to increasing achievement in all students.
      b.   school psychology is devoted to improving the schooling of students who have special needs, and educational psychology is devoted to better understanding of the entire educational system.
      c.   school psychology attempts to examine the entire educational process, and educational psychology looks at individual students.
      d.   educational psychology attempts to examine the entire educational process, and school psychology is devoted to assessing and correcting academic and school-related problems of students.

8. Which pair of individuals has been associated with functionalism?
   a. Leta Stetter Hollingworth and June Etta Downey
   b. Sigmund Freud and Wilhelm Wundt
   c. William James and John Dewey
   e. Wilhelm Wundt and William James

9. The _____ perspective of psychology places the greatest emphasis on the environment.
   a. neuroscience
   b. psychodynamic
   c. behavioral
   d. humanistic

10. In the past, Professor Kagan has conducted research on topics that include how genetics may influence particular behaviors and personality traits that persist in the population over time, such as shyness. Which of the following best describes Professor Kagan's research interests?
    a. Social psychology
    b. Industrial-organizational psychology
    c. Cross-cultural psychology
    d. Evolutionary psychology

11. When the drug manufacturers claim that a new sleeping aid is a safe drug and present studies that they paid to have done to support their claims, to what does this bear a strong resemblance?
    a. Self-help experts who claim that their system is best
    b. The self-help program that will solve major problems with a very low cost
    c. The expectation that there exists a universal cure for each major problem
    d. The view that the creators of an idea know best because they were expert enough to have the original idea

12. Erdem, Betsy, and Susie have volunteered to be subjects in a study. They are each, in turn, asked to concentrate on creating an image of a geometric shape. After forming the image, they are then required to describe how the image came to them. The researcher then asks them to imagine a triangle, then a square, and then several more complicated shapes. Which of the following have they been doing?
    a. Experimental psychology
    b. Introspection
    c. Gestalt psychology
    d. Functionalism

13. Which of the following would be **least** interested in cross-cultural studies?
    a. The neuroscience perspective
    b. The psychodynamic perspective
    c. The cognitive perspective
    d. The behavioral perspective

14. Studies of violence that suggest a cycle of violence, which is when violence in one generation is correlated with violence in the next generation, support which of the following sides in the key issues examined by psychology?
    a. Determinism
    b. Nature
    c. Individual differences
    d. Conscious control of behavior

15. Professor Cheetham is particularly interested in explanations of an individual's ability to make decisions based on free choice. She is exploring several factors that may influence or determine choices, but she is very hopeful that she can demonstrate that some nondetermined choices can be demonstrated. Which of the following combinations best represents the two perspectives that would be supported by her research?
    a. The psychoanalytic and neuroscience perspectives
    b. The behavioral and the humanistic perspectives
    c. The humanistic and cognitive perspectives
    d. The cognitive and behavioral perspectives

_____16. industrial-organizational psychology

_____17. health psychology

_____18. cross-cultural psychology

_____19. evolutionary psychology

_____20. clinical neuropsychology

a. The branch of psychology that investigates the similarities and differences in psychological functioning in various cultures and ethnic groups.

b. The emerging area that relates biological factors to psychological disorders.

c. The branch of psychology that seeks to identify behavior patterns that are a result of our genetic inheritance.

d. Applies psychology to helping people cope with stressful life events.

e. The branch of psychology that studies the psychology of the workplace, considering productivity, job satisfaction, and decision making.

21. A psychological approach that emphasizes the organization of perception and thinking as a whole rather than on individual elements of perception is _____ psychology.

22. _____was one of the early approaches to psychology that concentrated on what the mind does—the functions of mental activity—and the role of behavior in allowing people to adapt to their environment.

23. Companies sometimes hire _____ psychologists to improve group decision making, employee morale, worker motivation, and productivity.

24. Wilhelm Wundt asked his subjects to observe, analyze, and describe in detail what they were experiencing when they were exposed to a stimulus. This was known as _____.

25. _____, developed by Freud, proposed that patient's symptoms were caused by past conflicts, and emotional traumas were too threatening to be remembered consciously.

26. The _____ method attempts to find legitimate, valid answers to problems, rather than relying on intuition and speculation to find solutions.

27. Explain how you would respond to the comment that psychology is just common sense. Define critical thinking and demonstrate how it is used in psychological research.

■ ANSWER KEY: MODULES 1, 2, AND 3

Module 1:	Module 2:	Module 3:
[a] Psychology	[a] structuralism	[a] nurture
[b] Behavioral neuroscientists	[b] introspection	[b] unconscious
[c] Experimental	[c] functionalism	[c] observable behavior
[d] Cognitive	[d] Gestalt psychology	[d] determinism
[e] evolutionary psychology	[e] child development	[e] universally human
[f] clinical neuropsychology	[f] personality	[f] prevention
[g] clinical	[g] neuroscience	[g] public interest
[h] counseling	[h] psychodynamic	[h] cultural diversity
[i] social	[i] cognitive	
[j] cross cultural	[j] behavioral	Evaluate
[k] academic settings	[k] humanistic	1. e
[l] two-thirds	[l] free will	2. d
[m] Diversity		3. b
[n] doctorate		4. a
[o] master's degree	Evaluate	5. c
[p] social services	1. b	
	2. c	
	3. e	
Evaluate	4. a	
Test A Test B	5. d	
1. a 6. c		
2. d 7. a		
3. e 8. e		
4. c 9. d		
5. b 10. b		

Selected Rethink Answers

1-2 List those psychologists (e.g., behavioral neuroscientist, social, developmental, cognitive, cross-cultural, etc.) that you believe may study issues (e.g., poor nutrition, fear of being evaluated by others, lack of maturity, inability to perceive the written word correctly) related to a seven-year-old's inability to read. State the viewpoint/perspective that each would have about a seven-year-old's inability to read. Discuss how each would identify and correct the problem.

2-2 Identify a psychological perspective (e.g., the neuroscience perspective, the cognitive perspective, etc.). Research questions are then based on that perspective. For instance, a cognitive psychologist who is also interested in people's work lives might ask research questions such as: What sort of planning strategies do people use in planning for changes in their careers? How do people make decisions about the most effective use of their time at work?

Practice Test 1:

1.   d   mod. 3   p. 26
a.   Incorrect. Psychologists continue to become more specialized.
b.   Incorrect. New conceptual perspectives are unlikely.
c.   Incorrect. Psychologists are among the most politically and socially involved academics.

*d.   Correct. Of course, HMOs and managed care may alter the way this kind of treatment is delivered.

2.   a   mod. 3   p. 23
*a.   Correct. This is the focal interest of behaviorists and experimental psychologists.

b. Incorrect. Inner forces are the focal interest of psychodynamic psychologists.

c. Incorrect. Humanistic psychologists are interested in the individual's power to make choices on their own, in other words, the individual's free will.

d. Incorrect. Concepts are the domain of cognitive psychologists.

3. a   mod. 2   p. 8
*a. Corrrect. While not central, the learning process would be of some interest to psychodynamic psychologists.

b. Incorrect. While not central, the perceptions are of interest to psychodynamic psychologists.

c. Incorrect. As dreams reflect the activity of the unconscious elements of the mind, they would be of great interest to psychodynamic psychologists.

d. Incorrect. While not central, the functioning of the brain has been of some interest to some psychodynamic psychologists.

4. a   mod. 2   p. 19
*a. Correct. Above all things, Watson abhorred the use of information derived from consciousness and other unobservable phenomena.

b. Incorrect. If gathered through observable events, this is acceptable.

c. Incorrect. If gathered through observable events, this is acceptable.

d. Incorrect. If gathered through observable events, this is acceptable.

5. d   mod. 2   p. 19
a. Incorrect. The cognitive model focuses on understanding thought processes.

b. Incorrect. The psychodynamic model focuses on understanding the role of unconscious motivation and primitive forces in behavior.

c. Incorrect. The behavioral model focuses on understanding how behavior is conditioned and modified by stimuli and reinforcements.

*d. Correct. The biological model examines the role of genetics in all aspects of human behavior.

6. b   mod. 2   p. 18
a. Incorrect. This was an import from Germany.

*b. Correct. She coined the term "gifted" and also studied many women's issues.

c. Incorrect. Freud recognized this, as has everyone since.

d. Incorrect. This was pioneered by June Etta Downey.

7. c   mod. 2   p. 5

a. Incorrect. This statement is completely associated with gestalt psychology.

b. Incorrect. This statement is completely associated with gestalt psychology.

*c. Correct. This statement reflects the gestalt view that the mind organizes perceptions as it adds information to them.

d. Incorrect. This statement is completely associated with gestalt psychology.

8. b   mod. 3   p. 45
a. Incorrect. Psychologists are increasingly becoming interested in race in relation to psychology.

*b. Correct. There is quite a bit of disagreement over the use and meanings of the terms "race" and "ethnic group."

c. Incorrect. Cross-cultural research demonstrates that cultures can be quite different from one another.

d. Incorrect. Many psychologists take into account biology, environment, and culture when explaining behavior.

9. b   mod. 1   p. 8
a. Incorrect. Neuropsychology is specifically focused on the biological basis of behavior, although it may make contributions to all of the other alternatives.

*b. Correct. This describes the focus of developmental psychology.

c. Incorrect. This describes the interests and research focus of social psychology.

d. Incorrect. This describes the work of clinical psychology.

10. a   mod. 2   p. 19
*a. Correct. Psychodynamic psychology follows a coherent conceptual perspective.

b. Incorrect. Cross-cultural psychology involves a collection of approaches.

c. Incorrect. Experimental psychology involves a collection of theoretical approaches, although all utilize experimental methods.

d. Incorrect. Counseling psychology involves a wide range of approaches.

11. d   mod. 1   p. 8
a. Incorrect. Counseling psychology is dedicated to providing counseling to clients in need.
b. Incorrect. Health psychology may utilize such tests, but its focus is on understanding healthy lifestyles and promoting health.
c. Incorrect. Personality psychologists utilize testing and evaluation processes, but in the service of their research on personality structure and theory.
*d. Correct. The clinical psychologist is predominately focused on testing and evaluation as a bias for diagnosis and treatment of psychological disorders.

12. b   mod. 1   p. 8
a. Incorrect. Parenting skills comprise only a minor interest of developmental psychology.
*b. Correct. "Development" refers to growth, maturation, and change through life.
c. Incorrect. Peer relationships and marriage comprise only a minor interest of developmental psychology.
d. Incorrect. This too may be considered only a minor interest of developmental psychology.

13. b   mod. 1   p. 7
a. Incorrect. Experimental psychologists conduct controlled experiments, typically in laboratory settings, among other activities.
*b. Correct. Health psychologists would be very interested in stress and coping.
c. Incorrect. Developmental psychologists are mainly interested in how people grow and change over time.
d. Incorrect. Cognitive psychologists research how people think and solve problems.

14. d   mod. 2   p. 15
a. Incorrect. Freud did not have a laboratory, and his work began in the 1880s.
b. Incorrect. The APA was founded long after the beginning of psychology.
c. Incorrect. James established a lab in 1875, and some students conducted research in it.
*d. Correct. Wundt is given this credit because of his 1879 laboratory, complete with funding and graduate students.

15. d   mod. 1   p. 10
a. Incorrect. The effort must involve more than social psychologists.
b. Incorrect. Studies demonstrating the importance of cultural diversity may help, but they will not remedy the situation.

c. Incorrect. Being sensitive to ethnic origins of one's clients is important, but it will not remedy the problem.
*d. Correct. The only way to solve the problem of too little diversity is to recruit more individuals from diverse backgrounds.

16. e   mod. 2   p. 17
17. d   mod. 3   p. 27
18. a   mod. 2   p. 15
19. b   mod. 2   p. 16
20. c   mod. 2   p. 15

21. scientist   mod. 1   p. 12
22. increase   mod 2   p. 33
23. personality   mod. 1   p. 7
24. inaccurate and biased mod. 1   p. 24
25. nature, nurture   mod. 3   p. 41

26.
▪ Identify the key principle of the perspectives you have chosen. For instance, in the psychodynamic perspective, one of the key principles is unconscious motivation. For the neuroscience perspective, the focus is on the physiological and organic basis of behavior.

▪ Offer a reason, perhaps an example, that illustrates why you like this perspective. Asserting that you just "liked it" or that "it makes the most sense" is not a sufficient answer.

Practice Test 2:
1. c   mod. 1   p. 8
a. Incorrect. Experiments are conducted by almost every major specialty of psychology.
b. Incorrect. Cognitive psychology is very interested in studying learning and any other process related to mental life.
*c. Correct. Cognitive psychology began as a subspecialty of experimental psychology, although it is now a specialty in its own right.
d. Incorrect. It is the other way around.

2. b   mod. 1   p. 6
a. Incorrect. Not all psychologists seek to apply their knowledge to social situations.
*b. Correct. Mental processes and behavior constitute the area of study of psychology.
c. Incorrect. Few psychologists appear to respect the ideas of Freud.
d. Incorrect. Only special areas of psychology are interested in animal behavior.

3. d   mod. 1   p. 8
a. Incorrect. Forensic psychologists study legal issues.
b. Incorrect. Social psychologists study social behavior.
c. Incorrect. Cognitive psychologists study how we understand the world and solve problems.
*d. Correct. Health psychologists are focused on health issues such as obesity.

4. b   mod. 1   p. 8
a. Incorrect. Relationships with others and the influence of others does influence the scope of therapy, but researching these questions is not a concern of counseling psychologists.
*b. Correct. Social psychologists are quite interested in exploring topics of the influence of others on individuals and the way relationships affect our behavior.
c. Incorrect. Relationships with others and the influence of others does have a role in understanding abnormal behavior, but researching these questions is not a concern of clinical psychologists.
d. Incorrect. Relationships with others and the influence of others does influence health and wellness, but researching these questions is not a focal concern of health psychologists.

5. a   mod. 1   p. 8
*a. Correct. This is of interest to physiological and health psychology.
b. Incorrect. The ethics involved in experimentation affect every psychologist and would be of interest to all, although primarily experimental psychologists.
c. Incorrect. Environmental psychologists claim the study of crowding as their domain.
d. Incorrect. The determination of program effectiveness is the domain of psychologists concerned with program evaluation.

6. d   mod. 1   p. 11
a. Incorrect. Social psychologists are not directly interested in activities in organizations.
b. Incorrect. Counseling psychologists are not directly interested in organizations and their employees.
c. Incorrect. Clinical psychologists are not directly interested in organizations and their employees.
*d. Correct. Industrial-Organizational psychologists are interested in the well-being of employees in organizations.

7. c   mod. 1   p. 10

a. Incorrect. Figure 1–1 shows 22% self-employed.
b. Incorrect. Figure 1–1 shows 9% in private not-for-profit institutions.
*c. Correct. Figure 1–1 shows 33% in colleges or universities.
d. Incorrect. Figure 1–1 shows 19% in private for-profit institutions.

8. d   mod. 2   p. 16
a. Incorrect. This is probably an issue for existential and humanistic psychology.
b. Incorrect. This was structuralism's concern.
c. Incorrect. The neurological psychologist would be more interested in neuron function.
*d. Correct. The functionalists were primarily interested in the adaptive work of the mind.

9. d   mod. 1   p. 10
a. Incorrect. See answer d.
b. Incorrect. See answer d.
c. Incorrect. See answer d.
*d. Correct. There are currently more women students in graduate psychology programs than men.

10. c   mod. 2   p. 17
a. Incorrect. Much too early.
b. Incorrect. This is the date for Wundt's laboratory.
*c. Correct. Gestalt psychology has maintained a steady, although small interest in perceptual processes since its founding in the early 1900s.
d. Incorrect. The 1950s is more likely to be associated with the peak of behaviorism and the early beginnings of cognitive psychology.

11. a   mod. 2   p. 19
*a. Correct. Not only was he the first, but he was also the founder of the perspective called behaviorism.
b. Incorrect. Abraham Maslow and Carl Rogers share this honor.
c. Incorrect. Because this has to do with mind, Watson probably would reject such an association.
d. Incorrect. Not only does it have to do with mind, but psychoanalysis also attends to the unconscious mind, a double error for Watson.

12. b   mod. 2   p. 19
a. Incorrect. Cognitive psychologists would view these as information-processing errors.
*b. Correct. Psychodynamic psychologists are interested in issues of the unconscious.

c.   Incorrect. Biological psychologists would be more interested in the tongue itself.

d.   Incorrect. Humanistic psychologists would want the person to accept the conscious intent of the slip of the tongue.

13.   c   mod. 2   p. 19

a.   Incorrect. Behavioral experimental psychology has little interest in the unconscious whatsoever.

b.   Incorrect. The humanistic perspective has little interest in the unconscious whatsoever.

*c.   Correct. The psychodynamic approach explores the unconscious in order to understand behavior.

d.   Incorrect. A sports psychologist may have some interest in how the subconscious influences performance, but the role is not significant.

14.   a   mod. 2   p. 19

*a.   Correct. Dreams provide important insight into these subconscious forces because the powers that inhibit their expression are weakest during sleep.

b.   Incorrect. This reflects the interests of humanistic psychology more than psychoanalysis.

c.   Incorrect. This is an area of study of cognitive psychology.

d.   Incorrect. Biopsychology is concerned with inherited characteristics and their role in behavior.

15.   a   mod. 3   p. 27

*a.   Correct. Inexpensive solutions would be self-extinguishing!

b.   Incorrect. Few therapies are fast, and medical therapies are not typically among that group.

c.   Incorrect. This action would be unethical.

d.   Incorrect. More likely, the authors are less qualified than practitioners.

16. d   mod. 2   p. 17
17. c   mod. 1   p. 24
18. e   mod. 1   p. 26
19. a   mod. 1   p. 24
20. b   mod. 1   p. 25

21. behavioral neuroscience   mod. 2   p. 6
22. school   mod. 1   p. 7
23. Freud   mod. 2   p. 19
24. Wundt   mod. 2   p. 15
25. humanistic   mod. 2   p. 20

26.   For this answer, "freedom will versus determinism" is used as the example.

■   The selection of the freedom will side of this answer reflects how most people would choose.

However, it suggests that all of our actions are thus our responsibility, even boredom and mistakes. We should be unable to attribute any causes for our behavior to others than ourselves.

■   If the issue is resolved in favor of determinism, then we should be able to understand all of human behavior as flowing from some root cause. Many religions have this kind of view, and some theorists and philosophers believe that science should be able to find causes. For psychology, this view is most compatible with behaviorism and psychoanalysis.

Practice Test 3:

1.   d   mod. 1   p. 8

a.   Incorrect. A social psychologist would more likely study the prosocial behaviors (helping) exhibited shortly after an earthquake.

b.   Incorrect. An industrial-organizational psychologist might be interested in how efficiency of organizations is affected by the aftermath of a natural disaster.

c.   Incorrect. An educational psychologist might have an interest in how information regarding earthquakes could be transmitted most effectively.

*d.   Correct. A cognitive psychologist would be interested in memory phenomena, and an earthquake may have elements of such phenomena as the flashbulb memory.

2.   d   mod. 1   p. 8

a.   Incorrect. A social psychologist does not study traits directly, but may be interested in the role of groups as they may influence such a trait.

b.   Incorrect. The only interest that a cross-cultural psychologist may have is whether the trait was common to more than one cultural group.

c.   Incorrect. An educational psychologist would probably be interested in whether the trait could be acquired for learning purposes.

*d.   Correct. The study of traits is specifically the domain of personality psychologists.

3.   a   mod. 1   p. 8

*a.   Correct. The helping behavior studied by social psychologists is called prosocial behavior.

b.   Incorrect. A behavioral neuroscience psychologist would not be interested in this behavior.

c.   Incorrect. This would not be of interest to a clinical perspective.

d.   Incorrect. This would not be of interest to an I/O psychologist.

4.　d　mod. 1　p. 7
a. Incorrect. A clinical psychologist could not offer this kind of consultation.
*b. Correct. A school psychologist could help explain why success in school depends on many factors, including the environment and culture of the classroom.
c. Incorrect. A personality psychologist is more interested in traits that differentiate people.
d. Incorrect. Counseling psychologists are sometimes interested in people's adjustment in school settings, but do not necessarily specialize in school settings, as school psychologists do.

5.　d　mod. 2　p. 15
a. Incorrect. Cognition is a specialty area of psychology and refers to how we perceive, process, and store information; it is not a method of investigation.
b. Incorrect. Although it may lead to some kind of "mind expansion," such is not the psychological research technique.
c. Incorrect. Perception refers to any processing of sensory stimuli.
*d. Correct. This does define the concept of introspection and the way that Tichener sought to utilize the procedure.

6.　b　mod. 1　p. 4
a. Incorrect. Psychologists are not particularly interested in anecdotal evidence.
*b. Correct. Human behavior is complex and understanding it as completely as possible requires many different points of view.
c. Incorrect. Clinical psychology represents only one subfield of psychology, and can't be applied to all behavior.
d. Incorrect. Functionalism was most prominent in the early 1900s, and does not fully represent the field as it is today.

7.　d　mod. 1　p. 7
a. Incorrect. This response has the two types switched.
b. Incorrect. The school psychologist does more than promoting the needs of special students.
c. Incorrect. The difference is not one of a group versus the individual, as this option suggests.
*d. Correct. Both halves of this statement are true, and they reflect the broadest formulation of the goals of the two areas.

8.　c　mod. 2　p. 17
a. Incorrect. These are the two early psychologists who were also female.

b. Incorrect. Freud was associated with psychoanalysis, and Wundt is frequently identified as a major contributor to structuralism.
*c. Correct. Both James and Dewey contributed to the development of functionalism, although James more often thought of himself as a philosopher.
d. Incorrect. These two men hold in common the founding of the earliest psychology laboratories, and both are considered responsible for developments of the two early schools: James with functionalism and Wundt with structuralism.

9.　c　mod. 2　p. 19
a. Incorrect. The neuroscience perspective is associated with genetic and biological aspects of behavior.
b. Incorrect. The psychodynamic perspective focuses on inner, primitive forces that are hidden in the unconscious and manifest through behavior.
*c. Correct. In the behavioral perspective, the environment plays a critical role as the source of stimuli and reinforcements.
d. Incorrect. The humanistic perspective is focused on the capacity of the individual to direct behavior from within.

10.　d　mod. 1　p. 9
a. Incorrect. Social psychologists are not generally interested in genetic influences on behavior.
b. Incorrect. Only the aspect of women at work is relevant to I/O psychology.
c. Incorrect. To the extent that these may also be studied in various cultural contexts, there exists some similarity.
*d. Correct. The focus of Professor Kagan is centered on issues that illustrate how genetics influences behavior.

11.　a　mod. 3　p. 27
*a. Correct. Like the self-help experts, the drug companies have much to gain when the tests are in their favor.
b. Incorrect. Because such a self-help program would have little financial benefit, the comparison is fairly weak.
c. Incorrect. This view goes well beyond the current analogy.
d. Incorrect. This view lacks the necessary critical element, but includes the elements of bias of self-interest, because the claim can be made by others who have nothing to gain from the outcome.

12. b   mod. 2 p. 15
a.   Incorrect. While this may be part of an experiment, the subjects are not "doing" experimental psychology.
*b.   Correct. The subjects are each engaging in introspection, that is, examining their own thought processes.
c.   Incorrect. Gestalt psychology may be interested in how these representations are formed, but this example does not support the view that the subjects are somehow engaged in gestalt psychology.
d.   Incorrect. Functionalism was much more concerned with the processes that lead to adaption than to the internal processes of mental representation.

13. a   mod. 1 p. 9
*a.   Correct. Because the neuroscience perspective is interested in the common genetic inheritance that accounts for behavior, cross-cultural studies would be of least interest except where they may show universal patterns or localized variations.
b.   Incorrect. The psychodynamic perspective is interested in the cultural issues related to child development, dream symbolism, and other cultural artifacts.
c.   Incorrect. The cognitive perspective examines the different cultural patterns of such things as problem solving, perception, and language, among others.
d.   Incorrect. The behavioral perspective should be interested in the variations from one culture to another of stimuli and reinforcement.

14. a   mod. 3 p. 24
*a.   Correct. This is one of the ways that a behavior may be determined, that is, by its passage from one generation to the next.
b.   Incorrect. This would suggest that something genetic was at work here, affecting more family members.
c.   Incorrect. If individual differences were key here, then violence would not be passed from one generation to another, instead appearing without regard to family influence.
d.   Incorrect. If conscious control of behavior were at work, then this generational violence would not be as likely.

15. c   mod. 3 p. 20-21
a.   Incorrect. These two perspectives are both highly deterministic.

b.   Incorrect. The behavioral approach is highly deterministic, while the humanistic approach focuses on free choices.
*c.   Correct. Both of these approaches would accept self-determination in decision making.
d.   Incorrect. While the cognitive approach would allow for free will, the behavioral approach is highly determined.

16. e   mod. 1 p. 7
17. d   mod. 1 p. 7
18. a   mod. 1 p. 7
19. b   mod. 1 p. 7
20. c   mod. 1 p. 7

21. gestalt   mod. 1   p. 17
22. Functionalism   mod. 2   p. 16
23. industrial   mod. 1   p. 7
24. introspection   mod. 2   p. 15
25. Psychoanalysis   mod. 2   p. 19
26. scientific   mod. 1   p. 5

27.   Give examples of things that we believe because they are "common sense" or that you believe because of intuition.
▪   Critical thinking is the ability and willingness to assess claims and make objective judgments on the basis of well-supported reasons.
▪   Next, define the scientific approach. Explain how stating a hypothesis and then gathering information/facts to support the hypothesis through careful, methodical scientific methods will elicit a more exact measure of what is being studied.

Chapter 2: Psychological Research

Module 4: The Scientific Method
Module 5: Conducting Psychological Research
Module 6: Critical Research Issues

Overview

This set of modules focuses on the techniques psychologists use to refine and expand knowledge about the world around them. Psychologists pose questions of interest and then attempt to answer them through scientific research.

Module 4 examines the ways in which psychologists reach conclusions about the unknown. The scientific method is discussed in detail, focusing on the development of theories as the framework for understanding relationships, and is followed by a discussion about how hypotheses are used to test theories.

Module 5 offers a description of the way in which psychologists develop suppositions and test theories. Consideration is then given to the specific means that researchers use in doing research: archival research, naturalistic observation, survey research, case studies, correlational research, and experimental research. The major techniques used in carrying out research are discussed, as well as the benefits and limitations of each type of research. Particular attention is given to the features of experimental research, since this form of research is the only way psychologists can establish cause-and-effect relationships through research.

Module 6 discusses the ethics of doing psychological research, both on humans and animals. The treatment of subjects is examined, and a discussion on when it is and is not appropriate to design experiments using human subjects is presented. This module also describes two key threats to the validity of research – experimental bias and participant expectations. Finally, because none of us can turn on the television, listen to the radio, or pick up a newspaper or magazine without being bombarded with ideas about how to gain happiness and bliss, improve our lives, our work, and our futures, questions are posed that help the consumer scrutinize thoroughly what is valid and what is not in psychological research and the ways that we can become knowledgeable and critical consumers of research findings.

To further investigate the topics covered in this chapter, you can visit the related Web sites by visiting the following link: www.mhhe.com/feldmanup8.

Prologue: Why Did No One Help?
Looking Ahead

Module 4:
The Scientific Method

Theories: Specifying Broad Explanations
Hypotheses: Crafting Testable Predictions

- ***What is the scientific method?***
- ***What role do theory and hypotheses play in psychological research?***

The Scientific Method

A major aim of research in psychology is to discover which of our assumptions about human behavior are correct. First, questions that interest psychologists must be set into the proper framework so that a systematic inquiry may be conducted to find the answer to the question.

Psychologists use an approach called the **[a]** _____ to conduct their inquiry. The scientific method has three main steps: (1) identifying questions of interest; (2) formulating an explanation; and (3) carrying out research designed to support or refute the explanation.

[b] _____ are broad explanations and predictions about phenomena that interest the scientist. Because psychological theories grow out of the diverse models (presented in Chapter 1), they vary in breadth and detail. Psychologists' theories differ from our informal theories by being formal and focused. Latané and Darley proposed a theory of *diffusion of responsibility* to account for why bystanders and onlookers did not help Kitty Genovese.

After formulating a theory, the next step for Latané and Darley was to devise a way of testing the theory. They began by stating a(n) **[c]** _____ , a prediction stated in a way that allows it to be tested. Latané and Darley's hypothesis was "The more people who witness an emergency situation, the less likely it is that help will be given to a victim." Formal theories and hypotheses allow psychologists to organize separate bits of information and to move beyond the facts and make deductions about phenomena not yet encountered.

Evaluate

_____ 1. scientific research

_____ 2. hypothesis

_____ 3. theories

a. A prediction of future behavior that is based on observations and theories.

b. Careful observation of a phenomenon, statement of theories, hypotheses about future behavior, and then a test of the hypotheses through research.

c. Broad explanations and predictions concerning phenomena of interest.

Rethink

4-1   Starting with the theory that diffusion of responsibility causes lack of responsibility for helping among bystanders, Latané and Darley derived the hypothesis that the more people who witness an emergency situation, the less likely it is that help will be given to the victim. How many other hypotheses can you think of based on the same theory of diffusion of responsibility?

4-2   *From a lawyer's perspective:* Imagine that you are assigned to a case similar to the one of Kitty Genovese. Your supervisor, who is unfamiliar with psychological research, asks you to provide information (e.g., characteristics) about the eyewitnesses to explain why they did not help her. What would you include in your report?

Spotlight on Terminology and Language—ESL Pointers

Page 32 "Mike Petre wasn't thrilled about getting punched by six **thugs** aboard a light-rail train."

A **thug** is a slang term for someone who robs or attacks someone else in order to steal from them.

Page 32 "But what really hurt was the fact that none of the other passengers **lifted a finger** to help him."

To **lift a finger** is to provide help for someone else. In this case, and in the Kitty Genovese case presented later in the chapter no one **lifted a finger** or provided any help.

Page 32 "Mike said the six were **harassing** two young women."

When some one is **harassing** someone else they are bothering or attacking the other person.

Page 32 "In fact, if only one **bystander** had been present, the chances of that person intervening might have been fairly high. It turns out that the fewer the witnesses to an assault, the better the victim's chances of getting help."

A **bystander** is someone who is present but not taking part in an event. He or she would be a spectator.

Page 33 "**Birds of a feather flock together**"...or "opposites attract"?

"Birds of a feather flock together" is statement often used to mean that people will choose to be around people like themselves.

Page 33 "Psychologists—as well as scientists in other disciplines—meet the challenge of **posing** appropriate questions and properly answering them by relying on the scientific method."

When we **pose** a question we are asking a question. Scientists pose, or ask questions to begin the scientific process.

Page 33 "As illustrated in Figure 1 it consists of three main steps: (1) identifying questions of interest, (2) formulating an explanation, and (3) carrying out research designed to lend support to or **refute** the explanation."

To **refute** is to be able to prove something is false. In the courtroom, evidence and proof are used to **refute** statements. Psychological research is often used to **refute** assumptions people believe are true.

Page 34 "Psychologists Bibb Latané and John Darley, responding to the failure of **bystanders** to intervene when Kitty Genovese was murdered in New York, developed what they called a theory of **diffusion** of responsibility (Latané and Darley, 1970)."

Diffusion means to spread out and to make more widespread. When there is a **diffusion** of responsibility among a group of people, it means that so many people are witness to an event that each feels a lesser responsibility to report the event or to act on it because they can tell themselves the next person will do this. Have you experienced the phenomenon of **diffusion** of responsibility on a crowded road following an accident?

Page 34 "Hypotheses stem from theories; they help test the underlying **validity** of theories."

When a hypothesis has **validity**, the way the hypothetical prediction has been stated makes this statement capable of measuring, predicting, or representing what it has been designed to measure.

Page 34 "These hypotheses can range from **trivialities** (such as why our English instructor wears those weird shirts) to more meaningful matters (such as what is the best way to study for a test)."

A **triviality** is something that's really not important, or an event that is insignificant. Sometimes we are tempted to focus on **trivia** instead of on the larger picture.

Page 34 "Perhaps we try comparing two strategies: **cramming** the night before an exam versus spreading out our study over several nights."

Cramming means to study intensively in a short period of time. Many students will **cram** and study all night on the night before an exam.

Page 35 "For one thing, theories and hypotheses allow them to make sense of unorganized, separate observations and bits of information by permitting them to place the pieces within a structured and **coherent** framework."

When you are told you are thinking **coherently**, your thinking has logical consistency and an order to it. As you learn the psychological theories, you have a structured and **coherent** framework for explaining behavior.

Page 35 "In this way, theories and hypotheses provide a **reasoned** guide to the direction that future investigation ought to take (Howitt & Cramer, 2000; Cohen, 2003)."

A **reasoned** guide is a logical, rational direction for your thinking.

Module 5: Conducting Psychological Research

Archival Research
Naturalistic Observation
Survey Research

Applying Psychology in the 21st Century:
Secret Bias: Using the Implicit Association

The Case Study
Correlational Research
Experimental Research

- *What research methods do psychologists use?*
- *How do psychologists establish cause-and-effect relationships in research studies?*

Conducting Psychological Research

Research is systematic inquiry aimed at the discovery of new knowledge. It is the means of actually testing hypotheses and theories. In order to research a hypothesis, the hypothesis must be stated in a manner that is testable. A(n) **[a]** _____ is the translation of a hypothesis into specific, testable procedures that can be observed and measured. If we examine scientific methods closely, we can then make more critically informed and reasoned judgments about everyday situations.

[b] _____ requires examining existing records and collecting data regarding the phenomena of interest to the researcher. Latané and Darley would have begun by examining newspaper clippings and other records to find examples of situations like those they were studying.

[c] _____ involves the researcher observing naturally occurring behavior without intervening in the situation. Unfortunately, the phenomena of interest may be infrequent. Furthermore, when people know they are being watched, they may act differently.

In **[d]** _____, participants are chosen from a larger population and asked a series of questions about behavior, thoughts, or attitudes. Techniques are sophisticated enough now that small samples can be drawn from large populations to make predictions about how the entire population will behave. The potential problems are that some people may not remember how they felt or acted at a particular time, or they may give answers they believe the researcher wants to hear. Also, survey questions can be formulated in such a way as to bias the response.

When the phenomena of interest is uncommon, or there is very little prior information on the topic, psychologists may use a(n) **[e]** _____, an in-depth examination of an individual or small group of people. Insight gained through a case study must be done carefully because the individuals studied may not be representative of a larger group.

[f] _____ examines the relationship between two factors and the degree to which they are associated, or "correlated." The correlation is measured by a mathematical score ranging from +1.0 to -1.0. A positive correlation says that when one factor *increases*, the other correlated factor also *increases*. A negative correlation says that as one factor *increases*, the other negatively correlated factor *decreases*. When little or no relationship exists between two factors, the correlation is close to 0. Correlation can show that two factors are related and that the presence of one predicts another, but it cannot prove that one causes the other. Correlation research cannot rule out alternative causes when examining the relationship between two factors.

Experiments must be conducted in order to establish cause-and-effect relationships. A formal **[g]** _____ examines the relationship of two or more factors in a setting that is deliberately manipulated to produce a change in one factor and then to observe how the change affects other factors. This **[h]** _____ allows psychologists to detect the relationship between these factors. These factors, called **[i]** _____, can be behaviors, events, or other characteristics that can change or vary in some way. The first step in developing an experiment is to operationalize a hypothesis (as did Latané and Darley). At least two groups of participants must be observed. One group receives the **[j]** _____, the manipulated variable, and is called the **[k]** _____. The other group is called the **[l]** _____ and is not exposed to the manipulated variable. Latané and Darley created a bogus emergency and then varied the number of bystanders present, in effect creating several different treatment groups. The variable that is manipulated is the **[m]** _____—the condition that distinguishes the treatment groups—and in this example it was the number of people present. The **[n]** _____ is the variable that is measured to reveal the effect of the manipulation. In this example, the dependent variable was how long it took the *participant* to offer help.

In order to be assured that some characteristics of the participant do not influence the outcome of an experiment, a procedure called **[o]** _____ must be used to assign participants to treatment or control groups. The objective of random assignment is to make each group comparable.

Latané and Darley utilized a trained *confederate*, who feigned an epileptic seizure, to create the bogus emergency. The results of their experiment suggested that the size of the audience did influence the time it took for participants to offer help. They had to analyze their results according to statistical procedures to prove that it was unlikely that their results were caused by chance. Also, to be certain of their results, other psychologists must try to repeat the experiment under the same or similar circumstances and test other variations of the hypothesis. This process is called **[p]** _____.

Evaluate

_____ 1. naturalistic observation

a. The group in an experiment that receives the independent variable.

_____ 2. survey research

b. A precise definition that allows other researchers to replicate an experiment.

_____ 3. independent variable

c. The study of behavior in its own setting, with no attempt to alter it.

_____ 4. operational definition

d. The variable manipulated by a researcher to determine its effects on the dependent variable.

_____ 5. experimental group

e. Assignment of experimental participants to two or more groups on the basis of chance.

_____ 6. random assignment

f. A research method that involves manipulating independent variables to determine how they affect dependent variables.

_____ 7. correlation coefficient

g. An in-depth study of a single person that can provide suggestions for future research.

_____ 8. experimental research

h. A number ranging from +1.00 to -1.00 that represents the degree and direction of the relationship between two variables.

_____ 9. case study

i. A research method that involves collecting information from a group of people who represent a larger group.

Rethink

5-1   Can you describe how a researcher might use naturalistic observation, case study methods, and survey research to investigate gender differences in aggressive behavior at the workplace? First state a hypothesis, then describe your research approaches. What positive and negative features does each method have?

5-2   *From a health care worker's perspective:* Tobacco companies have asserted that no experiment has ever proved that tobacco use causes cancer. Can you explain this claim in terms of the research procedures and designs discussed in this module? What sort of research would establish a cause-and-effect relationship between tobacco use and cancer? Is such a research study possible?

Spotlight on Terminology and Language—ESL Pointer

Page 68 "*Research*—systematic inquiry **aimed** at the discovery of new knowledge—is a central ingredient of the scientific method in psychology."

Aimed at means that the inquiry was intended or directed at the discovery of new knowledge.

Page 68 "First, though, the hypothesis must be **restated** in a way that will allow it to be tested, a procedure known as operationalization."

Restated is to say it again - to paraphrase your hypotheses so that you have translated this hypothesis into a testable procedure that can be measured and observed.

Page 69 "Even people who do not have degrees in psychology, for instance, often carry out **elementary** forms of research on their own."

Elementary forms of research would suggest that these are straightforward or uncomplicated plans for research.

Page 69 "Each of these situations **draws on** the research practices we are about to discuss."

Here the phrase **draws on** means that the situation depends on the research practices.

Page 69 "The media constantly **bombard** us with claims about research studies and findings."

When a person gets **bombarded**, he or she feels attacked or assaulted. Students often question their professors persistently with questions on interesting topics; they may be **bombarding** their professors with questions as they delve into learning and understanding the material.

Page 70 "One of the first places you might turn to would be **historical** accounts."

Historical suggests you are looking at what has happened in the past- you are examining **historical** references.

Page 70 "By searching newspaper records, for example, you might find support for the **notion** that a decrease in helping behavior historically has accompanied an increase in the number of bystanders."

A **notion** is an idea or belief. Archival research can provide support for the idea that helping behavior decreases with the increase in the number of bystanders.

Page 70 "Of course, the use of existing data has several **drawbacks**."

Drawbacks are problems or weaknesses. When we have a **drawback** with the research we are conducting, it may mean that our very presence or behavior or questions are influencing the responses we are recording.

Page 70 "The information could be incomplete, or it could have been collected **haphazardly** (Simonton, 2000; Riniolo, Koledin, Drakulic, & Payne, 2003)."

Something that is **haphazard** occurs by chance. Data that is collected **haphazardly** is collected randomly rather then scientifically.

Page 71 "Most attempts at archival research are **hampered** by the simple fact that records with the necessary information often do not exist."

When something is **hampered**, it is held back, it is in an inferior position. Some college students enter college **hampered** and in a weak academic position because they have not yet developed strong study skills.

Page 71 "Furthermore, if people know they are being watched, they may alter their reactions, producing behavior that is not truly **representative**."

When something is **representative** it is a typical example of something.

Page 72 "There is no more **straightforward** way of finding out what people think, feel, and do than asking them directly."

When things are **straightforward** they are
Not complicated and easy to understand. Since surveys ask people questions they are the easiest (or the most **straightforward**) way to find out what a person is thinking.

Page 72 "In **survey research**, a *sample* of people chosen to represent a larger group of interest (a *population*) are asked a series of questions about their behavior, thoughts, or attitudes."

A *sample* is a small amount of something that is used as an example.

Page 72 "Survey methods have become so sophisticated that even with a very small sample researchers are able to **infer** with great accuracy how a larger group would respond."

When we **infer** a conclusion following the use of survey methods, we are using the survey research tool and drawing a conclusion from the information gathered.

Page 72 "Researchers investigating helping behavior might **conduct** a survey by asking people to complete a questionnaire in which they indicate their reasons for not wanting to come forward to help another individual."

To **conduct** something is to do something. When researchers **conduct** a survey they are doing the survey.

Page 72 "However, survey research has several potential **pitfalls.**"

Pitfalls are unexpected difficulties or problems.

Page 73 "To overcome participants' **reluctance** to be truthful, researchers are developing alternative, and often ingenious, research techniques, as we consider in the *Applying Psychology in the 21st Century* box."

When a person is **reluctant** to do something they are unwilling to do what was asked.

Page 74 "Her office decor **attested** to her passion for civil rights -- as a senior activist at a national gay rights organization, and as a lesbian herself, fighting bias and discrimination is what gets her out of bed every morning."

When we **attest** to something we are showing that something is true or valid.

Page 74 "The woman's index fingers **hovered** over her keyboard."

When the fingers **hovered** over the keyboard they floated in the air just above the keyboard.

Page 75 "Could you, like this woman, be **prejudiced** and not even know it?"

A **prejudice** occurs when someone holds negative, or unfavorable, opinions about someone or something that do not come from truthful information.

Page 75 "However, even though they may truly believe that they are unprejudiced, the reality is that they actually **routinely** differentiate between people on the basis of race, ethnicity, and sexual orientation."

Routine events are usual or typical. Research suggests that people typically or **routinely** differentiate between people based on race or ethnicity.

Page 75 "Direct questions such as, "Would you prefer interacting with a member of Group X rather than Group Y?" typically identify only the most **blatant** prejudices, because people try to censor their responses."

Blatant prejudices are those that are so obvious that they can not be hidden.

Page 76 "The results of the IAT show that almost 90 percent of test-takers have a pro-white **implicit bias**, and more than two-thirds of non-Arab, non-Muslim volunteers display implicit biases against Arab Muslims."

An **implicit bias** is a preference that is unspoken or hidden. Thus the IAT, or Implicit Association Test, is measuring unspoken or hidden preferences.

Page 76 "Of course, having an implicit bias does not mean that people will **overtly** discriminate, a criticism that has been made of the test."

When things are **overt** they are done openly. When prejudices are acted on overtly or openly, the act is called discrimination.

Page 77 "Case studies often include psychological testing, a procedure in which a carefully designed set of questions is used to gain some **insight** into the personality of the individual or group (Breakwell, Hammond, & Fife-Schaw, 2000; Gass et al., 2000)."

Insight involves the act of seeing into a situation, apprehending things intuitively.

Page 77 "Similarly, case studies of the Washington, D.C. area snipers who killed more than a dozen people in the early 2000s might help identify others who are **prone** to violence."

Prone means having a tendency toward; being likely to do something such as being **prone** toward domestic violence. Some drivers that claim they suffer from road rage say they are **prone** to violence.

Page 79 "When two variables are strongly correlated with each other, it is **tempting** to assume that one variable causes the other."

When we are **tempted** to do something we have a strong desire to do it. In the case of correlations, it is **tempting**, or desirous to assume that one variable causes the other.

Page 80 "Another example illustrates the critical point that correlations tell us nothing about cause and effect but **merely** provide a measure of the strength of a relationship between two variables."

Mere means by itself and without anything more. Correlations only provide a measure of the strength of a relationship between two variables.

Page 80 "We might find that children who watch a lot of television programs featuring high levels of aggression are likely to demonstrate a relatively high degree of aggressive behavior and that those who watch few television shows that **portray** aggression are **apt to** exhibit a relatively low degree of such behavior (see Figure 1).

To **portray** is to show. **Apt to** means "likely to". In this sentence the author is saying that the research shows that children who watch television shows with higher amounts of violence are **apt to**, or likely to show more aggression then children who watch television shows with low amounts of violence.

Page 80 "Clearly, then, any number of causal sequences are possible—none of which can be **ruled out** by correlational research.

To be **ruled out** is to exclude or to fail to include something. Correlational research cannot rule out, exclude any of the possible casual explanations for the relationship between variables.

Page 81 "Their first step was to formulate an operational definition of the hypothesis by **conceptualizing** it in a way that could be tested."

When we conceptualize we imagine or picture possibilities. Researchers create operational definitions of the hypothesis by imagining or **conceptualizing** the variables in a way that can be measured and tested.

Page 82 "To test her claim, she gives the medicine one day to a group of twenty people who have colds, and finds that ten days later all of them are cured. **Eureka**?"

Eureka is a term that is used to express pleasure or delight about the solving of a problem.

Page 82 "An observer viewing this **flawed** study might reasonably argue that the people would have gotten better even without the medicine."

Something **flawed** is imperfect or defective. If the way a research study is conducted is **flawed**, our interpretations of the research results will also be seriously **flawed.**

Page 83 "Through the use of control groups, then, researchers can **isolate** specific causes for their findings – and draw cause-and-effect inferences."

Through the use of control groups, researchers can find a cause of something. They are **isolating**, thereby identifying, which of a number of possible causes or factors is responsible for a particular phenomenon.

Page 83 "As their experimental manipulation, they decided to **vary** the number of bystanders present."

When the experimenters **varied** the number of bystanders in the research study they changed, or made different the number of people who were nearby.

Page 83 "Instead, they **settled** on a more complex procedure involving the creation of groups of three sizes—consisting of two, three, and six people—that could be compared with one another."

The researchers **settled** on, or decided that they needed to create three different size groups to test their hypothesis,

Page 84 "If they had done this, however, any differences they found in helping behavior could not be **attributed** with any certainty solely to group size, because the differences might just as well have been due to the composition of the group."

When we **attribute** a research outcome to a feature or aspect of a research study we give credit to that feature as causing the result.

Page 85 "Participants in each of the experimental groups **ought to** be comparable, and it is easy enough to create groups that are similar in terms of gender."

The term **ought to** indicates something we should do. In this research case the experimental groups should, or **ought to** be similar.

Page 85 "The problem becomes a bit more **tricky**, though, when we consider other participant characteristics."

When something is **tricky** it is problematic or difficult to deal with. Latané & Darley's research became tricky, or difficult to deal with when they started to take the subjects characteristics into account.

Page 85 "The experimenter might, for instance, **flip a coin** for each participant and assign a participant to one group when "heads" came up, and to the other group when "tails" came up."

The term **"flip a coin"** is used to mean to make a random choice.

Page 86 "To test their hypothesis that increasing the number of bystanders in an emergency situation would lower the **degree** of helping behavior, Latané and Darley placed the participants in a room and told them that the purpose of the experiment was to talk about personal problems associated with college."

The **degree** of something is the level or amount of the feature. Latané and Darley were testing whether or not the number of bystanders would change the amount or **degree** of helping behavior.

Page 87 "Each group included a trained *confederate*, or employee, of the experimenters. In each two-person group, then, there was only one real "bystander."

In research studies the term *confederate* is used to refer to a person who is knowingly helps the experimenter mislead the real subject.

Page 87 "As the participants in each group were holding their discussion, they suddenly heard through the intercom one of the other participants—the confederate having what sounded like an **epileptic seizure** and calling for help."

An **epileptic seizure** is a sudden attack of abnormal brain changes and possible loss of awareness often accompanied by a violent shaking of the body.

Page 87 "The dependent variable was the time that **elapsed** from the start of the "seizure" to the time a participant began trying to help the "victim.""

When time **elapses** it passes or goes by.

Page 88 "Of course, one experiment alone does not forever **resolve** the question of bystander intervention in emergencies.
When someone **resolves** something they make a decision. In the case of research however, one study does not resolve, or allow us to come to a firm decision about what factors influence the tendency for bystanders to intervene or help.

Page 89 "This three-step process **embodied** in the scientific method underlies all scientific inquiry, allowing us to develop a valid understanding of others'—and our own—behavior."

The three-step process that **embodies,** or makes up the scientific method is the basic aspects of all scientific thinking.

Module 6:
Critical Research Issues

The Ethics of Research

Exploring Diversity: Choosing Participants Who Represent the Scope of Human Behavior

Should Animals Be Used in Research?
Threats to Experiment Validity: Experimenter and Participant Expectations

Becoming an Informed Consumer of Psychology: Thinking Critically About Research

- *What major issues confront psychologists conducting research?*

Critical Research Issues

There are issues other than the quality of research that are of concern to psychologists. The ethics of certain research practices come into question when there exists a possibility of harm to a participant. Guidelines have been developed for the treatment of human and animal participants, and most proposed research is now reviewed by a panel to assure that guidelines are being met.

The concept of **[a]** _____ has become a key ethical principle. Before participating in an experiment, participants must sign a form indicating that they have been told of the basic outlines of the study and what their participation will involve. Following their participation, they must be given a(n) **[b]** _____ in which they are given an explanation for the study. For proper and meaningful generalizations of research results, a selection of participants that reflects the diversity of human behavior is necessary. Also, ethical guidelines call for assurance from researchers that they will make every effort to minimize discomfort, illness, and pain when animals are used in experiments.

Researchers must all address the issue of **[c]** _____, the factors that distort the experimenter's understanding of the relationship between the independent and dependent variables. **[d]** _____ *expectations* occur when the experimenter unintentionally conveys cues about how the participants should behave in the experiment.

[e] _____ *expectations* are the participant's expectations about the intended goal of the experiment. The participant's guesses about the hypothesis can influence behavior and thus the outcomes. One approach is to disguise the true purpose of the experiment. Another is to use a(n) **[f]** _____ with the control group so that the participants remain unaware of whether they are being exposed to the experimental condition. The *double-blind procedure* guards against these two biases by informing neither the experimenter nor the participant about which treatment group the participant is in.

Another major concern of psychologists who conduct research is aiming to obtain a sample of participants who are **[g]** _____ of the general population.

Evaluate

_____ 1. bias

_____ 2. placebo

_____ 3. informed consent

_____ 4. representative sample

a. A written agreement by the researcher in an experiment that is signed by the subject after receiving information about the researcher's specific procedures.

b. A sample that is selected to reflect the characteristics of a population the research is interested in studying.

c. Beliefs that interfere with a researcher's objectivity.

d. In drug research, the positive effects associated with a person's beliefs about a drug even when it contains no active ingredients.

Rethink

6-1   A researcher believes that college professors in general show female students less attention and respect in the classroom than male students. She sets up an experimental study involving the observation of classrooms in different conditions. In explaining the study to the professors and students who will participate, what steps should the researcher take to eliminate experimental bias based on both experimenter expectations and participant expectations?

6-2   Imagine that you pick up the newspaper and read an article about a new drug that claims to significantly prolong the life of terminally ill cancer patients. The article states: "Our study shows that patients who took the drug once a day lived longer than patients who did not take the drug." Based on the knowledge you learned in this module, are the results of the study valid? Why or why not?

6-3   *From a research analyst's perspective:* You are hired to study people's attitudes toward welfare programs by developing and circulating a questionnaire via the Internet. Is this study likely to accurately reflect the views of the general population? Why or why not?

Spotlight on Terminology and Language—ESL Pointers

Page 98 "We turn to the most fundamental of these issues; **ethics**."

Ethics are a basic and necessary component of psychological research, relating to and affecting the integrity of the research work.

Page 99 "How would you feel when you learned that the supposed victim was in reality a paid **accomplice**?"

An **accomplice** is somebody who is part of the plot or conspiracy. They knowingly help someone to commit an act considered morally wrong, or an undesirable act or an activity that involves breaking the law. Can you identify any recent news cases in which the **accomplice** has been named?

Page 99 "Although you might at first experience relief that there had been no real emergency, you might also feel some resentment that you had been **deceived** by the experimenter."

When you have been **deceived**, you are intentionally being misled. Can you suggest why **deception** – or the practice of deliberately making a research subject believe things that are not true - might be important in conducting some psychological research?

Page 99 "You might also experience concern that you had been placed in an embarrassing or **compromising** situation – one that might have **dealt a blow** to your self-esteem, depending on how you had behaved."

A **compromising** situation is a situation where it is likely you will be exposed to disgrace or humiliation.

When someone or something is **dealt a blow** they are undermined or weakened. When someone's self-esteem is **dealt a blow** their confidence in themselves is hurt or weakened.

Page 99 "Nonetheless, because research has the potential to violate the rights of participants, psychologists are expected to **adhere** to a **strict** set of ethical guidelines aimed at protecting participants (American Psychological Association, 2002)."

To **adhere** to something is to obey it or stick firmly to it. Strict guidelines are rigorous and precise. Psychologists adhere, or obey a **strict** or rigorous and precise set of ethical guidelines.

Page 99 "As **Interactivity 6-1** illustrates, those guidelines involve the following **safeguards**:"

Safeguards are protective measures that are intended to prevent undesirable outcomes from occurring.

Page 100 "Furthermore, after participation in a study, they must be given a **debriefing** in which they receive an explanation of the study and the procedures involved."

When subjects in a scientific research study are **debriefed** they take part in an interview in which they are informed about the purpose of the study and it procedure.

Page 100 "In fact, college students are used so frequently in experiments that psychology has been called - somewhat **contemptuously** – the "science of the behavior of the college sophomore" (Rubenstein, 1982)."

When you do something with **contempt**, you are suggesting that you have no respect or regard for it. **Contempt** here refers to disrespect for the research results conducted with the college sophomore research population. Persons **contemptuously** point out that the college student population is a very contained and limited grouping that is easy to involve in the research conducted at educational institutions.

Page 101 "Compared with older adults, their attitudes are likely to be less well formed, and they are more apt to be influenced by **authority figures** and **peers** (Sears, 1986)."

An **authority figure** is someone who holds power over another person. A **peer** is a person who is equal in standing with respect to age or social class.
Page 101 "College students are also **disproportionately** white and middle class."

When things are **disproportionate** they are unequal or out of proportion. Using college students for psychological research is a problem because the number of college students that are white and middle class is not the same or equal to that of the general population.

Page 101 "Because psychology is a science that **purports** to explain human behavior in general, something is therefore **amiss**."

To **purport** something is to claim something. Psychology claims to explain human behavior.

When something is **amiss**, there is a problem with it. In the case of scientific explanations for human behavior, something is faulty or **amiss** when a significant proportion of the population is not included in the sample population used to draw conclusions. This problem may produce research results that are not useful.

Page 102 "Not only must researchers **strive** to avoid causing physical discomfort, but they are also required to promote the *psychological* well-being of some species of research animals, such as primates (Novak & Petto, 1991; APA, 1993)."

To **strive** for something is to try hard to achieve it. Psychologists try hard to avoid causing harm or discomfort to their subjects, they **strive** to do so.

Page 102 "Research using animals has provided psychologists with information that has **profoundly** benefited humans."

Animal research has helped psychologists to penetrate and understand problems. The resulting valuable knowledge and insight has had a **profound** and significant impact on human lives and lifestyles. Do you think animal research involving cloning will have a **profound** effect on the societal perception of family?

Page 102 "For instance, it **furnished the keys** to detecting eye disorders in children early enough to prevent permanent damage, to communicating more effectively with severely retarded children, and to reducing chronic pain in people, to name just a few results (APA, 1988; Botting & Morrison, 1997)."
When research **furnishes the key** to something is said to provide the important information to solving the

problem.

Page 103 "For example, some critics believe that animals have rights no less significant than those of humans, and that the use of animals in studies is **unethical** because they are unable to give their consent."

Something is **unethical** when it conflicts with agreed standards of moral conduct.

Page 103 "Even the best-laid experimental plans are **susceptible** to experimental **bias** – factors that distort the way the independent variable affects the dependent variable in an experiment."

When something is **susceptible**, it has the capacity for being acted upon and impressed. Some young adults are very **susceptible** to the behavior of the leaders in their group.

Bias is a prejudice. When you have a **bias** you have a tendency or an inclination toward something. Have you ever found yourself having expectations for the difficulty of a class based on a professor's dress or lecturing style? Is so, you are exhibiting a **bias** as you have made prejudgments.

Page 104 "To guard against participant expectations biasing the results of an experiment, the experimenter may try to **disguise** the true purpose of the experiment."

When the experimenter **disguises** the purpose of the experiment they hide the purpose of it from the subject.

Page 104 "Suppose you were interested in testing the ability of a new drug to **alleviate** the symptoms of severe depression."

New drugs can make pain or depression more bearable, they **alleviate** the pain.

Page 104 "Because members of both groups are **kept in the dark** about whether they are getting a real or a false treatment, any differences in outcome can be attributed to the quality of the drug and not to the possible psychological effects of being administered a pill or other substance (Kirsch, 1999; Enserink, 1999, 2000a; Kim & Holloway, 2003)."

When someone is **kept in the dark** the details of the study are hidden from them. Researchers keep their subjects in the dark as to what group they are assigned so that they can make the needed comparisons.

Page 105 "By keeping both the participant and the experimenter who interacts with the participant **"blind"** to the nature of the drug that is being administered, researchers can more accurately assess the effects of the drug."

When participants in psychological research studies are **"blind"** they are unaware of the type of treatment they are receiving.

Page 105 "Instead, you would probably **mull** over the purchase, read about automobiles, consider the alternatives, talk to others about their experiences, and ultimately put in a fair amount of thought before you made such a major purchase."

To **mull** is to engage in a period of careful thought.

Page 105 "In contrast, many of us are considerably less **conscientious** when we expend our intellectual, rather than financial, assets."

Conscientious thought is thorough and persistent thought. Unfortunately people are often not **conscientious** when they think about most issues**.**

Page 105 "People often **jump to conclusions** on the basis of incomplete and inaccurate information, and only rarely do they take the time to **critically** evaluate the research and data to which they are exposed."

When people **jump to conclusions** they make a quick decision and do not think about the issues in much detail.

Critically does not need to mean to criticize or to see unfavorably. When you think **critically** about research, you are able to weigh all of the factors involved and use careful judgment and judicious evaluation skills.

Page 105 "Because the field of psychology is based on an **accumulated** body of research, it is crucial for psychologists to **scrutinize** thoroughly the methods, results, and claims of researchers."

When you have **accumulated** a body of research, you have a mass of research, a high quantity of research. **Accumulate** suggests an increasing quantity, which is why the research must be **scrutinized**, or examined closely. To **scrutinize** is to inspect and to evaluate.

Page 105 "Knowing how to approach research and data can be helpful in areas far **beyond the realm** of psychology."

Understanding research and data can be helpful **beyond the realm,** or outside the subject of psychology.

Page 106 "For instance, when the manufacturer of car X **boasts** that "no other car has a better safety record than car X," this does not mean that car X is safer than every other car."

When people **boast** about something they are speaking with excessive pride about something.

Page 106 "Expressed in the latter fashion, the finding doesn't seem worth **bragging** about."

When people **are bragging** about something they are boasting , or speaking with excessive pride about something.

Test your knowledge of the material presented in the modules by answering these questions. These questions have been placed in three Practice Tests. The first two tests consist of questions that will test your recall of factual knowledge. The third test contains questions that are challenging and primarily test for conceptual knowledge and your ability to apply that knowledge. Check your answers and review the feedback using the Answer Key that follows the tests.

PRACTICE TEST 1:

1. In the example of Kitty Genovese, how many bystanders probably heard her call for help?
   a. 38
   b. 2
   c. 1
   d. 107

2. One of the steps in _____ is formulating an explanation.
   a. naturalistic explanation
   b. experimenter bias
   c. an ethics review panel
   d. the scientific method

3. Theories tend to be _____, whereas hypotheses are _____.
   a. general statements; specific statements
   b. specific statements; general statements
   c. provable; impossible to disprove
   d. factual; based on speculation

4. Scientific research begins with:
   a. formulating an explanation.
   b. beginning the data-collection exercise.
   c. identifying a research question.
   d. confirming or disconfirming a hypothesis.

5. An operational definition requires that:
   a. data always be useful.
   b. procedures are followed exactly.
   c. variables are correctly manipulated.
   d. predictions be made testable.

6. When researchers obtain information by using the survey method, results are most likely to be inaccurate when:
   a. nearly everyone surveyed is willing to give a response.
   b. people are asked about socially sensitive subjects.
   c. questions about attitudes are included.
   d. only a few thousand people are surveyed to predict what millions think.

7. Researchers sometimes have the opportunity to conduct an in-depth interview of an individual in order to understand that individual better and to infer about people in general. This research method is called a:
   a. focused study.
   b. generalization study.
   c. case study.
   d. projection study.

8. Dr. Bianchi listed the strength of a relationship between length of time children spent in day care and the child's vocabulary level at age four by a mathematical score of +.87. This score means we are dealing with a:
   a. dependent variable.
   c. correlation.

b. manipulation.   d. treatment.

9. Although it is usually more expensive and time consuming, researchers like to do experiments whenever feasible because experiments:
    a. impress the public that psychology is really scientific.
    b. identify causal relationships.
    c. permit the application of statistical analyses to the data.
    d. are required in order for the study to get government funding.

10. Maura was part of an experiment and assigned to a group in a weight loss program that received no treatment. This program had several other groups that did receive treatment. Maura was:
    a. in a control group.   c. an independent variable.
    b. in a case study.   d. a measured variable.

11. In an experiment, the event that is measured and expected to change is the:
    a. dependent variable.   c. control variable.
    b. independent variable.   d. confounding variable.

12. The document signed by the participant in an experiment that affirms that the participant knows generally what is to happen is called:
    a. "in loco parentis."   c. informed consent.
    b. participant expectations.   d. experimenter expectation

13. A participant's interpretation of what behaviors or responses are expected in an experiment is called:
    a. the placebo effect.   c. participant expectations.
    b. experimenter expectations.   d. treatment condition.

14. Ingrid was part of an experimental drug research program and was given a pill without any significant chemical properties. The pill used in this experiment was called:
    a. a control.   c. a dependent variable.
    b. a placebo.   d. an independent variable.

15. When the results of a study cannot be replicated, then:
    a. the claimed effect is regarded with skepticism.
    b. cheating by the experimenter should be presumed.
    c. psychics have probably worked mischievously against the research.
    d. the data have probably been analyzed incorrectly.

_____ 16. scientific method

_____ 17. theories

_____ 18. hypothesis

_____ 19. research

_____ 20. operational definition

a. Systematic inquiry aimed at discovering new knowledge.

b. The assignment of participants to given groups on a chance basis alone.

c. A prediction stated in a way that allows it to be tested.

d. The process of translating a hypothesis into specific testable procedures that can be measured and observed.

e. The process of appropriately framing and properly answering questions, used by scientists to come to an understanding about the world.

f. Broad explanations and predictions concerning phenomena of interest.

21. Professor Gilbert stressed the importance of assigning participants to given groups based on a chance basis alone. This is referred to as _____.

22. The systematic inquiry aimed at discovering new knowledge is _____.

23. A(n) _____ is a prediction stated in such a way that allows it to be tested.

24. The process of appropriately framing and properly answering questions, used by scientists to come to an understanding about the world, is called _____.

25. _____ are defined as broad explanations and predictions concerning phenomena of interest.

26. Eating breakfast will increase the scores on a math test. Design an experiment to test the statement. Remember, your design must include a testable hypothesis, independent and dependent variables, and a method of establishing control. What problems will your research encounter?

PRACTICE TEST 2:

1. Identifying questions of interest is one of the steps of:
   a. survey research.
   b. case study methods.
   c. the scientific method.
   d. experimental design.

2. Conducting research designed to support or refute an explanation of a phenomenon is a main step in:
   a. the scientific method.
   b. developing theories.
   c. naturalistic observation.
   d. analysis of a significant outcome.

3. A hypothesis is:
   a. a broad explanation of phenomena of interest.
   b. the step of identifying phenomena of interest.
   c. observation that occurs without intervention by the observer.

d.   a prediction stated in such a way that it can be tested.

4.   Hypotheses are to predictions as:
      a.   explanations are to theories.   c.   explanations are to operational definitions.
      b.   theories are to explanations.   d.   operational definitions are to explanations.

5.   If you decide that love is measured by the amount of touching that a couple engages in, then you
      have _____ love.
      a.   archived   c.   theorized
      b.   operationalized   d.   correlationalized

6.   While shopping at the mall, Maria and her friends are often stopped by what they call "clipboard
      stalkers," who are questioning large numbers of shoppers to gather information concerning their
      views on a variety of different products and services. This method of gathering information is
      called
      a.   case study research.   c.   experimental research.
      b.   survey research.   d.   archival research.

7.   Dr. Radigan, a psychology professor, joined the circus and got a position working with the
      elephants in order to study the treatment of animals in the circus. Which research method is being
      applied?
      a.   Archival research   c.   Naturalistic observation
      b.   Correlational research   d.   Experimentation

8.   Which of the following statements is **not** true?
      a.   A correlation of 1.0 means that a strong positive relationship exists between two factors.
      b.   A correlation of 0.0 means that no systematic relationship exists between two factors.
      c.   Correlations describe a relationship between two factors.
      d.   Correlations tell us that one factor is caused by another.

9.   A variable is:
      a.   the experimental group receiving no treatment.
      b.   the experimental group receiving treatment.
      c.   a behavior or event that can be changed.
      d.   a participant in research.

10.   Omar's task was to establish groups for the smoking cessation study. In order for proper assignment
      of participants to be made to the conditions in the experiment, the assignments had to be determined
      by:
      a.   someone who does not know the participants.
      b.   chance.
      c.   someone who does know the participants.
      d.   factors relevant to the experiment.

11.   The variable that is manipulated by the experimenter is called the:
      a.   dependent variable.   c.   control variable.
      b.   independent variable.   d.   confounding variable.

12.   Whether a behavioral scientist uses human or animal participants in an experiment, the scientist
      must satisfy _____ in order not to violate the rights of the participants.

a. moral obligations   c. professional standards
b. religious principles   d. ethical guidelines

13. Deception—disguising the true nature of a study—is sometimes used in experiments in order to:
    a. eliminate participant expectations.   c. eliminate experimenter expectations.
    b. confuse the participant.   d. confuse the experimenter.

14. Neither the doctor nor the participants in the flu shot study are told which of the syringes have the real vaccine and which have only saline solution in order to:
    a. keep the confederate from influencing other participants.
    b. eliminate dependent variables.
    c. control the placebo effect.
    d. eliminate participant and experimenter expectations.

15. When a researcher reports that a study's outcome was statistically significant, this suggests that:
    a. efforts to replicate the results will succeed.
    b. a theory has been proven true.
    c. the results will have a noticeable social impact.
    d. the results were unlikely to have happened by chance.

_____ 16. experimental manipulation   a. The variable that is manipulated in an experiment.

_____ 17. experimental group   b. The experimental group receiving the treatment or manipulation.

_____ 18. control group

    c. The manipulation implemented by the experimenter to influence results in a segment of the experimental population.

_____ 19. independent variable

_____ 20. dependent variable

    d. The variable that is measured and is expected to change as a result of experimenter manipulation.

    e. The experimental group receiving no treatment.

21. A study carried out to investigate the relationship between two or more factors by deliberately producing a change in one factor and observing the effect that the change has on other factors is called _____ research.

22. Spending hundreds of hours interviewing and investigating the life of the notorious Charles Manson in order to understand him better and to infer criminal behavior in general is called a(n) _____.

23. _____ research is the examination of existing records information about a naturally occurring situation and does not intervene in the situation.

24. A behavior or an event that can be manipulated in an experiment is referred to as a(n) _____.

25. A(n) _____ is the change deliberately produced in an experiment to affect responses of behaviors in other factors to determine causal relationships between variables.

26. Imagine yourself in the Latané and Darley experiment as one of the participants who delays responding because of the diffusion of responsibility (you thought there were others around to help). After the experiment, you discover that your behavior has been deceptively manipulated and that the epileptic seizure was staged. What are your reactions to this deception? What are the ethical constraints on the researchers? Can you suggest alternatives to this kind of research? Is it justified?

PRACTICE TEST 3: Conceptual, Applied, and Challenging Questions

1. Which of the following would provide the **least** useful operational definition of the emotion "love"?
   a. The self-reports of children who consider themselves in love
   b. The change in heart rate when two people are together
   c. The number of letters written by lovers to each other
   d. The length of time a couple has been together

2. The method of sampling the attitudes of a small group of persons to use the information to predict those of the general population is called:
   a. situational research.   c. survey research.
   b. archival research.   d. experimentation.

3. Ashid used data he had collected on the previous incidence of cancer in the New York state community surrounding the Love Canal to see if there were patterns in the frequency of occurrence. This method of research is called:
   a. delayed naturalistic observation.   c. a survey.
   b. a case study.   d. archival.

4. In-depth examinations of the psychological aspects of the personalities of Ted Bundy and patterns of serial killers uses a method of research that relies on the use of:
   a. case studies.   c. dependent variables.
   b. correlational data.   d. naturalistic observation.

5. A prospective executive may undergo intensive interviews and extensive psychological testing. The executive may also have to provide references from previous and current occupational and personal sources. This process is most similar to:
   a. a survey.   c. naturalistic observation.
   b. an experimental study.   d. a case study.

6. A researcher finds a positive correlation between the amount of alcohol that pregnant women report drinking and the birth weight of their babies. This correlational finding means:
   a. drinking alcohol can cause lower birth weights.
   b. moms who drink less give birth to babies who have higher birth weights.
   c. drinking alcohol and birth weight are somewhat related, so one can be roughly predicted from the other.
   d. drinking alcohol gives babies a disadvantage over the babies whose moms don't drink.

7. Dr. Slocum has been studying the effects of music on the ability to soothe infants. Each experiment varies the conditions slightly, but usually only one factor is altered each time. Dr. Slocum is most likely trying to:
    a. develop a new statistical test.
    b. operationalize her hypothesis.
    c. formulate a new hypothesis.
    d. test the limits of her theory.

8. Research volunteers must be told in advance about any important details of a research project that might influence whether they want to serve. This is called the principle of:
    a. subject protection.
    b. behavioral privacy.
    c. informed consent.
    d. prevention of deception.

9. A graduate class in the School of Public Health has analyzed the death rates reported in several studies of SARS. They have compared the statistical results from each study and have been able to create a summary analysis. To complete their analysis, they most likely used:
    a. significant outcomes.
    b. meta-analysis.
    c. correlational research.
    d. experimental techniques.

10. Professor Krishniah uses a different tone of voice while speaking to groups of subjects in a problem-solving study: She speaks encouragingly to students in a class for the gifted and with a discouraging voice to a remedial class. This shows the experimental bias of:
    a. experimenter expectations.
    b. the double-blind procedure.
    c. randomization.
    d. the placebo effect.

11. Dr. Kent, a leading researcher in the area of voter behavior, is convinced that his theory claiming that voters are more easily influenced by negative campaign messages is correct. Which of the following would be his first step in demonstrating the theory to be correct?
    a. Dr. Kent must find ways to measure the negativity of messages and voter behavior.
    b. Dr. Kent must define the correlation coefficients.
    c. Dr. Kent must collect data about voters and campaigns.
    d. Dr. Kent must select the appropriate statistical analyses to utilize.

12. Which of the following statements requires the least modification in order to produce testable predictions?
    a. Decreases in physical exercise are associated with higher rates of heart-related diseases.
    b. Intelligence declines dramatically as people age.
    c. Disgruntled employees are likely to steal from their employers.
    d. Smiling can make you feel happy.

13. In an experiment, participants are placed in one of several rooms, each with a different color scheme. In each setting, the participants are given a problem-solving task that has been shown to be challenging and often results in increased tension while the problem solver attempts to solve the problem. Researchers have hypothesized that some colors may reduce stress and improve problem solving. In this study, the color schemes of the rooms would be considered:
    a. irrelevant.
    b. the independent variable.
    c. the dependent variable.
    d. the confounding variable.

14. In the previous study (number 13), the levels of stress experienced by the participants would be considered:
    a. a combination of the problem and the color schemes.
    b. the confounding variable.
    c. the independent variable.
    d. irrelevant.

15. In the previous study (number 13), the time required for each participant to solve the problem could be used as:
    a. the control condition.
    b. the independent variable.
    c. the dependent variable.
    d. the confounding variable.

_____ 16. archival research

_____ 17. naturalistic observation

_____ 18. survey research

_____ 19. case study

_____ 20. correlational research

a. Observation without intervention, in which the investigator records information about a naturally occurring situation and does not intervene in the situation.

b. The examination of existing records for the purpose of confirming a hypothesis.

c. An in-depth interview of an individual in order to understand that individual better and to make inferences about people in general.

d. Research to determine whether a relationship exists between two sets of factors, such as certain behaviors and responses.

e. Sampling a group of people by assessing their behavior, thoughts, or attitudes, then generalizing the findings to a larger population.

21. After participating in the university weight loss study, study participants are invited to receive a(n) _____, where they will receive an explanation of the study and the part they played in it.

22. When scientists use animals in research, they must strive to avoid physical discomfort to the animals and to promote their _____ well-being.

23. Occasionally, researchers argue that the use of _____ is sometimes necessary to prevent participants from being influenced by what they think the true purpose of the study might be.

24. A researcher will _____ a scientific study in order to increase confidence in the validity of the findings.

25. In the following experiment, identify (1) hypotheses, (2) the independent and dependent variables, (3) their operational definitions, and (4) experimental and control conditions.

A study was conducted on the effects of eating before a math exam and math exam performance. Experimental subjects were fed breakfast before the math exam. Subjects in the control group abstained from eating but still took the same exam. After the exam grades were recorded, calculations were done to see if there was a significant difference in the breakfast-eater group and the nonbreakfast group's math performance.

■ ANSWER KEY: MODULES 4, 5, AND 6

Module 4:	Module 5:	Evaluate	Module 6:
[a] scientific method	[a] operational definition	1. c	[a] informed consent
[b] Theories	[b] Archival research	2. i	[b] debriefing
[c] hypothesis	[c] Naturalistic observation	3. d	[c] experimental bias
	[d] survey research	4. b	[d] Experimenter
Evaluate	[e] case study	5. a	[e] Participant
1. b	[f] Correlational research	6. e	[f] placebo
2. a	[g] experiment	7. h	[g] fully representative
3. c	[h] experimental manipulation	8. f	
	[i] variables	9. g	Evaluate
	[j] treatment		1. c
	[k] experimental group		2. d
	[l] control group		3. a
	[m] independent variable		4. b
	[n] dependent variable		
	[o] random assignment to condition		
	[p] replication		

Selected Rethink Answers

4-1 Define the theory of diffusion of responsibility. Think about other explanations for why the people did not give assistance (e.g., people only help people like themselves, or older people are afraid of younger people).

5-1 State an operational definition for what you would consider aggression in the workplace. In naturalistic observation, researchers could get jobs at the workplace being studied in order to experience, or not, the aggression. In a case study, a thorough and detailed history of the situation could be taken from a selected few who had experienced this behavior. Design a survey to gather information from a wide group of people. List the positive and negative features of each approach. Which would you select and why?

6-3 The general population does not use the Internet; only a select portion of citizens fall into this survey group. Information gathered here would have to be presented as "People who use the Internet and filled out an attitude survey on welfare" had the following views on the topic. Your sample must reflect characteristics of the population being studied.

Practice Test 1:

1. a   mod. 4   p. 32
*a. Correct. Right! And of all these people, not one called the police.
b. Incorrect. Wrong number.
c. Incorrect. Wrong number.
d. Incorrect. Wrong number.

2. d   mod. 4   p. 33
a. Incorrect. Naturalistic observation (not explanation) does not have a prescribed step of formulating an explanation.
b. Incorrect. Experimenter bias is a phenomena related to unintended effects of the experimenter's expectations.
c. Incorrect. The ethics review panel reviews proposed studies to ensure that they do not violate the rights of animal or human subjects.

*d. Correct. The scientific method follows three steps according to the text, and the formulation of an explanation is the second step.

3. a   mod. 4   p. 33, 34
*a. Correct. Typically, theories are general statements about the relationships among the phenomena of interest, while hypotheses are specific statements about those relationships.
b. Incorrect. This is opposite the general trend.
c. Incorrect. All theories are potentially provable, but hypotheses can be disproved.
d. Incorrect. If it were a fact, it would not be a theory.

4. c   mod. 4   p. 33
a. Incorrect. This would come second.
b. Incorrect. This would follow formulating an explanation.
*c. Correct. First, one must identify what shall be studied.
d. Incorrect. The hypothesis can only be confirmed after data is collected.

5. d   mod. 5   p. 37
a. Incorrect. Much data collected by science is not useful to anyone.
b. Incorrect. Good scientific practice suggests that procedures be followed exactly, but this is not what is meant by operationalization.
c. Incorrect. Good scientific practice suggests that procedures be followed exactly and variables correctly manipulated, but this is not what is meant by operationalization.
*d. Correct. Operationalization means that the hypothesis and its prediction have been put in a form that can be tested.

6. b   mod. 5   p. 39
a. Incorrect. In almost every case, everyone is willing to give a response.
*b. Correct. Further research has indicated that sensitive issues result in the least accurate responses.
c. Incorrect. Surveys can be used to gather accurate information about attitudes
d. Incorrect. At about 1,500 participants, surveys become as accurate as possible for predicting behavior of a population, even millions of people.

7. c   mod. 5   p. 39
a. Incorrect. This is not a term in psychology, except as it may refer to the way students should study for exams.

b. Incorrect. Perhaps a learning theorist may conduct a study to test the generalization of stimuli or responses, but such would not fit the definition given.
*c. Correct. This definition describes a case study.
d. Incorrect. This is not a term in psychology.

8. c   mod. 5   p. 41
a. Incorrect. A dependent variable is the variable that changes as a result of changes in the independent variable.
b. Incorrect. The experimenter manipulates variables during an experiment.
*c. Correct. This defines a correlation.
d. Incorrect. The manipulation of variables is sometimes called a treatment.

9. b   mod. 5   p. 42
a. Incorrect. The public is unlikely to be impressed by such a move.
*b. Correct. Experiments are the only procedures that provide a definitive account of causal relationships.
c. Incorrect. Statistical methods can be applied to nonexperimental procedures.
d. Incorrect. Government funding is not contingent on experiments, only sound research practices.

10. a   mod. 5   p. 43
*a. Correct. The experiment must compare the behavior of one group to that of another in order to demonstrate that a specific variable caused the difference. The group receiving no treatment is one in which the variable should not change.
b. Incorrect. A case may refer to one instance of the event.
c. Incorrect. An independent variable is the variable that is changed in order to be "treated."
d. Incorrect. All variables should be measured, even those in the "no treatment" group.

11. a   mod. 5   p. 44
*a. Correct. The dependent variable changes as a result of a change in the independent variable.
b. Incorrect. The independent variable is manipulated by the experimenter, and it causes the change in the dependent variables.
c. Incorrect. The control involves a group that does not receive the treatment, and the dependent variable is not expected to change.
d. Incorrect. A confounding variable is a variable that causes change in the dependent variable unexpectedly.

12. c   mod. 6 p. 49
a.   Incorrect. This refers to someone who legally serves as a parent in absence of an actual parent.
b.   Incorrect. Subject expectations may result in the subjects behaving as they think the experimenter wants them to behave, thus spoiling the experiment.
*c. Correct. The subject signs the informed consent to indicate that he or she has been fully informed about the experiment, what to expect, and that he or she can withdraw at any time.
d.   Incorrect. When an experimenter accidentally reveals his or her expectations, thus gaining the compliance of the subjects and invalidating the outcome.

13. c   mod. 6 p. 52
a.   Incorrect. The placebo effect occurs whenever the subject responds to a nonexistent independent variable (a sugar pill rather than medicine).
b.   Incorrect. When an experimenter accidentally reveals expectations, thus gaining the compliance of the subjects and invalidating the outcome.
*c. Correct. Whenever the subject interprets expectations of the experimenter and behaves accordingly.
d.   Incorrect. The treatment condition is the group that is exposed to the independent variable.

14. b   mod. 6 p. 53
a.   Incorrect. The control is the group that does not receive the treatment.
*b. Correct. This is the term for a pill or any other event that has an effect only because the recipient thinks it should.
c.   Incorrect. The dependent variable changes as a result of a change in the independent variable.
d.   Incorrect. The independent variable is manipulated by the experimenter, and it causes the change in the dependent variables.

15. a   mod. 5 p. 47
*a. Correct. The ability of others to repeat a study is critical to its conclusions being accepted by the scientific community.
b.   Incorrect. Cheating is rare in the scientific community precisely because of the need to be able to replicate results.
c.   Incorrect. Not in this lifetime.
d.   Incorrect. The data are probably suspect.

16. d   mod. 4 p. 33
17. e   mod. 4 p. 33

18. b   mod. 4 p. 34
19. a   mod. 5 p. 37
20. c   mod. 5 p. 37

21. random assignment   mod. 5 p. 44
22. scientific method   mod. 4 p. 33
23. hypothesis   mod. 4 p. 34
24. critical thinking   mod. 5 p. 33
25. Theories   mod. 4 p. 33

26. Hypothesis: eating breakfast will increase the scores in a math test.
  ▪ Independent variable: eating breakfast
  ▪ Dependent variable: scores of math test
  ▪ Operational definition of eating breakfast, each student would eat cereal with milk, juice, and a donut a half an hour before the exam
  ▪ Experimental group: randomly selected would eat the breakfast
  ▪ Control group: would just sit for the exam without breakfast

Practice Test 2:
1. c   mod. 4 p. 33
a.   Incorrect. True, this is done in survey research, but it happens elsewhere too, making another alternative better.
b.   Incorrect. True, this is done in case study research, but it happens elsewhere too, making another alternative better.
*c. Correct. The scientific method incorporates the other methods listed in the alternatives, and identifying questions of interest is recognized as one of the key steps of the method.
d.   Incorrect. True, this is done in experimental design, but it happens elsewhere too, making another alternative better.

2. a   mod. 4 p. 33
*a. Correct. Three steps of the scientific method are given in the text, and this is one of them.
b.   Incorrect. A theory is an explanation that may be used to refute other explanations, but designing theories is not carrying out research.
c.   Incorrect. Naturalistic observation may include this element, but another alternative is more inclusive and thus a better choice.
d.   Incorrect. The analysis of a significant outcome occurs at the end of the research process and verifies that the results were not a matter of chance events.

3. d   mod. 4   p. 34
a. Incorrect. This stem defines a theory.
b. Incorrect. This is the first step in the scientific method, and it may lead to the formulation of a hypothesis.
c. Incorrect. This is the definition of naturalistic observation.
*d. Correct. A hypothesis formulates the theory into a testable prediction.

4. b   mod. 4   p. 34
a. Incorrect. This is the question backward.
*b. Correct. Hypotheses are testable versions of theories, and predictions are testable versions of explanations.
c. Incorrect. Both hypothesis and prediction are operationalizations of broader concepts of theory and explanation.
d. Incorrect. Both hypothesis and prediction are operationalizations of broader concepts of theory and explanation.

5. b   mod. 5   p. 37
a. Incorrect. "Archived" means to store in a secure place.
*b. Correct. "To operationalize" is to make something measurable and thus testable.
c. Incorrect. "To theorize" is to speculate about causal or other relationships.
d. Incorrect. This is not a word.

6. b   mod. 5   p. 38
a. Incorrect. A case study focuses on one or a few individuals to gain an in-depth description of a given phenomena.
*b. Correct. This is one technique of surveyors.
c. Incorrect. An experiment utilizes more exacting controls and would probably not use this technique.
d. Incorrect. Archival research involves the researchers using information that has been stored in a library, in an electronic form, or in some other form of data storage.

7. c   mod. 5   p. 38
a. Incorrect. Archival research involves searching records and libraries.
b. Incorrect. Correlational research involves a statistical analysis of pairs of data sets.
*c. Correct. One means of naturalistic observation is to blend into the situation and be unnoticed.
d. Incorrect. An experiment requires careful subject selection and control of variables.

8. d   mod. 5   p. 42
a. Incorrect. This statement is true, and it suggests the strongest possible positive correlation.
b. Incorrect. This statement is true, and it reflects the least amount of relationship whatsoever.
c. Incorrect. If a correlation is not 0.0, then it tells us about the relationship; if 0.0, then it tells us that there is no relationship.
*d. Correct. Only experiments can scientifically demonstrate cause-and-effect relationships.

9. c   mod. 5   p. 43
a. Incorrect. This is called the control group.
b. Incorrect. This is the experimental or treatment group.
*c. Correct. A variable is any behavior or event in an experiment that can be changed, either directly or indirectly.
d. Incorrect. This is a subject.

10. b   mod. 5   p. 44
a. Incorrect. Not knowing the subjects does not mean that potential biases resulting from other factors would not influence the selection.
*b. Correct. Only a selection by chance will ensure proper assignment of subjects.
c. Incorrect. Knowing the subjects may result in biased assignment to groups.
d. Incorrect. The factors of the experiment should not influence the assignment of subjects to a condition.

11. b   mod. 5   p. 43
a. Incorrect. The dependent variable changes as a result of the independent variable, not the manipulation of the experimenter.
*b. Correct. The experimenter manipulates levels of the independent variable in order to test its effect on the dependent variable.
c. Incorrect. The control variable should not be manipulated.
d. Incorrect. The confounding variable is one that unexpectedly appears and has an effect on the dependent variable.

12. d   mod. 6   p. 49
a. Incorrect. Moral refers to "right and wrong" and thus does not quite fit this context.
b. Incorrect. Behavioral scientists may choose not to undertake a kind of study on personal, religious grounds, but this does not describe the relationship to subjects.

c. Incorrect. "Professional standards" refers to a broad category of standards that apply to the conduct of a professional.

*d. Correct. The American Psychological Association has published a set of ethical guidelines that are meant to ensure the welfare of subjects in research.

13. a mod. 6 p. 52

*a. Correct. Sometimes subjects can determine the expected outcomes from the experimental conditions themselves, so deception is used to disguise the conditions.

b. Incorrect. Confusing the subject is not usually an intent of the design of research.

c. Incorrect. Deception may help eliminate the effect of experimenter expectations, but only double-blind procedures guarantee their elimination.

d. Incorrect. They are confused enough.

14. d mod. 6 p. 52

a. Incorrect. Often it is the goal of a confederate to influence subjects in an experiment.

b. Incorrect. An experiment must have dependent variables, otherwise it would not be an experiment.

c. Incorrect. The placebo effect can occur under many conditions, even the double-blind procedure.

*d. Correct. This is the only procedure that will guarantee that both subject and experimenter expectations are eliminated.

15. d mod. 5 p. 46

a. Incorrect. The results can be analyzed as significant, even if the study cannot be replicated.

b. Incorrect. The hypothesis may have been confirmed or disconfirmed, but the theory may still be up for grabs.

c. Incorrect. Statistical significance does not imply social importance.

*d. Correct. Statistical significance judges the probability that the results occurred due to chance.

16. c mod. 5 p. 42
17. b mod. 5 p. 43
18. e mod. 5 p. 43
19. a mod. 5 p. 43
20. d mod. 5 p. 44

21. experimentation mod. 5 p. 42
22. case study mod. 5 p. 39

23. Archival mod. 5 p. 38
24. independent variable mod. 5 p. 43
25. variable manipulation mod. 5 p. 46

26. For illustration, "Geniuses usually have poor social adjustment" has been chosen. The answer should include:

▪ A hypothesis must be stated, like: People with IQ scores above 130 have difficulty in new social situations. The hypothesis must establish a testable situation, in this case, a contrived social interaction that can be observed and rated. The control must be nongeniuses placed in the same situation for comparison.

▪ The independent variable would be the situation; the dependent variable would be the geniuses' social behaviors (behaviors determined to operationalize social adjustment).

▪ A discussion of potential problems must be included. In this case, it may be difficult to find individuals who have an IQ higher than 130.

Practice Test 3:

1. b mod. 5 p. 37

a. Incorrect. This may give some insight if systematically collected and analyzed.

*b. Correct. Two very angry people may have a change in heart rate, while two very in-love people might have a constantly high heart rate.

c. Incorrect. This could be a meaningful measure if used with other measures.

d. Incorrect. This may be the most useful operationalization of the group.

2. c mod. 5 p. 38

a. Incorrect. Situational research is not a formal method of research.

b. Incorrect. Archival research involves searching through records.

*c. Correct. This example describes a survey.

d. Incorrect. An experiment requires control over variables.

3. d mod. 5 p. 38

a. Incorrect. There is no such thing as "delayed" naturalistic observation.

b. Incorrect. A case study would involve in-depth analysis of one incident of cancer.

c. Incorrect. A survey requires living participants.

*d. Correct. The psychologist is searching "archives" and thus conducting archival research.

4. a   mod. 5 p. 39
*a. Correct. Case studies involve in-depth examinations of an individual or a group of individuals.
b. Incorrect. Correlational data are used to make comparisons between two variables.
c. Incorrect. Dependent variables are found in experiments, not case studies.
d. Incorrect. Because the examinations took place in the setting of therapy, this could not be considered naturalistic observation.

5. d   mod. 5 p. 39
a. Incorrect. A survey involves many subjects.
b. Incorrect. An experimental study would require greater controls and randomly selected subjects.
c. Incorrect. Naturalistic observation would require that the executive be observed in his or her natural setting (perhaps during actual work).
*d. Correct. The collection of in-depth information is most like a case study.

6. c   mod. 5 p. 41
a. Incorrect. Correlations cannot demonstrate causal relationships.
b. Incorrect. The factors of additional experiences were not included in the statement of correlation.
*c. Correct. The presence of one factor predicts the likelihood of the other factor being present too.
d. Incorrect. This conclusion is beyond the evidence of the correlation.

7. d   mod. 5 p. 47
a. Incorrect. No statistical test was mentioned or suggested in this scenario.
b. Incorrect. The amount of light and the levels of stress would need to be operationalized from the beginning.
c. Incorrect. A hypothesis would already need to be in place for this series of studies to have meaning.
*d. Correct. Researchers often repeat their studies with slight variations as they test the limits of their theories.

8. c   mod. 6 p. 49
a. Incorrect. This is not the correct phrase.
b. Incorrect. This is not the correct phrase.
*c. Correct. Without spoiling the research, participants should be fully aware of what they will encounter during the study.
d. Incorrect. This is not the correct phrase.

9. b   mod. 5 p. 47
a. Incorrect. Significant outcomes would have been reported in the studies, but so would results without significance.
*b. Correct. The use of other studies is the foundation for the procedure known as meta-analysis.
c. Incorrect. True, correlational data would be used, but as a part of the procedure known as meta-analysis.
d. Incorrect. Experimental techniques require controlled situations.

10. a   mod. 6 p. 52
*a. Correct. The experimenter's anticipation of favorable results can lead to subtle (and not-so-subtle) clues like those just described.
b. Incorrect. In this procedure, she would not know which group of participants was before her.
c. Incorrect. Randomization applies to participant selection.
d. Incorrect. The placebo effect is a participant bias, not an experimenter bias.

11. a   mod. 4 p. 34
*a. Correct. The first step after one has formulated a theory is to create a testable hypothesis.
b. Incorrect. One does not define correlation coefficients for specific studies.
c. Incorrect. True, but before collecting the data, it is necessary to define what data needs to be collected.
d. Incorrect. This will come after the data has been defined and collected.

12. a   mod. 4 p. 37
*a. Correct. Both the amount of physical exercise and the decline in heart-related disease can be measured and recorded.
b. Incorrect. "Dramatically" is not very well defined.
c. Incorrect. "Disgruntled" needs careful definition.
d. Incorrect. "Happy" is not well defined.

13. b   mod. 5 p. 43
a. Incorrect. If colors are a key to problem solving, then they must be relevant.
*b. Correct. The hypothesis suggests that color scheme influences tension, so varying the schemes would serve as the independent variable.
c. Incorrect. The level of tension is the dependent variable.
d. Incorrect. A confounding variable would be some factor not found in the experiment design.

14. a   mod. 5   p. 43
*a. Correct. Tension would depend on both the color scheme and the challenge of the problem.
b.   Incorrect. A confounding variable would be some factor not found in the experiment design.
c.   Incorrect. The color scheme is the independent variable.
d.   Incorrect. Levels of stress are quite relevant to the hypothesis.

15. c   mod. 5   p. 43
a.   Incorrect. The control would be something like a neutral color scheme.
b.   Incorrect. The color scheme is the independent variable.
*c. Correct. Time would indicate the amount of tension and how it impedes problem solving.
d.   Incorrect. A confounding variable would be some factor not found in the experiment design.

16. b   mod. 5   p. 38
17. a   mod. 5   p. 38
18. e   mod. 5   p. 38
19. c   mod. 5   p. 39
20. d   mod. 5   p. 41

21. debriefing   mod. 6   p. 50
22. psychological   mod. 6   p. 51
23. deception   mod. 6   p. 49
24 replicate   mod. 6   p. 47

25.
- Try to imagine yourself in this kind of situation. If you have had a similar experience (where you were deceptively manipulated), an example of your reactions would be appropriate.
- Psychologists are now expected to avoid harm, which can include undue stress, and to inform subjects to the extent possible. Also, informed consent suggests that a subject may discontinue at any point.
- In some cases, alternatives do exist, but in others, the only alternative is naturalistic observation, and the desired qualities of experimental research, such as establishing cause-and-effect relationships, are likely to be lost.

Chapter 3: Neuroscience and Behavior

Module 7: Neurons: The Basic Elements of Behavior
Module 8: The Nervous System and the Endocrine System
Module 9: The Brain

Overview

This set of modules focuses on the biological structures of the body that are of interest to biopsychologists.

Module 7 discusses nerve cells, called neurons, which allow messages to travel through the brain and the body. Psychologists are increasing their understanding of human behavior and are uncovering important clues in their efforts to cure certain kinds of diseases through their growing knowledge of these neurons and the nervous system.

Module 8 offers a review of the structure and the main divisions of the nervous system. This is followed by a discussion on how the different areas work to control voluntary and involuntary behaviors. The chapter also examines how the various parts of the nervous system operate together in emergency situations to produce lifesaving responses to danger. In addition, new information regarding the effects of heredity on various behaviors, such as those associated with psychological disorders, is discussed. Finally, the chemical messenger system of the body, the endocrine system, is examined.

Module 9 presents a discussion of the brain and explains neural activity by examining the brain's major structures and the ways in which these affect behavior. The brain controls movement, senses, and thought processes. It is also fascinating to focus on the idea that the two halves of the brain may have different specialties and strengths, so this area is discussed and the research presented. Potential gender and cultural differences with respect to brain lateralization are also discussed.

To further investigate the topics covered in this chapter, you can visit the related Web sites by visiting the following link: www.mhhe.com/feldmanup8.

Prologue: Out of Jail
Looking Ahead

Module 7: Neurons: The Basic Elements of Behavior

The Structure of the Neuron
How Neurons Fire
Where Neurons Meet: Bridging the Gap
Neurotransmitters: Multitalented Chemical Couriers

- *Why do psychologists study the brain and nervous system?*
- *What are the basic elements of the nervous system?*
- *How does the nervous system communicate electrical and chemical messages from one part to another?*

Neurons: The Basic Elements of Behavior

Psychologists' understanding of the brain has increased dramatically in the past few years.

Neuroscientists examine the biological underpinnings of behavior, and **[a]** _____ explore the ways the biological structures and functions of the body affect behavior.

Specialized cells called **[b]** _____ are the basic component of the nervous system. Every neuron has a nucleus, a cell body, and special structures for

communicating with other neurons. **[c]** _____ are the receiving structures

and **[d]** _____ are the sending structures. The message is communicated in one direction from the dendrites, through the cell body, and down the axon to the

[e] _____. A fatty substance known as the **[f]** _____ surrounds the axons of most neurons and serves as an insulator for the electrical signal being transmitted down the axon. It also speeds the signal. Certain diseases, such as multiple sclerosis, involve the deterioration of the myelin sheath. The axon thus becomes exposed, and results in messages between the brain and muscles being short-circuited.

The neuron communicates its message by "firing," which refers to its changing from a(n)

[g] _____ to a(n) **[h]** _____. Neurons express the

action potential following the **[i]** _____ law, that is, firing only when a certain level of stimulation is reached. Just after the action potential has passed, the neuron cannot fire again for a brief period. The thicker the myelin sheath and the larger the diameter of the axon, the faster the action potentials travel down the axons. Some neurons can fire as many as 1,000 times per second if the stimulus is very strong. However, the communicated message is a matter of how frequently or infrequently the neuron fires, not the intensity of the action potential, which is always the same strength.

The message of a neuron is communicated across the [j] _____ to the receiving neuron by the release of [k] _____. The synapse is the small space between the terminal button of one neuron and the dendrite of the next. Neurotransmitters can either excite or inhibit the receiving neuron. The exciting neurotransmitter makes

[l] _____ and the inhibiting neurotransmitter makes [m] _____.
Once the neurotransmitters are released, they lock into special sites on the receiving neurons.

They must then be reabsorbed through [n] _____ into the sending neuron or deactivated by enzymes.

About 100 chemicals have been found to act as neurotransmitters. Neurotransmitters can be either exciting or inhibiting, depending on where in the brain they are released. The most common neurotransmitters are *acetylcholine (ACh)*, *glutamate*, *gamma-amino butyric acid (GABA)*, *dopamine (DA)*, *serotonin*, and *endorphins*.

Evaluate

Part A

_____ 1.   neurons

_____ 2.   dendrites

_____ 3.   axon

_____ 4.   terminal buttons

_____ 5.   myelin sheath

a. Specialized cells that are the basic elements of the nervous system that carry messages.

b. Small branches at the end of an axon that relay messages to other cells.

c. A long extension from the end of a neuron that carries messages to other cells through the neuron.

d. An axon's protective coating, made of fat and protein.

e. Clusters of fibers at one end of a neuron that receive messages from other neurons.

Part B

_____ 1. acetylcholine (ACh)   a. Affects movement, attention, and learning.

_____ 2. glutamate   b. Similar to painkillers, they often produce euphoric feelings.

_____ 3. gamma-amino butyric acid (GABA)   c. Transmits messages to skeletal muscles.

_____ 4. dopamine   d. Plays a role in memory.

_____ 5. serotonin   e. Inhibitory transmitter that moderates behaviors from eating to aggression.

_____ 6. endorphins

f. Regulates sleep, eating, mood, and pain.

Rethink

7-1   How might psychologists use drugs that mimic the effects of neurotransmitters to treat psychological disorders?

7-2   _From the perspective of a health care provider:_ How would you explain the placebo effect and the role of endorphins to patients who wish to try unproven treatment methods that they find on the Web?

Spotlight on Terminology and Language—ESL Pointers

Page 114 "Later, when his legs began to shake and he had balance problems, his doctors informed him he had Parkinson's—a disorder marked by varying degrees of **muscular rigidity** and shaking."

When something is **rigid** it is stiff and firm. In Parkinson's disease **muscular rigidity** refers to a stiffening of the muscles in the arms and legs.

Page 115 "Because of the importance of the nervous system in controlling behavior, and because humans at their most basic level are biological beings, many researchers in psychology and other fields as diverse as computer science, zoology, and medicine have made the biological **underpinnings** of behavior their specialty."

Underpinnings refer to the foundation or the basic layer that we base a theory or idea on.

Page 117 "Watching Serena Williams hit a **stinging backhand**, Dario Vaccaro carry out a complex ballet routine, or Derek Jeter swing at a baseball, you may have marveled at the complexity—and wondrous abilities—of the human body."

A **stinging backhand** is a type of tennis move in which the tennis player hits the ball with a lot of force and skill.

Page 118 "Neurons are physically held in place by glial cells, which provide nourishment and **insulate** them (Bear, Connors, & Paradiso, 2000; Vylings, 2002)."

The glial cells **insulate** the neurons by shielding them and protecting them. To **insulate** is to place in a detached situation or in a state of isolation.

Page 119 "In certain diseases, such as **multiple sclerosis**, the myelin sheath surrounding the axon deteriorates, exposing parts of the axon that are normally covered."

Multiple sclerosis is a progressive disease of the central nervous system in which the myelin sheath of the neuron weakens.

Page 119 "The myelin sheath also serves to increase the **velocity** with which electrical impulses travel through axons."

Velocity is speed. The myelin sheath increases the rapidity of movement.

Page 121 "These complex events can occur at **dizzying** speeds, although there is great variation among different neurons."

When something occurs at a **dizzying speed,** it occurs at a very fast pace.

Page 122 "When a nerve impulse comes to the end of the axon and reaches a terminal button, the terminal button releases a chemical **courier** called a neurotransmitter."

The chemical **courier**, the neurotransmitter, carries messages. One of the most common neurotransmitters is acetylcholine. This neurotransmitter transmits messages related to our skeletal movement.

Page 123 "Like a boat that **ferries** passengers across a river, these chemical messengers move toward the **shorelines** of other neurons."

In this sentence the term **ferries** means to transport. Ferries are boats that transport people or things across a body of water.

Shorelines suggest a zone of contact.

Page 123 "In the same way that a jigsaw puzzle piece can fit in only one specific location in a puzzle, each kind of neurotransmitter has a distinctive **configuration** that allows it to fit into a specific type of receptor site of the receiving neuron."

Configuration has to do with the relative disposition or arrangement of parts – in this case the structure of the neurotransmitter.

Page 123 "**Excitatory** messages make it more likely that a receiving neuron will fire and an action potential will travel down its axon."

Excitatory messages are messages that are likely to induce action.

Page 123 "**Inhibitory** messages, in contrast, do just the opposite; they provide chemical information that prevents or decreases the likelihood that the receiving neuron will fire."

Inhibitory messages tend to reduce or suppress the activity of the receiving neuron.

Page 124 "If neurotransmitters remained at the site of the synapse, receiving neurons would be **awash in a continual chemical bath**, producing constant stimulation of the receiving neurons—and effective communication across the synapse would no longer be possible."

When the neurons are **awash in a continual chemical bath** they have more of the chemical then they can manage.

Page 124 "To solve this problem, neurotransmitters are either **deactivated** by enzymes or – more frequently – **reabsorbed** by the terminal button in an example of chemical recycling called reuptake."

When neurotransmitters are **deactivated**, they are made inactive or ineffective. Your body is basically deprived of the chemical activity that would be occurring.

When neurotransmitters are being **reabsorbed**, they are being reused.

Page 124 "Like a vacuum cleaner sucking up dust, neurons reabsorb the neurotransmitters that are now **clogging** the synapse."

When the synapse is being **clogged**, activity is restricted or halted.

Page 126 "In other instances, *over*production of dopamine produces negative consequences. For example, researchers have hypothesized that **schizophrenia** and some other severe mental disturbances are affected or perhaps even caused by the presence of unusually high levels of dopamine."

Schizophrenia is a psychological disorder in which patients show symptoms of emotional instability and a lack of interest in the real world. In some cases **Schizophrenics** will experience false sights & sounds.

Page 126 "A growing body of research points toward a broader role for serotonin, suggesting its involvement in such diverse behaviors as alcoholism, depression, suicide, **impulsivity**, aggression, and coping with stress (Smith, Williams, &Maris, 2002; Zalsman & Apter, 2002; Addolorato, Leggio, Abenavoli, & Gasbarrini, 2005)."

When a person is impulsive or shows **impulsivity** they have the tendency to act on sudden urges or desires.

Page 127 "Endorphins also may produce the **euphoric** feelings that runners sometimes experience after long runs."

Euphoria is a feeling of well-being or elation. What physical activities do you do that activate feelings of **euphoria**?

Page 127 "Although the research evidence is not firm, the exertion and perhaps the pain involved in a long run stimulate the production of endorphins, ultimately resulting in what has been called "**runner's high**" (Kremer & Scully, 1994; Kolata, 2002; Pert, 2002)."

A **runner's high** is a slang term used to describe the experience of intensive feelings of well-being or euphoria.

Page 129 "How might psychologists use drugs that **mimic** the effects of neurotransmitters to treat psychological disorders?

When drugs **mimic** the effects of neurotransmitters they imitate the action of the neurotransmitter.

Page 131 "Action potential: An electric nerve impulse that travels through a neuron when it is set off by a "**trigger**," changing the neuron's charge from negative to positive."

A **trigger** is a stimulus that set off an action or process.

Module 8: The Nervous System and the Endocrine System

The Nervous System
The Endocrine System: Of Chemicals and Glands

- *How are the structures of the nervous system linked together?*
- *How does the endocrine system affect behavior?*

The Nervous System and the Endocrine System

The nervous system is divided into the **[a]** _____—composed of the brain and the spinal cord—and the peripheral nervous system. The **[b]** _____ is a bundle of nerves that descends from the brain. The main purpose of the spinal cord is as a pathway for communication between the brain and the body. Some involuntary behaviors, called **[c]** _____, involve messages that do not travel to the brain but instead stay entirely within the spinal cord. **[d]** _____ neurons bring information from the periphery to the brain. **[e]** _____ neurons carry messages to the muscles and glands of the body. **[f]** _____, a third type of neuron, connect the sensory and the motor neurons, carrying messages between them. The spinal cord is the major carrier of sensory and motor information. Its importance is evident in injuries that result in *quadriplegia* and *paraplegia*. The **[g]** _____ branches out from the spinal cord. It is divided into the **[h]** _____, which controls muscle movement, and the **[i]** _____, which controls basic body functions like heartbeat, breathing, glands, and lungs.

The role of the autonomic nervous system is to activate the body through the **[j]** _____ and then to modulate and calm the body through the **[k]** _____. The sympathetic division prepares the organism for stressful situations, and the parasympathetic division calms the body to help the body recover after the emergency has ended.

The branch of psychology known as **[l]** _____ attempts to provide answers concerning how our genetic inheritance from our ancestors influences the structure and function of our nervous system and influences everyday behavior. The new field known as **[m]** _____ studies the effects of heredity on behavior.

The [n] _____ is a chemical communication network that delivers
[o] _____ into the bloodstream, which, in turn, influence growth and
behavior. Sometimes called the "master gland," the [p] _____ gland is the
major gland of the endocrine system. The hypothalamus regulates the pituitary gland.

Evaluate

_____ 1. peripheral nervous system

_____ 2. somatic division

_____ 3. autonomic division

_____ 4. sympathetic division

_____ 5. parasympathetic division

a. The part of the autonomic division of the peripheral nervous system that calms the body, bringing functions back to normal after an emergency has passed.

b. All parts of the nervous system *except* the brain and the spinal cord (includes somatic and autonomic divisions).

c. The part of the nervous system that controls involuntary movement (the actions of the heart, glands, lungs, and other organs).

d. The part of the autonomic division of the peripheral nervous system that prepares the body to respond in stressful emergency situations.

e. The part of the nervous system that controls voluntary movements of the skeletal muscles.

Rethink

8-1   In what ways is the "fight or flight" response helpful to organisms in emergency situations?

8-2   *From the perspective of a genetic counselor:* How would you explain the pros and cons of genetic counseling to someone who was interested in receiving genetic screening for various diseases and disorders?

Spotlight on Terminology and Language—ESL Pointers

Page 135 "Because each neuron can be connected to 80,000 other neurons, the total number of possible connections is **astonishing**.

When something is **astonishing** it is surprising or unbelievable.

Page 135 "However, connections among neurons are not the only means of communication within the body; as we'll see, the endocrine system, which secretes chemical messages that circulate through the blood, also communicates messages that influence behavior and many **aspects** of biological functioning (Kandel, Schwartz, & Jessell, 2000; Boahen, 2005; Forlenza, & Baum, 2004).

An **aspect** is a characteristic or feature of something.

Page 136 "As you can see from the **schematic** representation in Figure 1, the nervous system is divided into two main parts: the central nervous system and the peripheral nervous system."

When you see a **schematic**, you are seeing a diagram or a drawing that is being used to help illustrate what the author is discussing. It is important to look at all the **schematics** and review them.

Page 136 "An example is the way the knee **jerks** forward when it is tapped with a rubber hammer."

A jerk is a sudden movement. A **knee jerk** occurs when the leg suddenly moves after it is tapped.

Page 137 "In some cases, injury results in *quadriplegia*, a condition in which voluntary muscle movement below the neck is lost. In a less severe but still **debilitating** condition, *paraplegia*, people are unable to voluntarily move any muscles in the lower half of the body."

Quadriplegia is a total inability to move both arms and both legs.

A disease that is **debilitating** weakens someone's strength or energy.

Paraplegia is paralysis of the lower half of the body with involvement of both legs usually due to disease of, or injury to, the spinal cord.

Page 138 "As you look up, you see the **glint** of something that might be a knife."

A **glint** is a brief flash of daylight or something shiny.

Page 138 "As confusion **clouds your mind** and fear overcomes your attempts to think rationally, what happens to your body?"

When something is said to **cloud your mind** it means that things are becoming unclear or difficult to understand.

Page 138 "Your heart rate increases, you begin to sweat, and you develop **goose bumps** all over your body."

Goose bumps are pimples or bumps that appear on the skin of the arms. These bumps do not last very long and are often brought about by fear.

Page 139 "The **forerunner** of the human nervous system is found in the earliest simple organisms to have a spinal cord."

A **forerunner** is a something that goes ahead of something.

Page 139 "In fact, many animals, such as fish, still have a nervous system that is structured in roughly

similar fashion today."

Similar means alike. **Fashion**s are styles or shapes. Here the author is saying that many animals, including fish, have nervous systems that are styled or shaped alike.

Page 140 "Their work, in conjunction with the research of scientists studying genetics, biochemistry, and medicine, has led to an understanding of how our behavior is affected by heredity, our genetically-determined **heritage**."

Your genetically determined **heritage** is the things you inherit from your parents and grandparents. They are the things you are born with or born into.

Page 140 "In fact, evolutionary psychologists have **spawned** a new and increasingly influential field: behavioral genetics."

When some **spawns** an idea or a thing they have generated or created it. The research of evolutionary psychology has **spawned,** or created, new fields of study, one of them being behavioral genetics.

Page 140 "Behavioral genetics lies **at the heart** of the **nature-nurture** question, one of the key issues in the study of psychology."

Something that lies **at the heart of** something is the foundation or base of it.

The **nature-nurture** question in psychology refers to the question as to whether biological make-up or the environment you are raised in has more influence over a person's behavior.

Page 140 "Although no one would argue that our behavior is determined *solely* by inherited factors, evidence collected by behavioral geneticists does suggest that our genetic inheritance **predisposes** us to respond in particular ways to our environment, and even to seek out particular kinds of environments."

When we are **predisposed** toward something we are inclined to do it.

Page 141 "For example, researchers have found evidence that **novelty-seeking** behavior is determined, at least in part, by a certain gene."

A **novelty** is something new or original, thus **novelty-seeking** behavior occurs when a person continually tries to find new things.

Page 142 "Yet having the **variant** gene does not always lead to autism. More than 99.5 percent of people with the **variant** do not develop the disorder, and 60 percent of those with autism do not have the **variant**."

A **variant** is an alternative.

Page 143 "In examining the genetic roots of various behaviors, the study of behavior genetics has **stirred controversy**."

When something **stirs controversy** it generates or causes disagreement or debate.

Page 143 "In *gene therapy*, scientists inject genes meant to cure a particular disease into a patient's

bloodstream."

A patient's **bloodstream** refers to the flow of blood through the veins and arteries of the body.

Page 144 "Scientists have already developed genetic tests to determine whether someone is **susceptible** to certain types of cancer or heart disease, and it may not be long before analysis of a drop of blood can indicate whether a child—or potentially an unborn fetus—is susceptible to certain psychological disorders.

When someone is **susceptible** to a disease they are at risk for developing that illness.

Page 144 "Its job is to **secrete** hormones, chemical that **circulate** through the blood and affect the functioning or growth of other parts of the body."

Secreting is the process of producing a substance from the cells and fluids and discharging it.

Circulate refers to the flow of blood and hormones through the body.

Page 145 "Individual hormones can **wear many hats**, depending on circumstances."

To **wear many hats** is to be responsible for several different jobs.

Page 145 "The same hormone also seems to stimulate **cuddling** between species members."

Cuddling refers to the action of hugging or embracing another person.

Page 146 "There's even evidence that oxytocin is related to the development of trust in others, helping to **grease the wheels** of effective social interaction (Angier, 1991; Quadros et al., 2002; Kosfeld et al., 2005)."

To **grease the wheels** of something is to make it easy to do.

Page 146 "Although hormones are produced naturally by the endocrine system, the **ingestion** of artificial hormones has proved to be both beneficial and potentially dangerous."

To **ingest** something is to eat or drink something.

Page 146 "For example, before the early 2000s, physicians frequently prescribed hormone replacement therapy (HRT) to treat symptoms of **menopause** in older women."

Menopause is a period of the life of a woman during which her hormone levels drop and her ability to conceive children stops.

Page 146 "For athletes and others who want to **bulk up** their appearance, steroids provide a way to add muscle weight and increase strength."

When athletes **bulk up** they add muscles and gain weight in order to increase their strength.

Module 9: The Brain

Studying the Brain's Structure and Functions: Spying on the Brain

Applying Psychology in the 21st Century: Mind Reading: Harnessing Brainpower to Improve Lives

The Central Core: Our "Old Brain"
The Limbic System: Beyond the Central Core
The Cerebral Cortex: Our "New Brain"
Mending the Brain
The Specialization of the Hemispheres: Two Brains or One?

Exploring Diversity: Human Diversity and the Brain

The Split Brain: Exploring the Two Hemispheres

Becoming an Informed Consumer of Psychology: Learning to Control Your Heart—and Mind—through Biofeedback

- *How do researchers identify the major parts and functions of the brain?*
- *What are the major parts of the brain, and for what behaviors is each part responsible?*
- *How do the two halves of the brain operate interdependently?*
- *How can an understanding of the nervous system help us find ways to alleviate disease and pain?*

The Brain
Important advancements have been made that now allow a more precise examination of the brain than the traditional autopsy investigations of the past. Scanning techniques, such as the

[a] _____, which records the electrical activity of the brain; the [b]

_____, which shows biochemical activity in the brain on a moment-by-moment

basis; and the [c] _____, which provides a detailed three-dimensional image of the brain, have greatly improved both research and diagnosis. One of the newest types of scans is [d]

_____, which exposes tiny regions of the brain to a strong magnetic field, and then momentarily interrupts electrical activity. This type of scan has the potential to treat several types of psychological disorders, by directing brief magnetic pulses through the brain. These many advances in brain imaging have given rise to a new field called [e] _____, the application of brain science, behavioral genetics, and neural imaging to legal questions.

Because it evolved very early, the [f] _____ of the brain is referred to as the old brain. It is composed of the *medulla*, which controls functions like breathing and heartbeat; the *pons*, which transmits information helping to coordinate muscle activity on the right and left halves of the body; and the [g] _____, which coordinates muscle activity.

The [h] _____ is a group of nerve cells extending from the medulla and the pons that alert other parts of the brain to activity. The central core also includes the

[i] _____, which transmits sensory information, and the

[j] _____, which maintains *homeostasis* of the body's environment. The hypothalamus also plays a role in basic survival behaviors like eating, drinking, sexual behavior, aggression, and child-rearing behavior.

The [k] _____ is a set of interrelated structures that includes pleasure centers, structures that control eating, aggression, reproduction, and self-preservation. Intense pleasure is felt through the limbic system. The limbic system also plays important roles in learning and memory. The limbic system is sometimes called the "animal brain" because its structures and functions are so similar to those of other animals.

The [l] _____ is identified with the functions that allow us to think and remember. The cerebral cortex is deeply folded in order to increase the surface area of the covering. The cortex is divided into four main sections, or [m] _____. They are the *frontal, parietal, temporal,* and *occipital lobes.* The lobes are separated by deep groves called sulci. The cortex and its lobes have been divided into three major areas: the motor, sensory, and association areas.

The [n] _____ area of the brain is responsible for the control and direction of voluntary muscle movements.

Three areas are devoted to the [o] _____ area, that of touch, called the *somatosensory area*; that of sight, called the *visual area*; and that of hearing, called the *auditory area.* The [p] _____ area takes up most of the cortex and is devoted to higher mental processes like language, thinking, memory, and speech.

The two halves of the brain called [q] _____ are lateralized. The left hemisphere concentrates on verbal-based skills and controls the right side of the body. The right hemisphere deals with spatial understanding and pattern recognition and controls the left side of the body. This [r] _____ appears to vary greatly among individuals, and may also vary between the genders and cultural groups. One difference that has been discovered is that the connecting fibers between the two hemispheres, called the *corpus callosum,* have different shapes in men and women.

The brain continually reorganizes itself by a process of [s] _____. The number of neurons grows throughout life, and the interconnections between cells become more complex. In studies with rats, brain cells have been produced in test tubes.

Evaluate

Test A

_____ 1.   central core

_____ 2.   medulla

_____ 3.   pons

_____ 4.   cerebellum

_____ 5.   reticular formation

a. The part of the brain that joins the halves of the cerebellum, transmitting motor information to coordinate muscles and integrate movement between the right and left sides of the body.

b. The part of the central core of the brain that controls many important body functions, such as breathing and heartbeat.

c. The part of the brain that controls bodily balance.

d. The "old brain," which controls such basic functions as eating and sleeping and is common to all vertebrates.

e. A group of nerve cells in the brain that arouses the body to prepare it for appropriate action and screens out background stimuli.

Test B

_____ 1.   electroencephalogram (EEG)

_____ 2.   positron emission tomography (PET)

_____ 3.   functional magnetic resonance imaging (fMRI)

_____ 4.   transcranial magnetic stimulation (TMS)

_____ 5.   neuroergonomics

a. A new field which examines how objects and environments can be best designed to make use of the brain's capabilities.

b. A new type of scan which causes a momentary interruption of electrical activity in the brain.

c. Provides a detailed, three-dimensional, computer-generated image of brain structures.

d. Records electrical activity in the brain.

e. Shows the biochemical activity within the brain at any given moment.

Rethink

9-1   Before sophisticated brain-scanning techniques were developed, behavioral neuroscientists' understanding of the brain was largely based on the brains of people who had died. What limitations would this pose, and in what areas would you expect the most significant advances once brain-scanning techniques became possible?

9-2   Could personal differences in people's specialization of right and left hemispheres be related to occupational success? For example, might an architect who relies on spatial skills have a different pattern of hemispheric specialization than a writer?

9-3   *From the perspective of an educator:* How might you use different techniques to teach reading to boys and girls based on the brain evidence?

Spotlight on Terminology and Language—ESL Pointers

Page 153 "Despite its physical appearance, however, it ranks as the greatest natural **marvel** that we know and has a beauty and sophistication all its own."

To **marvel** is to wonder or be in awe of something.

Page 153 "The brain is responsible for our **loftiest** thoughts – and our most primitive urges. It is the **overseer** of the intricate workings of the human body."

To have **lofty** thoughts is to have great and superior thoughts. **Lofty** is often characterized by an elevation in character or speech.

The **overseer** is the person responsible for supervising the working of something.

Page 153 "The **sheer quantity** of nerve cells in the brain is enough to **daunt** even the most ambitious computer engineer."

The term "**sheer quantity**" is used to imply that there is a large amount of something.

Daunt refers to discouragement. The number of nerve cells in the brain is such a great number that it is **daunting** and intimidates many researchers.

Page 153 "However, it is not the number of cells that is the most **astounding** thing about the brain but its ability to allow the human intellect to **flourish** as it guides our behavior and thoughts."

When something is **astounding** it is amazing or surprising. **Flourish** means to thrive. Human intellect **flourishes** and increases.

Page 153 "Although we'll discuss specific areas of the brain in relation to specific behaviors, this approach is an **oversimplification.**"

An **oversimplification** is a generalization or statement that is too simple and does not take into account more complex aspects of the issue.

Page 153 "Our behavior, emotions, thoughts, hopes, and dreams are produced by a variety of neurons throughout the nervous system working **in concert**."

Things that are working **in concert** with each other are working together.

Page 154 "Today, however, brain-scanning techniques **provide a window** into the living brain."

The brain scanning images allow researchers to see the brain and observe its activity; thus, they are said to "**provide a window**" into the brain.

Page 154 "Using these techniques, investigators can take a "**snapshot**" of the internal workings of the brain without having to cut open a person's skull."

A snapshot is a photograph or a still picture.

Page 155 "By locating radiation within the brain, a computer can determine which are the more active regions, providing a **striking** picture of the brain at work."

A striking picture is one that is attractive or unusual.

Page 155 "For example, fMRI scans can show the operation of individual bundles of nerves by tracing the flow of blood, opening the way for improved diagnosis of **ailments** ranging from chronic back pain to nervous system disorders such as strokes, multiple sclerosis, and Alzheimers."

An **aliment** is an illness or disease. Multiple sclerosis, and Alzheimers disease are all illnesses, or **ailments**.

Page 155 "The procedure is sometimes called a "**virtual lesion**" because it produces effects analogous to what would occur if areas of the brain were physically cut."

The term "**virtual**" means artificial. In neuropsychology the term "**lesion**" is used to refer to any damage to the brain. Thus, when a procedure produces the same effect as actual brain damage with out physically damaging the brain, the procedure is referred to as a **virtual lesion**.

Page 156 "Advances in our understanding of the brain are also **paving the way** for the development of new methods for **harnessing** the brain's neural signals."

When someone or something "**paves the way**" for someone or something else they are creating a path that will make it easier for later discoveries.

Harnessing means to control and direct. What is some research you would like to see conducted to **harness** some of the functions of the brain?

Page 156 "We consider some of these **intriguing** findings in the *Applying Psychology in the 21st Century* box.

Intriguing findings are those that are interesting or exciting.

Page 157 "Just as his **attention begins to wander,** an alarm sounds, reminding him that he needs to focus more carefully.

When your **attention wanders** you are daydreaming and not paying attention to the environment around you.

Page 157 "Most now require that scans be carried out in large, body-**encompassing** equipment."

Encompassing means surrounding or encircling. Machines that are body-encompassing require that that the person's entire body be inside the machine.

Page 158 "For example, using EEG scanning techniques that react to the pattern of brain waves originating in the brain, one patient who suffered from paralysis learned to **boost** and **curtail** certain types of brain waves."

Boost means to increase or improve.

Curtail means to limit or restrict.

Page 158 "Although the method is slow and tedious—the patient can produce only about two characters per minute—it **holds great promise** (Birbaumer et al., 1999; Mitchener, 2001; Hinterberger, Birbaumer, & Flor, 2005).

When a treatment **holds great promise** it is showing signs that it will be useful.

Page 158 "Employers might use brain scans to **weed out** job applicants who are dishonest."

When we **weed out** something we discard them, or remove them from consideration.

Page 160 "A portion of the brain known as the central **core** is quite similar to that found in all vertebrates (species with backbones)."

Core is the innermost or most important part.

Page 160 " If we were to move up the spinal cord from the base of the skull to locate the structures of the central core of the brain, the first part we would come to would be the hindbrain, which contains the medulla, pons, and **cerebellum**."

The **cerebellum** is the brain structure responsible for coordination and regulation of complex voluntary muscular movement. The **cerebellum** is the brain region most involved in producing smooth, coordinated skeletal muscle activity.

Page 161 "Without the help of the cerebellum we would be unable to walk a straight line without **staggering** and **lurching** forward, for it is the job of the cerebellum to control bodily balance

When people **stagger and lurch** they walk unsteadily. They may stumble, sway and wobble.

Page 161 "In fact, drinking too much alcohol seems to depress the activity of the cerebellum, leading to the unsteady **gait** and movement characteristic of drunkenness."

Gait is a particular way of walking, or running, on moving on foot. **Gait** controls the speed at which we walk and run.

Page 161 "Like an ever-**vigilant** guard, the reticular formation is made up of groups of nerve cells that can activate other parts of the brain immediately to produce general bodily arousal."

Vigilant is to be on the alert, or watchful. Can you describe some situations in your life when you have felt the need to be especially **vigilant**?

Page 161 "Hidden within the forebrain, the *thalamus* acts primarily as a **relay station** for information about the senses.

A **relay station** is a place that collects incoming information and redirects it.

Page 162 "In an **eerie** view of the future, some science fiction writers have suggested that people someday will routinely have electrodes implanted in their brains."

An **eerie** view suggests a supernatural view that would be strange and mysterious.

Page 162 "Although **far-fetched**—and ultimately improbable—such a futuristic fantasy is based on fact."

Far-fetched ideas are ideas that are extremely unbelievable and unlikely.

Page 162 "Injury to the limbic system can produce **striking** changes in behavior."

In this case the term **striking** means obvious or extremely noticeable.

Page 162 "Such injuries can turn animals that are usually **docile and tame** into **belligerent** savages."

Animals that are **docile and tame** are quiet and submissive. **Belligerent** individuals are aggressive and argumentative.

Page 164 "Those unique features of the human brain – indeed, the very capabilities that allow you to come up with such a question in the first pace – are **embodied** in the ability to think, evaluate, and make complex judgments."

To **embody** is to gather and organize – to incorporate a number of things - into an organized whole

Page 164 "The principal location of these abilities, along with many others, is the **cerebral cortex**."

The **cerebral cortex** is the outer gray matter region of the cerebral hemispheres. The **cerebral cortex** accounts for the most sophisticated information processing in the brain.

Page 164 "It consists of a mass of deeply folded, **rippled, convoluted** tissue."

A ripple is a wrinkle. Convoluted means complex and complicated. Tissue that is rippled and convoluted is complexly wrinkled and folded upon itself.

Page 165 "Although we will discuss these areas as though they were separate and independent, keep in mind that this is an **oversimplification**."

When something is **over simplified** the explanation is made too simple and does not take into account the complexity of the issue.

Page 166 "Every portion of the motor area corresponds to a specific **locale** within the body."

A **locale** is a location.

Page 167 "For instance, the *somatosensory area* **encompasses** specific locations associated with the ability to perceive touch and pressure in a particular area of the body"

To **encompass** something is to include it.

Page 167 "It also appears that particular locations within the auditory area respond to specific **pitches** (deCharms, Blake, & Merzenich, 1998; Klinke et al., 1999; Hudspeth, 2000).

Pitch is a quality of sound. This will be discussed further in chapter 5.

Page 168 "The visual area provides another example of how areas of the brain are intimately related to specific areas of the body: specific structures in the eye are related to a particular part of the cortex—with, as you might guess, more area of the brain given to the most sensitive portions of the **retina** (Wurtz & Kandel, 2000)"

The **retina** is the light sensitive lining found at the back of the eye.

Page 168 "Twenty-five-year-old Phineas sone day in 1848 when an accidental explosion punched a 3-foot-long **spike**, about an inch in diameter, completely through his skull."

A **spike** is a sharp skewer shaped like a nail.

Page 168 "In fact, he was able to walk up a long **flight of stairs** before receiving any medical attention."

A **flight of stairs** is a section of a staircase**.**

Page 168 "Mentally, however, there was a difference: Once a careful and hard-working person, Phineas now became **enamored** with **wild schemes** and was **flighty** and often irresponsible."

To be **enamored** with something means to be in love with something.
Schemes are plans or ideas; wild schemes are plans or ideas that are crazy or foolish.

A **flighty** individual is someone whose behavior is erratic and inconsistent**.**

Page 168 "As one of his physicians put it, "Previous to his injury, though untrained in the schools, he possessed a well-balanced mind, and was looked upon by those who knew him as a **shrewd,** smart businessman, very energetic and persistent in executing all his plans of operation."

A **shrewd** person is someone who is smart and insightful.

Page 169 "In some cases, the injury
stemmed from natural causes, such as a tumor or a stroke, either of which would block certain blood vessels in the cerebral cortex."

Stems from means causes. When we say that a disease **stems from** natural causes we are saying that it was not caused by an artificial substance.

Page 169 "In other cases, accidental causes were the **culprits**, as was true of Gage."

A **culprit** is the reason, or the cause of a problem.

Page 170 "In *Broca's aphasia* (caused by damage to the part of the brain first identified by a French physician, Paul Broca, in 1861), speech becomes **halting, laborious,** and often ungrammatical."

When something is **halting** it contains many stops and starts.

When something is **laborious** it requires a lot of effort.

Page 170 "The speaker is unable to find the right words in a kind of **tip-of-the-tongue phenomenon** that we all experience from time to time.

The **tip-of-the-tongue phenomenon** occurs when you think you know something, but are not quite able to remember it.

Page 170 "People with aphasia, though, **grope** for words almost constantly, eventually **blurting out** a kind of "verbal telegram.""

When we **grope** for something we are fumbling, or searching with hesitation

When someone **blurts out** they suddenly say something out loud without thinking and without taking into account that someone else may be speaking.

Page 171 "Nothing could be done to prevent profound **retardation**."

Retardation is a term used to refer to a slowing of though processes.

Page 172 "The future also holds promise for people who suffer from the tremors and loss of motor control produced by Parkinson's disease, although the research is **mired** in controversy.

Mired means to be stuck in a difficult situation.

Page 172 "They seem to be **on the right track**."

When someone is **"on the right track"** they are heading in the right direction.

Page 173 "The issue has been **politicized,** and the question of whether and how stem cell research should be regulated is not clear (Rosen, 2005)."

To **politicize** something is to make it a political issue.

Page 173 "Although for many years **conventional wisdom** held that no new brain cells are created after childhood, new research finds otherwise."

Conventional means standard. **Conventional wisdom** refers to ideas that are standard, or typical beliefs.

Page 175 "For example, even before infants under the age of 1 year have developed real language skills, their **babbling** involves left hemisphere specialization (Holowka & Petitto, 2002).

Babbling are sounds like "ba ba ba," or "da da da" made by infants before they learn formal language,

Page 175 "However, it is important to keep in mind that the differences in specialization between the hemispheres are not great and that the degree and nature of **lateralization** vary from one person to another."

Lateralization refers to the idea that different behavior may be controlled by different sides of the brain.

Page 176 "Researchers have also **unearthed** evidence that there may be subtle differences in brain lateralization patterns between males and females."

When we **unearth** something we have uncovered or discovered something.

Page 176 "In contrast, women **display** less lateralization, with language abilities **apt** to be more evenly divided between the two -hemispheres (Gur et al., 1982; Shaywitz, Shaywitz, Pugh, Constable, et al., 1995; Kulynych, Vladar, Jones, & Weinberger, 1994).

To **display** something is to show it.

Apt means likely to. Women's language skill are more likely to be equally divided between the two hemispheres of the brain.

Page 177 "Such differences in brain lateralization may account, in part, for the superiority often displayed by females on certain measures of verbal skills, such as the **onset** and fluency of speech, and the fact that far more boys than girls have reading problems in elementary school (Kitterle, 1991)."

The **onset** of something is its start.

Page 178 "In turn, this greater early experience may **foster** the growth of certain parts of the brain."

To **foster** something is to encourage it.

Page 178 "The culture in which people are raised also may **give rise to** differences in brain lateralization.

To **give rise to** something is to create it.

Page 180 "In one experimental procedure, **blindfolded** patients touched an object with their right hand and were asked to name it."

When we **blindfold** someone we cover their eyes with a cloth so that they cannot see.

Page 181 "Tammy DeMichael was **cruising** along the New York State Thruway with her **fiancé** when he fell asleep at the wheel. The car slammed into the **guardrail** and flipped, leaving DeMichael with what the doctors called a "splattered C-6, 7"—a broken neck and crushed spinal cord."

When we **cruise along** we are traveling at a steady, relaxed rate of speed.

A **guardrail** is a rail or barrier along the side of a road to prevent cars from driving off the road.

Page 182 "Later, when she felt a headache starting, she could relax the relevant muscles and **abort** the pain."

Abort means to stop.

Page 182 "In DeMichael's case, biofeedback was effective because not all of the nervous system's connections between the brain and her legs were **severed.**"

When something is **severed** it is cut off.

Practice Tests

Test your knowledge of this set of modules by answering the following questions. These questions have been placed in three Practice Tests. The first two tests consist of questions that will test your recall of factual knowledge. The third test contains questions that are challenging and primarily test for conceptual knowledge and your ability to apply that knowledge. Check your answers and review the feedback using the Answer Key on the following pages of the *Study Guide*.

PRACTICE TEST 1:

1. The function of a neuron's dendrites is to:
   a. frighten potential cellular predators.
   b. make waves in the liquid that bathes the neurons.
   c. give personality or uniqueness to each neuron.
   d. receive incoming signals relayed from other neurons.

2. The specialized cells that allow the neurons to communicate with each other are called:
   a. glial cells.   c. somas.
   b. myelin sheaths.   d. dendrites and axons.

3. The _____ stores the neurotransmitters and is located at the end of the axon.
   a. terminal button   c. synapse
   b. cell body   d. refractory period

4. A neurotransmitter affects particular neurons, but not others, depending on whether:
   a. the receiving neuron expects a message to arrive.
   b. a suitable receptor site exists on the receiving neuron.
   c. the nerve impulse acts according to the all-or-none law.
   d. the receiving neuron is in its resting state.

5. The neural process of reuptake involves:
   a. the production of fresh neurotransmitters.
   b. the release of different neurotransmitter types by message-sending neurons.
   c. chemical breakdown of neurotransmitters by the receiving cell.
   d. soaking up of surplus neurotransmitters by the terminal button.

6. The portion of the nervous system that is particularly important for reflexive behavior is the:
   a. brain.   c. sensory nervous system.
   b. spinal cord.   d. motor nervous system.

7. Reflexes:
   a. are learned from infancy.
   b. involve the peripheral nervous system.
   c. always involve both the peripheral and central nervous systems.
   d. do not initially involve the cerebral cortex.

8. The autonomic nervous system controls:
   a. habitual, automatic movements such as applying the brakes of an automobile.
   b. the functions of the spinal cord.
   c. the body's response to an emergency or crisis.
   d. most of the spinal reflexes.

9. Which of the following is **not** likely to happen during activation of the sympathetic division of the nervous system?
   a. Increase in digestion
   c. Increase in sweating
   b. Increase in heart rate
   d. Increase in pupil sizes

10. Researchers involved in the study of teen drug abuse know that although "pleasure centers" are found at many brain sites, the most likely place to find them is in:
   a. the association areas of the cerebral cortex.
   c. the medulla.
   b. the limbic system.
   d. the cerebellum.

11. A car accident would probably lead to fatal results for the driver who damaged his _____, the part of the brain that controls important bodily functions such as heartbeat and breathing.
   a. medulla
   c. thalamus
   b. cerebellum
   d. hypothalamus

12. _____ in the cerebral cortex enhance(s) the most sophisticated integration of neural information by providing for much greater surface area and complex interconnections among neurons.
   a. Convoluted tissues
   c. Lateralization
   b. Mapping
   d. Hemispheric dominance

13. Andrew's recent stroke has left him unable to undertake purposeful, sequential behaviors. This condition is known as:
   a. dyslexia.
   c. apraxia.
   b. aphasia.
   d. paraplegia.

14. Sequential information processing is a characteristic of:
   a. the left cerebral hemisphere.
   c. the frontal lobes.
   b. the right cerebral hemisphere.
   d. the occipital lobes.

15. Which statement about the cerebral hemispheres does **not** apply to most right-handed people?
   a. The left hemisphere processes information sequentially.
   b. The right hemisphere processes information globally.
   c. The right hemisphere is associated with language and reasoning.
   d. Women display less hemispheric dominance than men, particularly with skills such as language.

____	16.	neurotransmitter	a. A chemical secretion that makes it more likely that a receiving neuron will fire and an action potential will travel down its axons.
____	17.	excitatory message	
____	18.	inhibitory message	b. A class of chemical secretions that behave like pain-killing opiates.
____	19.	endorphins	
____	20.	GABA	c. A chemical messenger that inhibits behaviors like eating and aggression.

d. A chemical secretion that prevents a receiving neuron from firing.

e. A chemical that carries the message from one neuron to another when secreted as the result of a nerve impulse.

21. The part of the brain's central core that transmits messages from the sense organs to the cerebral cortex and from the cerebral cortex to the cerebellum and medulla is the _____.

22. The major function of the _____ is to maintain homeostasis. It is located below the thalamus of the brain.

23. The _____ is a bundle of fibers that connects one-half of the brain to the other and is thicker in women than in men.

24. The major area of the brain that is responsible for voluntary movement of particular parts of the body is called the _____.

25. _____ is the area within the cortex corresponding to the sense of touch.

26. Describe the specific benefits of our knowledge of brain function and the effect of injury on the brain. What are the possible consequences of research in neurotransmitters, biofeedback, and even sex differences in the brain?

Practice Test 2:

1. A deficiency of acetylcholine is associated with:
   a. depression.
   b. Alzheimer's disease.
   c. Parkinson's disease.
   d. Huntington's chorea.

2. Neurons share many structures and functions with other types of cells, but they also have a specialized ability to:
   a. be active yet to consume almost no cellular energy.
   b. regenerate themselves even if injured seriously.
   c. send messages to specific targets over long distances.
   d. live for a long time even after the official death of the body.

3. Scientists have discovered that once an action potential has been fired, the neuron cannot fire again until:
   a. the resting state has been restored.
   b. the rising phase of the action potential has reached its peak.
   c. the reuptake of neurotransmitters has been complexed.
   d. the direction of the nerve impulse within the axon has been reversed.

4. Neural impulses generally travel:
   a. electrically between and within each neuron.
   b. chemically between and within each neuron.
   c. electrically between neurons and chemically within each neuron.
   d. chemically between neurons and electrically within each neuron.

5. Muscle tremors and rigidity associated with Parkinson's disease result from _____ in neural
   circuits.
   a. excessive ACh   c. excessive dopamine
   b. not enough ACh   d. not enough dopamine

6. The peripheral nervous system consists of:
   a. the spinal cord and brain.
   b. all neurons with myelin sheath.
   c. all neurons other than those in the spinal cord or brain.
   d. entirely efferent neurons.

7. Sympathetic division is to parasympathetic division as:
   a. fight is to flight.   c. arousing is to calming.
   b. central is to peripheral.   d. helpful is to hurtful.

8. The _____ records the brain's ongoing neural activities via electrodes attached externally to the skull.
   a. electroencephalogram (EEG)   c. transcranial magnetic stimulation (TMS) scan
   b. magnetic resonance imaging (MRI)   d. positron emission tomography (PET) scan

9. The capacities to think and remember probably best distinguish humans from other animals. These qualities are most closely associated with the function of the:
   a. cerebral cortex.   c. cerebellum.
   b. medulla.   d. limbic system.

10. The idea of neuroplasticity means that:
    a. the brain can change, reorganize, and develop new neural connections over the lifetime.
    b. there is flexibility in the motor functions that various parts of the brain control.
    c. plastic shields can be inserted into the corpus callosum of patients with epilepsy to keep the two halves of the brain from communicating during a seizure.
    d. certain areas of the brain are responsible for touch, temperature, and other physical stimulation.

11. Which area of the brain has the largest portion of the cortex?
    a. Motor area   c. Sensory area
    b. Somatosensory area   d. Association area

12. Erik has a deep appreciation of music, art, and dance, and an understanding of spatial relationships that are more likely to be processed in the:
    a. right side of the brain.   c. occipital lobes.
    b. left side of the brain.   d. temporal lobe.

13. Mr. Argulla is having difficulty with pattern-recognition tasks and spatial memory since his recent stroke. Damage to which of the following areas is most likely to have caused this difficulty?
    a. Frontal lobe   c. Right hemisphere
    b. Left hemisphere   d. Temporal lobe

14. In order to control internal biological states, doctors have used a system of biofeedback that works by:
    a. following the suggestions and strategies of a biologically trained facilitator or therapist.
    b. thinking positively about the biological responses to be modified.
    c. listening to a soothing audiocassette containing biorhythmic signals that alter biological responses in the brain.
    d. electronically monitoring biological responses and providing continuous feedback so that adaptive tactics for changing those responses can be applied.

15. In multiple sclerosis, the _____ deteriorates, exposing parts of the _____. The result is a short circuit between the nervous system and muscle, which leads to difficulties with walking, vision, and with general muscle coordination.
    a. cell body; nucleus   c. terminal button; nucleus
    b. dendrite; terminal button   d. myelin sheath; axon

_____ 16. synapse

_____ 17. acetylcholine

_____ 18. EEG

_____ 19. reflex

a. An imagining technique that involves monitoring the brain's metabolic activity.

b. The gap between neurons across which chemical messages are communicated.

c. Automatic behavior is response to a specific stimulus.

d. A chemical secretion that transmits messages relating to skeletal muscles and may also be related to memory.

20. The gap between neurons is called the _____.

21. The division of the nervous system that is particularly important for "fight or flight" is the _____.

22. The most likely place to find a "pleasure center" in the brain is the _____.

23. The _____ controls important bodily functions such as heartbeat and breathing.

24. The _____ areas of the brain deal with thinking, language, and speech.

25. Several recent developments raise important questions for ethical consideration. What are the problems that arise when surgery separates the two hemispheres? What are the potential dangers of transplanting fetal tissue into the brain? Discuss these ethical and moral issues. Are there other issues?

PRACTICE TEST 3: Conceptual, Applied, and Challenging Questions

1. One important purpose of glial cells is to:
   a. release neurotransmitters.
   b. clear metabolites from the cell.
   c. bring nourishment to the cell.
   d. regenerate an action potential after firing.

2. After neurotransmitters have sent their message to the receiving neuron, they are usually:
   a. deactivated by enzymes.
   b. reabsorbed by the terminal buttons.
   c. absorbed into the body and filtered through the kidneys.
   d. absorbed into the receiving neuron.

3. The word most closely associated with the function of the limbic system is:
   a. thinking.
   b. waking.
   c. emergency.
   d. emotion.

4. Which of the following may be the most critical structure for maintaining homeostasis, a steady internal state of the body?
   a. Hippocampus
   b. Cerebral cortex
   c. Hypothalamus
   d. Cerebellum

5. Damage to or lesions in which of the following brain structures would be most likely to cause dramatic changes in emotionality and behavior?
   a. Pons
   b. Medulla
   c. Cerebellum
   d. Limbic system

6. Which of the following is **true** of both the sensory and motor areas of the cortex?
   a. They both contain pleasure centers.
   b. More cortical tissue is devoted to the most important structures.
   c. Electrical stimulation produces involuntary movement.
   d. Destruction of any one area affects all of the senses.

7. Mr. Costello was a shrewd, energetic business executive who persistently carried out all of his plans of operation. After a head injury, he was no longer able to make plans or complete them. The dramatic changes in him after his accident suggest that which area of his cerebral cortex was injured?
   a. Neuromuscular
   b. Association
   c. Sensory-somatosensory
   d. Motor

8. Mr. McCarthy had a great deal of difficulty *understanding* the speech of others and producing coherent speech after his surgery. He suffered from:
   a. Wernicke's aphasia.
   c. Broca's aphasia.

b. Lou Gehrig's disease.   d. Phineas Gage's disease.

9. Left hemisphere is to _____ function as right hemisphere is to _____ function.
    a. sequential; successive   c. successive; sequential
    b. sequential; global   d. global; sequential

10. Wernicke's aphasia is to _____ as Broca's aphasia is to _____.
    a. spasticity; flaccidity
    b. motor cortex; sensory cortex
    c. overeating; irregular gait
    d. difficulty in comprehending words; searching for the correct word

11. One primary difference in the organization of male and female brains is that:
    a. logical abilities are on the opposite sides in males and females.
    b. language abilities are more evenly divided between the two hemispheres in females.
    c. the right hemisphere is almost always dominant in females.
    d. spatial abilities are on the opposite sides in males and females.

12. A split-brain patient has had:
    a. a stroke.   c. damage to one of the hemispheres.
    b. the nerves between the hemispheres cut. d. epilepsy.

13. Audry has just been diagnosed with a disease in which the myelin sheath deteriorates, causing messages sent from the brain to various muscles to be delayed or not received. The diagnosis is most likely:
    a. Alzheimer's disease.   c. multiple sclerosis.
    b. Parkinson's disease.   d. GABA disease.

14. In the middle of a sentence, Joseph becomes rigid and stares into space. After a few minutes, he shakes a little bit and then seems to return to the discussion. He explains that he has a common neural disorder related to a shortage of a neurotransmitter. His disorder is probably:
    a. Alzheimer's disease.   c. multiple sclerosis.
    b. Parkinson's disease.   d. GABA disease.

15. The neurologist recorded the activity of a set of neurons. As the neurons in the set increased their activity, surrounding neurons seemed to slow down. What kind of messages were these neurons most likely sending?
    a. Sensory   c. Inhibitory
    b. Motor   d. Autonomic

_____ 16. homeostasis

_____ 17. eating

_____ 18. terminal buttons

_____ 19. myelin sheath

_____ 20. reuptake

a. The limbic system regulates a variety of motivated behaviors such as _____.

b. Located at the end of the axon, their purpose is to store neurotransmitters before release.

c. Characterized by the functioning of an optimal range of physiological processes, it is the tendency of the body to maintain a balanced state.

d. Method of clearing the neurotransmitter from the synaptic cleft, transmitter returns to terminal buttons.

e. Specialized cells of fat and protein that wrap themselves around the axon.

21. The function of the neuron's _____ is to receive incoming signals relayed from other neurons.

22. The _____ is one of the major areas of the brain, the site of the higher mental processes, such as thought, language, memory, and speech.

23. The _____ hemisphere of the brain concentrates on tasks requiring verbal competence.

24. Music and emotional experiences are located in the _____ hemisphere.

25 Located in the occipital lobe, the _____ receives input of images from the eyes.

26. Discuss the role that the media might play in the research of certain brain research. Consider what well-known celebrities have done for the research of their particular illness (Michael J. Fox, Muhammad Ali, Janet Reno—Parkinson's disease; Christopher Reeve, spinal cord regeneration).

Module 7:	Module 8:	Module 9:	Evaluate
[a] biopsychologists	[a] central nervous system (CNS)	[a] (EEG)	Part A
[b] neurons	[b] spinal cord	[b] (PET) scan	1. d
[c] Dendrites	[c] reflexes	[c] (fMRI)	2. b
[d] axons	[d] Sensory (afferent)	[d] (TMS)	3. a
[e] terminal buttons	[e] Motor (efferent)	[e] neuroforensics	4. c
[f] myelin sheath	[f] Interneurons	[f] central core	5. e
[g] resting state	[g] peripheral nervous system	[g] cerebellum	
[h] action potential	[h] somatic division	[h] reticular formation	Part B
[i] all-or-none	[i] autonomic division	[i] thalamus	1. d
[j] synapse	[j] sympathetic division	[j] hypothalamus	2. e
[k] neurotransmitters	[k] parasympathetic division	[k] limbic system	3. c
[l] excitatory messages	[l] evolutionary psychology	[l] cerebral cortex	4. b
[m] inhibitory messages	[m] behavioral genetics	[m] lobes	5. a
[n] reuptake	[n] endocrine system	[n] motor	
	[o] hormones	[o] sensory	
Evaluate	[p] pituitary	[p] association	
Part A Part B		[q] hemispheres	
1. a 1. c	Evaluate	[r] lateralization	
2. e 2. d	1. b	[s] neuroplasticity	
3. c 3 e	2. e		
4. b 4. a	3. c		
5. d 5. f	4. d		
6 .b	5. a		

Selected Rethink Answers

7-1 A number of psychological disorders have been linked to imbalances in neurotransmitters. Patients could receive drugs that provide the proper balance of the neurotransmitters that they are either lacking, or have too much of. For instance, schizophrenia is linked to high dopamine, so sufferers could receive treatment to balance out dopamine levels or block the reception of dopamine. In another instance, depression is associated with improper serotonin levels, so patients could receive treatment to affect its balance.

8-1 Fight or Flight. Part of the sympathetic division that acts to prepare the body for action in the case of a stressful situation. It engages the organs' resources to respond to a threat: heart races, palms sweat, etc. Reactions occur at the physiological level.

9-2 Yes, it would seem that if people had somewhat unique brain lateralization, they could use this to their occupational success. For instance, some people may be more apt to use the right brain when processing information. This suggests they would process information in more non-verbal terms, thinking in terms of patterns, emotional expression, and spatial relationships. If so, they may be particularly good at occupations requiring those thinking styles, such as architecture, interior design, acting, and therapy. If someone was more apt to use the left brain in processing, they would be heavily reliant on reading, thinking, speaking, and reasoning as a way of information processing. Such people would probably make good scientists, teachers, public relations agents, and lawyers.

Practice Test 1:

1. d   mod. 7   p. 62
   a. Incorrect. Cellular predators cannot be frightened.
   b. Incorrect. The only waving done in the body is with the hand.
   c. Incorrect. Each neuron has a unique number and distribution of dendrites, but this is not the purpose of the dendrites.
   *d. Correct. Dendrites act as the receivers for the neuron.

2. d   mod. 7   p. 62
   a. Incorrect. Glial cells support neurons.
   b. Incorrect. The myelin sheath is the fatty substance that forms an insulating covering around axons.
   c. Incorrect. The soma is the cell body of the neuron.
   *d. Correct. Dendrites receive stimulation and axons convey information to the next neuron.

3. a   mod. 7   p. 62
   *a. Correct. This is the end of the axon branches.
   b. Incorrect. This part contains the nucleus and metabolic units of the neuron.
   c. Incorrect. The word "synapse" even means gap.
   d. Incorrect. A refractory period is the conclusion of an action potential during which the neuron cannot fire again.

4. b   mod. 7   p. 66
   a. Incorrect. Individual neurons do not exhibit the cognitive skill of "expectation."
   *b. Correct. Neurotransmitters lock into specific sites receptive to that type of neurotransmitter.
   c. Incorrect. All nerve impulses act according to the all-or-nothing law, thus this information would be irrelevant to the receiving neuron.
   d. Incorrect. If the neuron has the receptor sites, it always is affected by the neurotransmitter, whether it is firing or not.

5. d   mod. 7   p. 66
   a. Incorrect. The need for new production is minimized by reuptake.
   b. Incorrect. This is not reuptake.
   c. Incorrect. Some neurotransmitters are metabolized by enzymes in the synaptic cleft; this material may return to the neuron in another manner other than reuptake.
   *d. Correct. Reuptake is the reabsorption of unmetabolized neurotransmitters in the area of the synapse.

6. b   mod. 8   p. 71
   a. Incorrect. Actually, it could be said that the role of the brain is to override reflexes.
   *b. Correct. Many messages that are processed reflexively simply pass through the spinal cord and are not sent to the brain.
   c. Incorrect. We do sense the stimuli that cause reflexes, but we can actually have them without our sensation of them.
   d. Incorrect. However, without a motor system, we would not have reflexes.

7. d   mod. 7   p. 71
   a. Incorrect. Reflexes are inborn and not learned.
   b. Incorrect. They involve the peripheral nervous system and often the central nervous system.
   c. Incorrect. Some reflexes may not involve the central nervous system.
   *d. Correct. Fundamentally, reflexes are processed through the spinal cord or by lower parts of the brain.

8. c   mod. 7   p. 72
   a. Incorrect. These kinds of processes do involve the brain and the voluntary muscles.
   b. Incorrect. The autonomic nervous system is not responsible for spinal cord functions.
   *c. Correct. Of these choices, this is the only one included in the activity controlled by the autonomic system.
   d. Incorrect. The spinal reflexes involve the somatic system and voluntary muscles.

9. a   mod. 7   p. 73
   *a. Correct. The sympathetic division activates and energizes responses necessary for survival and quick responses, thus it shuts down the digestive processes.
   b. Incorrect. The sympathetic response increases heart rate in order to increase energy availability.
   c. Incorrect. The sympathetic response increases sweating in order to provide additional cooling.
   d. Incorrect. The sympathetic response increases pupil sizes, probably to increase the available detail about the visible world.

10. b   mod. 9   p. 84
   a. Incorrect. Memory is stored here.
   *b. Correct. Most of the structures related to pleasure, especially the hypothalamus and the amygdala, are part of the limbic system.
   c. Incorrect. The medulla controls things like breathing.
   d. Incorrect. The cerebellum controls voluntary muscle movements.

11. a   mod. 9   p. 82
*a. Correct. This is the medulla's role.
b.   Incorrect. The cerebellum helps control voluntary muscle and coordinate movement.
c.   Incorrect. The thalamus is responsible for handling incoming and outgoing messages for the cortex.
d.   Incorrect. The hypothalamus is responsible for regulating basic biological needs.

12. a   mod. 9   p. 85
*a. Correct. The convoluted tissues increase the surface area of the cortex dramatically.
b.   Incorrect. Mapping helps the neuroscientists but not the brain itself.
c.   Incorrect. Lateralization arises because of the cerebrum being divided into two hemispheres.
d.   Incorrect. Hemispheric dominance is not related to the amount of surface area of the cortex.

13. c   mod. 9   p. 88
a.   Incorrect. "Lexia" is related to the root of lexicon and refers to words.
b.   Incorrect. "Aphasia" refers to processing errors, like the inability to process language or the inability to produce speech.
*c. Correct. The root of "praxia" means practice or action.
d.   Incorrect. "Paraplegia" refers to paralysis in two limbs.

14. a   mod. 9   p. 91
*a. Correct. Logic, sequential, and many language functions are controlled in the left hemisphere.
b.   Incorrect. The right hemisphere has been associated more with spatial relations and emotional expression.
c.   Incorrect. The frontal lobes are more responsible for planning and physical movement.
d.   Incorrect. The occipital lobes are devoted to visual experience.

15. c   mod. 9   p. 91
a.   Incorrect. This is true of most right-handed people.
b.   Incorrect. This is true of most right-handed people.
*c. Correct. The left hemisphere is associated with language and reasoning.
d.   Incorrect. This applies to both left- and right-handed people.

16. e   mod. 7   p. 65
17. a   mod. 7   p. 65

18. d   mod. 7   p. 65
19. b   mod. 7   p. 68
20. c   mod. 7   p. 68

21. thalamus   mod. 9   p. 84
22. hypothalamus   mod. 9   p. 84
23. corpus callosum   mod. 9   p. 78
24. cerebellum   mod. 9   p. 83
25. The somatosensory area   mod. 9   p. 86

26.
▪ Knowledge of the brain leads to improved medical and psychological therapies of the injured and of stroke sufferers.
▪ Knowledge about brain function should provide greater knowledge about behavior.
▪ An understanding of neurotransmitter function can be applied to many phenomena, such as pain, drug abuse, healing processes, and thinking processes.
▪ Knowledge of male and female differences will help us understand differences and similarities among individuals as well.

Practice Test 2:
1.   b   mod. 9   p. 67
a.   Incorrect. Usually a lack of serotonin and dopamine.
*b. Correct. Lack of acetylcholine is a contributing factor.
c.   Incorrect. Parkinson's occurs when there is a lack of dopamine.
d.   Incorrect. Huntington's disease has a genetic component.

2.   c   mod. 7   p. 61
a.   Incorrect. Like any other cell, activity requires energy.
b.   Incorrect. Actually, they regenerate only in special circumstances.
*c. Correct. Many neurons have very long axons, and the axons are attached to specific targets.
d.   Incorrect. Neurons live no longer than any other cells.

3.   a   mod. 7   p. 63
*a. Correct. During the absolute refractory period before returning to the resting state, the neuron cannot fire.
b.   Incorrect. There is no "rising phase."
c.   Incorrect. Reuptake occurs continuously and independently of the firing of the neuron.
d.   Incorrect. The nerve impulse never reverses (though many neurons have feedback loops).

4.   d   mod. 7   p. 65
a.   Incorrect. A chemical process takes place between neurons.
b.   Incorrect. An electrical process carries the message within the neuron.
c.   Incorrect. The parts are reversed; try chemically between neurons and electrically within each neuron.
*d.   Correct. A neurotransmitter (chemical) passes between neurons; an electrical charge moves down neurons.

5.   d   mod. 7   p. 68
a.   Incorrect. The answer is insufficient dopamine.
b.   Incorrect. The answer is insufficient dopamine.
c.   Incorrect. The answer is insufficient dopamine.
*d.   Correct. The answer is insufficient dopamine, and these symptoms are linked to Parkinson's disease.

6.   c   mod. 7   p. 72
a.   Incorrect. This is the central nervous system.
b.   Incorrect. Neurons with myelin sheath can be found in both the central and peripheral nervous systems.
*c.   Correct. The peripheral system consists of the voluntary and involuntary control systems of the body.
d.   Incorrect. It also includes efferent neurons.

7.   c   mod. 7   p. 72
a.   Incorrect. Fight and flight are the options available whenever the sympathetic system is activated.
b.   Incorrect. Both sympathetic and parasympathetic divisions are part of the peripheral system.
*c.   Correct. The sympathetic division arouses and the parasympathetic division calms.
d.   Incorrect. Both divisions are necessary to survival (thus helpful).

8.   a   mod. 9   p. 80
*a.   Correct. EEG stands for electroencephalogram, or electrical recording of the brain.
b.   Incorrect. MRI scans use the magnetic fields of the object being scanned.
c.   Incorrect. TMS exposes the brain to a strong magnetic field, creating a "virtual lesion."
d.   Incorrect. PET scans utilize recordings of the metabolism of isotopes of a special glucose.

9.   a   mod. 9   p. 85
*a.   Correct. The cortex is rich in axons and dendrites that are very close together, thus supporting rapid processing of large amounts of information.
b.   Incorrect. The medulla controls unconscious functions like breathing and blood circulation.
c.   Incorrect. The cerebellum helps smooth and coordinate muscle movement.
d.   Incorrect. The limbic system includes a number of structures related to emotion, motivation, memory, pain, and pleasure.

10.   a   mod. 9   p. 87
*a.   Correct. This is the definition of neuroplasticity.
b.   Incorrect. This is not neuroplasticity, and moreover, there are certain structures in the brain which control certain functions.
c.   Incorrect. This doesn't exist, though it would be pretty neat if it did.
d.   Incorrect. This is true, though it is not the definition of neuroplasticity.

11.   d   mod. 9   p. 88
a.   Incorrect. Compared to the association areas, the motor area is quite small.
b.   Incorrect. Compared to the association areas, the somatosensory area is quite small.
c.   Incorrect. Compared to the association areas, the sensory areas are quite small.
*d.   Correct. All of the areas not specifically associated with an identified function, like sensation, motor activity, or language, are called association areas.

12.   a   mod. 9   p. 91
*a.   Correct. The right side of the brain is often associated with more global processing and emotional or expressive information.
b.   Incorrect. The left side of the brain is more often associated with linear and logical processing.
c.   Incorrect. The occipital lobes are necessary for the visual information about art and dance, but their role is more specialized to visual processing.
d.   Incorrect. The temporal lobes are primarily responsible for hearing, and they may contribute well to understanding dance and music, but less well to processing other forms of art.

13. c   mod. 9   p. 91
a.   Incorrect. The frontal lobe is responsible for higher-order thought and planning, among other activities.
b.   Incorrect. The left side of the brain is more often associated with linear and logical processing.
*c. Correct. The right side of the brain is often associated with more global processing, emotional or expressive information, and pattern recognition and spatial memory.
d.   Incorrect. The temporal lobes are primarily responsible for hearing.

14. d   mod. 7   p. 94
a.   Incorrect. In order to begin, one must attend to the directions of the person attaching the machine, but that is the only suggestion required.
b.   Incorrect. This may be part of the process, but it is not the technique.
c.   Incorrect. This may be feedback, but it is not biofeedback.
*d. Correct. The technique does involve focusing on electronic signals and attention to changes in them.

15. d   mod. 7   p. 62
a.   Incorrect. The myelin sheath deteriorates, and the axon is then exposed to stimulation from other axons.
b.   Incorrect. The myelin sheath deteriorates, and the axon is then exposed to stimulation from other axons.
c.   Incorrect. The myelin sheath deteriorates, and the axon is then exposed to stimulation from other axons.
*d. Correct. The myelin sheath breaks down and loses its insulating capacity, allowing the short circuits to occur.

16. b   mod. 7   p. 65
17. d   mod. 7   p. 67
18. a   mod. 7   p. 80
19. c   mod. 7   p. 71

20. synapse   mod. 7   p. 65
21. sympathetic-division mod. 7   p. 73
22. limbic system   mod. 9   p. 84
23. medulla   mod. 9   p. 82
24. Association   mod. 9   p. 88

25.
▪   Split-brain research may actually create the phenomena observed, yet many people wish to use it to substantiate strong differences between left- and right-brain dominant individuals. Also, this research depends on this operation.
▪   The danger of transplanting tissue is not that it will create some monster, but that tissue needed may come from sources that raise moral questions, like fetuses.
▪   You should identify moral and ethical reasons both for and against this research and related procedures.

Practice Test 3:
1. c   mod. 7   p. 62
a.   Incorrect. Neurotransmitters are released at the synapse as a result of an action potential.
b.   Incorrect. This is the work of other structures in the cell body.
*c. Correct. Some nourishment is brought to the cell body via the glial cells
d.   Incorrect. The action potential is regenerated in the refractory period by the sodium pump.

2. b   mod. 7   p. 66
a.   Incorrect. Deactivation by enzymes in the receiving cell happens to all neurotransmitters.
*b. Correct. Most are reabsorbed in the process called reuptake, some are broken down by enzymes in the area surrounding the synapse.
c.   Incorrect. Some, but not most, are processed out of the body this way.
d.   Incorrect. None are absorbed by the receiving neuron.

3. d   mod. 9   p. 84
a.   Incorrect. Thinking is associated with the frontal lobes.
b.   Incorrect. Waking is associated with the pons and the reticular formation.
c.   Incorrect. Emergencies are associated with the sympathetic nervous system.
*d. Correct. The limbic system is associated with emotions as well as pain and pleasure, motivation, and memory.

4. c   mod. 9   p. 84
a.   Incorrect. The hippocampus is associated with memory and motivation.
b.   Incorrect. The cerebral cortex is associated with thinking.
*c. Correct. This describes the primary role of the hypothalamus.
d.   Incorrect. The cerebellum is responsible for smoothing and coordinating voluntary muscle activity.

5. d   mod. 9   p. 84

a. Incorrect. Damage here might affect motor behavior but not emotion, and the individual would probably have difficulty waking up from the coma.
b. Incorrect. Damage here would affect breathing and circulation; however, emotional expression would be limited by the mobility of the heart-lung machine.
c. Incorrect. The cerebellum is responsible for smoothing and coordinating voluntary muscle activity.
*d. Correct. The limbic system is associated with emotions as well as pain and pleasure, motivation, and memory.

6. b   mod. 9   p. 86

a. Incorrect. Pleasure centers are in the limbic system.
*b. Correct. The amount of surface area correlates to the sensitivity or refinement of control of the associated function.
c. Incorrect. This is true only in the motor cortex.
d. Incorrect. Damage to the somatosensory area may affect all of the bodily sensation for the corresponding body area, but it will not affect the motor control.

7. b   mod. 9   p. 88

a. Incorrect. The neuromuscular area is not very close to the area affected.
*b. Correct. The areas affected must have been association areas because they are important for planning.
c. Incorrect. The damage described does not relate to damage to the somatosensory areas.
d. Incorrect. The damage described does not relate to damage to the motor areas.

8. a   mod. 9   p. 89

*a. Correct. Wernicke's aphasia is associated with the comprehension of speech.
b. Incorrect. Lou Gehrig's disease does affect speech, but it affects motor control, not the comprehension of speech.
c. Incorrect. Broca's aphasia results in difficulty producing speech, while the sufferer may be able to understand the speech of others perfectly well.
d. Incorrect. Phineas Gage did not have a disease; he had an accident that effectively gave him a frontal lobotomy.

9. b   mod. 9   p. 91

a. Incorrect. Successive functioning sounds a lot like sequential functioning.
*b. Correct. In broad terms, these two choices reflect the description of the styles of activity associated with the hemispheres.
c. Incorrect. Successive functioning sounds a lot like sequential functioning.
d. Incorrect. The choices are reversed.

10. d   mod. 9   p. 88-89

a. Incorrect. Probably not, although the terms have a technical ring to them.
b. Incorrect. Actually, Wernicke's area is closely aligned with the sensory cortex and Broca's area is closely aligned with the motor cortex.
c. Incorrect. Overeating would be associated with the hypothalamus and other limbic structures, while an irregular gait could be associated with motor cortex damage or damage to the cerebellum.
*d. Correct. These choices describe the correct aphasias. Both aphasias have an effect on the production of speech.

11. b   mod. 9   p. 92

a. Incorrect. Logic processing tends to occur in the left side of the brain for males and females.
*b. Correct. Language is more localized in males in the left hemisphere.
c. Incorrect. It may occasionally be dominant in left-handed people.
d. Incorrect. Spatial abilities tend to be processed in the right hemisphere for both males and females.

12. b   mod. 9   p. 93

a. Incorrect. The bundle of neural fibers called the corpus callosum has been severed in split-brain patients.
*b. Correct. The bundle of neural fibers called the corpus callosum has been severed in split-brain patients.
c. Incorrect. The bundle of neural fibers called the corpus callosum has been severed in split-brain patients, but not all patients had damage to a hemisphere.
d. Incorrect. The bundle of neural fibers called the corpus callosum has not been cut in all patients with epilepsy.

13. c mod. 7 p. 119
a. Incorrect. Alzheimer's disease has been associated with a deficiency of acetylcholine.
b. Incorrect. Parkinson's disease has been associated with an underproduction of dopamine.
* c. Correct. Multiple sclerosis involves the deterioration of the myelin sheath.
d. Incorrect. There is no disease called GABA disease.

14. b mod. 7 p. 126
a. Incorrect. Alzheimer's disease does not come and go.
*b. Correct. Parkinson's disease has been associated with a shortage of dopamine, and one of the symptoms is this on-and-off type of behavior.
c. Incorrect. Multiple sclerosis involves the deterioration of the myelin sheath.
d. Incorrect. There is no disease called GABA disease.

15. c mod. 7 p. 66
a. Incorrect. These kinds of messages do occur in sensory messages, but they do not define the sensory message.
b. Incorrect. These kinds of messages do occur in motor messages, but they do not define the motor message.
*c. Correct. This is what happens in inhibitory messages.
d. Incorrect. The autonomic system utilizes both inhibitory and excitatory messages.

16. c mod. 9 p. 84
17. a mod. 9 p. 84
18. b mod. 7 p. 62
19. e mod. 7 p. 62
20. d mod. 7 p. 66

21. dendrites   mod. 7 p. 62
22. association   mod. 9 p. 88
23. left   mod. 9 p. 91
24. right   mod. 9 p. 91
25. visual area   mod. 9 p. 87

26.
▪ The media helps us identify and understand different illnesses of the brain. News articles, movies of the week, and talk shows all make us aware of illnesses and their effects on human lives and the lives of their families.
▪ While it is unfortunate that famous people feel exploited, celebrity illnesses make good press. People like to read about those they know and like to watch their progress.
▪ Also, celebrities can successfully raise money for a particular cause (because they have access that many of us don't to people with money and influence).
▪ This has always been a lucrative avenue for those looking for research funding.

Chapter 4: Sensation and Perception

Module 10: Sensing the World Around Us
Module 11: Vision: Shedding Light on the Eye
Module 12: Hearing and the Other Senses
Module 13: Perceptual Organization: Constructing Our View of the World

Overview

This set of modules focuses on the nature of the information our body takes in through its senses and the way we interpret the information. Both sensation and perception are explored. Sensation encompasses the processes by which our sense organs receive information from the environment. Perception is the interpretation, analysis, and integration of stimuli involving our sense organs.

Module 10 introduces the major senses, including vision, hearing, balance, smell, taste, touch, and pain. It follows with an explanation of sensation and perception by exploring the relationships between the characteristics of a physical stimulus and the kinds of sensory responses they produce. This section defines absolute threshold, difference threshold, and the occurrence of sensory adaptation.

Module 11 illuminates the structure of the eye and the role each part of the eye plays in the production of sight. The process by which the eye sends messages to the brain is explained. This is followed by a discussion of color vision, the trichromatic theory of color vision, and the opponent-process theory of color vision.

Module 12 examines the structure of the ear as the center of sound, motion, and balance. The individual structures of the eardrum are discussed. This discussion is followed by an explanation of the physical characteristics of sound, its frequency, and amplitude. This module also explores the functions of taste and smell; the skin senses that are responsible for touch, pressure, temperature, and pain; and concludes with a discussion on the techniques used to alleviate pain.

Module 13 offers an explanation of our organization of the world. The principles that allow us to make sense of our environment include the gestalt laws of organization, feature analysis, top-down processing, and perceptual constancy. This is followed by a discussion on depth and motion perception. In conclusion, the module discusses visual illusions and the clues they provide about our understanding of perceptual mechanisms.

To further investigate the topics covered in this chapter, you can visit the related Web sites by visiting the following link: www.mhhe.com/feldmanup8.

Prologue: Feeling No Pain!
Looking Ahead

Module 10: Sensing the World Around Us

Absolute Thresholds: Detecting What's Out There
Difference Thresholds: Noticing Distinctions Between Stimuli
Sensory Adaptation: Turning Down Our Responses

- ***What is sensation, and how do psychologists study it?***
- ***What is the relationship between a physical stimulus and the kinds of sensory responses that result from it?***

Sensing the World Around Us

A(n) **[a]** _____ is the activity of the sense organ when it detects a stimulus. The difference between perception and sensation is that sensation involves the organism's first encounter with physical stimuli, and **[b]** _____ is the process of interpreting, analyzing, and integrating sensations.

We detect the world around us through our senses. A(n) **[c]** _____ is any physical energy that can be detected by a sense organ. Stimuli vary in type and intensity.

Intensity refers to the physical strength of the stimulus. **[d]** _____ studies the relationship between the strength of a stimulus and the nature of the sensory response it creates.

[e] _____ refers to the smallest amount of energy, the smallest intensity, needed to detect a stimulus. The absolute threshold for sight is illustrated by a candle burning at 30 miles away on a dark night; for hearing, the ticking of a watch 20 feet away in a quiet room; for taste, 1 teaspoon of sugar in 2 gallons of water; for smell, one drop of perfume in three rooms; and for touch, a bee's wing falling 1 centimeter onto a cheek. *Noise* refers to the background stimulation for any of the senses.

The smallest noticeable difference between two stimuli is called the **[f]** _____, or the **[g]** _____. The amount of stimulus required for the just noticeable difference depends on the level of the initial stimulus. **[h]** _____ states that the just noticeable difference is a constant proportion for each sense. Weber's law is not very accurate at extreme high or low intensities.

After prolonged exposure to a sensory stimulus, the capacity of the sensory organ adjusts to the stimulus through a process called **[i]** _____. The sensory receptor cells are most responsive to changes in stimuli, because constant stimulation produces adaptation. Context also affects judgments about sensory stimuli. People's reactions to sensory stimuli do not always accurately represent the physical stimuli that cause it.

Evaluate

_____ 1. sensation

_____ 2. intensity

_____ 3. absolute threshold

_____ 4. noise

_____ 5. difference threshold

a. The strength of a stimulus.

b. The smallest detectable difference between two stimuli.

c. The process of responding to a stimulus.

d. The smallest amount of physical intensity by which a stimulus can be detected.

e. Background stimulation that interferes with the perception of other stimuli.

Rethink

10-1   Do you think it is possible to have sensation without perception? Is it possible to have perception without sensation?

10-2   *From the perspective of a manufacturer:* How might you need to take psychophysics into account when developing new products or modifying existing ones?

Spotlight on Terminology and Language – ESL Pointers

Page 194 "Sure enough, an ophthalmologist discovered a **massive corneal abrasion**, a condition normally so painful that even an adult would be howling."

Massive means very large. An **abrasion** is a cut or scrape. A **corneal abrasion** is a cut or scrape of the eye.

Page 196 "To a psychologist interested in understanding the causes of behavior, sensation and perception are **fundamental** topics because so much of our behavior is a reflection of how we react to and interpret stimuli from the world around us."

Fundamental refers to something important or necessary.

Page 198 "Clearly, you would experience the dinner very differently than would someone whose sensory **apparatus** was intact."

Apparatus is the set of materials or equipment designed for a particular use. What are some of the ways in which you use your hearing and taste senses?

Page 198 "Although perhaps you were taught, as I was, that there are just five senses – sight, sound, taste, smell, and touch – that **enumeration** is too modest."

To **enumerate** is to list. This list of the senses is simply not complete. Which senses would you add to the list?

Page 198 "In formal terms, **sensation** is the activation of the sense organs by a source of physical energy."

Sensation is our first awareness of some outside stimulus.

Page 198 "**Perception** is the sorting out, interpretation, analysis, and integration of stimuli carried out by the sense organs and brain."

Perception is your brain assembling thousands on individual sensations into the experience of a meaningful pattern or image.

Page 198 "An absolute threshold is the smallest **intensity** of a stimulus that must be present for it to be detected."

Intensity refers to magnitude. Absolute threshold refers to the smallest amount of a stimulus that must be present for it to be determined that it exists.

Page 199 "In fact, our senses are so **fine-tuned** that we might have problems if they were any more sensitive."

Fine-tuned means precise or exact. When we ask how **fine-tuned** something is we are asking how precise or sensitive it is.

Page 199 "For instance, if our ears were slightly more **acute**, we would be able to hear the sound of air molecules in our ears knocking into the eardrum – a phenomenon that would surely prove distracting and might even prevent us from hearing sounds outside our bodies."

Acute means more discerning or more perceptive. **Acute** hearing is hearing that is responsive to slight impressions or stimuli.

Page 200 "The **din** of the crowd makes it hard to hear individual voices, and the smoke makes it difficult to see, or even taste, the food.

The **din** is the background noise made by a group of people.

Page 201 "The reason you **acclimate** to the odor is sensory adaptation."

When an organism **acclimates** to something, it makes a physiological adjustment to environmental changes.

Page 202 "Adaptation to the context of one stimulus (the size of the envelope) **alters** responses to another stimulus (the weight of the envelope) (Coren & Ward, 1989)."

When you **alter** something you make it different without changing it into something else.

Module 11:
Vision: Shedding Light on the Eye

Illuminating the Structure of the Eye
Color Vision and Color Blindness: The Seven-Million-Color Spectrum

- ***What basic processes underlie the sense of vision?***
- ***How do we see colors?***

Vision: Shedding Light on the Eye

The stimulus that produces vision is light. Light is the electromagnetic radiation that our visual apparatus is capable of detecting. The range of light that is visible to humans is called the **[a]** _____.

Light enters the eye through the **[b]** _____, a transparent, protective window. It then passes through the **[c]** _____, the dark opening in the iris. The iris is the pigmented muscle that opens and closes the pupil depending on how much light is in the environment. The narrower the pupil is, the greater is the focal distance for the eye. After the pupil, the light passes through the *lens*, which then bends and focuses the light on the back of the eye by changing its thickness, a process called **[d]** _____. The light then strikes the **[e]** _____, a thin layer of nerve cells at the back of the eyeball.

The retina is composed of light-sensitive cells called **[f]** _____, which are long and cylindrical, and **[g]** _____, which are shorter and conical in shape. The greatest concentration of cones is in the *fovea*, an area that is extremely sensitive. Cones are responsible for color vision, and rods are insensitive to color and play a role in *peripheral vision*, the ability to see objects to our side, and in night vision.

When a person goes into a dark room from a well-lit space, the person becomes, after a time, accustomed to the dark and experiences **[h]** _____, an adjustment by the eyes to low levels of light. The changes that make this adjustment are chemical changes in the rods and cones.

Rods contain **[i]** _____, a complex substance that changes chemically when struck by light. This chemical change sets off a reaction. The response is then transmitted to two other kinds of cells, first to the *bipolar cells* and then to *ganglion cells*. The ganglion cells organize and summarize the information and then convey it to the **[j]** _____. Where the optic nerve goes from the retina back through the eyeball, there are no rods or cones, which results in the blind spot.

The optic nerves from both eyes meet behind the eyes at the **[k]** _____, where each optic nerve splits. Nerve impulses from the right half of each eye go to the right side of the brain, and nerve impulses from the left half of each eye go to the left half of the brain. The visual message is processed from the beginning by ganglion cells, and continues to the visual cortex, where many neurons are highly specialized. Their roles are specialized to detect certain visual features, and the process is called **[l]** _____.

Evaluate

_____ 1. pupil

_____ 2. cornea

_____ 3. iris

_____ 4. lens

_____ 5. retina

a. The colored part of the eye.

b. The part of the eye that converts the electromagnetic energy of light into useful information for the brain.

c. A dark hole in the center of the eye's iris that changes size as the amount of incoming light changes.

d. A transparent, protective window into the eyeball.

e. The part of the eye located behind the pupil that bends rays of light to focus them on the retina.

Rethink

11-1 If the eye had a second lens that "unreversed" the image hitting the retina, do you think there would be changes in the way people perceive the world?

11-2 *From the perspective of an advertising specialist:* How might you market your products similarly or differently to those who are color-blind versus those who have normal color vision?

Spotlight on Terminology and Language—ESL Pointers

Page 207 "Our visual capabilities permit us to admire and react to scenes ranging from the beauty of a sunset, to the **configuration** of a lover's face, to the words written on the pages of a book.

A **configuration** is a pattern or design.

Page 208 "Light waves coming from some object outside the body (such as the tree in Figure 2) are sensed by the only organ that is capable of responding to the visible **spectrum**: the eye.

A **spectrum** is the range of possible values. The **visible spectrum** is the range of light waves (colors) that the human eye can detect.

Page 208 "The ray of light we are tracing as it is reflected off the tree in Figure 2 first travels through the cornea, a **transparent**, protective window."

When something is **transparent**, it has the property of transmitting light without appreciable scattering.

Page 208 "After moving through the cornea, the light **traverses** the pupil."

To **traverse** something is to pass through it. The light passes through the pupil as it enters the eye.

Page 209 "The **dimmer** the surroundings are, the more the pupil opens to allow more light to enter."

When you **dim** the lights, you reduce the light. You provide only a limited or insufficient amount of light when you **dim** the lights.

Page 209 "With a wide-open pupil, the range is relatively small, and details are harder to **discern**."

To **discern** something is to be able to tell the difference between it and something else.

Page 209 "The lens focuses light by changing its own thickness, a process called **accommodation**: It becomes flatter when viewing distant objects and rounder when looking at closer objects."

Accommodation is the change that occurs in existing experience or knowledge as a result of assimilating some new information.

Page 209 "Having traveled through the pupil and lens, our image of the tree finally reaches its ultimate destination in the eye – the **retina**."

The **retina** is a thin film lining the back of the eye. The **retina** consists of three layers, the third and deepest of which contains two kinds of photoreceptors, rods and cones, which change light waves into nerve impulses.

Page 210 "*Rods* are thin, **cylindrical** receptor cells that are highly sensitive to light."

Objects that are **cylindrical** are tube like in shape.

Page 210 "The **density** of cones declines just outside the fovea, although cones are found throughout the retina in lower concentrations."

Density refers to the degree of concentration or crowdedness. Areas that are **dense** contain a large number of items in a small area.

Page 210 "The rods play a key role in **peripheral** vision – seeing objects that are outside the main center of focus – and in night vision."

Peripheral vision is the outer part of the field of vision. Do you have good **peripheral** vision?

Page 211 "(Think of the experience of walking into a dark movie theater and **groping** your way to a seat but a few minutes later seeing the seats quite clearly.)"

When you are **groping** your way, you are feeling your way and guiding yourself using touch.

Page 211 "The distinctive abilities of rods and cones make the eye **analogous** to a camera that is loaded with two kinds of film."

Things that are **analogous** are alike or similar.

Page 211 "When light energy strikes the rods and cones, it starts a **chain of events** that transforms light into neural impulses that can be communicated to the brain.

A **chain of events** refers to a series of things that occurs one right after the other.

Page 212 "Normally, however, this absence of nerve cells does not interfere with vision because you automatically **compensate** for the missing part of your field of vision (Ramachandran, 1995)."

When we **compensate**, we are counterbalancing. We sometimes **compensate** for feelings of inferiority or failure in one field by achievement in another. We may **compensate** for an organic defect with the increased function of another organ.

Page 213 "Psychologists David Hubel and Torsten Wiesel won the Nobel Prize for their discovery that many neurons in the cortex are **extraordinarily** specialized, being activated only by visual stimuli of a particular shape or pattern – a process known as feature detection."

Extraordinary means exceptional to a very conspicuous degree. Some students have **extraordinary** powers of deduction; they have skills beyond what is usual in a college student.

Page 213 "Other cells are activated only by moving, as opposed to **stationary**, stimuli (Huber & Wiesel, 1979, Patzwahl, Zanker, & Altenmuller, 1994)."

When something is **stationary**, it is in a fixed mode. It is unchanging in condition. A **stationary** bicycle is one that is motionless.

Page 214 "Different parts of the brain seem to process nerve impulses in several individual systems **simultaneously**."

When something exists or occurs at the same time, it is occurring **simultaneously**.

Page 215 "For most people with color-blindness, the world looks quite **dull**."

Dull suggests a lack of sharpness or intensity. Vision that is **dull** may lack brightness or vividness.

Page 217 "When we stare at the yellow in the figure, for instance, our receptor cells for the yellow component of the yellow-blue pairing become **fatigued** and are less able to respond to yellow stimuli.

When something or someone is **fatigued,** they are exhausted or very tired.

Module 12: Hearing and the Other Senses

Sensing Sound

| **Applying Psychology in the 21st Century:**
Making Senses: New Technology for Restoring Sound and Sight |

Smell and Taste
The Skin Senses: Touch, Pressure, Temperature, and Pain
Interacting Senses

| **Becoming an Informed Consumer of Psychology:**
Managing Pain |

- *What role does the ear play in the senses of sound, motion, and balance?*
- *How do smell and taste function?*
- *What are the skin senses, and how do they relate to the experience of pain?*

Hearing and the Other Senses

[a] _____ is the movement of air that results from the vibration of objects. The outer ear collects sounds and guides them to the internal portions of the ear. Sounds are funneled into the auditory canal toward the [b] _____. Sound waves hit the eardrum, which in turn transmits its vibrations into the [c] _____. The middle ear contains three small bones: the hammer, the anvil, and the stirrup. These three bones transmit the vibrations to the [d] _____. The inner ear contains the organs for transmitting the sound waves into nerve impulses as well as the organs for balance and position. The [e] _____ is a coiled tube that contains the [f] _____. The basilar membrane is covered with [g] _____ that vibrate. Sound may also enter the cochlea through the bones that surround the ear.

Sound is characterized by *frequency*, or the number of waves per second, and *pitch* is our experience of this number as high or low. *Intensity* may be thought of as the size of the waves—how strong it is. Intensity is measured in *decibels*. The [h] _____ suggests that parts of the basilar membrane are sensitive to different pitches.

The **[i]** _____ suggests that the entire basilar membrane vibrates in response to any sound, and the nerves send signals that are more frequent for higher pitches and less frequent for lower pitches.

The inner ear is also responsible for the sense of balance. The structures responsible for balance are the **[j]** _____, three tubes filled with fluid that move around in the tubes when the head moves. The fluid affects **[k]** _____, small motion-sensitive crystals in the semicircular canals.

We are able to detect about 10,000 different smells, and women have a better sense of smell than do men. Some animals can communicate using odor. Odor is detected by molecules of a substance coming into contact with the _olfactory cells_ in the nasal passages. Each olfactory cell responds to a narrow band of odors. **[l]** _____ are chemicals that can produce a reaction in members of a species. These chemicals have a role in sexual activity and identification. Tastes, such as sweet, sour, salty, or bitter flavors, are detected by _taste buds_ on the tongue. A fifth category of taste has also been identified, called _umami_, though there is some controversy as to whether it is truly a fundamental taste. The experience of taste also includes the odor and appearance of food.

The **[m]** _____ include touch, pressure, temperature, and pain. Receptor cells for each of these senses are distributed all over the body, although each sense is distributed in varying concentrations. The major theory of pain is called the **[n]** _____. This theory states that nerve receptors send messages to the brain areas related to pain, and whenever they are activated, a "gate" to the brain is opened and pain is experienced. The gate can be shut by overwhelming the nerve pathways with nonpainful messages. It can also be closed by the brain producing messages to reduce or eliminate the experience of pain. **[o]** _____ may be explained by the first option, in which the needles shut off the messages going to the brain. Endorphins may also close the gate.

Evaluate

Test A

_____ 1. outer ear

_____ 2. auditory canal

_____ 3. eardrum

_____ 4. middle ear

_____ 5. oval window

a. The visible part of the ear that acts as a collector to bring sounds into the internal portions of the ear.

b. A tiny chamber containing three bones—the hammer, the anvil, and the stirrup—which transmit vibrations to the oval window.

c. The part of the ear that vibrates when sound waves hit it.

d. A thin membrane between the middle ear and the inner ear that transmits vibrations while increasing their strength.

e. A tubelike passage in the ear through which sound moves to the eardrum.

Test B

_____ 1. cochlea

_____ 2. basilar membrane

_____ 3. hair cells

_____ 4. frequency

_____ 5. pitch

a. The number of wave crests occurring each second in any particular sound.

b. A structure dividing the cochlea into an upper and a lower chamber.

c. A coiled tube filled with fluid that receives sound via the oval window or through bone conduction.

d. The characteristic that makes sound "high" or "low."

e. Tiny cells that, when bent by vibrations entering the cochlea, transmit neural messages to the brain.

Rethink

12-1   Much research is being conducted on repairing faulty sensory organs through such devices as personal guidance systems, eyeglasses, and so forth. Do you think that researchers should attempt to improve normal sensory capabilities beyond their "natural" range (for example, make human visual or audio capabilities more sensitive than normal)? What benefits might this bring? What problems might it cause?

12-2   *From the perspective of a social worker:* How would you handle the case of a deaf child whose hearing could be restored with a cochlear implant, but different family members had conflicting views on whether the procedure should be done?

Spotlight on Terminology and Language—ESL Pointers

Page 224 "The **blast-off** was easy compared with what the astronaut was experiencing now: space sickness.

A **blast-off** is the explosion that occurs when rocket ships go into space.

Page 225 "This sense allows people to navigate their bodies through the world and keep themselves **upright** without falling."

Upright is vertically upward. You are **upright** when you are standing.

Page 225 "The outer ear acts as a reverse **megaphone**, designed to collect and bring sounds into the internal portions of the ear (see Figure 1)."

A **megaphone** is a cone shaped objected used to increase the loudness of sound.

Page 225 "Sounds, arriving at the outer ear in the form of wavelike vibrations, are **funneled** into the *auditory canal*, a tube like passage that leads to the eardrum.

When things like sound waves are **funneled** they are being directed or guided somewhere.

Page 226 "When sound enters the inner ear through the oval window, it moves into the **cochlea**, a coiled tube that looks something like a snail and is filled with fluid that can vibrate in response to sound."

The **cochlea** is a coiled, fluid-filled structure in the inner ear that contains the receptors for hearing. The function of the **cochlea** is to transform vibrations into nerve impulses (electrical signals) that are sent to the brain for processing into sound sensations.

Page 226 "Inside the cochlea is the **basilar membrane**, a structure that runs through the center of the cochlea, dividing it into an upper chamber and a lower chamber."

The **basilar membrane** is a membrane within the cochlea that contains the auditory receptors, or hair cells.

Page 226 "Because the ear rests on a maze of bones in the skull, the cochlea is able to pick up **subtle** vibrations that travel across the bones from other parts of the head.

Vibrations that are **subtle** are faint or very weak in strength.

Page 227 "If you have ever seen an audio speaker that has no **enclosure**, you know that, at least when the lowest notes are playing, you can see the speaker moving in and out."

An **enclosure** is an area that is closed off from another area.

Page 227 "Air—or some other **medium**, such as water—is necessary to make the vibrations of objects reach us.

A **medium** is a substance.

Page 228 "Kathy Peck has some great memories of her days playing bass and singing with The Contractions, an all-female **punk band**.

"**Punk**" is a type of rock music.   A **punk band** is a group of musicians that play punk music.

Page 229 "The **delicacy** of the organs involved in hearing makes the ear vulnerable to damage.

Things that are **delicate** are frail and weak.

Page 229 "Exposure to intense levels of sound—coming from events ranging from rock concerts to overly loud earphones—eventually can result in hearing loss, as the hair cells of the basilar membrane lose their **elasticity** (see Figure 3).

Things with a high degree of **elasticity** have a lot of stretch to them. When the membranes lose their **elasticity** they lose their stretchiness and flexibility.

Page 230 "Ecklund's ability to hear is the result of a dramatic operation in which she received a **cochlear implant**.

A **cochlear implant** is a mechanical device that is placed in the cochlea to help correct hearing loss.

Page 232 "Similarly, the *penetrating auditory brainstem implant* (PABI) is an experimental technology that **sidesteps** the auditory nerve and sends sound stimuli directly to the auditory area of the brain stem.

When you **sidestep** something, you avoid or go around it.

Page 232 "By working directly at the brain stem, the new device **bypasses** the auditory nerves and nerve endings that often degenerate soon after people lose their hearing (LeVay, 2000; McCreery, Yuen, & Bullara, 2000)."

To **bypass** means to reroute, to avoid a place by traveling around it.

Page 232 "It's not just individuals with hearing impairments who are benefiting from technologies designed to **overcome** physical limitations.

When someone **overcomes** something they have defeated it.

Page 232 "The chips, which surgeons surgically implant **underneath** people's retinas, convert light into electrical energy that stimulates the damaged cells (Chow et al., 2004; Palanker et al., 2005).

The term **underneath** refers to the placement of an item below that of something else.

Page 235 "After an auditory message leaves the ear, it is transmitted to the auditory cortex of the brain through a complex series of neural **interconnections**."

Page 235 "Some neurons respond only to a specific pattern of sounds, such as a steady tone but not an **intermittent** one."

Page 235 "The semicircular canals of the inner ear consist of three tubes containing fluid that **sloshes** through them when the head moves, signaling rotational or angular movement to the brain.

When something **sloshes**, it moves with a splashing motion.

Page 236 "The *semicircular canals* of the inner ear (refer to Figure 1) consist of three tubes containing fluid that sloshes through them when the head moves, signaling **rotational** or **angular** movement to the brain."

When something **rotates** it goes around or moves in a circle. **Rotational** motion is circular motion.

Angular means pointed or sharp. **Angular** movement is motion with many sharp turns.

Page 237 "Although many animals have **keener** abilities to detect odors than we do, the human sense of smell (olfaction) permits us to detect more than 10,000 separate smells."

The **keen** sense of smell allows some animals to sense very minor differences and distinctions in smell.

Page 237 "We also have a good memory for smells, and long-forgotten events and memories can be brought back with the mere **whiff** of an odor associated with a memory (Gillyatt, 1997; Schiffman et al., 2002; DiLorenzo & Youngentob, 2003)."

A **whiff** is a slight or brief odor, just a trace of a smell of something. When you get a **whiff** of disinfectant, what is your immediate reaction?

Page 237 "We do know that the sense of smell is **sparked** when the molecules of a substance enter the nasal passages and meet *olfactory cells*, the receptor neurons of the nose, which are spread across the nasal cavity."

To **spark** something is to create it. The molecules of a substance spark, or create, the smell.

Page 238 "Although it seems reasonable that humans might also communicate through the release of pheromones, the evidence is still **scanty**."

Items that are **scanty** are scarce; there is too little of them.

Page 238 "Umami is a hard-to-translate Japanese word, although the English "**meaty**" or "**savory**" comes close."

Meaty refers to something that is substantial. **Savory** means full of flavor.

Page 239 "Ultimately, every taste is simply a combination of the basic flavor qualities, in the same way that the primary colors blend into a vast variety of shades and **hues** (Gilberson, Damak, & Margolskee, 2000; Dilorenzo & Youngentob, 2003)."

A **hue** is a shade of a color.

Page 239 "Some people, **dubbed** "supertasters," are highly sensitive to taste; they have twice as many taste receptors as "nontasters," who are relatively insensitive to taste."

To **dub** some one is to name them.

Page 240 "But even though the initial injury healed, the **excruciating**, burning pain accompanying it did not go away."

Excruciating pain is pain that hurts so much that it is unbearable.

Page 240 "Pain like Darling's can be **devastating**, yet a lack of pain can be equally bad."

When something is **devastating** it is overwhelmingly demoralizing or upsetting.

Page 242 "When these receptors are activated because of an injury or problem with a part of the body, a "**gate**" to the brain is opened, allowing us to experience the sensation of pain (Melzack & Katz, 2004)."

A **gate** is a door or opening.

Page 242 "Some of these variations are **astounding**."

When something is **astounding** it is so amazing it is unbelievable, or beyond belief.

Page 242 "What would seem likely to induce excruciating pain instead produces a state of celebration and near **euphoria**."

Euphoria is a state of great joy.

Page 119 "After an auditory message leaves the ear, it is **transmitted** to the auditory cortex of the brain through a complex series of neural interconnections."

Transmit is to pass something on, send something, or cause something to spread, from one person, thing, or place to another. Many diseases are transmitted by air-borne droplets.

Module 13: Perceptual Organization: Constructing Our View of the World

The Gestalt Laws of Organization
Feature Analysis: Focusing on the Parts of the Whole
Top-Down and Bottom-Up Processing
Perceptual Constancy
Depth Perception: Translating 2-D to 3-D
Motion Perception: As the World Turns
Perceptual Illusions: The Deceptions of Perceptions

Exploring Diversity: Culture and Perception

Subliminal Perception

- *What principles underlie our organization of the visual world and allow us to make sense of our environment?*
- *How are we able to perceive the world in three dimensions when our retinas are capable of sensing only two-dimensional images?*
- *What clues do visual illusions give us about our understanding of general perceptual mechanisms?*

Perceptual Organization: Constructing Our View of the World

Errors in perception occur because perception is an *interpretation* of sensory information. The distinction between *figure* and *ground* is crucial to perceptual organization. The tendency is to form an object in contrast to its ground, or background.

Through perception, we try to simplify complex stimuli in the environment. This tendency toward simplicity and organization into meaningful wholes follows basic principles called the

[a] _____. *Gestalt* refers to a "pattern." Basic patterns identified by the gestalt psychologists are (1) *closure*, groupings tend to be in complete or enclosed figures; (2) *proximity*, elements close together tend to be grouped together; (3) *similarity*, elements that are similar tend to be grouped together; and (4) *simplicity*, the tendency to organize patterns in a basic, straightforward manner.

The recent approach called **[b]** _____ suggests that we perceive first the individual components and then formulate an understanding of the overall picture. Specific neurons respond to highly specific components of stimuli, suggesting that each stimulus is composed of a series of component features. One theory has identified 36 fundamental components that form the basic components of complex objects. Treisman has proposed that perception requires a two-stage process: a *preattentive stage* and then a *focused-attention stage*.

Perception proceeds in two ways, through top-down or bottom-up processing. In **[c]** _____, perception is controlled by higher-level knowledge, experience, expectations, and motivation. Top-down processing helps sort through ambiguous stimuli or missing elements. Context is critical for filling in missing information. Isolated stimuli illustrate how context is important for top-down processing. **[d]** _____ consists of recognizing and processing information about individual components. If we cannot recognize individual components, recognizing the complete picture would be very difficult.

One phenomena that contributes to our perception of the world is that of **[e]** _____, the tendency for objects to be perceived as unvarying and consistent even as we see them from different views and distances. The rising moon is one example of how perceptual constancy works. The moon illusion is explained as resulting from the intervening cues of landscape and horizon, which give it context. When it rises, there are no context cues. Perceptual constancies occur with size, shape, and color.

The ability to view the world in three dimensions is called **[f]** _____. The two slightly different positions of the eyes create minute differences in the visual representation in the brain, a phenomenon called **[g]** _____. Discrepancy between the two images from the retinas gives clues to the distance of the object or the distance between two objects. The larger the disparity, the larger the distance. Other cues for visual depth perception can be seen with only one eye, so they are called **[h]** _____.

The Parthenon in Athens is built with an intentional illusion to give the building a greater appearance of straightness and stability. **[i]** _____ are physical stimuli that produce errors in perception. The *Poggendorf illusion* and the *Müller-Lyer illusion* are two of the more well-known illusions. Explanations of the **[j]** _____ focus on the apparatus of the eye and the interpretations made by the brain.

[k] _____ is the process of perceiving messages without our awareness of their being presented. Most research has shown that the subliminal message does not lead to substantial attitude or behavior change. Another controversial area is that of *extrasensory perception* (*ESP*). Claims of ESP are difficult to substantiate.

Evaluate

_____ 1. gestalts

_____ 2. closure

_____ 3. proximity

_____ 4. similarity

_____ 5. simplicity

a. The tendency to group together those elements that are similar in appearance.

b. Bits and pieces organized into patterns and studied by psychologists.

c. The tendency to perceive a pattern in the most basic, straightforward, organized manner possible— the overriding gestalt principle.

d. The tendency to group together those elements that are close together.

e. The tendency to group according to enclosed or complete figures rather than open or incomplete ones.

Rethink

13-1 In what ways do painters represent three-dimensional scenes in two dimensions on a canvas? Do you think artists in non-Western cultures use the same or different principles to represent three-dimensionality? Why?

13-2 *From the perspective of a corporate executive:* What arguments might you make if a member of your staff proposed a subliminal advertising campaign? Do you think your explanation would be enough to convince them? Why?

Spotlight on Terminology and Language—ESL Pointers

Page 245 "Now that an **alternative** interpretation has been pointed out, you will probably shift back and forth between the two interpretations."

When you have an **alternative** interpretation, you have a choice between two or more interpretations.

Page 245 "Known as **gestalt laws of organization**, these principles were set forth in the early 1900s by a group of German psychologists who studied patterns, or *gestalts* (Wertheimer, 1923)."

Gestalt is a German word that translates into form or pattern.

Page 247 "According to feature analysis, when we encounter a stimulus – such as a letter – the brain's perceptual processing system initially responds to its **component** parts."

A **component** part is often an element or a section of something bigger.

Page 249 "Treisman's perspective (and other approaches to feature analysis), compared with that of proponents of the gestaltist perspective, raises a fundamental question about the nature of perceptual processes: Is perception based mainly on consideration of the component parts of a stimulus, or is it **grounded** primarily in perception of the stimulus as a whole?"

When something is **grounded** on something else it is based on it.

Page 249 "If perception were based primarily on breaking down a stimulus into its most basic elements, understanding the sentence, as well as other **ambiguous** stimuli, would not be possible."

Ambiguous stimuli are stimuli that are vague, unclear or confusing.

Page 249 "You were able to figure out the meaning of the sentence with the missing letters because of your prior reading experience, and because written English contains **redundancies**."
When something is **redundant**, it is exceeding what is necessary or normal. Many times lectures are characterized by using more words than necessary. The speaker is **redundant**. A **redundant** message has parts that can be eliminated without the loss of essential information.

Page 250 "We would make no **headway** in our recognition of the sentence without being able to perceive the individual shapes that make up the letters."

If you are not able to make **headway**, you're not able to make progress toward achieving something. Oftentimes, student's find themselves unable to make **headway** with a project because the directions are not clear enough.

Page 250 "Bottom-up processing permits us to process the fundamental characteristics of stimuli, whereas top-down processing allows us to **bring our experience to bear** on perception."

When we **bring our experience to bear,** we are using our past to help us understand and create our current perception.

Page 251 "Perceptual constancy is a phenomenon in which physical objects are perceived as **unvarying** and consistent despite changes in their appearance or in the physical environment."

Unvarying means constant and unchanging.

Page 251 "When the moon is near the horizon, the perceptual cues of **intervening terrain** and objects such as trees on the horizon produce a misleading sense of distance."

Terrain refers to the way the ground or a piece of land is seen as related to its surface features - the physical features of a piece of land.

Page 252 "In addition to size constancy, other factors have been hypothesized to produce the moon **illusion**."

An **illusion** is something with deceptive appearance. In reference to perceptual constancy, an illusion is a misinterpretation of an experience of sensory perception.

Page 252 "The brain then integrates the two images into one **composite** view."

A **composite** view means a combined view.

Page 252 "The difference in the images seen by the left eye and the right eye is known as *binocular disparity*."

A **disparity** is a discrepancy or difference .

Page 254 "The monocular cue of ***texture gradient*** provides information about distance because the details of things that are far away are less **distinct**."

When something is **distinct** it is clear and well defined.

Page 257 "In contrast, a different explanation for the illusion suggests that we **unconsciously** attribute particular significance to each of the lines (Gregory, 1978; Redding & Hawley, 1993)."

When we do something **unconsciously** we do it automatically, or without thinking about it.

Page 259 "The **misinterpretations** created by visual illusions are ultimately due, then, to errors in both fundamental visual processing and the way the brain interprets the information it receives."

When we **misinterpret** something we make a mistake in understanding it.

Page 259 "**Subliminal** perception refers to the perception of messages about which we have no awareness."

Subliminal messages are brief auditory or visual messages that are presented below the absolute threshold, so that their chance of perception is less than fifty percent.

Page 260 "According to proponents of ESP, reliable evidence exists for an "**anomalous** process of information transfer," or psi."

Things that are **anomalous** are strange or out of the ordinary.

Test your knowledge of this set of modules by answering these questions. These questions have been placed in three Practice Tests. The first two tests consist of questions that will test your recall of factual knowledge. The third test contains questions that are challenging and primarily test for conceptual knowledge and your ability to apply that knowledge. Check your answers and review the feedback using the Answer Key on the following pages of the *Study Guide*.

PRACTICE TEST 1

1. A focus of interest on the biological activity of the sense organ is typical in:
    a. sensory psychology.
    b. perceptual psychology.
    c. gestalt psychology.
    d. illusionary psychology.

2. Absolute threshold is defined by psychophysicists as the:
    a. minimum amount of change in stimulation that is detectable.
    b. range of stimulation to which each sensory channel is sensitive.
    c. maximum intensity that is detectable to the senses.
    d. minimum magnitude of stimulus that is detectable.

3. Returning from the dentist, Tamara could not stop using her tongue to locate the new cap on her tooth, but two months later she does not notice the cap at all. This change has occurred because of the principle of:
    a. the difference threshold.
    b. sexual experience.
    c. bottom-up perceptual processing.
    d. sensory adaptation.

4. Feature detection is best described as the process by which specialized neurons in the cortex:
    a. identify fine details in a larger pattern.
    b. see things clearly that are far away.
    c. discriminate one face from another.
    d. recognize particular shapes or patterns.

5. The contemporary view of color vision is that the _____ theory is true only for early stages of visual processing, but the _____ theory applies correctly to both early and later stages.
    a. trichromatic; gate-control
    b. trichromatic; opponent-process
    c. place; gate-control
    d. opponent-process; trichromatic

6. Three tiny bones make up the middle ear. Their function is to:
    a. add tension to the basilar membrane.
    b. prevent the otoliths from becoming mechanically displaced.
    c. amplify sound waves being relayed to the oval window.
    d. minimize the disorienting effects of vertigo.

7. Compared with high-frequency sound, low-frequency sound:
    a. has more peaks and valleys per second.
    b. generates an auditory sensation of low pitch.
    c. has a lower decibel value.

d.   is heard by pets such as cats or dogs but not by humans.

8.   The theory that certain nerve receptors lead to specific areas of the brain that sense pain is the:
   a.   endorphin.   c.   opponent process.
   b.   opiate.   d.   gate control.

9.   The gestalt laws of organization are best described as:
   a.   patterns of perceiving determined by specific functions of neural receptors.
   b.   principles that describe how people perceive.
   c.   an explanation for how neural networks in the sensory system operate.
   d.   explanations of how people determine the quality of a work of art.

10. The fact that several instruments all blend together to form a symphony orchestra demonstrates:
   a.   a figure/ground relationship.
   b.   the law of similarity.
   c.   that the whole is more than the sum of its parts.
   d.   the law of perceptual constancy.

11. Perception that is guided by higher-level knowledge, experience, expectations, and motivations is called:
   a.   top-down processing.   c.   perceptual constancy.
   b.   bottom-up processing.   d.   feature analysis.

12. Officer Fazio is a police officer whose racial prejudices seem to influence whether she perceives the people on her beat as workers or vagrants. This would best demonstrate:
   a.   preattentive perceptual processing.   c.   gestalt perceptual organization.
   b.   bottom-up processing.   d.   top-down perceptual processing.

13. Binocular disparity refers to the fact that:
   a.   the world looks different with prescription glasses than without.
   b.   objects appear closer when they are larger.
   c.   the visual image on the retina of each eye is slightly different.
   d.   objects progressing into the distance, such as railroad tracks, appear to converge.

14. In the early days of movies, frames depicting popcorn and other snacks were often set into the movie reel without the moviegoers' knowledge. The perception of messages about which the person is unaware is called:
   a.   extrasensory perception.   c.   cognition in the Ganzfeld.
   b.   subliminal perception.   d.   otolithic preprocessing.

15. The signals that allow us to perceive distance and depth with just one eye are called:
   a.   the gestalt principle of figure/ground.   c.   monocular cues.
   b.   binocular disparity.   d.   motion parallax.

_____ 16. perceptual constancy

_____ 17. depth perception

_____ 18. binocular disparity

_____ 19. motion parallax

_____ 20. relative size

a. The ability to view the world in three dimensions and to perceive distance.

b. The change in position of the image of an object on the retina as the head moves, providing a monocular cue to distance.

c. The phenomenon by which, if two objects are the same size, the one that makes a smaller image on the retina is perceived to be farther away.

d. The phenomenon by which physical objects are perceived as unvarying despite changes in their appearance or the physical environment.

e. The difference between the images that reach the retina of each eye; this disparity allows the brain to estimate distance.

21. The _____ gets larger as the available light diminishes.

22. _____ is the process that causes the lens to focus light by changing its own thickness.

23. Cones are found primarily in the _____ of the retina.

24. A receptor called a(n) _____ is used in peripheral vision.

25. The sense of smell relies on receptor neurons called _____, which are spread across the nasal cavity.

26. Consider what it would be like if our senses were not within their present limits. What visual problems might we face? What would we hear if our hearing had a different range? What if we were more sensitive to smell? What about the other senses?

PRACTICE TEST 2:

1. A dog's nose is more sensitive to smells than is a human's nose. It then would be expected that the absolute threshold for smell will be _____ amount of odorant for a dog than for a person.
   a. a much larger
   b. a moderately larger
   c. about the same
   d. a smaller

2. The function of the retina is to:
   a. turn the image of the object upside down.
   b. redistribute the light energy in the image.
   c. convert the light energy into neural impulses.
   d. control the size of the pupil.

3. As Mrs. Bowman got older, she became aware that night driving was becoming more difficult. Along with many of her elderly friends, she has discovered that the _____, visual receptors most useful for night vision, are no longer adapting quickly enough for driving.
   a. buds
   b. cones
   c. ossicles
   d. rods

4. Dark adaptation refers to the fact that:
   a. our eyes are less sensitive to a dim stimulus when we look directly at it rather than slightly to the side of it.
   b. the color of objects changes at dusk as light intensity decreases.
   c. the eyes become many times more sensitive after being exposed to darkness.
   d. some people have great difficulty seeing things under low levels of illumination.

5. Afterimages can best be explained by the:
   a. opponent-process theory of color vision.
   b. trichromatic theory of color vision.
   c. place theory of color vision.
   d. receptive-field theory of color vision.

6. Luz often doesn't recognize her own voice on the telephone answering machine. She experiences her own voice differently from the way others hear it primarily because of:
   a. bone conduction.
   b. tympanic vibrations.
   c. low-frequency vibrations.
   d. gradual hearing loss associated with age.

7. Which statement about the taste buds is accurate?
   a. Each receptor is able to respond to many basic tastes and to send the information to the brain.
   b. More than 12 types of receptors for different basic flavors have been described.
   c. Taste receptors on the tongue, the sides and roof of the mouth, and the top part of the throat send complex information about taste to the brain, where it is interpreted.
   d. Receptors for the four well-accepted basic flavors are located on different areas of the tongue.

8. Look at these letters: *kkk kkk kkk kkk*. You see four groups, each containing three k's, rather than a single row of 12 k's because of the gestalt principle known as:
   a. similarity.
   b. proximity.
   c. closure.
   d. constancy.

9. Which principle of perceptual organization is used when we group items together that look alike or have the same form?
   a. Proximity
   b. Similarity
   c. Figure/ground
   d. Closure

10. Making sense of a verbal message by first understanding each word and then piecing them together is:
    a. top-down processing.
    b. bottom-up processing.
    c. selective attention.
    d. perceptual constancy.

11. When we perceive the characteristics of external objects as remaining the same even though the retinal image has changed, _____ has been maintained.

a. sensory adaptation
b. bottom-up processing
c. subliminal perception
d. perceptual constancy

12. The brain estimates the distance to an object by comparing the different images it gets from the right and left retinas using:
   a. the gestalt principle of figure/ground.
   b. binocular disparity.
   c. monocular cues.
   d. motion parallax.

13. The Parthenon in Athens looks as if it:
   a. is leaning backward from the viewer.
   b. is completely upright with its columns formed of straight lines.
   c. has bulges in the middle of the columns.
   d. is ready to fall over.

14. Mrs. Raehn's class is able to read the messages on the board even though part of each word has been erased. This is the gestalt principle of:
   a. figure/group.
   b. closure.
   c. proximity.
   d. similarity.

_____ 15. linear perspective

_____ 16. visual illusion

_____ 17. decibel

_____ 18. otoliths

_____ 19. figure/ground

a. Figure refers to the object being perceived, whereas ground refers to the background or spaces within the object.

b. A structure dividing the cochlea into an upper and a lower chamber.

c. The phenomenon by which distant objects appear to be closer together than nearer objects, a monocular cue.

d. A physical stimulus that consistently produces errors in perception (often called an optical illusion).

e. A measure of sound loudness or intensity.

20. The _____ holds that certain nerve receptors lead to specific areas of the brain that sense pain.

21. Perception that is guided by high-level knowledge, experience, expectations, and motivations is called _____.

22. _____ perspective makes railroad tracks appear to come closer together as they move away from the observer.

23. _____ is the study of the relationship between the physical nature of stimuli and a person's sensory responses to them.

24. The organ that gives your eyes their identifying color is the _____.

25. What are the basic differences between the gestalt organizational principles and the feature analysis approach to perception? Does one or the other approach explain some phenomena better? Are there phenomena that would be difficult for one approach to explain?

PRACTICE TEST 3: Conceptual, Applied, and Challenging Questions

1. _____ is to pinprick as _____ is to sharp pain.
   a. Threshold; just noticeable difference
   b. Stimulus; sensation
   c. Difference threshold; context
   d. Sensory adaptation; short-duration stimulation

2. Which statement about the rods and the cones of the retina is accurate?
   a. The rods are concentrated in the fovea of the retina; the cones are in the periphery.
   b. The rods are the receptors for dim illumination; the cones are for high illumination levels.
   c. The rods are responsible for the first 0–10 minutes of the dark adaptation curve; the cones are responsible for the remaining 11–40 minutes.
   d. Cones are found in larger numbers on the retina than are rods.

3. According to the text, the "blind spot" people notice is due to:
   a. an underproduction of rhodopsin.
   b. the lack of rods and cones in the area of the retina through which the optic nerve passes.
   c. binocular disparity associated with driving at night.
   d. an inability of the pupil to expand.

4. Suppose you could hear nothing but your own voice. Of the following, which might your physician suspect as the source of the problem?
   a. The cochlea
   c. The auditory cortex
   b. The basilar membrane
   d. The middle ear

5. On a piano keyboard, the keys for the lower-frequency sounds are on the left side; the keys for the higher-frequency sounds are on the right. If you first pressed a key on the left side of the keyboard and then a key on the right side, you might expect that:
   a. the pitch would depend on how hard the keys were struck.
   b. the pitch would be lower for the first key that was played.
   c. the pitch would be lower for the second key that was played.
   d. the pitch would be identical for each.

6. Intensity is to _____ as frequency is to _____.
   a. resonance; loudness
   c. acoustic nerve; auditory canal
   b. loudness; pitch
   d. external ear; consonance

7. The number of wave crests that occur in a second when a tuning fork is struck is referred to as:
   a. pitch.
   c. decibel level.
   b. intensity.
   d. frequency.

8. Frequency is to _____ as loudness is to _____.
   a. cycles per second; decibels
   c. cycles per second; wavelength
   b. millimicrometers; loudness
   d. cochlea; auditory nerve

9. Arial's father uses a BAHA to assist him in hearing. Which of the following types of hearing losses does he likely have?
   a. Full spectrum hearing loss
   b. Bone anchoring hearing loss
   c. Deafness in one ear
   d. Relaying hearing loss

10. The figure-ground principle:
    a. was formulated by gestalt psychologists to describe how objects seem to pop out from the background against which they are seen.
    b. states that figures are obscured by their backgrounds.
    c. suggests that elements that are located near to each other tend to be seen as part of the same perceptual unit, in most cases.
    d. states that individuals with attractive figures are likely to be viewed with interest.

11. An interesting reversible figure/ground stimulus for perceptual demonstrations:
    a. has a predominant ground.
    b. has a predominant figure.
    c. always gives the same dramatic visual image, no matter how it is viewed.
    d. has a figure and a ground that can alternate when viewed in certain ways.

12. Children at the Country Day Care Center are asked to sort geometric puzzle pieces, such as circles, squares, and triangles. This activity illustrates the gestalt principle of:
    a. figure/group.   c. proximity.
    b. closure.   d. similarity.

13. As you look at a car, you can see only the last part of the make, reading "mobile." You determine that the car is probably an Oldsmobile. This illustrates:
    a. top-down processing.   c. selective attention.
    b. bottom-up processing. d. feature analysis.

14. Which of the following statements concerning depth perception is **true**?
    a. It is not always necessary to use two eyes to perceive depth.
    b. Distant objects appear smaller because of linear perspective.
    c. The greater the discrepancy between two retinal images, the more difficult it is to reconcile depth.
    d. If two objects are the same size, the one that projects the smaller image on the retina is closer.

15. Suppose that you happened upon two buffalo grazing in an open field and one looked substantially larger than the other. Now suppose that the image of the smaller buffalo began to expand. You would probably assume that it was:
    a. growing.   c. moving away from you.
    b. running toward you.   d. turning sideways.

16. _____ is most important in order for major-league baseball players to be able to hit the ball when it reaches the plate.
    a. Tracking   c. Anticipation
    b. Focusing   d. Eye coordination

17. Abigail is trying to learn Spanish so that she can travel to Mexico during spring break, so she purchases some tapes to play while she is asleep. The concept that supports the notion of being able to learn in this manner is called _____. According to the text, will her tapes work?
    a. selective attention; Yes
    b. selective attention; No
    c. subliminal perception; Yes
    d. subliminal perception; No

18. Which alternative is **not** an important factor that influences illusions?
    a. Amount of formal education
    b. Cultural experiences
    c. Structural characteristics of the eye
    d. Interpretive errors of the brain

19. The visual receptors most useful for night vision are called _____.

20. _____ is potentially a fifth type of taste, though evidence is mixed on whether it is a fundamental one.

21. In the study of perception, patterns are referred to as "_____."

22. Filling in the gaps is known as _____.

23. Chemical molecules that promote communication among members of a species are called _____.

24. _____ is an organism's first encounter with a raw sensory stimulus.

25. The process by which the stimulus is interpreted, analyzed, and integrated with other sensory information is referred to as _____.

■ ANSWER KEY: MODULES 10, 11, 12, AND 13

Module 10:	Module 11:	Module 12:	Module 13:
[a] sensation	[a] visual spectrum	[a] Sound	[a] gestalt laws of
[b] perception	[b] cornea	[b] eardrum	organization
[c] stimulus	[c] pupil	[c] middle ear	[b] feature analysis
[d] Psychophysics	[d] accommodation	[d] oval window	[c] top-down processing
[e] Absolute threshold	[e] retina	[e] cochlea	[d] Bottom-up processing
[f] difference threshold	[f] rods	[f] basilar membrane	[e] perceptual constancy
[g] just noticeable	[g] cones	[g] hair cells	[f] depth perception
difference	[h] dark adaptation	[h] place theory of	[g] binocular disparity
[h] Weber's law	[i] rhodopsin	hearing	[h] monocular cues
[i] adaptation	[j] optic nerve	[i] frequency theory of	[i] Visual illusions
	[k] optic chiasm	hearing	[j] Müller-Lyer illusion
Evaluate	[l] feature detection	[j] semicircular canals	[k] Subliminal perception
1. c		[k] otoliths	
2. a	Evaluate	[l] Pheromones	Evaluate
3. d	1. c	[m] skin senses	1. b
4. e	2. d	[n] gate-control theory	2. e
5. b	3. a	of pain	3. d
	4. e	[o] Acupuncture	4. a
	5. b		5. c
		Evaluate	

Test A	Test B
1. a	1. c
2. e	2. b
3. c	3. e
4. b	4. a
5. d	5. d

Selected Rethink Answers

10-1   Sensory adaptation, an adjustment in sensory capacity following prolonged exposure to stimuli. Decline in sensitivity is caused by the inability of nerve receptors to constantly fire messages to the brain. Receptor cells are most responsive to changes in stimulation, and constant stimulation is not effective in producing a reaction. Adaptation to the context of one stimulus alters responses to another. If our senses were constantly bombarded by stimuli that was intense, we would have a constant high rate of stimulation.

12-1   Benefits of increased sensory capacity might allow us to see great distance. We may also be able to hear sounds from far away. Our sense of touch could cause us to have increased pain from cuts and burns. Science already has invented equipment that allows these things: "Sonic Ear" advertised to hear long distances, new surgery that improves eyesight, etc. These could be great scientific achievements, but to have our senses bombarded by increased stimuli doesn't seem to have overall advantages. How would we distinguish between necessary and unnecessary stimuli?

13-2   I would argue that scientific research demonstrates that people can be mildly influenced by stimuli they do not report being aware of, such as assigning a label to someone based on a prime. However, research has yet to demonstrate that people respond to subliminal messages with any substantial attitude or behavior change. I would need to explain the difference between systematic, scientific research using control and experimental groups, versus other kinds of research (e.g., correlational), in order to convince them of the weight of the research. It would probably take a while to convince them, especially given stories they've probably heard from the media, but the weight of scientific evidence would help in the argument.

Practice Test 1:

1. a   mod. 10 p. 101
*a. Correct. Sensory psychology focuses on sensation.
b. Incorrect. Perceptual psychology focuses on sensation and perception.
c. Incorrect. Gestalt psychology focuses primarily on perception.
d. Incorrect. Do not know of any such field.

2. d   mod. 10 p. 102
a. Incorrect. This defines a difference threshold.
b. Incorrect. This is referred to as the range of stimulation.
c. Incorrect. This would be some kind of maximum threshold.
*d. Correct. The absolute threshold is the smallest magnitude of a physical stimulus detectable by a sensory organ.

3. d   mod. 10 p. 103
a. Incorrect. The difference threshold would account for the initial detection of the new stimulus.
b. Incorrect. Sexual experience may alter his cognitive understanding of the ring, but not his sensory attention to it.
c. Incorrect. Actually, if this applies, it would be the top-down processing of ignoring the stimulus as described in answer d.
*d. Correct. This phenomenon is called sensory adaptation.

4. d   mod. 11 p. 109
a. Incorrect. This kind of recognition of details occurs in other processing areas.
b. Incorrect. The fovea is responsible for this capability.
c. Incorrect. The discrimination of faces occurs in the association areas of the brain.
*d. Correct. Feature detection is responsible for pattern recognition.

5. b   mod. 11 p. 111-112
a. Incorrect. Gate control relates to pain perception.
*b. Correct. Trichromatic accounts for the three different color spectrums to which the cones are responsive, whereas the opponent-process theory explains how four colors can be perceived with only three types of cones.
c. Incorrect. Place relates to hearing, and gate control to pain perception.
d. Incorrect. These are reversed.

6. c   mod. 12 p. 115
a. Incorrect. They are not connected to the basilar membrane.
b. Incorrect. Otoliths are found in the semicircular canal, not the middle ear.
*c. Correct. The bones transfer, focus, and amplify mechanical sound from the eardrum to the oval window.
d. Incorrect. Nothing can minimize these effects.

7. b   mod. 12 p. 117
a. Incorrect. This describes high-frequency, not low-frequency sound.
*b. Correct. Our perception of low frequency is low sound.
c. Incorrect. The decibel value applies to all sound, regardless of frequency.
d. Incorrect. Many pets can hear frequencies both higher and lower than their human attendants.

8. d   mod. 12 p. 125
a. Incorrect. Endorphins are neurotransmitters involved in reduction of the perception of pain.
b. Incorrect. Opiates are like endorphins and have similar effects on the neural pain messages.
c. Incorrect. Opponent processes are related to pain in the release of endorphins and the persistence of their effects after the pain stimulus has subsided.
*d. Correct. This is the name of the theory of pain.

9. b   mod. 13 p. 130
a. Incorrect. This refers to feature detection.
*b. Correct. The gestalt psychologists suggested that people organize their perceptions according to consistent principles of organization based on figure/ground relationships and simplicity.
c. Incorrect. Although some of these neural networks may work in this fashion, this is not the foundation of neural networks.
d. Incorrect. This shall remain a mystery for some time.

10. c   mod. 13 p. 130
a. Incorrect. In a figure/ground relationship, one instrument would stand out against the others.
b. Incorrect. The law of similarity applies to the similarity of items leading to their being grouped together.
*c. Correct. The fact that the orchestra creates a sound that is more complex than merely the sum of the sounds made by the individual instruments illustrates this concept.

d. Incorrect. Perceptual constancy applies to other phenomena altogether.

11. a   mod. 13 p. 133
*a. Correct. Top-down processing refers to processing that begins with a broad, general perspective and then completes details from this context.
b. Incorrect. Bottom-up processing builds the final picture from the details.
c. Incorrect. Perceptual constancy refers to our tendency to view an object as having a constant size, shape, color, or brightness, even when we see it in different environments or from different points of view.
d. Incorrect. Feature analysis refers to detection of patterns in an array of neural activity.

12. d   mod. 13 p. 133
a. Incorrect. See answer d.
b. Incorrect. See answer d.
c. Incorrect. See answer d.
*d. Correct. But this applies more to social perception than sensation and perception.

13. c   mod. 13 p. 135
a. Incorrect. This describes bifocal disparity.
b. Incorrect. This is retinal size.
*c. Correct. Because the eyes are a small distance apart, the images on the eyes vary slightly, and the disparity can be used to determine distance and depth.
d. Incorrect. This is called linear perspective, and it is a monocular cue.

14. b   mod. 13 p. 140
a. Incorrect. ESP typically involves messages about which only the perceiver is aware.
*b. Correct. Perceiving messages below the threshold of awareness is called subliminal perception.
c. Incorrect. Sounds good, but what is it?
d. Incorrect. Being tiny crystals, otoliths do not process anything.

15. c   mod. 13 p. 135
a. Incorrect. The gestalt principle of figure/ground suggests that we see an object in the context of its background.
b. Incorrect. Binocular disparity works on the basis of the slight disparity between the two images of the retinas because they have slightly different points of view.
*c. Correct. Monocular cues, by definition, come from only one eye.

d. Incorrect. Motion parallax arises when distant objects appear to move less than close objects when the observer moves by them.

16. d   mod. 13   p. 134
17. a   mod. 13   p. 135
18. e   mod. 13   p. 135
19. b   mod. 13   p. 135
20. c   mod. 13   p. 135

21. pupil   mod. 11   p. 106
22. Accommodation   mod. 11   p. 107
23. fovea   mod. 11   p. 107
24. rod   mod. 11   p. 107
25. olfactory cells mod. 11   p. 121-122

26. The major points that should be included in your answer are:
- Discuss the importance of sensory selectivity—of sense organs being sensitive to limited ranges of physical stimuli.
- Although we would probably adjust to the differences, additional information might create duplications.
- Describe the things we would be able to hear, smell, taste, and feel if our sensory ranges were broader.
- Reflect on the possibility that our ability at sensory adaptation might have to increase.

Practice Test 2:
1. d   mod. 10 p. 102
*a. Incorrect. See answer d.
b. Incorrect. See answer d.
c. Incorrect. See answer d.
d. Correct. Actually, the organ is the nasal epithelium, and the more area it has, the fewer odorant molecules are required to detect an odor.

2. c   mod. 11 p. 107
a. Incorrect. The lens turns the image upside down.
b. Incorrect. The light energy in the image is not redistributed, but it is converted to neural messages.
*c. Correct. This is the role of the retina, and the rods and the cones of the retina initiate the process.
d. Incorrect. The size of the pupil is controlled by the muscles of the iris.

3. d   mod. 11 p. 107
a. Incorrect. Buds occur on branches of dendrites, axons, and trees, and in the tongue, but they are not the name of visual receptors.

b. Incorrect. Cones are more responsive to bright light.

c. Incorrect. Ossicles are another pronunciation of the word "icicles."

*d. Correct. Rods are capable of detecting small amounts of light.

4. c   mod. 11 p. 107

a. Incorrect. This is because of the low number of rods in the fovea, our typical focal point in the eye in normal light.

b. Incorrect. This results from the low levels of light, making the operation of the cones less effective.

*c. Correct. Sensitivity changes in low levels of illumination and coming into bright light can be painful.

d. Incorrect. These people have what is known as night blindness caused by problems related to the rods or to processing information from rods.

5. a   mod. 11 p. 112

*a. Correct. The opponent color is activated to balance, or adapt, to the intensity of the initial color. When the initial color is removed, the opponent color is seen (the afterimage).

b. Incorrect. Trichromatic theory could not account for negative afterimages.

c. Incorrect. There is not a place theory of color vision, only one for hearing.

d. Incorrect. The receptive-field theory of color vision is yet to be developed.

6. a   mod. 12 p. 116

*a. Correct. The bone conducts sound differently from the air, and the only voice we hear through the bone is our own, so no one else hears it through your bone.

b. Incorrect. Everyone hears through tympanic vibrations.

c. Incorrect. Bone conduction is the reason we hear our voices differently from how others hear them.

d. Incorrect. But your voice changes too.

7. d   mod. 12 p. 122

a. Incorrect. Most receptors respond to only one taste.

b. Incorrect. Only four types are known.

c. Incorrect. Taste receptors are only on the tongue.

*d. Correct. The four basic tastes are sweet, sour, bitter, and salty.

8. b   mod. 13 p. 130

a. Incorrect. They are similar, but they are not selected from a larger set of dissimilar objects.

*b. Correct. Objects that are close together tend to be grouped together.

c. Incorrect. Closure would lead to filling in the missing p's in the sequence.

d. Incorrect. Constancy refers to the fact that we view P and p as the same object.

9. b   mod. 13 p. 130

a. Incorrect. Proximity applies to objects that are close to each other.

*b. Correct. Similar objects do tend to be grouped together.

c. Incorrect. Figure/ground refers to the tendency to see objects in contrast to their background.

d. Incorrect. Closure refers to our tendency to fill in missing or hidden parts of an object.

10. b   mod. 13 p. 133

a. Incorrect. Top-down processing would begin by understanding the sentence and then finding the missing words.

*b. Correct. Bottom-up processing identifies each part and then builds the larger picture.

c. Incorrect. Selective attention refers to our ability to ignore irrelevant information or sensory inputs and concentrate on a selected set of data.

d. Incorrect. Constancy refers to a principle of perception that concerns the tendency to view an object as if it is unchanged even when viewed from different points of view.

11. d   mod. 13 p. 134

a. Incorrect. This refers to habituation to a sensory stimulus.

b. Incorrect. In bottom-up processing, each new view would generate a new image and identity.

c. Incorrect. Subliminal perception may occur at the limits of conscious perception, but it does not influence perceptual constancy.

*d. Correct. When an object is perceived as not changing even though its visual image changes, perceptual constancy is at work.

12. b   mod. 13 p. 135
a. Incorrect. The gestalt principle of figure/ground suggests that we see an object in the context of its background.
*b. Correct. Binocular disparity works on the basis of the slight disparity between the two images of the retinas becausse they have slightly different points of view.
c. Incorrect. Monocular cues, by definition, come from only one eye.
d. Incorrect. Motion parallax arises when distant objects appear to move less than close objects when the observer moves by them.

13. b   mod. 13 p. 136
a. Incorrect. See answer b.
*b. Correct. Unseen bulges in the middle of the columns make it look more perfectly square and taller.
c. Incorrect. See answer b.
d. Incorrect. See answer b.

14. b   mod. 13 p. 130
a. Incorrect. There is no gestalt principle of "figure/group."
*b. Correct. Closure involves completing an incomplete figure by filling in missing components.
c. Incorrect. Proximity involves grouping elements that are close together.
d. Incorrect. This activity involves grouping according to similar features.

15. c   mod. 13   p. 136
16. d   mod. 13   p. 137
17. e   mod. 12   p. 118
18. b   mod. 12   p. 121
19. a   mod. 13   p. 129

20. Gate-control of pain theory   mod. 13 p. 125
21. top-down processing   mod. 13 p. 133
22. Linear   mod. 13 p. 136
23. Psychophysics   mod. 10 p. 101
24. Iris   mod. 11 p. 106

25.
▪ The major point is perception of wholes versus perception of parts. Top-down processing and bottom-up processing may also be used to distinguish the two approaches.
▪ Phenomena such as perception of objects when parts are hidden from view and the reading of words without having to identify each letter are

better explained by the gestalt approach. Identification of unusual objects by identifying and analyzing parts of the object is better accounted for by feature analysis.

Practice Test 3:
1. b   mod. 10 p.101
a. Incorrect. Just noticeable difference is inappropriate here.
*b. Correct. The pinprick is the stimulus and the pain is the sensation.
c. Incorrect. The pinprick does not represent a difference threshold.
d. Incorrect. Quite a few pinpricks would be needed to develop a sensory adaptation, especially if the pain is short in duration.

2. b   mod. 11 p. 107
a. Incorrect. This is reversed.
*b. Correct. Rods need little light to be activated; cones require much more.
c. Incorrect. The amount of rhodopsin is the relevant factor in dark adaptation, not the rod and cone differences.
d. Incorrect. This is the opposite as well.

3. b   mod 11 p. 109
a. Incorrect. Lack of rhodopsin wouldn't block a unique spot in the optic nerve.
*b. Correct. The optic nerve needs to pass through the retina. There is an opening in the retina where that occurs, and a consequent lack of rods and cones for any vision.
c. Incorrect. This refers to differences between the images seen in the right and left eye.
d. Incorrect. This would be a different problem, but not related to blind spots.

4. d   mod. 11 p. 116
a. Incorrect. If you could hear your own voice, then you could be hearing through bone conduction, and the cochlea, basilar membrane, and auditory cortex would be functioning properly.
b. Incorrect. See answer a.
c. Incorrect. See answer a.
*d. Correct. Some blockage would have had to occur in the middle ear, because you would be hearing through bone conduction, and the cochlea, basilar membrane, and auditory cortex would be functioning properly.

5.	b	mod. 12 p. 117
a.	Incorrect. Pitch does not depend on how hard the keys are struck on a piano.
*b.	Correct. The keys on the left side would have a lower frequency, and thus lower pitch, than the keys on the right side.
c.	Incorrect. The keys on the left side would have a lower frequency, and thus lower pitch, than the keys on the right side.
d.	Incorrect. Pitch is a function of frequency.

6.	b	mod. 12 p. 117
a.	Incorrect. Intensity may affect resonance, but frequency does not relate to loudness.
*b.	Correct. The greater the intensity, the louder the sound, and the higher the frequency, the higher the pitch.
c.	Incorrect. These do not have a match at all.
d.	Incorrect. Intensity will affect all of the ear, although the external ear will be affected least, yet consonance will be unaffected by frequency.

7.	d	mod. 12 p. 117
a.	Incorrect. However, pitch is how we perceive the differences between different frequencies.
b.	Incorrect. Intensity refers to loudness, or how tall the crests would be.
c.	Incorrect. This is intensity, or how tall the crests would be.
*d.	Correct. The count of the number of crests per second is the frequency of the sound.

8.	a	mod. 12 p. 117
*a.	Correct. Loudness is measured in decibels and frequency is measured in cycles per second.
b.	Incorrect. See answer a.
c.	Incorrect. See answer a.
d.	Incorrect. See answer a.

9.	c	mod. 12 p. 121
a.	Incorrect. Spectrums normally refer to light, rather than sound. Regardless, if he had full hearing loss, the BAHA would not be useful (see c, below).
b.	Incorrect. There is no such thing.
*c.	Correct. The purpose of BAHA is to redirect vibrations from a deaf ear to the good ear.
d.	Incorrect. There is no such thing.

10.	a	mod. 13 p. 129
*a.	Correct. This principle is central to the gestalt approach.
b.	Incorrect. Only in illusions.

c.	Incorrect. This is the principle of proximity.
d.	Incorrect. That is the physical attraction principle found in later chapters.

11.	d	mod. 13 p. 129
a.	Incorrect. The less predominant the ground, the easier it is to alternate figure and ground.
b.	Incorrect. The less predominant the figure, the easier it is to alternate figure and ground.
c.	Incorrect. Often the images are quite different, causing a dramatic effect.
*d.	Correct. If they can alternate, then the reversibility is possible.

12.	d	mod. 13 p. 130
a.	Incorrect. There is no gestalt principle of "figure/group."
b.	Incorrect. Closure involves completing an incomplete figure by filling in missing components.
c.	Incorrect. Proximity involves grouping elements that are close together.
*d.	Correct. This activity involves grouping according to similar features.

13.	a	mod. 13 p. 133
*a.	Correct. In top-down processing, incomplete information is completed by drawing on context and memory.
b.	Incorrect. Bottom-up processing would require all parts of the image.
c.	Incorrect. While selective attention may be involved (the car may have actually been a snowmobile), this example does not illustrate selective attention.
d.	Incorrect. Feature analysis helped you detect the word "mobile," but it was not used in completing the word.

14.	a	mod. 13 p. 135
*a.	Correct. There are many monocular, or single-eye, cues for depth.
b.	Incorrect. They appear smaller because of the physics involved.
c.	Incorrect. Actually, the greater discrepancy makes the depth determination easier.
d.	Incorrect. This is backward.

15.	b	mod. 13 p. 135
a.	Incorrect. Right, and it's about to explode.
*b.	Correct. Right, so you better take cover—the image is getting larger on your retina.
c.	Incorrect. No, it would have to be moving toward you.

d.   Incorrect. It could have started out sideways; if it is then turning sideways, it would be getting smaller.

16. c   mod. 13 p. 135
a.   Incorrect. The ball moves too quickly for the player to track the ball all the way to the plate.
b.   Incorrect. Focusing is less of a problem than tracking, and if the player cannot track the ball, he certainly cannot focus on it.
*c. Correct. The player must anticipate the location of the ball when it reaches the plate, because it approaches too quickly to be tracked all the way, and he must begin his swing before the ball reaches the plate.
d.   Incorrect. Eye coordination is critical, but he would not be a major-league player if he did not already have good coordination.

17. d   mod. 13 p. 140
a.   Incorrect. Try subliminal perception, and no, it probably will not work.
b.   Incorrect. Try subliminal perception, and no, it probably will not work.
c.   Incorrect. It is called subliminal perception, but it probably will not work.
*d. Correct. However, there is little evidence supporting the use of subliminal tapes for complex learning.

18. a   mod. 13 p. 137
*a. Correct. Educational level has no impact on the perception of illusions.
b.   Incorrect. Culture does appear to influence the perception of illusions, especially illusions involving objects or situations unfamiliar to members of the culture.
c.   Incorrect. The structure of the eye is one of the factors influencing how illusions work.
d.   Incorrect. Some illusions arise from incorrect interpretations at the level of the brain.

19. rods   mod. 11   p. 107
20. Umami   mod. 12   p. 105
21. gestalts   mod. 13   p. 130
22. closure   mod. 13   p. 130
23. Pheromone   mod. 12   p. 122
24. Sensation   mod. 10   p. 101
25. Perception   mod. 10   p. 10

Chapter 5: States of Consciousness

Module 14: Sleep and Dreams
Module 15: Hypnosis and Meditation
Module 16: Drug Use: The Highs and Lows of Consciousness

Overview

This set of modules focuses on the states of consciousness. Although some psychologists prefer to exclude studying the topic because of its reliance on "unscientific" introspections of experimental participants, contemporary psychologists support the view that several approaches permit the scientific study of consciousness. We can study brain wave patterns under conditions of consciousness ranging from sleep to waking to hypnotic trances. Also, understanding the chemistry of drugs such as marijuana and alcohol has provided insights into the way they provide pleasurable—as well as adverse—effects.

Another reason for the study of consciousness is the realization that people in many different cultures routinely seek ways to alter their states of consciousness. Consciousness may alter thinking. It may alter people's sense of time and perceptions about oneself or the world. This chapter considers several states of consciousness.

Module 14 focuses on what happens when we sleep. The REM stage of sleep is discussed, along with the manifest and latent content of dreams that occur during this sleep stage. The dreams-as-survival theory suggests that relevant information is reconsidered and reprocessed. Sleep disorders and their treatment, as well as a discussion of circadian rhythms, concludes this module.

Module 15 presents an explanation of both hypnosis, a heightened state of susceptibility, and the technique of meditation and its effects on consciousness. The fact that efforts to produce altered states of consciousness are widespread throughout many cultures is discussed.

Module 16 explains drug-induced states of consciousness. Stimulants arouse the nervous system, whereas depressants, alcohol, and barbiturates decrease arousal of the CNS. Narcotics such as morphine and heroin produce relaxation and reduce pain. Hallucinogens produce changes in perception. This module concludes with signals that indicate when drug use becomes abuse.

To further investigate the topics covered in this chapter, you can visit the related Web sites by visiting the following link: www.mhhe.com/feldmanup8.

Prologue: Violent Sleep
Looking Ahead

Module 14:
Sleep and Dreams

The Stages of Sleep
REM Sleep: The Paradox of Sleep
Why Do We Sleep, and How Much Sleep Is Necessary?

Applying Psychology in the 21st Century: Analyze This

The Function and Meaning of Dreaming
Sleep Disturbances: Slumbering Problems
Circadian Rhythms: Life Cycles
Daydreams: Dreams Without Sleep

Becoming an Informed Consumer of Psychology:
Sleeping Better

- *What are the different states of consciousness?*
- *What happens when we sleep, and what are the meaning and function of dreams?*
- *What are the major sleep disorders, and how can they be treated?*
- *How much do we daydream?*

Sleep and Dreams

[a] _____ is defined as our awareness of the sensations, thoughts, and feelings being experienced at any given moment. Consciousness can range from the perceptions during wakefulness to dreams. The variation in how we experience stimuli can be wide as well, and consciousness varies from active to passive states.

Much of our knowledge of sleep comes from the use of the [b] _____ to record brain activity throughout the cycles of sleep. The amplitude and frequency of the wavelike patterns formed by the EEG during sleep show regular and systematic patterns of sleep.

These patterns identify four stages of sleep. The first stage, called [c] _____, is the stage of transition to sleep, and the brain waves are rapid, low-voltage waves.

[d] _____ is characterized by slower, more regular waves and by occasional sharply pointed waves called spindles.

[e] _____ brain waves become slower with higher peaks and lower valleys. [f] _____ has even slower wave patterns. Stage 4 is experienced

soon after falling to sleep, and throughout the night, sleep becomes lighter and is characterized by more dreams.

The period of sleep associated with most of our dreaming is identified by the rapid back-and-forth movement of the eyes called [g] _____. REM sleep, which occupies about 20 percent of the total sleep time, is paradoxical because the body is in a state of paralysis even as the eyes are moving rapidly.

People who are deprived of sleep over long periods—up to 200 hours in some experiments—do not experience any long-term effects.

[h] _____ are the daily rhythms of the body, including the sleep and waking cycle, as well as the cycles of sleepiness throughout the day. Other functions, like body temperature, also follow circadian rhythms. *Seasonal affective disorder* and premenstrual syndrome (PMS) are two examples of rhythmic changes that have cycles longer than 24 hours.

[i] _____ are unusually frightening dreams. They occur sometimes in adults, but more frequently in children. Most dreams, however, involve daily, mundane events.

According to Freud's [j] _____, dreams are guides into the unconscious. The true meaning of these wishes was disguised, and Freud used the label of   [k] _____ because the meanings were too threatening. Freud called the story line of the dream the [l] _____. Freud sought to uncover the latent content by interpreting the symbols of the dream. Many psychologists reject this theory of dreams, instead preferring to interpret the content in terms of its more obvious references to everyday concerns. Another theory is the [m] _____, which suggests that dreams involve a reconsideration and reprocessing of critical information from the day. Dreams in this theory have meaning as they represent important concerns drawn from daily experiences. Research supports this idea that dreams help people reconsolidate memories, particularly memories related to [n] _____. Another influential theory is the [o] _____, which claims that dreams are by-products of biological processes. These processes are random firings related to changes in neurotransmitter production. These activities activate various, random memories, which the dreamer ultimately weaves into a logical story line. It is this story line produced by the dreamer that may provide a clue to his or her thoughts and emotions.

Evaluate

Test A

_____ 1. stage 1 sleep

_____ 2. stage 2 sleep

_____ 3. stage 3 sleep

_____ 4. stage 4 sleep

_____ 5. rapid eye movement (REM) sleep

a. The deepest stage of sleep, during which we are least responsive to outside stimulation.

b. Sleep characterized by increased heart rate, blood pressure, and breathing rate; erections; and the experience of dreaming.

c. Characterized by sleep spindles.

d. The state of transition between wakefulness and sleep, characterized by relatively rapid, low-voltage brain waves.

e. A sleep characterized by slow brain waves, with greater peaks and valleys in the wave pattern.

Test B

_____ 6. latent content of dreams

_____ 7. manifest content of dreams

_____ 8. latent content of dreams

_____ 9. dreams-for-survival theory

_____ 10. activation-synthesis theory

a. According to Freud, the "disguised" meaning of dreams, hidden by more obvious subjects.

b. Hobson's view that dreams are a result of random electrical energy stimulation and memories lodged in various portions of the brain, which the brain then weaves into a logical story line.

c. According to Freud, the threatening, disguised content of dreams.

d. The proposal that dreams permit information that is critical for our daily survival to be reconsidered and reprocessed during sleep.

e. According to Freud, the overt story line of dreams.

Rethink

14-1 Suppose that a new "miracle pill" is developed that will allow a person to function with only one hour of sleep per night. However, because a night's sleep is so short, a person who takes the pill will never dream again. Knowing what you do about the functions of sleep and dreaming, what would be some advantages and drawbacks of such a pill from a personal standpoint? Would you take such a pill?

14-2   *From the perspective of an educator:* How might you utilize the findings in sleep research to maximize student learning?

Spotlight on Terminology and Language—ESL Pointers

Page 146 "Awake, Jim Smith was an **amiable** and popular man."

Amiable describes someone who is friendly and cheerful.

Page 146 "In summer, he took his family pan-fishing for **crappie**."

Crappie is a type of small, fresh-water fish.

Page 146 "Wrapped in slumber, he would shout **obscenities**, kick the walls, punch the pillows."

When a person curses or says words in order to shock someone, the offending words are called **obscenities**.

Page 146 "People with the **malady** have been know to hit others, smash windows, punch holes in walls – all while fast asleep."

A **malady** is a problem. Would you say that people who suffer with the **malady** of REM sleep behavior disorder are suffering from a physical or psychological disorder or disease?

Page 146 "With the help of clonazepam, a drug that **suppresses** movement during dreams, his malady vanished, permitting him to sleep through the night undisturbed."

To **suppress** means to prevent something from happening.

Page 146 "In this view, it was philosophers—not psychologists—who should speculate on such **knotty issues** as whether consciousness is separate from the physical body, how people know they exist, how the body and mind are related to each other, and how we identify what state of consciousness we are in at any given moment (Rychlak, 1997; Gennaro, 2004)."

Ideas that are complex, where an answer is not easy because both sides of the question seem both good and bad are **knotty issues**, because, like a knot, you can't do one thing to solve the problem.

Page 147 "Most of us consider sleep a time of **tranquility** when we set aside the tensions of the day and spend the night in uneventful slumber."

Tranquility brings with it the ideas of peace and quiet; a **tranquil** person is undisturbed.

Page 147 "However, a closer look at sleep shows that a good deal of activity occurs throughout the night, and that what at first appears to be a **unitary** state is, in fact, quite diverse."

When something appears to be the same over and over again, it could be described as **unitary**.

Page 147 "When **probes** from an EEG machine are attached to the surface of a sleeping person's scalp and face, it becomes clear that the brain is active throughout the night."

A machine has **probes** to change energy into a form that can be seen or heard. The machine will make a graph or show numbers on a dial so that people understand what the energy is doing.

Page 147 "People progress through five distinct stages of sleep during a night's rest – known as stage 1 through stage 4 and REM sleep – moving through the stages in **cycles** lasting about ninety minutes."

A **cycle** is an interval of time during which a sequence or a recurring chain of events or phenomena is completed.

Page 147 "When people first go to sleep, they move from a waking state in which they are relaxed with their eyes closed into **stage 1 sleep**, which is characterized by relatively rapid, **low-amplitude** brain waves."

Amplitulde describes how much energy is in an electrical wave; a **low-amplitude** wave has less energy than a high-amplitude wave.

Page 147" This is actually a stage of **transition** between wakefulness and sleep and lasts only a few minutes."

A **transition** is a movement from one state to another.

Page 149 "**Paradoxically**, while all this activity is occurring, the major muscles of the body appear to be paralyzed – except in rare cases such as Donald Dorff's."

A **paradox** is something with seemingly contradictory qualities or phases. During REM sleep, it appears the major muscles of the body are paralyzed while at the same time this sleep period is characterized by increased heart rate, blood pressure, breathing rate and eye movement.

Page 149 "People deprived of REM sleep—by being awakened every time they begin to display the physiological signs of that stage—show a **rebound effect** when allowed to rest undisturbed."

When people are prevented from doing something, they will sometimes do more than normal when they are no longer restricted. This **rebound effect** is seen with medicine – sometimes if a medicine is stopped, the disease will be worse than it was before.

Page 150 "But—and this is an important but—a lack of sleep can make us feel **edgy**, slow our reaction time, and lower our performance on academic and physical tasks."

People that are **edgy** will be overly sensitive, easy to anger and overreact. Being on **edge** makes people nervous.

Page 151 "If you have had a similar dream—a surprisingly common dream among people involved in academic **pursuits**—you know how utterly convincing are the panic and fear that the events in the dream can bring about.

When you move toward a goal, you are **pursuing** it; the things you do with your life are your **pursuits**.

Page 152 "Whether dreams have a specific **significance** and function is a question that scientists have considered for many years, and they have developed several alternative theories."

Significance is meaning; it is something different enough to notice.

Page 152 "Sigmund Freud viewed dreams as a guide to the **unconscious** (Freud, 1900)."

The activities of a living mind that the mind is not aware of are in the **unconscious**. If you see a person you like, you may smile without thinking about it.

Page 152 "In his **unconscious wish fulfillment theory**, he proposed that dreams represent unconscious wishes that dreamers desire to see **fulfilled**."

When something happens that you wish for, that wish has been **fulfilled**. You **fulfill** your desires by working for them.

Page 152 "However, because these wishes are threatening to the dreamer's conscious awareness, the actual wishes – called the **latent** content of dreams – are disguised."

Latent content is something that is hidden, but is present and capable of becoming visible and obvious. A **latent** fingerprint at the scene of a crime would be one that is scarcely visible but could be developed for study.

Page 152 "The true subject and meaning of a dream, then, may have little to do with its apparent story line, which Freud called the **manifest** content of dreams."
When something is **manifest** it is clear and apparent; it is obvious. Information that is **manifest** would be clear to see or understand.

Page 153 "Using **positron emission tomography (PET)** scans that show brain activity, Braun's research team found that the limbic and paralimbic regions of the brain, which are associated with emotion and motivation, are particularly active during REM sleep."

Positron emission tomography (PET) is a method for looking inside the human body by using a machine that shows soft tissues, such as the brain, and blood.

Page 154 "Because we have a need to make sense of our world even while asleep, the brain takes these **chaotic** memories and weaves them into a logical story line, filling in the gaps to produce a rational scenario (Porte & Hobson, 1996; Hobson, 2005)."

When something makes no sense, and is not organized, it is said to be **chaotic**. **Chaos** is the opposite of order.

Page 154 "He suggests that the particular **scenario** a dreamer produces is not random but instead is a clue to the dreamer's fears, emotions, and concerns."

A **scenario** is a future or possible situation and the order of events that take place in that situation.

Page 155 "Just as she drifted off, Coutinho—her face and scalp dotted with electrodes, her head covered with a caplike device used for monitoring sleep—was **jolted** awake by a computerized voice asking her to "please report now" (Zook, 2004, p. 7)."

A **jolt** is a shock or bump that makes you jump or start. When you are **jolted**, your awareness suddenly changes.

Page 156 "The result is disturbed, **fitful** sleep, as the person is constantly reawakened when the lack of oxygen becomes great enough to trigger a waking response."

Fitful means restless, unable to relax or be comfortable.

Page 156 "Although night terrors initially produce great **agitation**, victims usually can get back to sleep fairly quickly."

Agitation is a state of great unrest, nervousness and upset. If you are **agitated**, you may become angry or fearful at anything.

Page 156 "Sleeping and waking, for instance, occur naturally to the beat of an internal **pacemaker** that works on a cycle of about twenty-four hours."

A **pacemaker** is something that produces a signal with a steady rhythm, such as a clock. A **pacemaker** causes regular action in the body, like a heartbeat.

Page 157 "The disorder appears to be a result of the **brevity** and gloom of winter days."

Brevity means brief and short lasting.

Page 157 "It is the stuff of magic: Our past mistakes can be wiped out and the future filled with **noteworthy** accomplishments."

Something that is special and should be rewarded can also be called **noteworthy**. It is worth remembering.

Page 158 "For example, around 2 to 4 percent of the population spends at least half their free time **fantasizing**."

Fantasizing is using your imagination to create possible future situations or events. **Fantasies** do not have to be real; you can fly like Superman, or they can be daydreams of what you actually could do.

Page 158 "As for the content of fantasies, most concern such **mundane**, ordinary events as paying the telephone bill, picking up the groceries, and solving a romantic problem" (Singer, 1975; Lynn & Rhue, 1988; Lynn et al., 1996).

Mundane refers to everyday things that do not surprise you.

Module 15: Hypnosis and Meditation

Hypnosis: A Trance-Forming Experience?
Meditation: Regulating Our Own State of Consciousness

Exploring Diversity: Cross-Cultural Routes to Altered States of Consciousness

- *What is hypnosis, and are hypnotized people in a different state of consciousness?*
- *What are the effects of meditation?*

Hypnosis and Meditation

[a] _____ is a state of heightened susceptibility to the suggestions of others. When people are hypnotized, they will not perform antisocial behaviors, carry out self-destructive acts, or reveal hidden truths about themselves, yet they are capable of lying. Between 5 and 20 percent of the population cannot be hypnotized at all, and about 15 percent are highly susceptible. Ernest Hilgard has argued that hypnosis does represent a state of consciousness that is significantly different from other states. The increased suggestibility, greater ability to recall and construct images, and ability to accept suggestions that contradict reality suggest that hypnotic states are different from other states. Some researchers have established that some people do pretend to be hypnotized. Moreover, adults do not have a special ability to recall childhood events while hypnotized. Hypnotism has been used successfully for the following: (1) controlling pain, (2) reducing or stopping smoking, (3) treating psychological disorders, (4) assisting in law enforcement, and (5) improving athletic performance.

[b] _____ is a learned technique for refocusing attention that brings about the altered state. Transcendental meditation (TM), which was brought to the United States by the Maharishi Mahesh Yogi, is perhaps the best-known form of meditation. TM uses a [c]

_____, a sound, word, or a syllable that is said over and over. In other forms, the mediator focuses on a picture, flame, or body part. In all forms, the key is to concentrate intensely. Following meditation, people are relaxed, they may have new insights, and in the long term, they may have improved health. The [d] _____ that accompany meditation are similar to relaxation: heart rate declines, oxygen intake declines, and brain-wave patterns change. The simple procedures of sitting in a quiet room, breathing deeply and rhythmically, and repeating a word will achieve the same effects as trained meditation techniques.

The cross-cultural aspects of altered states of consciousness are examined in the Exploring Diversity section. The search for experiences beyond normal consciousness is found in many cultures, and it may reflect a universal need to alter moods and consciousness.

Evaluate

_____1. hypnosis

_____2. meditation

_____3. Mesmer

_____4. ineffability

_____5. mantra

a. A technique for refocusing attention, it brings about an altered state of consciousness.

b. A sound, word, or syllable repeated over and over.

c. He argued that "animal magnetism" could be used to influence people and cure their illnesses.

d. An altered state of consciousness brought about by refocusing attention.

e. The inability to understand an experience rationally, as may be brought on by an altered state of consciousness.

Rethink

15-1   Why do you think people in almost every culture use psychoactive drugs and search for altered states of consciousness?

15-2   *From the perspective of a human resources specialist:* Would you allow (or even encourage) employees to engage in meditation during the work day? Why or why not?

Spotlight on Terminology and Language—ESL Pointers

Page 161 "People under hypnosis are in a **trancelike** state of heightened **susceptibility** to the suggestions of others."

A **trance** is a state of profound absorption, different than both sleeping states and waking states.

Susceptibility means easy to be affected by someone or something.

Page 161 "Despite their **compliance** when hypnotized, people do not lose all will of their own."

Compliance involves conforming to the statements of the hypnotherapy operator. **Compliance** is a disposition to follow suggestions.

Page 162 "The question of whether hypnosis is a state of consciousness that is **qualitatively** different from normal waking consciousness is controversial."

When something is **qualitatively** different, it means it is different in its essential character. This is not to be confused with quantitative, which involves measurements of quantity or amount.

Page 162 "More recent approaches suggest that the hypnotic state may best be viewed as **lying along a continuum** in which hypnosis is neither a totally different state of consciousness nor totally similar to normal waking consciousness" (Kirsch & Lynn, 1995; Kihlstrom, 2005).

Think of a **continuum** as a line, made up of an infinite number of points along that line. Each point is a member of the set, and differs from the next point only in value. Saying that two things are **lying on a continuum** means that they are alike in character but at different places on the scale.

Page 163 "For example, it may be employed to heighten relaxation, reduce anxiety, increase expectations of success, or modify **self-defeating** thoughts (Fromm & Nash, 1992; Zarren & Eimer, 2002)." **Self-defeating** thoughts are negative suggestions you give to yourself.

Page 163 "The **fundamentals** include sitting in a quiet room with the eyes closed, breathing deeply and rhythmically and repeating a word or sound – such as the word one – over and over."

The **fundamentals** are the essential and basic steps for experiencing the meditative state.

Page 164 "In fact, one **impetus** for the study of consciousness is the realization that people in many different cultures routinely seek ways to alter their states of consciousness."

An **impetus** is something that drives or compels you to do something. A good grade is an **impetus** for studying.

Page 164 "A group of Native American Sioux men sit naked in a steaming sweat lodge as a medicine man throws water on sizzling rocks to send **billows** of **scalding** steam into the air."

Billows are quickly spreading clouds of gas or steam; when steam or gas is hot enough to burn you, it is **scalding** hot.

Page 164 "Aztec priests **smear** themselves with a mixture of crushed poisonous herbs, hairy black worms, scorpions, and lizards.

When you rub or spread something soft, or liquid, on your skin or some other surface, you **smear** it; if you lean against a freshly painted wall, you would be **smeared** with paint.

Page 164 "Sometimes they drink the **potion**."

A **potion** is a drink that is said to have some kind of power, for instance, to give you strength or wisdom, or make you feel differently.

Page 164 "During the sixteenth century, a **devout Hasidic Jew** lies across the tombstone of a celebrated scholar."

The Jewish religion is divided into groups that believe in God in slightly different ways. A **Hasidic Jew** believes in constant communication with God in prayer, and with emotion. **Devout** means sincere and earnest.

Page 164 "If successful, he will attain a **mystical** state, and the deceased's words will flow out of his mouth."

Mystical refers to belief in meditation as a way to be with God.

Page 164 "Although they may seem exotic from the **vantage** point of many Western cultures, these rituals represent an apparently universal effort to alter consciousness (Furst, 1977; Fine, 1994; Bartocci, 2004)."

Vantage means a superiority, of being able to look over from a great height or commanding view.

Page 164 "Some scholars suggest that the **quest** to alter consciousness represents a basic human desire (Siegel, 1989)."

A **quest** is a search for something. What kinds of **quests** have you found yourself pursuing during your educational experience?

Module 16: Drug Use: The Highs and Lows of Consciousness

Stimulants: Drug Highs
Depressants: Drug Lows
Narcotics: Relieving Pain and Anxiety
Hallucinogens: Psychedelic Drugs

Becoming an Informed Consumer of Psychology:
Identifying Drug and Alcohol Problems

- *What are the major classifications of drugs, and what are their effects?*

Drug Use: The Highs and Lows of Consciousness

[a] _____ affect consciousness by influencing a person's emotions, perceptions, and behavior. Drug use among high school students has declined, as today about half of seniors have used an illegal drug in their lives. The most dangerous drugs are those that are addictive. [b] _____ produce psychological or biological dependence in the user, and the withdrawal of the drug leads to cravings for it.

Any drug that affects the central nervous system by increasing its activity and by increasing heart rate, blood pressure, and muscle tension is called a(n) [c] _____. An example of this kind of drug is *caffeine*, which is found in coffee, soft drinks, and chocolate. Caffeine increases attentiveness and decreases reaction time. Too much caffeine leads to nervousness and insomnia. *Nicotine* is the stimulant found in tobacco products.

[d] _____ and its derivative, crack, are illegal stimulants. This drug produces feelings of well-being, confidence, and alertness when taken in small quantities. Cocaine blocks the reuptake of excess dopamine, which in turn produces pleasurable sensations. Cocaine abuse makes the abusers crave the drug and go on binges of use.

[e] _____ are a group of very strong stimulants that bring about a sense of energy and alertness, talkativeness, confidence, and a mood "high." The amphetamines Dexedrine and Benzedrine are commonly known as speed, and excessive amounts of these drugs can lead to overstimulation of the central nervous system, convulsions, and death.

Drugs that slow the central nervous system are called [f] _____. Feelings of *intoxication* come from taking them in small doses.

One of the most disturbing trends among college students is [g] _____.

[h] _____ are a form of depressant drug used to induce sleep and reduce stress. They can be prescribed by physicians, but must be used carefully, as they are addictive and can be deadly when combined with alcohol.

[i] _____ increase relaxation and relieve pain and anxiety. *Morphine* and *heroin* are two powerful narcotics. Morphine is used to reduce pain, but heroin is illegal. Heroin effects include an initial rush followed by a sense of well-being. When this feeling ends, the heroin user feels anxiety and the desire to use the drug again. With each use, more heroin is needed to have any effect. A successful treatment for heroin addiction is the use of *methadone*, a drug that satisfies the cravings but does not produce the high. Methadone is biologically addicting.

[j] _____ are drugs capable of producing hallucinations, or changes in the perceptual processes, the most common of these being marijuana. Marijuana has various effects on people, and there are clear risks associated with long-term heavy marijuana use.

Evaluate

_____ 1. caffeine

_____ 2. nicotine

_____ 3. cocaine

_____ 4. amphetamines

_____ 5. alcohol

_____ 6. MDMA

a. An addictive stimulant present in cigarettes.

b. Strong stimulants that cause a temporary feeling of confidence and alertness but may increase anxiety and appetite loss and, taken over a period of time, suspiciousness and a feeling of persecution.

c. An addictive stimulant that, when taken in small doses, initially creates feelings of confidence, alertness, and well-being, but eventually causes mental and physical deterioration.

d. The most common depressant, which in small doses causes release of tension and feelings of happiness, but in larger amounts can cause emotional and physical instability, memory impairment, and stupor.

e. An addictive stimulant found most abundantly in coffee, tea, soft drinks, and chocolate.

f. A hallucinogen causing the user to feel empathic and relaxed, yet energetic.

Rethink

16-1   Why have drug education campaigns largely been ineffective in stemming the use of illegal drugs? Should the use of certain now-illegal drugs be made legal? Would it be more effective to stress reduction of drug use rather than a complete prohibition of drug use?

16-2   *From the perspective of a substance abuse counselor:* How would you explain why people start using drugs to the family members of someone who was addicted? What types of drug prevention programs would you advocate?

Spotlight on Terminology and Language—ESL Pointers

Page 167 "John Brodhead's **bio** reads like a script for an episode of **VH1's Behind the Music.**"

A **bio** is a biography, a story of a person's life.

VH1's Behind the Music is a television show about singers, songwriters and music producers.

Page 167 "A young **rebel** from the New Jersey **suburbs** falls in with a fast crowd, gets hooked on parties and booze and, with intensive counseling and a bit of tough love, manages to get his life back together."

A **rebel** is someone that opposes tradition or the current state of things. **Suburbs** are close to, but not in, larger cities, where people live in large areas of individual houses, rather than apartments, townhouses or on farms.

Page 167 "A large number of individuals have used more **potent** – and dangerous - psychoactive drugs than coffee and beer; for instance, surveys find that 41 percent of high school seniors have used an illegal drug in the last year."

Potent is powerful. **Potent** drugs are very chemically or medicinally effective.

Page 167 "**Addictive** drugs produce a biological or psychological dependence in the user, and withdrawal from them leads to a **craving** for the drug that, in some cases, may be nearly irresistible."

An **addiction** is a compulsive need for and use of a habit-forming substance, such as caffeine, nicotine, and alcohol.

A **craving** is an intense and urgent or abnormal desire or longing.

Page 167 "Furthermore, it takes longer to become addicted to some drugs than to others, even though the ultimate consequences of addiction may be equally **grave** (Wickelgren, 1988a; Thombs, 1999)."

When something is **grave**, it can cause or involve very bad consequences.

Page 168 "For instance, the alleged drug use of well-known role models (such as baseball player Darryl Strawberry and film star Robert Downey, Jr.), the easy availability of some illegal drugs, and **peer pressure** all play a role in the decision to use drugs."

People who are alike in many ways (age, job, education, etc) are **peers**, or equals. If your friends all try to get you to do something, they are applying **peer pressure**.

Page 168 "Finally, the sense of helplessness experienced by unemployed individuals trapped in lives of poverty may lead them to try drugs as a way of escaping from the **bleakness** of their lives."

Bleak is something that is grim, depressing. The situation was **bleak**; it was not hopeful or encouraging.

Page 169 "However, there is little accord on how to accomplish this goal. Even programs widely publicized for their effectiveness—such as **D.A.R.E. (Drug Abuse Resistance Education)**—are of questionable effectiveness."

D.A.R.E. teaches youths about how to stay away from alcohol and other harmful drugs, such as marijuana and cocaine.

Page 169 "Caffeine can also bring about an improvement in mood, most likely by **mimicking** the effects of a natural brain chemical, adenosine."

To **mimic** is to simulate and produce the same feelings.

Page 170 "Smokers develop a **dependence** on nicotine, and those who suddenly stop smoking develop strong cravings for the drug."

When you develop **a** dependence you develop a reliance on something. When this **dependence** is on drugs or caffeine, this may now constitute an addiction. Many workers have a **dependence** on caffeine to help alert them in the mornings.

Page 170 "When taken over long periods of time, amphetamines can cause feelings of being **persecuted** by others, as well as a general sense of **suspiciousness**."

If you feel that other people are trying to hurt you, you feel **persecuted**. A **suspicion** is a feeling of doubt or distrust; **suspiciousness** is the state of always thinking something is wrong or bad.

Page 170 "People taking amphetamines may lose interest in sex. If taken in too large a quantity, amphetamines overstimulate the central nervous system to such an extent that **convulsions** and death can occur."

Convulsions are abnormally violent and involuntary contractions of the muscles.

Page 170 ""Meth" is highly addictive and relatively cheap, and it produces a strong, **lingering** high.

Lingering refers to a feeling or condition that keeps going on and on.

Page 170 "It has made addicts of people across the social spectrum, ranging from **soccer moms** to **urban professionals** to poverty-stricken inner-city residents."

Women who live in the suburbs and have children that are involved in many activities are called **soccer moms** because they believe that their children, by having many activities, such as playing sports, will be better and happier children. **Urban** refers to the city, so an **urban professional** is someone who lives and works in the city at a job that requires much study.

Page 170 "Cocaine is inhaled or 'snorted' through the nose, smoked, or injected directly into the bloodstream."

Snorting is when you are forcing the drug into your system by inhalation.

Page 171 "However, there is a steep price to be paid for the pleasurable effects of cocaine."

A steep price is an extremely or excessively high price. Do you have knowledge of students who may have experienced a steep price for their use of stimulants or hallucinogens?

Page 171 "Over time, users deteriorate mentally and physically. In extreme cases, cocaine can cause hallucinations—a common one is of insects crawling over one's body."

A hallucination is when you think you see, hear or feel something that isn't there – your brain creates it.

Page 172 "Small doses result in at least temporary feelings of *intoxication*—drunkenness—along with a sense of euphoria and joy."

Intoxication is a state where your brain is affected by a drug, such as alcohol, so that it doesn't work normally – you react more slowly and feel different.

Page 172 "One of the more disturbing trends is the high frequency of binge drinking among college students."

If you drink a lot of alcohol over a period of many hours, or days, you are binge drinking, or on a binge.

Page 173 "Two-thirds of lighter drinkers said that they had had their studying or sleep disturbed by drunk students, and around one-third had been insulted or humiliated by a drunk student."

When someone is humiliated, this is a destructive insult to his or her self-respect and dignity.

Page 173 "It may be that physical reactions to drinking, which may include sweating, a quickened heartbeat, and flushing, are more unpleasant for East Asians than for other groups (Akutsu et al., 1989; Smith & Lin, 1996; Garcia-Andrade, Wall, & Ehlers, 1997)."

When you face turns red from fever, being embarrassed or physical activity, you are flushing.

Page 173 "Eventually they may fall into a stupor and pass out."

A stupor is a state when your brain has all but stopped working. You may be awake, but you do not know what you are doing.

Page 175 "*Rohypnol* is sometimes called the "date rape drug," because when it is mixed with alcohol, it can prevent victims from resisting sexual assault."

Date rape refers to sex between two people that know each other, but one of them does not desire sexual activity. Sometimes one person will give a date rape drug to the other person without their knowledge or consent to make them intoxicated, so that they cannot fight back with mind or body.

Page 175 "What do **mushrooms, jimsonweed,** and **morning glories** have in common?"

Certain types of **mushrooms**, along with a plant called **jimsonweed** and flowers called **morning glories,** contain drugs that can cause hallucinations.

Page 175 "The most common hallucinogen in widespread use today is *marijuana*, whose active ingredient—tetrahydrocannabinol (THC)—is found in a common **weed,** cannabis."

Weed is a slang term for marijuana.

Page 175 "Memory may be impaired, causing the user to feel pleasantly "**spaced out.**"

When your brain has been partially shut down by drugs, it causes a feeling of floating in space, or being "**spaced out**".

Page 176 "In addition, marijuana smoked during pregnancy may have lasting effects on children who are exposed **prenatally**, although the results are inconsistent."

When children are exposed to drugs **prenatally**, they are exposed before their birth. **Pre** is a prefix that means before, or earlier than.

Page 176 "Despite the possible dangers of marijuana use, there is little scientific evidence for the popular belief that users "**graduate**" from marijuana to more dangerous drugs."

When you **graduate**, you move on to other things.

Page 176 "Perceptions of colors, sounds, and shapes are altered so much that even the most **mundane** experience – such as looking at the knots in a wooden table – can seem moving and exciting."

Mundane is commonplace, like the **mundane** concerns of day-to-day life. What are some of the **mundane** activities of your daily existence?

Page 176 "Furthermore, people occasionally experience **flashbacks**, in which they hallucinated long after they initially used the drug (Baruss, 2003)."

Flashbacks are when past incidents recur vividly in the mind. A high proportion of the military personnel serving in Iraq are expected to experience **flashbacks** of this experience.

Page 177 "You can also get help from national **hotlines**."

Hotlines are direct telephone lines in constant operational readiness to facilitate immediate communication. A **hotline** is usually a toll-free telephone service available to the public for a specific purpose. What are some of the reasons you think college students might need to use a **hotline**?

Test your knowledge of this set of modules by answering these questions. These questions have been placed in three Practice Tests. The first two tests consist of questions that will test your recall of factual knowledge. The third test contains questions that are challenging and primarily test for conceptual knowledge and your ability to apply that knowledge. Check your answers and review the feedback using the Answer Key on the following pages of the *Study Guide*.

PRACTICE TEST 1:

1.   Consciousness is mainly:
     a.   our awareness of nervous system activity.
     b.   actions observable by others.
     c.   the deeply hidden motives and urges that influence our behavior in subtle ways but of which, for the most part, we are unaware.
     d.   our own subjective mental activity of which we are aware.

2.   Which stage represents the transition from wakefulness to sleep?
     a.   Stage 1   c.   Stage 3
     b.   Stage 2   d.   Rapid eye movement (REM)

3.   Which sleep stage is characterized by electrical signals with the slowest frequency, waveforms that are very regular, and a sleeper who is unresponsive to external stimuli?
     a.   Rapid eye movement (REM)   c.   Stage 3
     b.   Stage 2   d.   Stage 4

4.   REM sleep is considered paradoxical because:
     a.   brain activity is low but eye movement is high.
     b.   brain activity is low but muscle activity is high.
     c.   eye movement becomes rapid and brain activity is high.
     d.   the brain is active but body muscles are paralyzed.

5.   The increase in REM sleep during periods after a person has been deprived of it is called:
     a.   paradoxical sleep.   c.   latent dreaming.
     b.   the rebound effect.   d.   somnambulism.

6.   Freud concluded that dreams are reflections of:
     a.   day-to-day activities.
     b.   conscious activity.
     c.   unconscious wish fulfillment.
     d.   our evolutionary heritage.

7.   The average person has approximately _____ nightmares per year.
     a.   2   c.   24
     b.   10   d.   55

8. Insomnia is a condition in which a person:
    a. falls asleep uncontrollably.
    b. routinely sleeps more than 12 hours per night.
    c. has difficulty sleeping.
    d. exhibits abnormal brain-wave patterns during rapid eye movement (REM) sleep.

9. Caleb is having difficulty sleeping and breathing simultaneously. His problem is called:
    a. narcolepsy.   c. hypersomnia.
    b. sleep apnea.   d. insomnia.

10. Sudden infant death syndrome (SIDS) has been associated with:
    a. narcolepsy.   c. somnambulism.
    b. sleep apnea.   d. insomnia.

11. People who are easily hypnotized tend to:
    a. enroll in general psychology.   c. spend a lot of time daydreaming.
    b. be very aware of the outdoors.   d. be very good at biofeedback.

12. During transcendental meditation, a person repeats a(n) _____ over and over again.
    a. mantra   c. banta
    b. allegory   d. analogy

13. A psychoactive drug:
    a. affects a person's behavior only if he or she is receptive to mind-expanding experiences.
    b. influences thoughts and perceptions and is usually physically addictive.
    c. affects a person's emotions, perceptions, and behavior.
    d. acts primarily on biological functions such as heart rate and intestinal mobility.

14. _____ is the most common central nervous system depressant.
    a. Penobarbital   c. Valium
    b. Alcohol   d. Quaalude

_____ 15. rebound effect   a. An inability to get to or stay asleep.

_____ 16. nightterrors   b. Fantasies people construct while awake.

_____ 17. daydreams   c. Unusually frightening dreams accompanied by a
                                           strong physiological arousal.

_____ 18. insomnia
                                        d. A sleep disorder characterized by difficulty in
_____ 19. sleep apnea   breathing and sleeping simultaneously.

                                        e. An increase in REM sleep after one has been
                                           deprived of it.

20. Henry has been deprived of REM sleep and experiences a(n) _____, which means
    he spends more time in the REM stage when allowed to rest undisturbed.

21. There is wide _____ in the amount of sleep people need, some requiring seven or eight
    hours and others only three hours per night.

22. As far as we know, most people suffer no permanent consequences from temporary

    _____.

23. A biological rhythm with a period (from peak to peak) of about 24 hours is called

    _____.

24. Sleep periods characterized by eye movement, loss of muscle tone, and dreaming are called

    _____.

25. Discuss the competing theories of dreams. Are the theories actually incompatible? Which appears most convincing? Defend your answer.

PRACTICE TEST 2:

1. The deepest stages of sleep are generally experienced:
   a. during the first half of the sleep interval.
   b. during the second half of the sleep interval.
   c. during continuous periods averaging two hours each.
   d. while the sleeper dreams.

2. Within a single sleep cycle, as we progress through the stages of sleep toward deepest sleep, the EEG pattern gets:
   a. faster and more regular.
   b. faster and more irregular.
   c. slower and lower in amplitude.
   d. slower and more regular.

3. Irregular breathing, increased blood pressure, and increased respiration during sleep are characteristics of:
   a. stage 1 sleep.
   b. stage 2 sleep.
   c. rapid eye movement (REM).
   d. non-rapid eye movement (NREM).

4. The major muscles of the body act as if they are paralyzed during:
   a. stage 1 sleep.
   b. stage 3 sleep.
   c. stage 4 sleep.
   d. rapid eye movement (REM).

5. The viewpoint that dreams are the outcome of the random exercising of neural circuits in the brain is called the:
   a. unconscious wish fulfillment theory.
   b. dreams-for-survival theory.
   c. activation-synthesis theory.
   d. reverse learning theory.

6. Freud referred to the story line of a dream as its:
   a. libidinal content.
   b. unconscious content.
   c. manifest content.
   d. latent content.

7. Which of the following most closely describes the symptoms of seasonal affective disorder?
   a. Fatigue and irritability
   b. Allergic reactions associated with seasons
   c. Drowsiness during summer afternoons
   d. Despair and hopelessness during winter

8. People pass directly from a conscious, wakeful state to REM sleep if they suffer from:
   a. narcolepsy.
   b. insomnia.
   c. somnambulism.
   d. rapid eye movement (REM) showers.

9. The uncontrollable need to sleep for short periods that can happen at any time during the day is called:
   a. narcolepsy.
   b. sleep apnea.
   c. hypersomnia.
   d. insomnia.

10. _____ is the most common hallucinogen in use in the United States.
    a. PCP
    b. LSD
    c. Cocaine
    d. Marijuana

11. All of the following are typical suggestions for overcoming insomnia **except**:
    a. choose regular bedtimes.
    b. don't try to go to sleep.
    c. avoid drinks with caffeine.
    d. watch TV in bed.

12. Meditation is considered a way to achieve _____ by traditional practitioners of Zen Buddhism.
    a. hypnosis
    b. good fortune
    c. career goals
    d. spiritual insight

13. One downside to using methadone in drug therapy is:
    a. the patient is likely to become addicted to methadone.
    b. methadone eventually causes mental retardation in the patient.
    c. methadone patients are at risk of becoming alcoholics.
    d. methadone users find the marijuana high to be very appealing.

14. Caffeine, nicotine, cocaine, and amphetamines are considered:
    a. anesthetic agents.
    b. central nervous system stimulants.
    c. anti-anxiety drugs.
    d. hallucinogens.

15. The depressants Nembutal, Seconal, and phenobarbital are forms of:
    a. opiates.
    b. barbiturates.
    c. hallucinogens.
    d. hypnotics.

_____ 16. sudden infant death syndrome (SIDS)

_____ 17. narcolepsy

_____ 18. marijuana

_____ 19. lysergic acid diethylamide (LSD)

a. An uncontrollable need to sleep for short periods during the day.

b. A disorder in which seemingly healthy infants die in their sleep.

c. A common hallucinogen, usually smoked.

d. One of the most powerful hallucinogens, affecting the operation of neurotransmitters in the brain and causing brain cell activity to be altered.

20. Despite compliance when hypnotized, people will not perform antisocial behaviors or _____.

21. People _____ be hypnotized against their will.

22. People who are readily hypnotized often spend an unusual amount of time _____.

23. Psychologists working with seriously or chronically ill patients may use hypnosis to control _____.

24. The legal status of information gathered from a person in a hypnotic state is _____ because hypnotic recollections are sometimes inaccurate.

25. Debates regarding the legalization of drugs, especially marijuana, seem to come and go. If that debate were to arise today, what should psychology contribute? What are your feelings about the issue? Should some drugs be legalized or given through prescription? Defend your answer.

Practice Test 3: Conceptual, Applied, and Challenging Questions

1. Sleep involves four different stages. What is the basis for differentiating these stages of sleep?
   a. They are defined according to the electrical properties recorded by an electroencephalogram (EEG) attached to the sleeper.
   b. They are defined by the amount of time elapsed from the onset of sleep.
   c. They are based on the mental experiences described when sleepers are awakened and asked what they are thinking.
   d. They are characterized by patterns of overt body movements recorded with a video camera that is positioned over the sleeper.

2. Your friend Sandro comes to you concerned about his health after having stayed up for 36 hours straight studying. The most valid thing you could tell him is that:
   a. if he is going to stay up for so long, he should see a doctor regularly.
   b. if he continues to stay up for so long, he will probably get sick.
   c. there will probably be severe long-term consequences.
   d. research has demonstrated that lack of sleep will affect his ability to study.

3. Sharon dreams that Drew climbs a stairway and meets her at the top. According to Freudian dream symbols described in the text, this would probably suggest:
   a. that Sharon would like to start a friendship with Drew.
   b. that Sharon is really afraid to talk to Drew, although she would like to start a friendship.
   c. that Drew and Sharon probably work together in a building where there are stairs.
   d. that Sharon is dreaming of sexual intercourse with Drew.

4. If you had a dream about carrying grapefruits down a long tunnel, Freud would interpret the grapefruit as a dream symbol suggesting a wish to:
   a. take a trip to the tropics.
   b. caress a woman's body.
   c. caress a man's genitals.
   d. return to the womb.

5. Suppose that a study were done to show that people who are in new surroundings and involved in major unfamiliar activities have more dreams per night than others whose lives have been stable through the same intervals of the study. This study aims to test:
    a. the unconscious wish fulfillment dream theory.
    b. the dreams-for-survival dream theory.
    c. the activation-synthesis dream theory.
    d. the latent content dream theory.

6. During the movie, Tanya fantasized about running away and making love to Harrison Ford. She was experiencing a:
    a. nervous breakdown.   c. diurnal emission.
    b. daydream.   d. mantra.

7. Stephanie suffers from frequent sleepwalking. The doctor has told her all but which of the following statements about sleepwalking?
    a. Sleepwalkers will trip and stumble, so should always be awakened.
    b. Sleepwalking occurs in stage 4 sleep.
    c. Sleepwalkers are somewhat aware of their surroundings.
    d. Sleepwalking occurs most frequently in children.

8. In what way are meditation and hypnosis similar?
    a. They are both accompanied by changes in brain activity.
    b. They both result in a decrease in blood pressure.
    c. They are both based on Eastern religious practices.
    d. They both result in total relaxation.

9. Which of the following statements about addiction to drugs is **not** true?
    a. Addiction may be biologically based.
    b. Addictions are primarily caused by an inherited biological liability.
    c. All people, with few exceptions, have used one or more "addictive" drugs in their lifetime.
    d. Addictions may be psychological.

10. Valerie took a tablet someone gave her. She felt a rise in heart rate, a tremor in the hands, and a loss of appetite. She probably took a:
    a. megavitamin.   c. depressant.
    b. stimulant.   d. hallucinogen.

11. Which of the following is a hallucinogen?
    a. Heroin   c. Marijuana
    b. Cocaine   d. Morphine

12. Meghan dreams about wearing a man's leather jacket and parading around town. In Freud's view, the leather jacket and showing off are:
    a. latent content.   c. irrelevant to the meaning.
    b. manifest content.   d. day residues.

13. Meghan dreams about wearing a man's leather jacket and parading around town. If the leather jacket is seen as a sexual encounter and the parade as a form of exhibitionism, then in Freud's view, they would have provided insight into:
    a.   latent content.
    b.   manifest content.
    c.   activation processes.
    d.   day residues.

14. Betsy has just been hypnotized. Which of the following acts is she **least** likely to commit?
    a.   Completely undress
    b.   Flirt with her escort
    c.   Recall a past life
    d.   Stand on a chair and crow like a rooster

15. Which of the following are narcotic drugs?
    a.   LSD and marijuana
    b.   Morphine and heroin
    c.   Barbiturates and alcohol
    d.   Amphetamines and cocaine

_____ 16. barbiturates

_____ 17. morphine

_____ 18. heroin

_____ 19. methadone

_____ 20. hallucinogen

a.   A powerful narcotic, usually injected, that gives an initial rush of good feeling but leads eventually to anxiety and depression; extremely addictive.

b.   Addictive depressants used to induce sleep and reduce stress, the abuse of which, especially when combined with alcohol, can be deadly.

c.   A drug that is capable of producing changes in the perceptual process, or hallucinations.

d.   A chemical used to detoxify heroin addicts.

e.   Derived from the poppy flower, a powerful narcotic that reduces pain and induces sleep.

21.   Psychoactive drugs work primarily by affecting the _____.

22.   A very dangerous drug nicknamed the _____ can prevent victims from resisting sexual assault.

23.   Amphetamines, cocaine, caffeine, and nicotine are all examples of _____.

24.   The effects of drugs are often the result of their influence on the brain's _____ levels.

25.   Physical and _____ factors influence the way a particular individual reacts to the use of a drug.

26.   Describe the evidence regarding whether or not the experience of altered states of consciousness is similar across various cultures.

Module 14:	Evaluate	Module 15:	Module 16:
[a] Consciousness	Test A	[a] Hypnosis	[a] Psychoactive
[b] electroencephalogram (EEG)	1. d	[b] Meditation	drugs
[c] stage 1 sleep	2. c	[c] mantra	[b] Addictive drugs
[d] Stage 2 sleep	3. e	[d] biological	[c] stimulant
[e] Stage 3 sleep	4. a	changes	[d] Cocaine
[f] Stage 4 sleep	5. b		[e] Amphetamines
[g] rapid eye movement (REM)		Evaluate	[f] depressants
sleep	Test B	1. a	[g] Alcohol
[h] Circadian rhythms	6. a	2. d	[h] binge drinking
[i] Night terrors	7. e	3. c	[i] Barbiturates
[j] unconscious wish fulfillment	8. c	4. e	[j] Narcotics
theory	9. d	5. b	[k] Hallucinogens
[k] latent content of dreams	10. b		
[l] manifest content of dreams			Evaluate
[m] dreams-for-survival theory			1. e
[n] motor skills			2. a
[o] activation-synthesis theory			3. c
			4. b
			5. d
			6. f

Selected Rethink Answers

14-2 Students should be advised to get a full night's sleep every night, and how many hours that is depends very much on the individual student. Some may need seven hours, some may need 10 hours, etc. Students should get to know their sleep needs by assessing during the summer (when they don't need to wake up for school for several weeks at a time) how many hours they need each night without setting an alarm clock. Better sleep should lead to better concentration at school, and better learning.

15-1 Physical and Psychological Effects of Meditation—Studies show long-term meditation may improve health and longevity. Oxygen use decreases, heart and blood pressure decline.

Psychological Effects—although we feel relaxed when we meditate, it does not suggest that we are overburdened physically or psychologically, but it may suggest that there is a stronger mind-body connection than we previously realized. Meditation may allow us greater opportunities to relax and take time out from our day.

Practice Test 1:

1.   d   mod. 14 p. 148
a. Incorrect. We are not aware of the functioning of our nervous system.
b. Incorrect. Our individual consciousness is not observable by others.
c. Incorrect. These are unconscious forces.
*d. Correct. This is the definition of our personal conscious experience.

2.   a   mod. 14 p. 149
*a. Correct. The transition to sleep occurs in stage 1.
b. Incorrect. See answer a.
c. Incorrect. See answer a.
d. Incorrect. The occurrence of REM is associated with dreaming, while the transition to sleep normally occurs in stage 1.

3.   d   mod. 14 p. 150
a. Incorrect. REM sleep has very irregular waveforms; this describes stage 4 sleep.
b. Incorrect. Stage 2 is characterized by electrical signals that are faster than stages 3 or 4.

c.   Incorrect. Stage 3 is characterized by electrical signals that are faster than stage 4.
*d.   Correct. This is an accurate description of stage 4 sleep.

4.   d   mod. 14 p. 151
a.   Incorrect. Both brain activity and eye movement are high.
b.   Incorrect. Brain activity is high, and muscle activity is low.
c.   Incorrect. True, but this is not why it is called paradoxical.
*d.   Correct. The brain is active, but the body is completely inactive.

5.   b   mod. 14 p. 152
a.   Incorrect. Paradoxical sleep refers to the period of REM during which the brain is active and the body is paralyzed.
*b.   Correct. After sleep deprivation, the sleeper recovers lost REM time by having extra REM sleep for several nights.
c.   Incorrect. Latent dreaming would be hidden dreaming, which is not associated with REM.
d.   Incorrect. Somnambulism occurs most often in stage 4 sleep, and it is not a result of sleep deprivation.

6.   c   mod. 14 p. 155
a.   Incorrect. They include daily activities, but this is not what interested Freud.
b.   Incorrect. They tend to reflect unconscious activity.
*c.   Correct. Unconscious and repressed wishes often find their way into the content of dreams.
d.   Incorrect. Freud might accept this view, but he was interested in the content of current dreams.

7.   a   mod. 14 p. 160
a.   Inorrect. It would be very unusual to have this few nightmares each year.
b.   Incorrect. Ten nightmares is a somewhat low estimate.
*c.   Correct. Research indicates that on average, college students have approximately 24 nightmares per year.
d.   Correct. It would be unusual to have this many nightmares each year.

8.   c   mod. 14 p. 158
a.   Incorrect. Falling asleep uncontrollably is called narcolepsy.
b.   Incorrect. This is an unusual amount of sleep for an adult, but infants and small children sleep this much.
*c.   Correct. Insomnia simply refers to having difficulty falling asleep or returning to sleep once awakened during the night.
d.   Incorrect. This is not a condition associated with insomnia.

9.   b   mod. 14 p. 158
a.   Incorrect. The symptom of narcolepsy is falling into REM sleep uncontrollably.
*b.   Correct. Associated with snoring, the gasping for breath often awakens the person suffering from sleep apnea.
c.   Incorrect. This refers to excessive sleep.
d.   Incorrect. Insomnia is difficulty falling asleep and staying asleep.

10.   b   mod. 14 p. 158
a.   Incorrect. Narcolepsy has not been associated with sudden infant death syndrome.
*b.   Correct. Sleep apnea is thought to be the cause of sudden infant death syndrome—in effect, the child forgets to breathe.
c.   Incorrect. Somnambulism refers to sleep walking.
d.   Incorrect. Insomnia involves difficulties falling asleep.

11.   c   mod. 15 p. 163
a.   Incorrect. "You will encourage your friends to enroll in this class."
b.   Incorrect. Most of us are aware of the outdoors.
*c.   Correct. Frequent daydreamers do appear to be more easily hypnotized than infrequent daydreamers.
d.   Incorrect. This correlation has not been studied.

12.   a   mod. 15 p. 165
*a.   Correct. The repeated word is called a mantra.
b.   Incorrect. See answer a.
c.   Incorrect. See answer a.
d.   Incorrect. See answer a.

13.   c   mod. 15 p. 169
a.   Incorrect. The drug works without regard to the person's willingness to be affected.
b.   Incorrect. Not all psychoactive drugs are addictive.
*c.   Correct. Psychoactive drugs affect all three.

d. Incorrect. Psychoactive drugs affect emotions, perceptions, and behavior.

14. b   mod. 15 p. 175
a. Incorrect. The barbiturate phenobarbital is not as common as other depressants.
*b. Correct. Alcohol is the most common depressant.
c. Incorrect. Valium is an antianxiety drug that is commonly prescribed.
d. Incorrect. This is a common depressant, but not the most common.

15. e   mod. 14 p. 152
16. c   mod. 14 p. 159
17. b   mod. 14 p. 160
18. a   mod. 14 p. 158
19. d   mod. 14 p. 158

20. rebound effect   mod. 14 p. 152
21. variety   mod. 14 p. 152
22. sleep deprivation mod. 14 p. 152
23. circadian rhythm   mod. 14 p. 159
24. REM sleep   mod. 14 p. 151

25. The major positions that should be considered in your answer are the following:
▪ The psychoanalytic view argues that the symbols of dreams reflect deep meanings, many of which are unfulfilled wishes or repressed conflicts.
▪ The opposing views hold that dreaming is a natural process of cleaning excess material from the day, a survival mechanism, or a by-product of random electrical activity in the brain. These views may not necessarily be incompatible.

Practice Test 2:
1. a   mod. 14 p. 151
*a. Correct. Later in the night's sleep cycle, sleep is less deep.
b. Incorrect. See answer a.
c. Incorrect. See answer a.
d. Incorrect. Dreams occur at the least deep levels of sleep.

2. d   mod. 14 p. 151
a. Incorrect. It gets slower and more regular.
b. Incorrect. See answer a.
c. Incorrect. See answer a.
*d. Correct. The waveforms during the slowest phase are called delta waves.

3. c   mod. 14 p. 151
a. Incorrect. During stage 1, breathing becomes more regular, blood pressure drops, and respiration slows.
b. Incorrect. During stage 2, breathing continues to become more regular, blood pressure continues to drop, and respiration continues to slow.
*c. Correct. And this happens while the voluntary muscles are inhibited to the point of paralysis.
d. Incorrect. During non-REM sleep, breathing becomes more regular, blood pressure drops, and respiration slows.

4. d   mod. 14 p. 151
a. Incorrect. Paralysis occurs during REM sleep.
b. Incorrect. See answer a.
c. Incorrect. See answer a.
*d. Correct. Ironically, REM sleep is also characterized by irregular breathing, increased blood pressure, and increased respiration.

5. c   mod. 14 p. 157
a. Incorrect. This view sees dreams as a means for repressed desires to be expressed.
b. Incorrect. This approach understands dreams as a means of making sense of the information gathered throughout the day.
*c. Correct. This view accepts the notion of random activity as the source for dreams.
d. Incorrect. Reverse-learning implies undoing, or "cleaning," unnecessary information.

6. c   mod. 14 p. 155
a. Incorrect. Libidinal content would be sexual and may or may not be the obvious story line of the dream.
b. Incorrect. The unconscious content of dreams is most often the hidden, or latent, content.
*c. Correct. This is the term he used for the story line of the dream.
d. Incorrect. The latent content is the hidden content of the dream.

7. d   mod. 14 p. 292
a. Incorrect. These are symptoms of jet lag.
b. Incorrect. Allergic reactions are typically physiological, rather than psychologically-based.
c. Incorrect. Afternoon drowsiness is not a disorder.
*d. Correct. These are common symptoms of seasonal affective disorder, a form of severe depression experienced by some people when there is relatively less light from the sun.

8. a   mod. 14 p. 159
*a. Correct. A narcoleptic can fall asleep at any time, although stress does seem to contribute to the narcoleptic's symptoms.
b. Incorrect. Insomnia involves difficulty getting to sleep or staying asleep.
c. Incorrect. Somnambulism is also known as sleepwalking.
d. Incorrect. This concept is from some sci-fi movie, no doubt.

9. a   mod. 14 p. 159
*a. Correct. Narcolepsy is uncontrollable.
b. Incorrect. Sleep apnea will make one tired throughout the next day because of the frequent awakening through the night.
c. Incorrect. Hypersomnia is excessive sleep at night.
d. Incorrect. Insomnia involves difficulty getting to sleep or staying asleep.

10. d   mod. 15 p. 178
a. Incorrect. PCP is common, but not the most common.
b. Incorrect. LSD is common, but not the most common.
c. Incorrect. Cocaine is a stimulant, not a hallucinogen.
*d. Correct. Marijuana is by far the most commonly used hallucinogen.

11. d   mod. 14 p. 161
a. Incorrect. A regular bedtime makes for a habit of falling asleep.
b. Incorrect. Here we apply "reverse" psychology on ourselves.
c. Incorrect. Caffeine contributes to sleeplessness.
*d. Correct. The TV belongs in the living room, not the bedroom. TV is usually stimulating, not restful.

12. d   mod. 14 p. 304
a. Incorrect. Meditation is form of altering consciousness distinct from hypnosis.
b. Incorrect. It may be that good fortune ultimately comes from being focused and relaxed, and able to concentrate on one's work, however.
c. Incorrect. Again, it may be that career growth ultimately comes from being focused and relaxed, and able to concentrate on one's work, however.
*d. Correct. This is the major goal of meditation, according to Buddhism.

13. a   mod. 15 p. 178
*a. Correct. Methadone produces an addiction, but it does not have the psychoactive properties of heroin.
b. Incorrect. Methadone does not cause mental retardation.
c. Incorrect. Everyone is at risk, but methadone does not increase the risk.
d. Incorrect. Most drug users find the marijuana high to be appealing, but nothing about the methadone causes this.

14. b   mod. 15 p. 171
a. Incorrect. Because they stimulate the nervous system, they do not have an anesthetic effect.
*b. Correct. Each of these is considered a stimulant.
c. Incorrect. In some cases, even small doses of these drugs can cause anxiety.
d. Incorrect. With extreme doses, hallucinations are possible, but they do not occur in typical doses.

15. b   mod. 15 p. 177
a. Incorrect. An opiate is a narcotic.
*b. Correct. These are all classes of the depressant group known as barbiturates.
c. Incorrect. These drugs do not cause hallucinations under normal circumstances.
d. Incorrect. These drugs do not cause hypnosis.

16. b   mod. 14 p. 158
17. a   mod. 14 p. 159
18. c   mod. 15 p. 178
19. d   mod. 15 p. 179

20. self-destructive acts   mod. 15 p. 163
21. cannot   mod. 15 p. 163
23. daydreaming   mod. 15 p. 160
23. pain   mod. 15 p. 165
24. Unresolved   mod. 15 p. 165

25.
■ Identify the drugs that have been involved in this issue; include marijuana, but also, some have argued that drug use should be completely legalized and viewed as a medical or psychological problem.
■ State your view, identifying which drug(s) should be decriminalized and which should not. Many people suggest that the medical benefits of some drugs cannot be explored and used because of their status. Other reasons should be offered as well. For instance, the use of some drugs can be considered victimless, although the drug trade has many victims.

- If you believe that all drugs should remain illegal, then support your reasoning. Harm to society and to individuals is a common argument. Provide examples.

Practice Test 3:

1. a   mod. 14 p. 151
*a. Correct. The electrical properties are recorded as waveforms by the EEG, and thus are referred to as brain waves.
b. Incorrect. The time from sleep to stage is not a factor in defining the stages, and people go through several cycles of the stages each night.
c. Incorrect. Stage 4 and REM sleep have specific sleep events associated with them, but these are not used to define the stages.
d. Incorrect. With the exception of REM sleep, when the sleeper is quite still, the body movements are generally the same from one stage to another.

2. d   mod. 14 p. 152
a. Incorrect. There are no long-term effects from sleep deprivation.
b. Incorrect. He is unlikely to get sick, although he might make mistakes at work and be prone to accidents elsewhere.
c. Incorrect. There are no long-term consequences for staying awake 36 hours.
*d. Correct. If he is staying awake to study, then he might be jeopardizing his grade; it would be more effective to break the study into smaller parts and get some rest.

3. d   mod. 14 p. 156
a. Incorrect. Probably more than a friendship.
b. Incorrect. Nothing in the dream suggests any anxiety about talking to Jim.
c. Incorrect. This is a possible reading of the manifest content of the dream, but a Freudian approach would not differ from any other approach on this view.
*d. Correct. Climbing stairs is an act symbolic of sexual intercourse.

4. b   mod. 14 p. 156
a. Incorrect. This may be what it means, but it is a strange way of making the image clear, and besides, this is not what a Freudian would see.
*b. Correct. Grapefruits can generally be viewed as feminine bodies, but more specifically as breasts.
c. Incorrect. This is not a likely interpretation.
d. Incorrect. The trip down the tunnel may have a quality of a wish to return to the womb, but the grapefruits do not fit the image.

5. b   mod. 14 p. 157
a. Incorrect. Although the increase in anxiety would lead to additional wish-fulfillment types of dreams.
*b. Correct. The need to make sense of environmental, survival-oriented information makes this choice the better candidate.
c. Incorrect. The random activity would be just as random in either circumstance.
d. Incorrect. There is no latent content dream theory.

6. b   mod. 14 p. 160
a. Incorrect. This is not a common fantasy during nervous breakdowns.
*b. Correct. Fantasies about escape are common in daydreams.
c. Incorrect. Because she was in class, and probably not asleep, a nighttime emission is unlikely.
d. Incorrect. A mantra is a word repeated during meditation.

7. a   mod. 14 p. 159
*a. Correct. Sleepwalkers are often able to walk with agility, and don't necessarily need to be awakened unless something in their path poses a danger.
b. Incorrect. Sleepwalking most often occurs in stage 4 sleep.
c. Incorrect. If awakened, sleepwalkers can have a vague sense of where they are and what they were doing.
d. Incorrect. Sleepwalking is common throughout age groups.

8. a   mod. 15 p. 164
*a. Correct. The changes in brain activity can be recorded on an EEG.
b. Incorrect. They both may result in a decrease in blood pressure, but they may not.
c. Incorrect. Hypnosis is an invention of European origin.
d. Incorrect. "Total relaxation" is a bit overstated.

9. b   mod. 15 p. 169
a. Incorrect. Addiction may be either or both biologically and psychologically based.
*b. Correct. This may be true in cases of alcoholism, but other addictions arise from the nature of the body-drug interaction.
c. Incorrect. There is no foundation for this statement.
d. Incorrect. Addiction may be either or both biologically and psychologically based.

10. b   mod. 15 p. 171
a.   Incorrect. However, that must be some vitamin!
*b. Correct. This is what stimulants do.
c.   Incorrect. Depressants slow the heart rate.
d.   Incorrect. Among other things, a hallucinogen could cause these symptoms (among many others), but not necessarily.

11. c   mod. 15 p. 178
a.   Incorrect. Heroin is a narcotic.
b.   Incorrect. Cocaine is a stimulant.
*c. Correct. Marijuana is a hallucinogen.
d.   Incorrect. Morphine is a narcotic.

12. b   mod. 14 p. 155
a.   Incorrect. The latent content would be what the jacket and showing off might symbolize.
*b. Correct. This is what she actually did in her dream.
c.   Incorrect. The manifest content can be relevant to the meaning because it contains the symbols.
d.   Incorrect. These would be day residues only if this is what she did the day before.

13. a   mod. 14 p. 155
*a. Correct. As symbols, they hold the keys to the repressed or latent content of the dream.
b.   Incorrect. The wearing of the jacket and the parading were the manifest content.
c.   Incorrect. Activation process is not relevant to the dream interpretation.
d.   Incorrect. He would only need to ask Meghan about the daytime activities to make this determination.

14. a   mod. 15 p. 163
*a. Correct. Unless she is an exhibitionist, she would not undress.
b.   Incorrect. With slightly lowered inhibitions, she could easily flirt.
c.   Incorrect. She is likely to recall a past life, even if she does not have one.
d.   Incorrect. Making people do stupid animal tricks is a common hypnotic activity.

15. b   mod 16 p. 173
a.   Incorrect. These are hallucinogens.
*b. Correct. These are the two primary examples of narcotics given in the text.
c.   Incorrect. These are depressants.
d.   Incorrect. These are stimulants.

16. b   mod. 16 p. 177
17. e   mod. 16 p. 178
18. a   mod. 16 p. 178
19. d   mod. 16 p. 178
20. c   mod. 16 p. 178

21. consciousness   mod. 16 p. 169
22. date-rape drug   mod. 16 p. 322
23. stimulants   mod. 16 p. 171-172
24. neurotransmitter   mod. 16 p. 169
25. Psychological   mod. 16 p. 173

26. Research demonstrates that all humans share basic biological commonalities. Therefore, we would expect all humans to experience consciousness, including altered states, in the same way. However, research also suggests that people interpret consciousness in varied ways, depending on their culture. For instance, the experience of how quickly or slowly time passes varies between cultures.

Chapter 6: Learning

Overview

This set of modules presents the approaches that psychologists use in the study of learning. To understand what learning is, you must distinguish between performance changes caused by maturation and changes brought about by experience. Similarly, you must distinguish short-term changes in behavior caused by factors other than learning, such as declines in performance resulting from fatigue or lack of effort, from performance changes resulting from actual learning. Some psychologists have approached learning by considering it as simply any change in behavior.

Module 17 examines classical conditioning, the type of learning that explains responses ranging from a dog salivating when it hears the can opener to the emotions we feel when our national anthem is played. Concepts such as extinction, stimulus generalization, and stimulus discrimination are defined and explained.

Module 18 focuses on operant conditioning, a form of learning in which a voluntary behavior is strengthened or weakened through reinforcement. Theories that consider how learning is a consequence of rewarding circumstances are examined. Examples of primary and secondary reinforcers, along with an explanation of positive and negative reinforcers and punishment, are presented. The major categories of reinforcement schedules, shaping, and the biological constraints on the ability of the organism to learn are discussed.

Module 19 presents the cognitive and social-cognitive approaches to learning. Latent learning, cognitive maps, and the imitation of observed behavior are all discussed, with a focus on the impact a person's cultural background and unique pattern of abilities play in the learning process.

To further investigate the topics covered in this chapter, you can visit the related Web sites by visiting the following link: www.mhhe.com/feldmanup8.

Prologue: A Friend Named Minnic
Looking Ahead

Module 17:
Classical Conditioning

The Basics of Classical Conditioning
Applying Conditioning Principles to Human Behavior
Extinction
Generalization and Discrimination
Beyond Traditional Classical Conditioning: Challenging Basic Assumptions

- ***What is learning?***
- ***How do we learn to form associations between stimuli and responses?***

Classical Conditioning

[a] _____ is distinguished from *maturation* on the basis of whether the resulting change in behavior is a consequence of experience (learning) or of growth (maturation). Short-term changes in performance, the key measure of learning, can also result from fatigue, lack of effort, and other factors that are not reflections of learning. According to some people, learning can only be inferred indirectly.

Ivan Pavlov's studies concerning the physiology of the digestive processes led him to discover the basic principles of [b] _____, a process in which an organism learns to respond to a stimulus that did not bring about the response earlier. An original study involved Pavlov's training a dog to salivate when a bell was rung. In this process, the bell's sound is considered the [c] _____ because it does not bring about the response of interest.

The meat, which does cause salivation, is called the [d] _____. The salivation, when it occurs because of the presence of the meat (UCS), is called the [e] _____. The conditioning process requires repeated pairing of the UCS and the neutral stimulus. After training is complete, the neutral stimulus—now called the [f] _____—will now bring about the UCR, now called the [g] _____.

Pavlov noted that the neutral stimulus had to precede the UCS by no more than several seconds for the conditioning to be the most effective.

One of the more famous applications of classical conditioning techniques to humans is the case of the 11-month-old infant Albert. Albert was taught to fear a laboratory rat, to which he had shown no fear initially, by creating a loud noise behind him whenever he approached the rat.

The process of ending the association of the UCS and the CS is called **[h]** _____, which occurs when a previously learned response decreases and disappears. In Pavlov's experiment, if the bell is repeatedly sounded without the meat being presented, the dog will eventually stop salivating. Some war veterans suffer from **[i]** _____, because the response of fear and negative emotions associated with very loud noises (as occurs on battlefields) has never been extinguished. Systematic desensitization requires the repeated presentation of the frightening stimulus (a CS) without the presentation of the occurrence of the negative consequences.

When a CR has been extinguished, and a period of time has passed without the presentation of the CS, a phenomenon called **[j]** _____ can occur. The CS is presented and the previously extinguished response recurs, although it is usually weaker than in the original training and can be extinguished again more easily.

[k] _____ takes place when a conditioned response occurs in the presence of a stimulus that is similar to the original conditioned stimulus. In the case of Little Albert, the fear response was generalized to white furry things, including a white-bearded Santa Claus mask. **[l]** _____ occurs when an organism learns to differentiate (discriminate) one stimulus from another and responds only to one stimulus and not the others.

Many of the fundamental assumptions of classical conditioning have been challenged. One challenge has been to question the length of the interval between the neutral stimulus and the unconditioned stimulus. Garcia found that nausea caused by radiation, a state that occurred hours after exposure, could be associated with water drunk that has unusual characteristics or with water drunk in a particular place. Garcia's findings that the association could be made with delays as long as eight hours is a direct challenge to the idea that the pairing must be made within several seconds to be effective.

Evaluate

_____ 1.   neutral stimulus

a.   A stimulus that brings about a response without having been learned.

_____ 2.   unconditioned stimulus (UCS)

b.   A stimulus that, before conditioning, has no effect on the desired response.

_____ 3.   unconditioned response (UCR)

c.   A once-neutral stimulus that has been paired with an unconditioned stimulus to bring about a response formerly caused only by the unconditioned stimulus.

_____ 4.   conditioned stimulus (CS)

_____ 5.   conditioned response (CR)

d.   A response that, after conditioning, follows a previously neutral stimulus (e.g., salivation at the sound of a tuning fork).

e.   A response that is natural and needs no training (e.g., salivation at the smell of food).

Rethink

17-1   How likely is it that Little Albert, Watson's experimental subject, went through life afraid of Santa Claus? Describe what probably happened to prevent this behavior.

17-2   *From the perspective of an advertising executive:* How might knowledge of classical conditioning be useful in creating an advertising campaign? What, if any, ethical issues arise from this use?

Spotlight on Terminology and Language—ESL Pointers

Page 182 "The phone is his **lifeline**."

A **lifeline** is a support system.

Page 182 "She pulls the cord to open her cage, scampers to the kitchen floor, grabs the phone, **scales** Cook's leg and puts it back on his lap."

To **scale** something is to climb it.

Page 182 ""How **cool** is that?" Cook says, beaming like a proud father."

In this sentence **Cool** is a slang term meaning amazing or outstanding.

Page 182 "She turns lights on and off, opens soda bottles and retrieves **Hot Pockets** from the microwave...."

Hot Pockets are frozen sandwiches that are cooked in the microwave and eaten.

Page 182 "It is the result of **painstaking** training procedures—the same ones that are at work in each of our lives, illustrated by our ability to read a book, drive a car, play poker, study for a test, or perform any of the numerous activities that make up our daily routine."

Painstaking training is training that is done in a very through and careful way.

Page 182 "A developmental psychologist might inquire, "How do babies learn to **distinguish** their mothers from other people?" A clinical psychologist might wonder, "Why do some people learn to be afraid when they see a spider?" A social psychologist might ask, "How do we learn to believe that we've fallen in love?""

When we **distinguish** things we are making out the differences between them.

Page 183 "Does the mere sight of the **golden arches** in front of McDonald's make you feel pangs of hunger and think about hamburgers?"

In this sentence the term "**golden arches**" refers to the symbol of the fast food restaurant, McDonald's.

Page 183 "**Classical conditioning** is one of a number of different types of learning that psychologists have identified, but a general definition **encompasses** them all: Learning is a relatively permanent change in behavior that is brought about by experience."

Classical conditioning is also called Pavlovian conditioning.

Encompass is to include.

Page 183 "For example, some changes in behavior or performance come about through **maturation** alone, and don't involve experience."

Maturation refers to the biological process by which we age and grow.

Page 183 "It is clear that we are **primed** for learning from the beginning of life."

When we are **primed** for something we are ready or prepared for it.

Page 184 "Pavlov had been studying the secretion of stomach acids and **salivation** in dogs in response to the ingestion of varying amounts and kinds of food."

Salivation is the process by which we produce salvia.

Page 184 "While doing that, he observed a curious **phenomenon**: Sometimes stomach secretions and salivation would begin in the dogs when they had not yet eaten any food."

A **phenomenon** is an event or a happening.

Page 184 "**Classical conditioning** is a type of learning in which a neutral stimulus (such as the experimenter's footsteps) comes to **elicit** a response after being paired with a stimulus (such as food) that naturally brings about that response.

To **elicit** something is to extract it or bring it out.
Page 186 "Recall, for instance, the earlier illustration of how people may experience **hunger pangs** at the sight of McDonald's golden arches."

Pangs are spasms or brief contractions. **Hunger pangs** are spasms or contractions that indicate a need to eat.

Page 186 "In a now-**infamous** case study, psychologist John B. Watson and colleague Rosalie Rayner (1920) showed that classical conditioning was at the root of such fears by conditioning an 11-month-old infant named Albert to be afraid of rats."

Infamous means well-known, renowned. An **infamous** activity generally is one which is perceived negatively - something that has an extremely bad reputation. This **infamous** research study would not be allowed to be replicated in psychology laboratories today because of the questionable ethics of this research.

Page 186 "It is clear that Watson, the experimenter, has been **condemned** for using ethically questionable procedures and that such studies would never be conducted today."

You **condemn** something when you state that it's wrong, or unacceptable.

Page 188 "On the other hand, ***stimulus discrimination*** occurs if two stimuli are sufficiently distinct from one another that one **evokes** a conditioned response but the other does not."

To **evoke** is to elicit a response.

Page 188 "For example, according to Pavlov, the process of linking stimuli and responses occurs in a **mechanistic**, unthinking way.

When you explain behavior **mechanistically**, you're explaining it **mechanically**, explaining human behavior and other natural processes in terms of physical causes and processes.

Page 189 "The ease with which animals can be conditioned to avoid certain kinds of dangerous stimuli, such as **tainted** food, supports evolutionary theory."

Tainted food is contaminated fool, polluted food. When you eat **tainted** food, you often get sick.

Page 189 "Consequently, organisms that ingest **unpalatable** foods (whether coyotes that eat a carcass laced with a drug or humans who suffer food poisoning after eating spoiled sushi in a restaurant) are likely to avoid similar foods in the future, making their survival more likely (Steinmetz, Kim & Thompson, 2003)."

When food is **unpalatable**, it is not good food. It does not taste good. Have you ever put something in your mouth that you had to spit out right away, because the taste was bad? This food was **unpalatable**.

Module 18: Operant Conditioning

Thorndike's Law of Effect
The Basics of Operant Conditioning
Positive Reinforcers, Negative Reinforcers, and Punishment
The Pros and Cons of Punishment: Why Reinforcement Beats Punishment
Schedules of Reinforcement: Timing Life's Rewards
Discrimination and Generalization in Operant Conditioning
Shaping: Reinforcing What Doesn't Come Naturally

Applying Psychology in the 21st Century: A Nose for Danger: Saving Lives by Sniffing out Land Mines

Biological Constraints on Learning: You Can't Teach an Old Dog Just Any Trick

Becoming an Informed Consumer of Psychology: Using Behavioral Analysis and Behavior Modification

- *What is the role of reward and punishment in learning?*
- *What are some practical methods for bringing about behavior change, both in ourselves and in others?*

Operant Conditioning

[a] _____ is learning in which the response is strengthened or weakened according to whether it has positive or negative consequences. The term "operant" suggests that the organism *operates* on the environment in a deliberate manner to gain a desired result.

Edward L. Thorndike found that a cat would learn to escape from a cage by performing specific actions in order to open a door that allows it access to food, a positive consequence of

the behavior. Thorndike formulated the [b] _____, stating that responses with satisfying results would be repeated, and those with less satisfying results would be less likely to be repeated.

[c] _____ is the process by which a stimulus increases the probability that a preceding behavior will be repeated. In Skinner's experiments, releasing the food by

pressing a lever is a reinforcement, and the food is called a(n) [d] _____, which is any stimulus that increases the probability that a preceding behavior will be repeated. A

[e] _____ satisfies a biological need without regard to prior experience. A(n) [f]

183

_____ is a stimulus that reinforces because of its association with a primary reinforcer.

Reinforcers are also distinguished as positive or negative. **[g]** _____ bring about an increase in the preceding response. **[h]** _____ lead to an increase in a desired response when they are *removed*.

Negative reinforcement requires that an individual take an action to remove an undesirable condition. **[i]** _____ refers to a stimulus that *decreases* the probability that a behavior will be repeated. Punishment includes the application of an unpleasant stimulus, called **[j]** _____, such as spanking, as well as removal of something positive, called **[k]** _____, such as the loss of a privilege.

The frequency and timing of reinforcement depends on the use of **[l]** _____. With **[m]** _____, the behavior is reinforced every time it occurs. **[n]** _____ describes the technique of using reinforcement some of the time but not for every response. Partial reinforcement schedules maintain behavior longer than continuous reinforcement before extinction occurs.

A(n) **[o]** _____ delivers a reinforcement after a certain number of responses. A **[p]** _____ delivers reinforcement on the basis of a varying number of responses. The number of responses often remains close to an average. The fixed- and variable-ratio schedules depend on a *number* of responses, and the fixed- and variable-interval schedules depend on an *amount of time*. **[q]** _____ deliver reinforcements to the first behavior occurring after a set interval, or period, of time.

[r] _____ deliver reinforcement after a varying interval of time. Fixed intervals are like weekly paychecks; variable intervals are like pop quizzes.

Discrimination and generalization are achieved in operant conditioning through **[s]** _____. In stimulus control training, a behavior is reinforced only in the presence of specific stimuli. The specific stimulus is called a *discriminative stimulus*, one that signals the likelihood of a particular behavior being reinforced.

When a complex behavior is desired, a trainer may shape the desired behavior by rewarding closer and closer approximations of the behavior. Many complex human and animal skills are acquired through **[t]** _____.

Sometimes learning is constrained by behaviors that are biologically innate, or inborn. Not all behaviors can be taught to all animals equally well because of these *biological constraints*. Pigs might root a disk around their cages, and raccoons might horde and then clean similar disks.

[u] _____ refers to the formalized use of basic principles of learning theory to change behavior by eliminating undesirable behaviors and encouraging desirable ones. Behavior modification can be used to train mentally retarded individuals, to help people lose weight or quit smoking, and to teach people to behave safely. The steps of a typical behavior program include (1) identifying goals and target behaviors; (2) designing a data recording system and recording preliminary data; (3) selecting a behavior change strategy; (4) implementing the program; (5) keeping careful records after the program has been implemented; and (6) evaluating and altering the ongoing program.

Evaluate

_____ 1.   operant conditioning

_____ 2.   primary reinforcer

_____ 3.   secondary reinforcer

_____ 4.   positive reinforcer

_____ 5.   negative reinforcer

_____ 6.   punishment

_____ 7.   reward

a.   A stimulus that decreases the likelihood that the behavior will occur again.

b.   Similar to the idea of "positive reinforcer."

c.   A reward that satisfies a biological need (e.g., hunger or thirst) and works naturally.

d.   A stimulus added to the environment that brings about an increase in the response that preceded it.

e.   A stimulus that becomes reinforcing by its association with a primary reinforcer (e.g., money, which allows us to obtain food, a primary reinforcer).

f.   A stimulus whose removal is reinforcing, leading to a greater probability that the response bringing about this removal will occur again.

g.   A voluntary response is strengthened or weakened depending on its positive or negative consequences.

Rethink

18-1   Using the scientific literature as a guide, what would you tell parents who wish to know if the routine use of physical punishment is a necessary and acceptable form of child-rearing?

18-2   *From the perspective of an educator:* How would you utilize your knowledge of operant conditioning in the classroom to set up a program to increase the likelihood children will complete their homework more frequently?

Spotlight on Terminology and Language—ESL Pointers

Page 191 "Operant conditioning is at work when we learn that **toiling** industriously can bring about a raise or that studying hard results in good grades."

Toiling is working hard.

Page 192 "Thorndike's early research served as the foundation for the work of one of the twentieth century's most **influential** psychologists, B. F. Skinner, who died in 1990."

Influential means significant, prominent. An influential person is often a leader. Who have been some of your **influential** mentors?

Page 192 "You may have heard of the Skinner box,(shown in Figure 2), a **chamber** with a highly controlled environment that was used to study operant conditioning processes with laboratory animals."

A **chamber** is an enclosed space designed for experimental purposes.

Page 193 "Reinforcement is the process by which a stimulus increases the **probability** that a preceding behavior will be repeated."

When the **probability** of an act is increased, this means that the occurrence or circumstance is likely to occur again.

Page 194 "For instance, when a teenager is told she is "**grounded**" and will no longer be able to use the family car because of her poor grades, or when an employee is informed that he has been demoted with a cut in pay because of poor job evaluations, negative punishment is being administered."

When adolescents are **grounded**, their activities are confined to a limited area, often their home or their room.

Page 195 "For instance, a parent may not have a second chance to warn a child not to run into a busy street, and so punishing the first **incidence** of this behavior may prove to be wise."

An **incidence** is an occurrence of an action or situation.

Page 195 "Moreover, the use of punishment to **suppress** behavior, even temporarily, provides an opportunity to reinforce a person for **subsequently** behaving in a more desirable way."

Suppress is to stop behavior. **Subsequently** is following in time, coming later.

Page 195 "Punishment has several disadvantages make its routine **questionable**."

When something is **questionable** it is doubted and challenged.

Page 198 "Students' study habits often **exemplify** this reality."

To **exemplify** something is to create an example of it. Students' study habits are an example of this behavior.

Page 198 "Just before the exam, however, students begin to **cram** for it, signaling a rapid increase in the rate of their studying response.

To **cram** is to pack something into a small space. When students **cram** they pack all of their studying into a small amount of time.

Page 199 "There are many complex behaviors, ranging from auto repair to zoo management, that we would not expect to occur naturally as part of anyone's **spontaneous** behavior."

Spontaneous behavior is voluntary behavior that happens in a moment. It is not premeditated.

Page 199 "Shaping is the process of teaching a complex behavior by rewarding closer and closer **approximations** of the desired behavior."

An **approximation** is an inexact result coming closer in degree to the quality that is desired.

Page 200 "Instead, there are biological **constraints**, built-in limitations in the ability of animals to learn particular behaviors."

A **constraint** is something that restricts you from a given course of action. A biological **constraint** is a built-in restriction.

Page 204 "If the target behaviors are not **monitored**, there is no way of knowing whether the program has actually been successful."

To **monitor** something is to check systematically, usually for the purpose of collecting data. Do you see a purpose for public or governmental **monitoring** of any specific behaviors?

Module 19: Cognitive Approaches to Learning

Latent Learning
Observational Learning: Learning Through Imitation

Exploring Diversity:
Does Culture Influence How We Learn?

Applying Psychology in the 21st Century:
Violence in Television and Video Games:
Does the Media's Message Matter?

- *What is the role of cognition and thought in learning?*

Cognitive-Social Approaches to Learning

The approach that views learning in terms of thought processes is called

[a] _____. This approach does not deny the importance of classical and operant conditioning. It includes the consideration of unseen mental processes as well.

[b] _____ is behavior that is learned but not demonstrated until reinforcement is provided for demonstrating the behavior. Latent learning occurs when rats are allowed to wander around a maze without any reward at the end, but once they learn that a reinforcement is available, they will quickly find their way through the maze even though they were being reinforced for doing so in the past. The wandering around apparently leads them to

develop a(n) **[c]** _____ of the maze. Humans apparently develop cognitive maps of their surroundings based on landmarks.

Accounting for a large portion of learning in humans, **[d]** _____ is

learning that occurs by observing the behavior of another person, called the **[e]** _____.
The classic experiment involved children observing a model strike a Bobo doll, and then later those who had seen the behavior were more prone to act aggressively. Four processes are necessary for observational learning: (1) paying attention to critical features; (2) remembering the behavior; (3) reproducing the action; and (4) being motivated to repeat the behavior. We also observe the kinds of reinforcement that the model receives for the behavior. Observational learning has been related to how violence on television affects aggression and violence in children.

188

The Exploring Diversity section examines *learning styles* and how cultural differences are reflected in these different ways of approaching materials. Learning styles are characterized by cultural background and individual abilities.

Evaluate

_____ 1.   continuous reinforcement schedule

_____ 2.   partial reinforcement schedule

_____ 3.   schedules of reinforcement

_____ 4.   stimulus control training

_____ 5.   model

_____ 6.   relational learning style

a.   A process of understanding information by comprehending its entirety or the whole of the phenomenon.

b.   A person serving as an example to an observer; the observer may imitate that person's behavior.

c.   Reinforcing of a behavior every time it occurs.

d.   Reinforcing of a behavior some, but not all, of the time.

e.   The frequency and timing of reinforcement following desired behavior.

f.   Training in which an organism is reinforced in the presence of a certain specific stimulus, but not in its absence.

Rethink

19-1   The relational style of learning sometimes conflicts with the traditional school environment. Could a school be created that takes advantage of the characteristics of the relational style? How? Are there types of learning for which the analytical style is clearly superior?

19-2   *From the perspective of a social worker:* What advice would you give to families about children's exposure to violent media and video games?

Spotlight on Terminology and Language—ESL Pointers

Page 207 " In **latent** learning, a new behavior is learned but not demonstrated until some incentive is provided for displaying it (Tolman & Honzik, 1930)."

Latent is something present but not evident or active. A fingerprint that is difficult to see but can be made visible for examination is a **latent** fingerprint.

Page 209 "In the study, young children saw a film of an adult wildly hitting a five-foot-tall **inflatable** punching toy called a Bobo doll (Bandura, Ross, & Ross, 1963a, 1963b)."

Something **inflatable** is able to be blown up. Many **inflatable** Spiderman balloons, made of expandable material that could be filed with air, were sold following the successful Spiderman movie.

Page 209 "In one experiment, for example, children who were afraid of dogs were exposed to a model – **dubbed** the Fearless Peer – playing with a dog (Bandura, Grusec, & Menlove, 1967)."

The model was **dubbed**, or named, the Fearless Peer. The name, the Fearless Peer, was used as a descriptive nickname for the model.

Page 210 "Like other "media **copycat**" killings, the brothers' cold-blooded brutality raises a critical issue: Does observing violent and antisocial acts in the media lead viewers to behave in similar ways?"

A **copycat** is someone who imitates someone else's actions.

Page 210 "Finally, a continuous diet of aggression may leave us **desensitized** to violence, and what previously would have **repelled** us now produces little emotional response."

When we are **desensitized**, we become insensitive. Researchers are concerned that observing too much violence on television will **desensitize** us to physical aggression.

When something repels us, we find it disgusts us. Something that **repels** people causes an aversion. Is there any activity that previously would have **repelled** you, but now find you have become **desensitized** to?

Test your knowledge of this set of modules by answering these questions. These questions have been placed in three Practice Tests. The first two tests consist of questions that will test your recall of factual knowledge. The third test contains questions that are challenging and primarily test for conceptual knowledge and your ability to apply that knowledge. Check your answers and review the feedback using the Answer Key on the following pages of the *Study Guide*.

PRACTICE TEST 1:

1.　Which of the following statements concerning the relationship between nurture and learning is correct?
   a.　Learning refers to temporary change, whereas nurture is permanent.
   b.　Nurture results in only short-term changes in learned behavior.
   c.　Learning involves nature rather than nurture.
   d.　Nurture helps create learning.

2.　In order to understand when learning has occurred, we must differentiate it from:
   a.　measurable responses.
   b.　extinction.
   c.　maturation.
   d.　habituation.

3.　The _____ in Pavlov's experiment was the meat.
   a.　unconditioned stimulus
   b.　conditioned stimulus
   c.　unconditioned response
   d.　conditioned response

4.　Over time, when the conditioned stimulus is presented repeatedly without being paired with the unconditioned stimulus, the result will be:
   a.　learning.
   b.　perception.
   c.　habituation.
   d.　extinction.

5.　Spontaneous recovery can occur following:
   a.　operant conditioning.
   b.　token economy.
   c.　punishment.
   d.　extinction.

6.　Mrs. Tobin is used to turning off the lights to quiet the class, a classically conditioned behavior. This behavior can be extinguished by:
   a.　adding another conditioned stimulus to the pairing.
   b.　no longer presenting the unconditioned stimulus after the conditioned response.
   c.　using stimulus substitution.
   d.　reintroducing the unconditioned stimulus.

7.　Garcia's behavioral investigations of rats that were treated with doses of radiation illustrate that:
   a.　rats obey slightly different principles of classical conditioning than do humans.
   b.　some research findings involving classical conditioning do not appear to obey Pavlov's conditioning principles.
   c.　classical conditioning is a very robust form of learning because it is not weakened even by large doses of medication.
   d.　changes in classical conditioning are highly sensitive indicators of radiation effects.

8. The _____ states that we will continue to act in a manner that will lead to pleasing consequences.
    a. law of frequency   c. law of effect
    b. principle of similarity   d. principle of contiguity

9. The distinction between primary reinforcers and secondary reinforcers is that:
    a. primary reinforcers satisfy some biological need; secondary reinforcers are effective because of their association with primary reinforcers.
    b. organisms prefer primary reinforcers to secondary reinforcers.
    c. primary reinforcers are not effective with all organisms.
    d. primary reinforcers depend on the past conditioning of the organism; secondary reinforcers have a biological basis.

10. Ariel gives her dog a treat each time the dog comes when he is called. This stimulus that increases the likelihood that the preceding behavior will be repeated is called a(n):
    a. punisher.   c. response.
    b. reinforcer.   d. operant.

11. Negative reinforcement:
    a. is a special form of punishment.
    b. is a phenomenon that results when reward is withheld.
    c. involves the decrease or removal of an aversive stimulus.
    d. occurs in both classical and instrumental conditioning.

12. Constance receives checks from home to help subsidize her college activities. She never knows when or how much she will receive. In the variable schedule of reinforcement, the response rate is:
    a. always high.   c. easily extinguished.
    b. always constant and low.   d. highly resistant to extinction.

13. Because the number of lottery tickets a person must purchase before reinforcement occurs in the form of a winning ticket is not certain, he or she is working on a:
    a. variable-ratio schedule.   c. variable-interval schedule.
    b. fixed-ratio schedule.   d. fixed-interval schedule.

14. Learned taste aversions violate the traditional rules of classical conditioning because:
    a. people don't learn taste aversions, they are innate.
    b. universal biological constraints guide taste aversions.
    c. they depend on the neutral stimulus being presented before the unconditioned stimulus.
    d. people typically develop them even when there is a notable time lapse between eating the food and when they become ill.

15. Given the opportunity to explore a maze with no explicit reward available, rats will develop:
    a. a cognitive map of the maze.   c. an increased interest in the maze.
    b. an aversion to the maze.   d. a superstitious fear of the maze.

_____ 16.   cognitive learning theory   a.   The study of the thought processes that underlie learning.

_____ 17.   latent learning

                                          b.   Learning that involves the imitation of a model.

_____ 18.   observational learning

                                          c.   A new behavior is acquired but not readily demonstrated until reinforcement is provided.

_____ 19.   classical conditioning

_____ 20.   neutral stimulus   d.   A stimulus that, before conditioning, does not naturally bring about the response of interest.

                                          e.   A type of learning in which a neutral stimulus comes to bring about a response after it is paired with a stimulus that naturally brings about that response.

21.   _____ is the process of teaching a complex behavior by rewarding closer and closer approximations of the desired behavior.

22.   A(n) _____ stimulus is one that brings about a response without having been learned.

23.   A(n) _____ stimulus is a once-neutral stimulus that has been paired with an unconditioned stimulus to bring about a response formerly caused only by the unconditioned stimulus.

24.   A(n) _____ response is natural and needs no training.

25.   The use of physical punishment has become quite controversial. Most school systems now outlaw its use, and many parents try to find alternatives to it. Define the issues related to the use of punishment, and answer the question, "Is it wrong to use physical punishment to discipline children?" As you answer, consider whether there are circumstances that may require routine use, or whether it should be rare. Describe alternatives for use in normal disciplining of children.

PRACTICE TEST 2:

1.   Cognitive psychologists define learning as:
     a.   a change in behavior brought about by growth and maturity of the nervous system.
     b.   a measurable change in behavior brought about by conditions such as drugs, sleep, and fatigue.
     c.   a behavioral response that occurs each time a critical stimulus is presented.
     d.   a relatively permanent change in behavior brought about by experience.

2.   In classical conditioning, the stimulus that comes to elicit a response that it would not previously have elicited is called the:
     a.   classical stimulus.   c.   conditioned stimulus.
     b.   unconditioned stimulus.   d.   discriminative stimulus.

3.   Before the conditioning trials in which Watson planned to condition fear of a rat in Little Albert, the rat—which Albert was known not to fear—would have been considered:
     a.   an unconditioned stimulus.   c.   a discriminative stimulus.
     b.   an adaptive stimulus.   d.   a neutral stimulus.

4. Joanne is frustrated with her geometry teacher who keeps showing the students formulae for solving geometry problems, and then showing example problems. She wants to understand why and how one would use geometry, in general, before tackling the basic principles of the math needed in geometry. She probably uses a(n):
   a. relational learning style.
   b. analytic learning style.
   c. social learning style.
   d. phobic learning style.

5. When Tashiene's mother no longer pays any attention to her temper tantrums about getting ready for school, or when the conditioned stimulus is presented repeatedly without being accompanied by the unconditioned stimulus, _____ occurs.
   a. escape conditioning
   b. extinction
   c. stimulus generalization
   d. negative reinforcement

6. Pavlov's assumption that stimuli and responses were linked in a mechanistic, unthinking way has been challenged by:
   a. cognitive learning theorists.
   b. the animal trainers the Brelands.
   c. Edward Thorndike's law of effect.
   d. operant conditioning.

7. A reinforcement given for the first correct or desired response to occur after a set period is called:
   a. a fixed-ratio reinforcement schedule.
   b. a continuous reinforcement schedule.
   c. a fixed-interval reinforcement schedule.
   d. a variable-interval reinforcement schedule.

8. Which alternative below is **not** an example of operant conditioning?
   a. A cat pushes against a lever to open a door on its cage.
   b. A student drives within the speed limit to avoid getting another speeding ticket.
   c. A dog rolls over for a dog biscuit.
   d. A student's blood pressure increases when she anticipates speaking with her chemistry professor.

9. Which name below is **not** associated with classical conditioning or operant conditioning?
   a. Pavlov
   b. Skinner
   c. Wertheimer
   d. Thorndike

10. Typically, food is a _____, whereas money is a _____.
    a. discriminative stimulus; conditioned reinforcer
    b. need; motive
    c. primary reinforcer; secondary reinforcer
    d. drive reducer; natural reinforcer

11. Which of the following is most likely to be considered a primary reinforcer?
    a. Money
    b. Water
    c. Good grades
    d. A hammer

12. In which of the following situations would the use of punishment be most effective in reducing the undesired behavior?
    a. An employee is demoted for misfiling a report.
    b. A child is spanked for hitting her sister.
    c. A teenager is denied the opportunity to attend the Friday dance for staying out late on Monday.
    d. A child is spanked for running into the street.

13. Car sales, where a salesperson is paid for the number of cars sold, is an example of a:
    a. fixed-interval schedule of reinforcement.
    b. variable-interval schedule of reinforcement.
    c. variable-ratio schedule of reinforcement.
    d. fixed-ratio schedule of reinforcement.

14. With a fixed-interval schedule, especially in the period just after reinforcement, response rates are:
    a. speeded up.   c. relatively unchanged.
    b. extinguished.   d. relatively low.

15. Rewarding each step toward a desired behavior _____ the new response pattern.
    a. inhibits   c. disrupts
    b. shapes   d. eliminates

____ 16. extinction

____ 17. systematic desensitization

____ 18. spontaneous recovery

____ 19. stimulus generalization

____ 20. stimulus discrimination

a. The weakening and eventual disappearance of a conditioned response.

b. The reappearance of a previously extinguished response after a period of time, during which the conditioned stimulus has been absent.

c. Response to a stimulus that is similar to but different from a conditioned stimulus; the more similar the two stimuli, the more likely generalization is to occur.

d. The process by which an organism learns to differentiate among stimuli, restricting its response to one in particular.

e. A form of therapy in which fears are minimized through gradual exposure to the source of fear.

21. Learning that involves the imitation of a model is called _____.

22. The study of the thought processes that underlie learning is _____.

23. _____ is learning in which a voluntary response is strengthened or weakened depending on its favorable or unfavorable consequences.

24. _____ is the process by which a stimulus increases the probability that a preceding behavior will be repeated.

25. Three approaches to learning are described in the text. Classical and operant conditioning rely on external determinants of behavior, and cognitive learning depends in part on internal, mental activity. How can the differences between these three approaches be reconciled?

Practice Test 3: Conceptual, Applied, and Challenging Questions

1. Through conditioning, a dog learns to salivate at the sound of a bell because the bell signals that food is coming. In subsequent learning trials, a buzzer is sounded just before the bell. Soon the dog salivates at the sound of the buzzer. In this case, the bell acts as the:
   a. unconditioned stimulus.
   b. conditioned stimulus.
   c. unconditioned response.
   d. conditioned response.

2. Juanita uses a blender to prepare food for her daughter. Soon the baby knows that the sound of the blender signals that food is on the way. In this case, the food acts as:
   a. an unconditioned stimulus.
   b. a conditioned stimulus.
   c. an unconditioned response.
   d. a conditioned response.

3. In preparing to take his dog for a walk, Daniel puts on his running shoes. Soon the dog learns that the running shoes signal that she is going for a walk. In this case, the running shoes act as:
   a. an unconditioned stimulus.
   b. a conditioned stimulus.
   c. an unconditioned response.
   d. a conditioned response.

4. Rats are sometimes sickened by poisoned bait that resembles their favorite foods. Afterward, the rats avoid eating food that resembles the poisoned bait. The sickness caused by the poisoned bait is _____ in classical conditioning.
   a. an unconditioned response
   b. an unconditioned stimulus
   c. a conditioned response
   d. a conditioned stimulus

5. Kumar would like his dog to quickly learn the tricks required for the dog to compete in a dog competition this weekend. To reinforce the dog's learning while practicing the tricks, Kumar should use a(n) _____ when providing the dog with dog treats.
   a. variable-ratio schedule
   b. fixed-interval schedule
   c. extinction schedule
   d. shaping schedule

6. In order to stop smoking, "Big Joe" participates in aversive conditioning. Now he dislikes cigarettes and has also linked his dislike to the store where he used to buy them. This reaction illustrates:
   a. operant conditioning.
   b. stimulus discrimination.
   c. higher-order conditioning.
   d. systematic desensitization.

7. Katie is being taught colors and their names. When shown a red, pink, or yellow rose, the child correctly identifies the color of each flower. This is an example of:
   a. stimulus discrimination.
   b. stimulus generalization.
   c. spontaneous generalization.
   d. spontaneous recovery.

8. High schools have sometimes used dogs to search student lockers. Typically, the dogs are trained to sniff out a specific drug, such as cocaine, and to ignore all other drugs. The ability of the dogs to respond only to the specific drug they were trained to detect is an example of:
    a. stimulus discrimination.
    c. partial reinforcement.
    b. response generalization.
    d. spontaneous recovery.

9. Students generally study very hard before midterms and then slack off immediately afterward, which is characteristic of behavior reinforced on a:
    a. fixed-ratio schedule.
    c. fixed-interval schedule.
    b. variable-ratio schedule.
    d. variable-interval schedule.

10. A study in which children are given an opportunity to explore a complicated play area for a time and then are asked to locate a specific item in the room has been designed by professors at a local university. Researchers claim that children's speed and accuracy results from unseen mental processes that intervene in learning the area. Which of the following labels best describes the researchers?
    a. Personality psychologists
    c. Cognitive psychologists
    b. Sensory psychologists
    d. Biopsychologists

11. The existence of _____ supports the idea that learning may occur even though it is not yet evident in performance.
    a. partial reinforcement
    c. shaping
    b. classical conditioning
    d. latent learning

12. Kachtia's roommate is playing her stereo with the volume turned almost all the way up. In order to study, Kachtia puts on her own headphones and plays softer music to block out the loud music. Because the headphones result in the removal of the aggravating sound, the action would be called:
    a. punishment by application.
    c. negative reinforcement.
    b. positive reinforcement.
    d. punishment by removal.

13. Research studies that show a positive relationship between hours of viewed TV violence and viewers' personal aggressiveness show a methodological weakness in the sense that:
    a. only a few hundred persons serve as subjects in the study.
    b. the researchers interpret the results with bias favoring their own theoretical viewpoints.
    c. people lie habitually on surveys regarding their viewing habits.
    d. correlational data cannot prove that the TV viewing caused the violent behavior.

14. Steve tends to view information from the context of a broad perspective, usually taking an intuitive approach rather than a structured one in understanding information, and is also more task oriented. Based on this information, which of the following best describes Steve?
    a. He has a relational learning style.
    b. He tends to learn through classical conditioning.
    c. He will probably serve as a model in observational learning processes.
    d. He has a tendency toward implicit learning.

15. Which of the following options should Kent select **first** if he wants to improve his study skills?
    a. He should determine how effective his strategies have been so far.
    b. He should identify specific tests and class projects on which he can show improvement.
    c. He should implement the program of skill improvement.
    d. He should select a study skill to change.

_____ 16. fixed-ratio schedule

a. Reinforcement occurs after a varying number of responses rather than after a fixed number.

_____ 17. variable-ratio schedule

b. Reinforcement of a behavior every time it occurs.

_____ 18. fixed-interval schedule

_____ 19. variable-interval schedule

c. Reinforcement is given at various times, usually causing a behavior to be maintained more consistently.

_____ 20. continuous reinforcment schedule

_____ 21. discriminative stimulus

d. A stimulus to which an organism learns to respond as a part of stimulus control training.

e. Reinforcement is given at established time intervals.

f. Reinforcement is given only after a certain number of responses are made.

22. A(n) _____ is any stimulus that increases the probability that a preceding behavior will occur again.

23. A(n) _____ reinforcer is a stimulus added to the environment that brings about an increase in a preceding response.

24. _____ is a stimulus that decreases the probability that a previous behavior will occur again.

25. Using the theory of operant conditioning, illustrate the steps you might take in shaping a student's behavior to get him to stop leaving his seat, being disruptive, and acting out in class.

Module 17:	Module 18:	Evaluate
[a] Learning	[a] Operant conditioning	1. g
[b] classical conditioning	[b] law of effect	2. c
[c] neutral stimulus	[c] Reinforcement	3. e
[d] unconditioned stimulus (UCS)	[d] reinforcer	4. d
[e] unconditioned response (UCR)	[e] primary reinforcer	5. f
[f] conditioned stimulus (CS)	[f] secondary reinforcer	6. a
[g] conditioned response (CR)	[g] Positive reinforcers	7. b
[h] extinction	[h] Negative reinforcers	
[i] post-traumatic stress disorder	[i] Punishment	**Module 19:**
[j] spontaneous recovery	[j] positive punishment	[a] cognitive learning theory
[k] Stimulus generalization	[k] negative punishment	[b] Latent learning
[l] Stimulus discrimination	[l] schedules of reinforcement	[c] cognitive map
	[m] continuous reinforcement schedule	[d] observational learning
	[n] Partial reinforcement schedule	[e] model
	[o] fixed-ratio schedule	
Evaluate	[p] variable-ratio schedule	Evaluate
1. b	[q] Fixed-interval schedules	1. c
2. a	[r] Variable-interval schedules	2. d
3. e	[s] stimulus control training	3. e
4. c	[t] shaping	4. f
5. d	[u] Behavior modification	5. b
		6. a

Selected Rethink Answers

17-1   It is unlikely that Watson's subject went through life afraid of Santa Claus. After the experiment:
  • the conditioned response was no longer reinforced.
  • the subject probably had future experiences that involved white, furry objects that were not fearful.
  • the longer the CR was present without the CS, the less likely would be the conditioning; this is called extinction.

18-2   It would be relatively easy to set up reinforcements and punishments to increase the likelihood of children completing homework. Those reinforcements and punishments would need to be meaningful to the kids, and could include things like "teacher brings Mc Donald's lunch to the classroom for you" (reinforcement), or "must stay in during lunch" (punishment). Intermittent reinforcement would be difficult to institute because it might not seem fair from the kids' perspective. One could use continuous reinforcement, where kids get a "star" for every day of completed homework, and then can trade in their "stars" for a larger reinforcement (e.g., lunch) when they have earned enough of them. This would be similar to a token economy.

19-2   Quite a bit of research demonstrates a connection between viewing violence in the media or via video games, and aggressive behavior. Families should certainly limit, or curtail entirely, the amount of exposure kids get to this type of media or video games. In addition, kids may show "latent learning" of the aggressive behavior or violence; parents may not realize kids are learning this behavior until long after exposure, when for some reason, it is rewarding to the kids to show the behavior. So, parents need to be extra vigilant.

Practice Test 1:

1. d   mod. 17 p. 187
   a. Incorrect. Learning refers to relatively permanent changes.
   b. Incorrect. Nurture, which helps create learning, results in long-term changes.
   c. Incorrect. Learning is closely tied with nurture, or experience.
   *d. Correct. Nurture, or experience, creates learning.

2. c   mod. 17 p. 187
   a. Incorrect. Learning requires measurement of the response.
   b. Incorrect. Extinction refers to the idea of "unlearning" something.
   *c. Correct. Some changes in behavior occur simply because of maturational changes.
   d. Incorrect. Habituation is a primitive form of learning.

3. a   mod. 17 p. 188
   *a. Correct. Meat caused salivation to occur without any training and thus is "unconditioned."
   b. Incorrect. The conditioned stimulus originally did not cause any salivation.
   c. Incorrect. The response was salivation.
   d. Incorrect. The response was salivation.

4. d   mod. 17 p. 191
   a. Incorrect. Learning has already occurred in this scenario.
   b. Incorrect. Perception is a mental event related to understanding sensory stimuli.
   c. Incorrect. Habituation refers to a decrease in response to a stimulus.
   *d. Correct. When the CS is repeatedly presented without the UCS being paired with it, then the CS-CR connection becomes extinguished.

5. d   mod. 17 p. 191
   a. Incorrect. Operant conditioning does involve extinction.
   b. Incorrect. A token economy is a method that applies operant conditioning to discipline.
   c. Incorrect. Punishment is used in operant conditioning, and therefore would not involve extinction.
   *d. Correct. Spontaneous recovery may occur after extinction.

6. b   mod. 17 p. 191
   a. Incorrect. This method is unlikely to extinguish the initial response.
   *b. Correct. This is the standard method of extinction.
   c. Incorrect. This refers to the process of acquiring a UCS-CS connection initially.
   d. Incorrect. This will actually strengthen the CS.

7. b   mod. 17 p. 192
   a. Incorrect. The principles of classical conditioning are meant to apply uniformly to all organisms with the capacity to learn.
   *b. Correct. Garcia found that animals could be conditioned in open trial and that the time between the UCS and the CS could be quite long.
   c. Incorrect. This is not the point of Garcia's research.
   d. Incorrect. The effects can be achieved by spinning the rats, so this claim is not true.

8. c   mod. 17 p. 195
   a. Incorrect. The law of frequency suggests that conditioning requires frequent pairings.
   b. Incorrect. This is the gestalt principle of perception, not a rule for classical or operant conditioning.
   *c. Correct. The law of effect says that if a behavior has pleasing consequences, it is more likely to be repeated.
   d. Incorrect. The principle of contiguity in classical conditioning suggests that the CS and the UCS should be close together in time and space.

9. a   mod. 18 p. 197
   *a. Correct. Primary reinforcers are items like food and water; secondary are like praise and money.
   b. Incorrect. Organisms may differ in their preferences, but not in any uniform manner.
   c. Incorrect. For organisms that respond to operant conditioning, secondary reinforcers have an effect.
   d. Incorrect. This statement is reversed.

10. b   mod. 18 p. 197
    a. Incorrect. Punishers decrease the likelihood of a response being repeated.
    *b. Correct. This defines reinforcers.
    c. Incorrect. A response is the behavior, not the consequence.
    d. Incorrect. An operant is a kind of response.

11. c   mod. 18 p. 198
a.   Incorrect. It is a form of reinforcement, and it results in the increase of the desired behavior.
b.   Incorrect. Rewards are not withheld in negative reinforcement; in fact, the removal of the aversive stimulus is considered to be a reward.
*c.   Correct. The removal of the aversive stimulus is a pleasing consequence and will lead to the repetition of the behavior.
d.   Incorrect. Only instrumental conditioning utilizes reinforcement.

12. d   mod. 18 p. 201
a.   Incorrect. The rate depends on the schedule of reinforcement that has been chosen.
b.   Incorrect. The rate depends on the schedule of reinforcement that has been chosen.
c.   Incorrect. The response is actually difficult to extinguish.
*d.   Correct. The variability and the partial nature of the reinforcement results in behaviors that are highly resistant to extinction.

13. a   mod. 18 p. 201
*a.   Correct. The ratio of successful sales to attempts made varies from sale to sale.
b.   Incorrect. This would mean that the frequency of making a sale would be fixed at every fourth or every fifth attempt (or some number).
c.   Incorrect. A variable interval would mean that another sale would not take place until a set amount of time had passed.
d.   Incorrect. A fixed interval would mean that a sale would take place on a time schedule, say every hour or every two hours.

14. d   mod. 18 p. 203
a.   Incorrect. By definition, learned taste aversions are learned.
b.   Incorrect. Universal biological constraints related to learning are not in opposition to classical conditioning.
c.   Incorrect. A neutral stimulus being presented first follows traditional rules of classical conditioning.
*d.   Correct. Traditional classical conditioning indicates that there should be minimal time lapse between the conditioned and unconditioned stimulus.

15. a   mod. 18 p. 210
*a.   Correct. Quicker learning in later trials with reinforcement present suggests that some form of map or learning had developed.

b.   Incorrect. No aversion would occur unless the maze were filled with traps.
c.   Incorrect. Rat interest cannot yet be judged regarding mazes.
d.   Incorrect. Because rats are very superstitious, the maze would have little effect on their beliefs.

16. a   mod. 2 p. 209
17. c   mod. 2 p. 209
18. b   mod. 2 p. 211
19. e   mod. 1 p. 188
20. d   mod. 1 p. 188

21. Shaping   mod. 18 p. 203
22. unconditioned   mod. 17 p. 188
23. conditioned   mod. 17 p. 188
24. unconditioned   mod. 17 p. 188

25.
▪ Cite examples of the use of physical punishment. Describe alternatives for each use.
▪ Identify the conditions under which physical punishment may be necessary. These could include the need for swift and attention-getting action to prevent physical harm. Some parents use corporal punishment when children hit one another, and some do so to establish control when alternatives have failed.

Practice Test 2:
1.   d   mod. 17 p. 187
a.   Incorrect. This definition fits maturation better.
b.   Incorrect. This definition applies to circumstantial changes.
c.   Incorrect. This definition applies to reflex.
*d.   Correct. This is the definition given in the text.

2.   c   mod. 17 p. 188
a.   Incorrect. No such term is used in learning theory.
b.   Incorrect. The unconditioned stimulus elicits the unconditioned stimulus without any conditioning.
*c.   Correct. The term applied to this stimulus is the conditioned stimulus.
d.   Incorrect. This stimulus helps an organism in instrumental conditioning discriminate between times when a reinforcement would be given and times when a reinforcement is not available.

3.   d   mod. 17 p. 190
a.   Incorrect. Because the rat did not create a fear response, it could not have been considered an unconditioned stimulus for this study.

b.	Incorrect. This has another meaning in some other area of science.

c.	Incorrect. The discriminative stimulus helps an organism in instrumental conditioning discriminate between times when a reinforcement would be given and when it is not available.

*d.	Correct. Because it would not create the fear response, it would be considered neutral.

4.	a	mod. 17 p. 191

* a.	Correct. Someone using a relational learning style would appreciate understanding the "big picture" or entirety of the phenomenon, before focusing on its specific components, such as particular formulae.

b.	Incorrect. Someone using an analytic learning style would probably be happy with the teacher's approach.

c.	Incorrect. There is no such thing as a social learning style.

d.	Incorrect. There is no such thing as a phobic learning style.

5.	b	mod. 17 p. 191

a.	Incorrect. This does not describe escape conditioning.

*b.	Correct. The conditioned stimulus loses its value as a predictor of the unconditioned stimulus.

c.	Incorrect. This does not describe stimulus generalization.

d.	Incorrect. Negative reinforcement actually is intended to increase a desired behavior.

6.	a	mod. 18 p. 210

*a.	Correct. The cognitive learning theorists demonstrated that learning can occur as the transformation of mental processes, like the construction of a cognitive map that guides behavior.

b.	Incorrect. The Brelands primarily utilized operant conditioning and are concerned with other issues.

c.	Incorrect. Thorndike's law of effect does not repudiate classical ideas so much as add to them.

d.	Incorrect. Operant conditioning does not repudiate the ideas of classical conditioning, and in fact, is subject to the same challenges.

7.	c	mod. 18 p. 202

a.	Incorrect. See answer c.

b.	Incorrect. See answer c.

*c.	Correct. The period of time (interval) is set (fixed).

d.	Incorrect. See answer c.

8.	d	mod. 18 p. 188

a.	Incorrect. The consequence of the behavior is escape.

b.	Incorrect. The consequence of the behavior is the avoided speeding ticket.

c.	Incorrect. The consequence of the behavior is the biscuit reward.

*d.	Correct. The chemistry professor is a conditioned stimulus to which high blood pressure is the response.

9.	c	mod. 18 p. 188, 195

a.	Incorrect. Pavlov developed classical conditioning.

b.	Incorrect. Skinner developed operant conditioning.

*c.	Correct. Wertheimer was a gestalt psychologist.

d.	Incorrect. Thorndike developed the law of effect, a cornerstone of operant conditioning.

10.	c	mod. 18 p. 197

a.	Incorrect. Food is not considered to be a discriminative stimulus unless an organism has been trained to view it as such.

b.	Incorrect. Food satisfies a need, but it may also be a motive (as is true with money).

*c.	Correct. Because food satisfies a basic need, it is considered primary; because money must be conditioned to have any reinforcing value, it is a secondary reinforcer.

d.	Incorrect. Food may be a drive reducer, but money is not a natural reinforcer.

11.	b	mod. 18 p. 197

a.	Incorrect. Money requires conditioning to become a reinforcer.

*b.	Correct. Water satisfies a basic need, thus it is a primary reinforcer.

c.	Incorrect. Good grades require conditioning to become reinforcers.

d.	Incorrect. To be a reinforcer, the hammer would require some, though not much, conditioning.

12.	d	mod. 18 p. 197

a.	Incorrect. The employee would probably become angry for being punished for such a minor offense.

b.	Incorrect. The physical spanking reinforces the idea that violence is a way to make others cooperate.

c.	Incorrect. Punishment for a teenager can often become an opportunity for reinforcement through attention from friends.

*d. Correct. When self-endangerment occurs, quick and angerless punishment can make the child become attentive to the danger.

13. d   mod. 18 p. 201
a. Incorrect. The time interval for making each piece can change, but the rate is one payment for every three pieces.
b. Incorrect. Variable interval would suggest that the worker would not know when payment would come.
c. Incorrect. In this pattern, the payment would come after five, then three, then four, etc. pieces were made—not every three.
*d. Correct. This is a fixed-ratio schedule.

14. d   mod. 18 p. 202
a. Incorrect. They may speed up just before the interval has ended.
b. Incorrect. They do not become extinguished.
c. Incorrect. They slow down just after the reinforcement.
*d. Correct. The predictability of the interval leads the organism to pause just after the reinforcement.

15. b   mod. 18 p. 203
a. Incorrect. Reinforcement does not inhibit the desired behavior.
*b. Correct. Shaping is the technique of rewarding each successive behavior that gets closer to the desired behavior.
c. Incorrect. Reinforcement would not disrupt the targeted behavior.
d. Incorrect. Reinforcement would not eliminate the target behavior.

16. a   mod. 17 p. 191
17. e   mod. 17 p. 204
18. b   mod. 17 p. 191
19. c   mod. 17 p. 191
20. d   mod. 17 p. 192

21. observational learning   mod. 19 p. 211
22. cognitive learning   mod. 19 p. 209
23. Operant conditioning   mod. 18 p. 195
24. Reinforcement   mod. 18 p. 197

25.
▪ Describe each of the three approaches in such a way that they are clearly distinguished.
▪ Identify points of contradiction with each. In classical conditioning, the stimuli must precede the responses; in operant conditioning, the reinforcing stimuli comes after the response; in

observational learning, the behavior does not need to be practiced. Mental processes are also involved in observational learning.
▪ Observational learning may actually be reconciled with the other two once mental processes and reinforcement of the model (rather than the learner) are allowed.

Practice Test 3:
1. a   mod. 17 p. 188
*a. Correct. The bell is being used just as the unconditioned stimulus was in the earlier training.
b. Incorrect. While the bell is a conditioned stimulus, for the purpose of the second training event, it is an unconditioned stimulus.
c. Incorrect. The bell is not a response.
d. Incorrect. The bell is not a response.

2. a   mod. 17 p. 188
*a. Correct. The food elicits a response that has not been conditioned.
b. Incorrect. The juicer is the unconditioned response.
c. Incorrect. Food is not a response.
d. Incorrect. Food is not a response.

3. b   mod. 17 p. 188
a. Incorrect. The food is the unconditioned stimulus.
*b. Correct. The child has become conditioned to the blender as the signal for food.
c. Incorrect. The blender is not a response.
d. Incorrect. The blender is not a response.

4. a   mod. 17 p. 188
*a. Correct. The sickness occurs without any training, and should thus be considered the "unconditioned" response.
b. Incorrect. Sickness is a response, not a stimulus in this scenario.
c. Incorrect. As a response to the poison, the sickness is unconditioned.
d. Incorrect. If the response of sickness were to the sight of the bait, then it would be "conditioned."

5. a   mod. 18 p. 195
* a. Correct. A variable ratio schedule is likely to produce responses most quickly.
b. Incorrect. A fixed interval schedule is likely to produce slow responses for a period of time, with faster responses immediately prior to the end of the interval.
c. Incorrect. There is no such thing as an extinction schedule.

d.	Incorrect. Though Kumar may want to use shaping to encourage learning, there is no such thing as a shaping schedule.

6.	c	mod. 17 p. 191
a.	Incorrect. This appears to be a classically conditioned dislike.
b.	Incorrect. In stimulus discrimination, he would probably have only learned to dislike his favorite brand of cigarette.
*c.	Correct. This is an example of higher-order conditioning, where the store had once been a signal for buying the cigarettes; it is now a signal for the dislike of the cigarette.
d.	Incorrect. Systematic desensitization would have been used to eliminate a fear or other phobia, not a desired habit.

7.	a	mod. 17 p. 192
*a.	Correct. Of these choices, this best fits; the child learns to discriminate among different qualities of roses.
b.	Incorrect. With generalization, the discrimination of colors would decline.
c.	Incorrect. There is no such concept as spontaneous generalization.
d.	Incorrect. Spontaneous recovery occurs after extinction has been followed by a period of rest.

8.	a	mod. 17 p. 192
*a.	Correct. This is very discrete training and requires that the dog not respond to similar odors.
b.	Incorrect. If response generalization existed, this would not be it.
c.	Incorrect. Partial reinforcement may have been used in the training, but the ability indicates stimulus generalization.
d.	Incorrect. Spontaneous recovery requires extinction to occur.

9.	c	mod. 18 p. 202
a.	Incorrect. See answer c.
b.	Incorrect. See answer c.
*c.	Correct. The learner quickly identifies the apparent "wait time" that follows a reinforcement in a fixed-interval training schedule and thus does not respond for a period because no reinforcement will be forthcoming.
d.	Incorrect. See answer c.

10.	c	mod. 19 p. 210
a.	Incorrect. A personality psychologist would be more interested in traits than learned maps.

b.	Incorrect. A sensory psychologist would measure the sensory responses of the children.
*c.	Correct. He was demonstrating how children form cognitive maps and then demonstrate their knowledge at a later point in time.
d.	Incorrect. A biopsychologist might be interested in the underlying processes that account for the learning.

11.	d	mod. 19 p. 209
a.	Incorrect. Partial reinforcement supports the idea that not all performance needs to be reinforced.
b.	Incorrect. Classical conditioning depends on performance for evidence of learning.
c.	Incorrect. Shaping involves the gradual modification of behavior toward a desired form.
*d.	Correct. While performance is a measure of learning, the possibility of unmeasured learning is not ruled out.

12.	c	mod. 18 p. 198
a.	Incorrect. Playing the music loud in the first place was a form of punishment.
b.	Incorrect. Positive reinforcement refers to pleasant consequences for a target behavior (studying is the target behavior, not finding peace and quiet).
*c.	Correct. "Negative" in this case is the removal of an unwanted stimulus in order to increase a desired behavior (studying).
d.	Incorrect. She is being rewarded by removal, not punished.

13.	d	mod. 19 p. 213
a.	Incorrect. Some scientists make stronger claims with only 20 or 30 subjects.
b.	Incorrect. This cannot be determined from this statement.
c.	Incorrect. The study does not indicate how the viewing data was gathered.
*d.	Correct. This is correct only if the researchers claim or imply a causal relationship.

14.	a	mod. 19 p. 214
*a.	Correct. This describes the qualities of the relational learning style.
b.	Incorrect. Classical conditioning may help him learn, but the style described is the relational learning style.
c.	Incorrect. However, he could serve as a model, but this stem does not answer the question.
d.	Incorrect. The relational style does include explicit learning.

15.	b	mod. 19 p. 214

a.   Incorrect. Identifying which area to work on first should precede this step.

*b. Correct. Identifying objective goals is the first step in making a realistic attempt to improve learning.

c.   Incorrect. This is a later step of the program.

d.   Incorrect. After identifying which classes to work on, he could then identify a specific study skill.

16. f   mod. 18 p. 201
17. a   mod. 18 p. 201
18. e   mod. 18 p. 202
19. c   mod. 18 p. 202
20. b   mod. 18 p. 200
21. d   mod. 18 p. 203

22. reinforcer   mod. 18 p. 198
23. positive   mod. 18 p. 198
24. Punishment   mod. 18 p. 198

25.
- Establish what behaviors need to be changed.
- Use the concept of Skinner's "shaping" to reward successive approximations of the desired behavior.
- Decide what reward will be used to reinforce the change.
- Explain the type of reinforcement schedule that would be most effective.

Chapter 7: Memory

Module 20: The Foundations of Memory
Module 21: Recalling Long-Term Memories
Module 22: Forgetting: When Memory Fails

Overview

This set of modules looks at the nature of memory and the ways in which information is stored and retrieved.

Module 20 demonstrates the several ways that information is encoded, stored, and then later retrieved. The three systems of memory are discussed. An examination of the different kinds of memory is presented.

Module 21 presents a discussion about the causes and difficulties in remembering. The tip-of-the-tongue phenomenon, flashbulb memories, eyewitness testimony, and the process of recalling information in terms of schemas are all explanations of how remembering is facilitated.

Module 22 examines several processes that account for memory failure, including decay, interference, and cue-dependent forgetting. Finally, a discussion of some of the major memory impairments such as Alzheimer's disease, amnesia, and Korsakoff's syndrome is presented and followed by some techniques for improving memory.

To further investigate the topics covered in this chapter, you can visit the related Web sites by visiting the following link: www.mhhe.com/feldmanup8.

Prologue: Who Am I? And Who Are You?
Looking Ahead

Module 20: The Foundations of Memory

Sensory Memory
Short-Term Memory
Long-Term Memory

- *What is memory?*
- *Are there different kinds of memory?*
- *What is the biological basis of memory?*

The Foundations of Memory

Three processes comprise memory. **[a]** _____ is the process of placing

information in a form that can be used by memory. **[b]** _____ is the process

of retaining information for later use. **[c]** _____ is the process of

recovering information from storage. By definition, then, **[d]** _____ is the
sum of these three processes. Forgetting is an important part of memory because it allows us to
make generalizations and abstractions from daily life.

  The memory system is typically divided into three storage components or stages. The initial

storage system is that of **[e]** _____, where momentary storage of sensory

information occurs. **[f]** _____ includes information that has been given

some form of meaning, and it lasts for 15 to 25 seconds. **[g]** _____ is the
relatively permanent storage of memory. Although there are no locations in the brain of these
memory stages, they are considered abstract memory systems with different characteristics.

  Sensory memories differ according to the kind of sensory information, and the sensory
memory is thought of as several types of sensory memories based on the source of the sensory

messages. Visual sensory memory is called **[h]** _____, and its source is the

visual sensory system; auditory sensory memory is called **[i]** _____, and its
source is the auditory sensory system. Sensory memory stores information for a very short time.
Iconic memory may last no more than a second, and echoic memory may last for three to four
seconds. The duration of iconic memory was established by George Sperling's classic
experiment in which subjects were unable to recall an entire array of letters but could, on a cue
after the array was shown for one-twentieth of a second, recall any part of the array. Unless the
information taken into the sensory memories is somehow transferred to another memory system,
the sensory memories are quickly lost.

Sensory memories are raw information without meaning. In order to be transferred to the long-term memory, these sensory memories must be given meaning and placed in short-term memory. One view of this process suggests that the short-term memory is composed of verbal representations that have a very short duration. George Miller has identified the capacity of short-term memory as seven plus or minus two [j] _____, or meaningful groups of stimuli that are stored as a unit in the short-term memory. They can be several letters or numbers or can be complicated patterns, like the patterns of pieces on a chessboard. However, to be placed in a chunk, the board must represent a real or possible game.

Memory can be held in short-term memory longer by [k] _____, the repetition of information already in the short-term memory. Rehearsal is also the beginning of transferring short-term memory into long-term memory. The kind of rehearsal influences the effectiveness of the transfer to long-term memory. [l] _____ occurs whenever the material is associated with other information through placement in a logical framework, connection with another memory, the formation of an image, or some other transformation. The strategies for organizing memories are called [m] _____. Mnemonics are formal techniques for organizing information so that recall is more likely.

[n] _____ comes from Baddeley's theory that short-term memory has one organizing structure, the *central executive*, and three separate storage and rehearsal systems: the *visual store,* the *verbal store,* and the *episodic buffer.*

Two kinds of long-term memory have been identified: [o] _____ and [p] _____. Procedural memory includes the memory for skills and habits, like walking, riding a bicycle, and other physical activity. Declarative memory includes [q] _____, memories of specific events related to individual experiences, and [r] _____, those that consist of abstract knowledge and facts about the world. Psychologists suggest that [s] _____ are a way to represent how knowledge is stored. These networks can be thought of as clusters of interconnected information. When we think about a particular thing, related ideas are activated because of the association.

Neuroscientists have been searching for the [t] _____, the physical memory trace that corresponds to a memory. They have determined that the hippocampus, media temporal lobes, and amygdala are important brain structures involved in creating and storing memories. The ways in which memories are reflected in the neurons points to [u] _____, or the change in the excitability of a neuron at the synapse. As these changes occur, the work of [v] _____, or fixing and stabilizing of memories to long-term memories, takes place. In addition, biochemical processes assist in creating and storing memories. However, many of the neuroscience aspects of memory have yet to be learned.

Evaluate

_____ 1. storage

a. Locating and using information stored in memory.

_____ 2. retrieval

b. Relatively permanent memory.

_____ 3. sensory memory

c. Information recorded as a meaningless stimulus.

_____ 4. short-term memory

d. Working memory that lasts about 15 to 25 seconds.

_____ 5. long-term memory

e. The location where information is saved.

Rethink

20-1   It is a truism that "you never forget how to ride a bicycle." Why might this be so? In what type of memory is information about bicycle riding stored?

20-2   *From a marketing specialist's perspective:* How might ways of enhancing memory be used by advertisers and others to promote their products? What ethical principles are involved? Can you think of a way to protect yourself from unethical advertising?

Spotlight on Terminology and Language—ESL Pointers

Page 218 On February 15, Prigg, 17, one of the top high school **wrestlers** in Texas, was in the middle of a match in a town called the Colony, when he tumbled out of the ring and hit his head on the floor."

Wrestling is a sport in which two people struggle to force the opponent to the floor without puching or kicking.

Page 218 "It was like he was in a **trance**," says his father, John."

A **trance** is a dream like state in which the person is not responsive to others.

Page 218 "Since then John has found himself **marooned** in a strange **netherworld**."

When you are **marooned** you are stuck or isolated.

A **netherworld** is a false world that only exists in the shadows.

Page 218 "Stories like John Priggs's illustrate not only the important role memory plays in our lives, but also its **fragility**."

Fragility means delicate or easily broken.

Page 218 "Memory allows us to retrieve a **vast** amount of information."

A **vast** amount is a very large or limitless amount.

Page 219 "As you **rack your brain** for the answer, several fundamental processes relating to memory come into play."

When you **rack your brain** you are thinking very hard and stretching the limit of your memory.

Page 219 "The initial process of recording information in a form usable to memory, a process called *encoding*, is the first stage in remembering something."

To **encode** is to transfer information from one system into another. During the **encoding** stage, information is changed into usable form. In the brain, sensory information becomes impulses that the central nervous system reads and codes. On a computer, **encoding** occurs when keyboard entries are transformed into electronic symbols, which are then stored on a computer disk.

Page 219 "Memory also depends on one last process—*retrieval*: Material in memory storage has to be located and brought into **awareness** to be useful."

Awareness is attentiveness.

Page 219 "You can think of these processes as being **analogous** to a computer's keyboard (encoding), hard drive disk (storage), and software that accesses the information for display on the screen (retrieval)."

An **analogy** is a comparison between two situations. During the storage stage of memory, information is held in memory. This is the mind's version of a computer hard drive. During the retrieval stage, stored memories are recovered from storage, just as a saved computer program is called up by name and used again.

Page 219 "Historically, the approach has been extremely influential in the development of our understanding of memory, and—although new theories have **augmented** it—it still provides a useful **framework** for understanding how information is recalled

When you **augment** something you supplement or add to it.

A **framework** is an outline or structure.

Page 220 "A momentary flash of lightning, the sound of a **twig** snapping, and the sting of a **pinprick** all represent stimulation of exceedingly brief duration, but they may nonetheless provide important information that can require a response."

A **twig** is a small tree branch.
A **pinprick** is small puncture or a piercing.

Page 220 "Such stimuli are initially—and **fleetingly**—stored in sensory memory, the first repository of the information the world presents to us."

Things that are **fleeting** are very brief

Page 220 "However, despite the brief duration of sensory memory, its precision is high: Sensory memory can store an almost exact **replica** of each stimulus to which it is exposed (Darwin, Turvey, & Crowder, 1972; Long & Beaton, 1982; Sams et al., 1993)."

A **replica** is a copy or a duplicate.   Sensory memory can store a nearly exact replica of each stimulus to which it is exposed.

Page 221 " It was possible, then, that the information had initially been accurately stored in sensory memory, but during the time it took to **verbalize** the first four or five letters the memory of the other letters faded."

Verbalize is to state in words.

Page 221 "In sum, sensory memory operates as a kind of **snapshot** that stores information—which may be of a visual, auditory, or other sensory nature—for a brief moment in time."

A **snapshot** is a brief image, or picture.

Page 221 "Because the information that is stored briefly in sensory memory consists of representations of **raw** sensory stimuli, it is not meaningful to us."

Something that is **raw** is unprocessed.

Page 221 "If we are to make sense of it and possibly **retain** it, the information must be transferred to the next stage of memory: short-term memory."

When we **retain** something we hold on to or keep it.

Page 222 "If you've ever looked up a telephone number in a phone directory, repeated the number to yourself, put away the directory, and then forgotten the number after you've **tapped** the first three numbers into your phone, you know that information does not remain in short-term memory very long."

To **tap** something is to press it. When we **tap** numbers on a phone we are pressing them.

Page 222 "The transfer of material from short- to long-term memory proceeds largely on the basis of **rehearsal**, the **repetition** of information that has entered short-term memory."

Repetition the action of repeating, or doing something over and over.

Page 223 "Instead, as soon as we stop **punching** in the phone numbers, the number is likely to be replaced by other information and will be completely forgotten.

To punch something is to press or hit it. When we **punch** a button on a phone we are pressing the button.

Page 223 "*Elaborative rehearsal* occurs when the information is considered and organized in some **fashion**."

A **fashion** is a style or method.

Page 223 "For example, a list of vegetables to be purchased at a store could be **woven together** in memory as items being used to prepare an elaborate salad, could be linked to the items bought on an earlier shopping trip, or could be thought of in terms of the image of a farm with rows of each item."

Things that are **woven together** have been intertwined or connected one another.

Page 223 "For instance, when a beginning musician learns that the spaces on the music staff spell the word *FACE*, or when we learn the rhyme "Thirty days **hath** September, April, June, and November...," we are using mnemonics (Mastropieri & Scruggs, 2000; Bellezza, 2000; Goldstein et al., 1996; Schoen, 1996; Carney & Levin, 2003)."

Hath means have.

Page 223 "Rather than seeing short-term memory as an independent **way station** into which memories arrive, either to fade or to be passed on to long-term memory, many contemporary memory theorists conceive of short-term memory as far more active."

A **way station** is a place that travelers coming from all different directions pass through while on their routes.

Page 223 "Working memory is thought to contain a *central executive* processor that is involved in **reasoning** and decision making."

Reasoning is another word for thought based on facts.

Page 223 "The **episodic buffer** contains information that represents **episodes** or events (Baddeley, 2001; see Figure 4)."

A **buffer** is a temporary storage area for information being processed by the memory system.

An **episode** is an event.

The **episodic buffer** is the area in memory that holds information about events.

Page 223 "Although working memory aids in the recall of information, it uses a significant amount of cognitive resources during its operation. In turn, this can make us less aware of our **surroundings**— something that has implications for the debate about the use of cellular telephones in automobiles.

Our **surroundings** are the environment around use, including the people, events, objects and physical setting.

Page 224 "If a phone conversation requires thinking, it will **burden** working memory, leaving people less aware of their surroundings, an obviously dangerous state of affairs for the driver (deFockert et al., 2001; Wickelgren, 2001; Verhaeghen, Cerella, & Basak, 2004).

A **burden** is a problem or something that causes troubles or inconveniences someone.

Page 224 "In fact, one study found that students with the highest working memory capacity and greatest math ability were the ones who were most **vulnerable** to pressure to perform well."

When someone is **vulnerable** they are in a weak position and open to attack.

Page 225 "After fifteen seconds had gone by, recall **hovered** at around 10 percent of the material initially presented."

To **hover** is to stay around the same level.

Page 225 "Thus, semantic memory is somewhat like a mental **almanac** of facts."

An **almanac** is a book that is published annually and contains data and information relating to a subject.

Page 225 "You may think **otherwise** as you read the following **exchange** between a researcher and a participant in a study who was asked, in a memory experiment, what he was doing "on Monday afternoon in the third week of September two years ago.""

Otherwise means in other ways.

In this context an **exchange** is a conversation or discussion.

Page 225 "I remember he started off with the atomic table—a big **fancy** chart."

Something that is **fancy** is detailed and complex.

Page 226 "For many people, an apple **comes to mind** in both cases, since it fits equally well in each category."

When something **"comes to mind"** it is being thought about.

Page 226 "In this view, knowledge is stored in **semantic networks,** mental representations of **clusters** of interconnected information (Collins & Quillian, 1969; Collins & Loftus, 1975)."

Semantic refers to words and word meanings. A **network** is a system of things that are interconnected. Thus **semantic networks** are systems of interconnections between words and their meanings.

A **cluster** is a group

Page 226 "Can we **pinpoint** a location in the brain where long-term memories **reside**?"

To **pinpoint** something is to locate its exact location.

To **reside** is to live in.

Page 226 "Do memories leave an actual physical **trace** that scientists can view?

A **trace** is a mark; it is an indication that something or someone was there.

Page 228 "These changes reflect a process called *consolidation*, in which memories become **fixed** and stable in long-term memory."

Fixed means permanent or unchanging.

Page 228 "However, if they repeated the task with the same nouns several times, the activity in the brain **shifted** to another area."

To **shift** is to move.

Page 228 "Although memory researchers have made considerable **strides** in understanding the neuroscience behind memory, more remains to be learned—and remembered."

Strides are advances toward improving something.

Page 229 "Will our future **trips down memory lane** begin in the aisles of a drugstore?"

A "**trip down memory lane**" refers to the process of remembering your past.

Page 229 "This research is leading to the possibility that drugs may be designed to **enhance** our memory capabilities or even, perhaps, to suppress unwanted ones, such as memories of traumatic events."

To **enhance** something is to improve it.

Page 229 "Such "cosmetic neurology"—the use of drugs to improve our mental functioning (equivalent to the use of Botox to improve physical appearance)—may bring us closer to the day when healthy, normal individuals **pop a pill** to sharpen their memories prior to taking the SATs or heading out to a job interview (Begley, 2004; Chaterjee, 2004; Fields, 2005)."

To "**pop a pill**" refers to the act of is taking medication.

Page 229 "Compared with a control group of pilots who took a placebo pill, the pilots taking donepezil learned and remembered emergency **maneuvers** significantly better."

Maneuvers are movements that require skill and expertise.

Page 229 "These drugs, known as calcium channel modulators, counteract the reduction of neuronal activity that is associated with disorders such as Alzheimer's disease and other types of cognitive **impairment** associated with aging (Carmichael, 2004; Choudhary et al., 2005)."

An **impairment** is an injury or harm.

Page 229 "CREB inhibitors, drugs that affect the production of CREB—a protein responsible for establishment of memories—may eventually be used to prevent recurring, **intrusive,** unpleasant memories following a traumatic event."

Something that is **intrusive** is interfering and disturbing.

Page 229 "A person might even take such a drug *before* being exposed to a **grim** situation."

A **grim** situation is one that is one that is extremely unpleasant and distressing.

Page 229 "For instance, rescue workers (such as those who pulled victims from floodwaters surrounding New Orleans after Hurricane Katrina) might be given a drug before reaching the scene in order to reduce future **emotion-laden**, **grisly** memories (Chaterjee, 2004; Washburton et al., 2005)."

Something that is **emotion-laden** produces a large amount of feelings, or emotion.

Grisly refers to something that is horribly unpleasant and may create a sense of horror or fear.

Page 229 "Would the **eradication** of unpleasant memories also rob people of their identity?"

Eradication means to get rid of something completely so that there is no record that it ever existed.

Module 21: Recalling Long-Term Memories

Retrieval Cues
Levels of Processing
Explicit and Implicit Memory
Flashbulb Memories
Constructive Processes in Memory: Rebuilding the Past

Exploring Diversity: Are There Cross-Cultural Differences in Memory?

- *What causes difficulties and failures in remembering?*

Recalling Long-Term Memories

Retrieving information from long-term memory may be influenced by many factors. The

[a] _____ , where one is certain of knowing something but cannot recall it, represents one difficulty. The simple number of items of information that has been stored may

influence recall. We sort through this quantity with the help of **[b]** _____ . These are stimuli that allow recall from long-term memory. *Recall* consists of a series of processes—a search through memory, retrieval of potentially relevant information, then a decision whether the information is accurate, and a continuation of these steps until the right information is found. In contrast, *recognition* involves determining whether a stimulus that has been presented is correct, such as the selection of the stimulus from a list or determining whether the stimulus has been seen before.

A theory related to how well memories are recalled is the **[c]** _____ . This theory suggests that the difference in memories depends on the depth to which particular information is processed, that is, the degree to which information is analyzed and considered. The more attention information is given, the deeper it is stored and the less likely it is to be forgotten. Superficial aspects of information are given shallow processing, and when meaning is given, the processing is at its deepest level. This approach suggests that memory requires more active mental processing than was originally thought by memory researchers.

[d] _____ refers to exposing a person to a word or concept, thereby

making later recall of related items easier. **[e]** _____ refers to intentional or

conscious effort to recall memory, and **[f]** _____ refers to memories of which people are not consciously aware but nevertheless affect later performance and behavior. By priming people, psychologists are better able to study implicit memory.

217

In particularly intense events, we may develop **[g]** _____. A specific, important, or surprising event creates memories so vivid that they appear as if a snapshot of the event. Memories that are exceptional may be more easily retrieved than commonplace information. Research regarding flashbulb memories suggests that people recall quite a bit of detail about the event. However, some of that detail is likely to be inaccurate. For instance, when asked about their memories of the World Trade Center, 73 percent of respondents incorrectly recalled having seen initial television images of both planes on September 11. In fact, no video of the first plane was available on television until September 12.

Our memories reflect **[h]** _____, in which memories are influenced by the meaning we have attached to them. Guesses and inferences thus influence memory. Sir Frederic Bartlett first suggested that people remember in terms of **[i]** _____, which are general themes without specific details. Schemas were based on an understanding of the event, expectations, and the motivation of others.

The imperfection of memory has led to research into the accuracy of eyewitness testimony. The mistaken identification of individuals can lead to imprisonment. When a weapon is involved, the weapon draws attention away from other details. The wording of questions can also influence testimony in court. Children are especially prone to unreliable recollections.

The case of George Franklin illustrates the impact recovered memories can have (he was found guilty on the basis of these memories alone). Although childhood recollections can be forgotten and then recovered, the evidence does suggest that much distortion can take place as well, even to the point of fabricating false memories from childhood.

[j] _____ are our collections of information about our lives. People tend to forget information about the past that is incongruent with the way they currently see themselves. Depressed people tend to recall sad events more readily than happy ones from their past. More recent information also appears to be more affected than earlier recollections.

Evaluate

____ 1.	recall	a. Drawing from memory a specific piece of information for a specific purpose.
____ 2.	recognition	
		b. Having a memory for some material, but lack of recall as to where the information was encountered.
____ 3.	flashbulb memories	
____ 4.	priming	c. Memories of a specific event that are so clear they seem like "snapshots" of the event.
____ 5.	source amnesia	
		d. Acknowledging prior exposure to a given stimulus, rather than recalling the information from memory.
		e. Exposing someone to a word or concept, which later makes it easier to recall related information.

Rethink

21-1   Research shows that an eyewitness's memory for details of crimes can contain significant errors. How might a lawyer use this information when evaluating an eyewitness's testimony? Should eyewitness accounts be permissible in a court of law?

21-2   *From a social worker's perspective:* Should a child victim of sexual abuse be allowed to testify in court, based on what you've learned about children's memories under stress?

Spotlight on Terminology and Language—ESL Pointers

Page 428 "I can **kiss this job good-bye**."

When we "**kiss this job good-bye**" we quit or leave the job.

Page 428 "This common occurrence – known as the **tip-of-the-tongue** phenomenon – exemplifies the difficulties that can occur in retrieving information stored in long-term memory (Schwartz, Travis, Castro & Smith, 2000; Schwartz, 2001, 2002)."

Something that is on the **tip-of-the-tongue** is ready to be retrieved from your memory but cannot be brought forth at this time.

Page 429 "Many psychologists have suggested that the material that makes its way to long-term memory is relatively **permanent** (Tulving & Psotka, 1971)."

Permanent is something that is going to be remaining, something that continues and endures (as in the same state, status, or place) without fundamental or marked change. You think of something **permanent** as fixed. Can you describe some of your **permanent** memories?

Page 428 "For instance, if you are like the average college student, your vocabulary includes some 50,000 words, you know hundreds of mathematical "facts," and you are able to **conjure up** images – such as the way your childhood home looked – with no trouble at all."

To **conjure up** is to call up or invoke an image. You can **conjure up** many images.

Page 428 "For example, the smell of roasting turkey may **evoke** memories of Thanksgiving or family gatherings (Schab & Crowder, 1995)."

When you **evoke** a memory, you call it up. You are summoning or eliciting this material.

Page 430 "It suggests that the amount of information processing that occurs when material is initially encountered is **central** in determining how much of the information is ultimately remembered.

Things that **central** to something are the most important aspect or feature of it.

Page 431 "However, information to which we pay greater attention is processed more **thoroughly**."

To do something **thoroughly** is to do it completely.

Page 431 "At **shallow** levels, information is processed merely in terms of its physical and sensory aspects."

Shallow is having little depth; penetrating very lightly.

Page 431 "Those letters are considered in the **context** of words, and specific **phonetic** sounds may be attached to the letters."

When you consider items in **context**, you are examining the whole picture. You are looking at the interrelated conditions in which something exists or occurs.

Phonetic sounds represent the sounds and other phenomena, such as stress and pitch, of speech.

Page 431 "Although the concept of depth of processing has proved difficult to test experimentally and the levels-of-processing theory has its critics (e.g., Baddeley, 1990), it is clear that there are considerable practical **implications** to the notion that the degree to which information is initially processed affects recall."

To be able to make an **implication** means you are able to make an inference from this theory.

Page 432 "**Rote** memorization of a list of key terms for a test is unlikely to produce long-term recollection of information, because processing occurs at a shallow level."

Rote memorization is automatic repetition of what ever it is that is trying to be placed in memory.

Page 432 "Surgeons may be chatting with nurses about a new restaurant as soon as they **sew you up**."

When doctors' close up a patients wound it is said that they are "**sewing you up**."

Page 432 "However, it is very possible that although you had no conscious memories of the discussions on the **merits** of the restaurant, on some level, you probably did recall at least some information."

Merits are the value or benefits provided by something.

Page 433 "As we first discussed in the module on conducting psychological research, even though people may say and even believe they **harbor** no prejudice, assessment of their implicit memories may reveal that they have negative associations about members of minority groups."

When you **harbor** something you keep it in mind or believe it.

Page 434 "You **promptly** forget the name of the moon, at least consciously."

To do something **promptly** is to do it immediately, or right a way.

Page 435 "You will most likely **draw a blank** until this piece of information is added: February 1, 2003, was the date the Space Shuttle *Columbia* broke up in space and fell to Earth."

When people "**draw a blank**" they are unable to remember something.

Page 436 "Flashbulb memories illustrate a more general phenomenon about memory: Memories that are exceptional are more easily retrieved (although not necessarily accurately) than are those relating to events that are **commonplace**."

Things that are **commonplace** are usual or ordinary.

Page 437 "He suggested that people tend to remember information in terms of **schemas**, organized bodies of information stored in memory that **bias** the way new information is interpreted, stored, and recalled (Bartlett, 1932)."

To bias something is to be unfair or prejudice in your decisions.

Page 437 "One of the earliest demonstrations of schemas came from a classic study that involved a procedure similar to the children's **game of "telephone**," in which information from memory is passed sequentially from one person to another."

The **game of telephone** is a game in which a message is passed from one person to another in a whisper. The object is to see if the message started by the first person is the same message that the last person hears—usually the message changes as it gets passed from one person to the next.

Page 438 "The transformation of the Caucasian's razor into an African American's knife clearly indicates that the participants held a schema that included the **unwarranted** prejudice that African Americans are more violent than Caucasians and thus more apt to be holding a knife."

Things that are **unwarranted** are not justified or deserved.

Page 438 "Jackson was the victim of mistaken identity when two witnesses picked him out of a **lineup** as the **perpetrator** of a crime."
A **line-up** is a procedure used by police officers in which a number of people, including suspected criminals stand in a line so that a witness can identify the person responsible for the crime.

A **perpetrator** is a wrong doer or someone that commits a crime.

Page 439 "When a criminal perpetrator displays a gun or knife, it acts like a perceptual **magnet**, attracting the eyes of the witnesses."

A **magnet** is something, usually a piece of metal, which attracts things to it.

Page 439 "Even when weapons are not involved, eyewitnesses are **prone** to errors relating to memory."

When we are **prone** to something we are likely to be affected by it.

Page 439 "For instance, viewers of a twelve-second film of a **mugging** that was shown on a New York City television news program were later given the opportunity to pick out the assailant from a six-person lineup (Buckhout, 1974)."

A **mugging** is crime in which an attacker robs, or takes something away from a victim.

Page 439 "Some were then asked the question, "About how fast were the cars going when they *smashed* into each other?""

To **smash** something is to hit it very hard, so that it shatters or breaks into pieces.

Page 440 "Children's memories are especially **susceptible** to influence when the situation is highly emotional or stressful."

When someone is **susceptible** they are vulnerable or at risk.

Page 440 "For example, in trials in which there is significant pretrial publicity or in which **alleged** victims are questioned repeatedly, often by untrained interviewers, the memories of the alleged victims may be influenced by the types of questions they are asked (Scullin, Kanaya, & Ceci, 2002; Lamb & Garretson, 2003).

Alleged means suspected or claimed to done something, but there is not yet proof.

Page 440 "In short, the memories of witnesses are far from **infallible**, and this is especially true when children are involved (Howe, 1999; Goodman et al., 2002Schaaf et al., 2002)."

Infallible means fail-safe. Memories of witnesses are far from perfect.

Page 440 "But this case was different from most other murder cases: It was based on memories that had been **repressed** for twenty years."

When we **repress** something we block it from our awareness.

Page 441 "Franklin's daughter claimed that she had forgotten everything she had once known about her father's crime until two years earlier, when she began to have **flashbacks** of the event."

A **flashback** is a very vivid and detailed memory of a painful event that happened in the person's past.

Page 441 "On the basis of her memories, her father was convicted—and later cleared of the crime after an **appeal** of the conviction."

A **appeal** is formal request for the court system to rethink another court's decision.

Page 441 "Supporters of the notion of repressed memory (based on Freud's psychoanalytic theory) suggest that such memories may remain hidden, possibly throughout a person's lifetime, unless they are triggered by some current circumstance, such as the **probing** that occurs during psychological therapy."

When we **probe** something we do a complete investigation into it.

Page 441 "However, memory researcher Elizabeth Loftus (1998, 2003) maintains that so-called repressed memories may well be inaccurate or even **wholly** false—representing *false memory*."

Wholly means completely.

Page 442 "It's certainly not all that difficult to create false memories. In laboratory experiments, for example, participants asked to study a list of related words (tired, nap, **snooze,** and awake, for example) readily come to believe that a related word like "sleep" was in the initial list, even if it wasn't."

To **snooze** is to take a short nap.

Page 443 "For example, we tend to forget information about our past that is **incompatible** with the way in which we currently see ourselves."

Something that is **incompatible** is mismatched or conflicting.

Page 443 "One study found that adults who were well adjusted but who had been treated for emotional problems during the early years of their lives tended to forget important but troubling childhood events, such as being in **foster care**."

Foster care is a system in the United States in which children whose parents are unable to care for them are placed in the care of other families.

Page 443 "For example, although 61 percent of the questionnaire respondents said that playing sports and other physical activities was their favorite **pastime,** only 23 percent of the adults recalled it accurately (Offer et al., 2000)."

A **pastime** is a hobby or pleasurable activity.

Page 444 "Travelers who have visited areas of the world in which there is no written language often have returned with tales of people with **phenomenal** memories."

Something that is **phenomenal** is very unique or extra special.

Page 445 "Basic memory processes such as short-term memory capacity and the structure of long-term memory—the "**hardware**" of memory—are universal and operate similarly in people in all cultures."

Hardware refers to the tools and equipment that make up a computer.

Module 22: Forgetting: When Memory Fails

Proactive and Retroactive Interference: The Before and After of Forgetting
Memory Dysfunctions: Afflictions of Forgetting

Becoming an Informed Consumer of Psychology:
Improving Your Memory

- ### *Why do we forget information?*
- ### *What are the major memory impairments?*

Forgetting: When Memory Fails

Herman Ebbinghaus studied forgetting by learning a list of nonsense syllables and then timing how long it took him, at a later trial, to relearn the list. The most rapid forgetting occurs in the first nine hours. Three views concerning the forgetting of information have been developed. One theory explains forgetting by **[a]** _____ , or loss of information through nonuse.

The other theory proposes that **[b]** _____ between bits of information leads to forgetting. In interference, information blocks or displaces other information, preventing recall. Most forgetting appears to be the result of interference.

There are two kinds of interference. One is called **[c]** _____ *interference* that occurs when previously learned information blocks the recall of newer information.

[d] _____ *interference* is when new information blocks the recall of old information. Most research suggests that information that has been blocked by interference can eventually be recalled if appropriate stimuli are used.

The third reason why forgetting occurs is because of **[e]** _____ . When forgetting occurs for this reason, there are insufficient retrieval cues to help the person recall the information that is stored in memory.

It was originally thought that memories were evenly distributed throughout the brain. However, the current view suggests that the areas of the brain that are responsible for processing information about the world also store that information.

[f] _____ *disease* includes severe memory problems as one of its many symptoms. Initially, the symptoms appear as simple forgetfulness, progressing to more profound loss of memory, even failure to recognize one's own name and the loss of language abilities. The protein beta amyloid, which is important for maintaining neural connections, has been implicated in the progress of the disease. **[g]** _____ is another memory problem. Amnesia is a loss of memory occurring without apparent loss of mental function.

[h] _____ is memory loss for memories that preceded a traumatic event.

[i] _____ is a loss of memories that follow a traumatic event or injury. Long-term alcoholics who develop _Korsakoff's syndrome_ also have amnesia. Suffers of this syndrome may hallucinate or repeat the same story over and over. A perfect memory, one with total recall, might actually be very discomforting. A case studied by Luria of a man with total recall reveals that the inability to forget becomes debilitating.

The Informed Consumer of Psychology section outlines several mnemonic techniques and how they can be applied to taking tests. They include the _keyword technique_, in which one pairs a word with a mental image, or in the case of learning a foreign language, the foreign word with a similar-sounding English word. The _method of loci_ requires that one imagine items to be remembered as being placed in particular locations. Another phenomenon that affects memory is called **[j]** _____. Recall is best when it is attempted in conditions that are similar to the conditions under which the information was originally learned. The organization of text and lecture material may enhance memory of it. Practice and rehearsal also improve long-term recall. Rehearsal to the point of mastery is called _overlearning_. It should be noted that cramming for exams is ineffective; the better approach is to distribute practice over many sessions.

Evaluate

_____ 1. Alzheimer's disease

_____ 2. amnesia

_____ 3. retrograde amnesia

_____ 4. anterograde amnesia

_____ 5. Korsakoff's syndrome

a. An illness associated with aging that includes severe memory loss and loss of language abilities.

b. A memory impairment disease among alcoholics.

c. Memory loss unaccompanied by other mental difficulties.

d. Memory loss of the events following an injury.

e. Memory loss of occurrences before some event.

Rethink

22-1   What are the implications of proactive and retroactive inhibition for learning multiple foreign languages? Would previous language training help or hinder learning a new language?

22-2   _From a health care provider's perspective:_ Alzheimer's disease and amnesia are two of the most pervasive memory dysfunctions that threaten many individuals. What sorts of activities might health care providers offer their patients to help them combat memory loss?

Page 241 "Known in the scientific literature by the **pseudonym** H.M., he could remember, quite literally, nothing—nothing, that is, that had happened since the loss of his brain's temporal lobes and hippocampus during experimental surgery to reduce epileptic seizures."

A **pseudonym** is a name that is not the person's correct name, but is used by them as an alias, or fake name.

Page 241 "Using himself as the only participant in his study Ebbinghaus memorized lists of three-letter nonsense syllables – **meaningless** sets of two **consonants** with a vowel in between, such as FIW and BOZ."

Meaningless means unimportant and insignificant. These three letter syllables had no meaning.

A **consonant** is any letter of the alphabet except a vowel.

Page 241 "Despite his **primitive** methods, Ebbinghaus's study had an important influence on subsequent research, and his basic conclusions have been **upheld** (Wixted & Ebbesen, 1991)."

Primitive means very simple. The research design for this work was **primitive**. It did not involve relying on modern technology.

When a research conclusion is **upheld** it is maintained. Further replications of this research find the same result.

Page 244 "In decay, the old books are constantly crumbling and **rotting away**, leaving room for new arrivals."

When something **rots away** it is decomposing, or being broken down by the action of bacteria or fungus.

Page 244 "Finally, forgetting may occur because of cue-dependent forgetting, forgetting that occurs when there are insufficient retrieval cues to **rekindle** information that is in memory (Tulving & Thompson, 1983)."
To kindle interest means to arouse interest, to stir up interest. To **rekindle** this interest means to arouse it again.

Page 244 "If, for example, you have difficulty on a French achievement test because of your more recent exposure to Spanish, retroactive interference is the **culprit**."

A **culprit** is a cause of a problem.

Page 245 "Some researchers argue that a breakdown in working memory's central executive may result in the memory losses that are characteristic of Alzheimer's disease, the progressively **degenerative** disorder that produces loss of memory and confusion (Cherry, Buckwalter, & Henderson, 2002)."

A **degenerative** disorder is one that shows a gradual decline in the person's ability to function.

Page 245 "Usually, lost memories gradually reappear, although full **restoration** may take as long as several years."

Restoration means return.

Page 245 "A second type of amnesia is **exemplified** by people who remember nothing of their current activities."

Anterograde amnesia is **exemplified** or illustrated by people who have no recollection of their current activities.

Page 246 "Amnesia is also a consequence of **Korsakoff's syndrome**, a disease that **afflicts** long-term alcoholics."

Korsakoff's syndrome is a disorder that results from years of chronic alcoholism that produces severe memory loss.

A disease that **afflicts** someone troubles them or makes them miserable.

Page 246 "Such a skill at first may seem to be **enviable**, but it actually presented quite a problem."

Something that is **enviable** is desirable or lucky.

Page 246 "The man's memory became a **jumble** of lists of words, numbers, and names, and when he tried to relax, his mind was filled with images."

When things are **jumbled** they are in an untidy pile.

Page 246 "Partially as a consequence of the man's unusual memory, psychologist A. R. Luria, who studied his case, found him to be a "disorganized and rather **dull-witted person**" (Luria, 1968, p. 65)"

When a person is **dull-witted** they are slow in their thought processes and do not pay attention to details.

Page 247 "However, if you must take a test in a room different from the one in which you studied, don't **despair**: The features of the test itself, such as the wording of the test questions, are sometimes so powerful that they **overwhelm** the subtler cues relating to the original encoding of the material (Bjork & Richardson-Klarehn, 1989)."

Despair occurs when people lose hope and are despondent or depressed.

When something **overwhelm**s you it over powers you.

Page 247 "One proven technique for improving recall of written material is to **organize** the material in memory as you read it for the first time."

When you **organize** something you put things in order.

Test your knowledge of the material in these modules by answering these questions. These questions have been placed in three Practice Tests. The first two tests consist of questions that will test your recall of factual knowledge. The third test contains questions that are challenging and primarily test for conceptual knowledge and your ability to apply that knowledge. Check your answers and review the feedback using the Answer Key on the following pages of the *Study Guide*.

PRACTICE TEST 1:

1. The process of identifying and using information stored in memory is referred to as:
    a. storage.
    c. recording.
    b. retrieval.
    d. learning.

2. The process of recording information in a form that can be recalled is:
    a. encoding.
    c. decoding.
    b. storage.
    d. retrieval.

3. _____ stores information for approximately 15 to 25 seconds.
    a. Sensory memory
    c. Iconic memory
    b. Short-term memory
    d. Long-term memory

4. Researchers have discovered that short-term memory can hold approximately:
    a. five items.
    c. 10 items.
    b. seven items.
    d. 18 items.

5. Teresa's knack for storytelling keeps her friends highly entertained as she recalls the events of her childhood. This recall about what we have done and the kinds of experiences we have had best illustrates:
    a. periodic memory.
    c. semantic memory.
    b. episodic memory.
    d. serial production memory.

6. Saying things over and over, or repeating a task on numerous occasions is known as rehearsal, which:
    a. facilitates neither short-term memory nor long-term memory.
    b. has no effect on short-term memory duration, yet it facilitates the transfer of material into long-term memory.
    c. helps prolong information in short-term memory but has no effect on the transfer of material into long-term memory.
    d. extends the duration of information in short-term memory and assists its transfer into long-term memory.

7. You would be unable to _____ if your episodic long-term memory were disabled.
    a. remember details of your own personal life
    b. recall simple facts such as the name of the U.S. president
    c. speak, although you could still comprehend language through listening
    d. maintain information in short-term memory via rehearsal

8. Information from long-term memory is easier to access with the aid of:
   a. a retrieval cue.
   b. distractors.
   c. interpolated material.
   d. a sensory code.

9. Constructive processes are associated with all of the following **except**:
   a. episodic memory.
   b. motivation.
   c. procedural memory.
   d. organization.

10. The tip-of-the-tongue phenomenon exemplifies difficulties in:
    a. encoding.
    b. decoding.
    c. storage.
    d. retrieval.

11. Ebbinghaus, after memorizing a series of nonsense syllables, discovered that forgetting was most dramatic _____ following learning.
    a. two days
    b. an hour
    c. 10 days
    d. one day

12. Jonathan met a girl on the bus and repeatedly recited her phone number all the way home. This recitation:
    a. minimizes the effects of proactive interference.
    b. prevents trace decay from occurring.
    c. activates different brain areas than when the word sequence is spoken the first time.
    d. is a characteristic symptom of the disorder known as Korsakoff's syndrome; this symptom can, in most cases, be treated with drugs.

13. Which situation is characteristic of anterograde amnesia?
    a. A person has loss of memory for events before some critical event.
    b. A person receives a physical trauma to the head and has difficulty remembering things after the accident.
    c. A person forgets simple skills such as how to dial a telephone.
    d. A person begins to experience difficulties in remembering appointments and relevant dates such as birthdays.

14. Memories lost under retrograde amnesia sometimes are recovered later; this implies that the amnesia interfered with the process of:
    a. encoding.
    b. storage.
    c. retrieval.
    d. association.

15. The keyword technique is a memory aid that can be helpful in learning a foreign language. The first step is to identify:
    a. a word that has similar meaning in a familiar language and pair it with the foreign word to be learned.
    b. a word that has a similar sound in a familiar language to at least part of the foreign word and pair it with the foreign word to be learned.
    c. a word that suggests similar imagery in a familiar language and pair it with the foreign word to be learned.
    d. the first word to come to mind in a familiar language and pair it with the foreign word to be learned.

_____ 16.   echoic memory   a. Memory for skills and habits.

_____ 17.   episodic memories   b. Stored information relating to personal experiences.

_____ 18.   semantic memories   c. Stored, organized facts about the world (e.g., mathematical and historical data).

_____ 19.   declarative memory
                                      d. The storage of information obtained from the sense of hearing.
_____ 20.   procedural memory

                                      e. Memory for facts and knowledge.

21.   Recording information in a form usable to memory is _____.

22.   _____ memory is the storage of visual information.

23.   A stimulus such as a word, smell, or sound that aids recall of information located in long-term memory is a(n) _____.

24.   The _____ is when someone's ability to recall information in a list depends on where the item appears in the list.

25.   _____ help us recall information by thinking about related information.

26.   What role should psychologists play in helping the courts deal with repressed memories of abuse that have been recovered? Consider both the advantages and disadvantages of the answer you give.

PRACTICE TEST 2:

1.   Information deteriorates most quickly from:
     a. explicit memory.   c. sensory memory.
     b. short-term memory.   d. episodic declarative memory.

2.   Recording information in the memory system is referred to as:
     a. encoding.   c. decoding.
     b. storage.   d. retrieval.

3.   Information in short-term memory is stored according to its:
     a. meaning.   c. length.
     b. intensity.   d. sense.

4.   The process of grouping information into units for storage in short-term memory is called:
     a. similarity.   c. chunking.
     b. priming.   d. closure.

5.   Knowledge about grammar, spelling, historical dates, and other knowledge about the world best illustrates:
     a. periodic memory.   c. semantic memory.
     b. episodic memory.   d. serial production memory.

6. _____ may be necessary while information is in the short-term stage, in order to enhance consolidation of long-term memory.
   a. Massed practice
   b. Elaborative rehearsal
   c. Interpolation
   d. Interference

7. According to the levels-of-processing model, what determines how well specific information is remembered?
   a. The stage attained
   b. The meaning of the information
   c. The quality of the information
   d. The depth of information processing

8. Finding the correct answer on a multiple-choice test depends on:
   a. serial search.
   b. recall.
   c. mnemonics.
   d. recognition.

9. Your memory of how to skate is probably based on:
   a. procedural memory.
   b. semantic memory.
   c. elaborative rehearsal.
   d. declarative memory.

10. The detailed, vivid account of what you were doing when you learned of the *Challenger* disaster represents a:
    a. cognitive map.
    b. schema.
    c. flashbulb memory.
    d. seizure.

11. Which explanation has **not** been offered to account for how we forget information that was learned?
    a. Decay
    b. Interference
    c. Cue-dependency
    d. Inadequate processing during learning

12. All of the following have been associated with the biological basis of memory **except**:
    a. the hippocampus.
    b. sulci.
    c. neurotransmitters.
    d. long-term potentiation.

13. Which of the following syndromes is the **least** common?
    a. Retrograde amnesia
    b. Anterograde amnesia
    c. Alzheimer's disease
    d. Korsakoff's syndrome

14. The fundamental issue surrounding the controversy about repressed memories is whether the memories:
    a. are retrieved from long-term memory or from another type of memory.
    b. can be counteracted by therapy.
    c. have any noticeable effect on mental activities or behavior.
    d. are genuine recollections from the past.

15. Which alternative is **least** likely to help you do well on your next psychology quiz?
    a. Use a prioritized strategy by studying the material only the day before the quiz and avoiding any other subjects that might interfere.
    b. Overlearn the material.
    c. Take brief lecture notes that focus on major points and that emphasize organization.
    d. Ask yourself questions about the material as you study.

_____ 16. memory trace

a. The pairing of a foreign word with a common, similar-sounding English word to aid in remembering the new word.

_____ 17. proactive interference

_____ 18. retroactive interference

b. A physical change in the brain corresponding to the memory of material.

_____ 19. keyword technique

c. New information interferes with the recall of information learned earlier.

_____ 20. memory

d. The system used to store the results of learning.

e. Information stored in memory interferes with recall of material learned later.

21. The ability to retrieve and reproduce previously encountered material is called

_____.

22. _____ is the ability to identify previously encountered material.

23. _____ is the loss of ability to remember events or experiences that occurred before some particular point in time.

24. Breaking information into meaningful units of information is called _____.

25. Much of our knowledge about memory comes from strictly laboratory studies. Consider how the lack of "real-life" memory studies may bias the kinds of results obtained about how memory works in our daily lives. Do you have any suggestions for how psychologists might study memory in daily life?

PRACTICE TEST 3: Conceptual, Applied, and Challenging Questions

1. While Nick was watching a movie, his young son talked excitedly about the new bike his friend was getting. Somewhat frustrated, the boy exclaimed, "You're not paying attention to me!" At this point, Nick diverted his attention to his son and recited the last few things the boy had said. Which memory system is responsible for this ability?
   a. Episodic memory
   b. Echoic memory
   c. Iconic memory
   d. Short-term memory

2. Sensory memory is the information that is:
   a. held until it is replaced by new information.
   b. an accurate representation of the stimulus.
   c. an incomplete representation of the stimulus.
   d. lost if it is not meaningful.

3. A story is likely to be transformed when it has been told over and over and:
   a. ambiguous details become regularized to fit the person's expectations.
   b. distinctive features of the story are dropped out.
   c. engrams that were located will become lost.

    d.   the original story will become a "flashbulb," with excellent recall even after several serial reproductions.

4.   Older computer monitor screens sometimes have a brief persistence of the old image when the image is changed. This persistence of the monitor image is analogous to:
    a.   flashbulb memory.   c.   echoic memory.
    b.   iconic memory.   d.   declarative memory.

5.   Beth's basketball coach instructs her to practice a basic foul shot for about 30 minutes each day to improve her shot. After she does what the coach has suggested, she discovers that she can make a shot without any thought and with complete confidence. This is a demonstration of what kind of memory?
    a.   Working memory   c.   Autobiographical memory
    b.   Declarative memory   d.   Procedural memory

6.   After 20 years of not having been on a bicycle, the cycle-shop manager will allow Daniel's son to test a cycle only if Daniel rides one beside him. Within 10 seconds, Daniel has adjusted to the bicycle and is even more confident than his son, who has just learned to ride. This is a demonstration of which kind of memory?
    a.   Working memory   c.   Recovered, repressed memories
    b.   Procedural memory   d.   Autobiographical memory

7.   Who was responsible for the concept of schemas?
    a.   Sigmund Freud   c.   Frederic Bartlett
    b.   Jean Piaget   d.   Robert Feldman

8.   "The strength of a memory relates directly to the kind of attention given to it when the information was experienced." This statement most directly supports:
    a.   the three-stage model of memory.
    b.   the mental imagery model of memory.
    c.   the levels-of-processing model of memory.
    d.   the cultural diversity model of memory.

9.   You are asked to write your new address and phone number on the back of a check. Instead, you write your previous address and number. You are experiencing:
    a.   retroactive interference.   c.   amnesia.
    b.   fugue.   d.   proactive interference.

10.   Lyle learns the word-processing program "Easy Word" on his personal computer. Then he learns a second program, "Perfect Word," at work. He now finds it difficult to remember some of the commands when he uses his word processor at home. This is an example of:
    a.   work-induced interference.   c.   proactive interference.
    b.   retroactive interference.   d.   spontaneous interference.

11.   A server forgets a customer's order because 20 other orders have been completed during the intervening hour. The reduced recall of that customer's order reflects:
    a.   Alzheimer's disease.   c.   proactive interference.
    b.   decay.   d.   retroactive interference.

12. Alzheimer's disease is associated with deterioration of the:
    a. neurological connection between the spinal cord and muscles.
    b. connection between the hemispheres.
    c. manufacture of beta amyloid.
    d. basal ganglia and lower brain structures.

13. Which situation is most characteristic of retrograde amnesia?
    a. A person begins to experience difficulties in remembering appointments and relevant dates such as birthdays.
    b. A person receives a physical trauma to the head and has difficulty remembering things after the accident.
    c. A person forgets simple skills such as how to dial a telephone.
    d. A person has loss of memory for events before some critical event.

14. Samantha, the star of the soap opera *Days and Nights,* has found herself without any memory of her past life from a point in time only a few episodes ago. If her memory failure is real, which of the following types of memory loss best describes her condition?
    a. Retrograde amnesia   c. Infantile amnesia
    b. Anterograde amnesia   d. Korsakoff's syndrome

_____ 15. priming   a. A physical change in the brain corresponding to the memory of material.

_____ 16. keyword technique
                                   b. Memory of information is enhanced when recalled under the same conditions as when it was learned.
_____ 17. encoding specificity

_____ 18. recency effect   c. A technique of recalling information by having been exposed to related information at an earlier time.

_____ 19. engram
                                   d. When items presented later in a list are remembered best.

                                   e. The strategy of learning vocabulary by pairing one word with another similar sounding word.

20. _____ is the technique of recalling information by having been exposed to related information at an earlier time.

21. Scientists refer to changes in sensitivity at the neuron's synapse as _____.

22. One can create long-term memories by a process known as _____.

23. _____ are recollections of the facts about our own lives.

24. To increase the chance that information will be remembered, a person adds meaning to the information to be remembered, which is called _____.

25. List the factors that can reduce the accuracy of eyewitness testimony and describe how the misinformation effect works in memory dislocation.

■ ANSWER KEY: MODULES 20, 21, AND 22

Module 20:		Module 21:	Module 22:
[a] Encoding	[n] Working memory	[a] tip-of-the-tongue	[a] decay
[b] Storage	[o] declarative memory	phenomenon	[b] interference
[c] Retrieval	[p] procedural memory	[b] retrieval cues	[c] proactive
[d] memory	[q] episodic memories	[c] levels-of-processing	[d] Retroactive
[e] sensory memory	[r] semantic memories	theory	[e] cue-dependent forgetting
[f] Short-term memory	[s] semantic networks	[d] Priming	[f] Alzheimer's
[g] Long-term memory	[t] engram	[e] explicit memory	[g] Amnesia
[h] iconic memory	[u] long term	[f] implicit memory	[h] Retrograde amnesia
[i] echoic memory	potentiation	[g] flashbulb memories	[i] Anterograde amnesia
[j] chunks	[v] consolidation	[h] constructive	[j] encoding specificity
[k] rehearsal		processes	
[l] Elaborative rehearsal	Evaluate	[i] schemas	Evaluate
[m] mnemonics	1. e	[j] Autobiographical	1. a
	2. a	memories	2. c
	3. c		3. e
	4. d	Evaluate	4. d
	5. b	1. a	5. b
		2. d	
		3. c	
		4. e	
		5. b	

Selected Rethink Answers

20-1 Memories for motor skills are extremely long-lasting; they may be encoded and stored as kinesthetic (muscular) instructions.

22-2 These types of interference become especially difficult when learning a second foreign language. If someone's native language is English, and she learns French in high school and then Spanish in college, she might have trouble translating English words into Spanish; if proactive interference was occurring, she would likely come up with the correct French word, but not the Spanish word. On the other hand, if she eventually became quite proficient in Spanish but then traveled to France and had to speak French again, this could be difficult. Retroactive interference would be occurring if she couldn't come up with the correct French words, but instead spoke the correct Spanish words.

Practice Test 1:

1. b mod. 20 p. 223
a. Incorrect. Storage refers to the retention of the encoded memory.
*b. Correct. Retrieval is the recovery of stored, encoded information so that it can be used.
c. Incorrect. Recording is the work of committing information to a record, like taking notes, etc.
d. Incorrect. See Chapter 6.

2. a mod. 20 p. 223
*a. Correct. Encoding places the information in a manageable form.
b. Incorrect. Storage refers to the retention of the encoded memory.
c. Incorrect. Decoding must mean the removal of the code into which something has been encoded.

d. Incorrect. Retrieval is the recovery of stored, encoded information.

3. b mod. 20 p. 226
a. Incorrect. Sensory memory has a life of less than a second.
*b. Correct. Unless material is rehearsed, information is quickly lost from the short-term memory.
c. Incorrect. Iconic memory refers to visual sensory memory and has a duration of less than a quarter of a second.
d. Incorrect. The duration of long-term memory is indefinite.

4. b mod. 20 p. 228
a. Incorrect. It can hold up to nine items, but the average would be seven.

*b. Correct. Psychologists accept the view that we can hold about seven, plus or minus two items in short-term memory.
c. Incorrect. See answer b.
d. Incorrect. See answer b.

5. b   mod. 20 p. 233
a. Incorrect. No such memory concept.
*b. Correct. Memory of life events, or episodes, is one of the types of long-term memory.
c. Incorrect. Semantic memory is memory for declarative knowledge like words and definitions.
d. Incorrect. No concept like this has been used in contemporary psychology.

6. d   mod. 20 p. 228
a. Incorrect. Rehearsal facilitates all memory.
b. Incorrect. It does help short-term memory items persist in short-term memory.
c. Incorrect. It does aid in the transfer of memory to long-term storage.
*d. Correct. It helps both short-term duration and long-term consolidation.

7. a   mod. 20 p. 231
*a. Correct. Episodic memory is the storage of stories and details about life—that is, episodes.
b. Incorrect. Facts like these are considered semantic.
c. Incorrect. Episodic memory has little to do with speaking.
d. Incorrect. This would not affect short-term memory.

8. a   mod. 21 p. 238
*a. Correct. Retrieval cues are aspects—connections, similarities, etc.—of information that help us recall, or retrieve, the information.
b. Incorrect. Distractors are the stems of multiple-choice questions that are designed to confuse the test-taker.
c. Incorrect. This is not the answer.
d. Incorrect. The sensory code is relevant to short-term memory and our ability to manipulate that memory.

9. d   mod. 21 p. 240
a. Incorrect. See answer d.
b. Incorrect. See answer d.
c. Incorrect. See answer d.
*d. Correct. In terms of memory phenomena, construction processes apply to episodic memory, motivation, and procedural memory.

10. d   mod. 21 p. 238
a. Incorrect. Difficulties in encoding may make it impossible to retrieve any information.
b. Incorrect. Decoding is not a memory phenomenon.
c. Incorrect. A difficulty with storage would appear in the inability to form new memories.
*d. Correct. We may know that we know something, but not be able to retrieve it.

11. b   mod. 22 p. 247
a. Incorrect. After two days, the memory loss had settled down.
*b. Correct. Within an hour, a significant portion of the list had been forgotten.
c. Incorrect. Only a supermemory could remember the list 10 days later.
d. Incorrect. The most dramatic loss occurred within the first hour.

12. c   mod. 22 p. 250
a. Incorrect. May actually magnify if an error is repeated.
b. Incorrect. Trace decay may not occur anyway.
*c. Correct. Different brain areas are at work as the rehearsal begins to influence consolidation.
d. Incorrect. This is not a symptom of this disease.

13. b   mod. 22 p. 252
a. Incorrect. This is retrograde amnesia, which covers all the period prior to the trauma.
*b. Correct. This is common for head-injury patients, who lose the time following the accident.
c. Incorrect. This is an apraxia.
d. Incorrect. This is another kind of memory difficulty.

14. c   mod. 22 p. 252
a. Incorrect. Had they been encoded wrong, they could not be recovered.
b. Incorrect. Had they not been stored, they could never be recovered.
*c. Correct. Because they had not been destroyed, they could still be retrieved.
d. Incorrect. Association is not one of the traditional memory processes.

15. b   mod. 22 p. 253
a. Incorrect. The keyword technique suggests that a similar-sounding word would help in memory.
*b. Correct. In this description, a similar-sounding word is used.
c. Incorrect. One would already need to know the word to make similar imagery.
d. Incorrect. This is a free-association technique.

16. d   mod. 20 p. 227
17. b   mod. 20 p. 233
18. c   mod. 20 p. 232
19. e   mod. 20 p. 232
20. a   mod. 20 p. 232

21. encoding   mod. 20 p. 223
22. Iconic   mod. 20 p. 227
23. retrieval cue   mod. 21 p. 228
24. serial position effect mod. 22 p. 254
25. Semantic networks   mod. 20 p. 233

26.
- State the evidence supporting the existence of repressed memories and describe the problems that can arise from mistaken, recovered memories.
- One might argue that psychologists interfere with and compound the problem further by encouraging clients to "recover" memories that they may not have actually had, something like the demand characteristic in research. Consider whether there are ways to reduce false memories.

Practice Test 2:
1. c   mod. 20 p. 226
a. Incorrect. This is a form of long-term memory.
b. Incorrect. Short-term memory can last about 15 to 25 seconds
*c. Correct. Sensory memory lasts for less than a second.
d. Incorrect. This is a form of long-term memory.

2. b   mod. 20 p. 223
a. Incorrect. Encoding involves getting the information in a form that can be stored.
*b. Correct. Storage refers to the process of retaining the information for later use.
c. Incorrect. Memory has no decoding process.
d. Incorrect. Retrieval refers to the recovery of memory from storage.

3. a   mod. 20 p. 228
*a. Correct. With meaning, the items in short-term memory have greater duration.
b. Incorrect. Memory does not have an intensity except in the emotional sense.
c. Incorrect. Memories cannot be measured in terms of length, although their duration can.
d. Incorrect. Some visual memory will be coded verbally for easier manipulation.

4. c   mod. 20 p. 228

a. Incorrect. Similarity is the gestalt organizational principle.
b. Incorrect. Priming refers to a cognitive theory suggesting that memories, thoughts, and other cognitive material can be primed.
*c. Correct. The technical term is chunking, and it refers to grouping information together in any way that can be recalled.
d. Incorrect. Closure is a gestalt principle of perceptual organization.

5. c   mod. 20 p. 232
a. Incorrect. There is no form of memory known as periodic memory.
b. Incorrect. Episodic memory refers to the personal memories of experiences and life events.
*c. Correct. This is a definition of the form of declarative memory known as semantic memory.
d. Incorrect. None of the researchers have suggested a process called interpolation (yet).

6. b   mod. 20 p. 229
a. Incorrect. Massed practice is not an effective approach to enhancing long-term memory consolidation.
*b. Correct. Elaborative rehearsal strengthens the memory by providing a rich array of retrieval cues.
c. Incorrect. None of the researchers have suggested a process called interpolation (yet).
d. Incorrect. Interference will actually make consolidation more difficult.

7. d   mod. 21 p. 238
a. Incorrect. The stage of memory?
b. Incorrect. The meaning can be important and significant but still be forgotten.
c. Incorrect. Memories do not have qualities in a sense relevant to the levels-of-processing approach.
*d. Correct. The depth of processing is determined by the extent of elaboration and the kinds of information to which the new information was associated.

8. d   mod. 21 p. 238
a. Incorrect. This is a form of guessing, like your selecting this answer.
b. Incorrect. Recall refers to the free recall of information without any specific cues.
c. Incorrect. Mnemonics refers to the techniques or memory aids that can be used to improve memory.

*d. Correct. Because the answer is among the four items presented as alternatives, the test-taker only needs to recognize the right answer.

9. a   mod. 21 p. 232
*a. Correct. Procedural memories are skill-based memories, like riding a bicycle or skating.
b. Incorrect. A semantic memory is memory of words, definitions, procedures, grammatical rules, and similarly abstract information.
c. Incorrect. This is a kind of rehearsal that involves making many connections and relationships for an item being remembered.
d. Incorrect. Declarative memory combines episodic and semantic memory.

10. c   mod. 21 p. 239
a. Incorrect. A cognitive map is a more mundane memory item created while wandering about.
b. Incorrect. A schema is an organizational unit that gives structure or organization to a set of information.
*c. Correct. Significant events are often remembered in great detail and apparent specificity, as if a photograph were taken of the event (thus flashbulb memory).
d. Incorrect. A seizure is a traumatic experience and probably would not have this kind of memory associated with it.

11. d   mod. 22 p. 249
a. Incorrect. Decay theory says that we lose memories because they fade away.
b. Incorrect. Interference accounts for memory by the displacement of one memory by another.
c. Incorrect. Cue-dependency does cause forgetting, when people don't have adequate cues to help them remember.
*d. Correct. With inadequate processing, information would not likely have been committed to memory in the first place.

12. b   mod. 22 p. 251
a. Incorrect. The hippocampus is thought to play a role in the consolidation of short-term memories into long-term memories.
*b. Correct. The sulci have yet to be implicated in memory.
c. Incorrect. Neurotransmitters support the memory consolidation process.
d. Incorrect. Changes at the synapse that are relatively permanent are called long-term potentiation.

13. a   mod. 22 p. 252

*a. Correct. The loss of all memories before an accident is uncommon, although it is the most popularized form of amnesia.
b. Incorrect. See answer a.
c. Incorrect. See answer a.
d. Incorrect. See answer a.

14. d   mod. 21 p. 244
a. Incorrect. True only if "other type" refers to fabrication.
b. Incorrect. Usually they are recovered in therapy, not treated.
c. Incorrect. They do have a noticeable effect, but this is not an identifying feature.
*d. Correct. The problem faced by all is the ability to verify the genuineness of the memories.

15. a   mod. 22 p. 253
*a. Correct. This is called massed practice, and it is not very effective.
b. Incorrect. Overlearning is an effective form of study.
c. Incorrect. Organization helps memory by providing a meaningful scheme for the information.
d. Incorrect. This helps elaborate the material—putting it in your own words.

16. b   mod. 22 p. 248
17. e   mod. 22 p. 249
18. c   mod. 22 p. 249
19. a   mod. 22 p. 253
20. d   mod. 20 p. 223

21. recall   mod. 20 p. 238
22. Recognition   mod. 21 p. 238
23. Retrograde amnesia mod. 22 p. 252
24. Chunking   mod. 20 p. 228

25.
▪ Give several examples of laboratory research. The advantages include control over the experiment and the ability to document that prior memories do not influence the outcome.
▪ Identify experiences that are best examined in an everyday context. Much case study and archival research is based on reports that are made when an event occurs or on reports from several points of view and are thus a form of everyday memory research. Other examples should be given.
▪ As stated in the text, both of these techniques are needed to understand memory fully.

Practice Test 3:
1. d   mod. 20 p. 226

a. Incorrect. Episodic memory would mean that the items had been committed to long-term memory.
b. Incorrect. This is the sensory memory for hearing, and it only lasts about a second.
c. Incorrect. This is the sensory memory for vision, and it only lasts about a quarter of a second.
*d. Correct. Short-term memory would account for most of this ability of recollection. Some, however, think this is a special skill developed by husbands who watch football too much.

2. b   mod. 20 p. 226
a. Incorrect. This is difficult to judge because our sensory receptors are always active.
*b. Correct. The sensory information in the sensory memory has not been processed any further than the sensory register, thus it represents the information as it was taken in.
c. Incorrect. The sensory information in the sensory memory has not been processed any further than the sensory register, thus it represents the information as it was taken in; it is therefore as complete as the sensory system makes it.
d. Incorrect. The information will be lost if it is not processed, but some information can be processed and be meaningless.

3. a   mod. 21 p. 248
*a. Correct. This constructive may help give the memory its narrative quality.
b. Incorrect. We tend not to lose the distinctive features.
c. Incorrect. Engrams are not sheep.
d. Incorrect. Ambiguous details are not a hallmark of flashbulb memories.

4. b   mod. 20 p. 227
a. Incorrect. A flashbulb memory implies a photo-like recollection.
*b. Correct. The visual echo or afterimage of the screen is much like the sensory activation in iconic memory.
c. Incorrect. The parallel here would be the persisting buzz of a tube radio for the brief moment after it is turned off.
d. Incorrect. Declarative memory is very long term and does not appear to fade in this manner.

5. d   mod. 20 p. 232
a. Incorrect. Working memory applies to memories that soon become insignificant, like what we ate for lunch yesterday or where we parked our car yesterday (although where we parked it today is very important).

b. Incorrect. Declarative does not account for physical skills like this.
c. Incorrect. This contributes to our personal experiences and episodic memory.
*d. Correct. The basketball shot is a procedural skill and thus would be stored in procedural memory.

6. b   mod. 20 p. 232
a. Incorrect. Working memory is significant for only a few days.
*b. Correct. Procedural memory is just this kind of skill-based memory.
c. Incorrect. Only if he had been in a serious bicycle accident could the possibility of a repressed memory play a role.
d. Incorrect. This may be an important moment in the lives of Daniel and his son, but it is the procedural memory that contributes to Daniel's ability to recall this old skill.

7. c   mod. 21 p. 241
a. Incorrect. Freud did not introduce this idea.
b. Incorrect. Piaget used it, but it was introduced by someone else.
*c. Correct. This was Bartlett's contribution.
d. Incorrect. This is the author of the textbook.

8. c   mod. 21 p. 238
a. Incorrect. If attention means rehearsal, then this would be true.
b. Incorrect. There is no mental imagery model of memory.
*c. Correct. "Attention" would have an effect on how the memory was elaborated (thus given depth).
d. Incorrect. There is no specific cultural diversity model of memory.

9. d   mod. 22 p. 249
a. Incorrect. Try the opposite, where the first list influences the later list.
b. Incorrect. This is a dissociative state similar to amnesia.
c. Incorrect. This is a type of memory failure.
*d. Correct. In proactive interference, an earlier list interferes with a later list.

10. b   mod. 22 p. 249
a. Incorrect. This is not a recognized form of interference.
*b. Correct. In retroactive interference, a later list interferes with an earlier list.
c. Incorrect. In proactive interference, an earlier list interferes with a later list.

d.   Incorrect. This is not a recognized form of interference.

11. d   mod. 22 p. 249
a.   Incorrect. Alzheimer's disease would affect all of the transactions.
b.   Incorrect. Decay is not thought to be a significant factor, especially if the waiter would have remembered if the other transactions had not intervened.
c.   Incorrect. Proactive means the previous interfere with the current.
*d. Correct. Retroactive means the intervening events interfere with recall of the earlier event.

12. c   mod. 22 p. 252
a.   Incorrect. Try: the manufacture of beta amyloid.
b.   Incorrect. Try: the manufacture of beta amyloid.
*c. Correct. Platelets form and constrict brain tissue, causing it to die.
d.   Incorrect. Try: the manufacture of beta amyloid.

13. d   mod. 22 p. 252
a.   Incorrect. This sounds like Alzheimer's disease.
b.   Incorrect. This is anterograde amnesia.
c.   Incorrect. This sounds like advanced Alzheimer's disease or stroke victim.
*d. Correct. Memories are lost from before the accident.

14. a   mod. 22 p. 252
*a. Correct. Retrograde amnesia is marked by the loss of ability to recall events from before an accident or trauma.
b.   Incorrect. Anterograde amnesia involves the loss of memory from the point of an accident or trauma forward.
c.   Incorrect. This is a loss of memory from early childhood, usually before the development of language skills.
d.   Incorrect. This is a memory loss syndrome that results from severe, long-term abuse of alcohol.

15. c   mod. 20 p. 234
16. e   mod. 20 p. 233
17. b   mod. 22 p. 253
18. d   mod. 22 p. 254
19. a   mod. 21 p. 234

20. priming   mod. 20 p. 234
21. long-term potentiation   mod. 22 p. 250
22. Consolidation   mod. 22 p. 250
23. autobiographical memory   mod. 22 p. 244
24. elaborative rehearsal   mod. 20 p. 229

25. source confusion
▪   personal schema of the eyewitness
▪   power of the misinformation effect
▪   evidence related to the false memory syndrome
▪   relevant aspects of the encoding specificity theory.

Chapter 8: Cognition and Language

Module 23: Thinking and Reasoning
Module 24: Problem Solving
Module 25: Language

Overview

This set of modules focuses on cognitive psychology, the branch of psychology that studies higher mental processes, including thinking, language, memory, problem solving, knowing, reasoning, judging, and decision making. This unit concentrates on three broad topics: thinking and reasoning, problem solving, and creativity and language.

Module 23 offers a definition of thinking, the manipulation of mental representations of information. Mental images and concepts of categorization, along with syllogistic reasoning and the use of algorithms, are discussed.

Module 24 presents the three major stages in problem solving: preparation, production of solutions, and evaluation of solutions. Problem-solving strategies are discussed. Different strategies, such as creativity and skill at making judgments about solutions, may be useful tools in problem solving.

Finally, *Module 25* offers examples of how people use language. The production of language and the reinforcement and conditioning of language development are presented. How the innate language acquisition device guides the development of language is explained. A discussion on how language is developed and acquired is also presented.

To further investigate the topics covered in this chapter, you can visit the related Web sites by visiting the following link: www.mhhe.com/feldmanup8.

Prologue: The Sky's the Limit
Looking Ahead

Module 23: Thinking and Reasoning

Mental Images: Examining the Mind's Eye
Concepts: Categorizing the World
Reasoning: Making Up Your Mind
Computers and Problem Solving

- ***What is thinking?***
- ***What processes underlie reasoning and decision making?***

Thinking and Reasoning

The branch of psychology that studies problem solving and other aspects of thinking is called

[a] _____. The term [b] _____ brings together the higher mental processes of humans, including understanding the world, processing information, making judgments and decisions, and describing knowledge.

[c] _____ is the manipulation of mental representations—words, images, sounds, or data in any other modality—of information. Thinking transforms the representation in order to achieve some goal or solve some problem. The visual, auditory, and

tactile representations of objects are called [d] _____, and these are a key component of thought. The time required to scan mental images can be measured. Brain scans taken while people are forming and manipulating mental images are being used to study the

production and use of them. [e] _____ are categorizations of objects, events, or people that share common properties. Because we have concepts, we are able to classify newly encountered material on the basis of our past experiences. Ambiguous concepts

are usually represented by [f] _____, which are typical, highly representative examples of concepts. Concepts provide an efficient way of understanding events and objects as they occur in the complex world.

Reasoning, the process by which people use information to draw conclusions and make

decisions, is a topic of particular interest to cognitive psychologists. [g] _____ involves formal reasoning, beginning with asserting a general assumption, or premise, believed to be true, and then deriving specific implications, or conclusions, from that assumption.

242

A(n) **[h]** _____ is a rule that guarantees a solution if it is properly followed. Applying mathematical rules to equations will give us the answer even when we do not know why it works. A(n) **[i]** _____ is a rule of thumb or some other shortcut that may lead to a solution. Heuristics can help, but they often lead to erroneous solutions. People often use a(n) **[j]** _____ to determine whether something belongs to a category or not. The decision is based on whether an observed characteristic belongs in the category. The **[k]** _____ judges the probability of an event on how easily the event can be recalled from memory. We assume that events that are easier to remember must have happened more often and that similar events are more likely to recur.

A field which blends cognitive psychology with technology is **[l]** _____, in which people explore how to use technology to mimic human thinking, problem solving, and even creativity. Experts in that field have developed increasingly more sophisticated computers, that have come close, though not entirely identical, to approximating human thought processes.

Evaluate

_____ 1. mental image

_____ 2. algorithm

_____ 3. heuristic

_____ 4. representativeness heuristic

_____ 5. availability heuristic

a. A rule in which people and things are judged by the degree to which they represent a certain category.

b. A set of rules that, if followed, guarantees a solution, although the reason they work may not be understood by the person using them.

c. A rule for judging the probability that an event will occur by the ease with which it can be recalled from memory.

d. A rule of thumb that may bring about a solution to a problem but is not guaranteed to do so.

e. The mind's representation of an object or event.

Rethink

23-1   How might the availability heuristic contribute to prejudices based on race, age, and gender? Can awareness of this heuristic prevent this from happening?

23-2   _From the perspective of a human resources specialist:_ How might you use the research on mental imagery to improve employees' performance?

Spotlight on Terminology and Language—ESL Pointers

Page 252 "When the first American flew into space in 1961, Burt Rutan was a 17-year-old college **freshman**."

A **freshman** is a student who is in their first year of high school or college.

Page 252 "Listening to news of Alan Shepard's **groundbreaking suborbital** flight on the radio, Rutan was euphoric."

Things that are **groundbreaking** are new and original.

A **suborbital** flight is a flight of a rocket or spaceship that does not make a complete orbit of the Earth.

Page 252 "The nose is punctuated by **portholes**, like an ocean liner."

Portholes are small round windows.

Page 252 "Despite its **Flash Gordon** looks and unorthodox design… it became the first privately funded spacecraft."

Flash Gordon is a science fiction comic book character that was popular in the United States in the 1930's.

Page 252 "Thanks to the backing of two **starry-eyed** billionaires, SpaceShipOne is set to become the first in a new line of space-tourism craft coming in 2007."

When someone is **starry-eyed** they tend to be idealistic and impractical.

Page 252 "But whether or not SpaceShipOne revolutionizes space travel, it is clear that Rutan has the **elusive** quality that marks successful inventors: creativity."

It is difficult to understand and define, or identify, what is specifically happening when we think. The thinking process is hard to pin down. It is **elusive**. **Elusive** is when something is evasive; it tends to evade your grasp. Academic material can be considered **elusive** when it is not easily comprehended or defined.

Page 252 "More generally, how do people use information to **devise** innovative solutions to problems?"

To **devise** something is to think it up or develop the idea.

Page 252 "Clearly, the **realm** of cognitive psychology is broad."

The **realm** of something refers to its defined area of interest.

Page 253 "The **mere** ability to pose such a question underscores the distinctive nature of the human ability to think."

Mere means by itself and without any more.

Page 254 "They may visualize themselves taking a **foul shot**, watching the ball, and hearing the **swish** as it goes through the net."

A **foul shot** is an extra opportunity to shoot at the basket in a basketball game without any interference by the opponent.

A **Swish** is a whistling sound made by something moving quickly through air.

Page 254 "Such research suggests that children whose parents **nag** them about practicing an instrument, a dance routine, or some other skill can now employ a new excuse: They *are* practicing—mentally.'"

To **nag** is to ask someone something over and over again.

Page 255 "For example, we can **surmise** that someone tapping a handheld screen is probably using some kind of computer or PDA, even if we have never encountered that specific brand before."

When you **surmise**, you deduce or infer without certain knowledge. Rather, you make an inference or guess or conclusion that something is the case on the basis of only limited evidence or intuitive feeling.

Page 255 "For instance, most people in Western cultures consider cars and trucks good examples of vehicles, whereas elevators and **wheelbarrows** are not considered very good examples."

A **wheelbarrow** is an open container with one wheel in the front and two handles in the back that is used to carry tools and other things while tending a garden.

Page 256 "Their efforts have contributed to our understanding of formal reasoning processes as well as the cognitive shortcuts we routinely use – shortcuts that sometimes may lead our reasoning capabilities **astray**."

Astray is off track. When our reasoning goes **astray**, it is no longer logical – the path we followed to get to our conclusion does not make sense.

Page 258 "Such computer **mimicry** is possible because composers have a particular "signature" that reflects patterns, sequences, and combinations of notes."

To **mimic** is to imitate or copy someone else. **Mimicry** is the act of imitating other people's actions, voices and appearance and is often used for fun.

Page 259 "According to experts who study *artificial intelligence,* the field that examines how to use technology to imitate the outcome of human thinking, problem-solving, and creative activities, computers show **rudiments** of human-like thinking because of their knowledge of where to look—and where not to look—for an answer to a problem."

A **rudiment** is the beginning or early stage in the development of something.

Module 24:
Problem Solving

Preparation: Understanding and Diagnosing Problems
Production: Generating Solutions
Judgment: Evaluating the Solutions
Impediments to Solutions: Why Is Problem Solving Such a Problem?
Creativity and Problem Solving

Applying Psychology in the 21st Century:
Eureka! Understanding the Underpinnings of Creativity

Becoming an Informed Consumer of Psychology:
Thinking Critically and Creatively

- *How do people approach and solve problems?*
- *What are the major obstacles to problem solving?*

Problem Solving

Problem solving typically involves three major steps: preparation, production of solutions, and evaluation of solutions. Problems are distinguished as either well-defined or ill-defined. In a(n)

[a] _____, the problem and the information needed to solve it are clearly understood. The appropriate solution is thus easily identified. In a(n)

[b] _____, both the problem and what information is needed may be unclear.

    There are three categories of problem. [c] _____, like jigsaw puzzles, require the recombination or reorganization of a group of elements in order to solve the problem.

With [d] _____, the problem solver must identify a relationship between elements and then construct a new relationship among them. A common example is number sequence problems, where a test taker may be asked to supply the next number in the sequence.

The third kind of problem is [e] _____. Transformation problems have a desired goal and require a series of steps or changes to take place in order to reach the goal. The Tower of Hanoi problem described in the text in this chapter is a transformation problem. Once the kind of problem is understood, it is easier to determine how to represent and organize the problem.

    The creation of solutions may proceed at the simplest level as trial and error, but this approach may be inadequate for problems that have many possible configurations. The use of heuristics aids in the simplification of problems. The heuristic of [f] _____ proceeds by testing the difference between the current status and the desired outcome, and with each test, it tries to reduce the difference.

Another heuristic used to solve problems is to divide a problem into [g] _____, or intermediate steps. This allows the problem solver to focus on solving each, smaller step, rather than the problem as a whole. The downside is that some problems cannot be subdivided effectively.

The use of [h] _____ takes a slightly different approach to problem solving, requiring a reorganization of the entire problem in order to achieve a solution. The reorganization of existing elements requires prior experience with the elements.

The final step of problem solving is to evaluate the adequacy of a solution. If the solution is not clear, criteria to judge the solution must be made clear.

In the progress toward a solution, several obstacles can be met. [i] _____ refers to the tendency to think of an object according to its given function or typical use. Functional fixedness is an example of a broader phenomenon called

[j] _____, the tendency for old patterns of solutions to persist. Finally, sometimes people don't achieve a good solution because they are blocked by a(n) [k] _____, causing them to favor their initial hypotheses and assumptions, despite incoming contradictory information.

[l] _____ is usually defined as the combining of responses or ideas in novel

ways. [m] _____ refers to the ability to generate unusual yet appropriate

responses to problems. [n] _____ produces responses that are based primarily on knowledge or logic. *Cognitive complexity* is the use of elaborate, intricate, and complex stimuli and thinking patterns. Humor can increase creative output as well. Apparently, intelligence is not related to creativity, perhaps because the tests for intelligence evaluate convergent thinking rather than divergent thinking.

Evaluate

_____ 1. arrangement problems

_____ 2. problems of inducing structure

_____ 3. transformation problems

_____ 4. means-ends analysis

_____ 5. subgoals

a. Problems to be solved using a series of methods to change an initial state into a goal state.

b. A commonly used heuristic to divide a problem into intermediate steps and to solve each one of them.

c. Problems requiring the identification of existing relationships among elements presented so as to construct a new relationship among them.

d. Problems requiring the rearrangement of a group of elements in order to satisfy a certain criterion.

e. Repeated testing to determine and reduce the distance between the desired outcome and what currently exists in problem solving.

Rethink

24-1   Is the reasoning in the following logic correct or incorrect? Why? "Creative people often have trouble with traditional intelligence tests. I have trouble with traditional intelligence tests. Therefore, I am a creative person."

24-2   *From the perspective of a manufacturer:* How might you encourage your employees to develop creative ways to improve the products that you produce?

Spotlight on Terminology and Language—ESL Pointers

Page 261 "Psychologists have found that problem solving typically involves three major steps: preparing to create solutions, producing solutions, and evaluating the solutions that have been **generated**."

The solutions that are **generated** are the solutions that have been made, or created.

Page 261 "If the problem is a **novel** one, they probably will pay particular attention to any restrictions placed on coming up with a solution – such as the rule for moving only one disk at a time in the Tower of Hanoi problem."

Novel is new, original. The problem is **novel.** This would be a problem not seen before.

Page 261 "Thus, we can make **straightforward** judgments about whether a potential solution is appropriate."

Straightforward is clear and uncomplicated. When a problem is well defined, it is easier to make **straightforward** judgments about whether a potential solution is appropriate.

Page 263 "**Winnowing** out nonessential information is often a critical step in the preparation stage of problem solving."

Winnowing is removing, or getting rid of something undesirable or unwanted.

Page 264 "Our ability to represent a problem – and the kind of solution we eventually come to – depends on the way a problem is phrased, or **framed**."

Framed can mean conceived of or imagined. The difficulty of identifying a solution may arise depending on the way the problem is **framed** or stated.

Page 265 "Thomas Edison invented the light bulb only because he tried thousands of different kinds of materials for a **filament** before he found one that worked (carbon)."

A **filament** is a slim strand or fiber of material.

Page 266 "In a means-end analysis, each step brings the problem solver closer to a **resolution**."

A **resolution** is often a firm decision to do something. When a person chooses the path they will take for **resolution** of a problem, they now have to plan to **resolve** or respond to the problem.

Page 266 "In one of Köhler's studies, chimps were kept in a cage in which boxes and sticks were **strewn about**, and a bunch of tantalizing bananas hung from the ceiling, out of reach. "

When things are **strewn about** they are scattered, or spread around.

Page 267 "But then, in what seemed like a sudden **revelation**, they would stop whatever they were doing and stand on a box to reach the bananas with a stick."

A **revelation** is enlightenment. Like a surprise, all of a sudden, their behavior suggested this information was **revealed** to them.

Page 267 "Some researchers have suggested that the chimps' behavior was simply **chaining** together previously learned responses, no different from the way a pigeon learns, by trial and error, to peck a key (Epstein, 1987, 1996)."

Chaining is connecting. We often **chain** together bits of information.

Page 268 "**Impediments** to Solutions: Why is Problem Solving Such a Problem?"

An **impediment** is an obstacle. A serious **impediment** to our learning is the lack of study time.

Page 268 "You are given a set of **tacks**, candles, and matches each in a small box, and told your goal is to place three candles at eye level on a nearby door, so that wax will not drip on the floor as the candles burn [see Figure 7]."
Tacks are small nails that have a sharp point and a broad head.

Page 269 "For instance, functional fixedness probably leads you to think of this book as something to read, instead of its potential use as a doorstop or as **kindling** for a fire."

Kindling is something that could be used to start a fire.

Page 269 "It can prevent you from seeing beyond the apparent **constraints** of a problem."

In the activity presented in the text, the apparent **constraints** of the problem limited your creativity and problem-solving skills. **Constraints** are limitations.

Page 270 "If you had difficulty with the problem, it was probably because you felt **compelled** to keep your lines within the grid."

You may have felt that you were forced to do solve the problem only one way. You felt pressured or **compelled** to stay within certain boundaries that you had mentally established.

Page 270 "When the nuclear power plant at Three Mile Island in Pennsylvania suffered its initial malfunction in 1979, a disaster that almost led to a **nuclear meltdown**, the plant operators immediately had to solve a problem on the most serious kind."

Nuclear meltdown is the disastrous escape of radioactive materials or radiation into the environment.

Page 271 "You can put it on the sand if you had no towel, use it for bases in baseball, make paper airplanes with it, use it as a **dustpan** when you sweep, ball it up for the cat to play with, wrap your hands in it if it is cold (Ward, Kogan, & Pankove, 1972)."

A **dustpan** is a container with a flat base and open front that is used to collect dirt and dust.

Page 272 "**Eureka**!: Understanding the **Underpinnings** of Creativity"

Eureka is a term used to show pleasure or delight in solving a problem or discovering something. **Underpinnings** are things that supports or acts as a foundation for something.

Page 272 "The volunteers looked like electronic **Medusas**, with wires snaking from 30 electrodes glued to their scalps and recording their brain activity."

Medusa is a Greek mythological creature that had snakes for hair, and could turn anyone who looked at her to stone.

Page 272 "As they **peered** at a computer screen, a brainteaser flashed: Turn the incorrect Roman-numeral equation XI + I = X, made out of 10 sticks, into a correct one by moving as few sticks as possible."

When we **peer** at something we are looking at it very closely.

Page 272 "None could be solved by a **plug-and-chug approach;** all required insight and creativity (Begley, 2004, p. B1)."

A "**plug-and-chug approach**" involves picking different answers to a mathematical problem and trying each of them until the correct answer is found.

Module 25: Language

Grammar: Language's Language
Language Development: Developing a Way with Words
Understanding Language Acquisition: Identifying the Roots of Language
The Influence of Language on Thinking: Do Eskimos Have More Words for Snow Than Texans Do?
Do Animals Use Language?

Exploring Diversity: Teaching with Linguistic Variety: Bilingual Education

- *How do people use language?*
- *How does language develop?*

Language

[a] _____ is the systematic, meaningful arrangement of symbols. It is important for cognition and for communication with others. The basic structure of language is

[b] _____, the framework of rules that determines how thoughts are expressed.

The three components of grammar are (1) [c] _____, the smallest units of

sound, called [d] _____, that affect the meaning of speech and how words are

formed; (2) [e] _____, the rules that govern how words and phrases are

combined to form sentences; and (3) [f] _____, the rules governing meaning of words and sentences.

Language develops through set stages. At first, children [g] _____, producing speech-like but meaningless sounds. Babbling gradually sounds like actual speech, and by one year old, sounds that are not part of the language disappear. After the first year, children produce short, two-word combinations followed by short sentences.

[h] _____ refers to the short sentences that contain a critical message but sound as if written as a telegram, with noncritical words left out. As children begin to learn speech rules,

they will apply them without flexibility, a phenomenon known as [i]_____, where an "ed" might be applied to every past-tense construction. By the age of 5, most children have acquired the rules of language.

The [j] _____ to language acquisition suggests that the reinforcement and conditioning principles are responsible for language development. Praise for saying a word like "mama" reinforces the word and increases the likelihood of its being repeated. Shaping then makes child language become more adultlike. This approach has difficulty explaining the acquisition of language rules, because children are also reinforced when their language is incorrect. An alternative proposed by Noam Chomsky suggests that innate mechanisms are responsible for the acquisition of language. All human languages have a similar underlying structure he calls [k] _____ , and a neural system in the brain, the

[l] _____ , is responsible for the development of language.

Psychologists are also concerned whether the structure of language influences the structure of thought or whether thought influences language. The [m] _____ *hypothesis* suggests that language shapes thought, determining how people of a particular culture perceive and understand the world. In an alternative view, language may reflect the different ways we have of thinking about the world, essentially that thought produces language.

Children who enter school as non-native English speakers face several hardships. The debate over whether to take a bilingual approach or whether all instruction should be in English is a major controversy. Evidence suggests that bilingual children have cognitive advantages, being more flexible and able to understand concepts more easily than those who speak only one language. Bilingual students raise questions of the advantage of [n] _____ , in which a person is a member of two cultures. Some have argued that society should promote a(n)

[o] _____ , in which members of minority cultures are encouraged to learn both cultures.

Evaluate

_____ 1. grammar

_____ 2. phonology

_____ 3. phonemes

_____ 4. syntax

_____ 5. semantics

a. The framework of rules that determines how our thoughts can be expressed.

b. Rules governing the meaning of words and sentences.

c. The rules governing how words form sentences.

d. The study of how we use those sounds to produce meaning by forming them into words.

e. The smallest units of sound used to form words.

Rethink

25-1 Do people with two languages, one at home and one at school, automatically have two cultures? Why might people who speak two languages experience cognitive advantages over those who speak only one?

25-2 *From the perspective of a child care provider:* How would you encourage children's language abilities at the different stages of development?

Spotlight on Terminology and Language—ESL Pointers

Page 275 "Although few of us have ever come face to face with a tove, we have little difficulty in **discerning** that in Lewis Carroll's (1872) poem "Jabberwocky," the expression *slithy toves* contains an adjective, *slithy*, and the noun it modifies, *toves*."

When we discern something we are being very selective in our judgment, or opinion.

Page 276 "Semantic rules allow us to use words to convey the subtlest **nuances**."

A **nuance** is a tiny variation, just a shade of difference. You see a **nuance** as a very subtle distinction

Page 277 "Anyone who spends even a little time with children will notice the enormous **strides** that they make in language development throughout childhood."

Stride is a step in developmental advancement or progress. Children **stride** forward in their development of language skills.

Page 277 "Psychologists have offered two major explanations, one based on learning theory and the other based on **innate** processes."

Innate belongs to the essential nature of something. When a capability is **innate** in humans or other living organisms, these characteristics exist from birth.

Page 277 "To support the learning-theory approach, research shows that the more parents speak to their young children, the more **proficient** the children become in language use."

Proficient is skilled. The more parents speak to their young children, the more capable and competent the children become in language use.

Page 278 "Pointing to such problems with learning-theory approaches to language acquisition, linguist Noam Chomsky (1968, 1978, 1991) provided a **groundbreaking** alternative."

This **groundbreaking** theory was a new theory, a revolutionary theory. Your future research contributions may provide **groundbreaking** tools to treat mental and physical disease.

Page 279 "To **reconcile** such data, some theorists suggest the brain's **hardwired** language-acquisition device that Chomsky and geneticists **posit** provides the hardware for our acquisition of language, whereas the exposure to language in our environment that learning theorists observe allows us to develop the appropriate software."

When data is **reconciled**, we look at the conflicting ideas or interpretations, and work to make these apparently conflicting interpretations consistent or compatible.

If something is **hardwired**, this is affected by means of logic circuitry that is permanent.

To **posit** is to speculate, to hypothesize.

Page 280 "Further support for the point of view that language helps mold thinking comes from discoveries about language used by the Piraha, a tiny **hunter-gatherer** tribe in the Amazon."

A **hunter** is a person who seeks something.   A **gatherer** is a person who collects things. A **hunter-gatherer** is a member of a society of people that live by hunting and collecting only.

Page 281 "Many animals communicate with one another in **rudimentary** forms."

Rudimentary is basic. You would learn **rudiments**, or fundamental skills, during your early school years.

Page 281 "Even more impressively, Kanzi, a **pygmy** chimpanzee, has linguistic skills that some psychologists claim are close to those of a 2-year-old human being."

Pygmy means belonging top a small breed. **Pygmy** chimpanzees are a small breed of apes.

Page 281 "Proponents of bilingualism believe that students must **develop a sound footing** in basic subject areas and that, initially at least, teaching those subjects in their native language is the only way to provide them with that **foundation**."

To **develop a sound footing** is to have a strong base, or groundwork to build upon.

Foundation is the basis on which something stands or is supported.

Page 282 "Although the controversial issue has strong political **undercurrents**, evidence shows that the ability to speak two languages provides significant cognitive benefits over speaking only one language."

An **undercurrent** is an underlying feeling, often at odds with what is evident superficially.

Test your knowledge of the material in this set of modules by answering these questions. These questions have been placed in three Practice Tests. The first two tests consist of questions that will test your recall of factual knowledge. The third test contains questions that are challenging and primarily test for conceptual knowledge and your ability to apply that knowledge. Check your answers and review the feedback using the Answer Key on the following pages of the *Study Guide*.

PRACTICE TEST 1:

1. Manipulation of mental images is best demonstrated in research by subjects' abilities to:
    a.   use mental images to represent abstract ideas.
    b.   anticipate the exit of a toy train from a tunnel.
    c.   understand the subtle meanings of sentences.
    d.   mentally rotate one image to compare it with another.

2. A concept is defined as:
    a.   an idea or thought about a new procedure or product.
    b.   a group of attitudes that define an object, event, or person.
    c.   a categorization of people, objects, or events that share certain properties.
    d.   one of many facts that collectively define the subject matter for a specific area of knowledge (such as psychology).

3. Using a(n) _____ guarantees a solution, whereas using a(n) _____ is a shortcut that may lead to a solution.
    a.   concept; prototype   c.   heuristic; algorithm
    b.   prototype; concept   d.   algorithm; heuristic

4. When Isaac says that there is a high likelihood that a tornado will occur when he visits the Midwest, he may be relying on a(n) _____, since he remembers reading about tornados in the Midwest in the newspaper over the last several years.
    a.   syllogistic reasoning   c.   availability heuristic
    b.   prototype   d.   algorithm

5. All but which of the following are major steps in problem solving?
    a.   Evaluation of solutions generated
    b.   Preparation for the creation of solutions
    c.   Documentation of all solutions
    d.   Production of solutions

6. The Keane family has a passion for assembling jigsaw puzzles. This puzzle activity is an example of:
    a.   an overdefined problem.   c.   an undefined problem.
    b.   a well-defined problem.   d.   an ill-defined problem.

7. The most frequently used heuristic technique for solving problems is:
    a.   the availability heuristic.   c.   the representativeness heuristic.
    b.   categorical processing.   d.   means-ends analysis.

8. Which of the following is **not** associated with defining and understanding a problem?
    a. Discarding inessential information
    b. Simplifying essential information
    c. Dividing the problem into parts
    d. Clarifying the solution

9. Insight is a:
    a. sudden awareness of the relationships among various elements in a problem that previously appeared to be independent of one another.
    b. sudden awareness of the solution to a problem with which one has had no prior involvement or experience.
    c. sudden awareness of a particular algorithm that can be used to solve a problem.
    d. spontaneous procedure for generating a variety of possible solutions to a problem.

10. A simple computer program will include:
    a. trial-and-error solutions.
    b. a syllogism.
    c. a dozen or more heuristics.
    d. an algorithm.

11. Logic and knowledge are exemplified by _____ thinking.
    a. creative
    b. convergent
    c. divergent
    d. imaginal

12. Mary Ellen was able to think of 50 distinct uses for a plastic spoon in a 5-minute thinking interval; therefore, she:
    a. has an especially strong mental set.
    b. has superior intelligence.
    c. is especially prone to functional fixedness.
    d. is particularly good at divergent thinking.

13. The syntax of a language is the framework of rules that determines:
    a. the meaning of words and phrases.
    b. how words and phrases are combined to form sentences.
    c. the sounds of letters, phrases, and words.
    d. how thoughts can be translated into words.

14. Children sometimes use telegraphic speech. This refers to:
    a. speech that is rapid.
    b. seemingly nonessential words omitted from phrases and sentences.
    c. when the tonal quality of speech is limited.
    d. speech that may speed up, slow down, or contain pauses.

15. The Regents family is anxious to have little conversations with the newest member of their family, Emily. She will acquire most of the basic rules of grammar by:
    a. 2 years of age.
    b. 3 years of age.
    c. 4 years of age.
    d. 5 years of age.

_____ 16. concept

_____ 17. confirmation bias

_____ 18. creativity

_____ 19. divergent thinking

_____ 20. convergent thinking

a. Categorizations of objects, events, or people sharing some common properties.

b. A type of thinking that produces responses based on knowledge and logic.

c. The ability to generate unusual but appropriate responses to problems or questions.

d. A bias favoring an initial hypothesis and disregarding contradictory information suggesting alternative solutions.

e. The combining of responses or ideas in novel ways.

21. Using a rock as a hammer indicates a lack of _____.

22. You using a(n) _____ when you repeatedly test for differences between the desired outcome and the one that currently exists.

23. The rules of a language that govern how words are combined to form sentences is _____.

24. _____ speech is the two-word constructions typical of 2-year-olds.

25. Research supports the idea that _____ increases creativity and flexibility in solving problems.

26. Identify a major challenge that you anticipate facing in the next several years. It can involve choosing a career, getting married, selecting a major, choosing a graduate school, or one of many others. Describe the problem or challenge briefly, and then describe how you would apply the problem-solving steps presented in the text to the problem to generate solutions.

PRACTICE TEST 2:

1. Cognitive psychologists study all of the following **except** how:
    a. the sensory system takes in information.
    b. people understand the world.
    c. people process information.
    d. people make judgments.

2. Prototypes of concepts are:
    a. new concepts to describe newly emerging phenomena.
    b. new concepts that emerge within a language spontaneously and then are retained or discarded.
    c. representative examples of concepts.
    d. concepts from other languages that are incorporated into a native language if they appear useful.

3. In syllogistic reasoning, people:
   a. make reasoning errors by failing to use systematic techniques.
   b. use the representativeness heuristic humorously.
   c. draw a conclusion from a set of assumptions.
   d. create an analogy concerning the relationship between two sets of paired items, like "A is to B as C is to D."

4. Thomas relied on _____ by failing to solve a problem because he misapplied a category or set of categories.
   a. an availability heuristic
   c. functional fixedness
   b. a mental set
   d. a representativeness heuristic

5. Problems fall into one of three categories. Which of the following is **not** one of them?
   a. Arrangement
   c. Structure
   b. Affability
   d. Transformation

6. Identifying existing relationships among elements and constructing a new relationship is an example of:
   a. an inducing-structure problem.
   c. an arrangement problem.
   b. an organization problem.
   d. a transformation problem.

7. Problems that are solved by changing an initial state into a goal state are called:
   a. transformation problems.
   c. insight problems.
   b. problems of inducing structure.
   d. arrangement problems.

8. Patricia tells her roommate sardonically, "As a student, I measure success one midterm at a time." Her statement implies that her strategy for achieving a college degree is through:
   a. means-ends analysis.
   c. trial and error.
   b. achieving subgoals.
   d. application of algorithms.

9. Insight:
   a. is an unexplained discovery of a solution without prior experience with any elements of the problem.
   b. results from a methodical trial-and-error process.
   c. is a sudden realization of relationships among seemingly independent elements.
   d. is a solution that is independent of trial and error and experience.

10. Functional fixedness and mental set show that:
    a. the person's first hunches about the problem are typically correct.
    b. one's initial perceptions about the problem can impede the solution.
    c. convergent thinking is needed when the problem is well defined.
    d. the person who poses the problem is the one who solves it best.

11. A creative thinker often demonstrates which of the following characteristics?
    a. Convergent thought
    c. High intelligence
    b. Divergent thought
    d. Recurrent thought

12. The order of the words forming a sentence is generated by:
    a. synthetics.
    c. syntax.
    b. semantics.
    d. systematics.

13. Keenan has reached the age where babbling is a big part of his day. It is **not** true that babbling:
    a. occurs from 3 to 6 months of age.
    b. includes words such as "dada" and "mama."
    c. is speechlike.
    d. produces sounds found in all languages.

14. The fact that "mama" and "dada" are among the first words spoken in the English language:
    a. is unusual because these words do not contain the first sounds a child can make.
    b. suggests that they are responses the child is born with.
    c. is not surprising because these words are easy to pronounce, and the sound capabilities of the young child are limited.
    d. demonstrates that the sounds heard most frequently are the sounds spoken first.

15. According to Noam Chomsky, the brain contains a neural system designed for understanding and learning language called the:
    a. linguistic relativity system.
    b. language-acquisition device.
    c. limbic system.
    d. phonological linguistic device.

_____ 16. telegraphic speech

_____ 17. overgeneralization

_____ 18. babbling

_____ 19. universal grammar

_____ 20. language-acquisition device

a. A neural system of the brain hypothesized to permit understanding of language.

b. Sentences containing only the most essential words.

c. Applying rules of speech inappropriately.

d. An underlying structure shared by all languages.

e. Speechlike, but meaningless, sounds.

21. Producing many answers to the same question is called _____.

22. The notion that language determines our thought and feelings is called _____.

23. When you mentally manipulate information, it is called _____.

24. That there is a certain window of opportunity in which humans learn language is called the _____ of development.

25. Research shows that chimps can learn the meaning of _____.

26. Some psychologists consider language to be the capability that uniquely distinguishes us as human. Weigh the arguments for the language skills of specially trained chimpanzees and develop your position on this issue. Is language unique to humans? If so, how would you characterize the communication skills of chimpanzees? If not, then what capability does distinguish us from other animals?

PRACTICE TEST 3: Conceptual, Applied, and Challenging Questions

1. Which alternative does **not** fit within the text's definition of cognition?
    a. The higher mental processes of humans
    b. How people know and understand the world
    c. How people communicate their knowledge and understanding to others
    d. How people's eyes and ears process the information they receive

2. Concepts are similar to perceptual processes in that:
    a. concepts, like visual illusions, can produce errors in interpretation.
    b. concepts allow us to simplify and manage our world.
    c. concepts are to language what figure-ground relationships are to perception.
    d. some concepts and perceptual processes are innate.

3. You have had several troublesome, time-consuming, expensive, and emotionally trying experiences with telemarketers. Then you find out that your roommate for next term is a telemarketer. You are convinced, even without meeting your future roommate, that you should not be paired with this person. You have used the _____ heuristic to arrive at your conclusion.
    a. means-ends
    c. availability
    b. representativeness
    d. personality

4. Thinking of a George Foreman Grill in conventional terms may handicap your efforts to solve a problem when a possible solution involves using the grill for a novel use. This phenomenon is called:
    a. functional fixedness.
    c. awareness.
    b. insight.
    d. preparation.

5. The slight difference in meaning between the sentences "The mouse ate the cheese" and "The cheese was eaten by the mouse" is determined by the rules of:
    a. grammar.
    c. syntax.
    b. phonology.
    d. semantics.

6. Which of the following is the first refinement in the infant's learning of language?
    a. Production of short words that begin with a consonant
    b. Disappearance of sounds that are not in the native language
    c. Emergence of sounds that resemble words
    d. Production of two-word combinations

7. Generalizing from information presented in the text, which of the following two-word combinations is **least** likely to be spoken by a 2-year-old?
    a. Daddy up.
    c. I'm big.
    b. Mommy cookie.
    d. More, more.

8. Rabia exhibits a speech pattern characterized by short sentences, with many noncritical words missing. Which of the following is **not** true?
    a. Rabia is between 2 and 3 years old.
    b. Rabia is exhibiting telegraphic speech.
    c. Rabia is building complexity of speech.
    d. Rabia is using overgeneralization.

9. Dr. Slocum, a cognitive psychologist, has argued that the language of the child depends on exposure to the language of the parents. She would say that language is acquired through:
    a. classical conditioning.
    b. shaping.
    c. universal grammar.
    d. biological unfolding.

10. Which statement is **not** true about the language skills of humans and apes?
    a. Many critics believe that the language skills acquired by chimps and gorillas are no different from a dog learning to sit on command.
    b. The language skills of chimps and gorillas are equal to those of a 5-year-old human child.
    c. Sign language and response panels with different-shaped symbols have been used to teach language skills to chimps and gorillas.
    d. Humans are probably better equipped than apes to produce and organize language into meaningful sentences.

11. The Navaho have many names for the bluish, aquamarine color of turquoise. Based on how other, similar facts have been understood, this too could be used to support:
    a. the theory that language determines thought.
    b. the theory that thought determines language.
    c. the existence of the language-acquisition device.
    d. development of the nativistic position.

12. The notion that language shapes the way that people of a particular culture perceive and think about the world is called the:
    a. semantic-reasoning theory.
    b. cultural-language law.
    c. prototypical hypothesis.
    d. linguistic-relativity hypothesis.

13. Charise participates in a study in which she is asked to imagine a giraffe. After indicating that she has constructed the entire image, she is then asked to focus on the giraffe's tail. What should the experimenter be doing as she completes this task?
    a. Observing her reaction
    b. Timing each step
    c. Recording her respiration
    d. Getting the next subject ready

14. In a study concerned with concept formation and categorization, you are asked to think about a table. Which of the following would be considered a prototype if you were to have imagined it?
    a. Your grandmother's dining room table
    b. A four-legged, rectangular table
    c. The coffee table in the student lounge
    d. A round, pedestal-style oak table

_____ 15.   insight

_____ 16.   cognitive psychology

_____ 17.   prototypes

_____ 18.   linguistic relativity

_____ 19.   creativity

a. Typical, highly representative examples of a concept.

b. Sudden awareness of the relationships among various elements that had previously appeared to be independent of one another.

c. The branch of psychology that specializes in the study of cognition.

d. "Language determines thought."

e. Associated truth, divergent thinking, and playful thinking.

20.   When people repeatedly test for differences between desired outcomes and what currently exists, they are using _____.

21.   Intermediate steps to reach a goal are called _____.

22.   _____ occurs when the initial hypothesis is favored and alternative hypotheses are ignored.

23.   When Marcus applies rules even when doing so creates an error (such as "he walked" and "he runned"), it is called _____.

24.   A preference for elaborate, intricate thinking patterns is called _____.

25.   Discuss the controversy regarding bilingual education.

Module 23:	Module 24:	Module 25:	Evaluate
[a] cognitive psychology	[a] well-defined problem	[a] Language	1. a
[b] cognition	[b] ill-defined problem	[b] grammar	2. d
[c] Thinking	[c] Arrangement problems	[c] phonology	3. e
[d] mental images	[d] problems of inducing	[d] phonemes	4. c
[e] Concepts	structure	[e] syntax	5. b
[f] prototypes	[e] transformation problems	[f] semantics	
[g] syllogistic reasoning	[f] means-ends analysis	[g] babble	
[h] algorithm	[g] subgoals	[h] Telegraphic speech	
[i] heuristic	[h] insight	[i] overgeneralization	
[j] representativeness	[i] Functional fixedness	[j] learning-theory	
heuristic	[j] mental set	approach	
[k] availability heuristic	[k] confirmation bias	[k] universal grammar	
[l] artificial intelligence	[l] Creativity	[l] language-acquisition	
	[m] Divergent thinking	device	
Evaluate	[n] Convergent thinking	[m] linguistic-relativity	
1. e		[n] biculturalism	
2. b	Evaluate	[o] alternation model	
3. d			
4. a	1. d		
5. c	2. c		
	3. a		
	4. e		
	5. b		

Selected Rethink Answers

23-1   Define what is meant by the term *availability heuristic*. Knowing that we act on thoughts that we believe represent certain groups, negative thoughts about any race, age, or gender could lead to our developing a prejudice about that group. The media draws tragic events to our attention on a daily basis. If we believe these events to be true, we develop availability heuristics and use this information to guide future decision making (e.g., "People froze while hiking, so I shouldn't hike anymore."). Awareness can prevent this type of thinking by allowing us to assess what the real risks in a situation are and not rely on heuristics.

24-2   Use some of the strategies listed in the book, such as "redefine problems" and "consider the opposite." Employees can have productive brainstorming sessions using these strategies to increase creativity. In order for the sessions to work, there must be rules enforced, such as no criticism allowed and people are encouraged to describe ideas, even if they are only half-formed. A good moderator can help a brainstorming session.

25-1   It would make some sense to think that bilingual people have two cultures. Language allows us to express meanings and ultimately cultures. The same word in different cultures can have somewhat different meanings. Consequently, the same words could be the basis for somewhat differing cultures. This idea is related to the linguistic relativity hypothesis, which is somewhat controversial; there is evidence for both sides of the argument. People who speak two languages are apt to have more cognitive flexibility, which would be an advantage in problem-solving and creative endeavors.

Practice Test 1:

1.   d   mod. 23 p. 260
a.   Incorrect. This is difficult to document.
b.   Incorrect. This probably relates to spatial-temporal skills.
c.   Incorrect. This has to do with language skills.

*d.   Correct. Mental rotation and comparison is one technique used to study how people manipulate mental images.

2. c   mod. 23 p. 261
a. Incorrect. Concepts include more than new procedures and products.
b. Incorrect. The term "attitudes" is too restrictive, and this is a definition of a stereotype.
*c. Correct. Concepts are used to categorize thought.
d. Incorrect. Concepts can include natural objects as well as scientific knowledge.

3. d   mod. 23 p. 478
a. Incorrect. Prototypes and concepts are not used for generating solutions.
b. Incorrect. See above.
c. Incorrect. See below.
*d. Correct. These are the outcomes associated with using an algorithm and a heuristic.

4. c   mod. 23 p. 263
a. Incorrect. Syllogistic reasoning refers to a more formal set of steps in drawing conclusions.
b. Incorrect. Prototypes are not a process by which one draws conclusions.
*c. Correct. Availability heuristics draw conclusions from the most apparent (available). Isaac can easily recall instances of tornados, based on news reports, so he has likely used this cognitive shortcut.
d. Incorrect. Algorithms are rules for problem solution and guarantee a solution.

5. c   mod. 24 p. 265
a. Incorrect. This is an important step.
b. Incorrect. Good preparation is an important step in effective problem solving.
*c. Correct. To reach a solution, it is not necessary to document all possible solutions.
d. Incorrect. To solve a problem, one must produce at least one solution.

6. b   mod. 24 p. 266
a. Incorrect. Perhaps a problem could be so overdefined that it confused the problem solver.
*b. Correct. The answer as well as the means of solving the problem are clearly understood.
c. Incorrect. This is not a traditional way of understanding problem types.
d. Incorrect. If there were no picture on the puzzle, then it might be considered ill-defined.

7. d   mod. 24 p. 270
a. Incorrect. The text names means-ends analysis as the most common.
b. Incorrect. See answer a.
c. Incorrect. See answer a.

d. Correct. Consider how often we turn to the desired outcome and let it shape how we approach the problem.

8. d   mod. 24 p. 270
a. Incorrect. Removing the inessential may help make the definition of the problem clearer.
b. Incorrect. Making the information simpler, even putting it in a graphic form like a chart, helps make the problem easier to understand.
c. Incorrect. Dividing the problem into parts often helps define the whole problem more clearly.
*d. Correct. Clarifying the solution applies more to the later stages of solving the problem.

9. a   mod. 24 p. 271
*a. Correct. This is the definition of insight, where one becomes aware of a new or different arrangement of elements.
b. Incorrect. Insight does not suggest that an individual has no experience of a problem.
c. Incorrect. Although one might discover an algorithm for a problem through insight, it is not a necessary aspect of insight.
d. Incorrect. This refers more to brainstorming than insight.

10. d   mod. 23 p. 263
a. Incorrect. This requires complex programming.
b. Incorrect. This is an example of "d," thus not the best answer.
c. Incorrect. Heuristics require much more complicated programming.
*d. Correct. An algorithm is a set of rules that guarantees an answer.

11. b   mod. 24 p. 275
a. Incorrect. Creativity draws on knowledge and experience, but not necessarily so.
*b. Correct. Convergent thinking is defined as thinking exemplified by the use of logical reasoning and knowledge.
c. Incorrect. Divergent thinking often defies logic and is not dependent on a knowledge base.
d. Incorrect. The use of the imagination does not exemplify logical processes and is perhaps the least dependent knowledge.

12. d   mod. 24 p. 275
a. Incorrect. If the mental set is strong, it is not having any impeding effect.
b. Incorrect. Because intelligence and creativity have not been correlated, this is not necessarily true.
c. Incorrect. Exactly the opposite.

*d. Correct. Divergent thinking involves recognizing alternatives and optional uses.

13. b   mod. 25 p. 279
a. Incorrect. Semantics determines the meaning of words and phrases.
*b. Correct. Syntax refers to the meaningful structuring of sentences.
c. Incorrect. Phonology governs the production of sounds.
d. Incorrect. Somewhat broader than syntax, grammar governs the translation of thoughts into language.

14. b   mod. 25 p. 281
a. Incorrect. Speed and rate of speech are not factors in telegraphic speech.
*b. Correct. Like sending a telegraph, some words may be omitted, but the message is still clear.
c. Incorrect. The sound of the speech is not relevant to telegraphic speech.
d. Incorrect. Speed and rate of speech are not factors in telegraphic speech.

15. d   mod. 25 p. 281
a. Incorrect. At 2, children are just beginning to utilize speech and build vocabularies.
b. Incorrect. At 3, vocabulary and grammatical rules are still being acquired.
c. Incorrect. At 4, vocabulary and grammatical rules are still being acquired.
*d. Correct. By the age of 5, most children can produce grammatically correct speech.

16. a   mod. 24 p. 273
17. d   mod. 24 p. 275
18. e   mod. 24 p. 275
19. c   mod. 24 p. 275
20. b   mod. 24 p. 275

21. functional fixedness   mod. 24 p. 273
22. means-end analysis   mod. 23 p. 273
23. syntax   mod. 24 p. 279
24. Telegraphic   mod. 25 p. 281
25. Bilingualism   mod. 25 p. 287

26.
■ Describe your problem or challenge. It would be best to identify both the positive and negative aspects of the challenge (i.e., what is gained and what is given up).
■ Define the problem in terms of the steps that must be taken to achieve the solution.
■ State several possible solution strategies as they apply to your problem.

■ State how you will know when you have effectively solved the problem. Remember, if the problem is long-term, selecting one solution strategy may preclude using another.

Practice Test 2:
1. a   mod. 23 p. 258
*a. Correct. Perceptual psychologists focus on how the sensory system takes in information.
b. Incorrect. Our understanding of the world is a focal point of study for cognitive psychologists.
c. Incorrect. How we process information is a focal point of study for cognitive psychologists.
d. Incorrect. Decision making is a focal point of study for cognitive psychologists.

2. c   mod. 23 p. 261
a. Incorrect. While "prototype" may refer to a new or first type, it also refers to the template or standard.
b. Incorrect. Prototypes are neither spontaneous nor discarded quickly.
*c. Correct. In this sense, the prototype is the template or standard for a concept.
d. Incorrect. The concept described here is known as "cognate" or "loan words."

3. c   mod. 23 p. 263
a. Incorrect. Syllogistic reasoning is a formal, systematic process.
b. Incorrect. Not sure how one could use the representativeness heuristic with humor.
*c. Correct. Syllogistic reasoning does derive a conclusion from two premises, or assumptions.
d. Incorrect. An analogy may show a relationship between several concepts, but syllogistic reasoning is a form of logical reasoning; it goes beyond showing a relationship.

4. d   mod. 23 p. 263
a. Incorrect. In the availability heuristic, one applies the most available category to the situation.
b. Incorrect. A mental set is a set of expectations and inferences drawn from memory that may cause reasoning errors, but not in this manner.
c. Incorrect. Functional fixedness refers specifically to applying objects to a problem in the manner of their typical or common function, thus being fixated on a particular approach.
*d. Correct. The representative heuristic selects a category that may represent the situation but can be erroneously applied (or misapplied).

5.   b   mod. 23 p. 266
a.   Incorrect. Problems of arrangement may include puzzles and similar problems.
*b. Correct. No such type of problem!
c.   Incorrect. A problem of inducing structure involves finding relationships among existing elements.
d.   Incorrect. Transformation problems involve changing from one state to another (the goal state).

6.   a   mod. 24 p. 266
*a. Correct. True, this describes a problem of inducing structure.
b.   Incorrect. This is not one of the three types of problems and does not apply.
c.   Incorrect. An arrangement problem is more like a jigsaw puzzle, where elements are rearranged.
d.   Incorrect. A transformation problem involves moving from one state to another (goal state).

7.   a   mod. 24 p. 266
*a. Correct. Changing from one state to another is a transformation.
b.   Incorrect. This refers to another kind of problem.
c.   Incorrect. Insight is a means of solving a problem, not a type of problem (unless someone is without any insight).
d.   Incorrect. This refers to another kind of problem.

8.   b   mod. 24 p. 270
a.   Incorrect. A means-ends approach might be, "I know the steps I need to take, and I am taking them."
*b. Correct. Each step is a subgoal.
c.   Incorrect. Trial and error might be more: "I think I'll try this major next semester."
d.   Incorrect. Algorithmic approach might be, "I need three courses from this group, two from that, etc."

9.   c   mod. 24 p. 272
a.   Incorrect. Insight may be difficult to explain or articulate, and it may occur without prior experience, but these are not the defining elements.
b.   Incorrect. Insight does not result from trial-and-error processes.
*c. Correct. This sudden realization of relationship or recognition of patterns is key to insight.
d.   Incorrect. Insight may be founded on trial and error and experience, although the restructuring that occurs during insight may be independent; it may also be a result of experience or creative reorganization.

10. b   mod. 24 p. 273
a.   Incorrect. These hunches may actually make it difficult to see alternatives.
*b. Correct. Initial perceptions may include more conventional ways of using the elements of the problem and tools at hand to solve it.
c.   Incorrect. Although this is true, it does not apply to these two concepts.
d.   Incorrect. Not really sure what this means.

11. b   mod. 24 p. 275
a.   Incorrect. Convergent thinking involves logical reasoning and knowledge.
*b. Correct. Divergent thinking is the only consistently identified characteristic of creative thinking.
c.   Incorrect. Many creative thinkers are highly intelligent, but this is not a necessary characteristic.
d.   Incorrect. Recurrent thought does not characterize creativity.

12. c   mod. 25 p. 279
a.   Incorrect. Synthetics is a science fiction word used to describe synthetically produced biological organisms.
b.   Incorrect. Semantics is the study of the meanings of words.
*c. Correct. Syntax governs the order of words in a sentence.
d.   Incorrect. Systematics is a neologism (not really a word, but it sounds like one, and is probably used by a lot of people).

13. b   mod. 25 p. 280
a.   Incorrect. Babbling occurs from 3 to 6 months of age.
*b. Correct. "Dada" and "mama" are early words formed of babbling sounds.
c.   Incorrect. Babbling has many speech-like patterns.
d.   Incorrect. Babbling does produce all of the sounds humans make.

14. c   mod. 25 p. 280
a.   Incorrect. Actually, it is usual because they are among the first sounds made.
b.   Incorrect. We know of no words that are innate.
*c. Correct. These are easy and composed of sounds commonly heard in the babbling phase.
d.   Incorrect. Babies can even make sounds they have never heard before, especially if the parents' language does not include the sound.

15. b   mod. 25 p. 282
a. Incorrect. There is no linguistic relativity system; it is the linguistic relativity hypothesis, a theory about how language and thought interrelate.
*b. Correct. This is the term Noam Chomsky used to refer to this neural wiring.
c. Incorrect. The limbic system is the organization of several parts of the brain that is generally devoted to pleasure, emotion, motivation, and memory.
d. Incorrect. Sounds good, but this is not the term used, and it does not refer to any actual concept.

16. b   mod. 25 p. 281
17. c   mod. 25 p. 281
18. e   mod. 25 p. 282
19. d   mod. 25 p. 282
20. a   mod. 25 p. 282

21. divergent thinking   mod. 24 p. 275
22. linguistic relativity   mod. 25 p. 284
23. thinking   mod. 23 p. 259
24. critical period   mod. 25 p. 280
25. Symbols   mod. 25 p. 279

26.
- Chimpanzees acquire an ability to speak that is comparable to a 2-year-old child.
- The physical ability in humans to produce language has the greatest production capability.
- You may be familiar with research in dolphin and whale communication or work with other animals. Examples could be used to support your answer.
- What is meant by "unique" must be defined to complete this answer. Human language is unique, but other animals do communicate.

Practice Test 3:
1. d   mod. 23 p. 258
a. Incorrect. This is one of the components of the text's definition.
b. Incorrect. Cognition refers to the processes involved in how people come to know their world.
c. Incorrect. Cognition includes language and the interpretation of language.
*d. Correct. This statement describes the processes of sensation and perception; while not part of cognition, they are companion processes.

2. b   mod. 23 p. 261
a. Incorrect. Concepts may result from errors in some way, but they do not produce errors.
*b. Correct. Like perception, concepts help make the world understandable by simplifying and organizing it.
c. Incorrect. Even if this is true, it does not address the similarity between concepts and perception.
d. Incorrect. We know of no innate concepts.

3. b   mod. 23 p. 261
a. Incorrect. The means-ends does not apply here.
*b. Correct. Because your roommate is a member of the category of telemarketers, the representative heuristic suggests that somehow he might be representative of that group of people.
c. Incorrect. The availability heuristic would suggest that you utilized only currently available or the most prominent information about telemarketers and ignored other more important information that is easily recalled from memory. While true, you had no other information about your roommate.
d. Incorrect. There is no such heuristic.

4. a   mod. 24 p. 273
*a. Correct. Functional fixedness forces us to focus on the grill's traditional function, ignoring that it could be used as a weight or a clamp, or even an electrical conductor.
b. Incorrect. Insight is the restructuring of given elements.
c. Incorrect. Awareness seems to be restricted in this case.
d. Incorrect. Overpreparation may lead to functional fixedness by encouraging the habitual use of an object, but it is not the name of the phenomena.

5. d   mod. 24 p. 280
a. Incorrect. Grammar governs how a thought becomes language in a general sense, and a more precise possibility is given in the options.
b. Incorrect. Phonology governs the production of sounds.
c. Incorrect. Syntax refers to the structure of sentences and not their meaning.
*d. Correct. Semantics governs the use of words and sentences to make specific meanings, and would govern how the same words can be rearranged to make different meanings.

6.   b   mod. 25 p. 280
a.   Incorrect. This occurs shortly after the first major development of dropping sounds that the native language does not contain.
*b. Correct. The first thing that happens occurs when babbling sounds that are not in the native language disappear.
c.   Incorrect. This can happen at any time but becomes consistent after dropping sounds that the native language does not contain.
d.   Incorrect. This occurs after several other milestones.

7.   c   mod. 25 p. 281
a.   Incorrect. This two-word phrase has a telegraphic quality common to the language of 2-year-olds.
b.   Incorrect. This two-word phrase has a telegraphic quality common to the language of 2-year-olds.
*c. Correct. Contractions will not occur until later.
d.   Incorrect. Here is a holophrase meaning "I want you to get me more food now." It is repeated for emphasis.

8.   d   mod. 25 p. 281
a.   Incorrect. This commonly occurs in this age range.
b.   Incorrect. This is a description of telegraphic speech.
c.   Incorrect. The complexity of speech is built slowly, first by combining critical words and succeeding in communicating, and then by building on this foundation.
*d. Correct. Overgeneralization involves the use of a grammatically correct construction in more than the correct situation, like making the past tense by adding "-ed" to everything, producing the term "goed."

9.   b   mod. 25 p. 280
a.   Incorrect. Classical conditioning would be insufficient to account for language, because the language response must be, in effect, combined with new stimuli (and thus the language would need to be a preexisting response).
*b. Correct. As babbling may suggest, the language of the infant does progress through a process of successive approximations (shaping).
c.   Incorrect. A universal grammar would not require exposure to the language of the parents.
d.   Incorrect. Biological unfolding suggests an innate, rather than learned, process.

10. b   mod. 25 p. 281
a.   Incorrect. True, critics have compared the language skills of apes to other trained animals.
*b. Correct. The comparison has been made to a 2-year-old. A 5-year-old has most of the grammar skills of an adult.
c.   Incorrect. This describes one of the more common techniques used on training apes to produce communication.
d.   Incorrect. This reflects the major problem faced by apes: they do not have the correct physical apparatus for speech.

11. a   mod. 25 p. 284
*a. Correct. By having many names for turquoise, the Navaho may be able to make more refined distinctions about turquoise (thus think about it differently).
b.   Incorrect. This is a reverse statement of the linguistic relativity hypothesis and is the general view of how grammar works.
c.   Incorrect. The language-acquisition device does not address how having many words for an object would influence how we think.
d.   Incorrect. While the Navaho are considered Native Americans, this example does not support the nativist position.

12. d   mod. 25 p. 284
a.   Incorrect. If this theory existed, this might be a good definition of it.
b.   Incorrect. No such law has ever been stated.
c.   Incorrect. No such hypothesis has been named.
*d. Correct. The linguistic-relativity hypothesis states that language determines thought.

13. b   mod. 23 p. 261
a.   Incorrect. Reactions might be possible items to observe, but little about cognition could be gained from them in this study.
*b. Correct. Timing the process actually provides evidence of how different images can be formed and how people may produce images.
c.   Incorrect. After some study, the experimenter would probably find that respiration does not change much while imagining giraffes.
d.   Incorrect. Someone has been the subject of too many experiments!

14 a   mod. 23 p. 261
*a.   Correct. This example would probably come to mind more readily than the other options.
b.   Incorrect. This is not a specific example, but is instead a definition of one type of table.
c.   Incorrect. This specific table would be less familiar to you, but could serve as a prototype for someone else.
d.   Incorrect. This is not a specific example, but is instead a definition of one type of table.

15. b   mod. 24 p. 271
16. c   mod. 23 p. 258
17. a   mod. 23 p. 261
18. d   mod. 25 p. 284
19. e   mod. 24 p. 275

20. means-end analysis   mod. 24 p. 270
21. subgoals   mod. 24 p. 270
22. Confirmation bias   mod. 24 p. 275
23. overgeneralization   mod. 25 p. 281
24. cognitive complexity   mod. 24 p. 276

25. Positive:
  • Attempts to teach immigrants subject material in their own language and slowly adding English instruction.
  • Respecting their cultural differences by acknowledging their language illustrates value for their cultural heritage.
  • Supporters quote research stating that maintaining a native language will not interfere with learning English.
  • Bilingual children score higher on intelligence and achievement tests.
Negative:
  • Those not in favor say bilingual children will be left behind in school and the workplace.

Chapter 9: Intelligence

Module 26: What Is Intelligence?
Module 27: Variations in Intellectual Ability
Module 28: Group Differences in Intelligence: Genetic and Environmental Determinants

Overview

In this set of modules, we consider intelligence in many varieties. Intelligence represents a focal point for psychologists intent on understanding how people adapt to their environment. It is also a key aspect of how individuals differ from one another.

Module 26 deals with the various conceptions of intelligence that have been offered by psychologists and the efforts made to develop standardized tests to measure it. Fluid and crystallized intelligence, multiple intelligences, the information-processing approaches, and practical intelligence are discussed. Intelligence tests such as the Stanford-Binet, the Wechsler Adult Intelligence Test, and other achievement and aptitude tests are explained.

Module 27 discusses both the retarded and the gifted, two groups who display extremes in individual differences. Both their challenges and the programs developed to meet these challenges are presented.

Module 28 considers how and to what degree intelligence is influenced by heredity and by the environment and whether traditional intelligence tests are biased toward the dominant cultural groups in society.

To further investigate the topics covered in this chapter, you can visit the related Web sites by visiting the following link: www.mhhe.com/feldmanup8.

Prologue: Chris Burke and Sho Yano
Looking Ahead

Module 26:
What is Intelligence?

Theories of Intelligence: Are There Different Kinds of Intelligence?
The Biological Basis of Intelligence:
Practical Intelligence and Emotional Intelligence: Toward a More Intelligent View of Intelligence

> **Applying Psychology in the 21st Century:**
> How You Think About Intelligence Helps Determine Your Success

Assessing Intelligence

> **Becoming an Informed Consumer of Psychology:** Scoring Better on Standardized Tests

- ***What are the different definitions and conceptions of intelligence?***
- ***What are the major approaches to measuring intelligence, and what do intelligence tests measure?***

What Is Intelligence?

Laypersons have clear ideas about what constitutes intelligence, although their views are related to their culture. Psychologists have defined **[a]** _____ somewhat similarly to laypersons; most say it involves the capacity to understand the world, think rationally, and use resources effectively.

There are many different theories as to the ways to conceptualize intelligence. Early psychologists, such as Spearman, assumed that intelligence was composed of a single, general factor indicative of mental ability. This single factor was called **[b]** _____, and was thought to be the root of performance in all aspects of intelligence.

Recently, most psychologists have accepted the idea that intelligence is multidimensional, or composed of many factors. Some psychologists propose two different kinds of intelligence.

They are **[c]** _____, the ability to deal with new problems and situations, and

[d] _____, the store of information, skills, and strategies acquired through experience.

In an alternate formulation, Howard Gardner has a theory of eight **[e]** _____:
(1) musical intelligence; (2) bodily-kinesthetic intelligence; (3) logical-mathematical intelligence; (4) linguistic intelligence; (5) spatial intelligence; (6) interpersonal intelligence; (7) intrapersonal intelligence; and (8) naturalist intelligence. Gardner suggests that all people have

the same eight intelligences, although to varying degrees. He also suggests that these separate intelligences do not operate in isolation. Results from Gardner's work include the acceptance of more than one answer as correct on a test.

The **[f]** _____ to intelligence views intelligence as the ability to process information. New research in this area has demonstrated that people who score higher on intelligences tests generally spend more time in the encoding stage of problems as well as retrieve information from memory more quickly. Effective problem solvers have traditionally been those who also score high on intelligence tests.

[g] _____ grows from Sternberg's attention to the practical demands of everyday life. One of the problems is that although IQ tests predict performance in school, they do not correlate with career success. Several tests have been designed that measure practical intelligence in the business world. Sternberg also describes the importance of _analytical_ and _creative_ intelligences, which are distinct from practical intelligence.

Finally, some psychologists have focused on intelligence as it plays out in the emotional realm. **[h]** _____ involves the accurate assessment and evaluation of others' emotions, the effective expression of emotions, and regulation of emotions. It is the basis of empathy, self-awareness, and social skills.

Alfred Binet developed the first formal **[i]** _____ to identify the "dullest" students in the Parisian school system. His test was able to distinguish the "bright" from the "dull" and eventually made distinctions between age groups. The tests helped assign children a(n) **[j]** _____, the average age of children who achieved the same score. In order to compare individuals with different _chronological ages_, the

[k] _____ score was determined by dividing the mental age by the chronological age and multiplying by a factor of 100. Thus an IQ score is determined by the level at which a person performs on the test in relation to others of the same age.

The SAT is a(n) **[l]** _____ meant to determine the level of achievement of an individual; that is, what the person has actually learned. A(n) **[m]** _____ measures and predicts an individual's ability in a particular area. There is quite a bit of overlap among the IQ, achievement, and aptitude tests.

Psychological tests must have **[n]** _____; that is, they must measure something consistently from time to time. The question of whether a test measures the characteristic it is supposed to measure is called **[o]** _____. If a test is reliable, that does not mean it is valid. However, if a test is unreliable, it cannot be valid. A reliable test will produce similar outcomes in similar conditions. All types of tests in psychology, including intelligence tests, assessments of psychological disorders, and the measurement of attitudes, must meet tests of validity and reliability. **[p]** _____ are the standards of test performance that allow comparison of the scores of one test-taker to others who have taken it. This standard for a test is determined by calculating the average score for a particular group of people for whom the test is designed to be given. Then, the extent to which each person's score differs from the others can be calculated. The selection of the subjects who will be used to establish a norm for a test is critical.

273

Evaluate

_____ 1. intelligence tests

_____ 2. Stanford-Binet Test

_____ 3. Wechsler Adult
Intelligence Scale-III
(WAIS-III)

_____ 4. Wechsler Intelligence
Scale for Children-III
(WISC-III)

a. A test of intelligence consisting of verbal and nonverbal performance sections, providing a relatively precise picture of a person's specific abilities.

b. A test of intelligence that includes a series of items varying in nature according to the age of the person being tested.

c. A battery of measures to determine a person's level of intelligence.

d. An intelligence test for children consisting of verbal and nonverbal performance sections, providing a relatively precise picture of a child's specific abilities.

Rethink

26-1 What is the role of emotional intelligence in the classroom? How might emotional intelligence be tested? Should emotional intelligence be a factor in determining academic promotion to the next grade?

26-2 From the human resource specialist's perspective: Job interviews are really a kind of test. In what ways does a job interview resemble an aptitude test? An achievement test? Do you think job interviews can be made to have validity and reliability?

Spotlight on Terminology and Language—ESL Pointers

Page 289 "Although their destination may be just a small dot of land less than a mile wide, the Trukese are able to sail unerringly toward it without the aid of a compass, chronometer, **sextant**, or any of the other sailing tools that are indispensable to modern Western navigation."

A **sextant** is a tool used by sailors to plan and direct their travels.

Page 289 "They are able to sail accurately, even when prevailing winds do not allow a direct approach to the island and they must take a **zigzag** course (Gladwin, 1964; Mytinger, 2001)."

A **zigzag course** is one that repeatedly switches directions sharply.

Page 289 "Some might say that the inability of the Trukese to explain in Western terms how their sailing technique works is a sign of **primitive** or even unintelligent behavior."

Primitive behavior relates to an early or original state and is often marked by simplicity or an unsophisticated manner.

Page 289 "For years they have **grappled** with the issue of devising a general definition of intelligence."

When we **grapple** with something we are struggling or having difficulty accepting it.

Page 290 "Interestingly, **laypersons** have fairly clear ideas of what intelligence is, although the nature of their ideas is related to their culture."

A **layperson** is someone who has detailed knowledge about a topic, but who has not received specialized training in it.

Page 293 "For example, according to the findings of cognitive scientist John Duncan and colleagues, the brains of people completing intelligence test questions in both verbal and spatial domains show **activation** in a similar location: the lateral prefrontal cortex."

This means the lateral prefrontal cortex becomes **active**, begins to operate; things are set in motion.

Page 294 "People who are high in practical intelligence are able to learn general **norms** and principles and apply them appropriately."

A **norm** is a standard pattern of behavior that is considered normal in a particular society. Have you found that you are able to adapt to the **norms** of various cultures?

Page 294 "Some psychologists broaden the concept of practical intelligence even further beyond the intellectual **realm** and consider intelligence involving emotions."

Realm is the defined area of interest. Some psychologists are suggesting that practical intelligence is a robust characteristic.

Page 297 "If performance on certain tasks or test items improved with **chronological** or physical age, performance could be used to distinguish more intelligent people from less intelligent ones within a particular age group."

When something is arranged **chronologically**, it is arranged in order of time of occurrence. **Chrono** or **chron** is a prefix relating to time.

Page 297 "On the basis of this principle, Binet devised the first **formal** intelligence test, which was designed to identify the "dullest" students in the Paris school system in order to provide them with remedial aid."

Formal here relates to the official and prescribed nature of the design of this intelligence test.

Page 297 "By using mental age alone, for instance, we might assume that a 20-year-old responding at a 18-year-old's level would be as bright as a 5-year-old answering at a 3-year-old's level, when actually the 5-year-old would be displaying a much greater **relative** degree of slowness."

Relative means dependent on or interconnected with something else for significance or intelligibility. The text example expresses why mental age is **relative** to chronological age.

Page 298 "As you can see in Figure 5, when IQ scores from large numbers of people are **plotted** on a graph, they form a *bell-shaped distribution* (called "bell-shaped" because it looks like a bell when plotted)."

To **plot** something is to mark it on a graph.

Page 298 "**Remnants** of Binet's original intelligence test are still with us, although the test has been revised in significant ways."

Remnants are pieces. Some of the components of Binet's test remain in use today.

Page 298 "An examiner begins by finding a mental age level at which a person is able to answer all the questions correctly, and then moves on to **successively** more difficult problems."

Successively is to follow in order or sequence.

Page 300 "However, **sacrifices** are made in group testing that in some cases may **outweigh the benefits**."

Sacrifices are things that you forfeit for another thing thought to be of greater value. Students frequently **sacrifice** sleep and social activities to study and earn high grades.

If you have **outweighed the benefits**, you have sacrificed too much.

Page 301 "Finally, in some cases, it is simply impossible to **employ** group tests, particularly with young children or people with unusually low IQs (Aiken, 1996)."

To **employ** group tests would be to use them.

Page 302 "Test validity and reliability are **prerequisites** for accurate assessment of intelligence – as well as for any other measurement task carried out by psychologists."

A **prerequisite** is something that is required as a prior condition. To take many courses in college, you first must take a **prerequisite**, a course that teaches you the skills you must have to enter the next course.

Page 302 "**Norms** are standards of test performance that permit the comparison of one person's score on a test to the scores of others who have taken the same test."

Norms are standards that allow you to compare one item to another.

Page 303 "Because computerized adaptive testing **pinpoints** a test-taker's level of **proficiency** fairly quickly, the total time spent taking the exam is shorter than it is with a traditional exam."

When an exam **pinpoints** skill level, it is identifying skill level in a very precise and accurate manner.

Proficiency is the level at which you are able to perform. If you are highly **proficient** is a skill, you may be considered an expert.

Module 27: Variations in Intellectual Ability

Mental Retardation
The Intellectually Gifted

- **How can the extremes of intelligence be characterized?**
- **How can we help people reach their full potential?**

Variations in Intellectual Ability

More than 7 million people in the United States are classified as mentally retarded, and the populations that comprise the mentally retarded and the exceptionally gifted require special attention in order to reach their potential.

[a] _____ is defined by the American Association on Mental Retardation (2002) as a disability in which the person shows "significant limitations both in intellectual functioning existing and in conceptual, social, and practical adaptive skills." Despite this definition, mental retardation is difficult to measure, particularly the extent to which people lack conceptual, social, and practical skills. In terms of the relationship between retardation and scores on traditional, standardized intelligence tests, [b] _____ *retardation* includes individuals whose IQ scores fall in the 55 to 69 range. This comprises about 90 percent of the people with mental retardation. [c] _____ *retardation*, with scores ranging from 40 to 54; [d] _____ *retardation*, with scores from 25 to 39; and

[e] _____ *retardation*, with scores below 25, present difficulties that become more pronounced the lower the IQ score.

The moderately retarded typically require some supervision during their entire lives, and the severe and profound groups typically require institutionalization. One-third of the people classified as retarded suffer from biological causes of retardation, mostly from

[f] _____. Another major biological cause is [g] _____, a genetic disorder caused by an extra chromosome. [h] _____ occurs in cases when there is no biological cause but instead may be linked with a family history of retardation. This may be caused by environmental factors like severe poverty, malnutrition, and possibly a genetic factor that cannot be determined.

In 1975, Congress passed a law (Public Law 94–142) that entitles individuals who are mentally retarded to a full education and to education and training in the [i] _____. This law leads to a process of returning individuals to regular classrooms, called

[j] _____. The view is that by placing individuals in typical environments, they interact with individuals who are not retarded and benefit from the interaction.

The **[k]** _____ comprise about 2 to 4 percent of the population. This group is generally identified as those individuals with IQ scores higher than 130. Contrary to the stereotype, these individuals are usually outgoing, well-adjusted, popular people who do most things better than the average person. Lewis Terman conducted a well-known longitudinal study following 1,500 gifted children (with IQs above 140). They have an impressive record of accomplishments, although being gifted does not guarantee success.

Evaluate

_____ 1. severe retardation

_____ 2. profound retardation

_____ 3. Down syndrome

_____ 4. familial retardation

_____ 5. intellectually gifted

a. Characterized by an IQ between 25 and 39 and difficulty in functioning independently.

b. Mental retardation in which there is a history of retardation in a family but no evidence of biological causes.

c. Characterized by higher-than-average intelligence, with IQ scores above 130.

d. A common cause of mental retardation, brought about by the presence of an extra chromosome.

e. Characterized by an IQ below 25 and an inability to function independently.

Rethink

27-1   Why do you think negative stereotypes persist of gifted individuals and people with mental retardation, even in the face of contrary evidence? How can these stereotypes be changed?

27-2   What advantages and disadvantages do you think full-inclusion programs would present for students with mental retardation? For students without mental retardation?

Spotlight on Terminology and Language—ESL Pointers

Page 307 "Daniel responded, **deftly** punching in his answers on the computer's numeric key-pad."

Deftly is skillfully.

Page 307 "The computer **tallied** the results."

The results were computed, or added up; they were **tallied**.

Page 307 "Although sometimes thought of as a rare **phenomenon**, mental retardation occurs in 1 to 3 percent of the population."

A **phenomenon** is an occurrence.

Page 307 "There is wide variation among those labeled as mentally retarded, in large part because of the **inclusiveness** of the definition developed by the American Association on Mental Retardation (AAMR)."

Inclusiveness is completeness, thoroughness. The AAMR definition of mental retardation is extensive and comprehensive.

Page 308 "For people with moderate retardation, deficits are obvious early with language and motor skills **lagging** behind those of peers."

When a student is **lagging** behind, they are falling behind. Individuals with mental retardation develop or progress more slowly.

Page 308 "The law increased the educational opportunities for individuals with mental retardation, **facilitating** their integration into regular classrooms as much as possible – a process known as mainstreaming (Lloyd, Kameenui, & Chard, 1997; Katsiyannis, Zhang, & Archwamety, 2002)."

The law helped these students return to the regular classroom, if only for part of the school day. **Facilitating** is to make something easier to do.

Page 309 "However, full inclusion is a **controversial** practice, and it is not widely applied (Kavale, 2002; Hastings & Oakford, 2003; Praisner, 2003)."

When something is **controversial**, is provokes strong disagreements, or arguments. Can you identify some **controversial** topics that have been debated and discussed in your college classes?

Page 309 "Although special programs attempting to overcome the deficits of people with mental retardation **abound**, programs targeted at the intellectually gifted are rare."

Abound means that there are many of these special programs for those individuals with mental retardation.
Page 309 "More **enlightened** approaches, however, have acknowledged that without some form of special attention, the gifted become bored and frustrated with the pace of their schooling and may never react their potential."

Enlightened means open-minded. An **enlightened** person is often well informed and has access to all of the facts.

Module 28: Group Differences in Intelligence: Genetic and Environmental Determinants

Exploring Diversity: The Relative Influence of Genetics and Environment: Nature, Nurture, and IQ

Placing the Heredity-Environment Question in Perspective

- ***Are traditional IQ tests culturally biased?***
- ***Are there racial differences in intelligence?***
- ***To what degree is intelligence influenced by the environment, and to what degree by heredity?***

Group Differences in Intelligence: Genetic and Environmental Determinants

In the determination of the causes of individual differences, cultural differences in the framing of questions on a test can play an important role. On **[a]** _____, some culture and ethnic groups score lower than others, as with African Americans, who tend to score 15 points lower than whites. One view suggests that the tests are biased toward Western individualism and against African communalism. Because of the possibility of bias and discrimination, some jurisdictions have banned the use of traditional intelligence tests.

Attempts to develop a(n) **[b]** _____ IQ test that does not discriminate have led in some cases to even greater disparities in scores. The controversy based on ethnic and minority differences in intelligence tests reflects a greater concern of whether intelligence is predominantly a result of genetics or environment. On the genetics side, the explanation for lower performance by a population would be that they are less intelligent as a result of genetics. The debate reached a major peak with the publication of Murray and Herrnstein's

[c] _____, which argues that the difference between white and African-American IQ scores could not be explained by environmental differences because even when socioeconomic factors were considered, the difference did not disappear. Intelligence does show

a high degree of **[d]** _____, the measure of the extent to which a characteristic is related to genetic, inherited factors. The closer two people are linked genetically, the closer their IQ scores are likely to be. Critics of *The Bell Curve* have argued, with the support

of many psychologists, that such a factor as **[e]** _____ is highly variable from one household to another, even when group differences in SES are held constant.

Other research has demonstrated that African Americans raised in enriched environments similar to whites do not have lower IQ scores. The real differences between IQ scores cannot be examined in terms of differences in the mean scores between groups, such as racial or cultural groups, but must be understood as the difference between individuals.

The issue of genetics and environment is one in which experimental research that might establish causal relationships cannot be devised because of ethical issues. A question that should be of concern is how we can maximize the potential intellectual development of individuals.

Evaluate

_____ 1. *The Bell Curve*

_____ 2. culture-fair tests

_____ 3. Flynn effect

_____ 4. heritability

a. IQ tests in which questions assess experiences common in all cultures or do not make use of language.

b. The degree to which a characteristic can be explained by genetic factors.

c. A controversial book which described IQ differences between blacks and whites.

d. The significant rise in average IQ scores since the early 1900s.

Rethink

28-1   What ideas do you have for explaining the Flynn effect, the steady rise in IQ scores over the past half-century? How would you test your ideas?

28-2   *From a college admissions officer's perspective:* Imagine that you notice that students who are members of minority groups systematically receive lower scores on standardized college entrance exams. What suggestions do you have for helping these students improve their scores? What advice about their college applications would you give these students to help them be competitive applicants?

Spotlight on Terminology and Language—ESL Pointers

Page 311 "And if such types of questions were included on an IQ test, a critic could rightly **contend** that the test had more to do with prior experience than with intelligence."

A critic could argue or **contend** that the test was not fair.

Page 311 "Does this reflect a true difference in intelligence, or are the questions **biased** in regard to the kinds of knowledge they test."
Are the questions **biased**; are they unfair?

Page 311 "Furthermore, tests may include even **subtler** forms of bias against minority groups."

When something is **subtle**, it is slight and not very obvious.

Page 311 "For example, psychologist Janet Helms (1992) argues that assessments of cognitive ability developed in the United States are sometimes **constructed** to favor responses that implicitly reflect North American or European values, customs, or traditions."

These assessment tools are built, or **constructed**, in such a fashion as to favor one group over another.

Page 312 "More specifically, Helms suggests that the traditional Western value of "**rugged** individualism" means that correct answers to test items may require a test taker to reason independently of a particular social context."

A **rugged** individual would be strong and tough.

Page 312 "The efforts of psychologists to produce culture-fair measures on intelligence relate to a **lingering** controversy over differences in intelligence between members of minority and majority groups."

A **lingering** controversy is persistent and enduring. This **lingering** controversy has existed for a long time.

Page 312 "Richard Herrnstein, a psychologist, and Charles Murray, a sociologist, **fanned the flames** of the debate with the publication of their book *The Bell Curve* in the mid-1990s (Herrnstein & Murray, 1994)."

To **fan the flames** is to fuel the idea, to stir up the controversy.

Page 313 "Furthermore, no one can convincingly **assert** that the living conditions of blacks and whites are identical even when their socioeconomic status is similar."

No one can **assert** this declaration. They cannot convincingly declare this, or make the case that this is true.

Page 313 "Moreover, blacks who are raised in economically **enriched** environments have similar IQ scores to whites in comparable environments."

An **enriched** environment is an improved environment, an enhanced environment.

Page 313 "In short, the evidence that genetic factors play the major role in determining racial differences in IQ is not compelling, although the question still **evokes** considerable controversy (Neisser et al., 1996; Myerson et al., Fish, 2002)."

The debate on these questions and their theoretical support **evokes**, or stirs up, particular reactions and feelings.

Page 315 "The more critical question to ask, then, is not whether hereditary or environmental factors primarily underlie intelligence, but whether there is anything we can do to **maximize** the intellectual development of each individual."

To **maximize** is to make the most of. When you **maximize** a score, you make it as high as possible.

Practice Tests

Test your knowledge of the material in this set of modules by answering these questions. These questions have been placed in three Practice Tests. The first two tests consist of questions that will test your recall of factual knowledge. The third test contains questions that are challenging and primarily test for conceptual knowledge and your ability to apply that knowledge. Check your answers and review the feedback using the Answer Key on the following pages of the *Study Guide*.

PRACTICE TEST 1:

1.   The basic elements of intelligence include:
    a.   social competence, assertiveness, and innate knowledge.
    b.   algorithmic skill, verbal ability, and thrift.
    c.   perceptual speed, focal attention, and problem-solving skill.
    d.   capacity to understand, think rationally, and use resources effectively when facing challenges.

2.   The measure of intelligence that takes into consideration both mental and chronological age is called the:
    a.   achievement scale.   c.   intelligence quotient.
    b.   aptitude level.   d.   g-factor.

3.   To aid classroom teachers, school psychologists generally have relied on _____ in order to distinguish more intelligent from less intelligent people.
    a   intelligence tests   c.   achievement tests
    b.   genealogy   d.   projective tests

4.   On Alfred Binet's IQ test, suppose that an 8-year-old child can solve the problems that an average 10-year-old can solve. Her chronological age would be:
    a.   8.   c.   12.
    b.   10.   d.   impossible to judge from these data.

5.   The Wechsler Intelligence Tests provides scores in two areas:
    a.   visual and conceptual.   c.   performance and verbal.
    b.   spatial and verbal.   d.   performance and spatial.

6.   Andrew said, "I retook that last test three times, and my score was incredibly different each time." The test he described was:
    a.   invalid.   c.   culturally biased.
    b.   unreliable.   d.   subscaled.

7.   Maureen was asked to take a(n) _____ designed to measure her level of knowledge in a given subject area.
    a.   motor skills test   c.   aptitude test
    b.   personality test   d.   achievement test

8.   Crystallized intelligence is a reflection of a person's _____ .
    a.   heredity   c.   culture

b. nutrition and diet   d. native intelligence

9. Which is **not** one of Gardner's eight types of intelligence?
    a. Technical   c. Linguistic
    b. Interpersonal   d. Logical-mathematical

10. Which approach do cognitive psychologists use to understand intelligence?
    a. Structure-of-intellect   c. Aptitude-testing
    b. Deviation IQ   d. Information-processing

11. Sternberg's research in the area of intelligence has found that intelligence as traditionally measured and success in business:
    a. are strongly correlated.   c. cannot be correlated.
    b. are minimally correlated.   d. are inversely correlated.

12. Significant limitations in intellectual functioning accompanied by deficits in adaptive behavior defines:
    a. savant syndrome.   c. mental retardation.
    b. profound retardation.   d. severe retardation.

13. The biological cause of Down syndrome is:
    a. physical trauma to the fetus during pregnancy.
    b. poisoning of the mother by toxins during particular intervals of the pregnancy when the fetus is very sensitive to those chemicals.
    c. poisoning of the fetus by alcohol consumed by the pregnant mother.
    d. an extra chromosome segment in each cell of the body.

14. Familial retardation:
    a. results from hereditary factors.
    b. results from environmental factors.
    c. is a paradox because there are no known hereditary or environmental causes.
    d. may result from either hereditary or environmental factors, although there are no known biological causes.

15. Children who have been diagnosed as retarded have the opportunity to participate in mainstreaming, which means:
    a. more opportunities to relate to other students who are retarded.
    b. increased opportunities for education and socialization.
    c. the exclusion of other students who are retarded from the classroom.
    d. separating retarded and other students.

_____ 16. validity   a. Suggests a strong role of heredity in intelligence.

_____ 17. *The Bell Curve*   b. When a person is given the same test on two different occasions, test-retest.

_____ 18. cultural bias
                                   c. The extent to which a test measures what it is supposed to measure.
_____ 19. reliability

                                   d. Characteristics on tests that favor one group over

another.

20. _____ is characterized by an IQ of between 55 and 69 and the ability to function independently.

21. Frederick's mental age is the same as his chronological age. His IQ score is _____.

22. The WAIS III and the WISC-III intelligence tests are different fro, the Stanford-Binet because they include both a verbal score and a(n) _____ score.

23. Congress passed Public Law 94-172 to provide that people with mental retardation must be educated and trained in the _____ environment.

24. The Terman Study has followed 1,500 _____ for more than 60 years.

25. Describe and outline the definitions of intelligence offered in the text. Which of these do you find most acceptable? Support your view with examples or other evidence. What additional evidence would be required to strengthen the validity of the definition you have chosen?

PRACTICE TEST 2:

1. Intelligence is most clearly defined as:
    a. the ability to understand subject matters from different disciplines in an academic setting.
    b. a complex capability in humans and animals that allows them to think, act, and function adaptively.
    c. the capacity to understand the world, think rationally, and use resources effectively when faced with challenges.
    d. a multidimensional human capability that is determined by a person's heredity and environment.

2. The intelligence quotient was developed to:
    a. increase the reliability of the early intelligence tests.
    b. provide a way to compare the performance of French and American children on intelligence tests.
    c. permit meaningful comparisons of intelligence among people of different ages.
    d. correct a systematic scoring error in the first American intelligence tests.

3. The first IQ test was devised to:
    a. diagnose brain damage.
    b. identify slow learners for remedial teaching.
    c. screen applicants for medical school.
    d. select candidates for a school for the intellectually gifted.

4. Spearman's theoretical component that underlies mental ability is called:
    a. the g-factor.   c. the X-file.
    b. fluid intelligence.   d. crystallized intelligence.

5. The full range of scores on standardized IQ tests, ascribed to normal intelligence, is from:
    a. 50 to 150.   c. 0 to 100.

b.   85 to 115.   d.   70 to 130.

6. If an individual's test scores vary greatly from one session to the next, it is likely that the test is:
   a.   invalid but reliable.   c.   nomothetic.
   b.   unreliable.   d.   ideographic.

7. As part of the application process for college, Timothy was required to take an aptitude test designed to:
   a.   predict future performance.   c.   measure intelligence.
   b.   measure achievement in certain areas.   d.   calculate the g-factor.

8. Gardner suggested that we have eight types of intelligence. Which of the following is **not** among them?
   a.   General information intelligence   c.   Spatial intelligence
   b.   Musical intelligence   d.   Interpersonal intelligence

9. Among Gardner's suggested intelligences, which intelligence is described as "skill in interacting with others such as sensitivity to moods"?
   a.   Linguistic   c.   Interpersonal
   b.   Bodily-kinesthetic   d.   Intrapersonal

10. Mental retardation is primarily defined by:
    a.   ability to get along in the world and with other people.
    b.   deficits in intellectual functioning and adaptive behavior.
    c.   ability to perform in school.
    d.   ability to perform on intelligence tests.

11. The _____ approach to understanding intelligence emphasizes processes.
    a.   cognitive   c.   environmental
    b.   learning   d.   physiological

12. IQ scores falling below _____ fit one of the criterion for mental retardation.
    a.   80   c.   60
    b.   70   d.   50

13. Most cases of mental retardation are classified as being caused by:
    a.   Down syndrome.   c.   Kleinfelter syndrome.
    b.   familial retardation.   d.   traumatic injury.

14. Mentally retarded individuals who are classified as _____ retarded have the best prospects for successful mainstreaming.
    a.   mildly   c.   severely
    b.   moderately   d.   profoundly

15. Raphael and Alix were told that their youngsters have very high IQs and:
    a.   are gifted in every academic subject.
    b.   will have adjustment problems later in life.
    c.   should not be mainstreamed.
    d.   should show better social adjustment in school than others.

_____ 16. David Wechsler

_____ 17. Spearman

_____ 18. Howard Gardner

_____ 19. Binet

_____ 20. Sternberg

a. Suggested there were eight factors of intelligence called primary mental abilities.

b. First designed IQ tests with verbal and performance scales.

c. Argues for the importance of practical intelligence.

d. Assumed there was a general factor for mental ability, the g-factor.

e. Devised the first formal intelligence test.

22. Standards of test performance that permit comparison of one person's score on the test to the scores of others who have taken the same test are called _____.

23. A measure of intelligence that takes into account the person's mental and chronological ages is called _____.

24. _____ hypothesized that head configuration, being genetically determined, was related to brain size, and therefore related to intelligence.

25. The hypothesis of _____ stated that if performance on certain tasks or test items improved with chronological age, or physical age, then performance could be used to distinguish more intelligent from less intelligent ones within a particular age.

26. A person with an IQ score between 40 and 54 would be considered to have _____ retardation.

27. Outline the basic issues involved in the genetics versus environment debate. The text suggests that the more important concern is how to maximize intelligence. Considering the concepts introduced so far on the text, what methods ought to be considered in our efforts to reach our fullest intelligence potential?

PRACTICE TEST 3: Conceptual, Applied, and Challenging Questions

1. Helen is an 8-year-old child who has received a score on an IQ test that is usually achieved by a typical 10-year-old. Helen's IQ is:
   - a. 80.
   - b. 100.
   - c. 125.
   - d. 180.

2. Historically, the formula _____ is used to calculate ratio IQ.
   - a. $CA + MA \times 100 = IQ$
   - b. $CA \div MA \times .01 = IQ$
   - c. $MA \div CA \times 100 = IQ$
   - d. $(MA - CA) \div 100 = IQ$

3. Using standard testing procedures and the IQ formula, which of the following will have the highest IQ?
   - a. A 12-year-old with a mental age of 10
   - b. A 10-year-old with a mental age of 12
   - c. A 25-year-old with a mental age of 23
   - d. A 23-year-old with a mental age of 25

4. Of these first intelligence test statements, which is **not** correct?
   - a. It was designed to identify the "gifted" children in the school system.
   - b. It was developed by Alfred Binet in France.
   - c. It assumed that performance on certain items and tasks improved with age.
   - d. Many items were selected for the test when "bright" and "dull" students scored differently on them.

5. About two-thirds of all people have IQ scores of:
   - a. 95–105.
   - b. 90–110.
   - c. 85–115.
   - d. 70–110.

6. Which of the following is **not** one of the verbal subtests on the Wechsler intelligence scale?
   - a. Information
   - b. Similarities
   - c. Block design
   - d. Vocabulary

7. The administration of the Stanford-Binet test is ended when:
   - a. all items have been administered.
   - b. the person misses a total of five items.
   - c. the person misses a total of 10 items.
   - d. the person cannot answer any more questions.

8. Which of the following is **not** one of the performance subtests on the Wechsler intelligence scale?
   - a. Comprehension
   - b. Picture completion
   - c. Object assembly
   - d. Digit symbol

9. Solving a problem using your own experience as a basis for the solution uses:
   - a. availability heuristics.
   - b. crystallized intelligence.
   - c. fluid intelligence.
   - d. g-factors.

10. Robert Sternberg theorized that intelligence:
    - a. has three aspects: practical, analytic, and creative.
    - b. proposes that a brain organ is the central processor of intelligence.
    - c. emphasizes the importance of divergent reasoning in creativity.

d. was first developed from animal research and then applied to humans.

11. Which of the following situations best illustrates reliability as a quality of psychological tests?
    a. A prospective Air Force pilot takes a test, passes it, and becomes an excellent pilot.
    b. A college student studies diligently for an important exam and earns an A on it.
    c. A psychiatric patient takes a psychological test that yields the diagnosis that was suspected.
    d. A mentally retarded patient takes an intelligence test on Monday and again on Tuesday, getting the same result on each administration.

12. Johnny, who is an expert mason, takes a test that has been designed to assess brick-laying skills. He scores very poorly on the test. Because others have observed that he is an expert mason, the test he took could be said to have:
    a. good validity.
    b. poor validity.
    c. poor reliability.
    d. good reliability.

13. Professor Spielbauer has been developing a test that will predict how well his 20-year-old students will do in their intended careers. He has been attempting to correlate factors related to social relationships, emotional health, and initiative with later work success. His views are most compatible with which of the following concepts?
    a. Multiple intelligences
    b. Practical intelligence
    c. Information processing
    d. Constructive thinking

14. Jessica likes to organize activities for her brothers and her dolls. She often takes charge of playtime with other children her age. In Gardner's view, her social competence would be considered most like that of which of the following?
    a. A surgeon
    b. A scientist
    c. A musician
    d. Anne Sullivan

_____ 15. familial

_____ 16. standardization

_____ 17. gifted

_____ 18. practical intelligence

_____ 19. emotional intelligence

a. Three criteria required of an instrument for measuring intelligence are validity, reliability, and _____.

b. When there is no evidence of a physical cause, retardation is _____.

c. One who is precocious, independent, and seems driven to perfect her skills.

d. The set of skills that underlie the accurate assessment, evaluation, expression, and regulation of emotions.

e. Intelligence related to overall success in living.

20. Dr. Finelli insisted that Megan, a student with special needs, be integrated into regular classroom activities. This is called _____.

21. A main shortcoming of the Stanford-Binet IQ test is the focus on _____.

22. Most school systems administer group intelligence tests because the primary advantage is the _____ of administration.

23. The _____ is the phenomenon that demonstrates that the number of correct answers for the average person has risen significantly in the past several generations.

24. In Terman's longitudinal study of the gifted, he found that at 40 years of age, the _____ reported more life satisfaction than the _____.

25. Certain companies use measures of intelligence to exclude people from employment. Discuss both positive and negative aspects of this policy for child care workers, air traffic controllers, and health care professionals.

■ ANSWER KEY: MODULES 26, 27, AND 28

Module 26:		Module 27:	Module 28:
[a] Intelligence	[i] intelligence tests	[a] Mental retardation	[a] standardized
[b] g, or g-factor	[j] mental age	[b] Mild	intelligence test
[c] fluid intelligence	[k] intelligence	[c] Moderate	[b] culture-fair
[d] crystallized	quotient	[d] severe	[c] *The Bell Curve*
intelligence	[l] achievement test	[e] profound	[d] heritability
[e] multiple	[m] aptitude test	[f] Fetal Alcohol Syndrome	[e] socioeconomic
intelligences	[n] reliability	[g] Down syndrome	status
[f] information	[o] validity	[h] Familial retardation	
processing approach	[p] Norms	[i] least restrictive	Evaluate
[g] Practical		environment	1. c
intelligence	Evaluate	[j] mainstreaming	2. a
[h] Emotional	1. c	[k] intellectually gifted	3. d
intelligence	2. b		4. b
	3. a	Evaluate	
	4. d	1. a	
		2. e	
		3. d	
		4. b	
		5. c	

Selected Rethink Answers

26-2   To some extent, job interviews assess past knowledge, such as information mastered in school. In that way, they resemble achievement tests. However, employers are also interested in predicting how job candidates are likely to perform on the job in the future, so in that way, interviews resemble aptitude tests. Employers might give job candidates hypothetical scenarios of various job situations (e.g., for a sales job, "An irate customer is unhappy with a purchase, and is yelling loudly that she wants to return the item. What would you do to assist her? How would you behave?") to determine how job candidates are likely to perform on the job. Interviews can be made to have better reliability and validity if there is consistency in how questions are ordered and worded, and how responses interviewees provide are evaluated and scored.

27-2   **Full inclusion for students with mental retardation**
        Advantages: Social integration
                            Role models
                            Programs provide a challenge
        Disadvantages: Frustration that they can't keep up with peers
                            Risk of social isolation
        Full inclusion for students without mental retardation
        Advantages: Increasing awareness of the heterogeneous nature of the human race
                            Development of empathy
                            Peer tutoring may help them better understand materials themselves
        Disadvantages: Take extra time in class
                            Can be disruptive

Practice Test 1:

1. d   mod. 26 p. 294
a. Incorrect. Few people accept a notion of innate knowledge.
b. Incorrect. Thrift is not associated with intelligence.
c. Incorrect. These categories may be more acceptable to scientists trying to define intelligence for a scientific study.
*d. Correct. This is the definition given in the book.

2. c   mod. 26 p. 301
a. Incorrect. Achievement scales would only show levels of achievement.
b. Incorrect. Aptitude indicates areas of interest and inclinations toward certain areas of work.
*c. Correct. The intelligence quotient is calculated by dividing the mental age (as tested) by the chronological age.
d. Incorrect. The g-factor refers to the notion that one single factor of intelligence (a general factor) underlies different components of intelligence.

3. a   mod. 26 p. 300
*a. Correct. Intelligence tests have many faults, but they are successful predictors of performance in many kinds of activities, and they are standardized for large populations.
b. Incorrect. Genealogy does suggest family patterns, but familial, genetic traits do not always appear in each family member.
c. Incorrect. Achievement tests only indicate what an individual has been able to accomplish with his or her intellectual capacity, and they do not indicate what that capacity is.
d. Incorrect. Projective tests are useful indicators of certain personality traits and do not indicate intelligence levels.

4. a   mod. 26 p. 301
*a. Correct. The chronological age is the age in years.
b. Incorrect. See answer a.
c. Incorrect. See answer a.
d. Incorrect. See answer a.

5. c   mod. 26 p. 302
a. Incorrect. Neither fit, try another choice.
b. Incorrect. Spatial belongs to another test, and verbal is correct.
*c. Correct. The Wechsler tests assess nonverbal performance and verbal skills.
d. Incorrect. Performance is correct, but spatial belongs to another test.

6. b   mod. 26 p.305
a. Incorrect. The test may have tested what it sought to test, but generated different results on each taking.
*b. Correct. Typically, if a test produces different results for the same subject in different administrations, the test reliability is low.
c. Incorrect. Culturally biased tests do not account for variability in the score for the same subject.
d. Incorrect. Many tests have subscales, but this would not cause unreliability.

7. d   mod. 26 p. 302
a. Incorrect. Motor skills tests test a level of motor skill, not knowledge.
b. Incorrect. Personality tests assess personality traits and characteristics.
c. Incorrect. Aptitude tests predict an individual's interests and abilities in a certain area and line of work.
*d. Correct. Achievement tests measure the level of performance and knowledge in given areas, usually academic areas.

8. c   mod. 26 p. 294
a. Incorrect. Heredity may influence intelligence generally, but crystallized intelligence is more dependent on experience and its application.
b. Incorrect. Poor nutrition and diet may degrade intelligence, but crystallized intelligence does not depend on them.
*c. Correct. Crystallized intelligence reflects one's culture, which provides specific experiences and opportunities for the application of experience.
d. Incorrect. Native intelligence is a term used by some to refer to intellectual capacity (possibly genetic endowment).

9. a   mod. 26 p. 295
*a. Correct. The list of eight is musical, bodily kinesthetic, logical-mathematical, linguistic, spatial, interpersonal, intrapersonal intelligence, and naturalist.
b. Incorrect. See answer a.
c. Incorrect. See answer a.
d. Incorrect. See answer a.

10. d   mod. 27 p. 295
a. Incorrect. "Structure-of-intellect" is associated with another approach.
b. Incorrect. The deviation IQ is a formula introduced to adjust the conventional way of calculating IQ scores to fit any age.

c. Incorrect. Aptitude testing is used by school counselors and personnel counselors to guide job selection and placement.
*d. Correct. Cognitive psychologists use the information-processing approach because it addresses how people store, recall, and utilize information.

11. b   mod. 26 p. 298
a. Incorrect. They are only minimally correlated.
*b. Correct. This minimal correlation suggests that other types of intelligence may be responsible for business success.
c. Incorrect. They are minimally correlated.
d. Incorrect. They are minimally, positively correlated.

12. c   mod. 27 p. 311
a. Incorrect. This refers to the syndrome in which an individual, usually mentally retarded, has an extraordinary ability in one area, like mathematics, music, or art.
b. Incorrect. This defines mental retardation, and profound retardation is a category of mental retardation.
*c. Correct. This is the definition of mental retardation.
d. Incorrect. This defines mental retardation, and profound retardation is a category of mental retardation.

13. d   mod. 27 p. 312
a. Incorrect. This causes other forms of retardation.
b. Incorrect. Toxins in the environment have detrimental effects on the fetus, but they are not identified with Down syndrome.
c. Incorrect. Fetal alcohol syndrome has its own special set of symptoms and is not the same as Down syndrome.
*d. Correct. The extra chromosome is the definitive marker of Down syndrome

14. d   mod. 27 p. 312
a. Incorrect. It may result from hereditary factors, but these are unknown.
b. Incorrect. Environmental factors may play a role, but the actual cause is unknown.
c. Incorrect. It is not a paradox; the causes are simply unknown at this time.
*d. Correct. Familial retardation is characterized by having more than one retarded person in the immediate family group.

15. b   mod. 27 p. 312

a. Incorrect. Mainstreaming increases the opportunities to interact with nonretarded students.
*b. Correct. These opportunities are intended to improve educational access and remove the stigma of special classes.
c. Incorrect. The intent of mainstreaming is to include all persons in the classroom.
d. Incorrect. Mainstreaming is intended to end the separation of retarded and nonretarded students.

16. c   mod. 26 p. 307
17. a   mod. 28 p. 316
18. d   mod. 28 p. 316
19. b   mod. 26 p. 305

20. mild retardation   mod. 27 p. 312
21. 100   mod. 26 p. 301
22. performance   mod. 26 p. 302
23. least restrictive   mod. 27 p. 312
24. high IQ subjects   mod. 27 p. 313

25.
▪ Describe Binet's conception of intelligence, the g-factor view, Gardner's multiple intelligences, the triarchic theory, and the concepts of practical and emotional intelligence. (A good answer would not have to have all of these approaches.)
▪ State which you find most acceptable and for what reason. For instance, the concept of practical intelligence may be appealing because it focuses on something other than educational ability.
▪ The most important evidence predicts, but if a definition appears to agree with commonly held views, then it too will have some validity because people do act on these kinds of views.

Practice Test 2:
1. c   mod. 26 p. 294
a. Incorrect. This is not a definition of intelligence; perhaps it defines aptitude.
b. Incorrect. Though close, this is not the textbook's definition.
*c. Correct. Intelligence is generally accepted to include an individual's ability to utilize resources in the environment.
d. Incorrect. This sounds good, but it is not the definition given in the text.

2. c   mod. 26 p. 301
a. Incorrect. Other techniques were used to increase the reliability of earlier tests.
b. Incorrect. It does make this possible, but it was not the purpose of developing the intelligence quotient.
*c. Correct. The IQ is a standardized quotient, and it allows for comparisons between chronological ages.
d. Incorrect. This was not the purpose for developing the intelligence quotient.

3. b   mod. 26 p. 300
a. Incorrect. No IQ test has been devised for diagnosing brain damage.
*b. Correct. Binet was trying to develop a means of placing slower children in special classes.
c. Incorrect. This probably would not work anyway.
d. Incorrect. This is a common use today, but the original use was to identify slow learners.

4. a   mod. 26 p. 294
*a. Correct. Spearman introduced the g-factor to indicate general intelligence.
b. Incorrect. Others introduced this.
c. Incorrect. See Mulder and Scully about this one.
d. Incorrect. Others introduced this.

5. d   mod. 27 p. 301
a. Incorrect. See answer d.
b. Incorrect. See answer d.
c. Incorrect. See answer d.
*d. Correct. These scores represent the range that includes the first two standard deviations from the mean, and above 130 is considered gifted while below 70 is considered retarded.

6. b   mod. 26 p. 305
a. Incorrect. This is evidence of unreliability, but not invalidity.
*b. Correct. In taking the same test more than once, a wide variation in scores suggests that the test is inconsistent, or unreliable, unless other factors may account for the score differences.
c. Incorrect. Nomothetic refers to a type of study that involves many subjects and seeks to identify normative characteristics of a phenomena.
d. Incorrect. Ideographic refers to a type of research that focuses on a phenomenon in great detail, like a case study.

7. a   mod. 26 p. 305
*a. Correct. Aptitude tests are designed to predict future performance in specific skills and work areas.
b. Incorrect. Achievement tests measure achievement in a certain subject area.
c. Incorrect. Intelligence tests measure intelligence, not aptitude.
d. Incorrect. The g-factor is the general intelligence factor believed by some to underlie intelligence.

8. a   mod. 26 p. 295
*a. Correct. The list of eight is musical, bodily kinesthetic, logical-mathematical, linguistic, spatial, interpersonal, intrapersonal intelligence, and naturalist.
b. Incorrect. See answer a.
c. Incorrect. See answer a.
d. Incorrect. See answer a.

9. c   mod. 26 p. 296
a. Incorrect. This refers to linguistic capacity.
b. Incorrect. This refers to physical control skills, like dancers may have.
*c. Correct. Interpersonal skill is recognized as the skill of interaction with others.
d. Incorrect. Intrapersonal intelligence refers to the individual's self-awareness.

10. b   mod. 27 p. 311
a. Incorrect. Many people who are mentally retarded are capable of getting along in the world and with others.
*b. Correct. Intellectual and adaptive deficits define mental retardation.
c. Incorrect. Sometimes the intellectually gifted cannot perform in school.
d. Incorrect. Everyone (and anyone) can "perform" on an intelligence test.

11. a   mod. 26 p. 295
*a. Correct. Cognitive refers to mental processes like thought, memory, and problem solving, among others.
b. Incorrect. The learning approach emphasizes the role of reinforcements and observational learning.
c. Incorrect. An environmental approach would focus on the characteristics of the learning environment.
d. Incorrect. A physiological approach would focus on biological and genetic factors in intelligence.

12. b   mod. 27 p. 312
a.   Incorrect. Try 70.
*b. Correct. Any score below 70 is considered to indicate mental retardation.
c.   Incorrect. Any score below 70 is considered to indicate mental retardation, and the answer would be incorrect because all scores below 60 are considered, but other scores belong too.
d.   Incorrect. See answer c.

13. b   mod. 27 p. 312
a.   Incorrect. Down syndrome is the major biological cause of mental retardation, but biologically caused mental retardation comprises only about one-third of the cases.
*b. Correct. Familial retardation has no known biological or environmental cause.
c.   Incorrect. This is a fairly unusual cause of mental retardation.
d.   Incorrect. Traumatic injury may result in retardation, but it is not as common as familial retardation.

14. a   mod. 27 p. 312
*a. Correct. Of this list, this group suffers the least impairment and thus has the greatest chance for success in the "mainstreamed" environment.
b.   Incorrect. See answer a.
c.   Incorrect. See answer a.
d.   Incorrect. See answer a.

15. d   mod. 27 p. 313
a.   Incorrect. They may be gifted in only one subject, and they may not show academic achievement in any subject.
b.   Incorrect. They are typically well-adjusted.
c.   Incorrect. They are almost always in the mainstream setting.
*d. Correct. Intellectually gifted students have fewer social problems and adjustment problems than their peers.

16. b   mod. 26 p. 302
17. d   mod. 26 p. 294
18. a   mod. 26 p. 295
19. e   mod. 26 p. 300
20. c   mod. 26 p. 299

21. norms   mod. 26 p. 307
22. intelligence quotient   mod. 26 p. 301
23. Sir Frances Galton   mod. 26 p. 300
24. Alfred Binet   mod. 26 p. 300
25. Moderate   mod. 27 p. 312

26.
- Note that this returns to one of the major issues introduced in the beginning of the text and that there is no ready answer for the debate.
- The most fundamental issue is that we have a lot of evidence supporting the roles of both the environment and genetic factors. Psychologists do not want to select one over the other.
- Of particular relevance was the discussion of problem solving and creativity.
- The extent to which intelligence depends on the environment affects the possibility of developing a culture-fair test.

Practice Test 3:
1.   c   mod. 26 p. 301
a.   Incorrect. See answer c.
b.   Incorrect. See answer c.
*c. Correct. 8 divided by 10 equals 1.25; 1.25 times 100 equals 125, or the intelligence quotient for this individual.
d.   Incorrect. See answer c.

2.   c   mod. 26 p. 301
a.   Incorrect. See answer c.
b.   Incorrect. See answer c.
*c. Correct. This calculation is accurate for children, but the deviation IQ was developed to reflect the IQs of adolescents and adults.
d.   Incorrect. See answer c.

3.   b   mod. 26 p. 301
a.   Incorrect. 10 divided by 12 equals .83; .83 times 100 equals 83, or the intelligence quotient for this individual.
*b. Correct. 12 divided by 10 equals 1.2; 1.2 times 100 equals 120, or the intelligence quotient for this individual.
c.   Incorrect. 23 divided by 25 equals .92; .92 times 100 equals 92, or the intelligence quotient for this individual.
d.   Incorrect. 25 divided by 23 equals 1.09; 1.09 times 100 equals 109, or the intelligence quotient for this individual.

4. a   mod. 26 p. 300
*a. Correct. The original design was to distinguish between "bright" and "dull" students. Binet developed the test to help place students according to their tested skill level, and students who performed only as well as younger students were considered "dull."
b. Incorrect. See answer a.
c. Incorrect. See answer a.
d. Incorrect. See answer a.

5. c   mod. 26 p. 301
a. Incorrect. See answer c.
b. Incorrect. See answer c.
*c. Correct. Two-third includes the first standard deviation on either side of the average, which for IQ scores is between 85 and 115.
d. Incorrect. See answer c.

6. b   mod. 26 p. 304
a. Incorrect. See answer b.
*b. Correct. The subtests are information, comprehension, arithmetic, similarities, digit symbol, picture completion, and object assembly.
c. Incorrect. See answer b.
d. Incorrect. See answer b.

7. d   mod. 26 p. 302
a. Incorrect. The administration ends when the test-taker cannot answer any more questions, long before all items have been administered.
b. Incorrect. See answer d.
c. Incorrect. See answer d.
*d. Correct. Some tests end after a set number of questions have been missed in a row—often the number has been 5—but the Stanford-Binet ends when the person cannot answer any more questions.

8. a   mod. 26 p. 304
*a. Correct. The subtests are information, comprehension, arithmetic, similarities, digit symbol, picture completion, and object assembly; comprehension is a verbal subtest.
b. Incorrect. See answer a.
c. Incorrect. See answer a.
d. Incorrect. See answer a.

9. b   mod. 26 p. 294
a. Incorrect. You may utilize the availability heuristic, but not necessarily so.
*b. Correct. Crystallized intelligence comprises the knowledge individuals have acquired through experience.
c. Incorrect. Fluid intelligence is based on intellectual capacity, not experience.
d. Incorrect. The g-factor is the term used to represent the general intelligence factor that some believe underlies all intelligence.

10. a   mod. 27 p. 271
*a. Correct. These are the three components of his theory.
b. Incorrect. No such brain organ, although there is a "triune" theory of the brain.
c. Incorrect. This is someone else's idea.
d. Incorrect. Few theories of intelligence have begun with animal research.

11. d   mod. 26 p. 305
a. Incorrect. See answer d.
b. Incorrect. See answer d.
c. Incorrect. See answer d.
*d. Correct. Each time the test is given, it yields the same scores, suggesting that it is reliable from one situation to another. This example illustrates validity because this test clearly measured what it was supposed to measure.

12. b   mod. 26 p. 307
a. Incorrect. This is an example of poor validity because the test did not measure what it was intended to measure.
*b. Correct. This test clearly did not measure what it was supposed to measure.
c. Incorrect. Reliability cannot be judged with one use of the test.
d. Incorrect. See answer c.

13. b   mod. 27 p. 298
a. Incorrect. Although multiple intelligence approaches would be more compatible than some, the concept of practical intelligence is more appropriate.
*b. Correct. Practical intelligence reflects efforts to measure common sense, and common sense would be more appropriate to the career prediction.
c. Incorrect. The information-processing approach does not offer any special view of practical intelligence, which is described here.
d. Incorrect. The g-factor refers to the general intelligence factor, which some psychologists

believe underlies all intelligence; measures of
general intelligence have not been successful at
predicting job performance.

14. d   mod. 26 p. 296
a. Incorrect. A surgeon has good bodily kinesthetic
    intelligence.
b. Incorrect. A scientist would be high in logical-
    mathematical intelligence.
c. Incorrect. A musician would have good musical
    intelligence.
*d. Correct. Anne Sullivan, like Jessica, would be
    recognized for her interpersonal intelligence.

15. b   mod. 27 p. 312
16. a   mod. 26 p. 307
17. c   mod. 27 p. 313
18. e   mod. 26 p. 299
19. d   mod. 27 p. 299

20. mainstreaming   mod. 25 p. 312
21. performance   mod. 25 p. 302
22. ease   mod. 25 p. 302
23. Flynn effect   mod. 28 p. 318
24. gifted; nongifted mod. 27 p. 313

25. IQ tests to exclude:
- Child care workers: While under supervision,
  people with minimal intelligence often are
  excellent workers in this setting, but when
  situations arise that require decision making,
  lower intelligence scores may mean difficulty
  making these decisions.
- Air traffic controllers: The advantage of high
  intelligence here is the ability to make difficult
  decisions and be flexible while under a great deal
  of stress. A disadvantage might be that the
  tediousness of the job on an hourly basis may be
  difficult to contend with.
- Health care professionals are often asked to react
  on their own and deal effectively in crisis
  situations. This requires higher-functioning
  people. The disadvantage of hiring those with
  high IQs is that they may not have the training or
  authority to make decisions but may feel it is
  well within their skill range and may at times
  ignore superiors in favor of their own views.

Chapter 10: Motivation and Emotion

Module 29: Explaining Motivation
Module 30: Human Needs and Motivation: Eat, Drink, and Be Daring
Module 31: Understanding Emotional Experiences
Module 32: Nonverbal Behavior and the Expression of Emotions

Overview

This set of modules focuses on the major conceptions of motivation, discussing how the different motives and needs people experience jointly affect behavior. The theories of motivation draw on basic instincts, drives, levels of arousal, expectations, and self-realization as possible sources of motives.

Module 29 explores the factors that direct and energize behavior. Homeostasis, along with arousal, incentive, and cognitive approaches, are defined and discussed. Maslow's hierarchy is offered as an explanation of five basic needs and the motivation a person needs to fulfill these needs.

Module 30 offers a discussion of the factors that underlie hunger. Thirst and hunger are two motives that have a physiological basis. Social factors that play a role in the regulation of hunger are explored, along with factors related to obesity. Needs relating to achievement, affiliation, and power motivation are also presented here.

Module 31 offers a definition of emotions and illustrates how they have both a physiological and a cognitive component. Three major theories of emotion—the James-Lange Theory, the Cannon-Bard Theory, and the Schachter-Singer Theory—are presented, with recent approaches that are based on biology and neuroscience discussed as well.

Module 32 concludes the unit with a presentation on nonverbal behavior and the expression of emotion. Similarities in facial expressions and nonverbal behavior across cultures is investigated, and the facial-feedback hypothesis is explained.

To further investigate the topics covered in this chapter, you can visit the related Web sites by visiting the following link: www.mhhe.com/feldmanup8.

Prologue: Tour de Lance
Looking Ahead

Module 29: Explaining Motivation

Instinct Approaches: Born to Be Motivated
Drive-Reduction Approaches: Satisfying Our Needs
Arousal Approaches: Beyond Drive Reduction
Incentive Approaches: Motivation's Pull
Cognitive Approaches: The Thoughts Behind Motivation
Maslow's Hierarchy: Ordering Motivational Needs
Applying the Different Approaches to Motivation

- ***How does motivation direct and energize behavior?***

Explaining Motivation

The factors that direct and energize behavior comprise the major focus of the study of

[a] _____. Psychologists who study motivation seek to understand why people do the things they do. The study of emotions includes the internal experience at any given moment.

There are several approaches to understanding motivation. An early approach focused on

[b] _____ as inborn, biologically determined patterns of behavior. Proponents of this view argue that there exist preprogrammed patterns of behavior that are important for species survival.

[c] _____ *approaches to motivation* focus on behavior as an attempt to remedy the shortage of some basic biological requirement. In this view, a(n)

[d] _____ is a motivational tension, or arousal, that energizes a behavior to fulfill

a need. **[e]** _____ meet biological requirements, while **[f]** _____ have no obvious biological basis. Primary drives are resolved by reducing the need that underlies it.

Primary drives are also governed by a basic motivational phenomena of **[g]** _____, the goal of maintaining optimal biological functioning by maintaining an internal steady state. Drive-reduction theories have difficulty explaining behavior that is not directed at reducing a drive but may be directed instead at maintaining or increasing arousal. Also, behavior appears to be motivated occasionally by curiosity as well.

The theory that explains motivation as being directed toward maintaining or increasing

excitement is the **[h]** _____ *approach to motivation*. If the levels of stimulation are too low, arousal theory says that we will try to increase the levels.

In motivational terms, the reward is the **[i]** _____. **[j]** _____

approaches to motivation explain why behavior may be motivated by external stimuli.

[k] _____ *approaches to motivation* suggest that motivation is produced by

thoughts, expectations, and personal goals. **[l]** _____ refers to the value an

300

activity has in the enjoyment of participating in it, and **[m]** _____ refers to behavior that is done for a tangible reward. We work harder for a task that has intrinsic motivation. Also, as tangible rewards become available, intrinsic motivation declines and extrinsic motivation increases.

Maslow's theory describes motivations as being ordered in a hierarchy, with needs such as those related to physiology and safety being lower-order needs, and needs related to belongingness and esteem being higher-order needs. The highest-level need people aim to meet is **[n]** _____, the state of self-fulfillment in which people reach their unique and greatest potential. Maslow's theory of motivation has been very influential, though it has been difficult to validate empirically.

Evaluate

_____ 1. self-actualization

_____ 2. emotions

_____ 3. instinct

_____ 4. drive

_____ 5. primary drives

a. An inborn pattern of behavior that is biologically determined.

b. A state in which a person has achieved his or her highest potential.

c. The internal feelings experienced at any given moment.

d. Biological needs such as hunger, thirst, fatigue, and sex.

e. A tension or arousal that energizes behavior in order to fulfill a need.

Rethink

29-1   Which approaches to motivation are most commonly used in the workplace? How might each approach be used to design employment policies that can sustain or increase motivation?

29-2   _From the perspective of an educator:_ Do you think that giving students grades serves as an external reward that would decrease intrinsic motivation for the subject matter? Why or why not?

Page 320 "He **endured** surgery and intense chemotherapy."

When we **endure** something we allow something very unpleasant to happen to us.

Page 320 "At the same time, he refused to **give up** cycling, riding 20 to 50 miles a day even after enduring week-long rounds of chemotherapy."

To **give up** is to stop trying.

Page 320 "Armstrong **beat the odds**, in the same way he would go on to beat every challenger in the Tour de France after returning to racing."

When someone **beats the odds** something good that should not happen to them does.

Page 320 "When he retired after winning his seventh and final race, he left the sport not only as an example of an athlete at the top of his game but as a testament to **willpower,** drive, and the **undauntability** of the human spirit (Abt, 1999; Coyle, 2005; Wyatt, 2005)."

Willpower is self-discipline and determination.

To **daunt** is to make someone feel intimidated or anxious. The prefix **"un" means** "not." **Ability** menas talent or skill. Thus, **undauntability** is the ability or skill to not be intimidated or anxious in stressful times.

Page 320 "The satisfaction of achieving a long-**sought** goal?"

A goal that is **sought** after is a goal that is wanted.

Page 320 "Psychologists who study motivation seek to discover the particular desired goals—the motives—that **underlie** behavior."

When something **underlies** something else it is the cause of it.

Page 321 "An 800-pound **boulder** dislodged in a narrow canyon where Ralston was hiking in an isolated Utah canyon, pinning his lower arm to the ground."

A **boulder** is a large rock.

Page 321 "An experienced climber who had search-and-rescue training, he had **ample** time to consider his options."

Ample means plenty or a more than is needed.

Page 321 "He tried unsuccessfully to chip away at the rock, and he **rigged** up ropes and pulleys around the boulder in a vain effort to move it."

To **rig** something is to arrange or prepare it.

Page 321 "In acts of incredible bravery, Ralston broke two bones in his wrist, applied a **tourniquet**, and used a **dull** pen knife to amputate his arm beneath the elbow."

A **tourniquet** is a tight bandage that is usually used to stop severe bleeding.

Dull means blunt, or not sharp.

Page 322 "As a result of these **shortcomings**, newer explanations have replaced conceptions of motivation based on instincts."

Shortcomings are deficiencies or flaws. What were some of the **shortcomings** of the early explanations defining motivation?

Page 322 "We usually try to satisfy a primary drive by reducing the need **underlying** it."

Underlying means lying under or beneath. To satisfy the primary drive, we would identify the need.

Page 322 "Using feedback loops, **homeostasis** brings deviations in body functioning back to an **optimal** state, similar to the way a thermostat and a furnace work in a home heating system to maintain a steady temperature."

Homeostasis is the steady state of physiological equilibrium. It is the ability of a cell or an organism to maintain internal equilibrium by adjusting internal processes.

When things are **optimal** they are the best possible.

Page 322 "Both curiosity and thrill-seeking behavior, then, **shed doubt** on drive-reduction approaches as a complete explanation for motivation."

When something or someone **sheds doubt** on something they are unconvinced or uncertain about it.

Page 323 "When a **luscious** dessert appears on the table after a filling meal, its appeal has little or nothing to do with internal drives or the maintenance of arousal."

A **luscious** desert is one that has a rich, sweet taste.

Page 324 "**Incentive** approaches to motivation suggest that motivation stems from the desire to obtain valued external goals, or incentives."

An **incentive** is something that stimulates. Can both the fear of punishment and the expectation of reward be an **incentive**? What **incentives** do you find are the most effective in motivating you to set time aside for studying?

Page 325 "Although the theory explains why we may **succumb** to an incentive (such as a mouthwatering dessert) even though we lack internal cues (such as hunger), it does not provide a complete explanation of **motivation**, because organisms sometimes seek to fulfill needs even when incentives are not apparent."

When a person **succumbs**, they yield to an overwhelming desire or overpowering force.

Motivation is an inner state that energizes people toward the fulfillment of a goal. This would be the psychological process that arouses, directs and maintains behavior toward a goal.

Page 325 "**Intrinsic motivation** causes us to participate in an activity for our own enjoyment rather than for any concrete, **tangible** reward that it will bring us."

Intrinsic motivation is the inner drive that motivates people in the absence of external reward or punishment. What are some of your activities that are **intrinsically motivated**?

A **tangible** reward is something able to be perceived as materially existent. When you receive money for your efforts, you receive a **tangible** reward.

Page 325 "In contrast, **extrinsic motivation** causes us to do something for money, a grade, or some other concrete, tangible reward."

Extrinsic motivation is the desire to engage in an activity for money, recognition, or other tangible benefits. Describe some examples of how your educational institution helps to motivate you both intrinsically and **extrinsically**.

Page 326 "**Self-actualization** is a state of self-fulfillment in which people realize their highest **potentials**, each in his or her own unique way."

In Maslow's theory, **self-actualization** is the individual's predisposition to try to fulfill his or her **potential**.

Potential is the inherent ability or capacity for growth or development.

Page 326 "The important thing is that people **feel at ease** with themselves and satisfied that they are using their talents to the fullest.

When people **feel at ease** with themselves, they feel comfortable.

Page 326 "In a sense, achieving self-actualization reduces the striving and **yearning** for greater fulfillment that mark most people's lives and instead provides a sense of satisfaction with the current state of affairs (Jones & Crandall, 1991; Hamel, Leclerc & Lefrancois, 2003; Piechowski, 2003)."

When you **yearn** for something, you experience a strong desire. You want something very badly. Are there goals you **yearn** for?

Page 327 "Actually, many of the approaches are **complementary**, rather than **contradictory**."

Complement means something that completes or brings to perfection, such as the several theories of motivation are **complementary**, and provide a more complete analysis and understanding of motivation. Be cautious not to confuse this with "compliment," which means an expression of courtesy or praise, such as the professor paid the entire class a compliment on the quality of the grades they had earned on the exam.

When you **contradict** something, you express or assert the opposite of a statement. A **contradiction** is an inconsistency or discrepancy.

Module 30: Human Needs and Motivation: Eat, Drink, and Be Daring

The Motivation Behind Hunger and Eating
Eating Disorders

Becoming an Informed Consumer of Psychology: Dieting and Losing Weight Successfully

The Need for Achievement: Striving for Success
The Need for Affiliation: Striving for Friendship
The Need for Power: Striving for Impact on Others

- *What biological and social factors underlie hunger?*
- *How are needs relating to achievement, affiliation, and power motivation exhibited?*

Human Needs and Motivation: Eat, Drink, and Be Daring

One-third of Americans are considered more than 20 percent overweight and thus suffer from **[a]**

_____. Most nonhumans will regulate their intake of food even when it is abundant. Hunger is apparently complex, consisting of several mechanisms that signal changes in the body. One is the level of the sugar glucose in the blood. The higher the level of glucose,

the less hunger is experienced. The **[b]** _____ monitors the glucose levels in

the blood. A rat with a damaged **[c]** _____ will starve to death, and one with a

damaged **[d]** _____ will experience extreme overeating.

One theory suggests that the body maintains a(n) **[e]** _____. This set point controls whether the hypothalamus calls for more or less food intake. Differences in people's

metabolism may also account for being overweight. **[f]** _____ is the rate at which energy is produced and expended. People with high metabolic rates can eat as much food as they want and not gain weight. People with low metabolism eat little and still gain weight. As

an alternative to the set-point explanation, the **[g]** _____ proposes a combination of genetic and environmental factors. In addition, it is clear that social factors affect when and how much people eat.

[h] _____ is a disease that afflicts primarily young females, though rates for males are on the rise. Sufferers refuse to eat and may actually starve themselves to death. **[i]**

_____ is a condition in which individuals binge on large quantities of food and then purge with vomiting or laxatives. There are likely multiple causes of anorexia and bulimia, including a chemical imbalance in the hypothalamus or pituitary gland, as well as cultural values surrounding eating and ideal body shapes.

The [j] _____ is a learned characteristic involving the sustained striving for and attainment of a level of excellence. People with high needs for achievement seek out opportunities to compete and succeed. People with low needs for achievement are motivated by the desire to avoid failure.

The [k] _____ is used to test achievement motivation. It requires that the person look at a series of ambiguous pictures and then write a story that tells what is going on and what will happen next.

The [l] _____ refers to the needs we have of establishing and maintaining relationships with others. People who have high affiliation needs tend to be more concerned with relationships and to be with their friends more. The [m] _____ is a tendency to seek impact, control, or influence over others. People with a strong need for power tend to seek office more often than people with a weak need for power. Men tend to display their need for power through aggression, drinking, sexual exploitation, and competitive sports, whereas women who have a high need for power are more restrained.

Evaluate

_____ 1. body-mass index

_____ 2. self-actualization

_____ 3. need for achievement

_____ 4. need for affiliation

_____ 5. need for power

a. A tendency to want to seek impact, control, or influence over others in order to be seen as a powerful individual.

b. A need to establish and maintain relationships with other people.

c. A stable, learned characteristic, in which satisfaction comes from striving for and achieving a level of excellence.

d. A state of self-fulfillment in which people realize their highest potential.

e. The most widely used measure of obesity, involving a ratio of weight to height.

Rethink

30-1   In what ways do societal expectations, expressed by television shows and commercials, contribute to both obesity and excessive concern about weight loss? How could television contribute to better eating habits and attitudes toward weight? Should it be required to do so?

30-2   *From the perspective of a human resources specialist:* How might you use characteristics such as need for achievement, need for power, and need for affiliation to select workers for jobs? What additional criteria would you have to consider?

Spotlight on Terminology and Language—ESL Pointers

Page 329 ""It was extremely painful," says Arndt of those days... "But I was that desperate to make up for my **bingeing**.

A **binge** is a short period of time in which the person does a large amount of uncontrolled eating or drinking.

Page 329 "We begin with hunger, the primary drive that has received the most attention from researchers, and then turn to secondary drives – those uniquely human endeavors, based on learned needs and past experience, that help explain why people strive to achieve, to **affiliate** with others, and to seek power over others."

Affiliate means to associate with. Have you noticed that you choose to **affiliate** with particular people?

Page 329 "For instance, many contemporary Western cultures stress the importance of **slimness** in women—a relatively recent view."

To be **slim** is to be thin or small in size.

Page 330 "It's not just a matter of an empty stomach causing hunger pangs and a full one **alleviating** those pangs."

To **alleviate** is to relieve. We may work to **alleviate** mental suffering through the use of psychotherapy.

Page 331 "Increasing evidence suggests that the hypothalamus carries the primary responsibility for monitoring food **intake**."

Intake is an amount taken in.

Page 331 "They refuse food when it is offered, and unless they are **force-fed**, they eventually die."

To **force-feed** is to compel to take in nourishment. Sometimes people become so weak or so ill, they must be made to take in nutrition intravenously, or to swallow food, against their will.

Page 331 "Even people who are not deliberately monitoring their weight show only minor weight **fluctuations** in spite of substantial day-to-day variations in how much they eat and exercise."

Fluctuations are unpredictable changes in amount of something.

Page 331 "You've just finished a full meal and feel completely **stuffed**."

When you **feel stuffed** after eating it means that you are completely full and have eaten too much food.

Page 331 "Suddenly your host announces with great **fanfare** that he will be serving his "house specialty" dessert, bananas flambé, and that he has spent the better part of the afternoon preparing it."

When your host makes an announcement with great **fanfare**, he is making a showy and dramatic announcement. In this case he is marking the arrival of the dessert that he worked so hard to prepare for this event.

Page 332 "Similarly, we put **roughly** the same amount of food on our plates every day, even though the amount of exercise we may have had, and consequently our need for energy **replenishment**, varies from day to day.

Roughly means approximately, or almost.

A **replenishment** is something used to replace or refill something that has been used up.

Page 332 "Some of us head toward the refrigerator after a difficult day, seeking **solace** in a pint of Heath Bar Crunch ice cream."

We seek **solace** when we seek a source of comfort. Do you have any private "comfort food" that provides **solace**?

Page 332 "Eventually, we may have learned, through the basic mechanisms of classical and operant conditioning, to associate food with comfort and **consolation**."

Consolation is a source of support for someone who has been sad or upset.

Page 332 "One biological explanation is that obese individuals have a higher level of the hormone *leptin*, which appears to be designed, from an evolutionary **standpoint**, to "protect" the body against weight loss."

A **standpoint** is a point of view or the way a group of people thinks about something.

Page 333 "Instead, they suggest, the body has a *settling point*, determined by a combination of our genetic **heritage** and the nature of the environment in which we live."

Our **genetic heritage** refers to the genetic information that has been given to us by our parents and grandparents.

Page 333 "If high-fat foods are **prevalent** in our environment and we are genetically predisposed to obesity, we settle into an equilibrium that maintains relatively high weight."

Prevalent means common. Foods high in fat are prevalent, or a common part of our diets.

Page 333 "Some 10 percent of people with anorexia literally **starve** themselves to death."

When someone **starves** themselves they go hungry and refuse to eat.

Page 333 "After such a binge, sufferers feel guilt and depression and often **induce** vomiting or take laxatives to rid themselves of the food—behavior known as **purging**."

To **induce** something is to make it happen.

When we **purge** something they remove it. When people with eating disorders **purge**, they force them selves to remove the food they have eaten. They often do this by forcing themselves to vomit or by taking laxative medication.

Page 333 "Others believe that the cause has **roots** in society's valuation of **slenderness** and the parallel notion that obesity is undesirable."

When someone is **slender** they are thin.
The **root** of something refers to the cause or reason why something exists.

Page 333 "These researchers maintain that people with anorexia nervosa and bulimia become preoccupied with their weight and take to heart the **cliché** that one can never be too thin."

A **cliché** is an over used word or idea that is no longer as effective because it has been overused.

Page 333 "The complete explanations for anorexia nervosa and bulimia remain **elusive**."

When something is **elusive** it is difficult to find or understand.

Page 334 "Not only does watching television **preclude** other activities that burn calories (even walking around the house is helpful), people often **gorge on** junk food while watching."

 To **preclude** something is to prevent, or stop it from happening.

When we **gorge on** something we eat it to excess.

Page 334 "Wrap refrigerated foods in aluminum foil so that you cannot see the contents and be **tempted** every time you open the refrigerator."

When we are **tempted** we desire or crave something and we feel that we must have it.

Page 334 "*Avoid **fad** diets.*"

Fads are trends or fashion preferences that are popular for a short period of time.

Page 335 "Don't try to lose too much weight too quickly or you may **doom** yourself to failure."

To **doom** someone is to condemn or convict them to a terrible outcome.

Page 335 "In light of the difficulty of losing weight, psychologists Janet Polivy and C. Peter Herman suggest – **paradoxically** – that the best approach may be to avoid dieting in the first place."

A **paradox** is a seemingly contradictory statement that may nevertheless be true.

Page 335 "They recommend that people eat what they really want to eat, even if this means **indulging** in candy or ice cream every so often."

To **indulge** is to allow someone to have something very enjoyable.

Page 336 "But they are not **indiscriminate** when it comes to picking their challenges: They tend to avoid situations in which success will come too easily (which would be unchallenging) and situations in which success is unlikely."

When someone is **indiscriminate** they do not take care in making care choices or decisions.

In above sentence, since the author says that "They are *not indiscriminate…,*" he is actually saying that the people are very careful in their choices.

Page 336 "In the TAT, an examiner shows a series of **ambiguous** pictures, such as the one in Figure 4." An **ambiguous** picture or stimulus is one that is vague or unclear.

Page 336 "Few of us choose to lead our lives as **hermits**."

A **hermit** is a person who chooses to live alone and to have little contact with other people.

Page 336 "Individuals with a high need for affiliation write TAT stories that emphasize the desire to maintain or **reinstate** friendships and show concern over being rejected by friends."

To **reinstate** something is to restore it to its original form or return it to someone.

Page 337 "In addition, they seek to display the **trappings of power**."

Trappings of power are the dress, accessories and other outward things that show that someone is in a position of status or position.

Page 337 "Men with high power needs tend to show unusually high levels of aggression, drink heavily, act in a sexually **exploitative** manner, and participate more frequently in competitive sports—behaviors that collectively represent somewhat extravagant, **flamboyant** behavior.

Something that is **exploitative** makes use of someone in an abusive or unfair way.

Something that is **flamboyant** is showy or elaborate.

Page 337 "In contrast, women display their power needs with more restraint; this is **congruent** with traditional societal constraints on women's behavior."
When something is **congruent** it matches or is similar with something else.

Page 337 "Women with high power needs are more apt than men are to **channel** those needs in a socially responsible manner, such as by showing concern for others or displaying highly nurturing behavior (Winter, 1988, 1995; Maroda, 2004)."

To **channel** something is to guide or direct it along a specific path.

Module 31: Understanding Emotional Experiences

The Functions of Emotions
Determining the Range of Emotions: Labeling Our Feelings
The Roots of Emotions

> **Applying Psychology in the 21st Century:**
> The Truth About Lies: Detecting Deception in Terrorists and Your
> Next-Door Neighbor

- *What are emotions, and how do we experience them?*
- *What are the functions of emotions?*
- *What are the explanations of emotions?*

Understanding Emotional Experiences

Although difficult to define, [a] _____ are understood to be the feelings that have both physiological and cognitive aspects and that influence behavior. Physical changes occur whenever we experience an emotion, and we identify these changes as emotions.

Several important functions of emotions have been identified:

- *Preparing us for action.* Emotions prepare effective responses to a variety of situations.
- *Shaping our future behavior.* Emotions promote learning that will influence making appropriate responses in the future by leading to the repetition of responses that lead to satisfying emotional feelings.
- *Helping us to interact more effectively with others.* Emotions also help regulate interactions with others. The verbal and non-verbal communications associated with emotion can signal our feelings to observers.

Psychologists have been attempting to identify the most important fundamental emotions. Many have suggested that emotions should be understood through their component parts. There may be cultural differences as well, although these differences may reflect different linguistic categories for the emotions.

We have many ways to describe the experiences of emotion that we have. The physiological reactions that accompany fear are associated with the activation of the autonomic nervous system. They include (1) an increase in breathing rate; (2) an increase in heart rate; (3) a widening of the pupils; (4) widening pupils; and (5) a cessation of the functions of the digestive system.

Although these changes occur without awareness, the emotional experience of fear can be felt intensely. Whether these physiological responses are the cause of the experience or the result of the experience of emotion remains unclear.

The **[b]** _____ *theory of emotion* states that emotions are the perceived physiological reactions that occur in the internal organs. They called this *visceral experience*.

The **[c]** _____ *theory of emotion* rejects the view that physiological arousal alone leads to the perception of emotion. In this theory, physiological arousal and emotional experience are produced simultaneously by the same structure, a nerve stimulus. The thalamus signals the autonomic nervous system, which produces the visceral response. The thalamus simultaneously sends a message to the cortex which indicates the nature of the emotion.

The **[d]** _____ *theory of emotion* emphasizes that the emotion experienced depends on the environment and on comparing ourselves with others. We label our emotions accordingly.

Contemporary neuroscience perspectives on emotion underscore the importance of the *amygdala* and the *hippocampus* in creating emotion.

For each of the major theories, there is some contradictory evidence. Emotions are a complex phenomena that no single theory can yet explain adequately.

Evaluate

_____ 1.   James-Lange theory of emotion

_____ 2.   Cannon-Bard theory of emotion

_____ 3.   Schachter-Singer theory of emotion

_____ 4.   emotions

a.   Emotions are experienced by comparing our feelings with the feelings of others.

b.   The belief that emotions are determined jointly by a nonspecific kind of physiological arousal and its interpretation, based on environmental cues.

c.   The belief that emotional experience is a reaction to bodily events occurring as a result of an external situation.

d.   Feelings that generally have both physiological and cognitive elements and that influence behavior.

Rethink

31-1   If researchers learned how to control emotional responses so that targeted emotions could be caused or prevented, what ethical concerns might arise? Under what circumstances, if any, should such techniques be used?

31-2   *From the perspective of an advertising executive:* How might you use the findings produced by Schachter and Singer on the labeling of arousal to create interest in a product? Can you think of other examples whereby people's arousal could be manipulated, which would lead to different emotional responses?

Spotlight on Terminology and Language—ESL Pointers

Page 339 "He knew it could go either way; his grades were pretty good and he had been involved in some **extracurricular** activities, but his SAT scores had been not so terrific."

Extracurricular activities are clubs, sports and other things that students do outside of their school time.

Page 339 "With a **whoop** of excitement, Karl found himself jumping up and down **gleefully.**"

A **whoop** occurs when someone makes a loud howling cry of excitement.

When someone is **gleeful** they are very happy.

Page 339 "A rush of emotion overcame him as it **sank in** that he had, in fact, been accepted."

Sank is the past tense of sink. When something sinks in it is being slowly understood.

Page 339 "Perhaps we have felt the thrill of getting a sought-after job, the joy of being in love, sorrow over someone's death, or the **anguish** of **inadvertently** hurting someone."

When we **anguish** over something we experience extreme anxiety or stress over it.

When we do something **inadvertently** we have done it without intention or accidentally.

Page 339 "Although everyone has an idea of what an emotion is, formally defining the concept has proved to be an **elusive** task."

An **elusive** task is something that's hard to get a hold of, it is often not able to be defined.

Page 339 "Finally, the emotion probably encompasses cognitive elements: Our understanding and evaluation of the meaning of what is happening **prompts** our feelings of happiness."

To **prompt** someone is to encourage them to do something.

Page 339 "For instance, we may react with fear to an unusual or novel situation (such as coming into contact with an **erratic**, unpredictable individual), or we may experience pleasure over sexual excitation without having cognitive awareness or understanding of just what it is about the situation that is exciting."

Something that is **erratic** is not predictable or consistent.

Page 339 "This **school of thought** suggests that we must think about and understand a stimulus or situation, relating it to what we already know, before we can react on an emotional level (Lazarus, 1991a, 1991b, 1994, 1995)."

A **school of thought** is a way of thinking about a topic.

Page 339 "Proponents of both sides of this debate can **cite** research to support their viewpoints, and so the question is far from resolved."

When we **cite** something we are mentioning someone or something to use it as support for our position in an argument.

Page 340 "We may not know why we're afraid of mice, understanding objectively that they represent no danger, but we may still be **frightened out of our wits** when we see them (Lewis & Haviland-Jones, 2000)."

When we are **frightened out of our wits** we are so scared we cannot think.

Page 340 "Imagine what it would be like if we didn't experience emotion—no depths of despair, no depression, no **remorse**, but at the same time no happiness, joy, or love."

Remorse is a strong feeling of regret or guilt.

Page 340 "The role of the sympathetic division is to prepare us for emergency action, which **presumably** would get us moving out of the dog's way—quickly."

Presumably means "most probably" or that it would seem to be so.

Page 340 "The list would range from such obvious emotions as *happiness* and *fear* to less common ones, such as *adventurousness* and *pensiveness*."

Adventurousness is the tendency to be willing and eager to take part in dangerous or exciting things.

Pensiveness is tendency to think deeply or seriously about something.

Page 340 "In fact, some reject the question entirely, saying that *no* set of emotions should be **singled out** as most basic, and that emotions are best understood by breaking them down into their component parts."

When we **single out** someone out, we choose or select them from a group.

Page 341 "For instance, Germans report experiencing *schadenfreude*, a feeling of pleasure over another person's difficulties, and the Japanese experience *hagaii*, a mood of **vulnerable** heartache colored by frustration."

When some one is **vulnerable** they do not have enough protection and are open to possible damage.

Page 341 "In Tahiti, people experience *musu*, a feeling of reluctance to **yield** to unreasonable demands made by one's parents."

When we **yield** to someone we surrender, or give in to them.

Page 341 "I've never been so angry before; I feel my heart pounding, and I'm **trembling** all over... I don't know how I'll get through the performance."

To **tremble** is to uncontrollably and continuously shake with small movements

Page 342 "The James-Lange Theory: Do **Gut** Reactions Equal Emotions?"

Gut reactions are those reactions that you have instinctually, or automatically and without thinking.

Page 342 "The James-Lange theory has some serious **drawbacks**, however."

A **drawback** is a disadvantage, or an objectionable feature.

Page 342 "The James-Lange theory **poses** another difficulty: Physiological arousal does not invariably produce emotional experience."

To **pose** something is to be the cause of it.

Page 342 "Although some types of physiological changes are associated with specific emotional experiences, it is difficult to imagine how each of the **myriad** emotions that people are capable of experiencing could be the result of a unique visceral change."

Myriad is countless, innumerable.

Page 343 "In response to the difficulties **inherent** in the James-Lange theory, Walter Cannon, and later Philip Bard, suggested an alternative view."

When something is **inherent** it is basic or unable to be considered apart from other things.

Page 343 "Instead, the theory assumes that both physiological arousal and the emotional experience are produced simultaneously by the same nerve stimulus, which Cannon and Bard suggested **emanates** from the thalamus in the brain."

Emanate is originate; to come from.

Page 343 "Suppose that, as you are being followed down a dark street on New Year's Eve, you notice a man being followed by another **shady figure** on the other side of the street."

A **shady figure** is one that is suspicious and dishonest.

Page 344 "In one condition he acted angry and hostile, and in the other condition he behaved as if he were **exuberantly** happy."

When we are **exuberant** we are very excited.

Page 344 "Although later research has found that arousal is not as nonspecific as Schachter and Singer assumed, it is clear that arousal can **magnify**, and be mistaken for, many emotions."

To **magnify** something is to make it larger.

Page 344 "When Schachter and Singer carried out their **groundbreaking** experiment in the early 1960s, the ways in which they could evaluate the physiology that accompanies emotion were relatively limited."

Something that is **groundbreaking** is new and innovating.

Page 345 "For example, if we've once been attacked by a vicious **pit bull**, the amygdala processes that information and leads us to react with fear when we see a pit bull later—an example of a classically conditioned fear response (Adolphs, 2002; Miller et al., 2005)."

A **pit bull** is a type of dog that is known for its tendency to be very aggressive.

Page 345 "For one thing, emotions are not a simple phenomenon but are **intertwined** closely with motivation, cognition, neuroscience, and a host of related branches of psychology."

Intertwined is tangled, knotted. More than one factor must be examined when emotions are evaluated.

Page 346 "It was a gut reaction not to shoot—a **hunch** that at that exact moment he was not an **imminent** threat to me." (Gladwell, 2002, p. 38)."

A **hunch** is a premonition or a gut feeling about something.

Imminent is about to happen.

Page 346 "Because of the failure of traditional means of identifying liars, and **spurred on** by government efforts to identify terrorists, researchers are seeking to develop automated equipment that can instantly analyze the nonverbal behaviors of large numbers of people with the goal of identifying suspects who can then be further investigated."

To be **spurred on** is to be forced or strongly encouraged to do something.
Page 347 "In short, emotions are such complex phenomena, encompassing both biological and cognitive aspects, that no single theory has been able to explain fully all the **facets** of emotional experience."

Facets are the features, the components of emotional experience.

Module 32: Nonverbal Behavior and the Expression of Emotions

Exploring Diversity: Do People in All Cultures Express Emotion Similarly?

The Facial-Feedback Hypothesis: Smile, Though You're Feeling Blue

- *How does nonverbal behavior relate to the expression of emotions?*

Nonverbal Behavior and the Expression of Emotions

Facial expressions have been used to define six categories of emotional expression: happiness, anger, sadness, surprise, disgust, and fear. These are examined in the Exploring Diversity discussion. Paul Ekman has found that members of a jungle tribe in New Guinea were able to identify these emotions. Tribal members gave verbal and nonverbal responses that were similar to Western responses.

One explanation for this similarity is the hypothesis that a(n) **[a]** _____ exists at birth. The program is set in motion when the emotion is experienced, and then the appropriate expression is produced. The differences in how basic emotions are expressed in different cultures is attributed to display rules. **[b]** _____ are the guidelines that govern the appropriateness of showing emotion nonverbally, and they are often learned in childhood. **[c]** _____ is the explanation given for why there are subtle differences in emotional expressivity when comparing cultures. In the same way a particular language may have several dialects, so do non-verbal expressions of emotions.

The **[d]** _____ hypothesis argues that faces both reflect emotional experience and help determine how emotions are experienced. In a classic experiment, actors were asked to make facial expressions of emotions by describing the facial posture without mention of the actual emotion. When making the face for fear, the actors experienced an increase in heart rate and a decline in body temperature consistent with the experience of fear.

Evaluate

_____ 1.　visceral experience

_____ 2.　facial-affect program

_____ 3.　facial-feedback hypothesis

_____ 4.　display rules

a.　The belief that both physiological and emotional arousal are produced simultaneously by the same nerve impulses.

b.　The "gut" reaction experienced internally, triggering an emotion.

c.　The notion that facial expressions not only reflect, but also determine and help people identify, the experience of emotions.

d.　The guidelines that govern the appropriateness of showing emotion nonverbally.

Rethink

32-1　What might be the biological reasons for the fact that the six basic emotions are associated with universal facial expressions? The facial-affect program is said to be "universally present at birth"; can this be confirmed through experimentation?

32-2　*From the perspective of a business executive:* How could you use your knowledge of display rules when negotiating? How might your strategies vary depending on the cultural background of the person with whom you are negotiating?

Spotlight on Terminology and Language—ESL Pointers

Page 349 "It is particularly interesting that these six emotions are not unique to members of Western cultures; rather they **constitute** the basic emotions expressed **universally** by members of the human race, regardless of where individuals have been raised and what learning experiences they have had."

These six emotions **constitute**, or make up, the basic emotions.

Universally is across the world.

Page 350 "The facial-affect program – which is assumed to be universally present at birth – is **analogous** to a computer program that is turned on when a particular emotion is experienced."

Analogous means similar to. The facial affect program is like a computer program being activated.

Page 351 "For instance, you may observe slight differences in true and **sham** smiles when you compare the photos in Figure 2."

Sham is deceptive. The **sham** smile is not a genuine smile. A **sham** smile is often used for deception.

Page 351 "That is the implication of an **intriguing** notion known as the facial-feedback hypothesis."

When something is **intriguing**, it is fascinating. The facial-feedback hypothesis is interesting and **intriguing**.

Page 352 "Basically put, 'wearing' an emotional expression provides muscular feedback to the brain that helps produce an emotion **congruent** with that expression."

Congruent means compatible. This expression may cause you to match your feelings with your outward display of emotion.

Test your knowledge of the modules by answering these questions. These questions have been placed in three Practice Tests. The first two tests are composed of questions that will test your recall of factual knowledge. The third test contains questions that are challenging and primarily test for conceptual knowledge and your ability to apply that knowledge. Check your answers and review the feedback using the Answer Key in the following pages of the *Study Guide*.

PRACTICE TEST 1:

1. A newborn baby's behavior is based on primary drives, motives that:
    a. people rate as being most important to them.
    b. seem to motivate an organism the most.
    c. are least likely to be satisfied before self-actualization can occur.
    d. have a biological basis and are universal.

2. _____ correspond(s) to the factors which direct and energize behavior.
    a. Instinct   c. Emotion
    b. Motivation   d. Homeostatic energizers

3. _____ is the process by which an organism tries to maintain an optimal level of internal biological functioning.
    a. Primary drive equilibrium   c. Drive reduction
    b. Homeostasis   d. Opponent-process theory

4. The definition of a motivation behind behavior in which no obvious biological need is being fulfilled is:
    a. a primary drive.   c. a secondary drive.
    b. an achievement.   d. an instinct.

5. The desirable qualities of the external stimulus are the focus of:
    a. the incentive motivational approach.
    b. the drive-reduction motivational approach.
    c. the instinctive motivational approach.
    d. the cognitive motivational approach.

6. The incentive theory of motivation focuses on:
    a. instincts.
    b. the characteristics of external stimuli.
    c. drive reduction.
    d. the rewarding quality of various behaviors that are motivated by arousal.

7. Cognitive theories of motivation make distinctions between:
    a. drive reductions and positive incentives.
    b. rewards and punishments.
    c. intrinsic motivation and extrinsic motivation.
    d. hopes and disappointments.

8. Maslow believed that _____ must be met before people can fulfill any higher-order motivations.
   a. extrinsic needs
   c. primary needs
   b. intrinsic needs
   d. secondary needs

9. Kiana has experienced a major weight loss and has begun refusing to eat. She denies that she has an eating problem and does not recognize that she suffers from:
   a. hyperphagia.
   c. rolfing.
   b. bulimia.
   d. anorexia nervosa.

10. Which of the following is thought to be primarily involved in the physiological regulation of eating behavior?
    a. Cortex
    c. Hypothalamus
    b. Amygdala
    d. Hippocampus

11. Which alternative is **not** good advice for a person trying to lose weight?
    a. Exercise regularly.
    b. Reduce the influence of external cues and social behavior on your eating.
    c. Choose a diet program that gives rather rapid weight loss so you will stay motivated.
    d. Remember, when you reach your desired goal, you're not finished.

12. The _____ is used to measure an individual's need for achievement.
    a. Scholastic Assessment Test
    b. Intelligence Quotient Test
    c. Yerkes-Dodson Achievement Analysis
    d. Thematic Apperception Test

13. Which theory postulates that emotions are identified by observing the environment and comparing ourselves with others?
    a. Schachter-Singer theory
    c. James-Lange theory
    b. Cannon-Bard theory
    d. Ekman's theory

14. William James and Walter Lange suggested that major emotions correlate with particular "gut reactions" of internal organs. They called this internal response:
    a. a physiological pattern.
    c. an autonomic response.
    b. a psychological experience.
    d. a visceral experience.

15. The facial-affect program is:
    a. developed during early childhood.
    c. a technological breakthrough.
    b. unique to American culture.
    d. the activation of nerve impulses.

_____ 16. drive-reduction theory   a. Motivation by focusing on an individual's thoughts, expectations, and understanding of the world.

_____ 17. arousal approach to motivation   b. The theory that claims that drives are produced to obtain our basic biological requirements.

_____ 18. homeostasis

   c. The belief that we try to maintain certain levels of stimulation and activity, changing them as necessary.

_____ 19. incentive approach to motivation

   d. The theory explaining motivation in terms of external stimuli.

_____ 20. cognitive approaches to motivation

   e. The process by which an organism tries to maintain an internal biological balance.

21. The internal motivational state that is created by a physiological need is called a(n) _____.

22. The _____ model views motivated behavior as directed toward the reduction of a physiological need.

23. _____ is the body's mechanism for maintaining an optimum, balanced range of physiological processes.

24. Theories that stress the active processing of information are _____ of motivation.

25. Describe each of the main theories of motivation and attempt to explain a single behavior from the point of view of each theory.

PRACTICE TEST 2:

1. The main function of motivation is to:
   a. create tension.
   b. provide feeling.
   c. promote learning of survival behaviors.
   d. provide direction to behavior.

2. The best example of a drive that is common to both humans and animals is:
   a. power.
   b. hunger.
   c. cognition.
   d. achievement.

3. The compensatory activity of the autonomic nervous system, which returns the body to normal levels of functioning after a trauma, is called:
   a. homeostasis.
   b. biorhythmicity.
   c. biofeedback.
   d. transference.

4. In the drive-reduction motivation model, _____ is the drive related to the need for water.
   a. the drinking instinct
   b. thirst
   c. repetitive water-intake behavior
   d. water-balance in body tissues

5. Some psychologists feel that the incentive theory of motivation is strengthened when combined with complementary concepts drawn from:
   a. instinct theory.
   b. drive-reduction theory.
   c. arousal theory.
   d. cognitive theory.

6. Neuroscience has demonstrated that the _____, in the brain's temporal lobe, is important in the experience of emotions.
   a. amygdala
   b. semi-circular canal
   c. visual cortex
   d. corpus callosum

7. Which theory is **least** tied to biological mechanisms?
   a. Instinct theory
   b. Cognitive theory
   c. Drive-reduction theory
   d. Arousal theory

8. In Maslow's hierarchal pyramid of motivation, self-actualizers:
   a. are notably self-sufficient at all levels: growing their own food, finding their own friends, creating their own artwork, etc.
   b. depend on others but are inwardly focused.
   c. have achieved their major goals in life.
   d. encourage others to do their best while remaining modest themselves.

9. Based on the information given in the text, at which of the following ages would you imagine the amount of fat cells in the body usually stop declining?
   a. 24 years of age
   b. 20 years of age
   c. 12 years of age
   d. 2 years of age

10. An eating disorder usually affecting attractive, successful females between the ages of 12 and 40 who refuse to eat and sometimes literally starve themselves to death is called:
    a. metabolic malfunction.
    b. bulimia.
    c. anorexia nervosa.
    d. obesity.

11. Which of the following is **not** true of the need for achievement?
    a. Individuals with a high need for achievement choose situations in which they are likely to succeed easily.
    b. It is a learned motive.
    c. Satisfaction is obtained by striving for and attaining a level of excellence.
    d. High need for achievement is related to economic and occupational success.

12. Women, as opposed to men, tend to channel their need for power through:
    a. socially responsible ways.
    b. questionable means.
    c. quietly aggressive ways.
    d. uncharted, high-risk opportunities.

13. According to the James-Lange theory of emotion, _____ determines the emotional experience.
    a. physiological change
    b. a cognitive process
    c. an instinctive process
    d. the environment

14. There is convincing evidence that the way in which basic emotions are displayed and interpreted is:
    a. culture-specific.
    b. universal.
    c. gender-specific.
    d. learned.

15. The reflex that makes our facial expressions of emotions occur automatically when triggered is called:
    a. the facial-feedback hypothesis.
    b. the James-Lange theory.
    c. the display rules.
    d. the facial-affect program.

_____ 16. hypothalamus

_____ 17. lateral hypothalamus

_____ 18. ventromedial hypothalamus

_____ 19. metabolism

_____ 20. weight set point

a. The part of the brain that, when damaged, results in an organism's starving to death.

b. The particular level of weight that the body strives to maintain.

c. The part of the brain that, when injured, results in extreme overeating.

d. The structure in the brain that is primarily responsible for regulating food intake.

e. The rate at which energy is produced and expended by the body.

21. The view that basic needs must be met before an individual can move on to higher levels of satisfaction is illustrated by _____.

22. Kendra has been within 5 pounds of the weight she was in high school. This weight range maintained over time is referred to as the _____.

23. Louise is on the phone or having friends over during most of her waking hours. This behavior describes _____, the need to be with others and avoid being alone.

24. According to your text, Eleanor Roosevelt, Abraham Lincoln, and Albert Einstein all fulfilled the highest levels of motivational needs, Maslow's level of _____.

25. The _____ is the tiny brain structure primarily responsible for food intake.

26. Under what conditions might a polygraph test be considered fair? Outline the possible ethical and scientific concerns that arise from the use of a polygraph in support of your answer. In contrast, discuss the same concerns regarding the use of honesty, or integrity tests, by employers who attempt to discover the likelihood that job applicants would steal.

PRACTICE TEST 3: Conceptual, Applied, and Challenging Questions

1. Some college catalogs boast that their school offers generous financial aid packages, roommate selection, and smaller classes. These catalogs emphasize the concept of:
    a. opponent-process motivation.
    b. arousal motivation.
    c. drive-reduction motivation.
    d. extrinsic motivation.

2. Two friends, Damon, the thin one, and Jarrod, the obese one, had lunch just before boarding their plane. When flight attendants serve lunch, what will the two friends be expected to do, according to the external-cue theory?
    a. Neither will eat the lunch on the plane.
    b. The obese man will eat a second lunch, while the thin man may skip it.
    c. The thin man will eat a second lunch, but the obese man will skip it.
    d. Both men will eat a second lunch.

3. Which factor appears to play the **least** significant biological role in hunger for the American public?
    a. Blood chemistry
    c. Number and size of fat cells
    b. Stomach contractions
    d. Weight set point

4. Abby developed a cycle of binge eating, during which she consumed enormous quantities of high-calorie foods and then induced vomiting afterward. Dr. Slocum told Abby that she could do permanent damage to her health if she continued the behavior and that if she continued she could become:
    a. ischemic.
    c. volumetric.
    b. depressed.
    d. bulimic.

5. Tanya finished her college degree with honors and received a variety of excellent job offers. Instead, she decided to enter graduate school to acquire more advanced skills and get even better job offers. Tanya is demonstrating her:
    a. need for affiliation.
    c. fear of failure.
    b. need for achievement.
    d. need for power.

6. Emotions play an important role in all of the following **except**:
    a. making life interesting.
    b. helping us regulate social interaction.
    c. informing us of internal bodily needs.
    d. preparing us for action in response to the external environment.

7. Rudy, who devotes her efforts to maintaining her standing on the Dean's List, is highly motivated in her need for:
    a. affiliation.
    c. power.
    b. cognition.
    d. achievement.

8. The notion that the same nerve impulse triggers simultaneously the physiological arousal and the emotional experience is a hallmark of:
    a. the Cannon-Bard theory of emotion.
    c. the Schachter-Singer theory of emotion.
    b. the facial-affect theory of emotion.
    d. the James-Lange theory of emotion.

9. A polygraph is an electronic device that detects lying by measuring:
    a. brain waves.
    c. breathing patterns and sweating.
    b. brain waves and sweating.
    d. breathing patterns and brain waves.

10. Jan, a Korean American, has become good friends with Eugene, an African American. On some occasions, Jan has difficulty determining the emotion that Eugene is expressing, and vice versa. Which of the following is most likely to account for their difficulty in interpreting each other's emotions?
    a. The facial-feedback hypothesis
    c. The two-factor theory of emotions

b.   The facial-affect program   d.   Display rules

11. Which of the following is **not** one of the six basic categories of nonverbal emotion identified by Ekman?
    a.   Happiness   c.   Anger
    b.   Love   d.   Surprise

12. Which of the following is most typical of an individual who is high in the need for power?
    a.   Tina, who is aggressive and flamboyant
    b.   Daniel, who has joined the local chapter of a political party
    c.   Barbara, who shows concern for others and is highly nurturing
    d.   Mary, who enjoys competitive sports

13. Which of the following is most typical of an individual who is high in the need for affiliation?
    a.   Marie, who appears sensitive to others and prefers to spend all her free time with friends
    b.   Nicolas, who joins a local political group
    c.   Therese, who enjoys team sports and likes to attend parties
    d.   Michael, who is aggressive and controlling whenever he is in groups

14. If a theory claims that all emotions are universally determined by evolutionary forces, which of the following would be necessary to account for differences that arise from culture to culture?
    a.   The facial-feedback hypothesis   c.   The two-factor theory of emotions
    b.   The facial-affect program   d.   Display rules

15. Carlos is quite excited about keeping his new car cleaned and serviced, and he does it without being asked. His father then begins a system of rewarding his efforts with an additional allowance. According to the cognitive approach to motivation, what is the most likely response that Carlos will have?
    a.   His tendency to clean his car will be increased.
    b.   He will probably be less eager to clean his car.
    c.   He will be even more enthusiastic, but he will not clean his car any more frequently.
    d.   He will be unwilling to clean his car at all.

_____ 16.   secondary drives   a.   Anticipated rewards in motivation.

_____ 17.   intrinsic motivation   b.   Participating in an activity for a tangible reward.

_____ 18.   extrinsic motivation
                                           c.   Participating in an activity for its own enjoyment, not for a reward.
_____ 19.   incentive

_____ 20.   obesity   d.   Having weight that is more than 20 percent above the average weight for a person of a given height.

                                           e.   Drives in which no biological need is fulfilled.

21.   In order to increase your _____, the rate at which food is converted to energy, you need to increase exercise.

22. Parents who are demanding and overcontrolling may increase the likelihood that their daughters will develop _____.

23. Jason has the tendency to seek impact, control, and influence over his friends and the people he works with. This is called the _____.

24. There are cross-cultural differences in the _____, the guidelines that govern the appropriateness of nonverbal emotion.

25. Preparing us for action, shaping future behavior, and helping us act more effectively with others are all functions of _____.

26. Explain how parents can attempt to minimize the negative affects of a culture that demands an unreasonable focus on thinness for its youth, especially females.

Module 29:	Module 30:	Module 31:	Module 32:
[a] motivation	[a] obesity	[a] emotions	[a] facial-affect program
[b] instincts	[b] hypothalamus	[b] James-Lange	[b] Display rules
[c] Drive-reduction	[c] lateral hypothalamus	[c] Cannon-Bard	[c] dialect theory
[d] drive	[d] ventromedial hypothalamus	[d] Schachter-Singer	[d] facial-feedback
[e] Primary drives	[e] weight set point		
[f] secondary drives	[f] Metabolism	Evaluate	Evaluate
[g] homeostasis	[g] settling point	1. c	1. b
[h] arousal	[h] Anorexia nervosa	2. b	2. a
[i] incentive	[i] Bulimia	3. a	3. c
[j] Incentive	[j] need for achievement	4. d	4. d
[k] Cognitive	[k] Thematic Apperception Test (TAT)		
[l] Intrinsic motivation	[l] need for affiliation		
[m] extrinsic motivation	[m] need for power		
[n] self-actualization			
Evaluate			
1. b	Evaluate		
2. c	1. e		
3. a	2. d		
4. e	3. c		
5. d	4. b		
	5. a		

Selected Rethink Answers

29-1   The arousal approach might be seen in the workplace by employees who seek either a very high or a very low level of stimulation and activity. Individuals may self-select into jobs that meet this need. Employees should look for "goodness of fit" in employee–job matching. The incentive approach, the desire to obtain valued external goals, would encourage employers to find out what they can provide for employees to work toward. In the cognitive approach, employers should encourage the development of intrinsic motivation by rewarding employees for the job they do.

30-2   All of these characteristics could be important, depending on the job a person is applying for. You'd want people high in need for achievement in jobs which are very challenging and require a lot of hard work. These also might be jobs in which people can work independently, so they can show how well they, personally, have achieved. You'd want people high in need for affiliation in jobs where there are many people around. These might be jobs in which people need to work interdependently, in groups, and/or in jobs serving clients or customers. You'd want people high in need for power in executive-level positions, where people are required to make policy decisions, influence the future of the organization and the people in it, etc. Of course, all jobs require that people have the requisite knowledge, skills, and abilities to perform effectively, regardless of their motivations.

Practice Test 1:

1.   d   mod. 29 p. 328
a.   Incorrect. Because we may satisfy our primary drives without much difficulty, they may not hold much importance when compared with other types of drives.
b.   Incorrect. Other types of drives may motivate an organism more.

c.   Incorrect. They must be satisfied for self-actualization to occur.
*d. Correct. By definition, primary drives are those that have a biological basis.

2.   b   mod. 29 p. 327
a.   Incorrect. True, but "motivation" is a more comprehensive choice.
*b. Correct. This defines motivation.
c.   Incorrect. Emotions influence behavior, but refer more to feelings.
d.   Incorrect. These are currently unknown to earthling science.

3.   b   mod. 29 p. 328
a.   Incorrect. There is no concept such as "primary drive equilibrium."
*b. Correct. "Homeostasis" is the term used to describe a biological balance or equilibrium.
c.   Incorrect. But drive reduction might be used to achieve a state of homeostasis.
d.   Incorrect. Opponent-process theory is one of the theories that depends on the tendency toward homeostasis to account for many phenomena.

4.   c   mod. 29 p. 328
a.   Incorrect. A primary drive has a clear biological need that it satisfies.
b.   Incorrect. An achievement may or may not have a biological drive.
*c. Correct. By definition, secondary drives are not based on biological needs.
d.   Incorrect. An instinct is a species-specific behavior governed by genetics and is thus biological.

5.   a   mod. 29 p. 331
*a. Correct. External stimuli provide for "incentives" to act in a certain way.
b.   Incorrect. The drive-reduction model focuses on internal stimuli.
c.   Incorrect. Desirableness would be irrelevant to instincts.
d.   Incorrect. Although important for this theory, external stimuli would not be the focus.

6.   b   mod. 29 p. 331
a.   Incorrect. Instinct theory, not incentive theory, focuses on instincts.
*b. Correct. The characteristics of external stimuli provide the incentive, or promise of reinforcement, that governs incentive theory.
c.   Incorrect. Drive reduction is a core concept of drive theory.
d.   Incorrect. This refers to arousal theory.

7.   c   mod. 29 p. 331
a.   Incorrect. These two factors are taken from two other approaches to motivation.
b.   Incorrect. Both of these are typically extrinsic.

*c. Correct. Actually, motivations can only be one or the other of these two types.
d.   Incorrect. These would have more to do with feelings and how they connect to motivation.

8.   c   mod. 29 p. 332
a.   Incorrect. Some higher-order motivations may involve extrinsic motivations.
b.   Incorrect. Higher-order motivations would include many intrinsic needs.
*c. Correct. Primary needs must be satisfied before the individual can move on to higher-order motivation.
d.   Incorrect. Higher-order motivation includes many secondary drives.

9.   d   mod. 30 p. 339
a.   Incorrect. Hyperphagia would not account for the refusal to admit to the eating problem.
b.   Incorrect. Unlike the anorexic, the bulimic eats, and then regurgitates the meal.
c.   Incorrect. This is a deep massage technique.
*d. Correct. Someone suffering from anorexia refuses to eat and claims that she is overweight.

10. c   mod. 30 p. 337
a.   Incorrect. The cortex plays a role, but it is not central.
b.   Incorrect. In the limbic system but not correct.
*c. Correct. The hypothalamus monitors blood sugar and other body chemistry to regulate eating behavior.
d.   Incorrect. In the limbic system but not correct.

11. c   mod. 30 p. 340
a.   Incorrect. This is very good advice.
b.   Incorrect. A regular, internally driven eating behavior will minimize the effects of external cues.
*c. Correct. A slow diet will be more effective than a fast diet.
d.   Incorrect. This is good advice because weight management is a lifelong endeavor.

12. d   mod. 30 p. 342
a.   Incorrect. The SAT measures achievement.
b.   Incorrect. IQ tests measure IQ.
c.   Incorrect. This test is yet to be developed.
*d. Correct. The Thematic Apperception Test, or TAT, was used by McClelland to determine levels of achievement motivation in his research subjects.

13. a   mod. 31 p. 350
*a. Correct. Schachter and Singer proposed a theory of emotions that includes the cognitive element of interpretation of surroundings.
b. Incorrect. Cannon and Bard were critical of the James-Lange theory and proposed that exciting information went to the thalamus and then to the cortex and the physiological systems simultaneously.
c. Incorrect. The James-Lange theory is based on the perception of visceral changes.
d. Incorrect. Ekman's theory states that nonverbal responses to emotion-evoking stories seems to be universal.

14. d   mod. 31 p. 348
a. Incorrect. See answer d.
b. Incorrect. See answer d.
c. Incorrect. See answer d.
*d. Correct. Visceral refers to the internal organs.

15. d   mod. 32 p. 357
a. Incorrect. It may be innate.
b. Incorrect. It is found in every culture.
c. Incorrect. It is not a computer program.
*d. Correct. The "program" refers to the neural pathways involved in expressing an emotion.

16. b   mod. 29 p. 328
17. c   mod. 29 p. 329
18. e   mod. 29 p. 328
19. d   mod. 29 p. 331
20. a   mod. 29 p. 331

21. drive   mod. 29 p. 328
22. drive-reduction   mod. 29 p. 328
23. Homeostasis   mod. 29 p. 328
24. cognitive theories mod. 29 p. 331

25.
- Describe each of the main theories: instinct, drive reduction, arousal, incentive, opponent process, cognitive, and need theories.
- Select an activity—it could be anything from watching television to playing a sport—and describe the behavior involved from the point of view of the motivation theories (no more than one sentence each).
- Remember, some behaviors, like those satisfying basic needs, are easier to describe from the points of view of some theories, whereas others are easier to describe from other theories.

Practice Test 2:
1. d   mod. 29 p. 327
a. Incorrect. It may be focused on alleviating tension.
b. Incorrect. Feelings come from other aspects of behavior, although feelings and motivation may both be processed at least in part in the limbic system.
c. Incorrect. Many survival behaviors do not have to be learned, and many motivations are not survival-oriented.
*d. Correct. Motivation guides and energizes behavior.

2. b   mod. 29 p. 328
a. Incorrect. Some animals and some humans may not be interested in power.
*b. Correct. Hunger appears to be a rather universal drive among humans, animals, and insects.
c. Incorrect. Cognition is not considered a drive.
d. Incorrect. Achievement is a particularly human drive.

3. a   mod. 29 p. 328
*a. Correct. This is the activity of the parasympathetic system.
b. Incorrect. This new term may soon find its way into scientology.
c. Incorrect. Biofeedback requires intentional activity to control body processes.
d. Incorrect. This is a technical, psychoanalytic term that is not relevant to homeostasis.

4. b   mod. 29 p. 328
a. Incorrect. No such instinct exists.
*b. Correct. Actually, this is true in all approaches to motivation.
c. Incorrect. Sounds good, though.
d. Incorrect. The need for fluid in body tissues is important information for the brain's regulation of fluid in the body.

5. b   mod. 29 p. 331
a. Incorrect. Instinct theory focuses on innate drives and thus would not complement incentive theory.
*b. Correct. Incentives account for external factors, whereas drive reduction would account for internal factors.
c. Incorrect. Arousal theory says that we actually seek ways to increase stimulation (in contrast to drive reduction).
d. Incorrect. Cognitive theory suggests that motivation is a product of people's thoughts, expectations, and goals.

6. a   mod. 29 p. 331
*a. Correct. The amygdala is in the temporal lobe, and is related to emotion.
b. Incorrect. This is in the ear.
c. Incorrect. Reasonably, what you see could affect your emotions, but the visual cortex is separate from the temporal lobe.
d. Incorrect. This is the bundle of nerve fibers connecting the two brain hemispheres.

7. b   mod. 29 p. 331
a. Incorrect. Instinct theory requires the innate mechanisms known as instincts.
*b. Correct. Cognitive theory applies to our understanding of goals, their consequences, and our abilities to reach them.
c. Incorrect. Drive reduction depends on the biological concept of drives.
d. Incorrect. Arousal is biological.

8. c   mod. 29 p. 332
a. Incorrect. This is a gross overstatement of the idea of self-actualization.
b. Incorrect. Everyone is dependent on others for some aspect of living.
*c. Correct. Self-actualizers are striving toward goals and seeking to express their potential.
d. Incorrect. Self-actualizers are often not as concerned with the successes of others.

9. d   mod. 29 p. 338
a. Incorrect. The number of fat cells is fixed by the age of about 2.
b. Incorrect. See answer a.
c. Incorrect. See answer a.
*d. Correct. By 2, the number of fat cells stops declining.

10. c   mod. 29 p. 339
a. Incorrect. Try anorexia nervosa.
b. Incorrect. Bulimia is a similar disorder, but it involves binging and purging behavior to maintain or lose weight.
*c. Correct. Sufferers of this disorder often will not eat or will develop the disorder known as bulimia and then binge and purge.
d. Incorrect. But these females appear to have an extreme fear of obesity and will perceive themselves as obese even when they are dramatically underweight.

11. a   mod. 30 p. 342
*a. Correct. They are more likely to choose situations that are moderately challenging, not easy.
b. Incorrect. It is learned, or acquired.
c. Incorrect. Individuals with a high need for achievement do find satisfaction from attainment.
d. Incorrect. This is true as well.

12. a   mod. 29 p. 342
*a. Correct. Women tend to find power through socially acceptable ways more often than do men.
b. Incorrect. The means are rarely questionable and do tend to be socially acceptable.
c. Incorrect. The quality of aggression is not necessarily a matter of power.
d. Incorrect. This is much more likely with men than women.

13. a   mod. 31 p. 348
*a. Correct. The perception of a physiological change is the emotion for James and Lange.
b. Incorrect. However, because they argued that it was the perception of the physiological change that was the emotion, this answer is partially correct.
c. Incorrect. They did not turn to instinctive process.
d. Incorrect. The environment does not play a very big role in their theory.

14. b   mod. 31 p. 356
a. Incorrect. The evidence suggests universal patterns.
*b. Correct. The basic emotions are expressed and interpreted similarly across all cultures that have been studied.
c. Incorrect. See answer a.
d. Incorrect. See answer a.

15. d   mod. 32 p. 357
a. Incorrect. Close, but this hypothesis says that if we make the expression of an emotion, the feedback will cause us to experience the emotion.
b. Incorrect. James and Lange thought it was our perception of the bodily changes that was the emotion.
c. Incorrect. Display rules govern the variations of expression from one culture to another.
*d. Correct. This view suggests that we are programmed to express the basic emotions in the same manner from one group to another.

16. d   mod. 30 p. 337
17. a   mod. 30 p. 337
18. c   mod. 30 p. 337
19. e   mod. 30 p. 337
20. b   mod. 30 p. 337

21. Maslow's hierarchy   mod. 29 p. 332
22. weight set point   mod. 30 p. 337
23. Affiliation   mod. 30 p. 342
24. self-actualization   mod. 29 p. 332
25. Hypothalamus   mod. 30 p. 337

26.
- State the conditions for which you consider polygraph use to be appropriate. Give an example from your own experience, if you have one.
- Indicate the rationale that makes its use fair or appropriate. Are the rights of the test-taker protected? Would incrimination lead to damage to the individual?
- Is it fair to use a technique that has established scientific validity in specific areas in applications that go beyond the established validity?
- Integrity tests have now replaced the polygraph, and the issues now include concern for prejudging someone as "likely to steal." Like the polygraph, these honesty tests are considered of questionable validity.

Practice Test 3:
1. d   mod. 29 p. 331
a.   Incorrect. No opponent processes are indicated here.
b.   Incorrect. Arousal motivation suggests that we would seek an exciting college, not necessarily a high-quality one.
c.   Incorrect. However, the money may eventually lead to a reduction drive.
*d.   Correct. The extrinsic rewards are quite evident.

2. b   mod. 29 p. 338
a.   Incorrect. See answer b.
*b.   Correct. Because food is an external cue, the obese man is more likely to experience "hunger" as a result of the food, even though he already had lunch.
c.   Incorrect. The thin man is probably not so easily influenced by the external cue of another meal.
d.   Incorrect. Only if the thin man is one of those people who can eat all the time and gain no excess weight.

3. b   mod. 29 p. 337
a.   Incorrect. See answer b.
*b.   Correct. Blood chemistry, number and size of fat cells, and weight set point are more important factors than stomach contractions.
c.   Incorrect. See answer b.
d.   Incorrect. See answer b.

4. d   mod. 29 p. 339
a.   Incorrect. Interesting word, though.
b.   Incorrect. Depression is not the cause.
c.   Incorrect. Any type of measurement having to do with volume.
*d.   Correct. The disorder is known as bulimia.

5. b   mod. 29 p. 342
a.   Incorrect. A need for affiliation could be at work here, if she thought she would be isolated from friends once she began work.
*b.   Correct. This sounds most like a need for achievement.
c.   Incorrect. A fear of failure could be operative here, if she is avoiding beginning her career for fear of failure.
d.   Incorrect. Power can be achieved without education.

6. c   mod. 29 p. 345
a.   Incorrect. Life would probably be interesting without emotions, but far less so.
b.   Incorrect. Emotion plays a major role in regulating social interaction.
*c.   Correct. We are informed of our bodily needs through other mechanisms, mainly those related to motivation.
d.   Incorrect. Emotions are crucial for our preparation for actions, especially emergencies.

7. d   mod. 29 p. 342
a.   Incorrect. A need for affiliation would explain joining a sorority.
b.   Incorrect. The need for cognition might better explain a desire to know and solve problems.
c.   Incorrect. A need for power would account for a student running for student government offices.
*d.   Correct. If the effort is aimed at retaining the recognition of the Dean's List, then this describes a need for achievement.

8. a   mod. 31 p. 349
*a. Correct. Their position differed from that of James and Lange, who thought our perception of the bodily changes was the emotion.
b. Incorrect. This suggests that the facial changes result in emotional feelings.
c. Incorrect. Schachter and Singer thought that the emotion resulted from the interpretation of the perception of a bodily change.
d. Incorrect. James and Lange thought our perception of the bodily changes was the emotion.

9. c   mod. 31 p. 352
a. Incorrect. See answer c.
b. Incorrect. See answer c.
*c. Correct. The polygraph measures breathing rate, heart rate, blood pressure, and sweating, but not brain waves.
d. Incorrect. See answer c.

10. d   mod. 32 p. 358
a. Incorrect. The facial-feedback hypothesis suggests that information is linked to our self-perception of the emotion.
b. Incorrect. The facial-affect program is the pattern of neural responses that govern any given emotional expression.
c. Incorrect. The two-factor theory addresses how we utilize environmental information in evaluating our own emotional states.
*d. Correct. Display rules may affect how easily Eugene and Jan interpret each other's emotions and expressions, since they do have cultural elements.

11. b   mod. 32 p. 356
a. Incorrect. See answer b.
*b. Correct. The six emotions are happiness, anger, sadness, surprise, disgust, and fear.
c. Incorrect. See answer b.
d. Incorrect. See answer b.

12. c   mod. 29 p. 343
a. Incorrect. Being aggressive and flamboyant is not a typical approach for women who are high in the need for power.
b. Incorrect. Belonging to a political party is not a sign of a need for power.
*c. Correct. Women tend to display their need for power through socially acceptable methods, like concern for others and nurturing behavior.
d. Incorrect. Competitive sports are not themselves related to individual need for power.

13. a   mod. 29 p. 342
*a. Correct. Sensitivity to others and desires to spend time with friends reflect a need for affiliation.
b. Incorrect. Membership in a political group is not sufficient to indicate a need for affiliation.
c. Incorrect. Partying and sports are not signs of high need for affiliation.
d. Incorrect. Aggressive behavior does not signal a need for affiliation.

14. d   mod. 32 p. 358
a. Incorrect. Facial-feedback would be a support for the hereditary aspect of emotions.
b. Incorrect. A facial-affect program could be argued as part of the evolutionary aspect of emotions.
c. Incorrect. The two-factor theory of emotions would help account for how individuals differ in their interpretations, but not for the differences between cultures.
*d. Correct. Display rules are culturally defined, so they would be the means of accounting for cultural differences.

15. b   mod. 29 p. 331
a. Incorrect. See answer b.
*b. Correct. The shift from intrinsic to extrinsic rewards can undermine the behavior.
c. Incorrect. See answer b.
d. Incorrect. The shift from intrinsic to extrinsic rewards can undermine the behavior, but it will not necessarily destroy it.

16. e   mod. 29 p. 328
17. c   mod. 29 p. 331
18. b   mod. 29 p. 331
19. a   mod. 29 p. 331
20. d   mod. 29 p. 335

21. metabolism   mod. 29 p. 337
22. anorexia   mod. 29 p. 339
23. need for power   mod. 29 p. 343
24. display rules   mod. 32 p. 358
25. Emotions   mod. 31 p. 345

26.
▪ Discuss the biological and sociocultural viewpoints about weight control. Suggest behavioral alternatives.
▪ Allow children to select food and only eat until thy are full, not until they clean their plate. Don't use food as a reward, escape, or for consolation.
▪ Increase opportunities for exercise.
▪ Encourage individuals to focus on what they can do, not how they look.

Chapter 11: Sexuality and Gender

Module 33: Gender and Sex
Module 34: Understanding Human Sexual Response: The Facts of Life
Module 35: The Diversity of Sexual Behavior
Module 36: Sexual Difficulties: When Sex Goes Wrong

Overview

This set of modules presents the issues of human sexuality from several vantage points.

Module 33 explains how gender and sex are primarily the result of social expectations and cultural patterns. Sexual harassment and sexism on the job continue to impact how men and women are treated at work and in school settings. Very minor differences have been described regarding personality differences between the sexes. There is increasing evidence of minimal to no differences in cognitive skills between the sexes. Biological causes of sex differences are discussed, and an explanation of the evolutionary approach to gender differences is offered.

Module 34 presents information to help in the understanding of the human sexual response. Neuroscientists consider sexuality from the perspective of the relationship of the brain and the nervous system to the functioning of the sexual organs. This response is unique among humans, and the physiological response does follow a pattern.

Module 35 explains the variety of sexual behaviors, which include masturbation; premarital, marital, and extramarital heterosexual activity; and homosexual and bisexual activity.

Module 36 discusses the transmission of sexual disease as well as issues involved in sexual difficulties; nonconsensual sex, including rape, date rape, and sexual abuse are also discussed.

To further investigate the topics covered in this chapter, you can visit the related Web sites by visiting the following link: www.mhhe.com/feldmanup8.

Prologue: One Event, Two Perspectives
Looking Ahead

Module 33:
Gender and Sex

Gender Roles: Society's Expectations for Women and Men
Gender Differences: More Similar Than Dissimilar
Sources of Gender Differences: Where Biology and Society Meet

- **What are the major differences between male and female gender roles?**

Gender and Sex

[a] _____ is the sense of being male or female. From the very beginning of life, children are exposed to societal expectations that lead to the formation of

[b] _____, defined as the set of expectations that indicates appropriate behavior for men and women. The expectations differ significantly, and the result is that one sex stereotypes the other. [c] _____ is the process of making judgments and developing expectations about members of a group based on membership in the group.

Stereotypes based on gender roles result in [d] _____, which consists of negative attitudes and behavior toward a person based on that person's sex. In our society, the stereotype of the male is that he must be competent (independent, objective, and competitive), and the stereotype of the female is that she must be warm and expressive.

[e] _____ is defined by unwanted sexual attention, the creation of a hostile or abusive environment, or being coerced into participating in a relationship or unwanted sexual activity. Sexual harassment is more closely connected to the harasser's desire for power than for sex.

There are few clear personality or cognitive differences between men and women. However, both biological and environmental factors contribute to differences in how the genders behave. Hormones may play a role in the differences between male and female brains. Prenatal exposure to [f] _____, the male sex hormones, may slow the growth of the left hemisphere. The right hemisphere, responsible for mathematical problem solving, may then be strengthened.

When [g] _____, the female sex hormone, levels are high, women perform better on tasks requiring verbal skill and muscle coordination.

Environmental causes of gender differences include the amount and kind of interaction between parents and their children. Fathers play more roughly with their infant sons than daughters, and middle-class mothers talk more to their daughters. These differences lead to different personal experiences.

[h] _____ is the way individuals learn the rules and norms of socially appropriate behavior. The process includes information gained from television and the educational system. Boys are more likely to receive attention from teachers. Sandra Bem has suggested that this produces **[i]** _____, cognitive frameworks that organize and guide a child's understanding of gender-relevant information. In order to decrease their development, society must encourage **[j]** _____ activity, in which the gender roles include both male and female characteristics.

Evaluate

_____ 1.   gender roles

_____ 2.   stereotyping

_____ 3.   sexism

_____ 4.   gender schema

_____ 5.   androgynous

a.   Societal expectations about appropriate behavior for women and men.

b.   A cognitive framework that organizes and guides a child's understanding of gender.

c.   Beliefs and expectations about members of a group based on their membership in that group.

d.   A state in which gender roles encompass characteristics thought typical of both sexes.

e.   Negative attitudes toward a person based on that person's sex.

Rethink

33-1   The U.S. Congress has enacted laws prohibiting women in the armed forces from participating directly in combat, in the interest of keeping them out of harm's way. Do you think such laws are protective or sexist? Is this an example of "benevolent sexism"?

33-2   _From the perspective of a business executive:_ Evidence shows that sexism in the workplace is widespread. If you wanted to end sexism in organizational settings, can you think of ways to narrow the gap between men and women in terms of occupations and salary?

Spotlight on Terminology and Language—ESL Pointers

Page 356 "I figured she didn't want me to think that she was **"easy" or "loose."** "

"Easy" or "loose" refers to someone (usually female) that is willing to have sex with just about anybody without much persuasion.

Page 356 "Yet this example of date rape illustrates the emotion, confusion, and **downright** ignorance that often characterizes one of the most universal of behaviors: sexuality."

Downright means absolute or complete.

Page 356 "**Exemplifying** major personal, as well as societal, concerns, sex and the interrelated-topic of gender are also key topics for psychologists in a variety of specialties."

When something is **exemplified**, it is an ideal example of whatever category it belongs to.

Page 357 "**Gender roles** are the set of expectations, defined by a particular society, that indicate what is appropriate for men and women."

Gender roles are the societal expectations about how females and males should behave.

Page 358 "People in Western societies like ours generally hold well-defined stereotypes about men and women, which **prevail** regardless of age, economic status, and social and educational background."

These stereotypes **prevail**; they exist and often seem to be held by many.

Page 358 "Women continue to be viewed as best suited for traditionally female jobs: "**pink-collar**" jobs such as secretary, nurse, cashier, and other female-dominated professions that often feature low pay and low status."

Traditional office jobs were called "white-collar" jobs because the typical office workers wore white shirts & ties, as opposed to "blue-collar" workers with blue or denim work shirts. Since pink is a color associated with girls, "**pink-collar**" refers to jobs traditionally held by women.

Page 359 "On the other hand, attitudes are **shifting**."

Shifting means changing from one idea to another.

Page 359 "Even when women move into upper-level high-status positions, they may face significant **hurdles** in their efforts to move up the corporate ladder, eventually hitting what has come to be called the **glass ceiling**."

Hurdles are difficulties or barriers. Have you found your gender has played any role in the obstacles you may have encountered in your career search?

A **glass ceiling** is a barrier to career advancement. It is an unofficial but very real impediment to someone's opportunity for employment progress.

Page 361 "In some cases, harassment stems from **benevolent sexism**, stereotyped and restrictive attitudes that appear, on the surface, to be beneficial to women."

Benevolent means marked by or suggesting kind or charitable acts. **Sexism** is prejudice or discrimination based on sex. It is an arbitrary stereotyping of social roles based on gender.

Page 361 "Women's self-esteem is influenced to a large extent by their perception of their sense of **interdependence** and connection with others."

Interdependence is mutually dependent. Members of a family are often **interdependent**.

Page 362 "Women more often raise their **pitch** at the end of a sentence, and add 'tags' at the end of an opinion, rather than **stating the opinion outright**."

Pitch is the subjective quality of a sound, dependent primarily of the frequency and to a lesser extent on the intensity of the sound waves as produced by its source.
A **tag** is a speech fragment, used in speaking to soften the effect of words, or appear less certain of statement. **Tags** can also be used to add effect.

When you **state an opinion outright**, you state it openly and without qualification or reservation.

Page 363 "Women, however, are generally better than men at **decoding** the facial expressions of others (Ellyson, Dovidio, & Brown, 1992; Burgoon & Dillman, 1995; Coats & Feldman, 1996)."

Decoding is recognizing and interpreting.

Page 363 "That conclusion was accepted widely as one of the **truisms** of the psychological literature."

A **truism** is an undoubted or self-evident truth. It is often thought of as a fact that is too obvious to mention.

Page 364 "Some psychologists argue that **evolutionary** forces lead to certain differences between men's and women's behavior."

Evolution is a gradual process in which something changes into a different and usually better or more complex form.

Page 366 "The **potency** of television as an agent of socialization is underscored by data indicating that the more television children watch, the more sexist they become (Coltraine & Messineo, 2000; Furnham, Pallangyo, & Gunter, 2001; Turkel, 2002)."

The **potency** of television refers to the strength and effectiveness of television in influencing gender socialization.

Page 366 "On the basis of their **schemas** for appropriate and inappropriate behavior for males and females, children begin to behave in ways that reflect society's gender roles."

A **schema** is an organizational or conceptual pattern in the mind.

Page 366 "**Androgynous** individuals combine the psychological and behavioral characteristics thought typical of both sexes."

When someone is **androgynous,** they have both masculine and feminine characteristics. Do you think an **androgynous** individual, a feminine individual, or a masculine individual would survive best and thrive in our society today?

Module 34: Understanding Human Sexual Response: The Facts of Life

The Basic Biology of Sexual Behavior
Psychological Aspects of Sexual Excitement: What Turns People On?
The Phases of Sexual Response: The Ups and Downs of Sex

Exploring Diversity: Female Circumcision:
A Celebration of Culture—or Genital Mutilation?

- *Why, and under what circumstances, do we become sexually aroused?*

Understanding Human Sexual Response: The Facts of Life

Sexual behavior in humans is filled with meaning, values, and feelings. The basic biology of the sexual response helps us understand the importance of sexual behavior. Human sexual behavior is not governed by the genetic control that other animals experience. In males, the testes, part of

the male **[a]** _____, secrete **[b]** _____, beginning at puberty. Androgens increase the sex drive and produce secondary sex characteristics like body hair and voice change. When women reach puberty, the ovaries, the female reproductive organs,

produce **[c]** _____ and **[d]** _____, the female sex

hormone. Estrogen reaches its highest levels during **[e]** _____, the release of eggs from the ovaries. In many animals, the period of ovulation is the only time they are receptive to sex. Women remain receptive throughout their cycles. Although biological factors are important, we are also conditioned to respond to a wide range of stimuli that lead to arousal.

No areas of the body automatically lead to sexual arousal when touched. The

[f] _____, areas of the body that are dense in nerve endings, are sensitive to all kinds of touch, and what differs from one touch to another is the interpretation given to it.

The phases of the sexual response are (1) the **[g]** _____, during which the *penis* becomes erect and the *clitoris* swells. The *vagina* also becomes lubricated; (2) the

[h] _____, during which the body prepares for orgasm, with a maximum level of arousal being reached. In women, the breasts and the vagina swell. Heartbeat and pulse

rate increase; (3) **[i]** _____; although the sensation is difficult to describe, the physical process is a rhythmic muscular contraction. Males expel *semen*, the fluid containing sperm, in a process known as *ejaculation*; (4) and the final phase, the

[j] _____, occurring when the body returns to normal. In males, the

[k] _____ occurs, during which the males are unable to be aroused. Orgasm and

340

ejaculation are controlled by separate parts of the nervous system, so it is possible for some males to have multiple orgasms before ejaculation.

Evaluate

_____ 1. excitement phase

_____ 2. plateau phase

_____ 3. ejaculation

_____ 4. resolution stage

_____ 5. refractory period

a. A period in which the maximum level of arousal is attained, the penis and clitoris swell with blood, and the body prepares for orgasm.

b. Entered by a male after the resolution stage, a temporary period during which he cannot be sexually aroused again.

c. The final stage of sexual arousal, during which the body returns to its normal state.

d. The expulsion of semen through the penis.

e. A period during which the body prepares for sexual intercourse.

Rethink

34-1   Why do you think humans differ from other species in their year-round receptivity to sex and in the number and variety of sexual stimulants? What evolutionary purpose might this difference serve in humans?

34-2   *From the perspective of a sex counselor:* How do people learn to be aroused by the stimuli that their society considers erotic? When do they learn this, and where does the message come from?

Spotlight on Terminology and Language—ESL Pointers

Page 369 "When I started "**tuning out**," teachers thought I was sick—physically sick that is."

Tuning out is the act of withdrawing into your own thoughts and not paying attention to what is going on around you; you are daydreaming.

Page 369 "If I'd told them I was **carrying on** with Jennifer Lopez in their classes, while supposedly learning my Caesar and my Latin vocabulary, they'd have thought I was—well, delirious."

In this context, **carrying on** refers to being with someone and engaging in some type of sexual behavior, such as flirting or kissing.

Page 369 "Not only do **androgens** produce secondary sex characteristics, such as the growth of body hair and a deepening of the voice, they also increase the sex drive."

A general term for male sex hormones secreted by the testes is **androgens**.

Page 370 "Humans are considerably more **versatile**; not only other people but nearly any object, sight, smell, sound, or other stimulus can lead to sexual excitement."

Humans are more diversified in the stimuli that can lead to sexual excitement. They respond to a variety of stimuli.

Page 370 "Psychological Aspects of Sexual Excitement: **What Turns People On?**"

The phrase "**What Turns People On**?" is asking what makes people sexually excited.

Page 371 "Areas of the body, called erogenous zones, that have an unusually rich **array** of nerve receptors are particularly sensitive not just to sexual touch but to any kind of touch."

An **array** is a collection, a large number of nerves.

Page 375 "Furthermore, in some cases, more extensive surgery is carried out, in which additional parts of the female genitals are removed or are sewn together with **catgut** or thorns (French, 1977; Obermeyer, 2001; Lacey, 2002)."

Catgut is a tough thin cord made form the dried intestines of sheep and other animals. **Catgut** is used as the surgical thread.

Module 35:
The Diversity of
Sexual Behavior

Approaches to Sexual Normality
Surveying Sexual Behavior: What's Happening Behind Closed Doors?
Masturbation: Solitary Sex
Heterosexuality
Homosexuality and Bisexuality

Applying Psychology in the 21st Century:
Sexual Orientation: How Genes Matter

Transexualism

- *What is "normal" sexual behavior?*
- *How do most people behave sexually?*

The Varieties of Sexual Behavior

Sexual behavior is influenced by expectations, attitudes, beliefs, and the state of medical and biological knowledge. Defining what is normal can be approached by determining the deviation for an average or typical behavior, although many behaviors are unusual statistically but not abnormal. Another approach is to compare behavior against a standard or ideal form. However, the selection of a standard is difficult because it must be universally acceptable.

[a] _____ is sexual self-stimulation, and its practice is quite common. Males masturbate more often than females, with males beginning in early teens, although females start later and reach a maximum frequency later. Negative attitudes about masturbation continue, although it is perfectly healthy and harmless.

[b] _____ refers to sexual behavior between men and women. It includes all aspects of sexual contact—kissing, caressing, sex play, and intercourse. Premarital sex continues to be viewed by some through a(n) **[c]** _____, as something acceptable for males but unacceptable for females. The double standard appears to be changing toward an attitude of **[d]** _____, meaning that premarital intercourse is permissible if affection exists between the two persons.

With the increase in marital intercourse, there has also been an increase in **[e]** _____, or sexual activity between a married person and someone other than the spouse. Extramarital sex remains something that is consistently disapproved of.

Humans are not born with an innate attraction to the opposite sex. **[f]** _____
are individuals sexually attracted to members of the same sex, while **[g]** _____
are sexually attracted to both sexes. Many homosexual people prefer the terms *gay* or *lesbian* to
the more restrictive term *homosexual*. At least 20 to 25 percent of males and about 15 percent of
females have had an adulthood homosexual experience, and between 5 and 10 percent of both
males and females are exclusively homosexual.

Although people view homosexuality and heterosexuality as distinct orientations, Kinsey
places the two orientations on a scale from exclusively heterosexual behavior to exclusively
homosexual behavior.

Evaluate

_____ 1. heterosexuality

_____ 2. extramarital sex

_____ 3. homosexuality

_____ 4. bisexuality

a. A sexual attraction to a member of one's own sex.

b. Sexual behavior between a man and a woman.

c. Sexual activity between a married person and someone who is not his or her spouse.

d. A sexual attraction to members of both sexes.

Rethink

35-1 What societal factors have led to a reduction in the double standard by which sexuality in men and women is regarded differently? Do you think the double standard has completely vanished?

35-2 *From the perspective of a public opinion surveyor:* In what ways might a sample of respondents to a survey about sexual practices be biased? How might bias in such a survey be reduced?

Spotlight on Terminology and Language—ESL Pointers

Page 377 "Indeed, **trivia buffs** might be interested to learn that corn flakes owe their invention to a nineteenth-century physician, J. W. Kellogg, who believed that because the enjoyment of tasty food provoked sexual excitation, an alternative of "unstimulating" grains was needed."

Trivia buffs are people who enjoy learning and sharing facts that aren't known by many people, because these facts aren't considered important.

Page 378 "If some people prefer **portly** sexual partners, are they abnormal in a society that holds slimness in high regard?"

A **portly** person is heavy-set or fat.

Page 379 "For most of recorded history, the vast variety of sexual practices remained **shrouded** in ignorance."

To **shroud** means to shield or to hide.

Page 379 "However, in the late 1930s, biologist Albert Kinsey **launched** a series of surveys on the sexual behavior of people in the United States."

Albert Kinsey began conducting these surveys in the 1930's. **Launched** means started.

Page 379 "Kinsey and his colleagues interviewed tens of thousands of individuals, and the interview techniques they devised are still regarded as **exemplary** because of their ability to elicit sensitive information without causing embarrassment."

The interview techniques were excellent; they were **exemplary**.

Page 379 "However, by examining the common results **gleaned** from different samples of subjects, we now have a reasonably complete picture of contemporary sexual practices – to which we turn next."

To **glean** is to pick over information, bit by bit, in search of relevant material.

Page 380 "People often believe that the first time they have sexual intercourse they have achieved one of life's major **milestones**."

A **milestone** is used to measure distance along a road, or mark a significant spot. The word "**major**" means big or important. So, significant moments in a person's life, such as birth, death and marriage, are called **major milestones** of that person's life.

Page 381 "What may be most interesting about the patterns of premarital sex is that they show a **convergence** of male and female attitudes and behavior."

Convergence means a coming together. Both male and female attitudes in regard to premarital sex seem to be merging. Both sexes seem to be behaving similarly.

Page 381 "Where differing standards remain, the attitudes are almost always more **lenient** toward the male than toward the female (Sprecher & Hatfield, 1996)."

Lenient here means the attitudes are more relaxed for males.

Page 382 "To judge by the number of articles about sex in marriage, one would think that sexual behavior was the number one standard by which marital **bliss** is measured.

Bliss is pleasure, enjoyment.

Page 383 "Still, the possibility is real that some inherited or biological factor exists that **predisposes** people toward homosexuality, if certain environmental conditions are met (Veniegas, 2000; Teodorov et al., 2002; Rahman, Kumari, & Wilson, 2003)."

Predisposes means something specific inside you causes you to act a certain way.

Page 384 "**Analogously**, insertion of the female variant of the gene into male fruit flies made them avidly pursue other males."

An **analogy** is something that is similar to something else; in this case, the experiment with the fruit flies was similar to the other, and had the same kind of results.

Page 384 "The big problem came at **potty break**, when Alyn headed for the boys' room—and the teacher stepped in the way."

A toilet is sometimes called a **potty**. A scheduled time between activities is a **break**, so a **potty break** is a time between classes to use the toilet.

Module 36:
Sexual Difficulties:
When Sex Goes Wrong

Rape
Childhood Sexual Abuse
Sexually Transmitted Infections (STIs)
Sexual Problems

Becoming an Informed Consumer of Psychology: Lowering the Risks of Date Rape

- *How prevalent are rape and other forms of nonconsenting sex, and what are their causes?*
- *What are the major sexually transmitted infections?*
- *What sexual difficulties do people most frequently encounter?*

Sexual Difficulties: When Sex Goes Wrong

Sexual crimes have profound and long-lasting psychological consequences.

[a] _____ occurs when one person forces another to submit to sexual activity such as intercourse or oral-genital sex. Although rape is thought of by most as a crime committed by strangers, [b] _____ occurs when an acquaintance, first date, or casual date rapes an individual. Date rape is statistically more likely to occur than rape by a stranger. According to research, there is a 14- to 25-percent chance that a woman will be raped in her lifetime, and the chances are greater for African-American women and less for Latina women.

The risk of date rape can be lowered when women set clear limits, assert themselves when someone is pressuring them, and remain aware of risky situations. Men should be aware of their dates' views on sexual behavior, should not see a date as a possible "score," should understand "no" to mean "no," and should not assume that certain kinds of dress and behavior are an invitation to sex. Both men and women should realize that alcohol and drugs affect judgment and communication.

Diseases are classified as a(n) [c] _____ when they are transmitted through sexual contact. [d] _____ is a disease that produces no symptoms initially in women but a burning sensation during urination for men. [e] _____ is a virus related to cold sores. Small sores appear around the genitals and can break open and cause pain.

[f] _____ is an infection caused by a parasite that can cause pain during intercourse or urination and discharge from the vagina. [g] _____ can lead to

fertility problems and infection, and untreated *syphilis* can lead to brain and heart disease, can affect a fetus, and can be fatal. **[h]** _____ are small, lumpy warts on the genitals.

Sexual behavior in the last decade has changed because of **[i]** _____. Although AIDS was transmitted early among homosexuals, it now affects most populations. Casual sex is now less likely, and people use condoms more frequently. The only sure way to avoid getting AIDS from sexual activity is not to have any. Psychologists can contribute by finding ways to change behaviors that increase the risk for transmission of the disease.

Almost everyone will at some time in their lives experience a sexual problem. For males, one of the most common is **[j]** _____, or the inability to achieve or maintain an erection. **[k]** _____ refers to the inability of a male to delay orgasm as long as he wishes. **[l]** _____ occurs when a man is unable to ejaculate. Women experience **[m]** _____, or the lack of an orgasm.

[n] _____ refers to women who have never experienced an orgasm, and

[o] _____ refers to women who are currently unable to experience orgasm but have done so in the past, or who experience orgasm only under certain conditions. *Secondary orgasmic dysfunction* is so common in females that it is not considered dysfunctional, but merely a variant of female sexuality. Both males and females can experience **[p]** _____, which is described as a loss of motivation for sexual activity.

Evaluate

_____ 1. erectile dysfunction

_____ 2. anorgasmia

_____ 3. secondary orgasmic dysfunction

_____ 4. premature ejaculation

_____ 5. inhibited ejaculation

a. A female's having had an orgasm at some point, but no longer does.

b. A male's inability to ejaculate when he wants to, if at all.

c. A male's inability to achieve or maintain an erection.

d. A male's inability to delay ejaculation.

e. A female's lack of orgasm.

Rethink

36-1 Should women be free to dress any way they want without concerns about "giving off the wrong signals"? Is it reasonable for men to assume that women sometimes give off signals that indicate that they really want sex even when they say they don't?

36-2 *From the perspective of a politician:* What responsibilities do people who learn they have a sexually transmitted disease have to their sexual partners, and what responsibilities do public health officials have? Should legislation be designed to restrict sexual behavior for those who have STIs?

Spotlight on Terminology and Language—ESL Pointers

Page 388 "Finally, there is a common, although unfounded, societal belief that many women offer **token resistance** to sex, saying no to sex when they mean yes."

Token resistance refers to just symbolic or nominal resistance.

Page 388 "The **repercussions** of rape are **devastating** for the victims."

The **repercussions** of rape are the results and indirect effects created by this hostile act.

When someone feels **devastated**, they feel ruined. Immediate psychological interventions can help victims deal with the immediate and long-term repercussions of rape.

Page 389 "Estimates suggest that one of five people in the United States is infected with some form of STI, and at least one of four will probably **contract** an STI during their lifetimes."

When you **contract** something you catch it, you become infected with it.

Page 390 "People are less likely to engage in "**casual sex**" with new acquaintances, and the use of condoms during sexual intercourse has increased."

Casual sex refers to having sex with someone you don't know very well, or on the spur of the moment.

Page 392 "It is only when these problems persist, cause **undue** anxiety, and turn sex from play into work that they are cause for concern."

Undue anxiety would be excessive anxiety or too much anxiety.

Page 392 "As we have seen, surveys of college women make clear that the greatest danger of rape comes not from some unknown **assailant** but from a fellow student."

An **assailant** is a violent attacker.

Page 393 "Both men and women should understand that alcohol and drugs **cloud** judgment and hinder communication between them."

When you judgment is **clouded**, your judgment becomes very impaired. You're confused, your judgment is blurred and you don't make well-educated decisions.

Page 394 "Should women be free to dress any way they want without being concerned about "**giving off the wrong signals**"?"
The phrase "**giving off the wrong signals**" means you behave in some way that implies the opposite effect of what you mean.

Test your knowledge of the material in the modules by answering these questions. These questions have been placed in three Practice Tests. The first two tests consist of questions that will test your recall of factual knowledge. The third test contains questions that are challenging and primarily test for conceptual knowledge and your ability to apply that knowledge. Check your answers and review the feedback using the Answer Key in the following pages of the *Study Guide*.

PRACTICE TEST 1:

1. Sexism produces:
    a. negative attitudes and behavior toward a group.
    b. positive attitudes and behavior toward a group.
    c. positive and negative attitudes and behavior toward a group.
    d. negative attitudes and positive behavior toward a group.

2. One's sense of being male or female is known as:
    a. gender role.   c. sexual category.
    b. gender.   d. sex object choice.

3. Long-term research attempting to determine differences between males and females in measures of intelligence showed that males score higher than females in:
    a. high school mathematics.   c. diction and pronunciation of words.
    b. grammar and language arts.   d. music courses.

4. Socialization refers to the process by which an individual:
    a. learns the rules and norms for appropriate behavior.
    b. enters into relationships with other males and females.
    c. learns the roles and behaviors that are appropriate for sexual encounters.
    d. behaves in a cooperative and understanding manner to promote harmony in social situations.

5. The name for the male reproductive organ(s) is(are):
    a. androgen.   c. the penis.
    b. prostrate.   d. the testes.

6. Androgyny is:
    a. damaging to American youth.
    b. restricting the flexibility with which men and women can behave.
    c. behavior that encompasses both typical masculine and feminine roles.
    d. an inherited predisposition.

7. Human sexual behavior is unique compared with many nonhuman species in that:
    a. males reach their sexual peak much later than females.
    b. sexual drive is not cyclical.
    c. sexual behavior is confined to days 12 through 18 of the estrus cycle.
    d. resolution may be achieved before orgasm.

8. The erotic character of a stimulus is determined for the most part by:
   a. genetic history.
   c. society.
   b. whether it depicts nudity.
   d. hereditary factors.

9. Men are unable to be aroused or have orgasms during the:
   a. plateau phase of sexual response.
   c. orgasm phase of sexual response.
   b. excitement phase of sexual response.
   d. resolution phase of sexual response.

10. Masters and Johnson established in their research that an intense, highly pleasurable sexual experience that defies description occurs during the:
    a. resolution phase.
    c. excitement phase.
    b. orgasm phase.
    d. plateau phase.

11. Which of the following statements about masturbation is **true**?
    a. All of society views masturbation as a healthy, normal activity.
    b. Most people surveyed have masturbated at least once.
    c. Males and females begin masturbation at puberty.
    d. Psychologists view people who masturbate as poorly adjusted.

12. Tanisha and her brother have different rules, established by their parents and based on society's customs around the issue of premarital sex. This double standard in Western society means:
    a. twice as many men have premarital sex as women.
    b. premarital sex is discouraged for both men and women.
    c. even people who are marrying for a second time should refrain from sex before their remarriage.
    d. premarital sex is discouraged for women but not for men.

13. Researchers believe that childhood sexual abuse is undoubtedly more common than expected because:
    a. only the most extreme cases tend to be reported to the authorities.
    b. deciding what constitutes abuse is highly subjective.
    c. in many instances, the child has done something to provoke the abuse.
    d. standards of acceptable sexual conduct are relative to social norms, which change over decades.

14. Which statement about marital sexual intercourse is correct?
    a. There are few differences in the frequency of marital sex for younger and older couples.
    b. The average frequency of marital sex is 1.3 times per week.
    c. The frequency of marital sex is closely related to happiness in the marriage.
    d. Marriage partners are often concerned about the frequency or type of sex they have.

15. Which of these male sexual disorders most likely has a physical cause rather than a psychological cause?
    a. Premature ejaculation
    c. Erectile dysfunction
    b. Inhibited ejaculation
    d. Secondary orgasmic dysfunction

351

_____ 16.   testes   a.   The male and female sex organs.

_____ 17.   genitals   b.   The monthly release of an egg from an ovary.

_____ 18.   progestin   c.   A female sex hormone.

_____ 19.   ovulation   d.   The male organs responsible for secreting androgens.

_____ 20.   clitoris   e.   The small and very sensitive organ in the female's
                                        external genitals.

21.   The _____ is when men are unable to develop another erection, post-orgasm.

22.   Sexual coercion based on promised rewards, threatened punishments, or creation of a hostile
      workplace environment is known as _____.

23.   _____ teach women to be passive and dependent and men to be
      assertive and independent.

24.   Research has demonstrated that math scores for females are higher than those for males until
      _____.

25.   The fluid ejaculated from the penis during an orgasm is called _____.

26.   Discuss the factors that contribute to the existence and prevalence of female circumcision. Is this a
      violation of a female's human rights or acceptable as part of the societal customs that are imposed
      on the individual?

PRACTICE TEST 2:

1.   Which alternative is **not** a practice consistent with "safe sex"?
     a.   Avoid intercourse and engage in anal sex or oral-genital sex.
     b.   Use condoms.
     c.   Know your sexual partner well.
     d.   Consider the benefits of monogamy.

2.   _____ are beliefs and expectations about members of a group based on their membership
     in that group.
     a.   Sexisms   c.   Stereotypes
     b.   Sexual identities   d.   Sexual orientations

3.   Unwanted sexual advances, in which a worker is asked repeatedly to begin a sexual relationship with
     her boss, is an example of:
     a.   sexual schemas.   c.   sexism.
     b.   male flirtation and chauvinism. d.   sexual harassment.

4.   Gender differences are determined by:
     a.   societal forces.   c.   biological sex forces.
     b.   cultural forces.   d.   biological and environmental forces.

5. Sandra Bem's research on gender issues found that the cognitive framework that organizes and guides a child's understanding of gender is called:
   a. sex role.
   b. gender role.
   c. gender schema.
   d. stereotyping.

6. A single male parent must show resolve and affection, assertiveness and love. To do so, he would most likely develop:
   a. bisexuality.
   b. androgyny.
   c. sexism.
   d. gender schema.

7. At what point in life does the human male secrete the greatest amount of androgen?
   a. Just after birth
   b. Just after puberty
   c. Upon entering young adulthood
   d. Upon entering middle adulthood

8. Erogenous zones are:
   a. areas of the body especially sensitive to sexual arousal.
   b. areas of the body with a rich array of nerve receptors.
   c. the same as erotic zones.
   d. necessarily stimulated in order for excitement to occur.

9. During the excitement and plateau phases, the penis and clitoris swell with:
   a. semen.
   b. androgen.
   c. blood.
   d. estrogen.

10. The most intensive body movements and maximum arousal occur during the _____ phase of the sexual response cycle.
   a. orgasm
   b. plateau
   c. resolution
   d. excitement

11. Which alternative is **not** a criterion for sexual abnormality?
   a. A standard or ideal
   b. Frequency of the behavior
   c. Deviation from the average
   d. Psychological consequences

12. Masturbation is:
   a. always viewed as inappropriate behavior.
   b. practiced more by men than women.
   c. more common in older men than younger men.
   d. commonly regarded by experts as counterproductive to learning about one's sexuality.

13. Which of the following trends was most pronounced between the mid-1960s and mid-1980s in America?
   a. An increased percentage of females engaged in premarital sex
   b. An increased percentage of males engaged in extramarital sex
   c. A decreased percentage of males engaged in premarital sex
   d. A decreased percentage of females engaged in extramarital sex

14. Which of the following is **not** characteristic of child molestation and sexual abuse?
   a. The child abuser is generally a man 50 years of age or older.
   b. Most children are molested when they are about 10 years old.
   c. The abuser is more likely to be a relative or acquaintance than a stranger.
   d. Victims often experience sexual difficulties later in life.

15. Relative to animals, the stimuli that arouse sexual desire in humans are:
   a. more varied.
   b. more clearly biological.
   c. more closely timed to occur during ovulation.
   d. experienced mainly during the resolution phase.

____ 16. acquired immune deficiency syndrome

a. An STD that, if untreated, may affect brain, heart, and a developing fetus, and can be fatal.

____ 17. chlamydia

b. An STD that leads to infertility and infection.

____ 18. genital herpes

c. A noncurable virus producing small blisters or sores around the genitals; symptoms disappear but often recur.

____ 19. gonorrhea

____ 20. syphilis

d. A fatal STD that is caused by a virus that destroys the body's immune system and has no known cure.

e. An STD that initially produces no symptoms in women but that can lead to pelvic inflammation and sterility, and produces in men painful urination and discharge from the penis.

21. A(n) _____ is the peak of excitement, during which rhythmic muscular contractions occur in genitals.

22. Women's ovaries produce two hormones, estrogen and _____.

23. The possession of both male and female behavioral characteristics is referred to as _____.

24. Mothers exposed to high levels of _____ during pregnancies are more likely to give birth to girls who play with toys that are stereotypically selected by young boys.

25. In female _____, the clitoris is removed, resulting in a permanent inability to experience sexual pleasure.

26. Discuss ways that young men and women can reduce the likelihood of rape.

PRACTICE TEST 3: Conceptual, Applied, and Challenging Questions

1. The threat of AIDS has prompted several large-scale changes in sexual behavior. Which alternative is **not** one of them?
   a. People are less likely to engage in casual sex with new acquaintances.
   b. Use of condoms during sexual intercourse has increased.

    c.   The practice of celibacy is more common.
    d.   The frequency of rape has decreased.

2.   There is no cure for:
    a.   chlamydia.   c.   genital herpes.
    b.   gonorrhea.   d.   syphilis.

3.   Current thinking on differences in verbal skills between men and women suggests that:
    a.   men are superior to women in verbal skills.
    b.   women are superior to men in verbal skills.
    c.   there are no notable differences in verbal skills between men and women.
    d.   men are superior in verbal skills until adolescence, when women gain superiority for the rest of their lives.

4.   Which is the best example of a culturally determined stereotype?
    a.   Redheads have short tempers.
    b.   Men are taller than women.
    c.   Advanced education leads to greater income.
    d.   Computers will be used more and more in the future.

5.   Two sex hormones produced by the ovaries to regulate fertility are:
    a.   estrogen and progesterone.   c.   progesterone and insulin.
    b.   androgen and estrogen.   d.   insulin and adrenaline.

6.   Which of the following is **not** true about sexual arousal?
    a.   What people find to be sexually arousing changes with history.
    b.   What people find to be sexually arousing changes with culture.
    c.   Only in Western culture do men find large breasts to be arousing.
    d.   In America, women find a large male chest to be arousing.

7.   Which alternative is correct about the role of biological factors in the female sex drive?
    a.   The female sex drive is related to the level of estrogen, which is greatest when a woman is 25 to 38 years old; sex drive is lower before and after this period.
    b.   Estrogen levels vary dramatically each month; however, female sex drive occurs anytime during the month and appears greatly influenced by psychological and situational factors.
    c.   The sex drive is related to the level of estrogen, which is greatest soon after sexual maturity; short-term variations in estrogen are minor.
    d.   The female sex hormone, estrogen, fluctuates each month; female sex drive is usually strongest midcycle, when levels are greatest.

8.   Marissa frequently experiences several orgasms, many of which occur by cycling from the:
    a.   excitement to the resolution stage.   c.   orgasmic to the excitement stage.
    b.   plateau to the orgasmic stage.   d.   resolution to the orgasmic stage.

9.   Psychologists widely agree that homosexuals:
    a.   have had stressful childhood experiences but should not be blamed or punished for those experiences.
    b.   have biological defects but must not be blamed or punished.
    c.   are as psychologically healthy as heterosexuals.
    d.   are psychologically disordered and need psychotherapy.

10. Standards of normal sexual behavior are:
    a. applicable universally to discern normal from abnormal practices.
    b. unchanging because they are based on the body's biological limits.
    c. relative because they depend on social attitudes, expectations, and medical knowledge of each society.
    d. unchangeable because scriptural teachings are valid eternally.

11. Of the following, which is **least** likely to represent the motivations of a rapist?
    a. The desire for sexual gratification
    b. Revenge for past mistreatment by a member of the opposite sex
    c. Demonstration of power or control over the victim
    d. The notion that women want forced sex

12. Towanda's father always longed for a son. In fact, she had been expected to be her father's first son. As Towanda grew older, she was competitive and aggressive and liked playing sports, going fishing, mowing the lawn, and repairing automobiles. Towanda's behavior is consistent with her father's:
    a. stereotype for her.   c. sex role for her.
    b. sexism toward her.   d. gender role for her.

13. Which of the following is **true** about how men and women differ?
    a. Men are more intelligent than women.
    b. Women are more intelligent than men.
    c. Women rate their academic abilities more harshly, and more men think they are above average.
    d. Men rate their academic abilities more harshly, and fewer women think they are above average.

14. Seth, a teenage male, has discovered that he is fascinated with the male body and finds it sensual. However, he knows that he still likes girls. Which of the following presents the most accurate descriptions of Seth's orientation?
    a. Kinsey's view that sexual orientation is on a gradient from heterosexuality to homosexuality.
    b. The cultural view that you are either heterosexual or homosexual.
    c. The early view that masturbation is harmful and leads to harmful consequences.
    d. Masters and Johnson's view that sexual response goes through a set pattern no matter what the stimulus.

15. Imagine that an alien race visits the Earth, and psychologists discover that they share all tasks equally among their three sexes. What would this prove about the division of labor in human societies?
    a. Genetics must govern our tendency to have some tasks be associated with a specific gender.
    b. Learning must govern our tendency to have some tasks be associated with a specific gender.
    c. The division of labor in human societies must then be a result of both genetic and environmental forces.
    d. The aliens' division of labor has nothing to do with our division of labor. Their equality is proof they are from another planet.

16. Erin goes on a first date with Chris, whom she likes very much. They go to a movie, then to dinner, and finally to a bar. When he returns her to her apartment, he insists on coming in and talking for a while. After a brief period, he becomes aggressive and coerces Erin into sexual activity. According to the concepts described in the text, this act was:
    a. normal for American young people.
    b. date rape.
    c. promiscuity with affection.
    d. a result of Erin not being careful.

_____ 17. anorgasmia
       a. A female's long-term inability to achieve orgasm.

_____ 18. primary orgasmic dysfunction
       b. A condition in which the motivation for sexual activity is restrained or lacking.

_____ 19. secondary orgasmic dysfunction
       c. A female's temporary inability to achieve orgasm or her ability to achieve orgasm only under certain conditions (such as masturbation).

_____ 20. inhibited sexual desire
       d. A female's lack of orgasm.

21. _____ refers to the behaviors considered appropriate for males and females in a given culture.

22. When men and women develop masculine and feminine characteristics as a function of their accumulated experiences, it is referred to as _____.

23. The _____ is an invisible barrier within an organization that, because of gender discrimination, may prevent women from being promoted beyond a certain level.

24. _____ is the process by which an individual learns the rules and norms of appropriate behavior.

25. Attitudes that place women in stereotyped and restrictive roles that appear on the surface to be positive are referred to as _____.

26. What factors have led to the recent changes in sexual attitudes? How have they changed since the sexual revolution began in the late 1960s?

Module 33:	Module 34:	Module 35:	Module 36:
[a] Gender	[a] genitals	[a] Masturbation	[a] Rape
[b] gender roles	[b] androgens	[b] Heterosexuality	[b] date rape
[c] Stereotyping	[c] estrogen	[c] double standard	[c] sexually transmitted infections
[d] sexism	[d] progesterone	[d] permissiveness with	(STI)
[e] Sexual harassment	[e] ovulation	affection	[d] Chlamydia
[f] androgens	[f] erogenous zones	[e] extramarital sex	[e] Genital herpes
[g] estrogen	[g] excitement phase	[f] Homosexuals	[f] Trichomoniasis
[h] Socialization	[h] plateau phase	[g] bisexuals	[g] Gonorrhea
[i] gender schema	[i] orgasm		[h] Genital warts
[j] androgynous	[j] resolution stage		[i] acquired immune deficiency
	[k] refractory period	Evaluate	syndrome (AIDS)
Evaluate		1. b	[j] erectile dysfunction
1. a	Evaluate	2. c	[k] Premature ejaculation
2. c	1. e	3. a	[l] Inhibited ejaculation
3. e	2. a	4. d	[m] anorgasmia
4. b	3. d		[n] Primary orgasmic dysfunction
5. d	4. c		[o] secondary orgasmic dysfunction
	5. b		[p] inhibited sexual desire
			Evaluate
			1. c
			2. e
			3. a
			4. d
			5. b

Selected Rethink Answers

33-1   Armed forces: Laws may be both protective and sexist. Protective in that some people, particularly men, may need to see themselves as the stronger sex. Sexist in that an assumption that the skills needed to be a soldier can only be acquired by men. Yes, this is an example of benevolent sexism. It places women in stereotypical and restrictive roles that appear, on the surface, to be positive.

34-2   That people "learn" to be aroused suggests that the experience of being aroused is based on experience. People may gain experience about what constitutes erotic stimuli from all sorts of places, including images on television and in the media, information gained from peers at school, and conversations overheard or had directly with parents. Much of this information is apt to be learned early, though learning continues throughout the life cycle.

35-2   Survey responses are always biased by the fact that only those who voluntarily participate make up the sample. People likely to voluntarily participate in a survey about sex, which to some extent is considered a very private act, probably share some common characteristics. Among them might be extroversion, self-confidence, curiosity, or even arrogance (about their own sexual prowess) or mental health problems (such as obsession with perverted sexual acts). Bias might be reduced through asking people to participate in a written or telephone survey, rather than a face-to-face survey; the former modes would allow for more anonymity, which may induce a wider variety of people to be willing to respond.

Practice Test 1:

1. a   mod. 33 p. 365
*a. Correct. Sexism typically refers to the negative, gender-specific attitudes and behavior.
b. Incorrect. See answer a.
c. Incorrect. See answer a.
d. Incorrect. See answer a.

2. b   mod. 33 p. 365
a. Incorrect. See answer b.
*b. Correct. This is the definition of "gender."
c. Incorrect. See answer b.
d. Incorrect. Homosexuals do not have alternative gender identities; males still view themselves as male even if their sexual object choice differs from most members of their gender.

3. a   mod. 33 p. 371
*a. Correct. Other than high-school math, the differences were very small.
b. Incorrect. The differences in grammar and language skills is insignificant.
c. Incorrect. The differences in diction and pronunciation have not been explored.
d. Incorrect. Music courses have not been studied.

4. a   mod. 33 p. 373
*a. Correct. Socialization is the means by which social and cultural practices are passed from one generation to another.
b. Incorrect. This option refers to "socializing."
c. Incorrect. Sexual encounters are rarely the focal subject of the socialization process, although forming relationships may be governed by socialization.
d. Incorrect. This option refers to being sociable.

5. d   mod. 34 p. 377
a. Incorrect. Androgen is a male hormone.
b. Incorrect. The prostrate is a gland that produces seminal fluid that carries sperm.
c. Incorrect. The penis is a sexual organ, but it is not the reproductive organ.
*d. Correct. Sperm are produced in the testes, making them the reproductive organs.

6. c   mod. 33 p. 374
a. Incorrect. Androgyny would be helpful to American youth.
b. Incorrect. Androgyny increases the flexibility.
*c. Correct. Androgyny refers to behaviors that are cross-gender in terms of the cultural views.
d. Incorrect. Androgyny does not refer to a genetic disposition.

7. b   mod. 34 p. 377
a. Incorrect. In many primate species, males reach sexual activity much later in life than do females.
*b. Correct. All of the primates, except humans, have an estrus cycle that governs sexual activity and receptivity.
c. Incorrect. Sexual behavior in human females is not limited to any part of the monthly cycle.
d. Incorrect. Resolution must follow orgasm in all bisexual species that use sexual reproduction, because resolution is defined as a period following orgasm.

8. c   mod. 34 p. 378
a. Incorrect. Genetic history does not determine erotic qualities of a stimulus.
b. Incorrect. A stimulus can be erotic without nudity.
*c. Correct. The erotic nature of a stimulus does appear to be socially determined.
d. Incorrect. Hereditary factors do not determine the character of erotic stimuli.

9. d   mod. 34 p. 382
a. Incorrect. Orgasms typically occur after this phase, but they can occur during this phase.
b. Incorrect. Orgasms typically occur after this phase, but they can occur during this phase.
c. Incorrect. Orgasms occur during this phase.
*d. Correct. During this phase, which follows orgasm, another orgasm cannot occur.

10. b   mod. 34 p. 380
a. Incorrect. It occurs one phase earlier.
*b. Correct. And it is called an orgasm.
c. Incorrect. It typically comes after this phase.
d. Incorrect. It typically comes after this phase.

11. b   mod. 35 p. 387
a. Incorrect. The views on masturbation in our society are quite mixed.
*b. Correct. Most of that number have done it more than once.
c. Incorrect. Masturbation can begin much earlier, and some people begin much later than puberty.
d. Incorrect. Masturbation is a normal, healthy activity.

12. d   mod. 35 p. 389
a. Incorrect. However, does this mean that there are a large number of unmarried women or just a few very busy women?
b. Incorrect. This would be a single standard.
c. Incorrect. This would be a single standard.

*d. Correct. A double standard means that one group is held to one standard and another group is held to another standard.

13. a   mod. 36 p. 397
*a. Correct. Authorities are suspicious that vast numbers of mild cases go unreported.
b. Incorrect. While this is true, the authorities in charge have specific definitions.
c. Incorrect. This blame-the-victim approach went out long ago.
d. Incorrect. This may not have anything to do with sexual abuse of children.

14. d   mod. 35 p. 390
a. Incorrect. The frequency of sexual intercourse declines for married couples as they grow older.
b. Incorrect. For most married couples, the frequency is between one and three times a week.
c. Incorrect. There appears to be little relationship between how often a couple engages in intercourse and how happy they are together.
*d. Correct. Sex is often a standard couples use to judge their marital happiness, so they often worry about their sex lives.

15. c   mod. 36 p. 399
a. Incorrect. The equipment works, but too fast.
b. Incorrect. Ejaculation is still possible (thought physically sound) but does not occur in certain situations.
*c. Correct. People respond to this problem with medication, suggesting that it is biologically based.
d. Incorrect. This occurs in females.

16. d   mod. 34 p. 377
17. a   mod. 34 p. 377
18. c   mod. 34 p. 377
19. b   mod. 34 p. 377
20. e   mod. 34 p. 379

21. refractory period   mod. 34 p. 379
22. sexual harassment   mod. 33 p. 368
23. Gender stereotypes   mod. 33 p. 366
24. high school   mod. 33 p. 371
25. Semen   mod. 34 p. 380

26.
▪   Consider whether you believe that the individual right to self-determination overrides cultural views that place the social order before the individual. Violation of these social rules have

psychological consequences for others as well as the affected individual.
▪   Consider whether this is a human-rights issue or a cultural issue. Should societies that practice female circumcision be condemned for their beliefs?

Practice Test 2:
1. a   mod. 36 p. 399
*a. Correct. Anal sex is probably more dangerous than intercourse because of the possibility of direct contact with blood.
b. Incorrect. Condoms are reasonably effective as protection against the transmission of HIV.
c. Incorrect. Knowing your partner is extremely important, although it only takes one act of infidelity to become infected.
d. Incorrect. Monogamy is one certain way to avoid HIV transmission, as long as both partners are free of HIV before the beginning of the relationship.

2. c   mod. 33 p. 366
a. Incorrect. Sexism is a special class of stereotypes.
b. Incorrect. Sexual identity may work this way, but the stem does not define it.
*c. Correct. This is the definition for stereotype, and it includes racism, sexism, ageism, and many others.
d. Incorrect. Sexual orientations describe the sexual object-choice differences from person to person.

3. d   mod. 33 p. 368
a. Incorrect. A sexual schema is a view of how a particular gender should behave and interact.
b. Incorrect. To some, any flirtation is harassment, but this activity in the workplace is not flirtation.
c. Incorrect. Not all sexism results in overt behaviors.
*d. Correct. An unwanted sexual advance or sexually charged suggestion is considered harassment.

4. d   mod. 33 p. 371
a. Incorrect. Societal forces determine only some of the gender differences.
b. Incorrect. Cultural forces determine only some of the gender differences.
c. Incorrect. Biological sex forces determine only a few of the gender differences.
*d. Correct. Gender differences result from both biological and environmental pressures.

5. c   mod. 33 p. 374

a. Incorrect. She used the term "gender schema" to describe this cognitive framework.
b. Incorrect. See answer a.
*c. Correct. This cognitive framework guides our understanding of gender.
d. Incorrect. See answer a.

6. b   mod. 33 p. 374
a. Incorrect. Bisexuality is not likely to arise from parenting styles.
*b. Correct. These characteristics would suggest someone with an androgynous approach.
c. Incorrect. Sexism refers to negative gender stereotyping.
d. Incorrect. A gender schema is a cognitive framework, according to Bem, that organizes and guides a person's understanding of gender-relevant information.

7. b   mod. 34 p. 377
a. Incorrect. The greatest amount of androgen is secreted just after puberty.
*b. Correct. Just after puberty, many changes occur in males, and androgens play an important role in these changes.
c. Incorrect. See answer a.
d. Incorrect. See answer a.

8. b   mod. 34 p. 379
a. Incorrect. What makes these areas sensitive is a rich array of nerve receptors as suggested by another alternative.
*b. Correct. This rich array of nerve receptors makes these areas sensitive to sensual contact.
c. Incorrect. "Erotic zones" is not a term used in the study of sexual behavior.
d. Incorrect. Erogenous zones do not have to be stimulated for arousal to occur.

9. c   mod. 34 p. 379
a. Incorrect. Semen is stored in the seminal vesicle until use.
b. Incorrect. Androgen is a hormone released in the body in quantities too small to engorge the penis or the clitoris.
*c. Correct. Blood causes the swelling, or engorgement, of the penis and the clitoris.
d. Incorrect. Estrogen is a hormone released in the body in quantities too small to engorge the penis or the clitoris.

10. a   mod. 34 p. 380
*a. Correct. Orgasm is so intense that few people can offer coherent descriptions of it.
b. Incorrect. See answer a.

c. Incorrect. See answer a.
d. Incorrect. See answer a.

11. b   mod. 35 p. 386
a. Incorrect. Sexual abnormality can be judged by comparing the behavior to a standard or ideal behavior.
*b. Correct. How often someone engages in a sexual behavior can be used to judge abnormality only in the most extreme cases, and then it is not the behavior that is considered abnormal, but the frequency.
c. Incorrect. Deviations from the average can be used to judge abnormality.
d. Incorrect. The way someone feels about the sexual activity does have a major impact on how the behavior is judged.

12. b   mod. 35 p. 387
a. Incorrect. Masturbation is a healthy behavior, although there are many situations in which its practice would be inappropriate (in public, for instance).
*b. Correct. Men report that they masturbate more often than women report.
c. Incorrect. Masturbation is more common in younger men than older men.
d. Incorrect. Masturbation is an excellent way to learn about one's sexuality.

13. a   mod. 35 p. 389
*a. Correct. Of all the trends, the change in the frequency of female premarital sexual activity was the most significant.
b. Incorrect. This number was small in comparison to the changes in female rates.
c. Incorrect. Males did not decrease their rate of premarital sexual activity; instead it increased slightly.
d. Incorrect. Females did not decrease their rate of premarital sexual activity; instead it increased dramatically.

14. a   mod. 36 p. 396
*a. Correct. The child abuser can be any age and typically is about 20 years older than the victim.
b. Incorrect. The age of 10 is particularly vulnerable.
c. Incorrect. The victim usually knows the abuser.
d. Incorrect. Victims do often have sexual problems later, though they are not any more likely to be sexual abusers.

15. a   mod. 34 p. 378
*a. Correct. Humans can be aroused by untold
     varieties of stimuli.
b.   Incorrect. Most animals respond to stimuli in a
     manner strongly linked by biology.
c.   Incorrect. This is true of animals, not humans.
d.   Incorrect. Not true for animal or human sexual
     behavior.

16. d   mod. 36 p. 398
17. e   mod. 36 p. 397
18. c   mod. 36 p. 397
19. b   mod. 36 p. 398
20. a   mod. 36 p. 398

21. orgasm   mod. 34 p. 380
22. progesterone   mod. 34 p. 377
23. Androgyny   mod. 33 p. 374
24. androgens   mod. 33 p. 372
25. Circumcision   mod. 34 p. 382

26.
Women
   ▪ Should have the right to set limits.
   ▪ Be assertive under pressure.
   ▪ Be aware of "risky" situations.
   ▪ Keep tabs on what they drink and who they
      drink with.
Men
   ▪ Should be aware of their date's views on
      sexual behavior.
   ▪ Understand "no" means "no."
   ▪ Not assume behaviors/dress are invitations
      to sex.

Practice Test 3:
1. d   mod. 36 p. 399
a.   Incorrect. Casual sex has become less common.
b.   Incorrect. Condom use has increased.
c.   Incorrect. Celibacy and monogamous
     relationships are more common.
*d. Correct. The frequency of rape has remained
     unaffected by the threat of AIDS.

2. c   mod. 36 p. 398
a.   Incorrect. Chlamydia can be cured with
     antibiotics.
b.   Incorrect. Gonorrhea can be cured with
     antibiotics.
*c. Correct. Genital herpes is a virus, and there is
     currently no cure for the infection.
d.   Incorrect. Syphilis can be cured with antibiotics.

3. c   mod. 33 p. 371
a.   Incorrect. See answer c.
b.   Incorrect. See answer c.
*c. Correct. It was once thought that women had
     better verbal skills than men, but no differences
     exist today.
d.   Incorrect. See answer c.

4. a   mod. 33 p. 365
*a. Correct. The association of a physical
     characteristic with a personality characteristic
     results from stereotypes developed in cultural
     settings.
b.   Incorrect. This statement reflects biological
     tendencies.
c.   Incorrect. This statement reflects demographic
     trends resulting more from skills than cultural
     stereotypes.
d.   Incorrect. This statement reflects trends in
     technology.

5. a   mod. 34 p. 377
*a. Correct. These are the female sexual hormones.
b.   Incorrect. Androgen is the male sexual hormone.
c.   Incorrect. Insulin is the blood sugar hormone.
d.   Incorrect. Adrenaline is produced in the adrenal
     glands and is released during stress.

6. c   mod. 34 p. 379
a.   Incorrect. At one time, plump and even obese
     women were found attractive; at another time,
     thin women were found attractive.
b.   Incorrect. One culture may prize large women
     and fat men, and another culture may consider
     baldness especially appealing.
*c. Correct. Large breasts are arousing to men in
     many cultures, and they are often associated with
     fertility.
d.   Incorrect. Of the buttocks, legs, chest, and penis,
     women find moderately large chests most
     arousing.

7. b   mod. 34 p. 377
a.   Incorrect. The female sex drive is somewhat
     independent of the level of estrogen.
*b. Correct. The female sex drive is somewhat
     independent of the level of estrogen, especially
     in comparison with the close link between sexual
     responsiveness and the estrus cycle in other
     primates.
c.   Incorrect. Estrogen levels vary throughout the
     estrus cycle, while sexual activity depends more
     on psychological and situational factors.
d.   Incorrect. The sex drive in females is not
     strongest at any time of the month.

8. d   mod. 34 p. 381
a.   Incorrect. To have an orgasm, Marissa would need to cycle to the orgasm stage.
b.   Incorrect. After an orgasm, Marissa would go into the resolution phase, not the plateau stage.
c.   Incorrect. After an orgasm, Marissa would go into the resolution phase, not the plateau stage.
*d. Correct. After orgasm, Marissa goes into the resolution stage and then back to the orgasmic stage.

9. c   mod. 35 p. 393
a.   Incorrect. Homosexuals have childhoods as ordinary and as confused as any other group.
b.   Incorrect. Biological differences have not been fully established, much less to claim there are "defects."
*c. Correct. The variety of psychological health exhibited in the heterosexual world is equally present in the homosexual population.
d.   Incorrect. See answer c.

10. c   mod. 35 p. 386
a.   Incorrect. Universal standards of sexual behavior would hinder our ability to adapt.
b.   Incorrect. They are not limited by biology.
*c. Correct. They do vary from society to society.
d.   Incorrect. Whose scripture applies universally?

11. d   mod. 36 p. 396
a.   Incorrect. Sexual gratification is part of the motivation for rape, although power and aggressive motivations may be more influential.
b.   Incorrect. Rape is often a means of getting back at a parent or other person who is perceived as having mistreated the rapist at some point.
c.   Incorrect. Power and control are the strongest themes in the motivation of rapists.
*d. Correct. The belief that women want forced sex is often given as an after-the-fact explanation, but it is not part of the motivation of most rapists.

12. d   mod. 33 p. 365
a.   Incorrect. A female stereotype would not have included these activities.
b.   Incorrect. A sexist attitude would not have included these activities.
c.   Incorrect. A sex role would have been a socially defined female role for Towanda.
*d. Correct. Towanda's father has given her a male gender role (although not a male gender identity).

13. c   mod. 33 p. 370
a.   Incorrect. No evidence exists suggesting that males are more intelligent than females or the other way around.
b.   Incorrect. No evidence exists suggesting that females are more intelligent than males or the other way around.
*c. Correct. Women tend to be far more self-critical in regard to their academic skills, and males have an overly optimistic view of their abilities.
d.   Incorrect. This is reversed.

14. a   mod. 35 p. 391
*a. Correct. Kinsey's view is that everyone falls somewhere on a gradient between complete homosexual orientation to complete heterosexual orientation.
b.   Incorrect. This view would suggest that Seth must either be homosexual or heterosexual, not a mixture.
c.   Incorrect. While this old view did suggest that masturbation led to deviant sexual behavior, it would not account for Seth's mixed feelings.
d.   Incorrect. This is not relevant to Masters and Johnson's conceptualization of the sexual response cycle.

15. d   mod. 33 p. 373
a.   Incorrect. What alien division of labor would have to do with human division of labor is a good question.
b.   Incorrect. While this is true, a visit by aliens would not prove it.
c.   Incorrect. While this is true, a visit by aliens would not prove it.
*d. Correct. Enough said.

16. b   mod. 36 p. 395
a.   Incorrect. It may be viewed as normal by some, but it is still date rape.
*b. Correct. This is an increasing phenomenon on American college campuses and in high schools.
c.   Incorrect. Coercion is not affection.
d.   Incorrect. While Erin needs to be more careful, her actions were not the cause of the rape.

17. d   mod. 36 p. 399
18. a   mod. 36 p. 399
19. c   mod. 36 p. 399
20. b   mod. 36 p. 401

21. gender roles   mod. 35 p. 365
22. gender schema   mod. 33 p. 377
23. glass ceiling   mod. 33 p. 367
24. Socialization   mod. 33 p. 373

25. benevolent sexism   mod. 33 p. 369

26.
- Social acceptance of sexual activity and increased visibility of activity in the media have contributed to the increase in activity.
- AIDS and campaigns for safer sex have caused some populations to reconsider risky sexual practices.
- The double standard has changed slightly.
- The 1960s were marked by a sexual freedom that has been affected to some extent by AIDS and by the aging of the population.

Chapter 12: Development

Overview

The fundamental issue for developmental psychology is the interaction between nature and nurture in human development. Development from conception to birth illustrates the nature-nurture interaction.

Module 37 discusses various topics of study within the field of developmental psychology, with an emphasis on the nature-nurture issue. This is followed by a discussion of research methods. Cross-sectional research compares people of different ages with one another, and longitudinal research traces the behavior of one or more individuals as they become older. Finally, sequential research combines the two methods.

Module 38 explains the nature of human development before birth. Genetic abnormalities and environmental influences that affect prenatal development are listed.

Module 39 offers an explanation of the reflexes and sensory abilities of newborns. Both the physical development and the social development of newborns are discussed in detail and include the concepts of attachment, peer social interactions, parenting styles, Erikson's psychosocial developmental stages, and Piaget's theory of cognitive development.

Module 40 examines development during adolescence. The module on adolescence covers the physical, emotional, moral, and cognitive changes that occur during the transition to adulthood.

Module 41 focuses on adulthood. These years are marked by the formation of a family, the establishment and success (or failure) in work, and the gradual progress toward old age. Finally, the module shows how old age does not conform to our myths about it. Many elderly people are still quite capable of leading active and happy lives. An examination of the physical, intellectual, and social changes that occur at this time of life shows both improvements and declines in various types of functioning.

To further investigate the topics covered in this chapter, you can visit the related Web sites by visiting the following link: www.mhhe.com/feldmanup8.

Prologue: Test-Tube Baby Birthday
Looking Ahead

Module 37: Nature and Nurture: The Enduring Developmental Issue

Determining the Relative Influence of Nature and Nurture
Developmental Research Techniques

- • **_How do psychologists study the degree to which development is an interaction of hereditary and environmental factors?_**

Nature and Nurture: The Enduring Developmental Issue

[a] _____ is the branch of psychology focused on explaining the similarities and differences among people that result from the growth and change of individuals throughout life.

   Developmental psychologists are interested in a fundamental question of distinguishing the causes of behavior that are _environmental_ from the causes that result from _heredity_. This question is identified as the **[b]** _____. However, both nature and nurture are involved, and it is not a question of nature or nurture. Some theories focus on learning and the role of the environment, and other theories focus on the role of growth and

[c] _____, or the development of biologically predetermined patterns, in causing developmental change. Environment plays a role in enabling individuals to reach the potential allowed by their genetic background. Developmental psychologists take a(n)

[d] _____ position, arguing that behavior and development are determined by genetic and environmental influences.

   One approach used by developmental psychologists is the study of **[e]** _____. Different behaviors displayed by identical twins must have some environmental component. Many studies seek to find identical twins that were separated at birth by adoption. Non-twin siblings who are raised apart also make contributions to these kinds of studies. The opposite approach takes people of different genetic backgrounds and examines their development and behavior in similar environments.

Evaluate

_____ 1. environment

_____ 2. heredity

_____ 3. genetic makeup

_____ 4. maturation

_____ 5. interactionist

a. The unfolding of biologically predetermined behavior patterns.

b. Influences on behavior that occur in the world around us—in family, friends, school, nutrition, and others.

c. Biological factors that transmit hereditary information.

d. Influences on behavior that are transmitted biologically from parents to a child.

e. Combination of genetic predisposition and environmental influences determines the course of development.

Rethink

37-1   When researchers find similarities in development between different cultures, what implications might such findings have for the nature-nurture issue?

37-2   *From the perspective of a child care provider:* Consider what factors might determine when a child learns to walk. What kinds of environmental influences might be involved? What kinds of genetic influences might be involved? What recommendations might you make to the child's parents about the situation?

Spotlight on Terminology and Language—ESL Pointers

Page 398 "If Louise Brown's conception was unconventional, her life has **unfolded** in more traditional ways."

When things **unfold** they develop overtime.

Page 398 "We begin by examining the approaches developmental psychologists use to study the environmental and genetic factors: the **nature–nurture** issue."

The **nature–nurture issue** refers to the debate over what portion of our behavior is due to our genetics (nature) and what portion is the result of learning (nurture).

Page 399 "How many bald, six-foot-six, 250-pound volunteer firefighters in New Jersey wear **droopy** mustaches, aviator-style eyeglasses, and a key ring on the right side of the belt?"

When something is **droopy** it is limp and floppy.

Page 399 "Levey went to college, studying forestry; Newman planned to study **forestry** in college but instead took a job **trimming** trees.

Forestry is the study of planting and growing trees in a forest.

To **trim** something (like trees or hair) is to make it look neat by cutting it.

Page 399"This question **embodies** the nature-nurture issue."

This question pretty much sums up the nature-nurture issue. The nature-nurture issue is **embodied**, or represented, by the question, "How can we distinguish between the environmental causes of behavior and the hereditary causes of behavior."

Page 399 "Although the question was first **posed** as a nature-versus-nurture issue, developmental psychologists today agree that both nature and nurture interact to produce specific developmental patterns and outcomes."

The question was first **posed**, or presented, a bit differently.

Page 399 "Consequently, the question has **evolved** into, how and to what degree do environment and heredity both produce their effects?"

The question has **evolved** into, or advanced into, one that better reflects the awareness of the influence of the two factors.

Page 399 "However, the debate over the **comparative** influence of the two factors remains active, with different approaches and theories of development emphasizing the environment or heredity to a greater or lesser degree (de Waal, 1999; Pinker, 2002)."

Comparative is proportional.

Page 400 "Despite their differences over theory, developmental psychologists **concur** on some points."

Developmental psychologists **concur**, or agree, on some points.

Page 400 "They agree that genetic factors not only provide the potential for particular behaviors or traits to emerge, but also place limitations on the **emergence** of such behavior or traits."

Emergence is the appearance of, or coming out, of some traits.

Page 401 "Studies of nontwin siblings who are raised in totally different environments also **shed some light** on the issue."

When we **shed some light** on an issue we are adding information that will help us understand the issue better.

Page 401 "Researchers can also take the opposite **tack**."

A **tack** is an approach or a method of doing something.

Age 757 "Instead, the scores may reflect differences in the educational **attainment** of the cohorts represented."

Attainment refers to an achievement or the accomplishment of something.

Page 401 "Longitudinal research **traces** the behavior of one or more participants as the participant's age."

To trace something is to follow or track down something. Longitudinal research **traces**, or follows the behavior of the research participants.

Page 402 "Unfortunately, longitudinal research requires an enormous **expenditure** of time (as the researcher waits for the participants to get older), and participants who begin a study at an early age may drop out, move away, or even die as the research continues."

Expenditure of time refers to the outlay of time that is necessary for longitudinal research.

Module 38: Prenatal Development: From Conception to Birth

The Basics of Genetics

Applying Psychology in the 21st Century: Gene Therapy and the Coming Medical Revolution

The Earliest Development

- ***What is the nature of development prior to birth?***
- ***What factors affect a child during the mother's pregnancy?***

Prenatal Development: Conception to Birth

From a biological perspective, development begins at the point of **[a]** _____ when the male's sperm penetrates the female's egg. The fertilized egg is at this point called a(n)

[b] _____. It contains 23 pairs of **[c]** _____, one-half from the father and the other half from the mother. Each chromosome contains thousands of

[d] _____, the individual units that carry genetic information. Genes are responsible for the development of the systems of the body, heart, circulatory, brain, lungs, and

so on. At four weeks, the zygote becomes a structure called the **[e]** _____. It has a rudimentary heart, brain, intestinal tract, and other organs. By the eighth week, the embryo has arms and legs. From the end of the eighth week on, the individual is called a(n) **[f]**

_____. It is responsive to touch, and can bend its fingers when touched on the hand. At 16 to 18 weeks, many new mothers begin to feel the movement of the fetus. At the 24th week, the fetus has many of the characteristics that newborns display, such as grasping, sucking, looking around, and crying. Many infants are even able to survive if born prematurely

at approximately 22 weeks, considered the **[g]** _____. At 28 weeks, the fetus will weigh about three pounds. Research demonstrates that infants at this age are even capable of learning.

Other research suggests that there are *critical* or **[h]** _____ during the various stages of fetal development. These are key time periods during which the fetus is particularly sensitive to various stimuli, such as drug use by the mother.

Though genetics influence fetal development, environmental factors can affect its development as well. Development can be adversely affected by **[i]** _____ such as drugs, chemicals, and viruses; these influences can result in birth defects.

Evaluate

_____ 1.   teratogens

_____ 2.   zygote

_____ 3.   chromosomes

_____ 4.   genes

_____ 5.   embryo

_____ 6.   fetus

a.   A zygote that has a heart, a brain, and other organs.

b.   The one-celled product of fertilization.

c.   A developing child, from nine weeks after conception until birth.

d.   Structures that contain basic hereditary information.

e.   The parts of a chromosome through which genetic information is transmitted.

f.   Environmental toxins that produce birth defects.

Rethink

38-1   Given the possible effects of the environment on the developing fetus, do you think pregnant women should be prosecuted for the use of alcohol and other drugs that can seriously harm their unborn children? Defend your position.

38-2   *From the perspective of an educator:* How would you utilize your knowledge of sensitive periods in language to improve students' learning? Would you want to teach children more than one language during this time?

Spotlight on Terminology and Language—ESL Pointers

Page 403 "A routine prenatal test brought Jennifer and Brian Buchkovich **horrifying** news: Their unborn baby, Ethan, was afflicted with spina bifida, a failure of the spine to close over the spinal cord."

News that is **horrifying** is bad news that is unexpected and shocking.

Page 403 "But doctors offered the Windber, Pennsylvania, couple a **glimmer** of hope—an experimental operation designed to reduce the damage and to eliminate or delay the need for a surgically implanted **shunt** to drain excess fluid from the brain."

A **glimmer** is a small amount of something.

A **shunt** is a tube that is used to change the flow of fluid within the body.

Page 403 "The **hitch**: The surgery would have be performed while Ethan was still inside Jennifer's womb (People Weekly, 2000, p. 117).

A **hitch** is an obstacle or a problem with a plan.

Page 403 "Our increasing understanding of the first **stirrings** of life spent inside a mother's womb has permitted significant medical advances like those that helped Ethan Buchkovich."

Stirrings are slight movements.

Page 403 "Let's consider how an individual is created by looking first at the genetic **endowment** that a child receives at the moment of conception."

An **endowment** is a gift.

Page 403 "Each chromosome contains thousands of **genes** – smaller units through which genetic information is transmitted."

The **genes** transmit, or convey genetic information. The **genes** pass on the genetic information.

Page 403 "Composed of **sequences** of DNA (deoxyribonucleic acid) molecules, genes are the biological equivalent of 'software' that programs the future development of all parts of the body's hardware."

The **sequence** is the order, or the succession of related genes.

Page 404 "The zygote starts out as a microscopic **speck**."

A **speck** is a very small spot.

Page 405 "A pediatrician rubs a cotton **swab** across Meghan Johannsen's inside cheek in order to get a DNA sample of the month-old girl and hands it to a technician."

When someone **swabs** your cheek they are wiping the cheek.

Page 405 "When the gene arrives at the location of a problem (or potential problem), it leads the body to produce chemicals that can **alleviate** the danger."

Alleviate means to lessen or to improve something.

Page 405 "It also may be possible to "**harvest**" defective cells from a child prior to birth."

When we **harvest** something we are gathering or collecting it.

Page 405 "In fact, after they initially seem to be cured, some recipients of gene therapy have **relapsed**, and some have suffered from unpleasant side effects (Nakamura, 2004; Wagner et al., 2004; Harris, 2005)."

When someone **relapses** they suddenly become ill again after seeming to have recovered.

Page 405 "The result would be **offspring** genetically identical to the parent except for the genetic defect. (Weiner, 2000; Smith, 2004; Allhoff, 2005)."

A person's **offspring** are their children.

Page 405 "As an embryo develops through an **intricate**, preprogrammed process of cell division, it grows 10,000 times larger by 4 weeks of age, attaining a length of about one-fifth of an inch."

Things that are **intricate** are complex and have a lot of details to them.

Page 406 "Such newborns, who may weigh as little as two pounds at birth, are in **grave** danger because they have immature organs; they have less than a 50-50 chance of survival."

These infants in **grave** danger are in serious danger.

Page 407 "Poorly **nourished** babies are also more susceptible to disease, and a lack of **nourishment** may have an adverse impact on their mental development (Adams & Parker, 1990; Ricciuti, 1993; Sigman, 1995; Zigler, Finn-Stevenson, & Hall, 2002; Najman et al., 2004)."

To **nourish** someone is to provide food to them. Babies that are poorly **nourished** are not given a lot of food.

Page 408 "Mothers who are anxious and tense during the last months of their pregnancies are more apt to have **irritable** infants who sleep and eat poorly."

When someone is **irritable** they are bad-tempered and made angry easily.

Module 39: Infancy and Childhood

The Extraordinary Newborn
The Growing Child: Infancy through Middle Childhood

- *What are the major competencies of newborns?*
- *What are the milestones of physical and social development during childhood?*
- *How does cognitive development proceed during childhood?*

Infancy and Childhood

At birth, the newborn baby is called a(n) **[a]** _____. The neonate looks strange because the journey through the birth canal squeezes and shapes the skull. The neonate is

covered with **[b]** _____, a white, greasy material that protects the skin before

birth, and soft hair called **[c]** _____. The neonate is born with several **[d]**

_____, unlearned, involuntary responses. Most are necessary for survival and maturation. The

[e] _____ fans out the toes when the edge of the foot is touched. These reflexes are lost within a few months and replaced by more complex behaviors.

   In the first year of life, children triple their birth weight, and their height increases by 50 percent. From 3 to 13 years of age, the child adds an average of 5 pounds and 3 inches per year. The proportion of body and body parts changes throughout the time period as well. In addition to physical and perceptual growth, infants grow socially as well.

   [f] _____ refers to the positive emotional bond between a child and a particular individual. Harry Harlow demonstrated the importance of attachment by showing that baby monkeys preferred a terrycloth "mother" to a wire "mother," even though the wire version provided food and the terrycloth one did not. Infants play an active role in the development of the bond. Recently, the father's role in children's development has been researched. Fathers spend less time caring for their children, but the attachments can be just as strong.

   [g] _____ with peers are crucial for a preschooler's social development. Play increases social competence, provides a perspective on the thoughts and feelings of others, and helps teach children self-control.

   Diana Baumrind has proposed four main parenting styles: **[h]** _____ are

rigid and punitive and expect unquestioning obedience. **[i]** _____ are lax and

inconsistent although warm. **[j]** _____ set limits and are firm, but as their children

get older, they reason and explain things to them. Finally, **[k]** _____ demonstrate little interest in their children, and are somewhat emotionally detached.

Children of authoritarian parents tend to be unsociable, unfriendly, and withdrawn. Children of permissive parents are immature, moody, and dependent with low self-esteem. Children of authoritative parents are likable, self-reliant, independent, and cooperative. Children of uninvolved parents probably fare the worst, as the children feel unloved, and physical as well as cognitive development is hampered.

Children are born with **[l]** _____, or basic, innate dispositions. The temperament can elicit a certain child-rearing style. The child-rearing styles may be applicable to American culture, where independence is highly valued. For instance, Japanese parents encourage dependence to promote values of community and cooperation.

Erik Erikson has proposed an eight-stage theory of social development. Each stage of **[m]** _____ involves a basic crisis or conflict. Although each crisis is resolved as we pass through the stages, the basic conflict remains throughout life.

[n] _____ refers to the developmental changes in a child's understanding of the world. Theories of cognitive development attempt to explain the intellectual changes that occur throughout life. Jean Piaget proposed that children pass through four distinct stages of cognitive development, and that these stages differ in both the quantity of information acquired and the quality of knowledge and understanding. Maturation and relevant experiences are needed for children to pass through the stages.

An alternative to Piaget's theory is **[o]** _____, which examines how people take in, use, and store information. According to the Russian developmental psychologist Lev Vygotsky, children's cognitive abilities increase when they are exposed to information that falls into their **[p]** _____, which he describes as the level at which a child can almost, but not fully, comprehend or perform a task on his or her own. Parents, teachers, and peers provide supportive information that serves as **[q]** _____ for the child's development.

Evaluate

Part A

_____ 1. authoritarian parents

_____ 2. permissive parents

_____ 3. authoritative parents

_____ 4. temperament

_____ 5. psychosocial development

a. Parents who are lax, inconsistent, and undemanding, yet warm toward their children.

b. Development of individuals' interactions and understanding of one another and their knowledge and understanding of themselves as members of society.

c. Basic, innate disposition.

d. Parents who are rigid and punitive and who value unquestioning obedience from their children.

e. Parents who are firm, set clear limits, and reason with and explain things to their children.

Part B

_____ 1. sensorimotor stage

_____ 2. object permanence

_____ 3. preoperational stage

_____ 4. principle of conservation

_____ 5. concrete operational stage

a. Objects do not cease to exist when they are out of sight.

b. Little competence in representing the environment.

c. Characterized by language development.

d. Characterized by logical thought.

e. Quantity is unrelated to physical appearance.

Rethink

39-1 Do you think the widespread use of IQ testing in the United States contributes to parents' views that their children's academic success is due largely to their children's innate intelligence? Why? Would it be possible (or desirable) to change this view?

39-2 *From the perspective of a child care provider:* If a parent wasn't sure whether to enroll his or her child in your program, what advice would you give about the possible positive and negative consequences about day care?

Spotlight on Terminology and Language—ESL Pointers

Page 411 "In addition to a **shock** of black hair on his head, his body was covered with dark, fine hair known as "lanugo.""

A shock is a large amount of thick , long and tangled hair.

Page 411 "Yet ask any parents: Nothing is more beautiful or exciting than the first **glimpse** of their newborn."

A **glimpse** is a brief look.

Page 411 "The skin secretes *vernix*, a white, greasy covering, for protection before birth, and the baby may have *lanugo*, a soft **fuzz**, over the entire body for a similar purpose."

Fuzz is a group of short fine hairs.

Page 411 "Even more impressive are the capabilities a neonate begins to display from the moment of birth—capabilities that grow at an **astounding** rate over the **ensuing** months."

An **astounding** rate is one that is surprising.

Ensuing means subsequent or those that follow.

Page 411 "Critical for survival, many of those reflexes **unfold** naturally as part of an infant's ongoing maturation."

When things **unfold** they open up or expand over time.

Page 411 "Among other reflexes are a *gag reflex* (to clear the throat), the startle reflex (a series of movements in which an infant **flings** out the arms, fans the fingers, and arches the back in response to a sudden noise), and the *Babinski reflex* (a baby's toes **fan out** when the outer edge of the sole of the foot is **stroked**)."

When we **fling** something we throw it with a lot of force.

When toes **fan out** they are spread apart.

To **stroke** something is to gently caress or touch it.

Page 412 "However, researchers have devised a number of **ingenious** methods, relying on the newborn's biological responses and innate reflexes, to test perceptual skills."

Their **ingenious** methods are clever and imaginative methods of perceptual assessment.

Page 412 "For instance, infants who see a **novel** stimulus typically pay close attention to it, and, as a consequence, their heart rates increase."

When the infant sees a **novel** stimulus, a fresh or unusual stimulus, their heart rates increase.

Page 413 "A change in the rate and **vigor** with which the babies suck helps researchers infer that babies can perceive variations in stimuli."

Vigor is strength or force.

Page 413 "At birth, babies prefer patterns with **contours** and edges over less distinct patterns, indicating that they can respond to the configuration of stimuli."

Contours are outline or edges.

Page 414 "Otherwise a **model of decorum**, Russell had somehow learned how to unzip the Velcro chin strap to his winter hat."

Someone who is a **model of decorum** is an ideal example of good behavior.

Page 414 "He would remove the hat whenever he got the **urge**, seemingly oblivious to the potential health problems that might follow."

An **urge** is a strong need to do something.

Page 414 "To the **chagrin** of the teachers in the day care center, not to speak of the children's parents, soon other children were following his lead, removing their own caps at will."

Chagrin is distress and annoyance.

Page 414 "Russell's mother, made aware of the **anarchy** at the day care center – and the other parents' distress over Russell's behavior – **pleaded** innocent."

Anarchy is lawlessness, rebellion. The children in the day care center were creating chaos with the constant removal of their caps.

When someone **pleads** they are asking for something in a very emotional way, they are begging.

Page 414 ""He learned by trial and error, and the other kids saw him do it one day when they were getting dressed for an **outing**" (Goleman, 1993a, C10)."

An **outing** is a walk or day trip that takes place outside.

Page 415 "As anyone who has seen an infant smiling at the sight of his or her mother can guess, at the same time that infants grow physically and **hone** their perceptual abilities, they also develop socially."

When we hone our abilities we are practicing and improving them. The infants are **honing** their perceptual abilities; they are practicing and improving these capabilities.

Page 415 "Lorenz focused on newborn **goslings**, which under normal circumstances instinctively follow their mother, the first moving object they perceive after birth."

A **gosling** is a young goose.

Page 415 "Lorenz found that goslings whose eggs were raised in an incubator and which viewed him immediately after **hatching** would follow his every movement, as if he were their mother."

Hatching is the process of coming out of an egg.

Page 416 " They spent most of their time clinging to the warm cloth 'monkey,' although they made occasional **forays** to the wire monkey to nurse."

A **foray** is a short trip to a place, usually for a specific purpose.

Page 418 "For example, Korean American children engage in a higher proportion of parallel play than their Anglo-American counterparts, while Anglo-American preschoolers are involved in more **pretend** play (Farver, Kim, & Lee-Shin, 1995; Farver & Lee-Shin, 2000; Bai, 2005; Drewes, 2005)."

To **pretend** is to make believe or act as if something made up is true and real.

Page 418 "They may engage in **elaborate** games involving teams and rigid rules."

Things that are **elaborate** have many parts and are very detailed and complex.

Page 418 "Research on the importance of social interaction is **corroborated** by work that examines the benefits of child care out of the home, which is an important part of an increasing number of children's lives."

When we **corroborate** things we confirm or give evidence as to the truthfulness of them.

Page 418 "They may also be more **compliant** and regulate their own behavior more effectively, and their mothers show increased sensitivity to their children (Lamb, 1996; NICHD Early Child Care Research Network, 1997, 1998, 1999, 2001)."

Someone who is **compliant** is one who is always ready to agree.

Page 419 "The key to the success of nonparental child care is its quality. High-quality child care produces benefits; low-quality child care provides little or no gain, and may even **hinder** children's development."

To **hinder** someone is to delay or hold them back.

Page 420 "In contrast, permissive parents' children show immaturity, **moodiness**, dependence, and low self-control."

Moodiness is the tendency to change mood or your frame of mind without any warning.

Page 420 "The children of authoritative parents **fare** best: With high social skills, they are likable, self-reliant, independent, and cooperative."

To **fare** is to happen to turn out in a specific way.

Page 420 "Such children display unusual social skills: **outgoingness**, intelligence, and a feeling that they have control over their lives."

Outgoingness is the tendency to be secure and friendly in social settings.

Page 420 "In sum, a child's **upbringing** results from the **child-rearing** philosophy parents hold, the specific practices they use, and the nature of their own and their child's personalities."

A person's **upbringing** is the way they have been brought up in early life.

Child-rearing refers to act of parenting or the upbringing of children.

Page 421 "Although his theory has been criticized on several **grounds**—such as the imprecision of the concepts he employs and his greater emphasis on male development than female development—it remains influential and is one of the few theories that encompass the entire life span."

Grounds are reasons why something would be true.

Page 421 "Yet despite this seeming sophistication, there are deep **gaps** in children's understanding of the world."

Gaps are holes or an area where something is missing.

Page 423 "Thus, children's stories and explanations to adults can be **maddeningly** uninformative, as they are delivered without any context."

Something that is **maddening** is annoying or frustrating.

Page 423 "In a number of other ways, some quite **startling**, the failure to understand the principle of conservation affects children's responses."

When something is **startling** it is surprising.

Page 423 "Research demonstrates that principles that are obvious to and unquestioned by adults may be completely misunderstood by children during the preoperational period, and that it is not until the next stage of cognitive development that children **grasp** the concept of conservation."

When we **grasp** something we understand it.

Page 423 "Although children make important advances in their logical capabilities during the concrete operational stage, their thinking still displays one major limitation: They are largely **bound to** the concrete, physical reality of the world."

To be **bound to** something means to be limited by it or tied to it.

Page 423 "The way in which children approach the "**pendulum** problem" devised by Piaget (Piaget & Inhelder, 1958) illustrates the emergence of formal operational thinking."

A **pendulum** is a weight on a string or pole that swings freely from a fixed point.

Page 425 "For instance, some evidence suggests that infants as young as 5 months have **rudimentary** mathematical skills (Wynn, 1995, 2000; Wynn, Bloom, & Chiang, 2002)."

Rudimentary means basic or simple.

Page 425 "For example, Piaget suggests that individuals cannot increase their cognitive performance unless both cognitive **readiness** brought about by maturation and appropriate environmental stimulation are present."

Readiness is the state of being prepares for something to happen.

Page 425 "If cognitive development does not proceed as a series of stages, as Piaget suggested, what does underlie the enormous growth in children's cognitive abilities that even the most **untutored** eye can observe?"

Untutored refers to someone who has not been taught or someone who has not had any formal education or training.

Page 425 "From this perspective, children become increasingly **adept** at information processing, much as a computer program may become more sophisticated as a programmer modifies it on the basis of experience."

When we are **adept,** we are skilled.

Page 426 "Vygotsky argues that cognitive development occurs as a consequence of social interactions in which children work with others to **jointly** solve problems."

When we do something **jointly** we work together with others.

Page 426 "This type of assistance, called *scaffolding*, provides support for learning and problem solving that encourages independence and growth."

A *scaffolding* is a temporary framework that is used to support workers.

Module 40: Adolescence: Becoming an Adult

Physical Development: The Changing Adolescent
Moral and Cognitive Development: Distinguishing Right from Wrong
Social Development: Finding Oneself in a Social World

Exploring Diversity: Rites of Passage:
Coming of Age around the World

- *What major physical, social, and cognitive transitions characterize adolescence?*

Adolescence: Becoming an Adult

Development continues throughout life, from adolescence to adulthood and old age. The major biological changes that begin with the attainment of physical and sexual maturity and the changes in social, emotional, and cognitive function that lead to adulthood mark the period

called **[a]** _____.

The dramatic physical changes of adolescence include a growth in height, the development of breasts in females, the deepening of the male voice, the development of body hair, and intense sexual feelings. The growth spurt begins around age 10 for girls and age 12 for boys. The development of the sexual organs begins about a year later. There are wide individual variations, however. Better nutrition and medical care in Western cultures is probably the cause of the

decreasing age of onset of **[b]** _____. Early-maturing boys have an advantage over later-maturing boys, doing better in athletics and being more popular, although they do have more difficulties in school. Early-maturing girls are more popular and have higher self-concepts than those who mature late, but the obvious changes in breasts can cause separation from peers and ridicule. Late-maturers suffer because of the delay, with boys being ridiculed for their lack of coordination and girls holding lower social status in junior high and high school.

Erikson's theory of psychosocial development (introduced in module 39) identifies the

beginning of adolescence with his fifth stage, called the **[c]** _____ *stage*.

During this stage, individuals seek to discover their abilities, skills, and **[d]** _____.
If one resolves this stage with confusion, then a stable identity will not be formed, and the individual may become a social deviant or have trouble with close personal relationships later. The stage is marked by a shift from dependence on adults for information and the turn toward the peer group for support.

During college, the **[e]** _____ *stage* describes the basic conflict. This stage focuses on developing relationships with others. Middle adulthood finds people in the

[f] _____ *stage*. The contribution to family, community, work, and society comprise generativity; and feelings of triviality about one's activities indicate the difficulties of the stage and lead to stagnation. The final stage is the **[g]** _____ *stage*, which is marked by a sense of accomplishment if a person has been successful in life or a sense of despair if one regrets what might have been.

Kohlberg has also written about development for adolescents, though focused on moral development. He suggests that the highest stage of moral development involves the application of abstract, carefully considered principles to solving moral problems. Carol Gilligan, on the other hand, suggests that the moral development of boys and girls, and men and women, differ. Women's morality centers around **[h]** _____ , and the highest level of morality involves compassionate concern for the welfare of others.

Evaluate

_____ 1. identity vs. role
           confusion stage

_____ 2. intimacy vs. isolation
           stage

_____ 3. generativity vs.
           stagnation stage

_____ 4. ego integrity vs. despair
           stage

a. A period from late adulthood until death during which we review life's accomplishments and failures.

b. A period in middle adulthood during which we take stock of our contributions to family and society.

c. A period during early adulthood that focuses on developing close relationships with others.

d. A time in adolescence of testing to determine one's own unique qualities.

Rethink

40-1 In what ways do school cultures help or hurt teenage students who are going through adolescence? What school policies might benefit early-maturing girls and late-maturing boys? Explain how same-sex schools help, as some have argued.

40-2 *From the perspective of a social worker:* How might you determine if an adolescent was at risk for suicide? What strategies would you use to prevent the teen from committing suicide? Would you use different strategies depending on the teenager's gender?

Spotlight on Terminology and Language—ESL Pointers

Page 429 "Trevor Kelson, Age 15: "Keep the Hell Out of my Room!" says a sign on Trevor's bedroom wall, just above an **unmade** bed, a desk littered with dirty T-shirts and candy wrappers, and a floor covered with clothes."

An **unmade** bed is one that is messy and untidy

Page 429 "I went to a National Honor Society **induction**."

An **induction** is an initiation experience.

Page 429 "It is a time of profound changes and, occasionally, **turmoil**."

Turmoil is a period of extreme confusion, agitation, or commotion.

Page 429 "At the same time, and **rivaling** these physiological changes, important social, emotional and cognitive changes occur as adolescents strive for independence and move toward adulthood."

When something is **rivaled**, it is in competition with competing forces.

Page 429 "Furthermore, adolescents spend considerably less time with their parents, and more with their peers, than they did several **decades** ago."

A **decade** is a period of ten years.

Page 429 "Finally, the **ethnic** and cultural diversity of adolescents as a group is increasing dramatically."

Ethnic refers to the sharing of unique cultural characteristics.

Page 429 "A third of all adolescents today are of non-European **descent**, and by the year 2050 the number of adolescents of Hispanic, African American, Native American, and Asian origin will have grown significantly (Carnegie Council on Adolescent Development, 1995; Dreman, 1997)."

Your **descent** refers to your ancestry or your heritage.

Page 429 "A **spurt** in height, the growth of breasts in girls, deepening voices in boys, the development of body hair, and intense sexual feelings cause curiosity, interest, and sometimes embarrassment for individuals entering adolescence."

A **spurt** is a short sudden increase in something.

Page 430 "The physical changes that occur at the start of adolescence result largely from the **secretion** of various hormones, and they affect virtually every aspect of an adolescent's life."

Secretion refers to the process of producing and releasing substances from cells.

Page 431 "For example, early breast development may set them apart from their peers and be a source of **ridicule** (Simmons & Blyth, 1987; Ge, Conger, & Elder, 1996; Nadeem & Graham, 2005)."

To **ridicule** someone is to laugh at or make fun of them.

Page 431 "Adolescents, however, can **reason** on a higher **plane**, having typically reached Piaget's formal operational stage of cognitive development."

To **reason** is to think. See chapter 8 for a more detailed discussion of **reasoning**.

Reasoning on a higher **plane** refers to a higher level of consciousness or intellectual and moral development.

Page 431 "Because they are able to comprehend broad moral principles, they can understand that morality is **not always black and white** and that conflict can exist between two sets of socially accepted standards."

In this context the term "**not always black and white**" is being used to imply that something that something is not clear cut.

Page 432 "One glaring **shortcoming** of Kohlberg's research is that he primarily used male participants."

A **shortcoming** is a limitation or a weakness.

Page 432 "In contrast, women see it in terms of responsibility toward individuals and **willingness** to make sacrifices to help a specific individual within the context of a particular relationship."

Willingness refers to the tendency to be ready to do something without being forced.

Page 432 "Compassion for individuals is a more **salient** factor in more behavior for women than it is for men."

A **salient** factor is something that stands out conspicuously.

Page 433 "They attempt to discover who they are, what their strengths are, and what kinds of roles they are best **suited** to play for the rest of their lives—in short, their **identity**."

When someone is **suited** for something, they are appropriate or well-matched for it.

Your **identity** is how you define your self; who you think you are.

Page 433 "A person confused about the most appropriate role to play in life may lack a stable identity, adopt an unacceptable role such as that of a social **deviant**, or have difficulty maintaining close personal relationships later in life (Brendgen, Vitaro, & Bukowski, 2000; Updegraff et al., 2004; Vleioras & Bosma, 2005)."

A **deviant** is someone who is abnormal or acts in a way that is very different from the accepted cultural behaviors.

Page 434 "The identity-versus-role-confusion stage has another important characteristic: declining reliance on adults for information, with a **shift** toward using the peer group as a source of social judgments."

A **shift** is a change or a move in a different direction.

Page 434 "According to Erikson, the identity-versus-role-confusion stage marks a **pivotal** point in psychosocial development, **paving the way** for continued growth and the future development of personal relationships."

Something that is **pivotal** is critical; it is vitally important

When we "**pave the way**" for something we are doing things to prepare for it and these things make it easier for that thing to happen.

Page 434 "In sum, adolescence is not an end point but rather a **way station** on the path of psychosocial development (Whitbourne et al., 1992; McAdams et al., 1997)."

A **way station** is an intermediate stopping place.

Page 434 "Although Erikson's theory provides a broad outline of identity development, critics have pointed out that his approach is **anchored** in male-oriented concepts of individuality and competitiveness."

An **anchor** is a device used to hold ships in place. When things are **anchored** they are securely linked or connected.

Page 434 "Does puberty invariably **foreshadow** a **stormy**, rebellious period of adolescence?"

When an event **foreshadows** something, it warns of, or indicates, the next event.

Something that is **stormy** it is unsettled and wild.

Page 434 "At one time, psychologists thought most children entering adolescence were beginning a period **fraught** with stress and unhappiness."

When something is **fraught** with something it is full of problems.

Page 434 "However, research now shows that this characterization is largely a **myth**, that most young people pass through adolescence without **appreciable** turmoil in their lives, and that parents speak easily—and fairly often—with their children about a variety of topics (Klein, 1998; van Wel, Linssen, & Abma, 2000; Granic, Hollenstein, & Dishion, 2003)."

A **myth** is an ancient story or fairy tale that is sometimes untrue but answers some kind of question about mankind.

Appreciable means a large or important enough to be noticed.

Page 434 "In most families with adolescents, the amount of arguing and **bickering** clearly rises."

When people **bicker** they are having a petty, or unimportant argument.

Page 435 "One reason for the increase in **discord** during adolescence appears to be the **protracted** period in which children stay at home with their parents."

386

Discord is the increase in conflict and friction.

Protracted is the much longer and drawn out period children are now staying at home.

Page 435 "Current social trends even hint at an extension of the conflicts of adolescence beyond the teenage years, because a significant number of young adults—known as *boomerang children*—return to live with their parents after leaving home for some period."

A **boomerang** is a curved piece of wood that returns to the person who throws it. **Boomerang children** return to live with their parents after leaving home for some period.

Page 435 "Another source of **strife** with parents lies in the way adolescents think."

Strife is a bitter conflict or struggle.

Page 435 "Furthermore, they develop *personal fables,* the belief that their experience is unique, exceptional, and shared by no one else."

Fables are stories that teach a lesson.

Page 435 "Typically, adolescents change schools at least twice (from elementary to middle school or junior high, then to senior high school), and relationships with friends and peers are particularly **volatile**."

Something that is **volatile** is unpredictable and is prone to sudden extreme changes.

Page 436 "One factor is depression, characterized by unhappiness, extreme **fatigue**, and—a variable that seems particularly important—a profound sense of hopelessness."

Fatigue is a state of extreme mental or physical tiredness or exhaustion.

Page 436 "In other cases, adolescents who commit suicide are perfectionists, **inhibited** socially and prone to extreme anxiety when they face any social or academic challenge (Ayyash-Abdo, 2002; Goldston, 2003; CDC, 2004; see Figure 4; Richardson, Bergen, Martin, Roeger, & Allison, 2005)."

When we **inhibit** something we prevent, or stop it from happening.

Page 436 "A long-standing history of conflicts between parents and children may lead to adolescent behavior problems, such as **delinquency**, dropping out of school, and aggressive tendencies."

Delinquent means not following rules or laws. **Delinquency** refers to illegal behavior done by teenagers or someone who is young.

Page 437 "Several warning signs indicate when a teenager's problems may be severe enough to **warrant** concern about the possibility of a suicide attempt."

To **warrant** something is to have a reason for it.

Page 437 "First come **whippings** with sticks and prickly branches, both for the boys' own past misdeeds and in honor of those tribesmen who were killed in warfare."

A **whipping** is a punishment in which someone is hit with a whip or rope.

Page 437 "Other cultures have less **fearsome**, although no less important, ceremonies that mark the passage from childhood to adulthood."

Something that is **fearsome** is frightening.

Page 437 "For instance, when a girl first menstruates in traditional Apache tribes, the event is marked by dawn-to-dusk **chanting.**"

Chanting occurs when someone repeats a series of word in a rhythmic, or regular pattern.

Page 437 "Western religions, too, have several types of celebrations, including bar and bat mitzvahs at age 13 for Jewish boys and girls and confirmation ceremonies for children in many Christian **denominations** (Myerhoff, 1982; Dunham, et al., 1986; Rakoff, 1995)."

Denominations are religious groupings within a faith that have specific beliefs and practices that differ from other groupings with that faith.

Page 437 "The **renowned** anthropologist Margaret Mead remarked, only partly in jest, that the **preponderance** of male ceremonies might reflect the fact that "the worry that boys will not grow up to be men is much more **widespread** than that girls will not grow up to be women" (1949, p. 195)."

When someone or something is **renowned** they are famous or well-known.

Preponderance means the majority.

When something is **widespread** it is common.

Module 41: Adulthood

Physical Development: The Peak of Health
Social Development: Working at Life
Marriage, Children, and Divorce: Family Ties
The Later Years of Life: Growing Old
Physical Changes in Late Adulthood: The Aging Body
Cognitive Changes: Thinking About—and During—Late Adulthood
The Social World of Late Adulthood: Old But Not Alone

Becoming an Informed Consumer of Psychology: Adjusting to Death

- ***What are the principal kinds of physical, social, and intellectual changes that occur in early and middle adulthood, and what are their causes?***
- ***How does the reality of late adulthood differ from the stereotypes about the period?***
- ***How can we adjust to death?***

Adulthood

Early adulthood is generally considered to begin at about 20 years of age and to last until about 40 to 45 years, and middle adulthood lasts from 40 to 45 to about 65 years of age. These ages have been studied less than any other. Fewer significant physical changes occur, and the social changes are diverse.

The peak of physical health is reached in early adulthood, and quantitative changes begin at about 25 years as the body becomes less efficient and more prone to disease through time. The major physical development is the female experience of [a] _____, the cessation of menstruation and the end of fertility. The loss of estrogen may lead to hot flashes, a condition that can be successfully treated with artificial estrogen. Problems that were once blamed on menopause are now seen as resulting from the perceptions of coming old age and society's view of it. Although men remain fertile, the gradual decline of physical abilities has similar effects to menopause, causing the man to focus on the social expectations of youthfulness.

One model of adult development suggests that in the formative stages of adulthood, people focus on entering the world of work, envisioning life goals, and developing an adult identity which often corresponds with their careers. At about 40 or 45, people enter a period called the [b] _____, during which past accomplishments are assessed, and, in some cases, the assessment leads to a(n) [c] _____, in which the signs of physical aging and a sense that the career will not progress combine to force a reevaluation of and an effort to remedy their dissatisfaction. Most people go through the midlife transition without any difficulties. During their fifties, people become more accepting of others and their own lives. They realize that death is inevitable and seek to understand their accomplishments in terms of how they understand life.

[d] _____ study development and the aging process from the age of about 65. Gerontologists reexamine our understanding of aging, suggesting that the stereotype of aging is inaccurate. Napping, eating, walking, and conversing are the typical activities of both the elderly and college students. The obvious physical changes that appear in old age include thinning and graying hair, wrinkling and folding skin, and a loss of height. Vision and hearing become less sharp, smell and taste are less sensitive, reaction time slows, and oxygen intake and heart-pumping abilities decrease. Two types of theories have been offered to account for these

changes. One group includes the [e] _____ *theories of aging*, which suggest that there are preset time limits on the reproduction of human cells governed by genetics. The

other group includes the [f] _____ *theories of aging*, which suggest that the body simply stops working efficiently. By-products of energy production accumulate, and cells make mistakes in their reproduction.

The view that the elderly are forgetful and confused is no longer considered an accurate

assessment. Tests show declines in [g] _____ in old age, but

[h] _____ remains stable or even increases in some. Fluid intelligence may be more sensitive to changes in the nervous system than crystallized intelligence.

One assumption about the elderly is that they are more forgetful. Evidence suggests that forgetfulness is not inevitable. The progressive decline in cognitive abilities associated with old

age is called [i] _____, but this is now viewed as a symptom caused by other

factors, like [j] _____, anxiety, depression, or even overmedication.

Loneliness is a problem for only a small portion of the elderly, although social patterns do change in old age. Two theories account for how people approach old age. The

[k] _____ *theory of aging* views aging as a gradual withdrawal from the world on physical, psychological, and social levels. Energy is lower and interaction lessens. This view

sees aging as an automatic process. The [l] _____ *theory of aging* suggests that the happiest people are ones who remain active and that people should attempt to maintain the activities and interests they develop during middle age. The nature of the activity is the most important factor, not the quantity. Regardless of how aging progresses, most people conduct a

[m] _____ later in life, in which they examine and evaluate their lives, often developing a better understanding of themselves and gaining wisdom in the process.

Death requires major adjustments, as the death of those near you causes changes in life and makes you consider the possibility of your own death. Elisabeth Kübler-Ross outlined five stages

of the death process: (1) [n] _____, the person denies the fact that he or she is

dying; (2) [o] _____, the person becomes angry at people who are healthy, angry at the medical profession for not being able to help, and angry at God; (3)

[p] _____, after anger, the person may try to postpone death through a bargain

in exchange for extended life; (4) [q] _____, once bargaining fails, the person experiences depression, realizing that death is inevitable; and (5) [r] _____, which is signaled by the end of mourning one's own life, becoming unemotional and noncommunicative as if at peace with oneself.

Evaluate

Part A

_____ 1. Erik Erikson

_____ 2. Lawrence Kohlberg

_____ 3. Jean Piaget

_____ 4. Elisabeth Kübler-Ross

_____ 5. Arlie Hochschild

a. Moral development.

b. Death and dying.

c. Psychosocial development.

d. Cognitive development.

e. The "second shift."

Part B

_____ 1. genetic preprogramming theories of aging

_____ 2. wear-and-tear theories of aging

_____ 3. disengagement theory of aging

_____ 4. activity theory of aging

a. Theories that suggest that the body's mechanical functions cease efficient activity and, in effect, wear out.

b. A theory that suggests that the elderly who age most successfully are those who maintain the interests and activities they had during middle age.

c. Theories that suggest a built-in time limit to the reproduction of human cells.

d. A theory that suggests that aging is a gradual withdrawal from the world on physical, psychological, and social levels.

Rethink

41-1 Is the possibility that life might be extended for several decades a mixed blessing? What societal consequences might an extended life span bring about?

41-2 *From the perspective of a health care provider:* What sorts of recommendations would you make to your older patients about how to deal with aging? How would you handle someone who believed that getting older had only negative consequences?

Spotlight on Terminology and Language—ESL Pointers

Page 439 "After going twelve years in professional football and twelve years before that in amateur football without ever having surgery performed on me, the last two seasons of my career I **went under the knife** three times."

The phrase "**went under the knife**" is a slang term for having a medical procedure involving surgery.

Page 439 "In addition, the **diverse** social changes that arise during this period **defy** simple categorization."

Diverse means varied or having many differences.

To **defy** is to disobey someone.

Page 439 "For most people, early adulthood marks the **peak** of physical health."

Peak means best or highest.

Page 440 "However, hormone therapy poses several dangers, such as an increase in the risk of breast cancer, blood **clots**, and heart disease."

A **clot** is a sticky lump of thickened liquid.

Page 440 "These uncertainties make the routine use of HRT **controversial** (Kittell & Mansfield, 2000; National Heart, Lung, & Blood Institute, 2002; Rymer, Wilson, & Ballard, 2003)."

The routine use of hormone replacement therapy is **controversial**; there are many arguments both for and against the use of HRT.

Page 440 "Menopause was once **blamed** for a variety of psychological symptoms, including depression and memory loss."

To be **blamed** is to be responsible for something wrong that has happened.

Page 440 "According to **anthropologist** Yewoubdar Beyene (1989), the more a society values old age, the less difficulty its women have during menopause."

An **anthropologist** is a person who studies people. **Anthropologists** study all human beings, studying cultures and human development.

Page 440 "Once again, though, any psychological difficulties associated with these changes are usually brought about not so much by physical deterioration as by the inability of an aging individual to meet the exaggerated standards of **youthfulness.**"

To be **youthful** is to have the characteristics of someone who is not very old.

Page 440 "People come to accept the fact that death is **inevitable**, and they try to understand their accomplishments in terms of the broader meaning of life."

When something is **inevitable**, it is unavoidable, it will happen no matter what you do.

Page 441 "In the typical fairy tale, a **dashing** young man and a beautiful young woman marry, have children, and live happily ever after."

Dashing is handsome, good-looking

Page 441 "The percentage of U.S. **households** made up of unmarried couples has increased dramatically over the last two decades."

A **household** refers to the group of people that live together in a single home.

Page 441 "Before they are 18 years old, two-fifths of children will experience the **breakup** of their parents' marriages."

A **breakup** is the coming apart of something.

Page 441 "In South Korea, for example, the divorce rate **quadrupled** from 11 percent to 47 percent in the 12-year period ending in 2002 (Schaefer, 2000; Lankov, 2004; Olson & DeFrain, 2005)."

When something **quadruples** it increase by a factor of four.

Page 441 "Furthermore, in most single-parent families, it is the mother, rather than the father, with whom the children **reside**—a phenomenon that is consistent across racial and ethnic groups throughout the industrialized world (U.S. Bureau of the Census, 2000)."

Reside means to live with.

Page 442 "In fact, children may be more successful growing up in a harmonious single-parent family than in a two-parent family that **engages** in continuous conflict (Harold et al., 1997; Clarke-Stewart et al., 2000; Kelly, 2000; Olson & DeFrain, 2006)."

To **engage** is to take part in something.

Page 442 "The number of hours put in by working mothers can be **staggering.**"

When something is **staggering** it is hard to believe.

Page 442 "It is not surprising that some wives feel **resentment** toward husbands who spend less time on child care and housework than the wives had expected before the birth of their children (Stier & Lewin-

Epstein, 2000; Kiecolt, 2003; Gerstel, 2005).”

Resentment is the feeling of anger or bitterness toward someone.

Page 443 “By focusing on the period of life that starts at around age 65, **gerontologists** are making important contributions to **clarifying** the capabilities of older adults.”

Gerontologists are scientists that study aging.

When we **clarify** something we make it clearer and easier to understand.

Page 443 “It probably doesn't surprise you that these relatively nonstrenuous activities represent the typical **pastimes** of late adulthood.”

Pastimes are hobbies or interests that someone does in their spare time.

Page 443 “These theories suggest that after a certain time cells stop dividing or become harmful to the body—as if a kind of automatic **self-destruct** button had been pushed.”

To **self-destruct** means to act in a way so that you will destroy or ruin yourself.

Page 444 “Yet if we looked a little more closely at the specific test, we might find that that conclusion was **unwarranted**.”

Something that is **unwarranted** is unnecessary or not needed.

Page 444 “Other difficulties **hamper** research into cognitive functioning during late adulthood.”

When something is **hampered** it is hindered or blocked from happening.

Page 445 “For instance, losses tend to be limited to **episodic** memories, which relate to specific experiences in people's lives.”

A **episode** is a section or limited period of time. See Refer back to chapter 7 for a detailed description of **episodic memories**.

Page 445 “For instance, it is not surprising that a retired person, who may no longer face the same kind of consistent intellectual challenges encountered on the job, may be less practiced in using memory or even be less motivated to remember things, leading to an **apparent** decline in memory.”

Something that is **apparent** is obvious or noticeable.

Page 445 “Even in cases in which long-term memory declines, older adults can usually profit from **compensatory** efforts.”

Compensate means to counteract or offset. **Compensatory efforts** are things that make up for negative effects of something else.

Page 445 “Training older adults to use the **mnemonic** strategies developed by psychologists studying memory not only may prevent their long-term memory from deteriorating, but may actually improve it

(Verhaeghen, Marcoen, & Goossens, 1992; West, 1995)."

A **mnemonic** is a memory aid. See chapter 7 for a more detailed explanation of **mnemonics.**

Page 446 "However, such disengagement serves an important purpose, providing an opportunity for increased **reflectiveness** and decreased emotional investment in others at a time of life when social relationships will inevitably be ended by death."

Reflectiveness refers to the tendency to be thoughtful.

Page 446 "Evidence shows that positive self-perceptions of aging are associated with increased **longevity** (Charles, Reynolds, & Gatz, 2001; Levy et al., 2002; Levy & Myers, 2004)."

Longevity is the length or duration of your life.

Page 446 "Remembering and reconsidering what has occurred in the past, people in late adulthood often come to a better understanding of themselves, sometimes resolving lingering problems and conflicts, and facing their lives with greater wisdom and **serenity**."

Serenity is a state of calmness with out worry or stress.

Page 447 "A generation ago, talk of death was **taboo**."

Something that is **taboo** is forbidden or not allowed to occur.

Page 447 "That changed, however, with the pioneering work of Elisabeth Kübler-Ross (1969), who brought the subject of death into the open with her observation that those facing **impending** death tend to move through five broad stages:"

Something that is **impending** is imminent or about to happen any minute.

Test your knowledge of the modules by answering these questions. These questions have been placed in three Practice Tests. The first two tests consist of questions that will test your recall of factual knowledge. The third test contains questions that are challenging and primarily test for conceptual knowledge and your ability to apply that knowledge. Check your answers and review the feedback using the Answer Key in the following pages of the *Study Guide*.

PRACTICE TEST 1:

1. When theories stress the role of heredity in their explanations of change in individual development, the focus of their accounts would be on:
    a. maturation.
    c. environmental factors.
    b. nurture.
    d. social growth.

2. A study in which several different age groups are examined over different points in time is called:
    a. cross-sectional.
    c. longitudinal.
    b. maturational.
    d. cross-sequential.

3. Hereditary information is represented in thousands of _____, which are tiny segments of stringy material called _____.
    a. zygotes; embryos
    c. genes; neonates
    b. chromosomes; zygotes
    d. genes; chromosomes

4. In prenatal development, the age of viability is a developmental stage in which:
    a. the eyes and other sense organs are functional.
    b. the fetus can survive if born prematurely.
    c. development has advanced sufficiently so that the fetus is capable of learning from environmental cues.
    d. the sexual organs of the fetus are differentiated.

5. Which of the following is caused by genetic birth defects?
    a. Phenylketonuria (PKU)
    c. Diethylstilbestrol (DES)
    b. AIDS
    d. Fetal alcohol syndrome

6. The infant's later temperament is known to be affected by the mother's:
    a. consumption of "junk foods" during pregnancy.
    b. sleep patterns during early fetal development.
    c. attitude about whether the baby is wanted or unwanted.
    d. emotional state during the late fetal period.

7. Which reflex helps the newborn infant position its mouth onto its mother's breast when it feeds?
    a. Rooting reflex
    c. Gag reflex
    b. Startle reflex
    d. Surprise reflex

8. Erikson's theory of development:
   a. was based on experiences of psychotic women.
   b. covers an entire lifetime.
   c. takes a behaviorist approach.
   d. was derived from Piaget's cognitive approach to development.

9. What changes in perception do **not** take place in the first six months after birth in human infants?
   a. They develop discrimination of tastes and smells.
   b. They can recognize two- and three-dimensional objects.
   c. They can discriminate all sounds important for language production.
   d. They understand their native language.

10. In order to proceed from one of Piaget's stages of cognitive development to another, it is necessary for children to achieve a certain level of:
    a. perceptual and cognitive development.
    b. maturation and experience.
    c. memory capacity and physical development.
    d. social and cognitive development.

11. Which of the following is a possible reason for the steadily decreasing age at which adolescents reached puberty during the last century?
    a. Nutrition and medical care have increased.
    b. Cultural prohibitions about sexuality have weakened.
    c. Sexual promiscuity among children has increased.
    d. Puberty rituals have been abandoned in most Western societies.

12. If a person's behavior reflected the desire to please other members of society, he or she would be considered to be at Kohlberg's:
    a. preconventional level of moral reasoning.
    b. conventional level of moral reasoning.
    c. postconventional level of moral reasoning.
    d. nonconventional level of moral reasoning.

13. The most noteworthy feature of Erikson's theory of psychosocial development is that:
    a. both men and women are included in its descriptions of developmental changes.
    b. it accurately describes developmental changes that people in other cultures also experience.
    c. it has greatly increased understanding of infant development.
    d. it suggests that development is a lifelong process.

14. Several warning signs indicate that a teenager may attempt suicide. Which alternative is **not** one of them?
    a. Loss of appetite or excessive eating
    b. Withdrawal from friends or peers
    c. A preoccupation with death, the afterlife, or what would happen "if I died"
    d. An increase in praying, going to church, or other religious behavior

15. The primary cause of a midlife crisis tends to be:
    a. an awareness of the detrimental physical changes associated with aging.
    b. a series of disappointments and shortcomings in a person's children.

c.   a recognition that a person's reproductive capabilities are decreasing or will soon end.

d.   a failure to achieve desired career goals and objectives.

16.   Which kind of development seems to show important differences between men and women according to development researcher Carol Gilligan?

a.   Culmination   c.   Moral

b.   Cognitive   d.   Reality

17.   Genetic preprogramming theories suggest which of the following about physical decline of aging?

a.   Women live four to 10 years longer than men.

b.   The body, like a machine, eventually wears out.

c.   There is a built-in time limit to the ability of human cells to reproduce.

d.   Physical aging is a biological process in which all physical functions decline.

18.   Fluid intelligence provides the capabilities for many adaptive and functional human behaviors. Which alternative correctly describes a person's fluid-intelligence capabilities?

a.   Fluid intelligence increases after birth until early adulthood.

b.   Fluid intelligence is high all through a person's lifetime.

c.   Fluid intelligence increases more slowly during late adulthood and old age.

d.   Fluid intelligence remains fairly constant until a person's death.

19.   What is the most accurate statement regarding genetic preprogramming theories of aging and wear-and-tear theories of aging?

a.   There is more support for genetic preprogramming theories.

b.   There is more support for wear-and-tear theories.

c.   There is evidence in support of both theories.

d.   Aging is probably explained by some other, as yet undiscovered, theory.

20.   A pattern of reduced social and physical activity as well as a shift toward the self rather than a focus on others characterizes the:

a.   deactivation theory of aging.   c.   withdrawal theory of aging.

b.   activity theory of aging.   d.   disengagement theory of aging.

Part A

_____ 21.   trust vs. mistrust stage   a.   The stage of psychosocial development where children can experience self-doubt if they are restricted and overprotected.

_____ 22.   autonomy vs. shame and doubt stage

     b.   The first stage of psychosocial development, occurring from birth to 18 months of age.

_____ 23.   initiative vs. guilt stage

_____ 24.   industry vs. inferiority stage

     c.   The period during which children may develop positive social interactions with others or may feel inadequate and become less sociable.

     d.   The period during which children experience conflict between independence of action and the sometimes negative results of that action.

Part B

_____ 25. adolescence

_____ 26. identity

_____ 27. menopause

_____ 28. midlife transition

_____ 29. midlife crisis

a. The point at which women stop menstruating, generally at around 45 years of age.

b. The stage between childhood and adulthood.

c. The negative feelings that accompany the realization that we have not accomplished all that we had hoped.

d. The distinguishing character of the individual: who each of us is, what our roles are, and what we are capable of.

e. Beginning around age 40, a period during which we come to realize that life is finite.

30. Considering the discussion of the nature-nurture issue at the beginning of the chapter, what is your assessment of the role of child-rearing practices in the development of the person as a unique individual? Are certain styles more likely to help individuals reach their potential?

31. Describe the factors that contribute to problems between parents and teenagers and suggest ways that these may be overcome. Are the recent changes in childhood and adolescence that result in changes in the family to blame for some of these factors?

PRACTICE TEST 2:

1. The philosophical view that infants are born with a blank slate favors which of the following as a dominant influence on development?
    a. Interactionism
    b. Nature
    c. Nurture
    d. Dualism

2. Identical twins are especially interesting subjects for developmental studies because they:
    a. communicate via telepathy (i.e., direct mental transfer of ideas).
    b. have typically shared their lives together in their parents' home.
    c. have identical genetic makeup since they developed from one zygote.
    d. are highly cooperative in their dealings with psychologists.

3. What is the next stage the organism progresses through after the zygote has developed at conception?
    a. Embryo
    b. Neonate
    c. Fetus
    d. Fertilization

4. The unborn fetus has many of the features and characteristics of a newborn as early as:
    a. 8 weeks.
    b. 12 weeks.
    c. 16 weeks.
    d. 24 weeks.

5. A genetic defect that leads to a very short life because of a breakdown in strategic metabolic processes and occurs most frequently among Jews of Eastern European descent is called:
   a. Tay-Sachs disease.
   b. Down syndrome.
   c. meningitis.
   d. phenylketonuria (PKU).

6. The presence of an extra chromosome results in the developmental disorder called:
   a. Down syndrome.
   b. sickle-cell anemia.
   c. Tay-Sachs disease.
   d. phenylketonuria (PKU).

7. Rubella is also known as:
   a. Down syndrome.
   b. German measles.
   c. phenylketonuria (PKU).
   d. sickle-cell anemia.

8. A neonate is:
   a. a prenatal infant in its 30th to 38th week of development.
   b. a newborn infant.
   c. an infant born with deformities because of chromosomal abnormalities.
   d. a premature baby up to the time at which the normal due date passes.

9. A researcher compares visual abilities in four groups of infants of ages 1 month, 3 months, 5 months, and 7 months. This is an application of:
   a. the longitudinal research method.
   b. the critical period research method.
   c. the cross-sectional research method.
   d. the cross-sequential research method.

10. According to research by Diana Baumrind's categories of parental styles, _____ parents are those who are firm and set limits and goals, reasoning with their children and encouraging their independence.
    a. Authoritarian
    b. Permissive
    c. Militaristic
    d. Authoritative

11. Carol Gilligan demonstrated in her research that the beginning level of moral reasoning for women is the stage of:
    a. goodness equated with self-sacrifice.
    b. self-worth and self-respect.
    c. orientation toward individual survival.
    d. morality of nonviolence.

12. In Erikson's developmental stage, college-age people typically contend with the conflicts found in the:
    a. intimacy vs. isolation stage.
    b. generativity vs. stagnation stage.
    c. ego integrity vs. despair stage.
    d. identity vs. role confusion stage.

13. Multiple research studies have demonstrated that the "storm and stress" of adolescence:
    a. is a myth for most teenagers.
    b. is lessened because teenagers remain under parental supervision for a longer time frame than is the case in other societies.
    c. is reflected in the concerns of the industry vs. inferiority stage.
    d. characteristically applies to all teenagers.

14. A major developmental task for people age 40 to 50 years old who are experiencing the initial stages of middle adulthood is to:
    a. maintain harmonious relationships with their children.
    b. accept that the die has been cast and that they must come to terms with circumstances.
    c. carefully choose goals so that all major career advances can still be realized before old age.
    d. adjust to changes brought about by menopause and physical deterioration.

15. Professor Costello, a 46-year-old female, reviews her past actions and failed personal goals. She devoted her efforts to her academic career rather than to marriage or children, yet she now realizes that her colleagues regard her research as trivial and uninspired. She feels old and knows that she has accomplished little in her life. She is experiencing:
    a. menopause.
    c. midlife transition.
    b. delayed identity crisis.
    d. midlife crisis.

16. According to Erikson, generativity is the ability to contribute to:
    a. one's family.
    b. one's community.
    c. one's workplace.
    d. all of the above.

17. The _____ theory of aging states that aging involves a gradual withdrawal from the world on multiple levels.
    a. wear-and-tear
    c. disengagement
    b. genetic preprogramming
    d. activity

18. Which type of intelligence can actually increase with age?
    a. Fluid intelligence
    c. Basic intelligence
    b. Verbal intelligence
    d. Crystallized intelligence

19. The reaction of women to menopause is:
    a. better in cultures that value old age more than youth.
    b. universally negative because of its effects on female reproduction.
    c. positive if the woman is single but negative if she is married.
    d. positive for heterosexuals but negative for lesbians.

Part A

____ 20. rooting reflex

____ 21. sucking reflex

____ 22. gag reflex

____ 23. startle reflex

a. The reflex in response to a sudden noise where the infant flings its arms, arches its back, and spreads its fingers.

b. A neonate's tendency to turn its head toward things that touch its cheek.

c. A reflex that prompts an infant to suck at things that touch its lips.

d. An infant's reflex to clear its throat.

Part B

_____ 24. egocentrism

_____ 25. personal fables

_____ 26. sexual attraction

_____ 27. formal operations

_____ 28. caring

a. Piaget's stage of cognitive development where the individual is able to think abstractly and see things from another point of view.

b. A state of self-absorption in which the world is viewed from one's own point of view.

c. Gilligan's theory of morality suggests that women display a morality of more _____.

d. An adolescent's view that what happens to him or her is unique, exceptional, and shared by no one else.

e. Begins early in adolescence as sexual organs mature.

29. Define Vygotsky's cognitive theory and explain how his Zone of Proximal Development (ZPD), with the assistance of scaffolding, promotes better learning.

30. Apply the disengagement and activity theories of aging to the question of mandatory retirement. Should there be a mandatory retirement age, and what are the exceptions and who shall judge?

PRACTICE TEST 3: Conceptual, Applied, and Challenging Questions

1. One-tenth of the African-American population in the United States has the possibility of passing on _____, which leaves the newborn with a variety of health problems and very short life expectancy.
    a. hypertension
    b. sickle-cell anemia
    c. phenylketonuria
    d. Tay-Sachs disease

2. Which statement about the sensory and perceptual capabilities of infants is **not** true?
    a. At 4 days of age, they can distinguish between closely related sounds such as "ba" and "pa."
    b. At 60 days of age, they can recognize their mother's voice.
    c. After 6 months of age, they are capable of discriminating virtually any difference in sounds that is relevant to the production of language.
    d. They prefer sweetened liquids to unsweetened liquids.

3. Attachment between the baby and its mother and father are different in that:
    a. mothers spend more time directly nurturing their children, whereas fathers spend more time playing with them.
    b. mothers spend more time playing with their children, whereas fathers spend more time nurturing them.
    c. mothers generally are identified as primary caregivers, so the attachment is stronger.
    d. fathers spend more time doing things with their children than mothers.

4. A father's typical attachment to his children:
   a. is superior to the mother's attachment in most situations.
   b. is aloof and detached.
   c. is generous with affection, especially during verbal interaction.
   d. is qualitatively different, but comparable to the mother's attachment.

5. Play in young children has many consequences. Which alternative is **not** one of them?
   a. They become more competent in their social interactions with other children.
   b. They learn to take the perspective of other people and to infer others' thoughts and feelings.
   c. They learn to control emotional displays and facial expressions in situations where this is appropriate.
   d. They become more independent of other children from ages 2 to 6.

6. Dr. Liefeld, a developmental psychologist, is evaluating a young child's cognitive development. Dr. Liefeld shows the child two separate arrangements of red disks. Eight disks are laid in a straight line in one arrangement. Another eight disks are arranged in a random "scatter" pattern in the other. The psychologist asks, "Is the amount of disks in each arrangement the same?" Dr. Liefeld is testing the child's understanding of:
   a. spatial reversibility.   c. spatial inertia.
   b. conservation.   d. reorganization.

7. Jess and Kelly were playing with two balls of clay. Kelly was molding a cake and Jess was making a bowl. Jess then suggested they get new balls of clay so they could make something different. Kelly informed her that no new clay was necessary; the clay could be remolded to make different objects. What principle was Kelly teaching to Jess?
   a. The principle of conservation   c. The principle of egocentric thought
   b. The principle of reversibility   d. The principle of logic

8. The last time Shareen used her personal computer, she observed that several files were not copied onto the floppy disk as she had expected. She carefully checked her sequence of operations and considered the characteristics of the software. After evaluating alternative explanations for what had happened, she correctly deduced why the files were not copied. Shareen is in Piaget's:
   a. concrete operational stage of cognitive development.
   b. preoperational stage of cognitive development.
   c. sensorimotor stage of cognitive development.
   d. formal operational stage of cognitive development.

9. Piaget found that _____ is mastered early in the _____ for most children.
   a. reversibility; sensorimotor stage   c. object permanence; formal operational stage
   b. conservation; concrete operational stage   d. abstraction; preoperational stage

10. Jason thinks, "If I hit my brother, I will get sent to my room." In which level of moral development is this child functioning?
    a. Amorality   c. Conventional morality
    b. Preconventional morality   d. Postconventional morality

11. Mary Margaret leads a group that has as its focus rape prevention and assistance in recovery from rape. The group represents moral development consistent with Gilligan's notion of:
    a. morality of nonviolence.   c. goodness as self-sacrifice.
    b. orientation toward individual survival.   d. preconventional morality.

12. Which factor does not contribute to the stresses experienced by adolescents outside the home that may cause stress at home?
    a. The number of school changes made
    b. Volatile relationships with friends and other peers
    c. Frequent arguments about money with family members
    d. Holding a part-time job while maintaining studies

13. Divorce produces many changes in the emerging single-parent family. Which alternative is **not** one of them?
    a. Time is always at a premium.
    b. The painful experience of divorce may hinder the building of close relationships throughout life.
    c. Children in a single-parent family develop interpersonal skills, so they are less likely to divorce.
    d. High levels of parental conflict before the divorce may produce increased anxiety and aggressive behavior in the children.

14. When a child's mother and father work, the mother is generally still viewed as holding the main child-rearing responsibility. According to research, one consequence of this is:
    a. women who work are more likely to resent husbands for not assisting in the "second shift" at home.
    b. women who work play a greater role in the decisions that affect the lives of their families.
    c. women who work enjoy more responsibility than those who don't work, yet allow their husbands valuable time alone with their children.
    d. women who work have better-developed social lives.

15. Dr. Perini is an authority on Egyptian mummies and has been retired for 13 years. He was recently asked to speak at a monthly faculty luncheon. If he gives one of his "canned" presentations on mummies to the faculty, he will be drawing heavily from his:
    a. crystallized intelligence.   c. fluid intelligence.
    b. common sense.   d. practical intelligence.

16. Marcus is satisfied with his teaching position, is quite comfortable with his single lifestyle, and has begun to expand his reflections on the subject he has taught and researched to consider its broader implications for society. He hopes to write a book that appeals to a wider audience than the typical academic book. Which of the following best describes Marcus's situation?
    a. Disengagement theory of aging   c. Generativity vs. stagnation
    b. Concrete operations   d. Conventional morality

17. Marta has reached a point where she says, "If I can only live to see my Ginny graduate from college, I will devote the rest of my time to the church." Marta is expressing which of the following?
    a. Kübler-Ross's stage of bargaining
    b. The wear-and-tear theory of aging
    c. Erikson's stage of ego integrity vs. despair
    d. Kübler-Ross's stage of acceptance

18. Why do so many rites of passage seem to be focused on males?
    a. Societies need to know when children have become adults.
    b. Menarche serves to demarcate female achievement of adulthood.
    c. It is important for males to be able to stand up to ridicule and face pain.
    d. The rituals are devised and administered by men.

Part A

_____ 19. phenylketonuria (PKU)

_____ 20. sickle-cell anemia

_____ 21. Tay-Sachs disease

_____ 22. Down syndrome

_____ 23. rubella

_____ 24. fetal alcohol syndrome

a. A disease of the blood that affects about 10 percent of America's African-American population.

b. German measles.

c. A disorder caused by the presence of an extra chromosome, resulting in mental retardation.

d. An inherited disease that prevents its victims from being able to produce an enzyme that resists certain poisons, resulting in profound mental retardation.

e. A genetic defect preventing the body from breaking down fat and typically causing death by the age of 4.

f. An ailment producing mental and physical retardation in a baby as a result of the mother's behavior.

Part B

_____ 25. forgetfulness

_____ 26. crystallized intelligence

_____ 27. fluid intelligence

_____ 28 senility

_____ 29. life review

a. An examination and evaluation of one's life.

b. A broad, imprecise term typically applied to older persons with progressive deterioration of mental abilities.

c. Intelligence such as reasoning, memory, and information processing.

d. Not the issue in old age that it was once believed to be.

e. Intelligence based on information, skills, and problem solving.

30. One of the main points of the chapter is that developmental psychologists are interested in finding ways that the individual potential can be maximized. Children can be stimulated through contact with parents, through play, and while at day care, and they can be encouraged to explore by having the appropriate attachments. What would the world of a perfectly "enriched" child look like? Is it possible to overstimulate children?

31. What does the author of the text suggest are some reasons for the high rates of suicide in adolescence? What are some of the signs that may suggest to friends and family that a teen is contemplating taking his or her own life?

■ ANSWER KEY: MODULES 37, 38, AND 39

Module 37:	Module 38:	Module 39:	[l] temperaments	Part A
[a] Developmental psychology	[a] conception	[a] neonate	[m] psychosocial development	1. d
[b] nature-nurture issue	[b] zygote	[b] vernix	[n] Cognitive development	2. a
[c] maturation	[c] chromosomes	[c] lanugo	[o] information processing	3. e
[d] interactionist	[d] genes	[d] reflexes	[p] zone of proximal development, or ZPD,	4. c
[e] identical twins	[e] embryo	[e] Babinski reflex	[q] scaffolding	5. b
	[f] fetus	[f] Attachment		
Evaluate	[g] age of viability	[g] Friendships		Part B
1. b	[h] sensitive periods	[h] authoritarian parents		1. b
2. d	[i] teratogens	[i] Permissive parents		2. a
3. c		[j] Authoritative parents		3. c
4. a	Evaluate	[k] Uninvolved parents		4. e
5. e	1. f			5. d
	2. b			
	3. d			
	4. e			
	5. a			
	6. c			

■ ANSWER KEY: MODULES 40 AND 41

Module 40:	Module 41:	[n] denial
[a] adolescence	[a] menopause	[o] anger
[b] puberty	[b] midlife transition	[p] bargaining
[c] identity vs. role confusion	[c] midlife crisis	[q] depression
[d] identity	[d] Gerontologists	[r] acceptance
[e] intimacy vs. isolation	[e] genetic preprogramming	
[f] generativity vs. stagnation	[f] wear-and-tear	Part A
[g] ego integrity vs. despair	[g] fluid intelligence	1. c
[h] caring	[h] crystallized intelligence	2. a
	[i] senility	3. d
Evaluate	[j] Alzheimer's disease	4. b
1. d	[k] disengagement	5. e
2. c	[l] activity	
3. b	[m] life review	Part B
4. a		1. c
		2. a
		3. d
		4. b

Selected Rethink Answers

37-2   When considering how a child learns to walk, include environmental factors such as the influence of parents, siblings, school, and nutrition, and activity levels and experiences the developing child is exposed to. Consider also the genetic makeup by looking at family developmental histories that provide clues about growth and development throughout life. Encourage parents to take a wait-and-see approach, as each child has his or her own developmental timetable. Parents and physician should continue to monitor child's progress. The vast majority of children ultimately learn to walk.

38-1   The medical model states that substance abuse/addiction is a medical problem. The prosecution of pregnant women for alcohol and drug abuse might open the door that would allow for the prosecution of anyone who engaged in behavior that can be proven as harmful to a person's health. Obesity, smoking, and lack of exercise have become potentially life-threatening behaviors. Victims of heart disease, diabetes, cancer, etc. cost insurance companies, employee absenteeism, and the potential for early death to young parents. Where would this end?

41-2   Aging involves both a balance of gains and losses. Older people should be alerted to this, so they can anticipate both the difficulties associated with loss, and the positive things associated with the gains. For instance, there may be a decline in fluid intelligence, but this may be balanced against the gain associated with developing wisdom. In addition, older people need to be mindful not to fall victim to the negative stereotypes others might hold about them. Older people need to stay abreast of research into later life development, such as the fact that college students and older people share in common many typical pastimes, including napping, eating, walking, and conversing, so they can actively combat the negative stereotypes.

Practice Test 1:

1.   a   mod. 37 p. 409
*a.   Correct. Maturation involves, to a large extent, the unfolding of genetic code.
b.   Incorrect. Nurture refers to the element of environmental influence, not heredity.
c.   Incorrect. Environmental factors are not hereditary.
d.   Incorrect. Social growth would reveal environmental, nurturing types of factors and some hereditary factors.

2.   d   mod. 37 p. 412
a.   Incorrect. A cross-sectional study examines several groups at one given point in time.
b.   Incorrect. There is no type of study called "maturational."
c.   Incorrect. A longitudinal study follows a single group through a given span of time, taking measurements at points along the way.
*d.   Correct. The cross-sequential study combines longitudinal and cross-sectional approaches by studying different groups in a longitudinal fashion, often allowing for a shorter timeframe to complete the study.

3.   d   mod. 38 p. 413
a.   Incorrect. Zygotes and embryos refer to different stages of the fetus.
b.   Incorrect. Zygotes are fetuses, not genes.
c.   Incorrect. Neonates are newborn, not chromosomes.
*d.   Correct. Each of our 46 chromosomes is composed of thousands of genes.

4.   b   mod. 38 p. 416
a.   Incorrect. Many sense organs are functional long before the fetus reaches a level of physical maturity that would allow it to survive if born.
*b.   Correct. This age continues to be earlier and earlier as medical technology evolves.
c.   Incorrect. Viability and learning are independent of each other in that viability depends on the ability of the fetus to function physically independent of the mother, and this may be highly reflexive.
d.   Incorrect. Sexual organs are differentiated long before viability.

5.   a   mod. 38 p. 417
*a.   Correct. This disease is inherited and causes mental retardation through the accumulation of toxins.
b.   Incorrect. AIDS results from HIV infection.
c.   Incorrect. This is a hormone that was prescribed in the 1960s and has resulted in abnormalities in the cervix and vagina in the daughters of women who took the hormone.
d.   Incorrect. This syndrome occurs in children who are exposed to high levels of alcohol as fetuses.

6.   d   mod. 38 p. 418
a.   Incorrect. Junk food might affect some other aspect of development, but this link has not been established.
b.   Incorrect. This link has not been established.
c.   Incorrect. This is more likely to affect the marriage and the child's later behavior.
*d.   Correct. Research suggests that this is true, possibly because the chemicals in the mother's system enter and influence the child's temperament.

7. a   mod. 39 p. 421
*a. Correct. Whenever the baby's cheek is stroked, it will turn its head in the direction of the stroked cheek.
b. Incorrect. The startle reflex is a pattern of actions related to being startled in which the baby flings out its arms, spreads its fingers, and arches its back.
c. Incorrect. This reflex helps the baby clear its throat.
d. Incorrect. The startle reflex would probably be considered a "surprise" reflex, but there is not a reflex officially named this.

8. b   mod. 39 p. 431
a. Incorrect. It was based on the normal development of normal individuals.
*b. Correct. The eight stages he proposed cover life from birth to death.
c. Incorrect. As a psychoanalyst, his approach is anything but behavioral.
d. Incorrect. Actually, Erikson's views predate those of Piaget and are partially derived from the ideas of Freud.

9. d   mod. 39 p. 424
a. Incorrect. Taste and smell discriminations occur throughout the six months.
b. Incorrect. From birth, infants refine their ability to distinguish different shapes and objects.
c. Incorrect. As early as four days after birth, infants can distinguish sounds like *ba* and *pa*.
*d. Correct. Within the first six months, infants do not develop an understanding of their native language.

10. b   mod. 39 p. 432
a. Incorrect. Only the first stage of Piaget's developmental scheme utilizes perceptual development.
*b. Correct. The child must develop a level of maturation and experience appropriate to the stage he or she is currently completing before moving on to the next stage; in fact, experience and maturation are the forces that create the concerns of the next stage.
c. Incorrect. Memory organization, not capacity, plays a role in Piaget's scheme, and physical growth is only a minor element in the earliest stage.
d. Incorrect. The social development that is associated with the cognitive development is not one of the necessary elements of cognitive development, rather a by-product of it.

11. a   mod. 40 p. 441
*a. Correct. Nutrition and medical care are the commonly assumed causes of this change.
b. Incorrect. Cultural prohibition about sexuality would have nothing to do with this physical change.
c. Incorrect. Sexual promiscuity would have little to do with this physical change.
d. Incorrect. The timing of a puberty ritual does not affect the timing of puberty.

12. b   mod. 40 p. 442
a. Incorrect. In the preconventional stage, people are more likely to be motivated by rewards and avoidance of punishment.
*b. Correct. The conventional stage is marked by a desire to get along socially.
c. Incorrect. Individuals in the postconventional stage are not likely to be concerned with how others think about them.
d. Incorrect. Kohlberg did not define a nonconventional stage.

13. d   mod. 40 p. 443
a. Incorrect. Many of the other theories are inclusive of both males and females.
b. Incorrect. Cross-cultural studies have not supported or rejected a universal application of Erikson's views.
c. Incorrect. Erikson does not place any special emphasis on understanding infant development in comparison to the rest of the life span.
*d. Correct. Erikson has been a leader in placing emphasis on the entire life span.

14. d   mod. 40 p. 447
a. Incorrect. Changes in regular habits are important signals that something is wrong.
b. Incorrect. Suicide often follows a withdrawal from friends and peers.
c. Incorrect. A common and persistent theme among those contemplating suicide is the nature of death and the afterlife.
*d. Correct. People contemplating suicide do not increase their attendance at church or amount of prayer (these may actually be signs of hope and contrary to suicidal thoughts).

15. d   mod. 41 p. 450
a. Incorrect. The detrimental changes are only beginning to occur, and this does not seem to be a major issue during a midlife crisis.
b. Incorrect. These disappointments can occur at any time and are not necessarily associated with midlife crises.
c. Incorrect. For males, the reproductive capability does not end.
*d. Correct. More often than other reasons, the midlife crisis is a result of a recognition of failure to meet many personal goals.

16. c   mod. 41 p. 450
a. Incorrect. Culmination is not a relevant aspect of Gilligan's theory.
b. Incorrect. Though morality is part of cognition, this is not what Gilligan focused on.
*c. Correct. Women and men have different understandings of what constitutes a "moral" choice.
d. Incorrect. Everyone has difficulty with reality.

17. c   mod. 41 p. 454
a. Incorrect. The genetic preprogramming approach would suggest that this results from genetic programming, but this is not what they would say about the decline.
b. Incorrect. This is the point of view of the wear-and-tear theorists.
*c. Correct. The preprogramming theories suggest that cells can only reproduce a certain number of times, and then they begin to decline.
d. Incorrect. This view is held by many, and is not exclusive to the genetic preprogramming theories.

18. a   mod. 41 p. 455
*a. Correct. Fluid intelligence and its adaptive power are most needed during the earlier part of life.
b. Incorrect. Fluid intelligence does begin a decline after middle adulthood.
c. Incorrect. Fluid intelligence actually declines slowly during these periods.
d. Incorrect. Fluid intelligence increases early and declines later.

19. c   mod. 41 p. 454
a. Incorrect.
b. Incorrect.
*c. Correct. Both processes seem to contribute to aging.
d. Incorrect. There may be other important theories, though the two mentioned have significant support.

20. d   mod. 41 p. 457
a. Incorrect. Deactivation theory sounds good, but its actual name is "disengagement."
b. Incorrect. Activity theory sounds good, but its actual name is "disengagement."
c. Incorrect. Withdrawal theory sounds good, but its actual name is "disengagement."
*d. Correct. This defines the disengagement theory of aging.

21. b   mod. 39 p. 431
22. a   mod. 39 p. 431
23. d   mod. 39 p. 431
24. c   mod. 39 p. 431

25. b   mod. 40 p. 439
26. d   mod. 40 p. 444
27. a   mod. 41 p. 450
28. e   mod. 41 p. 450
29. c   mod. 41 p. 450

30.
▪   Identify the relative importance of nature and nurture for your views. Do you see them as equal or is one stronger than the other?
▪   Each of the styles may imply a view of the nature-nurture debate. The authoritarian style, for instance, may see children as naturally unruly and in need of strict discipline to come under control. The permissive parent may expect the child to find his or her own potential, such that exploration is natural.
▪   The view that sees nature and nurture as interacting would suggest that the parenting style is the place that an inherited potential can be realized, so child-rearing practices are crucial.

31.

- Note that the text considers the notion of excessive stress to be unsupported.
- Describe specific instances where parents and adolescents have conflicts (e.g., rules, self-determination, school performance), and describe the nature of the disagreements. Identify things either parents or children can do to solve the problem. Are some of the problems an effort to assert a sense of self and identity?
- Home life has changed significantly, and many adolescents are growing up in single-parent homes.

Practice Test 2:

1. c   mod. 37 p. 409
a. Incorrect. Interactionism admits to genetic (not a blank slate) influences.
b. Incorrect. The "nature" element is that of heredity, suggesting that some aspects of development are influenced by one's disposition.
*c. Correct. Nurture implies the forces of the environment, including the caregiving and socializing influences, so nurture would be the dominant influence for someone with such a view.
d. Incorrect. Dualism refers to the philosophical perspective of the duality of the mind and body, not the duality of nature and nurture.

2. c   mod. 37 p. 411
a. Incorrect. Only those born of alien parents.
b. Incorrect. Non-twin siblings have shared their lives just as much.
*c. Correct. Having identical genes makes the difference.
d. Incorrect. Most subjects are highly cooperative in their dealings with psychologists.

3. a   mod. 38 p. 416
*a. Correct. The next stage is an embryo, which is followed by the stage known as a fetus.
b. Incorrect. A neonate is a newborn, and an embryo would not survive birth.
c. Incorrect. A fetus is the stage that follows embryo, which follows zygote.
d. Incorrect. Fertilization precedes the zygote phase.

4. d   mod. 38 p. 416
a. Incorrect. At eight weeks, only arms, legs, and face are discernible.
b. Incorrect. At this stage, the face does not have any characteristics of later life to it, and eyes do not open, among many other differences.
c. Incorrect. At this stage, the fetus can move noticeably, the face has characteristics it will have later, and major organs begin to function.
*d. Correct. At 24 weeks, most of the characteristics that will be seen in the newborn are present: eyes will open and close, it can cry, grasp, and look in directions.

5. a   mod. 38 p. 417
*a. Correct. Children with Tay-Sachs disease are unable to break down fat, and they die by the age of 4.
b. Incorrect. Down syndrome can occur in any child, but it is more frequent with children of older parents.
c. Incorrect. Meningitis is not a genetic disease.
d. Incorrect. Phenylketonuria, or PKU, is a genetic disease that can afflict anyone, and it does not result in early death; rather, it results in retardation if not treated properly.

6. a   mod. 38 p. 417
*a. Correct. Down syndrome children have an extra chromosome, which results in mental retardation and unusual physical features.
b. Incorrect. Sickle-cell anemia is a recessive trait common among people of African descent.
c. Incorrect. Children with Tay-Sachs disease are unable to break down fat, and they die by the age of 4.
d. Incorrect. Phenylketonuria, or PKU, is a genetic disease that results in retardation if not treated properly.

7. b   mod. 38 p. 418
a. Incorrect. Down syndrome children have an extra chromosome, which results in mental retardation and unusual physical features.
*b. Correct. This disease can cause serious malformation and prenatal death.
c. Incorrect. Phenylketonuria, or PKU, is a genetic disease that results in retardation if not treated properly.
d. Incorrect. Sickle-cell anemia is a recessive trait common among people of African descent.

8. b   mod. 39 p. 421
a.   Incorrect. A neonate is a newborn.
*b. Correct. This is the official term used to refer to newborns in their first week.
c.   Incorrect. A neonate is any newborn.
d.   Incorrect. A neonate is a newborn, and can be early, late, or on time.

9. c   mod. 37 p. 411
a.   Incorrect. Longitudinal method follows one group through many years.
b.   Incorrect. However, the length of funding for the project would probably define the critical period.
*c. Correct. The researcher is comparing different age groups at the same time to compare the different abilities shown by each group.
d.   Incorrect. This combines longitudinal and cross-sectional, following several groups for an extended period.

10. d   mod. 39 p. 430
a.   Incorrect. However, children of authoritarian parents are also quite well behaved.
b.   Incorrect. Children of permissive parents tend to be unpleasant and demanding of attention.
c.   Incorrect. This is not one of the presumed types, but militaristic parents would get this behavior from their children as well.
*d. Correct. According to this view, children of authoritative parents are well behaved.

11. c   mod. 40 p. 442
a.   Incorrect. See answer c.
b.   Incorrect. See answer c.
*c. Correct. The stages, in order, are orientation toward individual survival, goodness as self-sacrifice, and morality of nonviolence.
d.   Incorrect. See answer c.

12. a   mod. 40 p. 444
*a. Correct. In college, the stage of intimacy vs. isolation begins as the individual begins to experience self-defined roles and independence.
b.   Incorrect. See answer a.
c.   Incorrect. See answer a.
d.   Incorrect. See answer a.

13. a   mod. 40 p. 444
*a. Correct. Highly troubled adolescence is fairly rare.
b.   Incorrect. This would probably increase the storm and stress if it occurred very much at all.
c.   Incorrect. This stage is before adolescence, so it should not have much to do with storm and stress.

d.   Incorrect. Applies to only a few; see answer a.

14. b   mod. 41 p. 450
a.   Incorrect. Most people maintain harmonious relationships with their children.
*b. Correct. It is the prospect that personal goals and dreams may not be completely fulfilled and that there is now less chance for achieving them.
c.   Incorrect. All major career advances may no longer be possible.
d.   Incorrect. Menopause and physical deterioration may be yet to come, and not all females experience problems with menopause, and certainly physical deterioration is not evident in every 40- to 50-year-old.

15. d   mod. 41 p. 450
a.   Incorrect. No evidence of menopause here.
b.   Incorrect. The term for this is "midlife crisis," in which one examines one's identity.
c.   Incorrect. This is too traumatic to be considered a mere transition.
*d. Correct. Unlike the milder form of transition, this sounds like a crisis.

16. a   mod. 41 p. 452
a.   Incorrect. Generativity concerns this, but other areas of life as well.
b.   Incorrect. See answer a.
c.   Incorrect. See answer a.
d.   Incorrect. Generativity can concern all of these areas.

17. c   mod. 41 p. 457
a.   Incorrect. The wear-and-tear theories suggest that the body wears out.
b.   Incorrect. The genetic preprogramming theories suggests that the body is programmed to slow and die.
*c. Correct. The disengagement theory says that people age because they consciously withdraw.
d.   Incorrect. The activity theory of aging suggests that people who remain active have a more successful old age.

18. d   mod. 41 p. 455
a.   Incorrect. Fluid intelligence declines with age.
b.   Incorrect. Verbal intelligence may increase as crystallized intelligence increases.
c.   Incorrect. Basic intelligence is not defined adequately to suggest that it exists, much less changes with age.
*d. Correct. As described, crystallized intelligence increases as the experiences and memories

become more important aspects of intelligent behavior in later adulthood.

19. a   mod. 41 p. 450
*a. Correct. In cultures that value old age, a menopausal woman has reached "old age."
b.   Incorrect. It varies from culture to culture.
c.   Incorrect. There is little or no evidence to support this claim.
d.   Incorrect. There is no difference between the way lesbians and heterosexuals handle menopause.

20. b   mod. 39 p. 421
21. c   mod. 39 p. 422
22. d   mod. 39 p. 422
23. a   mod. 39 p. 422

24. b   mod. 40 p. 445
25. d   mod. 40 p. 445
26. e   mod. 40 p. 441
27. a   mod. 40 p. 442
28. c   mod. 40 p. 443

29.
▪ Vygotsky theorized that the culture in which one is raised has an important influence on our cognitive development.
▪ Cognitive developmental occurs as a consequence of social interactions with others to jointly solve problems.
▪ ZPD is the level at which children can almost learn, but not quite, on their own.
▪ Scaffolding occurs when parents, teachers, and skilled peers assist by presenting information that is both new and within the ZPD.

30.
• First, describe each of these two theories and offer an example of how they differ.
• The activity theory suggests that a successful retirement would require a level of activity that would allow continuity.
• Retirement serves as an important marker of age in the disengagement theory.
• Describe the benefits (such as making room for people entering the job market) or costs (loss of expertise) of mandatory retirement in order to support your answer.

Practice Test 3:
1. b   mod. 38 p. 417
a.   Incorrect. While hypertension has some genetic disposition, it is not identifiable enough to be said to be directly transmitted, and it does not cause a short life expectancy.
*b. Correct. This disease results from recessive genes (passed on by both parents), and the red blood cells have a deformed, sickle shape.
c.   Incorrect. Children with Tay-Sachs disease are unable to break down fat, and they die by the age of 4, but they are usually of Jewish descent.
d.   Incorrect. Phenylketonuria, or PKU, is a genetic disease that can afflict anyone, and it does not result in early death; rather, it results in retardation if not treated properly.

2. b   mod. 39 p. 424
a.   Incorrect. And the infant's production of speech sounds and recognition of sounds continues to grow rapidly.
*b. Correct. Infants can recognize their mother's voice as early as three days.
c.   Incorrect. This too is true.
d.   Incorrect. The sweet tooth must be built in.

3. a   mod. 39 p. 428
*a. Correct. The style of interaction between mother and child differs from that of father and child.
b.   Incorrect. This is reversed.
c.   Incorrect. The attachment is not stronger or weaker, but of a different style.
d.   Incorrect. Fathers probably spend less time with their children, but this is not universally true.

4. d   mod. 39 p. 428
a.   Incorrect. Few would describe the difference as one of superiority.
b.   Incorrect. Rather than aloof and detached, fathers are often quite physical and in close contact with their children.
c.   Incorrect. While affectionate, fathers do not express this as verbally as do mothers.
*d. Correct. Due to the differences in how fathers and mothers interact with their children, the best description is that the attachment differs in quality.

5. d   mod. 39 p. 428
a.   Incorrect. See answer d.
b.   Incorrect. See answer d.
c.   Incorrect. See answer d.
*d. Correct. Play may actually increase mutual dependence and support. Play builds social competence, encourages taking the perspective of others, and requires emotional control.

6. b   mod. 39 p. 433

a. Incorrect. Reversibility would refer to the ability to reverse an operation.
*b. Correct. This test describes an effort to determine the ability of the child to conserve a number even if the objects are arranged differently.
c. Incorrect. A developmental psychologist would not test for spatial inertia.
d. Incorrect. Reorganization is not one of the principles that could be tested by a developmental psychologist.

7. b   mod. 39 p. 434
a. Incorrect. The principle of conservation would be applied to whether a lump of clay was more if it was long or short and fat—even if it was the same ball of clay.
*b. Correct. As simple as it sounds, Jess is learning that he can reverse his bowl back into a ball of clay.
c. Incorrect. If egocentric thought were at work, Jess might simply decide that the cake Kelly made was a pot of soup for her bowl.
d. Incorrect. Logic will come much later.

8. d   mod. 39 p. 434
a. Incorrect. See answer d.
b. Incorrect. See answer d.
c. Incorrect. See answer d.
*d. Correct. This sequential and systematic problem-solving approach is most common of someone in the formal operations stage.

9. b   mod. 39 p. 433
a. Incorrect. Reversibility is mastered in the concrete operations stage, not the sensorimotor stage.
*b. Correct. Conservation is one of the major accomplishments of the stage.
c. Incorrect. Object permanence occurs in the sensorimotor stage.
d. Incorrect. Abstraction occurs in the formal stage.

10. b   mod. 40 p. 442
a. Incorrect. Amorality has been used to describe the period before when cognitive processes are much involved in behavior, but it does not describe the phase illustrated in the question.
*b. Correct. The preconventional level of morality is driven by rewards and punishments.
c. Incorrect. The conventional level of morality is marked by efforts to please others and becoming a good member of society.
d. Incorrect. People in the postconventional level of morality make judgments according to moral principles that are seen as broader than society.

11. a   mod. 40 p. 443
*a. Correct. Rape prevention and mutual assistance is not only the survival of an earlier stage, but the principle that views violence as immoral.
b. Incorrect. Prevention may be focused on survival, but mutual assistance focuses on higher concerns.
c. Incorrect. Rape awareness does not specifically call on self-sacrifice.
d. Incorrect. This is not one of Gilligan's stages, and preconventional morality would understand rape through the punishment it deserves.

12. c   mod. 40 p. 445
a. Incorrect. The number of school changes does affect stress in the home.
b. Incorrect. Volatile relationships with peers do increase stress at home.
*c. Correct. Arguments about money with family members is not a stress outside the home.
d. Incorrect. Holding part-time jobs causes stress and may lead to stress at home.

13. c   mod. 41 p. 452
a. Incorrect. Since the parent must work as well as care for children and maintain the household, time is always at a premium.
b. Incorrect. This is one of the effects of divorce on children, a later fear of repeating the same "mistakes" of the parents.
*c. Correct. All children develop interpersonal skills, and these skills do not seem to prevent divorce.
d. Incorrect. The stress before divorce can often be as bad as the stress of divorce.

14. a   mod. 41 p. 452
*a. Correct. The "second shift" is a tremendous, and exhausting, problem for many women, and can be the root of resentment.
b. Incorrect. This is not always true.
c. Incorrect. The amount of time spent by husbands with children does not increase as the time the wife spends working outside the home increases.
d. Incorrect. There is no evidence for this, and given the amount of time required for household work, one wonders where the social life would fit.

15. a   mod. 41 p. 455
*a. Correct. Crystallized intelligence depends on memory and experience.
b. Incorrect. Common sense would not have us all informed about Egyptian mummies.

413

c.   Incorrect. Fluid intelligence is used earlier in life to help people adapt to new challenges.

d.   Incorrect. Practical intelligence refers to a type of intelligence that helps one survive and thrive in domains like work and social life.

16. c   mod. 40 p. 444

a.   Incorrect. The disengagement theory of aging would predict that Marcus would withdraw from society.

b.   Incorrect. Concrete operations occurs at the ages of 6 to 11.

*c. Correct. Marcus is considering becoming productive in a broad sense of making a contribution to society, rather than stagnating in his comfortable position.

d.   Incorrect. Conventional morality would be the level of morality focused on getting along with the social group, not necessarily contributing to it.

17. a   mod. 41 p. 458

*a. Correct. She is bargaining with death.

b.   Incorrect. The wear-and-tear theory of aging does not address the rationalizations we make in order to finish life.

c.   Incorrect. This bargain does not sound like ego integrity.

d.   Incorrect. Allison has not yet accepted her impending death.

18. b   mod. 40 p. 450

a.   Incorrect. While this may be true, it would apply to males and females.

*b. Correct. Since menarche makes the female passage easy to identify, a rite is necessary to make the male passage as clear.

c.   Incorrect. Not all rites of passage involve ridicule and pain.

d.   Incorrect. This may be true, but it would then suggest that females would undergo similar rites more often.

19. d   mod. 38 p. 417
20. a   mod. 38 p. 417
21. e   mod. 38 p. 417
22. c   mod. 38 p. 417
23. b   mod. 38 p. 418
24. f   mod. 38 p. 419

25. d   mod. 41   p. 456
26. e   mod. 41   p. 455
27. c   mod. 41   p. 455
28. b   mod. 41   p. 456
29. a   mod. 41   p. 458

30.
- Describe the factors that you consider important for early exposure. Can a child's later learning be enhanced through early exposure to academic skills like spelling and math? Or should the focus be on processes like imagination and creative work?
- What criteria would you use to identify overstimulation? Keep in mind that the child must feel safe and have a secure attachment in order to explore the environment freely.

31. Factors that put adolescents at risk are:
- Depression
- Unhappiness
- Extreme fatigue
- Profound hopelessness

Warning signs are when teens exhibit:
- Loss of appetite
- Self-destructive behavior
- Signs of depression
- Preoccupation with death
- Putting affairs in order
- Explicit announcement of thoughts of suicide

Chapter 13: Personality

Overview

This set of modules introduces both the approaches to the understanding of personality along with methods psychologists use to assess individual personality characteristics.

Module 42 defines personality as the sum of the enduring characteristics that differentiate individuals and provide the stability in a person's behavior across situations and time. First, the psychoanalytic approach to personality is discussed. Psychoanalysis understands personality in terms of how a person manages the unconscious that seeks to dominate behavior. Freud's psychoanalytic theory suggests that personality develops in stages. Defense mechanisms are unconscious strategies that reduce anxieties. The neo-Freudian theories of Jung, Adler, and Horney conclude this module.

Module 43 investigates five major alternatives to the psychoanalytic approach: trait approaches, learning approaches, biological approaches, evolutionary approaches, and humanistic approaches. The substantial differences in these theories focus on the various aspects of personality and the overall complexity of personality.

Module 44 illustrates several ways that personality can be assessed. Psychological tests that demonstrate both reliability and validity and also have standardized norms are studied. The most frequently given assessments include the MMPI, the Rorschach test, and the TAT.

To further investigate the topics covered in this chapter, you can visit the related Web sites by visiting the following link: www.mhhe.com/feldmanup8.

Prologue: The Dapper Don
Looking Ahead

Module 42: Psychodynamic Approaches to Personality

Freud's Psychoanalytic Theory: Mapping the Unconscious Mind
The Neo-Freudian Psychoanalysts : Building on Freud

- *How do psychologists define and use the concept of personality?*
- *What do the theories of Freud and his successors tell us about the structure and development of personality?*

Psychodynamic Approaches to Personality

The field of psychology known as **[a]** _____ studies the characteristics that make a person unique and attempts to explain what makes a person act consistently across situations and through time.

[b] _____ are concerned with understanding the hidden forces that govern people's behavior and remain outside of awareness. These forces have their roots in childhood experiences. This theory, called **[c]** _____, was developed by Sigmund Freud. Slips of the tongue are examples of how thoughts and emotions are held in the

[d] _____, the part of the personality that remains beyond the person's awareness. Slips reflect these hidden concerns. The unconscious also contains *instinctual drives*, which include infantile wishes, desires, demands, and needs that remain hidden because of the conflicts they can cause. Freud described conscious experience as the top of an iceberg, suggesting that the larger part of our personality is unconscious. In order to understand personality, these unconscious elements must be illuminated. The contents of the unconscious are disguised, thus requiring that slips of the tongue, fantasies, and dreams be interpreted in order to understand how unconscious processes direct behavior.

Freud described a general model of the personality that contains three interacting structures.

The **[e]** _____ is the raw, unorganized, inherited part of the personality aimed at reducing the tension caused by basic drives of hunger, sex, aggression, and irrational impulses.

The drives are powered by **[f]** _____, and the id operates according to the **[g]**

_____, or the desire for immediate gratification of all needs. Reality limits the expression of these id impulses. The **[h]** _____ is responsible for constraining the id. It serves as a buffer between reality and the pleasure-seeking demands of the id. The ego

operates on the **[i]** _____, in which restraint is based on the safety of the individual and an effort to integrate into society. The ego is the seat of the higher cognitive functions.

The **[j]** _____ represents the rights and wrongs of society as represented by the

parents. The superego includes the **[k]** _____, which prevents us from behaving immorally. Both the superego and the id make unrealistic demands. The ego must compromise between the moral-perfectionist demands of the superego and the pleasure-seeking gratification sought by the id.

Freud proposed a theory of development that accounted for how the adult personality comes into existence. Difficulties and experiences from a childhood stage may predict adult behaviors, and each stage focuses on a biological function. The first period of development is the

[l] _____ **stage,** during which the baby's mouth is the focus of pleasure. This suggested to Freud that the mouth is the primary site of sexual pleasure. Though most people

advance beyond this stage, Freud said that some adults develop a(n) [m] _____ , meaning that they show concerns or conflicts related to a particular stage. An orally fixated adult, for instance, would likely smoke a lot, chew gum, and indulge in too much food. At about

12 to 18 months until the age of 3, the child is in the [n] _____ **stage**. The major source of pleasure moves to the anal region, and the child derives pleasure from the retention and expulsion of feces. If toilet training is particularly demanding, fixation can occur. Fixation can lead to unusual rigidity and orderliness or the extreme opposite of disorder or sloppiness.

At the age of 3, the [o] _____ **stage** begins and the source of pleasure moves to the genitals. In the end, Freud suggests that boys' task is to identify with their fathers, and girls

must identify with their mothers. The next period is called the [p] _____ **period,** beginning around 5 or 6 and lasting to puberty. Sexual concerns become latent. The final period,

the [q] _____ **stage,** begins at puberty. Mature adult sexuality emerges during this period.

Anxiety, an intense, negative emotional experience, arises as a signal of danger to the ego. Although anxiety may arise from realistic fears, the *neurotic anxiety* arises because of the irrational impulses from the id that threaten to break into consciousness. The ego has developed

unconscious strategies to control the impulses called [r] _____ . *Regression* involves using behavior from earlier stages of development to deal with the anxiety. *Displacement* is the process of redirecting the unwanted feeling onto a less threatening person. *Rationalization* occurs when reality is distorted by justifying events with explanations that protect our self-esteem. *Denial* occurs when a person simply refuses to acknowledge the existence of an anxiety-producing piece of information. *Projection* involves protecting oneself by attributing unwanted impulses and feelings to someone else. *Sublimation* is the diversion of unwanted impulses to socially acceptable behaviors. According to Freud, these mechanisms are used to some degree by everyone, although some people devote a large amount of energy to dealing with unacceptable impulses to the extent that daily life becomes hampered. He identified this tendency as *neurosis.*

Neo-Freudians have contributed to personality theory in many ways; all shared in common

the focus on the ego, rather than the id. Jung developed the idea of the [s] _____ , which is a universally shared unconscious that impacts behavior worldwide. For instance, in widely diverse cultures there is a common love of mother, and belief in a supreme being. Jung

proposed that the collective unconscious contains [t] _____ , universal symbols of people, objects, and experiences. Horney was a neo-Freudian who focused on the development of personality in the context of social relationships and particularly familial relationships.

417

Evaluate

___ 1. unconscious

___ 2. instinctual drives

___ 3. id

___ 4. superego

___ 5. fixation

a. Behavior reflecting an earlier stage of development.

b. Infantile wishes, desires, demands, and needs hidden from conscious awareness.

c. A person is unaware of this determinant of behavior.

d. The raw, unorganized, inherited part of personality created by biological drives and irrational impulses.

e. The structure of personality, according to Freud, involving the conscience.

Rethink

42-1 Can you think of ways in which Freud's theories of unconscious motivations are commonly used in popular culture? How accurately do you think such popular uses of Freudian theories reflect Freud's ideas?

42-2 *From the perspective of an advertising executive:* How might you use Jung's concepts of archetypes in designing your advertisements? Which of the archetypes would you use?

Spotlight on Terminology and Language—ESL Pointers

Page 452 "His hair was always freshly **barbered**, and his nails were meticulously manicured."

A **barber** is someone who is trained to cut men's hair. Hair that is "freshly **barbered**" is hair that has recently been neatly cut by a professional.

Page 452 "A **ruthless**, **greedy** mobster, willing to do anything to keep control of his crime family?"

Someone who is **ruthless** is a person who is cruel.

Some one who is **greedy** is a person who has an extreme desire to always have more of something.

Page 453 "The college student was **intent** on making a good first impression on an attractive woman he had spotted across a crowded room at a party."

Someone who is **intent** on something is determined to do it.

Page 453 "As he walked toward her, he **mulled** over a line he had heard in an old movie the night before:

'I don't believe we've been properly introduced yet.'"

When we **mull something** over; we think about and give consideration.

Page 453 "After **threading** his way through the crowded room, he finally reached the woman and **blurted out**, "I don't believe we've been properly seduced yet.""

When we **thread** through something we are pass through it very carefully.

To **blurt** something out is to sat it suddenly, as if by accident.

Page 453 "Like the unseen mass of a floating iceberg, the memories, knowledge, beliefs, and feelings in the unconscious far **surpass** in quantity the information about which we are aware."

To **surpass** is to exceed. This theory proposes we have much more information in the unconscious than just the information about which we are aware.

Page 453 "But because the unconscious **disguises** the meaning of the material it holds, the content of the unconscious cannot be observed directly."

Disguises are changes in someone's appearance so that they are not recognized.

Page 454 "The unconscious provides a '**safe haven**' for our recollections of threatening events."

A **safe haven** is a place of safety.

Page 454 "If personality consisted only of primitive, instinctual **cravings** and **longings**, it would have just one component: the id. The <u>id</u> is the raw, unorganized, inborn part of personality."

Cravings are a strong desire for something.

Longings are a strong desire for something or someone that we are unable to have.

Page 455 "Such conflicts may be due to having needs ignored or (**conversely**) being **overindulged** during the earlier period."

Conversely means the opposite of something.
When we **overindulge** we give into our cravings and allow ourselves to take in too much.

Page 455 "The sequence Freud proposed is **noteworthy** because it explains how experiences and difficulties during a particular childhood stage may predict specific characteristics in the adult personality."

Something that is **noteworthy** is important and deserving of being noticed.

Page 455 "In the first psychosexual stage of development, called the *oral stage*, the baby's mouth is the **focal point** of pleasure (see Figure 2 for a summary of the stages)."

A **focal point** is the center of attention.
Page 456 "Fixation at the oral stage might produce an adult who was unusually interested in oral

419

activities—eating, talking, smoking—or who showed symbolic sorts of oral interests: being either "**bitingly**" **sarcastic** or very **gullible** ("**swallowing**" anything)."

Something that is **biting** is clever and cruel.

Something that is **sarcastic** makes fun of someone and is characterized by words that mean the opposite of what they seem to mean.

Someone who is **gullible** is very trusting and will believe anything they are told.

To **swallow** something is to believe it.

Page 456 "Fixation during the anal stage might result in unusual rigidity, orderliness, punctuality—or extreme disorderliness or **sloppiness**—in adulthood."

Things that are **sloppy** lack order; they are messy.

Page 456 "Now interest focuses on the genitals and the pleasures derived from **fondling** them."
When we **fondle** something we stroke it in a loving way."

Page 456 "During this stage the child must also negotiate one of the most important **hurdles** of personality development,: the *Oedipal conflict*."

Hurdles are difficulties that need to be overcome.

Page 456 "Furthermore, according to Freud, at this time the male unconsciously begins to develop a sexual interest in his mother, starts to see his father as a **rival**, and harbors a wish to kill his father—as Oedipus did in the ancient Greek tragedy."

A **rival** is an enemy or opponent in a competition.

Page 456 "During this period, sexual interests become **dormant**, even in the unconscious."

When things become **dormant** they are temporarily not active.

Page 456-457 "Although anxiety can arise from realistic fears—such as seeing a poisonous snake about to strike—it can also occur in the form of *neurotic anxiety*, in which irrational impulses **emanating** from the id threaten to burst through and become uncontrollable."

To **emanate** from something is to come from it.

Page 457 "The feelings remain **lodged** within the unconscious, because acknowledging them would provoke anxiety."

When something is **lodged** somewhere it is stuck in that place.

Page 457 "If repression is ineffective in **keeping anxiety at bay**, other defense mechanisms may be used."

When we "**keeping something at bay**" we are preventing it from influencing us.

Page 457 "Yet some people **fall prey** to them to such an extent that a large amount of psychic energy must constantly be directed toward hiding and rechanneling unacceptable impulses."

When we **"fall prey"** to something we have allowed something to influence us.

Page 457 "The **vague** nature of Freud's theory also makes it difficult to predict how certain developmental difficulties will be displayed in an adult."

Something that is **vague** is unclear.

Page 458 "His theory was based almost entirely on upper-class Austrian women living in the strict, **puritanical** era of the early 1900s who had come to him seeking treatment for psychological and physical problems."

Puritanical means to obey or follow a strict code of moral beliefs.

Page 460-461 "Her conceptualizations, developed in the 1930s and 1940s, laid the **groundwork** for many of the central ideas of feminism that emerged decades later Eckardt, 2005)."

Groundwork is basic work that helps prepare for a larger project.

Module 43: Trait, Learning, Biological, Evolutionary, and Humanistic Approaches to Personality

Trait Approaches: Placing Labels on Personality
Learning Approaches: We Are What We've Learned

Applying Psychology in the 21st Century:
The Downside of High Self-Esteem

Biological and Evolutionary Approaches: Are We Born with Personality?
Humanistic Approaches: The Uniqueness of You
Comparing Approaches to Personality

- *What are the major aspects of trait, learning, biological and evolutionary, and humanistic approaches to personality?*

Other Major Approaches to Personality: In Search of Human Uniqueness

A number of theories take a different approach than that of psychoanalysis. These include

[a] _____, which assumes that individuals respond to different situations in a

fairly consistent manner. **[b]** _____ are the enduring dimensions of personality characteristics along which people differ. Trait theories assume that all people have certain traits, and the degree to which a trait applies to a specific person varies.

Gordon Allport identified 18,000 separate terms that could be used to describe personality, which he then reduced to 4,500 descriptors. In order to make sense of this number, he defined

three basic categories of traits. A(n) **[c]** _____ is a single characteristic that directs most of a person's activities. Most people do not have cardinal traits; instead, they have

five to 10 **[d]** _____ that define major characteristics.

[e] _____ are characteristics that affect fewer situations and are less influential than cardinal or central traits. Preferences would be secondary traits.

The statistical technique called **[f]** _____, in which relationships among a large number of variables are summarized into smaller, more general patterns, has been used to identify fundamental patterns or combinations of traits. Raymond Cattell suggested that there are 16 *source traits* that represent the basic dimensions of personality. He then developed the Sixteen Personality Factor Questionnaire (16 PF).

Hans Eysenck used factor analysis to identify three major dimensions.

[g] _____ is the dimension marked by the degree of sociability one shows.

[h] _____ is the dimension marked by the degree of emotional stability one demonstrates. **[i]** _____ refers to the degree to which reality is distorted. Recent research has developed what has become the most influential trait theory of personality—the "Big Five" theory. It suggests that there are five underlying traits we all possess to some degree: *openness to experience, conscientiousness, extraversion, agreeableness*, and *neuroticism* (or, *emotional stability*).

According to B. F. Skinner, personality is a collection of learned behavior patterns. Similarities across situations are caused by a similarity of reinforcements. Strict learning theorists are less interested in the consistency issue than they are in finding ways to modify behavior. In their view, humans are quite changeable.

[j] _____ *approaches* emphasize the role of a person's cognitions in determining personality. According to Albert Bandura, people are able to foresee the outcomes of behaviors before carrying them out by using the mechanism of **[k]** _____.

Bandura considers **[l]** _____, the expectations of success, to be an important factor in determining the behaviors a person will display. Other social-cognitive theorists have focused on the role of **[m]** _____, or our positive and negative evaluations of ourselves, in determining the outcomes of our behavior. Traditional learning theories have been criticized for ignoring internal processes and reducing behavior to stimuli and responses.

[n] _____ *approaches* to personality suggest that important components of personality are inherited. The study of **[o]** _____, the basic innate disposition that emerges early in life, is studied through the biological approach. Research on temperament indicates that general activity level and mood are determined very early in life, and form the basis of what might be viewed as personality characteristics, such as easygoingness or irritability.

[p] _____ *approaches to personality* emphasize the basic goodness of people and their tendency to grow to higher levels of functioning. Carl Rogers is a major representative of this approach. The positive regard others have for us makes us see and judge ourselves through the eyes of other people. The views others have of us may not match our own *self-concept*. If the difference is great, we may have problems with daily functioning. The discrepancy is overcome by support from another person in the form of **[q]** _____, defined as an attitude of acceptance and respect no matter what the person says or does. Rogers and Maslow view the ultimate goal of personality growth to be **[r]** _____.

The criticisms of humanistic theory are centered on the difficulty of verifying the basic assumptions of the theory. The assumption that all people are basically "good" is unverifiable and injects nonscientific values into scientific theories.

Evaluate

_____ 1. cardinal trait

_____ 2. central traits

_____ 3. secondary traits

_____ 4. self-esteem

_____ 5. self-efficacy

a. A single trait that directs most of a person's activities.

b. Our belief in our own capabilities.

c. Our positive and negative evaluations of self.

d. Traits less important than central and cardinal traits.

e. A set of major characteristics that compose the core of a person's personality.

Rethink

43-1 If personality traits are merely descriptive and not explanatory, of what use are they? Can assigning a trait to a person be harmful—or helpful? Why or why not?

43-2 *From the perspective of a substance abuse counselor:* Many alcohol and substance abuse programs attempt to raise their clinets' sense of self-worth by communicating "feel-good messages." Do you expect these messages to be beneficial or detrimental to a client? Why or why not? Can you think of alternative ways to assist and support individuals who have a drug or alcohol addiction?

43-3 *From the perspective of an educator:* How might you encourage your students' development of self-esteem and self-efficacy? What steps would you take to ensure that their self-esteem did not become over-inflated?

Spotlight on Terminology and Language—ESL Pointers

Page 463 "He's the friendliest guy I know—**goes out of his way** to be nice to everyone."

When someone "**goes out of their way**" they go above what is expected on them.

Page 463 "He's just so **even-tempered**, no matter what's happening."

Even-tempered is calm. He is not likely to get flustered.

Page 463 "He seems to have **boundless** energy, much more than I have."

Something that is **boundless** is endless or limitless.

Page 463 ""He is so self-centered and arrogant that it **drives me crazy**.""

When something is said to **"drive me crazy"** it is annoying.

Page 463 "Trait theory seeks to explain, in a **straightforward** way, the consistencies in individuals' behavior."

Something that is **straightforward** is truthful and to the point.

Page 464 "When personality psychologist Gordon Allport systematically **pored over** an **unabridged** dictionary, he came up with some 18,000 separate terms that could be used to describe personality."

To **pore over** something is to read it studiously or attentively.

The **unabridged** version is the complete version, the full-length of the document.

Page 464 "Although he was able to **pare** down the list to a mere 4,500 descriptors after eliminating words with the same meaning, he was left with a problem crucial to all trait approaches: Which of those traits were the most basic?

To **pare** down something is to cut back or reduce.

Page 465 "In short, a growing **consensus** exists that the "Big Five" represent the best description of personality traits we have today."

A **consensus** is an agreement or compromise.

Page 465 "Trait approaches have several **virtues**."

A **virtue** is a beneficial quality moral quality.

Page 465 "However, trait approaches also have some **drawbacks**."

A **drawback** is the downside of this approach, the negative aspect or shortcomings of the trait approach.

Page 466 "The psychodynamic and trait approaches we've discussed concentrate on the "inner" person— the **fury** of an unobservable but powerful id or a hypothetical but critical set of traits."

Fury is a violent anger.

Page 467 "According to Albert Bandura, one of the main **proponents** of this point of view, people can foresee the possible outcomes of certain behaviors in a particular setting without actually having to carry them out."

A **proponent** of something is a supporter of it.

Page 467 "If we try **snowboarding** and experience little success, we'll be less likely to try it again."

Snowboarding is a sport in which the person slides down a snow slope on a board.

Page 467 "Although people have a general level of self-esteem, it is not **unidimensional**."

Something that is **unidimensional** is basic and unsophisticated, or simple.

Page 467 "Although almost everyone goes through periods of low self-esteem (after, for instance, an **undeniable** failure), some people are **chronically** low in self-esteem."

Something that is **undeniable** is unquestionable; it cannot be contested.

Something that is **chronic** is constant.

Page 468 "Of course, some of these criticisms are **blunted** by social cognitive approaches, which explicitly consider the role of cognitive processes in personality."

These criticisms are weakened, or dulled. They are **blunted**.

Page 468 "As in psychoanalytic theory (which suggests that personality is determined by the unconscious forces) and trait approaches (which view personality in part as a mixture of genetically determined traits), learning theory's reliance deterministic principles deemphasizes the ability of people to **pilot** their own course through life."

To **pilot** something is to steer it or be in charge of it.

Page 468 "The degree of success of these treatments is a testimony to the **merits** of learning theory approaches to personality."

Merits are the qualities or worth of something.

Page 469 "When their unwarranted positive view of themselves is contradicted, they may feel so threatened that they **lash out**, sometimes violently."

When someone **lashes out** at something they yell impulsively.

Page 469 "In the same way, efforts to increase self-esteem so as to improve the performance of academically challenged students may **backfire**."

When things **backfire** they do not go as planned.

Page 469 "Feel-good messages that seek to **instill** higher self-esteem in everyone ("we're all special" and "we applaud ourselves") may be off the target, leading people to develop unwarranted self-esteem."

To **instill** something is to impress ideas or teachings on someone else.

Page 470 "In the study, each twin was given a **battery** of personality tests, including one that measured eleven key personality characteristics."

A **battery** of tests is a series or set of tests.

Page 470 "Similarly, some are relatively easygoing, while others are irritable, easily upset, and difficult to **soothe**."

When we **soothe** someone we calm them down.

Page 470 "These thrill seekers tend to be extroverted, impulsive, **quick-tempered**, and always in search of excitement and novel situations (Hamer et al., 1993; Zuckerman & Kuhlman, 2000)."

Someone who is **quick-tempered** is easily angered.

Page 471 "In contrast, the parents of a **cranky**, fussy baby may be less inclined to smile at the child; in turn, the environment in which that child is raised will be a less supportive and pleasant one."

A **cranky** baby is one that is easily irritated and grouchy.

Page 472 "You may have experienced the power of unconditional positive regard when you **confided** in someone, revealing embarrassing secrets because you knew the listener would still love and respect you, even after hearing the worst about you (Snyder, 2002)."

When you **confide** in someone you tell them private things that you would not tell anyone else.

Page 472 "Although humanistic theories suggest the value of providing unconditional positive regard toward people, unconditional positive regard toward humanistic theories has been less **forthcoming**."

Things that are **forthcoming** are open and available when needed.

Page 472 "Humanistic approaches have also been criticized for making the assumption that people are basically "good"—a notion that is **unverifiable**—and, equally important, for using nonscientific values to build supposedly scientific theories."

Things that are **unverifiable** are not able to be proven to be true.

Module 44: Assessing Personality: Determining What Makes Us Distinctive

- *How can we most accurately assess personality?*
- *What are the major types of personality measures?*

Assessing Personality: Determining What Makes Us Special

The intentionally vague statements that introduce the topic of assessment suggest that measuring different aspects of personality may require great care and precision. The assessment of personality requires discriminating the behavior of one person from that of another. **[a]** _____ are standard measures that assess aspects of behavior objectively.

Psychological tests must have **[b]** _____, that is, they must measure something consistently from time to time. A reliable test will produce similar outcomes in similar conditions. The question of whether a test measures the characteristic it is supposed to is called

[c] _____. If a test is reliable, that does not mean it is valid.

[d] _____ are the standards of test performance that allow comparison of the scores of one test-taker to others who have taken it. The norm for a test is determined by calculating the average score for a particular group of people for whom the test is designed to be given.

Instead of conducting a comprehensive interview to determine aspects of childhood, social relationships, and success and failures, the use of **[e]** _____ allows individuals to respond to a small sample of questions, which psychologists use to infer the presence of various personality characteristics. The most frequently used self-report measure is the **[f]**

_____. Originally developed to distinguish people with psychological disturbances from people without disturbances, the MMPI scores have been shown to be good predictors of such things as whether college students will marry within 10 years and whether they will get an advanced degree. The test has 567 true-false items covering categories such as mood, opinions, and physical and psychological health. The interpretation of the responses is important, but there are no right or wrong answers. The test is scored on 10 scales and includes a lie scale for people trying to falsify their answers. The MMPI has undergone a procedure called

[g] _____ by which the test authors have determined which items best differentiate among groups of people, like differentiating those suffering from depression from normal subjects.

[h] _____ *tests* require the subject to describe an ambiguous stimulus. The responses are considered to be projections of what the person is like. The best known is the

[i] _____ *test*, which consists of symmetrical stimuli. The **[j]** _____ consists of a series of pictures about which the person is asked to write a story. Inferences about the subject are then based on these stories. These tests are criticized because too much inference depends on the scorer.

In order to obtain an objective test based on observable behavior, a(n)

[k] _____ may be conducted either in a natural setting or in a laboratory under controlled conditions. The assessment requires quantifying behavior as much as possible.

Evaluate

____ 1. Minnesota Multiphasic Personality Inventory-2 (MMPI-2)

____ 2. test standardization

____ 3. projective personality test

____ 4. Rorschach test

____ 5. Thematic Apperception Test (TAT)

a. Used to identify people with psychological difficulties.

b. Consists of a series of ambiguous pictures about which a person is asked to write a story.

c. Uses inkblots of indefinite shapes.

d. Uses ambiguous stimuli to determine personality.

e. Validates questions in personality tests by studying the responses of people with known diagnoses.

Rethink

44-1 Should personality tests be used for personnel decisions? Should they be used for other social purposes, such as identifying individuals who are at risk for certain types of personality disorders? What sorts of policies would you devise to ensure that such tests were used ethically?

44-2 *From the perspective of a politician:* Imagine that you had to vote on a law that would require institutions and organizations to perform race norming procedures on standardized performance tests. Would you support such a law? Why or why not? In addition to race, should norming procedures take other factors into account? Which ones and why?

Spotlight on Terminology and Language—ESL Pointers

Page 475 "Although you have some personality weaknesses, you generally are able to **compensate** for them."

You **compensate** for your personality weaknesses by making up for these weaknesses in other ways or with other behaviors.

Page 475 "You prefer a certain amount of change and variety and become dissatisfied when **hemmed in** by restrictions and limitations."

When you're **hemmed in**, you're restricted or constrained. You can't respond or behave in the manner you would like.

Page 475 "You have found it unwise to be too **frank** in revealing yourself to others."

Frank is open and forthright. You may have found it unwise to be too honest when speaking with others.

Page 475 "Most college students think that the descriptions are **tailored** just to them."

Tailored is custom-made, personalized. Most college students identify very closely with these descriptions.

Page 475 "The ease with which we can agree with such **imprecise** statements **underscores** the difficulty in coming up with accurate and meaning assessments of people's personalities (Johnson et al., 1985; Prince & Guastello, 1990)."

An **imprecise** statement is a vague statement.

Underscores means emphasizes or highlights.

Page 917 "The establishment of appropriate norms is not a simple **endeavor**."

An **endeavor** is a directed activity or undertaking.

Page 476 "The problem that **sparked** the controversy is that African Americans and Hispanics tend to score lower on the test, on average, than do members of other groups."

A **spark** is a factor that sets off or produces something.

Page 476 "Critics of the adjusted norming system suggest that such a procedure discriminates in favor of certain racial and ethnic groups at the expense of others, thereby **fanning the flames** of racial **bigotry**."

When we "**fan the flames**" we are heating things up or encouraging them to develop.

Bigotry is prejudice or an intolerance toward people who are different in appearance or viewpoint.

Page 476 "However, proponents of race norming continue to argue that norming procedures that take race into account are an **affirmative action** tool that simply permits minority job seekers to be placed on an **equal footing** with white job seekers."

430

Affirmative action is a US policy aimed at fighting discrimination in employment and education.

When people are on **equal footing** they are of the same status or are on the same level.

Page 476 "It suggested that the unadjusted test norms are not terribly useful in predicting job performance, and that they would tend to **screen out** otherwise qualified minority-group members."

When we **screen out** something we are eliminating or deleting them from being considered.

Page 477 "The issue of establishing norms for tests is further complicated by the existence of a **wide array** of personality measures and approaches to assessment."

A "**wide array**" means that there are a large number of choices available for use.

Page 478 "The questions cover a variety of issues, ranging from mood ("I feel useless at times") to opinions ("People should try to understand their dreams") to physical and psychological health ("I am bothered by an upset stomach several times a week" and "I have strange and **peculiar** thoughts")."

Peculiar means strange and unusual.

Page 478 "For example, there is a "lie scale" that indicates when people are falsifying their responses in order to present themselves more **favorably** (through items such as "I can't remember ever having a bad night's sleep") (Butcher, 1999, 2005; Graham, 1999; Stein & Graham, 2005)."

Favorable things are things that are promising

Page 479 "For instance, employers who use it as a **screening tool** for job applicants may interpret the results improperly, relying too heavily on the results of individual scales instead of taking into account the overall patterns of results, which require skilled interpretation."

A job **screening tool** would be an assessment inventory or application process used to select or eliminate job applicants.

Page 479 "Furthermore, critics point out that the individual scales **overlap**, making their interpretation difficult."

Things that **overlap** lie on top of each other.

Page 479 "The shape in the figure is representative of **inkblots** used in projective personality tests, in which a person is shown an ambiguous stimulus and asked to describe it or tell a story about it."

A **inkblot** is one of the abstract patterns used in the Rorschach test.

Page 480 "For instance, **respondents** who see a bear in one inkblot are thought to have a strong degree of emotional control, according to the scoring guidelines developed by Rorschach (Aronow, Reznikoff, & Moreland, 1994; Weiner, 2004)."

A **respondent** is a person who answers questions.

Page 480 "Instead, you would be more apt to use behavioral assessment—direct measures of an individual's behavior designed to describe characteristics **indicative** of personality."

Things that are **indicative** of something show or point out that something exists.

Page 480 "Regardless of the setting in which behavior is observed, an effort is made to ensure that behavioral assessment is **carried out** objectively, quantifying behavior as much as possible."

When something is **carried out** it is done or completed.

Page 480 "Another method is to measure the duration of events: the duration of a **temper tantrum** in a child, the length of a conversation, the amount of time spent working, or the time spent in cooperative behavior."

A **temper tantrum** is a childish outburst of anger.

Page 480 "It provides a means of assessing the specific nature and incidence of a problem and subsequently allows psychologists to determine whether **intervention** techniques have been successful."

An **intervention** is an action taken to change what is happening or what might happen in someone else's affairs.

Page 481 "Wanted: People with "kinetic energy," "emotional maturity," and the ability to "deal with large numbers of people in a fairly **chaotic** situation.""

Something that is **chaotic** is disordered or disorganized.

Page 481 "Although this job description may seem most appropriate for the job of **cohost** of *Wheel of Fortune*, in actuality it is part of an advertisement for managers for American MultiCinema's (AMC) theaters."

A **cohost** is one of two or more people who introduce guests on a TV show.

Page 481 "For example, potential Microsoft employees have been asked **brain-teasers** like "If you had to remove one of the 50 U.S. states, which would it be?""

Brain-teasers are puzzles that challenge a person to think.

Page 481 "No single test can provide an understanding of the **intricacies** of someone's personality without considering a good deal more information than can be provided in a single testing session (Gladwell, 2004; Paul, 2004)."

Things that are **intricate** are complex and have many details.

Test your knowledge of the modules by answering these questions. These questions have been placed in three Practice Tests. The first two tests consist of questions that will test your recall of factual knowledge. The third test contains questions that are challenging and primarily test for conceptual knowledge and your ability to apply that knowledge. Check your answers and review the feedback using the Answer Key in the following pages of the *Study Guide*.

PRACTICE TEST 1:

1. Sigmund Freud believed that the _____ harbors repressed emotions and thoughts as well as instinctual drives.
   a. unconscious
   b. collective unconscious
   c. conscience
   d. conscious

2. Which of the following is **least** likely to involve making unrealistic demands on the person?
   a. The id
   b. The ego
   c. The superego
   d. The pleasure principle

3. The most important mental factors in Freud's psychoanalytic theory were:
   a. those that the person consciously controls or manipulates.
   b. associated with the latency developmental stage.
   c. those about which the person is unaware.
   d. based on social learning and influence.

4. Freud's concept of the conscience refers to:
   a. infantile wishes, desires, demands, and needs hidden from conscious awareness.
   b. the part of the superego that prevents us from behaving in morally improper ways.
   c. the part of personality that provides a buffer between the id and the outside world.
   d. the part of the ego that prevents us from doing what is morally wrong.

5. A child who is in the midst of toilet training is probably in the:
   a. genital psychosexual stage.
   b. anal psychosexual stage.
   c. phallic psychosexual stage.
   d. oral psychosexual stage.

6. Which of the following defense mechanisms is considered the primary one?
   a. Repression
   b. Sublimation
   c. Rationalization
   d. Projection

7. Unconscious strategies, called defense mechanisms, are what people use to:
   a. decrease their reliance on the reality principle.
   b. reduce anxiety.
   c. increase the superego's power to regulate behavior.
   d. prevent Freudian slips.

8.   Trait theorists believe that:
      a.   everyone has the same traits, but in different amounts.
      b.   everyone has different traits that do not change with time.
      c.   everyone has different traits, and they change with time.
      d.   everyone has different traits, but they cannot be measured.

9.   Which of the psychologists listed is **not** a trait theorist?
      a.   Albert Bandura   c.   Raymond B. Cattell
      b.   Gordon Allport   d.   Hans Eysenck

10.   From the perspective of learning theorists such as B.F. Skinner, consistencies of behavior across
      situations relate to:
      a.   stable individual characteristics called personality traits.
      b.   the dynamics of unconscious forces.
      c.   the rewards or punishments received by the person previously.
      d.   any conflict between the person's experiences and his or her self-concept.

11.   Factor analysis is:
      a.   a method of recording data that requires sophisticated equipment.
      b.   a method of understanding how the unconscious works.
      c.   a statistical method of finding common traits.
      d.   a sociometric method of determining personality traits in a group.

12.   Carl Rogers would argue that prisons should offer rehabilitation programs because humanistic
      theories of personality assume that:
      a.   man's basic goodness is contrasted with an evil unconscious.
      b.   man is self-sufficient and that society corrupts the individual.
      c.   man is basically good and desires to improve.
      d.   man's fundamental depravity may be offset through education.

13.   Alcoholics Anonymous relies on the conscious, self-motivated personal ability to improve, which is
      the core of:
      a.   the learning theory of personality.
      b.   the neo-Freudian psychoanalytic theory of personality.
      c.   the humanistic theory of personality.
      d.   the trait theory of personality.

14.   Which one of the following tests is designed to uncover unconscious content?
      a.   MMPI   c.   The Behavioral Assessment Inventory
      b.   TAT   d.   Edwards Personal Preference Schedule

15.   A student retakes the SAT. Despite her claim that she did poorly the first time because she was
      very sleepy that day, her score is within 2 percent of her first score. This outcome supports the
      notion that the SAT is:
      a.   a standardized assessment tool.   c.   a reliable assessment tool.
      b.   an academic ability assessment tool.   d.   a valid assessment tool.

_____ 16.   pleasure principle   a.   Provides a buffer between the id and the outside world.

_____ 17.   ego   b.   The principle by which the id operates.

_____ 18.   reality principle   c.   Prevents us from doing what is morally wrong.

_____ 19.   superego   d.   Represents the morality of society as presented by
                                              parents, teachers, and others.
_____ 20.   conscience
                                         e.   The principle by which the ego operates.

21.   The state of fulfillment in which people realize their unique potential is called

      _____.

22.   A phenomenon whereby adults have continuing feelings of weakness and insecurity is referred to
      as having a(n) _____.

23.   _____ is when unpleasant id impulses are pushed back into the unconscious.

24.   The refusal to accept anxiety-producing information is known as _____.

25.   Allport suggests three basic categories of traits: cardinal, central, and _____.

26.   Given that Freud's theory appears to be primarily focused on male development and thus on a
      male personality, identify the areas of Freud's theory that are the weakest with regard to female
      psychological issues. Defend your response with other points of view presented in the text.

PRACTICE TEST 2:

1.   _____ suggests that a person's desire to improve is self-motivated behavior and is
     triggered largely by powerful forces found in the unconscious.
     a.   Humanistic theory   c.   Psychoanalytic theory
     b.   Learning theory   d.   Trait theory

2.   Freud's structure of personality has three major parts. Which alternative is **not** one of them?
     a.   Archetype   c.   Superego
     b.   Id   d.   Ego

3.   In Freud's explanation of personality development, which of the following controls thought, solves
     problems, and makes decisions?
     a.   Id   c.   Superego
     b.   Ego   d.   Conscience

4.   Freud's theory of psychosexual development illustrates that a child who is constantly putting things
     in its mouth is most likely at the:
     a.   genital stage.   c.   phallic stage.
     b.   anal stage.   d.   oral stage.

5. Freud's stages theory of mature sexual relationships begin to occur at which psychosexual stage?
   a. Phallic
   b. Oral
   c. Genital
   d. Anal

6. Defense mechanisms are:
   a. unconscious.
   b. instinctive.
   c. learned.
   d. reflexive.

7. Victims of child abuse, rape, or incest attacks might not recall the incident or may remember only scant details. Freud suggested that the reason for this is that the defense mechanism of _____ was applied.
   a. sublimation
   b. repression
   c. denial
   d. projection

8. For Gordon Allport, _____ traits are so distinct that having only one of these traits will define a person's personality.

   a. general
   b. secondary
   c. central
   d. cardinal

9. What are the three important categories defined in Allport's theory of personality dimensions?
   a. Primary, secondary, and tertiary
   b. Factors, traits, and features
   c. Source, surface, and circumscript
   d. Cardinal, central, and secondary

10. The basic assumption shared by trait personality theorists is that:
    a. the traits are consistent across situations.
    b. the unconscious mind is the underlying source of the traits we have.
    c. traits are learned habits that are modified by reinforcers.
    d. people possess the traits to the same degree but differ in how they choose to apply them.

11. According to Bandura, we can modify our own personalities through the use of:
    a. defense mechanisms.
    b. drive reduction.
    c. psychoanalysis.
    d. self-reinforcement.

12. Temperament is presumed to originate from the child's:
    a. personally chosen interests and ideas.
    b. source traits.
    c. early learning experiences with the primary caregiver or mother.
    d. genetic predisposition.

13. If a test provides a consistent score for a particular individual over repeated administrations, the test is said to be:
    a. accurate.
    b. valid.
    c. reliable.
    d. statistical.

14. The MMPI was originally developed to:
    a. identify personality disorders.
    b. uncover unconscious thoughts.
    c. locate traits.
    d. conduct behavioral assessments.

15. Test stimuli are the most ambiguous on the:
   a. TAT.   c. Rorschach.
   b. California Psychological Inventory.   d. MMPI.

_____ 16. oral stage   a. A child's attempt to be similar to the same-sex parent.

_____ 17. anal stage   b. An infant's center of pleasure is the mouth.

_____ 18. phallic stage   c. A child's interest focuses on the genitals.

_____ 19. identification   d. A child's pleasure is centered on the anus.

_____ 20. penis envy   e. A girl's wish that she had a penis.

21. According to Freud, children's sexual concerns are temporarily put aside during the
     _____.

22. A defense mechanism identified by an unwanted feeling directed toward a weaker object is
     _____.

23. When a person attributes his inadequacies or faults to someone else, it is known as
     _____.

24. _____ is the diversion of unwanted impulses into acceptable thoughts,
     feelings, and behaviors.

25. _____ is defined as supportive behavior for another individual.

26. State one issue or situation that most adolescents tend to deal with during their high school years.
     Looking over Freud's defense mechanisms, describe how each of three of the mechanisms might
     be used by the adolescent to "protect one's psyche" from the anxiety produced by the stated
     situation.

PRACTICE TEST 3: Conceptual, Applied, and Challenging Questions

1. Listed below are four alternatives. Three of the four give pairs of items that are related. Which
    alternative below gives items that are **not** related?
    a. Ego; reality principle   c. Superego; "executive" of personality
    b. Sigmund Freud; Viennese physician d. Id; pleasure principle

2. Dr. Kasha viewed the thumb-sucking of 7-year-old Maureen as:
    a. behavior of a normal youngster.
    b. fixated at the oral stage of development.
    c. having been breastfed as an infant.
    d. ready to enter the phallic stage of development.

3. According to the psychoanalytic perspective, a rapist would be considered to have:
    a. unconditioned positive regard for his victim.
    b. a well-developed ego-ideal.
    c. a deficient superego.
    d. brain damage.

4. Rupert kept his clothes hung up and neatly pressed, whereas his roommate Renita rarely laundered or hung up his clothes. Freud might have suggested that both men were fixated at the:
    a. anal stage.   c. phallic stage.
    b. oral stage.   d. genital stage.

5. Tina accepted a date from a young man she greatly admired. At the time of the date, however, the man didn't show up. In response, she exclaimed, "I didn't want to go out with him anyway!" This illustrates:
    a. rationalization.   c. regression.
    b. denial.   d. repression.

6. Freud's stages of psychosexual development:
    a. emphasize adolescence as the key interval in personality development.
    b. designate the oral stage as the highest in the sequence.
    c. identify parts of the body that are biological pleasure zones toward which gratification is focused.
    d. relate to the same behaviors described in Piaget's theory.

7. The _____ approach emphasizes voluntary conscious aspects of personality, while the _____ approach emphasizes unconscious aspects.
    a. biological; learning   c. humanistic; psychoanalytic
    b. trait; humanistic   d. trait; humanistic

8. Listed below are four alternatives. Three of the four list pairs of items that are related. Which alternative contains items that are **not** related?
    a. Jung; collective unconscious
    b. Horney; women do not have penis envy
    c. Adler; inferiority complex
    d. Cattell; striving for superiority

9. A trait theorist would most likely make which of the following statements:
    a. He really hurt her feelings, but he's rationalizing it away.
    b. He really could have gone a long way, but his inferiority complex destroyed any confidence he had.
    c. These are five stages in the process of his development toward fulfilling his highest potential.
    d. He is a sensitive, warm, and considerate person.

10. Various approaches to personality have names and concepts uniquely associated with them. Three of the four alternatives below list pairs of items that are related. Which alternative contains items that are **not** related?
    a. Trait theory; assessment of traits that comprise personality
    b. Learning theory; experiences with situations in the environment
    c. Learning theory; Skinner
    d. Psychoanalytic theory; consistency of behavior across situations

11. Kate loves working with animals and wants to study veterinary science in college. Her boyfriend wants her to be a computer analyst and criticizes her for her love of animals. According to Carl Rogers, this conflict will lead to:
    a. Kate learning to love being a computer analyst.
    b. anxiety on Kate's part.
    c. Kate becoming a fully functioning person.
    d. unconditional positive regard.

12. Which of the following situations best illustrates reliability as a quality of psychological tests?
    a. A prospective Air Force pilot takes a test, passes it, and becomes an excellent pilot.
    b. A college student studies diligently for an important exam and receives an A on it.
    c. A psychiatric patient takes a psychological test that yields the diagnosis the patient had suspected.
    d. A mentally retarded patient takes an intelligence test on Monday and again on Tuesday, getting the same result on each administration.

13. Which of the following statements about Freud's theories is **not** a criticism given by psychologists?
    a. The theory has several vague concepts, making it difficult to make predictions.
    b. Freud derived his theory from a diverse sample, making its applicability questionable.
    c. Current research demonstrates that personality change and development can occur later than Freud thought, into adolescence and adulthood.
    d. There is little clear evidence for Freud's conception of the structure of personality.

14. According to researchers who explore the role of biology in personality:
    a. there is a gene that is linked to thrill-seeking.
    b. many personality traits can be explained wholly by biology.
    c. temperament is stable throughout adulthood.
    d. social closeness can be well-explained by genetic components.

15. Which of the following would be a confounding variable for studies that are attempting to demonstrate which traits parents pass on to their children genetically?
    a. The fact that social traits like religiosity rate high in twin studies, even when this trait is entirely dependent on traditional cultural practices.
    b. When twins are separated at birth, they always express similar traits.
    c. The role of parents in shaping the environment.
    d. Evidence that some traits appear more heritable than others.

_____ 16. anxiety

_____ 17. neurotic anxiety

_____ 18. defense mechanisms

_____ 19. collective unconscious

_____ 20. archetypes

a. The concept that we inherit certain personality characteristics from our ancestors and the human race.

b. Anxiety caused when irrational impulses from the id threaten to become uncontrollable.

c. Universal, symbolic representations of a particular person, object, or experience.

d. A feeling of apprehension or tension.

e. Unconscious strategies used to reduce anxiety by concealing its source from oneself and others.

21. The _____ is defined by marked mature sexual behavior.

22. A defense mechanism identified by the justification of a negative situation to protect one's self-esteem is called _____.

23. Behavior that is reminiscent of an earlier stage of development is called _____.

24. _____ is learning by viewing the actions of others.

25. Psychologists refer to the realization of one's highest potential as _____.

26. A major issue that will affect virtually everyone is the creation of norms for different minority and ethnic groups. Describe the issues involved and discuss whether the use of different norms will be helpful, harmful, or a mixture of both.

Module 42:	Module 43:	Module 44:
[a] personality	[a] trait theory	[a] Psychological tests
[b] Psychodynamic personality theorists	[b] Traits	[b] reliability
	[c] cardinal trait	[c] validity
[c] psychoanalytic theory	[d] central traits	[d] Norms
[d] unconscious	[e] Secondary traits	[e] self-report measures
[e] id	[f] factor analysis	[f] Minnesota Multiphasic
[f] psychic energy	[g] Extroversion	Personality Inventory-2
[g] pleasure principle	[h] Neuroticism	(MMPI-2)
[h] ego	[i] Psychoticism	[g] test standardization
[i] reality principle	[j] Social-cognitive	[h] Projective personality
[j] superego	[k] observational learning	[i] Rorschach
[k] conscience	[l] self-efficacy	[j] Thematic Apperception Test
[l] oral	[m] self-esteem	(TAT)
[m] Fixation	[n] Biological and evolutionary	[k] behavioral assessment
[n] anal	[o] temperament	
[o] phallic	[p] Humanistic approaches to	Evaluate
[p] latency	personality	1. a
[q] genital	[q] unconditional positive	2. e
[r] defense mechanisms	regard	3. d
[s] collective unconscious	[r] self-actualization	4. c
[t] archetypes		5. b
	Evaluate	
Evaluate	1. a	
1. c	2. e	
2. b	3. d	
3. d	4. c	
4. e	5. b	
5. a		

Selected Rethink Answers

43-1   Traits are enduring dimensions of personality characteristics along which people differ. Because each person probably possesses certain traits, what makes individuals different is the degree to which a given trait applies to a single person. Traits allow us to compare one person with another and provide an explanation for a person's behavioral consistency. Assigning certain negative traits to a person may cause a person to be stigmatized by others. Assigning other, more positive traits to a person may raise people's expectations of them and cause them undo pressure in many situations.

44-1   Personality tests might be useful to both the employer and the employee as one more source of information in trying to make employment decisions. Test should be used to find ways to include people and place them in appropriate work situations. In this way, both parties would gain. No single test should be used alone to exclude anyone from obtaining a position. Tests are helpful to distinguish personality disorders when they arc one of several assessment tools. They are not accurate enough to make conclusive judgments on their own. Anyone who is going to be excluded from a job, placed in, or excluded from a program should have a means to appeal the decision and have other means of assessment available to determine if the decision is valid.

Practice Test 1:

1.   a   mod. 42 p. 467
*a.   Correct. Repressed wishes, desires, anxiety, and conflict are found in the realm Freud called the unconscious.
 b.   Incorrect. This was a concept introduced by Freud's follower, Carl Jung.
 c.   Incorrect. The conscience is to be found in the superego.
 d.   Incorrect. The conscious contains our awareness of the world.

2.   b   mod. 42 p. 468
 a.   Incorrect. The id is always making demands on the person that are unrealistic, even sometimes dangerous.
*b.   Correct. It is the ego's role to manage the competing demands of the id and the superego, and it responds according to the reality principle.
 c.   Incorrect. The superego's demands of moral perfection and ego-ideal are unrealistic and in conflict with the id.
 d.   Incorrect. The pleasure principle is the principle that animates the id, making its demands very unrealistic.

3.   c   mod. 42 p. 468
 a.   Incorrect. While important, they are not at the center of his theory.
 b.   Incorrect. More likely the earlier stages.
*c.   Correct. The mental factors of which we are least aware can have the most grave effects on our personality.
 d.   Incorrect. This theory came long after Freud.

4.   b   mod. 42 p. 468
 a.   Incorrect. This describes the id.
*b.   Correct. This is the definition of the conscience, which is housed in the superego.
 c.   Incorrect. This is the role of the ego.
 d.   Incorrect. There is no part of the ego that does this.

5.   b   mod. 42 p. 469
 a.   Incorrect. The genital stage is the last stage in the sequence, and it occurs long after toilet training.
*b.   Correct. During the anal stage, the child learns self-control, and one of the manifestations of self-control is toilet training.
 c.   Incorrect. The phallic stage is marked by the Oedipal conflict, and it occurs after the stage that includes toilet training.
 d.   Incorrect. The oral stage is the first stage, and it is marked by a focus on pleasure taken from the mouth.

6.   a   mod. 42 p. 471
*a.   Correct. Repression forces conflict into the unconscious, and is quite commonly used, according to Freud.
 b.   Correct. Sublimation converts repressed desire, especially sexual desire, into socially acceptable forms, like work.
 c.   Incorrect. Rationalization involves creating self-justifying reasons after the fact.
 d.   Incorrect. Projection places unacceptable impulses onto a safe object.

7.   b   mod. 42 p. 470
 a.   Incorrect. Probably just the opposite.
*b.   Correct. Anxiety is a great threat to the ego, so the ego's defense mechanisms help protect it.
 c.   Incorrect. The ego, at times, needs protection against the superego as well.
 d.   Incorrect. Sometimes defense mechanisms cause Freudian slips.

8.   a   mod. 43 p. 475
*a.   Correct. For most trait theorists, everyone has the major traits to some extent, and the amount of these traits tends to be stable through time.
 b.   Incorrect. See answer a.
 c.   Incorrect. See answer a.
 d.   Incorrect. See answer a.

9.   a   mod. 43 p. 476-477
*a.   Correct. Albert Bandura is the leading social learning theorist.
 b.   Incorrect. Allport is known for the cardinal, central, and secondary traits.
 c.   Incorrect. Cattell is known for the 16 factor theory, distinguishing source from surface traits.
 d.   Incorrect. Eysenck proposed three main trait characteristics: extroversion, neuroticism, and psychoticism.

10. c   mod. 43 p. 479
 a.   Incorrect. This terminology is that of the trait theorists.
 b.   Incorrect. This terminology is from the psychodynamic perspective.
*c.   Correct. As Skinner is a behaviorist, "traits" are explained in behavioral terms.
 d.   Incorrect. This terminology is from the humanistic perspective.

11. c   mod. 43 p. 477
a. Incorrect. It is an analytic technique, and it requires no special equipment.
b. Incorrect. Used by trait theorists, this use is unlikely.
*c. Correct. Factor analysis identifies common patterns in data and was used by Cattell to identify the source traits in his theory.
d. Incorrect. While it might help identify personality traits in a group (if that is possible), it is only a statistical technique.

12. c   mod. 43 p. 484
a. Incorrect. Humanistic theories tend not to judge the unconscious as evil.
b. Incorrect. Society is not generally viewed by humanistic theories as a corrupting force.
*c. Correct. Humans have within themselves the ability to heal their own psychological disorders and resolve their conflicts.
d. Incorrect. No psychological view holds to this thesis of fundamental depravity.

13. c   mod. 43 p. 485
a. Incorrect. Learning theory depends on conditioning and reinforcement.
b. Incorrect. The psychodynamic theory focuses on unconscious forces.
*c. Correct. The humanistic approach focuses on the abilities of the individual to engage in self-actualization.
d. Incorrect. The trait theory searches for long-term, consistent behavior patterns.

14. b   mod. 44 p. 492
a. Incorrect. The MMPI asks the test-taker to respond to questions concerning items of which the test-taker has an awareness.
*b. Correct. The Thematic Apperception Test (TAT) asks that respondents tell a story about a picture and through that story, they may reveal unconscious concerns.
c. Incorrect. Though there are many behavioral assessments, there is probably no Behavioral Assessment Inventory. Regardless, it wouldn't be directed at the unconscious.
d. Incorrect. This is probably another self-report instrument.

15. c   mod. 44 p. 487
a. Incorrect. It is a standardized test, but the scenario does not support this notion.
b. Incorrect. It is supposed to be an academic ability assessment tool, but this scenario does not question that.
*c. Correct. Since it measured her performance and knowledge the same in both circumstances, the assessment is quite reliable.
d. Incorrect. It may be valid, but this story does not support that claim.

16. b   mod. 42 p. 468
17. a   mod. 42 p. 468
18. e   mod. 42 p. 468
19. d   mod. 42 p. 468
20. c   mod. 42 p. 468

21. self-actualization   mod. 42 p. 468
22. inferiority complex   mod. 42 p. 473
23. Repression   mod. 42 p. 471
24. denial   mod. 42 p. 471
25. secondary   mod. 43 p. 477

26.
- The weakest area is Freud's developmental stages, particularly with the Oedipus complex. Freud's concept of penis envy is not well accepted by many.
- Just as Gilligan contests Kohlberg's views of moral development, one could argue that Freud's concept of a genital stage rests on masculine norms.

Practice Test 2:
1. c   mod. 42 p. 467
a. Incorrect. Humanistic theory is concerned with the person recognizing his or her own potential and finding ways to achieve self-actualization.
b. Incorrect. Learning theory is concerned with the kinds of reinforcements and punishments that have contributed to the formation of the current patterns of behavior of an individual.
*c. Correct. Psychoanalytic theory considers the hidden contents of the unconscious to be powerful forces in the shaping of personality.
d. Incorrect. Trait theory seeks to identify and measure the consistent patterns of traits manifested by people.

2. a   mod. 42 p. 468
*a. Correct. The archetype is a concept from Jung's theory of the collective unconscious. Freud was concerned with the id, ego, and superego.
b. Incorrect. See answer a.
c. Incorrect. See answer a.
d. Incorrect. See answer a.

3. b   mod. 42 p. 468
a. Incorrect. The id seeks to satisfy the pleasure principle and is not concerned with thought, decisions, or solving problems.
*b. Correct. The ego is responsible for balancing the demands of the id and the superego, and thus must solve problems, think, and make decisions.
c. Incorrect. The superego seeks to present a moralistic, ego-ideal and a judgmental conscience to the ego.
d. Incorrect. The conscience is one of the two components of the superego; the other is the ego-ideal.

4. d   mod. 42 p. 469
a. Incorrect. See answer d.
b. Incorrect. See answer d.
c. Incorrect. See answer d.
*d. Correct. This child is seeking pleasure from the mouth, and is thus in the oral stage.

5. c   mod. 42 p. 469
a. Incorrect. The child is only about 6 years old during this stage, and thus unlikely to participate in mature sexual relations.
b. Incorrect. The child is less than 2 years old during this stage, and thus will not be engaging in any mature sexual relations.
*c. Correct. This was the name Freud gave to the stage in which sexual maturity develops.
d. Incorrect. This stage occurs when the child is between 2 and 4 years of age, and thus mature sexual relations are unlikely.

6. a   mod. 42 p. 470
*a. Correct. Defense mechanisms operate below the level of awareness as part of their role in protecting the ego from anxiety and conflict.
b. Incorrect. There are two instincts (drives) in Freud's view: eros (love) and the death drive.
c. Incorrect. Freud did not describe whether the defense mechanisms were learned or innate.
d. Incorrect. After they have been utilized, they may become reflexive, but they respond to complex stimuli rather than the simple stimuli typically associated with reflexes.

7. b   mod. 42 p. 471
a. Incorrect. Sublimation does not apply here.
*b. Correct. Repression is a form of intentional forgetting.
c. Incorrect. Denial is one means of dealing with this kind of trauma, but the core mechanism is repression.
d. Incorrect. After repression, the victims of child abuse may project fears onto other people.

8. d   mod. 43 p. 476
a. Incorrect. Allport did not identify any traits as "general."
b. Incorrect. Allport's concept of secondary traits is that people have many of these, and they govern such things as the style and preference of many everyday behaviors.
c. Incorrect. In Allport's view, everyone has several central traits, but these do not dominate the personality.
*d. Correct. Allport called these cardinal traits, and they dominate the personality of the individual.

9. d   mod. 43 p. 477
a. Incorrect. See answer d.
b. Incorrect. See answer d.
c. Incorrect. See answer d.
*d. Correct. The cardinal trait controls and dominates the personality, while at the other end, secondary traits define style and preferences.

10. a   mod. 43 p. 475
*a. Correct. If traits exist, then by definition they need to persist.
b. Incorrect. Trait theories did not commonly offer a theory for the existence of traits.
c. Incorrect. To only a few are traits learned in the traditional operant conditioning approach.
d. Incorrect. People do not choose to apply traits.

11. d   mod. 43 p. 480
a. Incorrect. This is Freud's idea.
b. Incorrect. This belongs to other drive theorists, like Clark Hull.
c. Incorrect. Bandura may agree that psychoanalysis will modify our personality, but not by using any of Bandura's concepts.
*d. Correct. Self-reinforcement is an important component of the social learning theory of Bandura.

12. d   mod. 43 p. 482
a.   Incorrect. Since it appears long before the child has an opportunity to form interests, this answer is incorrect.
b.   Incorrect. Temperament might be considered a source trait.
c.   Incorrect. Temperament is present before the opportunity to have early learning experience.
*d.   Correct. This is the current view of temperament, that it is genetically disposed.

13. c   mod. 44 p. 487
a.   Incorrect. If the test does not measure what it should, it would not be very accurate.
b.   Incorrect. If the test made the same measure each time, it would still have to measure what it is supposed to measure to be considered valid.
*c.   Correct. Even if the test failed to measure what it was supposed to measure, yet it made the same measurement each time, then the test would be reliable.
d.   Incorrect. A statistical test would have to measure some kind of statistics, would it not?

14. a   mod. 44 p. 489
*a.   Correct. The MMPI measures tendencies toward psychological difficulties, but it can be taken by anyone and it does produce meaningful results for people who do not have psychological problems.
b.   Incorrect. The MMPI is a self-report test, and thus unlikely to reveal many thoughts that are not within the awareness of the test-taker.
c.   Incorrect. The MMPI does not locate "traits" and is not specific to any trait theory.
d.   Incorrect. The MMPI is a self-report test, and thus it cannot be used for a behavioral assessment except for the selection of true or false on the test.

15. c   mod. 44 p. 492
a.   Incorrect. The TAT uses ambiguous pictures, but they are not as ambiguous as the inkblots used on the Rorschach.
b.   Incorrect. The California Psychological Inventory and the MMPI both use statements that require a direct and unambiguous response to a rather unambiguous item.
*c.   Correct. The Rorschach inkblots are probably the most ambiguous test stimuli used in this manner.
d.   Incorrect. See answer b.

16. b   mod. 42 p. 469
17. d   mod. 42 p. 469
18. c   mod. 42 p. 469
19. a   mod. 42 p. 470
20. e   mod. 42 p. 470

21. latency period   mod. 42 p. 470
22. displacement   mod. 42 p. 471
23. projection   mod. 42 p. 471
24. Sublimation   mod. 42 p. 471
25. Unconditional positive regard   mod. 43 p. 484

26. Adolescents want autonomy and attempt to negotiate with their parents for more freedom to make their own decisions:
   ▪ Regression allows them to scream and yell and carry on when they don't get their own way. They act as they did when they were younger in order to avoid the real conflict and get their way.
   ▪ Rationalization would involve creating self-justifying excuses after the fact.
   ▪ Projection places unacceptable impulses onto a safe object.

Practice Test 3:
1.   c   mod. 42 p. 468
a.   Incorrect. The ego does operate on the reality principle as it tries to balance demands of the id and the superego.
b.   Incorrect. Sigmund Freud was a Viennese physician.
*c.   Correct. The ego is considered the executive of the personality, not the superego.
d.   Incorrect. The id follows the pleasure principle as it seeks to satisfy desires and wishes.

2.   b   mod. 42 p. 469
a.   Incorrect. This is unusual, yet not abnormal for a child of this age.
*b.   Correct. Thumb sucking is an oral behavior, so the youngster must be fixated in the oral stage.
c.   Incorrect. Breast feeding is not relevant to later thumb sucking.
d.   Incorrect. The child is probably already in the phallic stage, but the fixation or regression to the oral stage is present.

3. c   mod. 42 p. 470
a. Incorrect. The concept of unconditioned positive regard is from humanistic theory, and the rapist is the last person who would have such regard for another person.
b. Incorrect. Only if the ego-ideal was that of a rapist.
*c. Correct. The superego provides a sense of right and wrong, and a rapist is clearly missing this dimension of morality.
d. Incorrect. A psychoanalyst would not attribute the behavior of a rapist to brain damage.

4. a   mod. 42 p. 469
*a. Correct. The extremes of neatness and messiness have been associated with the anal stage, with the neat person overdoing anal retention and the messy person rejecting order.
b. Incorrect. The messy person could be fixated in the oral stage, but not the neat one.
c. Incorrect. Fixation in the phallic stage does not result in messiness or neatness.
d. Incorrect. Freud did not describe what fixation would be like for stages in which we are currently occupied.

5. b   mod. 42 p. 471
a. Incorrect. Rationalization would involve making an explanation that would protect the self through after-the-fact justification.
*b. Correct. The young woman is denying that she had any interest in the young man in the first place.
c. Incorrect. Regression would require that she regress to an earlier developmental stage.
d. Incorrect. Repression requires that she force her anxiety and anger into the unconscious.

6. c   mod. 42 p. 469
a. Incorrect. Many researchers in addition to Freud saw earlier childhood as critical for the development of the personality.
b. Incorrect. The first in the sequence, but highest only if you stand up.
*c. Correct. Infants, children, and adults seek physical pleasure.
d. Incorrect. Piaget's sensorimotor stage is similar to Freud's oral stage, but the others differ.

7. c   mod. 43 p. 484
a. Incorrect. The biological view would not be that interested in conscious decisions.
b. Incorrect. The trait approach does not consider traits within the person's ability to choose, and the humanistic approach certainly focuses on conscious behavior.
*c. Correct. The humanistic approach rests on the person's ability to be rational and self-motivated while the psychodynamic approach assumes the power of the irrational and unconscious forces in the person.
d. Incorrect. The biological view would not be that interested in conscious decisions, and the humanistic approach certainly focuses on conscious behavior.

8. d   mod. 43 p. 477
a. Incorrect. Jung proposed the idea of a collective unconscious.
b. Incorrect. Horney argued that women do not have penis envy.
c. Incorrect. Adler did develop the idea of an inferiority complex.
*d. Correct. Striving for superiority is Adler's idea, not Cattell's.

9. d   mod. 43 p. 476
a. Incorrect. Sounds psychoanalytic.
b. Incorrect. Sounds like Adler's idea of inferiority complex.
c. Incorrect. Sounds like Maslow's hierarchy of needs.
*d. Correct. A trait theorist would describe someone in terms of traits, like warm and considerate.

10. d   mod. 43 p. 477
a. Incorrect. Trait theory proposes that traits can be assessed and a picture of the person composed.
b. Incorrect. Learning theory suggests that the environment is a major force in shaping the personality.
c. Incorrect. Skinner is associated with learning theory.
*d. Correct. While psychoanalytic theory would suggest that behavior would be consistent across situations, this is a major issue for trait theorists.

11. b   mod. 43 p. 484
a.   Incorrect. This is unlikely, except if she compromises her own desires.
*b. Correct. The incongruency between Kate and her boyfriend could lead to anxiety.
c.   Incorrect. If this incongruency becomes a condition of worth, then Kate cannot become a fully functioning person.
d.   Incorrect. Unconditional positive regard requires more acceptance than this.

12. d   mod. 44 p. 487
a.   Incorrect. This suggests that the test was a valid measure of pilot potential.
b.   Incorrect. This suggests that studying is a valid means of preparing for an exam.
c.   Incorrect. The test has validated the suspicion.
*d. Correct. Repeating a test and getting the same or nearly the same score on each administration demonstrates reliability.

13. b   mod. 43 p. 483
a.   Incorrect. This is a criticism many have made.
*b. Correct. Freud developed his ideas based on a sample which was very limited in diversity. It was an upper-middle-class group of Austrian women.
c.   Incorrect. This is also an important criticism.
d.   Incorrect. This, too, is an important criticism.

14. a   mod. 43 p. 483
*a. Correct. It is the dopamine-4 receptor gene.
b.   Incorrect. Even biological psychologists recognize the role of the environment in shaping personality.
c.   Incorrect. Tempermant is relatively stable until adolescence, but environmental input can change it, even into adulthood.
d.   Incorrect. Social closeness is only weakly explained by genetics.

15. c   mod. 43 p. 483
a.   Incorrect. Traditionalism has been shown to be heritable.
b.   Incorrect. This would actually indicate something about the dependent variable, not a confounding variable.
*c. Correct. When trying to separate parental genes from environmental forces, one must accept the confounding aspect of the parent's role in shaping the environment.
d.   Incorrect. This is not a confounding element.

16. d   mod. 42 p. 470
17. b   mod. 42 p. 470
18. e   mod. 42 p. 470
19. a   mod. 42 p. 472
20. c   mod. 42 p. 473

21. genital stage   mod. 42 p. 469
22. rationalization   mod. 42 p. 471
23. regression   mod. 42 p. 471
24. Observational learning mod. 43 p. 480
25. self-actualization   mod. 43 p. 484

26.
-   Some people argue that any kind of separation of a group from the larger society is detrimental.
-   One major problem is the use of norms or averages to prepare job "profiles." These are still average and composite pictures of the individual and may unfairly discriminate against those who do not fit the profile. With these kinds of norms, negative reactions can and have occurred by those excluded from the special normed group. Recent court cases will change how this is viewed as well.

Chapter 14: Health Psychology: Stress, Coping, and Well-Being

Overview

This set of modules discusses the ways in which psychological factors affect one's health. Health psychology investigates the prevention, diagnosis, and treatment of medical problems.

Module 45 focuses on the causes and consequences of stress, as well as the means of coping with it. Classes of events that provoke stress, including cataclysmic events, personal stressors, background stressors, and daily stressors are discussed. In addition, the consequences of stress are explained by Selye's general adaptation syndrome.

Module 46 explores the psychological aspects of several major health problems, including heart disease, cancer, and smoking.

Module 47 offers insight into patient and physician interactions to see how they influence our health. Suggestions are offered for increasing patients' compliance with behavior that will improve their well-being. The characteristics of happy people are also presented.

To further investigate the topics covered in this chapter, you can visit the related Web sites by visiting the following link: www.mhhe.com/feldmanup8.

Prologue: So Much to Do, So Little Time to Do It
Looking Ahead

Module 45:
Stress and Coping

Stress: Reacting to Threat and Challenge
Coping with Stress

Applying Psychology in the 21st Century:
The Value of Social Support: Sick and Lonely – Why the Two Go
Together

Becoming an Informed Consumer of Psychology:
Effective Coping Strategies

- *How is health psychology a union between medicine and psychology?*
- *What is stress, how does it affect us, and how can we best cope with it?*

Stress and Coping

[a] _____ focuses on the application of psychology to the prevention, diagnosis, and treatment of medical problems. Health psychologists view the mind and the body as closely linked. Good health and the ability to stay healthy are affected by how a person manages stress and the person's health habits. Health psychologists have been particularly interested in the [b]

_____ , which is our bodies' natural defense in fighting disease, and is affected by attitudes and emotional state. Health psychology has changed the view of disease from a purely biological problem, and it has had to help people cope with the problems associated with

adjustment to diseases that last for a long time. [c] _____ is the study of the relationship between psychological factors and the immune system.

The response to events that threaten or challenge a person is called [d] _____, and the events are called *stressors*. There are many types of stressors, from personal to global. What is felt as stressful by one person may not be felt as stressful by another. There are three

general classes of events that are considered stressors. The first is [e] _____, strong stressors that affect many people at the same time. The stress of these events is usually dealt with well because so many people experience the event and share the problem. The second

class of stressor is [f] _____, which include life events of a personal or individual nature, like the death of a parent or spouse, the loss of a job, or a major illness. Typically, personal stressors cause an immediate major reaction that tapers off. Sometimes, though, the effects can last for a long time, such as the effects of being raped. Some people experience prolonged problems caused by either catastrophic events or severe personal stressors, and this is called [g] _____. People may experience flashbacks or dreams during which they reexperience the event. The symptoms can include a numbing of emotional experience, sleep difficulties, problems relating to others, and drug problems, among others. The third class of stressors is called [h] _____, and they include standing in long lines, traffic jams, and other [i] _____. Daily hassles can add up, causing unpleasant emotions and moods. A critical factor is the degree of control people have over the daily hassles. When they have control, the stress reactions are less. On the other side of daily hassles are [j] _____, positive events that lead to pleasant feelings.

The class of medical problems called [k] _____, caused by the interaction of psychological, emotional, and physiological problems, are also related to stress. High levels of stress interfere with people's ability to cope with current and new stressors.

Hans Selye proposed that everyone goes through the same set of physiological responses no matter what the cause is, and he called this the [l] _____. The first stage is the [m]_____, during which the presence of a stressor is detected and the sympathetic nervous system is energized. The second stage is the [n] _____, during which the person attempts to cope with the stressor. If coping is inadequate, the person enters the [o] _____. The person's ability to cope with stress declines and the negative consequences appear. These include illness, psychological symptoms like the inability to concentrate, and possibly disorientation and losing touch with reality.

GAS has provided a model that explains how stress leads to illness. The primary criticism has focused on the fact that the model suggests that every stress response is physiologically the same. If people are to consider an event stressful, they must perceive it to be threatening and must lack the ability to cope with it adequately. The same event may not be stressful for everyone. The perception of stress may depend on how one attributes the causes for events.

In an environment in which control is seen as impossible, one can experience [p] _____. Victims of learned helplessness have decided that there is no link between the responses they make and the outcomes that occur. When elderly people in nursing homes were given control over simple aspects of their lives, they were less likely to experience an early death. Not everyone experiences helplessness.

Our efforts to control, reduce, or learn to tolerate stress are known as [q] _____. Many of our responses are habitual. The [r] _____ are unconscious strategies that help control stress by distorting or denying the actual nature of the situation. Denying the significance of a nearby geological fault is an example. [s] _____ is another example in which a person does not feel emotions at all. Another means of dealing with stress is the use of direct and positive means. These include [t] _____, the conscious regulation of emotions, and [u] _____, the management of the stressful stimulus. People use both strategies, but they are more likely to use the emotion-focused strategy when they perceive the problem as unchangeable.

People can be described as having coping styles. **[v]** _____ refers to the style associated with a low rate of stress-induced illness, consisting of three components: commitment, challenge, and control. *Commitment* is a tendency to be involved in whatever we are doing with a sense that it is important and meaningful. *Challenge* refers to the view that change is the standard condition of life. *Control* refers to the sense of being able to influence events. The hardy person is optimistic and approaches the problem directly.

Relationships with others help people cope with stress. The knowledge of a mutual network of concerned, interested people helping individuals experience lower levels of stress is called

[w] _____. Social support demonstrates the value of a person to others and provides a network of information and advice. Also, actual goods and services can be provided through social support networks. Even pets can contribute to this support.

Stress can be dealt with through several steps: Turn stress into a challenge, make the threatening situation less threatening by changing attitudes about it, change goals in order to remove oneself from an uncontrollable situation, and take physical action.

Evaluate

_____ 1. immune system

_____ 2. stressors

_____ 3. psychophysiological disorders

_____ 4. alarm and mobilization

_____ 5. resistance

a. Circumstances that produce threats to well-being.

b. A person's initial awareness of the presence of a stressor.

c. The stage of coping with the stressor.

d. Medical problems caused by an interaction of psychological, emotional, and physical difficulties.

e. The body's natural defenses that fight disease.

Rethink

45-1 Why are cataclysmic stressors less stressful in the long run than other types of stressors? Does the reason relate to the coping phenomenon known as social support? How?

45-2 *From the perspective of a social worker:* How would you help people deal with and avoid stress in their everyday lives? How might you encourage people to create social support networks?

Spotlight on Terminology and Language—ESL Pointers

Page 487 "Some people would find jumping off a bridge while attached to a slender rubber **tether** extremely stressful."

To **tether** is to tie things together.

Page 488 "One reason is that natural disasters have a clear **resolution**."

When something has a clear **resolution**, it has a clear solution.

Page 488 "Typically, personal stressors produce an immediate major reaction that soon **tapers off**."

As the reaction **tapers off**, it is gradually reduced. It is becoming smaller in size or amount.

Page 489 "**Exemplified** by standing in a long line at a bank and getting stuck in a traffic jam, daily hassles are the minor irritations of life that we all face time and time again: delays, noisy cars and trucks, broken appliances, other people's irritating behavior, and so on."

When you **exemplify** something, you are giving an example in order to make something clearer.

Page 492 "Selye's theory has not gone **unchallenged**."

Things that are **unchallenged** are accepted and are not called in to question.

Page 492 "They believe that people's biological response is specific to the way they **appraise** a stressful event."

The way people evaluate or **appraise** a stressful event may be an important factor.

Page 492 "This perspective has led to an increased focus on **psychoneuroimmunology** (Lazarus, 2000; Taylor et al., 2000; Gaab, Rohleder, Nater, & Ehlert, 2005)."

Psychoneuroimmunology is the study of the connection among the central nervous system, the endocrine system, and psychosocial factors such as cognitive reactions to stressful procedures, the individual's personality traits, and social pressures.

Page 493 "In normal circumstances, our bodies produce lymphocytes, specialized white blood cells that fight disease, at an extraordinary rate – some 10 million every few seconds – and it is possible that stress can **alter** this level of production (Ader, Felten, & Cohen, 2001; Miller & Cohen, 2001; Cohen et al., 2002)."

To **alter** is to change.

Page 494 "For example, in one experiment, volunteers were taken as simulated **hostages** in a highly stressful situation in which the **terrorists** were convincingly **portrayed** by FBI agents."

Hostages are people that are held as prisoner for a ransom or some other demand.

A **terrorist** is somebody who uses violence to intimidate or threaten people, often for political purpose.

To **portray** something is to show it visually.

Page 494-495 "For example, one study examined California college students who lived in dormitories close to a **geological fault**."

A **geological fault** is a crack in the crust of the earth along which there is often movement of the rocks on either side.

Page 495 "Have you ever faced an **intolerable** situation that you just couldn't resolve, where you finally just gave up and accepted things the way they were?"

Intolerable is very unpleasant or annoying.

Page 495 "Most of us cope with stress in a **characteristic manner**, employing a *coping style* that represents our general tendency to deal with stress in a specific way."

A **characteristic** is a defining feature or quality that makes somebody or something recognizable.

A **manner** is the way something is done.
A **characteristic manner** is the defining way that something is done.

Page 496 "They are usually independent, and they have a sense of control over their own **destiny**—even if fate has dealt them a **devastating** blow."

Someone's **destiny** is their preordained future.

Something that is **devastating** is very upsetting and harmful.

Page 496 "For instance, such support demonstrates that a person is an important and valued member of a **social network**."

Social networks are made up of the people that we socialize with and that we can call on for support in stressful times.

The A's, B's, and D's of Coronary Heart Disease
Psychological Aspects of Cancer
Smoking

Exploring Diversity: Hucksters of Death:
Promoting Smoking Throughout the World

- *How do psychological factors affect such health-related problems as coronary heart disease, cancer, and smoking?*

Psychological Aspects of Illness and Well-Being

Two characteristic behavior patterns have been identified that are associated with coronary heart disease. **[a]** _____ is seen in individuals who are competitive, have a sense of urgency about time, are aggressive, and are driven regarding their work.

[b] _____ is seen in individuals who are less competitive, less time-oriented, and not aggressive, driven, or hostile. In an extensive study, people with Type A behavior developed heart disease twice as often as Type B individuals. One theory says that Type A individuals become excessively aroused when they are placed in stressful situations, and that this arousal increases the hormones epinephrine and norepinephrine, in turn leading to higher blood pressure and heart rate. Long-term damage then results. The evidence supporting the connection between Type A behavior and coronary heart disease is not conclusive. The data are correlational, and a clear association between Type A and heart disease has not been established for women. One new piece of evidence relating personality styles to heart problems describes the **[c]** _____ personality. People with this personality type tend to be distressed, anxious, insecure, and have negative outlooks, which puts them at risk for heart attacks.

[d] _____ is the second leading cause of death after **[e]** _____. Although its causes remain unknown, the progress of cancer is from altered cell to tumor, and the tumor robs nutrients from healthy tissue, eventually impairing normal function. Evidence is growing that the emotional response to cancer influences the disease's progress. Fighters appear more likely to recover than pessimists. Survival rates for women with breast cancer were higher among those who fought the disease or even denied it than for those who stoically accepted the illness or who accepted their fate. Evidence suggests that the patient's immune system may be affected by **[f]** _____. Positive emotional responses may help increase the natural "killer" cells. **[g]** _____ may suppress these kinds of cells. Other studies have found that positive emotional states improve longevity of cancer patients. Social support and cancer have also been linked. One study found that individuals who receive psychotherapy live longer than those who do not.

Although the link between smoking and cancer is well-established, millions of people continue to smoke. Most smokers agree that smoking damages their health, but they continue to smoke. Mostly caused by [h] _____, the habit of smoking develops through several phases, including thinking it's "cool" to it being a rite of passage:

Quitting smoking is very difficult. Only about 15 percent of those trying to stop smoking will have long-term success. Behavioral strategies for quitting view smoking as a learned habit that needs to be unlearned. Social norms will also eventually lead to reduced smoking, as smoking is banned in more and more public places and society begins to change its attitude about those who smoke. Still, more than one-quarter of the population smokes, and those who begin do so at an earlier age.

Cigarette manufacturers have turned to new markets as the number of smokers in the United States declines. The new markets include targeted campaigns toward people of Latin American countries, Hong Kong, and places such as India, Ghana, and Jamaica.

Evaluate

_____ 1. emotion-focused coping   a. The conscious regulation of emotion as a means of dealing with stress.

_____ 2. problem-focused coping

     b. Characterized by noncompetitiveness, nonaggression, and patience in times of potential stress.

_____ 3. hardiness

_____ 4. Type A behavior pattern

     c. Characterized by competitiveness, impatience, a tendency toward frustration, and hostility.

_____ 5. Type B behavior pattern

     d. Characterized by commitment, challenge, and control.

     e. The management of a stressful stimulus as a way of dealing with stress.

Rethink

46-1 Is there a danger of "blaming the victim" when we argue that the course of cancer can be improved if a person with the disease holds particular beneficial attitudes or beliefs? Why?

46-2 *From the perspective of a health care provider:* What type of advice would you give to your patients about the connections between personality and disease? For example, would you encourage Type A people to become "less Type A" in order to decrease their risk of heart disease?

Spotlight on Terminology and Language—ESL Pointers

Page 499 "They nod in **tacit understanding**, eight women sitting in a loose circle of chairs here in a small, sparely furnished room at Stanford University Medical Center."

Tacit understanding is unspoken understanding.

Page 499 "All of them have been diagnosed with **recurrent** breast cancer."

Recurrent breast cancer is breast cancer that has returned after treatment.

Page 499 "As recently as two decades ago, most psychologists and health-care providers would have **scoffed at** the notion that a discussion group could improve a cancer patient's chances of survival."

When you **scoff at** something, you make fun of it, you ridicule it.

Page 499 "How could the driver **dawdle** like that?"

To **dawdle** is to waste time.

Page 500 "Have you, like Tim, ever **seethed** impatiently at being caught behind a slow-moving vehicle, felt anger and frustration at not finding material you needed at the library, or experienced a sense of competitiveness with your classmates?"

When you **seethe** impatiently, you are furious; you are boiling with rage.

Page 500 "Many of us experience these sorts of feelings at one time or another, but for some people they represent a **pervasive**, characteristic set of personality traits known as the Type A behavior pattern."

They represent a **pervasive** or persistent, always present, personality characteristic.

Page 501 "Why is hostility so **toxic**?"

Toxic is poisonous, deadly.

Page 501 "Although a diagnosis of cancer is not as **grim** as one might at first suspect – several kinds of cancer have a high cure rate if detected early enough – cancer remains the second leading cause of death after coronary heart disease."

When something is **grim**, it's bleak and dismal.

Page 501 "For example, one experiment found that people who adopt a fighting spirit are more likely to recover than are those who **pessimistically** suffer and resign themselves to death (Pettingale et al., 1985)."

Pessimistically is gloomily, negatively.

Page 502 "Women who **stoically** accepted their fate, trying not to complain, and those who felt the situation was hopeless and that nothing could be done showed the lowest survival rates; most of those women were dead after ten years."

Someone who is **stoic** tends to remain unemotional and unaffected by emotion.

Page 503 "Would you walk into a **convenience store** and buy an item with a label warning you that its use could kill you?"

A **convenience store** is a small store that sells food and general supplies and is usually open all day and night.

Page 504 "The long-term effect of the **barrage** of information regarding the negative consequences of smoking on people's health has been substantial; overall, smoking has declined over the last two decades, particularly among males."

A **barrage** is a continuous attack that overwhelms someone or something.

Page 504 "In Dresden, Germany, three women in miniskirts offer **passersby** a pack of Lucky Strikes and a leaflet that reads: "You just got hold of a nice piece of America.""

A **passerby is** someone who happens to walk by a place.

Page 504 "At a video arcade in Taipei, free American cigarettes are **strewn** atop each game."

Things that are **strewn** are scattered.

Module 47: Promoting Health and Wellness

Following Medical Advice
Well-Being and Happiness

Applying Psychology in the 21st Century: Happy Thoughts: Thinking Positively May Help You Live Longer

- *How do our interactions with physicians affect our health and compliance with medical treatment?*

- *What leads to a sense of well-being?*

Promoting Health and Wellness

How the patient and the physician communicate can influence the effectiveness of the diagnosis and medical treatment. Many patients are reluctant to tell their physicians their symptoms. The prestige and power of the physician intimidates many patients. On the other side, physicians have difficulties getting their patients to provide the proper information. The technical nature of their questions does not mesh with the personal nature of the individual's concerns. The reluctance can prevent the health-care giver from understanding the full nature of the problem, and often the patient sees the physician as all-knowing. Patients who do not understand their treatment cannot ask questions about it. Many patients do not know how long they should take their medication, and many do not know the purpose of the drug. The use of professional jargon to communicate technical information does not help the patient understand the treatment. Sometimes medical practitioners use "baby talk" and talk down to the patient. The number of patients seen makes it difficult for many physicians to determine how much each patient can understand. Patients often construct their own theories about their illnesses that have little to do with reality. The problem can be dealt with by training patients to ask more direct questions. Physicians who are taught simple rules of courtesy, like saying hello, addressing the patient by name, and saying goodbye, are better perceived by their patients.

One major consequence of the difficulties in communication between the physician and the patient is the lack of compliance with medical advice. Noncompliance can include failing to meet appointments, not following diets, discontinuing medication, and other behaviors. Patients may practice **[a]** _____, in which they adjust their treatments themselves.

Sometimes noncompliance results from **[b]** _____, a disagreeable emotional and cognitive reaction that results from the restriction of one's freedom and can be associated with medical regimens. Compliance is linked to the degree of satisfaction a patient has with the physician. Satisfied patients tend to comply better than dissatisfied patients.

Compliance is also affected when physicians use **[c]** _____, that is, they communicate health-related information in such a way that patients come to understand that a

459

change in their behavior will lead to a gain. By contrast, **[d]** _____ suggest what patients will lose by not performing a behavior. Positively-framed messages seem most effective in creating behaviors that will lead to detecting disease, while negatively-framed messages are best for creating preventive behavior.

The vast majority of people want to be informed about the details of their illnesses. Patients prefer to be well-informed, and their degree of satisfaction is linked to how well the physician is able to convey the nature of the illness and its treatment.

A measure of how happy people are is **[e]** _____. Research demonstrates that happy people, assumedly those with a positive sense of well-being, share several characteristics. They have high self-esteem, a firm sense of control, strong optimism, and like to be around others. Fortunately, most people rate themselves at least moderately happy most of the time.

Evaluate

_____ 1. creative nonadherence

_____ 2. reactance

_____ 3. subjective well-being

_____ 4. noncompliance

_____ 5. increase of compliance

a. Negative emotional and cognitive reaction that results from the restriction of one's freedom.

b. Patient discontinues medication, misses appointments, doesn't follow treatment.

c. Occurs when patient is friendly and satisfied with a physician.

d. Patient adjusts a treatment prescribed by a physician relying on their own medical judgment.

e. People's evaluations of their lives based on thoughts and emotions.

Rethink

47-1   Do you think stress plays a role in making communication between physicians and patients difficult? Why?

47-2   _From the perspective of a health care provider:_ How would you try to better communicate with your patients? How might your techniques vary depending upon the patient's background, gender, age, and culture?

47-3   If money doesn't buy happiness, what can you do to make yourself happier? As you answer, consider the research findings on stress and coping, as well as on emotions.

Spotlight on Terminology and Language—ESL Pointers

Page 507 "Let's take a closer look at two areas they have **tackled**: producing compliance with health-related advice and identifying the determinants of well-being and happiness."

To **tackle** something is to deal with it.

Page 507 "As many as 85 percent of patients do not fully **comply with** a physician's recommendations."

To **comply with** is to obey, or to meet the terms of. Do you **comply** 100% with your instructor's recommendations for academic success?

Page 508 "I was lying on a **gurney**, trying to prepare myself for a six-hour breast-reconstruction surgery."

A **gurney** is a wheeled stretcher or bed used to carry patients in a hospital.

Page 508 "But as the surgeon diagramed **incision** points on my chest with a felt-tip pen, my husband asked a question: 'Is it really necessary to transfer this back muscle?' (Halpert, 2003, p. 63)."

Incision points are the points where the surgeon will make the cuts.

Page 508 "But after a hurried consultation with her husband, the patient **opted for** the less invasive procedure."

The patient **opted for**, or chose, this procedure.

Page 508 "Furthermore, the relatively high **prestige** of physicians may intimidate patients."

Prestige is esteem. In the American society, we give a lot of **prestige**, or esteem to persons in the medical profession. We hold these individuals in high regard.

Page 509 "Although **compliance** with medical advice does not guarantee that a patient's medical problems will go away, it does optimize the possibility that the patient's condition will improve." **Compliance** with medical advice would be fulfilling the directions for treatment as prescribed by the physician.

Page 509 "One strategy is to provide clear instructions to patients regarding drug **regimens**."

A drug **regimen** is the schedule for the medication.

Page 509 "Patients generally prefer to be well informed – even if the news is bad – and their degree of satisfaction with their medical care is **linked** to how well and how accurately physicians are able to convey the nature of their medical problems and treatments (Hall, Roter, & Katz, 1988; Haley, Clair, & Saulsberry, 1992.)"

Their satisfaction is **linked**, or connected, to the honest and accurate delivery of information.

Page 510 "The way in which a message is **framed** also can result in more positive responses to health-related information."

The way a person uses language and examples will impact the way in which a message is **framed** or stated.

Page 511 "Furthermore, life-altering events that one might expect would produce long-term **spikes** in happiness, such as winning the lottery, probably won't make you much happier than you already are, as we discuss next."

A **spike** is a sudden brief increase in something.

Page 512 "For example, when asked, "Who of the following people do you think is the happiest?" survey respondents answered "**Oprah Winfrey**" (23 percent), "**Bill Gates**" (7 percent), "the Pope" (12 percent), "**Chelsea Clinton**" (3 percent), and "yourself" (49 percent), with 6 percent saying they didn't know (Black & McCafferty, 1998)."

Oprah Winfrey is a TV talk show host. **Bill Gates** is the founder of the Microsoft company. **Chelsea Clinton** is the daughter of a former US president.

Practice Tests

Test your knowledge of the material in this set of modules by answering these questions. These questions have been placed in three Practice Tests. The first two tests consist of questions that will test your recall of factual knowledge. The third test contains questions that are challenging and primarily test for conceptual knowledge and your ability to apply that knowledge. Check your answers and review the feedback using the Answer Key in the following pages of the *Study Guide*.

PRACTICE TEST 1:

1. The system of organs and glands that forms the body's natural defense against disease is called:
   a. the limbic system.
   b. the endocrine system.
   c. the immune system.
   d. the sympathetic system.

2. Which alternative is **not** a stage of Selye's general adaptation syndrome?
   a. Resistance
   b. Challenge
   c. Alarm and mobilization
   d. Exhaustion

3. _____ is a circumstance that produces threats to people's well-being.
   a. A stressor
   b. A mobilization state
   c. A defense mechanism
   d. An inoculation

4. The alarm and mobilization stage of Selye's general adaptation syndrome is characterized by:
   a. preparing to react to the stressor.
   b. increased resistance to disease.
   c. emotional and physical collapse.
   d. becoming aware of the presence of a stressor.

5. Events that are strong stressors and that occur suddenly and affect many people simultaneously are called:
   a. cataclysmic stressors.
   b. background stressors.
   c. uplifts.
   d. personal stressors.

6. Uplifts are defined as:
   a. minor irritations of life that are encountered daily.
   b. minor positive events that make a person feel good.
   c. exhilarating experiences that leave a person in a dazed state.
   d. major positive life events.

7. High blood pressure, ulcers, or eczema are common:
   a. defense mechanism disorders.
   b. life-crisis disorders.
   c. hardiness disorders.
   d. psychophysiological disorders.

8. A person's ability to tolerate, control, or reduce threatening events is called:
   a. defense.
   b. arousal.
   c. coping.
   d. adaptation.

463

9. Michael has been classified as hardy. This means he is:
    a. unable to cope with stress at all.
    b. unlikely to develop stress-related disease.
    c. unlikely to view stress as a challenge.
    d. affected mostly by hard emotional choices.

10. Which personality type is most highly associated with heart disease, independent of other single factors?
    a. Type A   c. Hardy personality
    b. Type B   d. Cataclysmic

11. Which behavior or personality type is best described by the following traits: feeling driven, competitiveness, and hostility?
    a. Type B behavior   c. Helpless personality
    b. Hardy personality   d. Type A behavior

12. Which of the following strategies does **not** work well when trying to quit smoking?
    a. Using drugs that replace nicotine, such as the patch
    b. Developing a view of smoking as a learned habit
    c. Quitting cold-turkey
    d. Adhering to changing social attitudes and public policies toward smoking

13. Which of the following is **not** a reason for communication difficulties between doctor and patient?
    a. Physicians may ask patients questions that are highly technical.
    b. Physicians have difficulty encouraging patients to give helpful information.
    c. Physicians sometimes simplify things too much and talk down to patients.
    d. Patients have the primary responsibility for discussing their medical problems, and they are often unskilled in initiating discussions about their problems.

14. The accuracy with which physicians present information about the nature of medical problems is related to the degree of patient:
    a. suffering.   c. discontent.
    b. anxiety.   d. satisfaction.

15. What should a physician do to enhance the physician-patient relationship?
    a. Be courteous and supportive toward the patient.
    b. Use simplistic explanations.
    c. Explain the diagnosis in professional jargon.
    d. Encourage the patient to construct a personal theory to account for the reported symptoms.

_____ 16. cataclysmic events

_____ 17. personal stressors

_____ 18. background stressors

_____ 19. daily hassles

_____ 20. uplifts

a. The same as background stressors.

b. Strong stressors that occur suddenly, affecting many people at once (e.g., natural disasters).

c. Events, such as the death of a family member, that have immediate negative consequences that generally fade with time.

d. Minor positive events that make one feel good.

e. Events such as being stuck in traffic that cause minor irritations but have no long-term ill effects unless they continue or are compounded by other stressful events.

21. Commitment, control, and challenge seem to make _____ people more resistant to negative stressors.

22. The fight-or-flight response is also known as the _____ stage.

23. Several months after his wife was diagnosed with Alzheimer's disease, Sam's own body lost its ability to respond or adjust. He had reached the _____ stage of GAS.

24. Lazarus, in his research, described stressors as _____, things like lost keys, rude sales clerks, and bad hair days.

25. Calculate the degree of stress in your life using Interactivity 45-1. Interpret the results using the scoring information. What do the results say about the cause of illness and the role of stress in your health?

PRACTICE TEST 2:

1. The branch of psychology devoted to exploring psychological factors and principles in treatment, diagnosis, and prevention of physical illness is called:
   a. health psychology.
   b. physiological psychology.
   c. forensic psychology.
   d. organizational psychology.

2. _____ developed the general adaptation syndrome model.
   a. Martin Seligman
   b. Hans Selye
   c. B. F. Skinner
   d. Sigmund Freud

3. The general adaptation syndrome (Selye) states that:
   a. stress generates biological responses in animals that differ from those in humans.
   b. stressful situations produce many different responses in individuals.
   c. the same set of physiological reactions to stress occur regardless of the situation.
   d. immobilization happens when the organism confronts a stressor.

4. Myron has been coping with the death of his wife. He has been hospitalized for an acute respiratory infection, fatigue, and physical collapse. He is likely experiencing the _____ stage of the general adaptation syndrome.
   a. resistance
   b. alarm and mobilization
   c. exhaustion
   d. challenge

5. The best predictor of breast cancer victims' survival time was a factor of mental resilience and vigor, also labeled as:
   a. acceptance.
   b. hardiness.
   c. fatalism.
   d. joy.

6. Background stressors do not require much coping or response, but continued exposure to them may produce:
   a. an inability to use problem-focused techniques.
   b. as great a toll as a single, more stressful incident.
   c. as great a toll as a cataclysmic event.
   d. psychosomatic illness.

7. According to Seligman, _____ occurs when one concludes that unpleasant or annoying stimuli cannot be controlled.
   a. learned helplessness
   b. hysteria
   c. cataclysmic stress
   d. posttraumatic stress

8. What two types of strategies do people use when consciously attempting to regulate a stressful situation?
   a. Control-oriented or defensive coping strategies
   b. Emotion-focused or problem-focused coping strategies
   c. Emotional insulation or denial coping strategies
   d. Conscious or unconscious coping strategies

9. Which of the following traits is characteristic of a Type B personality?
   a. Relaxed
   b. Aggressive
   c. Scheduled
   d. Competitive

10. Frequently experiencing negative emotions has been linked to _____ and also to the _____ personality.
    a. hypertension; Type B
    b. lowered incidence of heart failure; Type A
    c. eczema; Type B
    d. coronary disease; Type A

11. Some evidence suggests that, rather than focusing on Type A behavior as the cause of heart disease, a more effective approach should concentrate on:
    a. Type A behaviors that affect the immune system.
    b. Type B behaviors that appear critical to the prevention of heart disease.
    c. Type A behaviors that can be altered instead of eliminated.
    d. Type B behaviors that work with the immune system.

12. Although about _____ of smokers agree that they would like to quit, only about _____ are able to achieve long-term successes in their efforts to stop smoking.
    a. 95 percent; 40 percent
    b. 80 percent; 30 percent
    c. 75 percent; 15 percent
    d. 30 percent; 15 percent

13. Which behavior personality type would best be described as someone who is resilient to stress and does not get stress-related diseases?
    a. Type A behavior
    b. Hardy personality
    c. Helpless personality
    d. Type B behavior

14. Patients' erroneous theories about their own illnesses:
    a. reinforce their confidence in the physician's wisdom.
    b. lead them to disobey the doctor's prescribed course of treatment.
    c. are actually correct in an amazingly large number of cases.
    d. relate closely to their improvements from prior medical treatment.

15. Which of the following is **not** likely to bring you the best possible health care?
    a. Choose physicians who communicate well.
    b. Ask questions until you fully understand your treatment.
    c. Accept some responsibility for your treatment.
    d. Do anything necessary to gain the attention of the health-care providers.

____ 16. learned helplessness   a. Preparation for stress before it is encountered.

____ 17. coping   b. The efforts to control, reduce, or learn to tolerate the threats that lead to stress.

____ 18. defense mechanisms

____ 19. social support   c. A learned belief that one has no control over the environment.

____ 20. inoculation   d. Unconscious strategies people use to reduce anxiety by concealing its source from themselves and others.

e. Knowledge of being part of a mutual network of caring, interested others.

21. The _____ is the complex of organs, glands, and cells that make up our body's natural line of defense.

22. Adjusting one's own medical treatment so that it is somewhat different from that prescribed by a physician is called _____.

23. The tendency to throw ourselves into whatever we are doing with a sense that the activity is important is called _____.

24. One characteristic of hardiness is the anticipation of change that serves as an incentive rather than a threat. This is called _____.

25. _____ is comfort provided by other humans as well as pets.

26. Smoking is a serious habit with both psychological and physiological addictions. Should smoking be banned in public places? Discuss the problems posed by such a ban and the benefits that should be expected by enforcing it.

PRACTICE TEST 3: Conceptual, Applied, and Challenging Questions

1. Which alternative about health psychology is **not** correct?
    a. Health psychology uses treatments such as prescription medications, surgery, and radiation therapy when indicated.
    b. Health psychology is concerned with changing people's habits and lifestyles to help them prevent disease.
    c. Health psychology recognizes that health is interwoven with psychological factors.
    d. Health psychology recognizes that psychological factors may affect the immune system and have beneficial or detrimental effects upon health.

2. Health psychologists take the position on the mind-brain problem that:
    a. the mind-brain problem is an eternal mystery that will never be solved.
    b. mind and brain are separate and operate independently.
    c. mind and brain are separate but work with perfect synchrony, like two clocks that are set to give synchronized time readings.
    d. mind and brain interact with each other.

3. Carlos realized that he had failed to reach his sales goals at the end of the year, so he set new goals for the following year. Carlos' behavior is typical for a person at the _____ stage of the general adaptation syndrome.
    a. resistance
    b. exhaustion
    c. alarm and mobilization
    d. repression

4. For those involved, the terrorist bombing of an office building is which type of stressor?
    a. Personal stressor
    b. Background stressor
    c. Daily hassle
    d. Cataclysmic event

5. Upon visiting the doctor's office and going through extensive testing, Michael finds out that he has a lung disease. Which type of stress is Michael likely to experience?
    a. Cataclysmic stress
    b. Personal stress
    c. Posttraumatic stress
    d. Background stress

6. A physician uses his assistants to regulate in-patients' every activity. By the end of their time in his clinic, the patients take no initiative. This demonstrates:
    a. the general adaptation syndrome.
    b. daily hassles.
    c. the inferiority complex.
    d. learned helplessness.

7. Your boss learns that he exhibits Type A behavior pattern while attending a company-sponsored stress workshop. Which alternative is correct?
    a. Nothing can be done to change your boss's Type A behavior pattern.
    b. Your boss should remember that the relationship between the Type A behavior pattern and heart attacks or development of coronary heart disease is correlational.
    c. There is little hope for your boss because the Type A behavior pattern has been found to cause heart attacks or development of heart disease.
    d. Your boss is fortunate because women with Type A behavior patterns are at greater risk.

8. In a study that placed patients with advanced breast cancer in either psychotherapy or a control that did not receive psychotherapy, what were the results?
    a. The psychotherapy group felt better, and they lived longer.
    b. The psychotherapy group felt better, but there was no impact on their survival rate.
    c. The psychotherapy group became more depressed because of their increased awareness of the cancer, but they also lived longer.
    d. The study proved that psychotherapy increased the survival rate of cancer patients.

9. Aunt Nina, who is 87 years old, is in the hospital for minor surgery. However, because she is older, she realizes that even minor surgery can be risky. Her surgeon, apparently trying to calm her fears, says "We'll just pop right in there and sneak back out." The problem with his comments appears to be quite common in that:
    a. they treat Nina as if she were either a child or senile.
    b. they don't go far enough in minimizing the risk factors.
    c. when spoken to in this manner, patients get an exaggerated sense of the surgeon's ability.
    d. they reflect techniques taught in medical school.

10. Kiesha, who is 35 years old, has been smoking for 15 years. She knows it is extremely unhealthy for her and wants to stop but is having difficulty doing so. What may prove to be the most effective means to help Kiesha to stop smoking?
    a. The "cold-turkey" method
    b. Banning smoking in all public places
    c. Behavior strategies that concentrate on changing the smoking response
    d. Changing societal norms and attitudes about smoking

11. The malfunction of the Three Mile Island plant in the early 1980s exposed people to a potential nuclear meltdown. This produced emotional, behavioral, and psychological consequences that lasted more than a year. This would be considered a(n):
    a. cataclysmic event.   c. uplift.
    b. background stressor.   d. personal stressor.

12. A patient decides that she will do better by maintaining her exercise and taking the rest of some medication she had been given earlier instead of carefully following the prescribed regimen of rest and antibiotics for an infection. This is an example of:
    a. reactance.   c. preventive medicine.
    b. Type A behavior.   d. creative nonadherence.

13. In a group therapy session with alcoholics, the counselor describes the range of personal issues that are aggravated by alcohol; this approach is meant to promote:
    a. hardiness.   c. learned helplessness.
    b. problem-focused coping.   d. stress inoculation.

14. Whenever Pablo measures his blood pressure at the drug store, where they have free blood-pressure checks, his pressure is always in the normal range. However, whenever he goes to his physician, he gets nervous and anxious, and his blood pressure usually measures in the high range. This could best be explained by:
    a. reactance.   c. Type B behavior.
    b. Type A behavior.   d. creative nonadherence.

15. Social support is an effective means of coping with all of the following types of stress. However, based on the descriptions in the text, in which one of the following is social support most likely to occur as a matter of the nature of the stressor?
    a. Personal stressors
    b. Events leading to posttraumatic stress disorder
    c. Cataclysmic events
    d. Uplifts

_____ 16. general adaptation syndrome (GAS)   a. When patients modify a physician's treatment.

_____ 17. posttraumatic stress disorder (PTSD)   b. A set of symptoms that occurs after disturbing events: trouble concentrating, anxiety, guilt, and sleep difficulties.

_____ 18. creative nonadherence

_____ 19. reactance   c. Typical series of responses to stressful situations that includes alarm, resistance, and exhaustion.

     d. A negative emotional and cognitive reaction to a restriction of one's freedom.

20.   Most people _____ agree with the statement, "Cigarette smoking frequently causes disease and death."

21.   People smoke in an effort to regulate both emotional states and _____ in the blood.

22.   Research on well-being shows that happy people have high _____.

23.   _____ helps individuals to persevere at tasks and ultimately to achieve more.

24.   One explanation for the stability of subjective well-being is that people may have a general _____ for happiness.

25.   Define the personality characteristic of hardiness. Discuss how parents can encourage the development of hardiness in their children.

Module 45:	[p] learned	Module 46:	Module 47:
[a] Health psychology	helplessness	[a] Type A behavior	[a] creative nonadherence
[b] immune system	[q] coping	pattern	[b] reactance
[c] Psychoneuroimmunology	[r] defense	[b] Type B behavior	[c] positively-framed
[d] stress	mechanisms	pattern	messages
[e] cataclysmic events	[s] Emotional	[c] Type D	[d] negatively-framed
[f] personal stressors	insulation	[d] cancer	messages
[g] posttraumatic stress	[t] emotion-focused	[e] coronary heart	[e] subjective well-being
disorder, or PTSD	coping	disease	
[h] background stressors	[u] problem-focused	[f] emotional state	Evaluate
[i] daily hassles	coping	[g] Negative response	1. d
[j] uplifts	[v] Hardiness	[h] environmental	2. a
[k] psychophysiological	[w] social support	factors	3. e
disorders			4. b
[l] general adaptation		Evaluate	5. c
syndrome (GAS)	Evaluate	1. a	
[m] alarm and mobilization	1. e	2. e	
stage	2. a	3. d	
[n] resistance stage	3. d	4. c	
[o] exhaustion stage	4. b	5. b	
	5. c		

Selected Rethink Answers

45-1   Cataclysmic stressors are strong stressors that occur suddenly and affect many people. They produce less stress in the long run because they have a clear resolution. Social support, the sharing of the event with others, helps reduce stress because there are others who know how you are feeling.

46-1   Yes, there is definitely a danger of blaming the victim. The research regarding how cancer progresses only says that a patient's emotional response and coping styles can impact the course of the disease, not that it definitely will have an impact. As with most research in psychology, there is only evidence for an "average" positive effect, but the case for any one individual may be good or bad (that's how we get an average). So, if any one person doesn't have a good outcome, even with a positive emotional style and good coping strategies, he or she should not be blamed.

47-1   Stress has a number of psychological effects. Among them are causing difficulty concentrating and creating unrealistic views of the environment (e.g., a person views things in a somewhat distorted way). Both of these outcomes could make it difficult for patients and physicians to communicate. Physicians, who are under time and workload pressure may not be able to effectively concentrate on developing a caring, thoughtful interaction with a patient. Patients, who may be under the stress of hearing about a disease they have developed, or may be under other work or family-related stress, may hear the diagnosis and treatment information in a distorted, unrealistic way.

Practice Test 1:
1.   c   mod. 45 p. 498
a.   Incorrect. The limbic system is part of the brain.
b.   Incorrect. The endocrine system is the system of hormone-secreting organs, and it is part of the larger system that defends against disease.
*c. Correct. The immune system includes the endocrine system, the sympathetic system, and parts of the limbic system, as well as other organs.

d.   Incorrect. The sympathetic system is part of the nervous system, and it is part of the larger immune system.

2. b   mod. 45 p. 501
a. Incorrect. See answer b.
*b. Correct. The stages of Selye's general adaptation syndrome are alarm and mobilization, resistance, and exhaustion.
c. Incorrect. See answer b.
d. Incorrect. See answer b.

3. a   mod. 45 p. 499
*a. Correct. Stressors present threats or challenges to a person and require some type of adaptive response.
b. Incorrect. A mobilization state is not a threat to a person's well-being.
c. Incorrect. A defense mechanism is used by the ego to protect against unconscious conflict.
d. Incorrect. An inoculation is a medical intervention that builds the immune system response.

4. d   mod. 45 p. 501
a. Incorrect. The stage is part of the reaction to a stressor, not just a preparation to react.
b. Incorrect. Increased resistance to the stressor occurs in the next stage, during which the ability to resist disease declines.
c. Incorrect. This describes the final stage of the general adaptation syndrome.
*d. Correct. The "alarm" involves the psychological awareness of the stressor.

5. a   mod. 45 p. 503
*a. Correct. Cataclysmic stressors include man-made and natural disasters, like earthquakes and terrorist attacks.
b. Incorrect. Background stressors are the ongoing demands made on the individual all the time.
c. Incorrect. Uplifts are the positive challenges that contribute to a sense of accomplishment or completion.
d. Incorrect. Personal stressors are the demands that are unique to the person and typically not shared with others (like being fired from a job).

6. b   mod. 45 p. 505
a. Incorrect. These are described as hassles.
*b. Correct. These minor positive events may be just as demanding and stressful on the individual as are hassles, but they leave the person feeling good rather than drained.
c. Incorrect. Uplifts, by definition, would not be exhilarating.
d. Incorrect. Uplifts, by definition, would not be major.

7. d   mod. 45 p. 500
a. Incorrect. These disorders can appear as a result of the extended operation of the resistance phase of the GAS and are sometimes called disorders of defense (but not of the psychodynamic ego defense mechanisms).
b. Incorrect. These do not immediately threaten life.
c. Incorrect. Hardy people appear to have fewer of these disorders than the less hardy.
*d. Correct. These disorders often have psychological origins in stress and are thus considered psychophysiological.

8. c   mod. 45 p. 507
a. Incorrect. In the psychoanalytic view, "defense" would apply to unconscious events that threaten the ego.
b. Incorrect. Arousal is not the appropriate adjective.
*c. Correct. "Coping" is used to describe the ability to deal with stress and the techniques used.
d. Incorrect. However, coping is a form of adaptation.

9. b   mod. 45 p. 508
a. Incorrect. Hardy individuals are quite capable of coping with stress.
*b. Correct. The hardy individual is resilient to stress and does not get stress-related diseases.
c. Incorrect. The hardy individual does recognize the challenge of stress.
d. Incorrect. Everyone is affected in some way by emotional choices, especially if they are difficult.

10. a   mod. 46 p. 512
*a. Correct. Type A behavior pattern is most associated with heart disease.
b. Incorrect. Type A, not Type B, is most associated with heart disease.
c. Incorrect. The hardy personality is actually more resistant to stress-related heart disease.
d. Incorrect. There is no personality type known as cataclysmic (although you may know someone who would fit such a description).

11. d   mod. 46 p. 511
a. Incorrect. Type B behavior is not related to these.
b. Incorrect. The hardy individual is resistant to stress-related diseases.
c. Incorrect. A helpless person would not be competitive or driven to succeed.
*d. Correct. These traits describe the Type A behavior pattern.

12. c   mod. 46 p. 515
a.   Incorrect. These kinds of drugs, many of which can be obtained over-the-counter, are highly effective.
b.   Incorrect. Behavioral strategies are also effective, with an initial "cure" rate of 60 percent.
*c. Correct. This is the least effective approach, particularly when you "go at it alone."
d.   Incorrect. Social norms and policies are powerful influences on behavior.

13. b   mod. 47 p. 520
a.   Incorrect. Physicians apparently have difficulty asking questions in such a way that the patient can answer them with information that is useful.
*b. Correct. Patients often begin the discussion, and when they do take responsibility, communication with the physician often improves.
c.   Incorrect. A common response with the elderly is to act as if they are children and condescend to them.
d.   Incorrect. Physicians often ask questions that patients have difficulty understanding, or they understand them in other ways.

14. d   mod. 47 p. 520
a.   Incorrect. Suffering results from the disease.
b.   Incorrect. See answer d.
c.   Incorrect. See answer d.
d.   Correct. The accuracy of the communication seems to improve the patient's satisfaction with treatment and lessens anxiety about the disease and discontent with the physician.

15. a   mod. 47 p. 522
*a. Correct. Simple courtesy goes a long way.
b.   Incorrect. Simplistic answers and explanations make understanding the problem more difficult.
c.   Incorrect. Professional jargon is the greatest barrier to improved communication.
d.   Incorrect. Patients will do this if the explanation they receive is not well understood.

16. b   mod. 45 p. 503
17. c   mod. 45 p. 504
18. e   mod. 45 p. 504
19. a   mod. 45 p. 504
20. d   mod. 45 p. 505

21. hardy   mod. 45 p. 510
22. Alarm and mobilization   mod. 45 p. 502
23. resistance   mod. 45 p. 502
24. Hassles   mod. 45 p. 506

25.
▪   Tabulate your stress score using Table 15-1.
▪   Determine whether you are at risk or normal. Do the events that contribute to your score seem part of the normal course of life, or have you experienced an unusual number of stressful things recently?
▪   Identify any recent illnesses that would have been influenced by the stress.

Practice Test 2:
1.   a   mod. 45 p. 498
*a. Correct. Health psychology includes all of the psychological aspects of health.
b.   Incorrect. Physiological psychology is focused on the various psychological aspects of our biological organism.
c.   Incorrect. Forensic psychology is the use of psychology in the legal system.
d.   Incorrect. Organizational psychology attends to the study of behavior in organizations.

2.   b   mod. 45 p. 501
a.   Incorrect. Seligman is responsible for the concept of learned helplessness.
*b. Correct. A Canadian physician, Hans Selye, proposed and researched this universal pattern of stress reaction.
c.   Incorrect. Skinner is responsible for operant conditioning.
d.   Incorrect. Freud developed psychoanalytic theory.

3.   c   mod. 45 p. 501
a.   Incorrect. See answer c.
b.   Incorrect. The psychological responses vary considerably, but the physiological responses differ only by degree.
*c. Correct. Selye believed and demonstrated through his research that the physiological stress response pattern was pretty much universal.
d.   Incorrect. This happens rarely and with extreme stressors.

4.   c   mod. 45 p. 501
a.   Incorrect. This is the middle stage, during which the individual puts up a fight.
b.   Incorrect. This is the earliest stage of initial response, and it does not have these symptoms.
*c. Correct. The conditions described suggest that the man has reached the final stage of the GAS.
d.   Incorrect. There is no "challenge" stage.

5.   d   mod. 46 p. 514

a. Incorrect. Acceptance does not have an influence on survival of cancer.
b. Incorrect. Hardiness does not have an influence on survival of cancer.
c. Incorrect. Fatalism has a negative impact on survival of cancer.
*d. Correct. Researchers defined this as joy, and it was correlated to higher survival rates.

6. b   mod. 45 p. 504
a. Incorrect. This ability depends on factors other than the presence of background stressors.
*b. Correct. The effect of background stress, and any stress, can accumulate, with the sum of many small stressors having the same effect as one large one.
c. Incorrect. This would be difficult to judge.
d. Incorrect. Background stressors would be unlikely to cause a psychosomatic illness.

7. a   mod. 45 p. 506
*a. Correct. Seligman applied this term to the perception that a situation was beyond the individual's control.
b. Incorrect. Hysteria refers to a psychological disorder treated by Freud.
c. Incorrect. Cataclysmic stress refers to major stressful events that affect many people.
d. Incorrect. Posttraumatic stress disorder refers to the long-term effects of highly stressful events.

8. b   mod. 45 p. 507
a. Incorrect. See answer b.
*b. Correct. The two types are emotion-focused and problem-focused coping. Emotion-focused coping is used more in situations in which circumstances appear unchangeable.
c. Incorrect. See answer b.
d. Incorrect. See answer b.

9. a   mod. 46 p. 512
*a. Correct. Of the traits given, relaxed best fits the Type B personality. Aggressive, scheduled, and competitive are Type A characteristics.
b. Incorrect. See answer a.
c. Incorrect. See answer a.
d. Incorrect. See answer a.

10. d   mod. 46 p. 513
a. Incorrect. Type B personalities tend to have less hypertension than Type A.
b. Incorrect. This may be true only of second heart attacks.
c. Incorrect. Eczema is not associated with Type A or B patterns.

*d. Correct. The Type A behavior that correlates most with CHD is negative emotions.

11. b   mod. 46 p. 513
a. Incorrect. It appears that all Type A behaviors have an effect on the immune system.
*b. Correct. Those Type B behaviors that are associated with healthy results can be taught to the Type A person.
c. Incorrect. This approach has not been successful.
d. Incorrect. Rather than those that work with the immune system (if they can be isolated), the approach has been to focus on those that are successful with heart conditions.

12. c   mod. 46 p. 515
a. Incorrect. See answer c.
b. Incorrect. See answer c.
*c. Correct. Smoking is one of the most difficult habits to break.
d. Incorrect. See answer c.

13. b   mod. 47 p. 508
a. Incorrect. The need for achievement, competitiveness, and commitment sometimes leads to illness.
*b. Correct. The hardy individual is less affected by stress.
c. Incorrect. An individual would not be competitive or driven but not protected from illness, still affected by stress.
d. Incorrect. The person who is not competitive or driven may be less likely to get illness than a Type A person.

14. b   mod. 47 p. 519
a. Incorrect. They probably did not receive any of their physician's wisdom.
*b. Correct. They become their own physicians and change their regime of treatment.
c. Incorrect. Simply not true.
d. Incorrect. Perhaps one accidental correct guess may lead them to think they know better.

15. d   mod. 47 p. 519
a. Incorrect. Better communication reduces anxiety and improves recovery after surgery.
b. Incorrect. Never give up, these answers make a difference in your health.
c. Incorrect. The more responsibility you accept, they better your chances of recovery.
*d. Correct. This may result in some detrimental effects, including being ignored when a true emergency occurs.

16. c   mod. 45 p. 506

17. b   mod. 45 p. 507
18. d   mod. 45 p. 507
19. e   mod. 45 p. 509
20. a   mod. 45 p. 507

21. immune system   mod. 45 p. 502
22. creative nonadherence   mod. 45 p. 508
23. commitment   mod. 45 p. 508
24. challenge   mod. 45 p. 508
25. Social support   mod. 45 p. 509

26.
- Identify whether you believe that public places should ban smoking.
- Under which conditions should a person be allowed or not allowed to smoke in public?
- Describe the difficulties and problems that would be involved with enforcing a complete ban.

Practice Test 3:
1. a   mod. 45 p. 498
*a. Correct. Health psychology may promote the effective use of medical treatments, but it is not involved in using the treatments.
b. Incorrect. Health psychology can contribute to changing habits by implementing behavior modification strategies, among other strategies.
c. Incorrect. Some health psychologists have taken a holistic view of mind and body, suggesting that the two are inseparable.
d. Incorrect. The role of the immune system and the way psychological factors can affect it is a major interest for health psychology.

2. d   mod. 45 p. 500
a. Incorrect. The mind-brain problem is a mystery created by modern philosophy.
b. Incorrect. True only among philosophers.
c. Incorrect. This is a view reminiscent of the philosopher Leibniz.
*d. Correct. Without this basic assumption, attention to the physical health of the brain as an organ (and the rest of the body as well) would have no impact on the mind.

3. c   mod. 45 p. 501
a. Incorrect. This is a new stress, so Carlos is probably at the alarm and mobilization stage.
b. Incorrect. Exhaustion would only appear in this circumstance after many years of failing to meet goals.
*c. Correct. Because this is a new recognition, Carlos has mobilized his energies and already begun to cope with the stress of not meeting this year's goals.

d. Incorrect. In repression, Carlos would probably ignore his failure to meet this year's goals and make no effort to compensate for next year.

4. d   mod. 45 p. 503
a. Incorrect. Personal stressors are major life events like marriage or death.
b. Incorrect. Background stressors include everyday annoyances like traffic.
c. Incorrect. Daily hassles are also known as background stressors, and they include everyday annoyances like traffic.
*d. Correct. The traumatic experience would be classed as cataclysmic.

5. b   mod. 45 p. 504
a. Incorrect. Cataclysmic stress involves many people, such as during war, earthquakes, and terrorist attacks.
*b. Correct. This is considered a major personal stressor.
c. Incorrect. Posttraumatic stress disorder actually follows a significant period of traumatic stress.
d. Incorrect. Background stress includes the many small and insignificant worries and challenges one faces each day.

6. d   mod. 45 p. 506
a. Incorrect. This does not illustrate the GAS.
b. Incorrect. Daily hassles will not account for their not taking any initiative.
c. Incorrect. If they come to believe that they are inferior, then the answer would be "d" anyway.
*d. Correct. They have learned that they are totally under the control of the assistant coaches, thus helpless.

7. b   mod. 46 p. 513
a. Incorrect. Certainly, he can change a number of his behavior patterns or he can take measures to improve his health practices.
*b. Correct. The correlation does not mean that he will definitely develop coronary heart disease.
c. Incorrect. With precautions, he will have just as good an outlook as anyone else.
d. Incorrect. Women are not at greater risk with these patterns.

8. a   mod. 46 p. 514
*a. Correct. They had a more positive outlook, and in early studies, they extended their lives significantly.
b. Incorrect. There apparently was a link between how they felt and their survival rate.
c. Incorrect. They were less depressed.
d. Incorrect. The study did not prove the relationship; it only suggested that more study was necessary.

9. a   mod. 47 p. 520-521
*a. Correct. This condescending approach is extremely common among physicians.
b. Incorrect. They go too far in minimizing the risks involved.
c. Incorrect. If they are not entirely put off, patients may develop expectations of success that are not realistic.
d. Incorrect. They reflect that for many physicians, techniques for communicating with patients have not been taught at all.

10. c   mod. 46 p. 516
a. Incorrect. The cold-turkey method is effective in only a few cases.
b. Incorrect. Banning smoking in public places helps nonsmokers, but it does not help smokers.
*c. Correct. Behavior strategies have proven to be the most effective, but they still require perseverance.
d. Incorrect. This will help others avoid starting the habit, but it will not help Kiesha.

11. d   mod. 45 p. 504
a. Incorrect. Although they occur suddenly and affect many people, they usually have a clear resolution.
b. Incorrect. Minor irritations that are sometimes called daily hassles. Require little coping.
c. Incorrect. Positive events that make one feel good.
*d. Correct. Major life events where the effects produce an immediate major reaction but that can sometimes linger for long periods.

12. d   mod. 47 p. 519
a. Incorrect. Reactance is the disagreeable emotional and cognitive reaction to being restricted to a medical regimen.
b. Incorrect. Type A behavior does not predict compliance to medical prescriptions.
c. Incorrect. It may prevent physicians from losing their jobs because she will probably have to visit them again.

*d. Correct. The term for her actions is creative nonadherence.

13. b   mod. 45 p. 507
a. Incorrect. Hardiness may be improved by shifting to a problem-focused coping approach.
*b. Correct. Attention to problems that can be addressed and resolved.
c. Incorrect. Therapists should not promote learned helplessness.
d. Incorrect. Stress inoculation would focus more on what is about to happen, not what has already surfaced.

14. a   mod. 47 p. 519
*a. Correct. Reactance is the disagreeable emotional and cognitive reaction to being restricted to a medical regimen, and it can cause higher reading on blood pressure because of increased anxiety about the physician.
b. Incorrect. Reactance is independent of Type A or Type B behavior.
c. Incorrect. Reactance is independent of Type A or Type B behavior.
d. Incorrect. Creative nonadherence occurs when a patient creates his or her own course of treatment, often ignoring the prescribed treatment.

15. c   mod. 45 p. 503
a. Incorrect. Personal stressors are not shared unless someone seeks out support.
b. Incorrect. One element of posttraumatic stress disorder is the failure of the support systems in the first place.
*c. Correct. Because many others have just experienced the same major stressor, the social support group is already defined.
d. Incorrect. Uplifts are personal background stressors that result in the person feeling good.

16. c   mod. 45 p. 501
17. b   mod. 45 p. 504
18. a   mod. 45 p. 519
19. d   mod. 47 p. 519

20. do   mod. 46 p. 515
21. nicotine levels mod. 46 p. 515
22. self-esteem   mod. 47 p. 523
23. Optimism   mod. 45 p. 508
24. set point   mod. 47 p. 523

25.

- Hardiness is the coping style whose characteristics are associated with a lower rate of stress-related illness.

- Parents can encourage their children to be optimistic, to commit themselves to activities that are important and meaningful to them.
- Children should understand that change rather than stability is the standard condition of life.
- Parents can allow children a sense of control over the events in their lives.

Chapter 15: Psychological Disorders

Module 48: Normal Versus Abnormal: Making the Distinction
Module 49: The Major Psychological Disorders
Module 50: Psychological Disorders in Perspective

Overview

In this set of modules, you see that abnormality is difficult to define, and it is best to consider behavior as on a continuum from normal to abnormal.

Module 48 presents the contemporary perspectives that attempt to explain abnormal behavior. They are the medical perspective, the psychoanalytical perspective, the behavioral perspective, the cognitive perspective, the humanistic perspective, and the sociocultural perspective. The system used by most professionals to classify mental disorders is the *DSM-IV-TR*.

Module 49 helps us identify the anxiety disorders, the somatoform disorders, and the dissociative disorders. Also included in this module are discussions on mood disorders and one of the most severe mental illnesses, schizophrenia. The personality disorders, those that cause little or no personal distress but do present difficulty in trying to function as a normal member of society, are also discussed. These include antisocial personality disorder, borderline personality disorder, and the narcissistic personality. This module finishes with a presentation of the major childhood disorders with a focus on attention-deficit hyperactivity disorder.

Module 50 explains that about half the people in the United States are likely to experience a disorder at some time in their lives. It is important to keep in mind that disorders develop within a social and cultural context, so that incidence rates and symptoms vary across cultures and eras. The signals that indicate a need for professional help are discussed. These include long-term feelings of psychological distress, inability to cope, prolonged depression or hopelessness, phobias, compulsions, and the inability to interact with others.

To further investigate the topics covered in this chapter, you can visit the related Web sites by visiting the following link: www.mhhe.com/feldmanup8.

Prologue: Chamique Holdsclaw
Looking Ahead

Module 48: Normal Versus Abnormal: Making the Distinction

Defining Abnormality

Applying Psychology in the 21st Century:
Terrorist Suicide Bombers: Normal or Abnormal?

Perspectives on Abnormality: From Superstition to Science
Classifying Abnormal Behavior: The ABCs of *DSM*

- *How can we distinguish normal from abnormal behavior?*
- *What are the major perspectives on psychological disorders used by mental health professionals?*
- *What classification system is used to categorize psychological disorders?*

Normal Versus Abnormal: Making the Distinction

A passage from James Joyce's *Ulysses* suggests that madness cannot be determined by a small sample of a person's behavior. The text examines the following approaches to the definition of abnormal behavior:

- *Abnormality as deviation from the average.* This definition uses the statistical definition of behavior to define "abnormal" as behavior that is statistically unusual or rare. The problem with this approach is that simply being unusual or rare does not define abnormal: Individuals with high IQs are rare, but they are not considered abnormal.
- *Abnormality as deviation from the ideal.* This definition classifies behavior as abnormal if it deviates from the ideal or standard behavior. However, society has very few standards on which everyone agrees.
- *Abnormality as a sense of personal discomfort.* This approach focuses on the consequences of behavior that make a person feel discomfort. However, some people who engage in what others would consider abnormal behavior do not experience discomfort.
- *Abnormality as the inability to function effectively.* People who are unable to adjust to the demands of society and unable to function in daily life are considered abnormal in this view. An unemployed homeless woman would be classified as abnormal in this view even if the choice to live on the streets were her own.
- *Abnormality as a legal concept.* The legal system uses the concept of insanity to distinguish normal from abnormal behavior. Insanity refers generally to whether the defendant could understand the difference between right and wrong when the act was committed. The precise definition and how it is used varies from one jurisdiction to another.

None of the five approaches is broad enough to include all possibilities of abnormal behavior, and the line between normal and abnormal remains unclear. The best way to solve the problem is to consider normal and abnormal as on a continuum, or scale, of behavior rather than to consider them to be absolute states. In the past, abnormal behavior has been attributed to superstition, witchcraft, or demonic possession. The contemporary approach includes six major perspectives on abnormal behavior:

- The **[a]** _____ of abnormality views the cause of abnormal behavior to have a physical origin such as a hormone or chemical imbalance or a physical injury.

- The **[b]** _____ of abnormality maintains that abnormal behavior comes from childhood. The conflicts of childhood that remain unresolved can cause abnormal behavior in adulthood.

- The **[c]** _____ of abnormality views the behavior as the problem, understanding that behavior is a response to stimuli that one finds in one's environment.

- The **[d]** _____ of abnormality assumes that *cognitions* are central to a person's abnormal behavior, which can then be changed by learning new and more adaptive ways of thinking.

- The **[e]** _____ of abnormality emphasizes the control and responsibility people have for their own behavior. This model considers people to be basically rational, oriented to the social world, and motivated to get along with others.

- The **[f]** _____ of abnormality assumes that behavior is shaped by the family group, society, and culture. The stresses and conflicts people experience promote and maintain abnormal behavior.

One standard classification system has been accepted by most professionals for classifying mental disorders. Devised by the American Psychiatric Association, the system is known as the

[g] _____. The manual has more than 200 diagnostic categories. It evaluates behavior according to five dimensions called *axes*. The first three axes address the primary disorder exhibited, the nature of any personality disorders or developmental problems, and any physical disorders. The fourth and fifth axes address the severity of stressors and the general level of functioning. The *DSM-IV-TR* attempts to be descriptive and to avoid suggestions of cause. The objective is to provide precise description and classification.

Criticisms include the fact that it reflects categories that assume a physiological view of causes (arising from the fact that it was developed by psychiatrists, who, as physicians, tend to follow a medical model) and that the categories are inflexible. In other views, the labeling of an individual as deviant is seen as a lifelong, dehumanizing stigma. A classic study by Rosenhan illustrated how the stigma of being labeled mentally ill can linger. Eight people, including Rosenhan, presented themselves to mental hospitals complaining of only one symptom, hearing voices. Although they did not complain of the symptom again, they stayed for an average of 19 days and were released with labels like "schizophrenia in remission." None of the impostors was detected by the staff. Despite its drawbacks, the *DSM-IV-TR* does provide a reliable and valid way to classify psychological disorders.

Evaluate

_____ 1. medical perspective

_____ 2. psychoanalytic perspective

_____ 3. behavioral perspective

_____ 4. cognitive perspective

_____ 5. humanistic perspective

_____ 6. sociocultural perspective

a. Suggests that abnormality stems from childhood conflicts over opposing desires regarding sex and aggression.

b. Suggests that people's behavior, both normal and abnormal, is shaped by family, society, and cultural influences.

c. Suggests that people's thoughts and beliefs are a central component to abnormal behavior.

d. Suggests that when an individual displays symptoms of abnormal behavior, the cause is physiological.

e. Suggests that abnormal behavior is the problem to be treated, rather than viewing behavior as a symptom of some underlying medical or psychological problem.

f. Suggests that abnormal behavior results from an inability to fulfill human needs and capabilities.

Rethink

48-1 Do you agree or disagree that the *DSM* should be updated every several years? What makes abnormal behavior so variable? Why can't there be one definition of abnormal behavior?

48-2 *From the perspective of an employer:* Imagine that a well-paid employee was arrested for shoplifting a $15 sweater. What sort of explanation for this behavior would be provided by the proponents of each perspective on abnormality: the medical perspective, psychoanalytic perspective, behavioral perspective, cognitive perspective, humanistic perspective, and sociocultural perspective? Based on the potential causes of the shoplifing, would you fire the employee? Why or why not?

Spotlight on Terminology and Language—ESL Pointers

Page 516 "We begin by discussing the difference between normal and abnormal behavior, which can be surprisingly **fuzzy**."

Something that is **fuzzy** is blurred and not clear enough to be understood.

Page 517 "Universally that person's **acumen** is esteemed very little perceptive concerning whatsoever matters are being held as most profitable by mortals with **sapience** endowed to be studied who is ignorant of that which the most in doctrine **erudite** and certainly by reason of that in them high mind's ornament deserving of **veneration** constantly maintain when by general consent they affirm that other circumstances being equal by no exterior **splendour** is the prosperity of a nation..."

Acumen is insight or the ability to make quick accurate judgments.

Sapience means full of wisdom.

Erudite means very knowledgeable through study.

Veneration is a feeling of respect for someone or something.

Splendour is the condition of being brilliant or impressive.

Page 517 "It would be easy to conclude that these are the **musings** of a madman."

Musings are thoughts about something.

Page 517 "Actually this passage is from James Joyce's classic Ulysses, **hailed** as one of the major works of twentieth-century literature (Joyce, 1934, p. 377)."

Hailed is acclaimed and praised. This is one of the premier works of the twentieth-century.

Page 517 "To employ this statistically based approach, we simply observe what behaviors are rare or occur infrequently in a particular society or culture and label those **deviations** from the norm 'abnormal.'"

Deviation is a departure from the norm.

Page 517 "Similarly, such a concept of abnormality unreasonably labels a person who has an unusually high IQ as abnormal, simply because a high IQ is **statistically rare**."

Statistically rare would be unlikely, uncommon.

Page 518 "The definition of insanity varies from one **jurisdiction** to another."

Jurisdiction is the limits, or boundaries within which authority exists.

Page 518 "Behavior should be evaluated in terms of **gradations,** ranging from completely normal functioning to extremely abnormal behavior."

Gradations are steps, or stages of an activity.
They are a series of gradual, successive stages.

Page 519"What kinds of people are willing to strap explosives to their bodies and blow themselves—and as many others as possible—to **smithereens**?"

Smithereens are very small broken pieces of something.

Page 519 "However, although terrorist leaders **orchestrate** strategy, suicide bombers are not focused only on political objectives; they are also motivated by commitment to a particular group or cause."

To **orchestrate** something is to organize a situation.

Page 519 "Contemporary approaches take a more **enlightened** view."

These approaches take a more progressive, or tolerant view. An **enlightened** view uses knowledge based on theoretical perspectives to understand psychological disorders.

Page 520 "Whereas the medical perspective suggests that biological causes are at the **root of** abnormal behavior, the psychoanalytic perspective hold that abnormal behavior stems from childhood conflicts over opposing wishes regarding sex and aggression."

At the **root of**, means the cause or origin of something.

Page 520 "To understand the roots of people's disordered behavior, the psychoanalytic perspective **scrutinizes** their early life history."

The psychoanalysts pore over, analyzing and **scrutinizing** the details of their childhood experiences. When you scrutinize something, you inspect and observe it carefully and critically.

Page 521 "For instance, suppose a student forms the **erroneous** belief that 'doing well on this exam is crucial to my entire future' whenever he or she takes an exam."

Erroneous is mistaken, wrong. Sometimes our cognitive thoughts are based on unrealistic or **erroneous** thinking.

Page 521 "Psychologists who **subscribe to** the humanistic perspective emphasize the responsibility people have for their own behavior, even when such behavior is seen as abnormal."

Subscribe to means to support something. These psychologists ascribe to, or support the humanistic perspective.

Page 522 "For instance, diagnoses of **schizophrenia** tend to be higher among members of lower socioeconomic groups than among members of more affluent groups."

Schizophrenia is a psychiatric disorder in which the patient shows symptoms of emotional instability and detachment from reality.

Page 524 "**Conning** the Classifiers: The Shortcomings of DSM-IV-TR. "

When we **con** someone we trick them.

Page 524 "In short, each of the **pseudo-patients** acted in a "normal" way (Rosenhan, 1973)."

Pseudo-patients are people that look and act like real patients but are not real patients.
Page 524 "For instance, some critics argue that labeling an individual as abnormal provides a dehumanizing, lifelong **stigma**."

A **stigma** is the mark of shame or dishonor that results when someone does something that is socially unacceptable.

Module 49: The Major Psychological Disorders

Anxiety Disorders
Somatoform Disorders
Dissociative Disorders
Mood Disorders
Schizophrenia
Personality Disorders
Childhood Disorders
Other Disorders

- ***What are the major psychological disorders?***

The Major Psychological Disorders

Everyone experiences *anxiety,* a feeling of apprehension or tension, at some time. When anxiety occurs without external reason and interferes with daily functioning, the problem is known as

anxiety. [a] _____ refers to the disorder in which an individual experiences long-term consistent anxiety without knowing why. The anxiety makes the person unable to

concentrate, and life becomes centered on the anxiety. [b] _____ is distinguished by attacks that may last a few seconds or several hours. In a panic attack, the individual feels anxiety rise to a peak and gets a sense of impending doom. Physical symptoms of increased heart rate, shortness of breath, sweating, faintness, and dizziness may be experienced.

[c] _____ has as its primary symptom a(n) [d] _____, an irrational fear of specific objects or situations. Exposure to the stimulus may cause a full-blown panic attack. (A list of several types of phobias is given in Figure 1 of this chapter.) Phobias may be minor, or they may cause extreme suffering.

[e] _____ is characterized by unwanted thoughts and the impulse to carry out a certain action. [f] _____ are thoughts or ideas that keep recurring. Although everyone has some, when they continue for days and months and include bizarre images, they make it

difficult for the individual to function. [g] _____ are urges to repeat behaviors that seem strange and unreasonable even to the person who feels compelled to act. If they cannot carry out the action, extreme anxiety can be experienced. The cleaning ritual described in the text is a good example of a compulsion. Carrying out the action usually does not reduce the anxiety.

The causes of anxiety disorders are not fully understood. A tendency for both identical twins to have an anxiety disorder if one of them has the disorder suggests that there may be a biological cause. Some chemical deficiencies in the brain have also been linked to the disorder, as well as an overactive autonomic nervous system.

The behavioral approach suggests that anxiety is a learned response to stress and that the anxiety is reinforced by subsequent encounters with the stressor. The cognitive approach suggests that anxiety grows out of inappropriate and inaccurate cognitions.

[h]_____ involves a constant fear of illness, and physical sensations are misinterpreted as disease symptoms. The symptoms are not faked—hypochondriacs actually experience the symptoms. Hypochondriasis belongs to a class of disease known as

[i]_____, which are psychological difficulties that take physical form. There are no underlying physical problems to account for the symptoms, or if one does exist, the person's

reaction exaggerates it. A major somatoform disorder is [j]_____, in which actual physical symptoms are caused by psychological problems. These disorders usually have a rapid onset—a person may awaken one morning totally blind or with a numb hand (called "glove anesthesia"). One characteristic is that individuals with conversion disorders seem relatively unconcerned with the symptoms. Generally, conversion disorders occur when an emotional stress can be reduced by having a physical symptom.

[k]_____ have been the most dramatized disorders, including the multiple-personality stories of *The Three Faces of Eve* and *Sybil*. The central factor is the dissociation, or splitting apart, of critical parts of the personality. There are three major dissociative disorders.

[l]_____ occurs when two or more distinct personalities are present in the same individual. Each personality is a separate person with desires and reactions to situations. Even vision can change when the personality changes. Because the personalities reside in only one body, they must take turns, causing what appears to be sometimes radically inconsistent

behavior. [m]_____ is a failure or inability to remember past experiences. The information has not been forgotten; it simply cannot be recalled. In some cases, memory loss can be total, as illustrated in the case of Raymond Power, Jr., who had no memory of his wife of 30

years or his children. [n]_____ is a state in which people may take an impulsive, sudden trip and assume a new identity. After a period of time, they realize they are in a strange place. They often do not recall what they did while wandering.

Changes in mood are a part of everyday life. However, mood changes can be extreme enough to cause life-threatening problems and to cause an individual to lose touch with reality. These

situations result from [o]_____, disturbances in mood severe enough to interfere with daily life. Major depression is one of the more common mood disorders. As many as 15 million people experience major depression at any time. Twice as many women as men experience major depression, and one in four females will encounter it at some time. Depression is not merely sadness, but involves feelings of uselessness, worthlessness, loneliness, and despair. Major depression is distinguished by the severity of the symptoms.

[p]_____ refers to an extended state of intense euphoria and elation. Also, people experience a sense of happiness, power, invulnerability, and energy. They may be involved with wild schemes. When this is paired with bouts of depression, it is called a bipolar disorder. The swings between highs and lows can occur every several days or can be over a period of years. Typically, the depression lasts longer than the mania.

Major depression and bipolar disorder seem to have strong genetic and biochemical causes. For instance, in depression, imbalanced levels of the neurotransmitters serotonin and norepinephrine have been identified as causes. The cognitive approach draws on the experience of **[q]**_____, a state in which people perceive that they cannot escape from or cope with stress. According to this view, depression is a response brought on by helplessness. Aaron Beck has suggested that depression involves faulty cognitions held by the sufferer about themselves. Theories about the cause of depression have not explained why twice as many women get it as men. One theory suggests that the stress for women is higher at certain times of life. Women are also more subject to physical and sexual abuse, earn less money than men, and report greater unhappiness with marriage.

Schizophrenia is a class of disorders in which severe distortion of reality occurs. Thinking, perception, and emotion deteriorate, there is a withdrawal from social interaction, and there may be bizarre behavior. The characteristics of schizophrenia include:

- *Decline from a previous level of functioning.*
- *Disturbances of thought and language*, in which logic is peculiar, thoughts do not make sense, and linguistic rules are not followed.
- *Delusions* are unshakable beliefs that have no basis in reality, involving thoughts of control by others, persecution, or the belief that thoughts are being broadcast to others.
- *Perceptual disorders* occur in which schizophrenics do not perceive the world as everyone else does, and they may have **[r]** _____, the experience of perceiving things that do not actually exist.
- *Emotional disturbances* include a lack of emotion or highly inappropriate emotional responses.
- Schizophrenics tend to *withdraw* from contact with others.

The symptoms follow two courses: process schizophrenia develops symptoms early in life, with a gradual withdrawal from the world; and **[s]** _____ has a sudden and conspicuous onset of symptoms. Reactive schizophrenia responds well to treatment; process schizophrenia is more difficult to treat.

Schizophrenia is recognized to have both biological and psychological components at its root. The biological components are suggested by the fact that schizophrenia is more common in some families than others. This suggests a genetic link to the disease. Another biological explanation suggests the presence of a chemical imbalance or a structural defect. The

[t] _____ suggests that schizophrenia occurs when there is an excess activity in the areas of the brain that use dopamine to transmit signals across nerve cells. Drugs that block dopamine action are effective in reducing symptoms. *Glutamate,* another neurotransmitter, may also be a problem in this disorder. Structural differences in the brains of schizophrenics have also been found. Importantly, the **[u]** _____ suggests that schizophrenia develops as a result of the interaction between nature and nurture. Specifically, developing schizophrenia is most likely when people have an inherited predisposition, which is triggered by stressful factors in the environment. This is currently the predominant explanation for schizophrenia.

Other forms of abnormal behavior described by the *DSM-IV-TR*, and related to information considered elsewhere in the book, include **[v]** _____, **[w]** _____, and **[x]** _____.

Evaluate

____ 1.	hypochondria	a.	Characterized by actual physical disturbances.
____ 2.	somatoform disorder	b.	A pattern of lacking a clear sense of self, emotional volatility, and self-destructiveness.
____ 3.	conversion disorder		
____ 4.	antisocial personality disorder	c.	A pattern of lack of regard for morals, ethics, or the rights of others.
		d.	A misinterpretation of normal aches and pains.
____ 5.	borderline personality disorder	e.	Psychological difficulties that take on physical form.

Rethink

49-1   What cultural factors might contribute to the rate of anxiety disorders found in a culture? How might the experience of anxiety differ among people of different cultures?

49-2   *From the perspective of a social worker:* Personality disorders are often not apparent to others, and many people with these problems seem to live basically normal lives and are not a threat to others. Because these people often appear from the outside to function well in society, why should they be considered psychologically disordered?

Spotlight on Terminology and Language—ESL Pointers

Page 527 "Sally experienced her first panic attack **out of the blue**, 3 weeks after completing her senior year in college."

When something happens "**out of the blue**" it is unexpected.

Page 527 "In the restaurant, she began to feel **dizzy**."

When someone feels **dizzy** they are unsteady and feel as if they are about to lose their balance.

Page 527-528 "Clothes shopping is done only when necessary, **lest** static on garments send her running from the store."

Lest means "in case." She only does clothes shopping when she cannot avoid it, just in case the static from the clothes scares her.

Page 528 "Although the objective danger posed by an anxiety-producing stimulus (which can be just about anything, as you can see from the list in Figure 1) is typically small or **nonexistent**, to the individual suffering from the phobia the danger is great, and a full-blown panic attack may follow exposure to the stimulus."

Something that is **nonexistent** is absent or does not exist.

Page 528 "Instead, during an attack, such as the ones experienced by Sally in the case described earlier, anxiety suddenly – and often without warning – rises to a peak, and an individual feels a sense of **impending**, unavoidable doom."

The event is **impending**; it is imminent. The event is approaching rapidly.

Page 528 "Although the physical symptoms differ from person to person, they may include heart **palpitations,** shortness of breath, unusual amounts of sweating, faintness and dizziness, an urge to urinate, **gastric** sensations, and—in extreme cases—a sense of imminent death.

Heart **palpitations** are a fast or irregular heartbeat. Heart **palpitations** may occur in response to anxiety.

Gastric sensations are those that come from the stomach.

Page 529 "In other cases, though, people with the disorder feel that something dreadful is about to happen but can't identify the reason, experiencing '**free-floating**' anxiety."

Free-floating anxiety is anxiety without an apparent or identifiable cause.

Page 529 "In obsessive-compulsive disorder, people are **plagued** by unwanted thoughts, called obsessions, or feel that they must carry out actions, termed compulsions, against their will."

These symptoms **plague** the recipient; they're very bothersome.

Page 529 "As part of an obsessive-compulsive disorder, people may also experience compulsions, **irresistible** urges to repeatedly carry out some act that seems strange and unreasonable, even to them."

Irresistible urges are overwhelming urges – a person plagued with **irresistible** urges finds they must carry out some compulsion.

Page 529 "She would then thoroughly scrub her body, starting at her feet and working **meticulously** up to the top of her head, using certain washcloths for certain areas of her body."

Meticulously is to so something painstakingly, or very carefully.

Page 530 "Although such **compulsive rituals** lead to some immediate reduction of anxiety, in the long term the anxiety returns."

A **compulsive ritual** is a habit or behavior that must be performed.

Page 530 "In fact people with severe cases lead lives filled with **unrelenting** tension (Goodman, Rudorfer, & Maser, 1999; Penzel, 2000)."

Unrelenting is insistent and merciless.

Page 531 "For example, people with anxiety disorders may view a friendly puppy as a **ferocious** and **savage** pit bull, or they may see an air disaster **looming** every moment they are in the vicinity of an airplane."

Something that is **ferocious** behaves in a very fierce or savage way.

A **savage** is a wild violent or vicious person ore beast.

When something is **looming** it refers to the fact that something threatening or bad is about to happen.

Page 531 "It is not that the "symptoms" are faked; instead, it is the misinterpretation of those sensations as evidence of some serious illness—often in the face of **inarguable** medical evidence to the contrary—that characterizes hypochondriasis (Noyes et al., 1993, 2002, 2003; Fallon & Feinstein, 2001)."

When something is **inarguable** it is impossible to deny or take an opposing view about it.

Page 531 "For instance, a person in good health who wakes up blind may react in a **bland**, matter-of-fact way."

They may react in a **bland** way; they may react very mildly to this symptom.

Page 533 "Women are twice as likely to experience major depression as men, with one-fourth of all females **apt** to encounter it at some point during their lives."

Apt means likely to do it again.

Page 534 "He purchased a large number of **cuckoo clocks** and then an expensive car, which he planned to use as a mobile showroom for his wares, anticipating that he would make a great deal of money."

A **cuckoo clock is** a clock that tells time with sounds like a cuckoo bird's call, usually accompanied by the appearance of a mechanical bird from behind a door.

Page 536 "By focusing on the negative side of situations, they feel **inept** and unable to act constructively to change their environment. In sum, their negative cognitions lead to feelings of depression (Newman et al., 2002)."

Someone who is **inept** is unable to do their job.

Page 536 "Brain imaging studies suggest that people with depression experience a general **blunting** of emotional reactions."

A **blunting** of emotional response refers to a lessening or weakening of that response.

Page 536 "Other recent explanations of depression **derive** from evolutionary psychology, which considers how behavior is influenced by our genetic inheritance from our ancestors."

Derive means to come from a something.

Page 537 "When people **fruitlessly** pursue an ever-elusive goal, depression begins, ending pursuit of the goal."

When something is **fruitless** it produces nothing or is unproductive

Page 537 "The various theories of depression have not provided a complete answer to an elusive question that has **dogged** researchers: Why does depression occur in approximately twice as many women as men—a pattern (shown in Figure 7) that is similar across a variety of cultures?"

When someone does something **doggedly** they are determined to continue and will not give up, even when faced with problems and obstacles.

Page 537 "I use **Cover Girl** creamy natural makeup."

Cover Girl is a brand of cosmetics or make-up sold in U.S. stores.

Page 537 **Oral Roberts** has been here to visit me...This place is where **Mad magazine** is published."

Oral Roberts is a U.S. television religious personality.

Mad magazine is a magazine that became popular in the U.S. during the 1960's. It uses humor and satire to make fun of popular culture.

Page 537 "The **Nixons** make Noxon metal polish."

Richard Nixon was the 37 th president of the U.S and was the only president to resign from office.

Page 538 "He's down to the **smokestack**, looking through the smoke trying to get the balloon gassed up you know."

A **smokestack** is pipe used to vent smoke or steam out of an engine.

Page 538 "As this selection illustrates, although the basic grammatical structure may be intact, the substance of thinking characteristic of schizophrenia is often illogical, **garbled**, and lacking in meaningful content (Holden, 2003; see Figure 9)."

When something is **garbled** it is jumbled or distorted.

Page 539 "For example, a person with schizophrenia may laugh **uproariously** at a funeral or react with anger when being helped by someone."

Something **uproarious** is very loud and funny.

Page 543 "Their emotional **volatility** leads to impulsive and self-destructive behavior."

Because of their emotional **volatility** their moods and tempers are unpredictable and changeable.

Page 554 "Although they are not out of touch with reality in the way that people with schizophrenia are, people with personality disorders lead lives that put them on the **fringes** of society (Millon et al., 2000;

Trull & Widiger, 2003).”

The **fringe** of something is its outer edge.

Page 544 “Rather than showing profound sadness or hopelessness, childhood depression may produce the expression of exaggerated fears, **clinginess**, or avoidance of everyday activities.”

Clinginess occurs when something sticks closely to someone or something else.

Module 50: Psychological Disorders in Perspective

Prevalence of Psychological Disorders: The Mental State of the Union
The Social and Cultural Context of Psychological Disorders

Exploring Diversity: *DSM* and Culture—and the
Culture of *DSM*

Becoming an Informed Consumer of Psychology:
Deciding When You Need Help

- *How prevalent are psychological disorders?*
- *What indicators signal a need for the help of a mental-health practitioner?*

Psychological Disorders in Perspective

Psychological disorders are surprisingly common in the United States. Though determining the number of people with signs of psychological disorders is a difficult task, our best estimates is that the rates are rather high. A survey of 8,000 Americans found that 30 percent currently had a mental disorder, and a total of 48 percent had experienced a disorder at some time in their lives. Some people experience more than one disorder simultaneously, known as [a] _____.

The disorders in the *DSM-IV-TR* reflect late-twentieth-century thinking. There was also significant controversy during its development. One controversial disorder was [b] _____, which referred to people in abusive relationships. This disorder was not placed in the *DSM-IV-TR*. The other disorder was [c] _____, or premenstrual syndrome. This disorder was included, despite protests that it reflects normal female experience. The Exploring Diversity section discusses the differences between cultures in the nature of abnormal behavior. Also, disorders that appear in non-Western cultures, but not as of yet in Western cultures, are described.

The decision concerning if and when to seek help for psychological disorders is difficult, but several guidelines should help. If the following signals are present, help should be considered: long-term feelings of distress that interfere with functioning, occasions when stress is overwhelming, prolonged depression, withdrawal from others, chronic physical problems, a fear or phobia that prevents normal functioning, feelings that other people are talking about the person or are out to get the person, or the inability to interact effectively with others.

Evaluate

_____ 1. premenstrual disphoric disorder

_____ 2. anxiety disorder

_____ 3. *Diagnostic and Statistical Manual IV, TR*

_____ 4. depression

_____ 5. self-defeating personality disorder

a. Directory where the specific nature of the disorders is a reflection of 20th-century Western values.

b. Removed from *DSM-IV-TR*, applied to cause in which individuals in unpleasant or demeaning situations take no action.

c. Controversial inclusion to *DSM-IV-TR*.

d. One of four categories found in all cultures includes schizophrenia, bipolar disorder, depression.

e. Most common of all psychological disorders.

Rethink

50-1   Why is inclusion in the *DSM-IV-TR* of "borderline" disorders such as self-defeating personality disorder and premenstrual dysphoric disorder so controversial and political? What disadvantages does inclusion bring? Does inclusion bring any benefits?

50-2   *From the perspective of a college counselor:* What indicators might be most important in determining whether a college student is experiencing a psychological disorder? Do you believe that all students who show signs of a psychological disorder should seek professional help? How might your responses change if the students were from a different culture (e.g., an African society)?

Spotlight on Terminology and Language—ESL Pointers

Page 547 "That's the conclusion drawn from a **massive study** on the prevalence of psychological disorders."

A **massive study** would be a study based on a large population.

Page 547 "In addition, 30 percent experience a disorder in any particular year, and the number of people who experience **simultaneous** multiple disorders (known as comorbidity) is significant (Kessler et al., 1994; Welkowitz et al., 2000)."

Simultaneous disorders are problems occurring or existing at the same time.

Page 547 "Furthermore, there are economic **disparities** in treatment, such that more affluent people with mild disorders receive more and better treatment than poor people who have more severe disorders (see

Figure 2; The WHO World Mental Health Survey Consortium, 2004)."

A **disparity** is a lack of equality between things or people.

Page 549 "Furthermore, some critics complained that use of the label had the effect of **condemning** targets of abuse for their **plight** – a blame-the-victim phenomenon – and as a result, the category was removed from the manual."

When you **condemn** someone, you consider them guilty. You blame that person for something.

Plight is a difficult or dangerous situation or predicament.

Page 549 "Yet some **Plains Indians** routinely hear the voices of the dead calling to them from the afterlife."

The term **"Plains Indians"** refers to the members of any of the tribes of Native American people that lived on the great plains of the United States.

Page 550 "Most often, of course, your concerns will be **unwarranted**."

Unwarranted is uncalled-for, or unjustifiable.

Page 551 "On the other hand, many people do have problems that **merit** concern, and in such cases it is important to consider the possibility that professional help is warranted."

When something **merits** thinking about, it deserves more consideration.

Test your knowledge of the material in this set of modules by answering these questions. These questions have been placed in three Practice Tests. The first two tests consist of questions that will test your recall of factual knowledge. The third test contains questions that are challenging and primarily test for conceptual knowledge and your ability to apply that knowledge. Check your answers and review the feedback using the Answer Key in the following pages of the *Study Guide*.

PRACTICE TEST 1:

1. Mr. Smith reports that he suffers from the constant fear of illness, and he misinterprets normal aches and pains. He suffers from:
    a.   conversion disorder.
    b.   hypochondriasis.
    c.   somatoform disorder.
    d.   phobic disorder.

2. When the *Titanic* sank in 1912, some male passengers saved themselves at the expense of women and children, contrary to the Victorian standard of manly heroism. This behavior was abnormal because it was:
    a.   very different from average.
    b.   insane.
    c.   opposed to an ideal.
    d.   severely uncomfortable.

3. The therapists have assured his family that Kenneth's abnormal behavior is related to an endocrine system malfunction. His problem best fits the:
    a.   medical model of abnormality.
    b.   psychoanalytic model of abnormality.
    c.   behavioral model of abnormality.
    d.   sociocultural model of abnormality.

4. The _____ perspective of abnormality suggests that when an individual displays the symptoms of abnormal behavior, the diagnosed causes are physiological.
    a.   humanistic
    b.   medical
    c.   psychoanalytic
    d.   sociocultural

5. Which of the following approaches of abnormality is **least** likely to view the therapist as the "expert" who cures the patient?
    a.   The behavioral approaches
    b.   The humanistic approaches
    c.   The medical approaches
    d.   The psychoanalytic approaches

6. Tory and Dave Joshal, siblings who grew up in a very disruptive environment, have discovered that the sources of their strange beliefs or actions are hidden conflicts that are carried over from their childhood, according to:
    a.   the psychoanalytic approaches.
    b.   the humanistic approaches.
    c.   the cognitive approaches.
    d.   the behavioral approaches.

7. Many people with psychological disorders come from broken homes and low-income backgrounds. To understand the effects of these and similar conditions on abnormal behavior, a comprehensive diagnosis must include insights from the:
    a.   behavioral approaches.
    b.   psychoanalytic approaches.
    c.   humanistic approaches.
    d.   sociocultural approaches.

8.   In the *DSM-IV-TR,* there are approximately _____ different disorders identified.
    a.   50   c.   200
    b.   100   d.   500

9.   Kirsten has been told by her therapist that her nervousness and fears that have no apparent justification and impair her normal daily functioning are symptoms of a(n):
    a.   psychosomatic disorder.   c.   anxiety disorder.
    b.   personality disorder.   d.   neurotic disorder.

10. The main character in the movie *Sybil* suffered from:
    a.   schizophrenia.   c.   disordered personality.
    b.   psychogenic personality.   d.   dissociative identity disorder.

11. Kiesha often has feelings of impending doom or even death paired with sudden and overwhelming bodily reactions. These are typical symptoms of:
    a.   obsessive-compulsive disorder.   c.   personality disorder.
    b.   panic disorder.   d.   generalized anxiety disorder.

12. Isaiah, a Chicago native, was unable to account for his actions in the past three weeks or figure out how he arrived in Tucson, Arizona, but could recall memories before his amnesia. This description exemplifies:
    a.   dissociative identity disorder.   c.   hypochondriasis.
    b.   dissociative fugue.   d.   panic disorder.

13. An individual who has a bipolar disorder is one who has:
    a.   opposing phobias.   c.   a split personality.
    b.   alternation of mania and depression. d.   alternation of phobia and panic.

14. _____ schizophrenia is characterized by gradual onset, general withdrawal from the world, blunted emotions, and poor prognosis.
    a.   Paranoid   c.   Process
    b.   Catatonic   d.   Reactive

15. The belief that Bigfoot enters the house during the night and contaminates any food that has been left in the refrigerator would be regarded as a(n):
    a.   compulsion.   c.   delusion.
    b.   hallucination.   d.   early sign of narcissism.

_____ 16.   dissociative fugue

_____ 17.   anxiety

_____ 18.   mood disorder

_____ 19.   mania

_____ 20.   bipolar disorder

a. A disorder in which a person alternates between euphoric feelings of mania and bouts of depression.

b. Affective disturbance severe enough to interfere with normal living.

c. A condition in which people take sudden, impulsive trips, sometimes assuming a new identity.

d. An extended state of intense euphoria and elation.

e. A feeling of apprehension or tension.

21. A constant fear of illness and the misinterpretation of normal aches and pains would be considered
_____.

22. The _____ study illustrated that placing labels on individuals influences how their actions are perceived and interpreted.

23. The intense but real fear Megan felt at just the thought of an airplane flight is known as a(n)
_____.

24. Men and women whose lives seem to center around their worry may suffer from
_____ _____.

25. People experiencing _____ feel intense happiness, power, invulnerability, and energy.

26. Discuss the implications of Rosenhan's study, in which he and seven other individuals faked mental illness in order to test the ability of mental hospitals to distinguish abnormal from normal behavior and the effects of labeling. What are the scientific issues related to his study? Are there any ethical issues?

PRACTICE TEST 2:

1.   "Mental illness" as a description of a person implies that:
   a.   demons and devils exert their evil influence on the body through medical ailments, especially ailments of the nervous system.
   b.   the target person suffers a lack of unconditional positive regard.
   c.   the person has bizarre thoughts but not bizarre behavior.
   d.   the speaker or writer accepts the medical model.

2.   The main difference between panic disorder and generalized anxiety disorder is that generalized anxiety is:
   a.   more intense than panic.
   b.   continuous, whereas panic is short-term.
   c.   triggered by alcohol, whereas panic is triggered by social events.
   d.   dissociative, whereas panic is schizophrenic.

3.　Which of the following approaches in the study of abnormality is likely to hold most strongly to the concept that the patient has little control over his or her actions?
　　a.　The medical approaches　　　　　c.　The behavioral approaches
　　b.　The sociocultural approaches　　　d.　The humanistic approaches

4.　According to the psychoanalytic model of abnormality, abnormal behavior derives from:
　　a.　failure to develop logical thought processes.
　　b.　physiological malfunctions.
　　c.　unresolved childhood conflicts.
　　d.　confusion in the collective unconscious.

5.　Which of the following models of abnormality is most likely to emphasize the patient's responsibility and participation in the treatment?
　　a.　The medical model　　　　　　　c.　The behavioral model
　　b.　The psychoanalytic model　　　　d.　The humanistic model

6.　Proponents of which therapeutic approach are most likely to take the position that there is no such thing as abnormal behavior?
　　a.　The sociocultural approach　　　　c.　The behavioral approach
　　b.　The psychoanalytic approach　　　d.　The medical approach

7.　Dr. Gaipo uses the *DSM-IV-TR* classifications primarily to:
　　a.　show the causes of and to treat abnormality.
　　b.　classify and identify causes of abnormality.
　　c.　classify and describe abnormality.
　　d.　describe and treat abnormality.

8.　The Rosenhan (1973) study in which normal individuals were admitted to mental hospitals showed that:
　　a.　therapeutic techniques that improve disordered patients can be applied by normal people to make them even better adjusted than they were at first.
　　b.　mental patients served as models for each others' strange behaviors.
　　c.　the "mental patient" label affects how ordinary acts are perceived.
　　d　the *DSM-IV-TR* categories are prone to stability and change.

9.　Which of the following is **not** a reasonable criticism of the *DSM-IV-TR* ?
　　a.　Mental disorders are classified into a "category" rather than along a continuum.
　　b.　The *DSM-IV-TR* materials usually do not reflect changing views in society about mental disorders, since the manual is updated only every 15 years.
　　c.　The *DSM-IV-TR* system of classification may be too heavily influenced by the medical model.
　　d.　A diagnosis may become an explanation for a problem.

10.　Mr. Carney has been diagnosed with a disorder that shares a common feature with all other dissociative disorders in that:
　　a.　their hereditary basis is well-known and documented.
　　b.　an obsessive-compulsive disorder usually precedes the onset of any dissociative disorder.
　　c.　they tend to occur in persons who are poor and have large families.
　　d.　they allow the person to escape from anxiety-producing situations.

11. Hannah has been suffering from psychological difficulties that take on a physical form, but doctors have found no actual physical or physiological abnormality. These difficulties are called:
    a. somatoform disorders.   c. psychophysical disorders.
    b. psychological disorders.   d. freeform disorders.

12. Together, dissociative identity disorder, amnesia, and dissociative fugue are called:
    a. depressive disorders.   c. somatoform disorders.
    b. schizophrenic disorders.   d. dissociative disorders.

13. Mania and bipolar disorder differ mainly in:
    a. the sense that mania applies to both genders but bipolar applies to men.
    b. the fact that mania has a psychological origin but bipolar is biological.
    c. the stability of the emotional state.
    d. the sense that one is a personality disorder, whereas the other is a mood disorder.

14. Convicted murderers like Ted Bundy and John Wayne Gacy have been diagnosed as sociopaths. They were able to fool the lie detector test because they:
    a. feel stress or anxiety more or less continuously.
    b. are psychologically sophisticated; many have studied the *DSM-IV*.
    c. feel no guilt or remorse.
    d. have lost touch with reality.

15. Which mental disturbance is most likely to result in the afflicted person's using language in ways that do **not** follow conventional linguistic rules?
    a. Schizophrenia   c. Dissociative fugue
    b. Dissociative identity disorder d. Depressive disorder

_____ 16. learned helplessness

_____ 17. process schizophrenia

_____ 18. reactive schizophrenia

_____ 19. dopamine hypothesis

_____ 20. predisposition model of schizophrenia

a. Suggests that individuals may inherit tendencies that make them vulnerable to environmental stress factors.

b. Onset of symptoms is sudden and conspicuous.

c. Symptoms begin early in life and develop slowly.

d. Suggests that schizophrenia occurs when excess activity occurs in certain areas of the brain.

e. A state in which people give up fighting stress, believing it to be inescapable, leading to depression.

21. Together, dissociative identity disorder, amnesia, and dissociative fugue are called

_____.

22. Critics suggest that the _____ compartmentalizes people into inflexible all-or-nothing categories.

23. _____, which are brought about by specific objects or situations, can last from a few seconds to hours.

24. A person with _____ may actually carry several pairs of eyeglasses because vision changes with each personality.

25. One approach used to explain the disorder depression is the _____ approach, which suggests that depression is the result of feelings of loss.

26. What can research with groups of twins, some reared together and some reared apart, tell researchers about the causes of schizophrenia?

PRACTICE TEST 3: Conceptual, Applied, and Challenging Questions

1. Schizophrenia produces many dramatic and debilitating changes in a person affected with this disorder. Which alternative is **not** one of them?
   a. Delusions
   b. Dissociative identity disorder
   c. Decline from an earlier level of functioning
   d. Withdrawal

2. Which statement is **not** consistent with the sociocultural model of abnormality?
   a. Behavior is shaped by our family, by society, and by the culture in which we live.
   b. There is something wrong with a society that is unwilling to tolerate deviant behavior.
   c. Competing psychic forces within the troubled individual erode personal standards and values.
   d. Abnormal behaviors are more prevalent among some social classes than others.

3. Caroline was beginning her SAT exams when she suddenly became extremely anxious and felt a sense of impending, unavoidable doom. Her heart beat rapidly, she was short of breath, she became faint and dizzy, and she felt as if she might die. Caroline was experiencing:
   a. phobic disorder.
   b. panic disorder.
   c. generalized anxiety disorder.
   d. obsessive-compulsive disorder.

4. "The kinds of stresses and conflicts that people experience in their daily interactions with others can promote and maintain abnormal behavior." This statement is consistent with the _____ model of abnormality.
   a. sociocultural
   b. behavioral
   c. humanistic
   d. psychoanalytic

5. Dr. Keane, a psychiatrist, listened patiently as Myriah revealed a series of episodes involving irrational fears of snakes. Dr. Keane probably labeled Myriah's symptoms as:
   a. schizophrenic reactions.
   b. phobic reactions.
   c. organic reactions.
   d. obsessive-compulsive reactions.

6. Scott is terrified to ride in an elevator in any building. He is especially bothered by the small, confined space and the fact that he is "trapped" until the elevator doors open. Usually, he avoids this unpleasantness by refusing to ride in elevators. Scott is experiencing:
   a. phobic disorder.
   b. panic disorder.
   c. obsessive-compulsive disorder.
   d. tension disorder.

7. Mr. Lombardi, a lawyer in a large, prosperous law practice, finds that two or three hours before an important appearance in court, he cannot talk. The firm's doctor cannot find any medical reason for this problem. The doctor is also surprised that the lawyer seems unconcerned. If the lawyer's symptoms are the result of a psychological disorder, it would most likely be diagnosed as:

a.   somatoform disorder.   c.   panic disorder.
b.   conversion disorder.   d.   obsessive-compulsive disorder.

8.   Marlane has been tense and anxious during her professors' lectures, and it is causing her to have a difficult time at college. She has been much better lately because she distracts herself by counting the number of times her professors say "the" during their lectures. Marlane's "counting" suggests she is experiencing:
    a.   panic disorder   c.   obsessive-compulsive disorder.
    b.   phobic disorder.   d.   generalized anxiety disorder.

9.   The most frequent mental disorder in America after depression is:
    a.   bipolar disorder.   c.   paranoid schizophrenia.
    b.   obsessive-compulsive disorder.   d.   alcohol dependence.

10.   What is one difference between dissociative fugue and dissociative amnesia?
    a.   In fugue, memory can be restored with drugs.
    b.   In amnesia, the memory loss is temporary.
    c.   In fugue, past memory is typically eventually regained.
    d.   In amnesia, the memories are physically lost.

11.   Process schizophrenia is different from reactive schizophrenia because with reactive schizophrenia, the patient:
    a.   experiences a sudden and conspicuous onset of symptoms.
    b.   is less withdrawn.
    c.   may be dangerously aggressive and abusive to others.
    d.   is less likely to have a hereditary basis for the disorder.

12.   When minor symptoms of schizophrenia follow a severe case or episode, the disorder is called:
    a.   disorganized schizophrenia.   c.   paranoid schizophrenia.
    b.   catatonic schizophrenia.   d.   residual schizophrenia.

13.   Which of the following accounts of schizophrenia assumes that inappropriate behavior is learned by attending to stimuli that are not related to normal social interaction?
    a.   Learned helplessness hypothesis   c.   Predisposition model
    b.   Dopamine hypothesis   d.   Learned-inattention theory

14.   Personality disorder is best characterized by:
    a.   firmly held beliefs with little basis in reality.
    b.   a mixture of symptoms of schizophrenia.
    c.   a set of inflexible, maladaptive traits.
    d.   an extended sense of euphoria and elation.

15.   Tanisha is uncooperative, refuses to speak to her coworkers, and frequently disrupts meetings with distracting questions and irrelevant challenges. However, she is fully capable of doing all her work and maintains a reasonable family life. She uses her status as a female to threaten her superiors with "harassment" if they question what she is doing, and she exploits anyone who is unwitting enough to be caught in her self-promotion schemes. Because she believes she can do whatever she can get away with doing, which of the following categories best fits her?
    a.   Sociopathic personality disorder   c.   Premenstrual dysphoric disorder
    b.   Self-defeating personality disorder   d.   Dissociative identity disorder

_____ 16. personality disorder

a. Characterized by a set of inflexible, maladaptive traits that keep a person from functioning properly in society.

_____ 17. antisocial or sociopathic personality disorder

b. Inability to develop a secure sense of self.

_____ 18. narcissistic personality disorder

c. Characterized by an exaggerated sense of self and an inability to experience empathy for others.

_____ 19. borderline personality disorder

d. Individuals display no regard for moral and ethical rules or for the rights of others.

20. The _____ perspective suggests that when an individual displays symptoms of abnormal behavior, the cause will be found in a medical exam.

21. Nyringian feels apprehensive or tense every time he has to speak publicly; he is experiencing _____.

22. Big Joe suffers from _____, which often causes him such anxiety that he is unable to leave his home.

23. The term _____ is sometimes used to describe the lost memories of dissociative amnesia.

24. The psychologist _____ has proposed that faulty cognitions underlie people's depressed feelings.

25. Describe the types of schizophrenia, its symptoms, and its causes. Compare the differing theories concerning the cause of schizophrenia.

Module 48:	Module 49:	[m] Dissociative amnesia	Module 50:
[a] medical perspective	[a] Generalized anxiety	[n] Dissociative fugue	[a] comorbidity
[b] psychoanalytic	disorder	[o] mood disorders	[b] self-defeating
perspective	[b] Panic disorder	[p] Mania	personality disorder
[c] behavioral	[c] Phobic disorder	[q] learned helplessness	[c] premenstrual
perspective	[d] phobia	[r] hallucinations	dysphoric disorder
[d] cognitive perspective	[e] Obsessive-	[s] reactive schizophrenia	
[e] humanistic	compulsive disorder	[t] dopamine hypothesis	Evaluate
perspective	[f] Obsessions	[u] predisposition model of	1. c
[f] sociocultural	[g] Compulsions	schizophrenia	2. d
perspective	[h] Hypochondriasis	[v] psychoactive substance-	3. a
[g] *Diagnostic and*	[i] somatoform disorders	use disorder	4. e
Statistical Manual of	[j] conversion disorder	[w] eating disorders	5. b
Mental Disorders,	[k] Dissociative disorders	[x] sexual disorders	
Fourth Edition, Text	[l] Dissociative identity		
Revision (DSM-IV-TR)	disorder		
		Evaluate	
Evaluate		1. d	
1. d		2. e	
2. a		3. a	
3. e		4. c	
4. c		5. b	
5. f			
6. b			

Selected Rethink Answers

48-2   Proponents of each perspective on the topic of shoplifting:

Medical—might view shoplifting as arising from organic, physiological conditions.

Psychoanalytic—would view shoplifting as a conflict in the unconscious and the adequacy of ego development.

Cognitive—would focus on the irrational conscious thoughts that preceded the shoplifting.

Humanistic—would suggest that the individual take control and responsibility for the shoplifting.

Sociocultural—shoplifting was the result of sociocultural forces such as income or a broken home.

An employer would likely fire the employee either way, as it is likely against the rules described in an employee handbook. However, an employer might consider suspending the employee until he or she sought help for and recovered from the shoplifing "problem" via therapy.

49-3   People who have personality disorders have maladaptive personality traits that do not permit them to function appropriately as members of society. They have no regard for the moral and ethical rules of society or the rights of others. They are manipulative and deceptive; have a lack of guilt or anxiety over wrong-doing; are often impulsively distrustful and controlling, demanding, eccentric, obnoxious, or difficult.

Practice Test 1:

1. b   mod. 49 p. 545

a. Incorrect. This is a form of somatoform disorder.

*b. Correct. Hypochondriacs suffer every ache as a major disease.

c. Incorrect. This is the disorder in which psychological problems are manifest as physical systems.

d. Incorrect. Phobic disorder is a fear of a specific event or stimulus.

2. c   mod. 48 p. 535

a. Incorrect. It probably was not different from how people would behave on average.

b. Incorrect. Such behavior is quite sane.

*c. Correct. The ideal was for men to sacrifice themselves for their wives and children.

d. Incorrect. Although many were probably uncomfortable after the fact, they were still alive.

3. a   mod. 48 p. 534
*a. Correct. The medical model views abnormal behavior as arising from organic, physiological conditions.
b. Incorrect. The psychoanalytic view of abnormality depends on the extremes of conflict in the unconscious and the adequacy of ego development.
c. Incorrect. The behavioral model of abnormality views abnormality as a result of inappropriate, learned behaviors.
d. Incorrect. The sociocultural view of abnormality views abnormality as the result of sociocultural forces, often with the view that social systems are themselves abnormal.

4. b   mod. 48 p. 534
a. Incorrect. The humanistic view would understand abnormality as the self in conflict.
*b. Correct. The medical approach seeks to understand abnormality as a result of organic, physiological causes.
c. Incorrect. The psychoanalytic view of abnormality depends on the extremes of conflict in the unconscious and the adequacy of ego development.
d. Incorrect. The sociocultural view of abnormality views abnormality as the result of sociocultural forces, often with the view that social systems are themselves abnormal.

5. b   mod. 48 p. 536
a. Incorrect. The behavioral model utilizes a behavioral expert who can help modify behavior.
*b. Correct. The humanistic model views the client as the person capable of effecting a cure; the humanistic therapist is there to facilitate.
c. Incorrect. The medical model depends on a medical professional.
d. Incorrect. The psychoanalytic model requires a trained psychoanalyst.

6. a   mod. 48 p. 535
*a. Correct. Psychodynamic views depend on hidden or unconscious conflicts as the cause of most behavior.
b. Incorrect. The humanistic view would embrace the notion of "open" rather than hidden conflicts.
c. Incorrect. The cognitive model would accept the idea of strange beliefs, but it would focus on the irrational conscious thoughts.
d. Incorrect. The behavioral model would suggest that all strange behaviors are learned.

7. d   mod. 48 p. 536

a. Incorrect. However, a behaviorist should be able to identify the system of rewards and punishments that contribute to these patterns.
b. Incorrect. The psychoanalyst is unlikely to be concerned with the socioeconomic status in which the conditions occur.
c. Incorrect. The humanistic model would not be interested in the socioeconomic conditions in which the abnormality occurs.
*d. Correct. The sociocultural model emphasizes the contributions made by social and economic factors such as income and broken homes.

8. c   mod. 48 p. 537
a. Incorrect. Try 200.
b. Incorrect. Try 200.
*c. Correct. The 200 categories suggest an increasing attention to a wide range of diseases.
d. Incorrect. Try 200.

9. c   mod. 49 p. 541
a. Incorrect. A psychosomatic disorder involves a physical symptom with no apparent physical cause.
b. Incorrect. A personality disorder involves a long-standing, habitual, and maladaptive personality pattern.
*c. Correct. This describes an anxiety disorder.
d. Incorrect. The term "neurotic disorder" is no longer used.

10. d   mod. 49 p. 546
a. Incorrect. Schizophrenia involves disordered thought, not multiple personalities.
b. Incorrect. Not quite sure what this is, but Sybil did not have it.
c. Incorrect. This is not an official diagnostic category.
*d. Correct. Once called "multiple personality," this problem is increasingly common.

11. b   mod. 49 p. 542
a.   Incorrect. In obsessive-compulsive disorder, the sufferer has uncontrollable thoughts and compulsions to act.
*b. Correct. The panic attack can be without warning and without apparent cause.
c.   Incorrect. A personality disorder involves a long-standing, habitual, and maladaptive personality pattern.
d.   Incorrect. A generalized anxiety disorder involves long-standing, consistent anxiety without an apparent cause or source.

12. b   mod. 49 p. 547
a.   Incorrect. A dissociative identity disorder is marked by the presence of two or more personalities, not the dissociative fugue described.
*b. Correct. In dissociative fugue, the individual disappears, often just wondering off, and later reappears, without any knowledge of why he or she left.
c.   Incorrect. Someone suffering hypochondriasis has symptoms without physical illness.
d.   Incorrect. Panic attack is marked by feelings of impending doom or even death, paired with sudden and overwhelming bodily reactions.

13. b   mod. 49 p. 549
a.   Incorrect. Or maybe, alternating fears of penguins and polar bears?
*b. Correct. The "bipolar" aspect is the swing from the high mood of mania to the depths of depression.
c.   Incorrect. See answer b.
d.   Incorrect. See answer b.

14. c   mod. 49 p. 553
a.   Incorrect. Paranoid schizophrenia is characterized by delusions of persecution or grandeur.
b.   Incorrect. Catatonic schizophrenia is characterized by waxy flexibility and autistic withdrawal.
*c. Correct. This statement describes process schizophrenia.
d.   Incorrect. Reactive schizophrenia usually has a quicker onset and has a better prognosis than the process schizophrenia described in the item.

15. c   mod. 49 p. 553
a.   Incorrect. A compulsion is an idea that seems to have a life of its own—the sufferer gets up every night to hide the remote.

b.   Incorrect. The hallucination is just seeing Bigfoot.
*c. Correct. Very delusional. Everyone knows Bigfoot belongs in garages.
d.   Incorrect. Only if you are Bigfoot.

16. c   mod. 49 p. 547
17. e   mod. 49 p. 541
18. b   mod. 49 p. 547
19. d   mod. 49 p. 548
20. a   mod. 49 p. 549

21. Hypochondriasis   mod. 49 p. 545
22. Rosenhan   mod. 48 p. 539
23. phobia   mod. 49 p. 542
24. generalized anxiety disorder   mod. 49 p. 541
25. Mania   mod. 49 p. 548

26.
▪   The Rosenhan study suggested that mental health workers label their clients with rather unshakable labels. The labels also lead to interpretations of behavior that continue to confirm the diagnosis (note that some stayed for many weeks even though they only complained of the symptom once on admission to the hospital).
▪   The issues of deception and the use of a subject who had not given consent are major problems.
▪   A brief examination of the study does not explain the contexts involved: Few people voluntarily walk into a mental hospital and complain of a major symptom. The sudden disappearance of the symptom could be considered abnormal as well.

Practice Test 2:
1.   d   mod. 48 p. 534
a.   Incorrect. Centuries ago, maybe.
b.   Incorrect. Rogers never intended for this to be a meaning of his concept.
c.   Incorrect. The person may have bizarre behavior as well.
*d. Correct. The notion of psychological disorders being an "illness" suggests the medical view.

2.   b   mod. 49 p. 543
a.   Incorrect. Panic is probably the more intense.
*b. Correct. Panic involves symptoms that last for a brief period and then disappear until the next incident.
c.   Incorrect. Generalized anxiety disorder is not caused by alcohol.
d.   Incorrect. Panic disorder is not schizophrenic, although persons suffering from schizophrenia may experience panic.

3. a mod. 48 p. 534

*a. Correct. If the disease is organic and physiological, then abnormal behaviors are beyond the individual's control.

b. Incorrect. The sociocultural model would accept that the individual has control over his or her actions, even though those actions may be present partly because of sociocultural forces.

c. Incorrect. The behavioral model allows for the individual to take control of his or her actions through behavior modification and self-regulation.

d. Incorrect. The humanistic model suggests that the individual must ultimately take control and responsibility for his or her actions.

4. c mod. 48 p. 535

a. Incorrect. This explanation is more consistent with a cognitive model.

b. Incorrect. This explanation is more consistent with the medical model.

*c. Correct. Unresolved childhood conflicts would be repressed in the unconscious, and their efforts to be expressed and the costs of keeping them repressed can lead to abnormalities.

d. Incorrect. The unconscious is confused and confusing for both healthy and psychologically disturbed individuals.

5. d mod. 48 p. 536

a. Incorrect. The medical model is currently focused on treatment through medication, and the only role the patient has is to take the drugs.

b. Incorrect. The psychoanalyst directs the patient toward an understanding of the problem.

c. Incorrect. The behavioral model depends on the application of different reward systems to alter the problem.

*d. Correct. The humanistic model views the patient as capable of self-healing and control and having responsibility over his or her actions.

6. a mod. 48 p. 536

*a. Correct. Some proponents of the sociocultural model claim that the society is sick, not the individual.

b. Incorrect. See answer a.

c. Incorrect. See answer a.

d. Incorrect. See answer a.

7. c mod. 48 p. 537

a. Incorrect. Treatment is not part of the manual.

b. Incorrect. The causes of abnormality are identified with specific theories, so they have not been addressed in the manual.

*c. Correct. The purpose of the manual is classification and description without implied theories.

d. Incorrect. The manual does not offer treatment.

8. c mod. 48 p. 539

a. Incorrect. While this may be true in some cases, it is not the conclusion of the Rosenhan study.

b. Incorrect. This may be true, but it was not addressed by the Rosenhan study.

*c. Correct. Labeling carries a stigma that is difficult to erase.

d. Incorrect. The *DSM-IV* categories have little to do with stability and change.

9. b mod. 48 p. 537

a. Incorrect. Some prefer a continuum approach and are critical of the category approach.

*b. Correct. The manual is updated with greater frequency, and the update is highly sensitive to changing views of society about mental disorders.

c. Incorrect. This is a common complaint, especially among psychologists who prefer a less medical orientation.

d. Incorrect. Often, the diagnosis is viewed as if it provided an analysis of the cause of a disorder.

10. d   mod. 49 p. 546
a. Incorrect. The anxiety that gives rise to them is environmental, but the cause of the illness remains open.
b. Incorrect. Not so.
c. Incorrect. They are equal opportunity disorders.
*d. Correct. They all have some form of escape from anxiety.

11. a   mod. 49 p. 545
*a. Correct. These include hypochondriasis and conversion disorders.
b. Incorrect. The stem describes a psychological disorder known as somatoform disorder, and not all psychological disorders have these symptoms.
c. Incorrect. A disorder related to the study of psychophysics?
d. Incorrect. No such disorder has been recognized.

12. d   mod. 49 p. 546
a. Incorrect. Depressive disorders include major and minor depression.
b. Incorrect. Schizophrenia does not share these disorders with the dissociative category.
c. Incorrect. Somatoform disorders involve a physical symptom without a physical cause, not the dissociation of part of the personality.
*d. Correct. Each of these disorders involves the separation of some part of the personality or memory.

13. c   mod. 49 p. 549
a. Incorrect. Bipolar disorders appear in men and women.
b. Incorrect. Both can have either origin.
*c. Correct. In mania, the state remains high-pitched all the time.
d. Incorrect. Both are mood disorders.

14. c   mod. 49 p. 557
a. Incorrect. They feel stress and anxiety to the same extent that normal individuals experience stress and anxiety.
b. Incorrect. A rare sociopath has bothered to study the *DSM-IV*.
*c. Correct. Guilt or remorse are necessary to trigger the physiological reaction that the polygraph measures.
d. Incorrect. They are quite in touch with reality.

15. a   mod. 49 p. 552
*a. Correct. Some people with schizophrenia have their own private language.
b. Incorrect. People with dissociative identity disorder appear quite normal on the surface.

c. Incorrect. The fugue state results in wandering off, not incoherence.
d. Incorrect. Depressive individuals can become incoherent, but not because of unconventional language use.

16. e   mod. 49 p. 550
17. c   mod. 49 p. 553
18. b   mod. 49 p. 553
19. d   mod. 49 p. 554
20. a   mod. 49 p. 554

21. dissociative disorders   mod. 49 p. 546
22. *DSM-IV-TR*   mod. 48 p. 537
23. Panic attacks   mod. 49 p. 542
24. dissociative identity disorder   mod. 49 p. 546
25. Psychoanalytic   mod. 48 p. 535

26. Schizophrenia has both biological and environmental origins.
   • Being more common in families suggests genetic factors seem to be involved.
   • Biochemical or structural abnormality (dopamine hypothesis) or exposure to a virus during pregnancy are suggested causes.
   • Regression to earlier experiences and stages; lack of strong ego, id acts with no concern for reality—inability to cope.
   • Another theory suggests high levels of expressed emotion.
   • Genetic factors may become evident in twins who are reared apart if genetic factors held when environments changed.
   • Different family lifestyles may indicate certain factors that precipitate the condition in twins who have been identified with genetic factors that predispose them to schizophrenia.

Practice Test 3:
1. b   mod. 49 p. 553
a. Incorrect. This is one of the major symptoms.
*b. Correct. Dissociative identity disorder, also known as multiple personality disorder, is not associated with schizophrenia.
c. Incorrect. This is a common symptom of schizophrenia.
d. Incorrect. This is a common symptom of schizophrenia.

2.   c   mod. 49 p. 536
a.   Incorrect. This statement is consistent with the sociocultural model.
b.   Incorrect. See answer a.
*c. Correct. The sociocultural model recognizes that many aspects of abnormal behavior arise from the conditions of society; even psychic forces within the individual would reflect conflicts in society.
d.   Incorrect. See answer a.

3.   b   mod. 49 p. 542
a.   Incorrect. A phobic disorder is an irrational fear of a specific situation or object.
*b. Correct. This describes a panic attack.
c.   Incorrect. Generalized anxiety disorder is very similar to this condition, but it occurs without the rapid heartbeat, shortness of breath, and becoming faint (that is, without the panic).
d.   Incorrect. Obsessive-compulsive disorder is marked by uncontrollable thoughts and compulsions to carry out ritualistic behaviors, not by panic.

4.   a   mod. 48 p. 536
*a. Correct. The sociocultural model of abnormality emphasizes the interactions between people as well as the conditions of society as contributors to abnormal behavior.
b.   Incorrect. The behavioral model would attribute abnormal behavior to faulty learning.
c.   Incorrect. The humanistic model would attribute abnormal behavior to conflicts within the self.
d.   Incorrect. The psychoanalytic model would attribute abnormal behavior to inner psychic conflicts.

5.   b   mod. 49 p. 542
a.   Incorrect. It is possible for someone with schizophrenia to have irrational fears of snakes, but this kind of fear is more likely a phobia.
*b. Correct. A phobia is a persistent, irrational fear of an object or situation.
c.   Incorrect. While the psychiatrist is more prone to using a medical model, the term "organic reactions" is not used to describe any known ailment.
d.   Incorrect. Obsessive-compulsive disorder is marked by uncontrollable thoughts and compulsions to carry out ritualistic behaviors, not by panic.

6.   a   mod. 49 p. 542
*a. Correct. A phobia is a persistent, irrational fear of an object or situation.

b.   Incorrect. Panic disorder involves extreme anxiety and a sense of impending, unavoidable doom accompanied by rapid heartbeat, shortness of breath, and becoming faint and dizzy.
c.   Incorrect. Obsessive-compulsive disorder is marked by uncontrollable thoughts and compulsions to carry out ritualistic behaviors, not by panic.
d.   Incorrect. There is no category called tension disorder.

7.   b   mod. 49 p. 545
a.   Incorrect. This falls in the class of somatoform disorders, but another choice offers the specific disorder.
*b. Correct. In a conversion disorder, psychological problems are converted into physical problems, often without the sufferer showing the concern one might expect if the situation were a truly serious physical condition.
c.   Incorrect. Panic disorder involves extreme anxiety and a sense of impending, unavoidable doom accompanied by rapid heartbeat, shortness of breath, and becoming faint and dizzy.
d.   Incorrect. Obsessive-compulsive disorder is marked by uncontrollable thoughts and compulsions to carry out ritualistic behaviors, not by loss of voice.

8.   c   mod. 49 p. 543
a.   Incorrect. Panic disorder involves extreme anxiety and a sense of impending, unavoidable doom accompanied by rapid heartbeat, shortness of breath, and becoming faint and dizzy.
b.   Incorrect. A phobia is a persistent, irrational fear of an object or situation.
*c. Correct. Obsessive-compulsive disorder is marked by uncontrollable thoughts and compulsions to carry out ritualistic behaviors, like counting the number of times the professor says "the" in the lecture.
d.   Incorrect. Generalized anxiety is the feeling that something bad is about to happen without any direct object causing the fear or anxiety.

9.   d   mod. 49 p. 551
a.   Incorrect. Less than 1 percent at any given time.
b.   Incorrect. Less than 1 percent at any given time.
c.   Incorrect. Less than 1 percent at any given time.
*d. Correct. As many as 7 percent of the population may experience alcohol dependence each year.

10. c   mod. 49 p. 547
a.   Incorrect. Drugs are not typically used in this state, because the condition is not typically recognized until the memory is recovered.
b.   Incorrect. In dissociative amnesia, the loss can be permanent.
*c.   Correct. The fugue state helps the person escape an anxiety-producing situation, and sometime after the escape, memory can be recovered.
d.   Incorrect. In dissociative amnesia, the memories are considered present, but psychologically blocked.

11. a   mod. 49 p. 553
*a.   Correct. Reactive schizophrenia also has a better treatment outlook.
b.   Incorrect. Although process schizophrenia is marked by gradual withdrawal, reactive schizophrenia can be just as withdrawn.
c.   Incorrect. No type of schizophrenia is necessarily aggressive or abusive.
d.   Incorrect. Neither type has been shown to be more hereditary than the other.

12. d   mod. 49 p. 552
a.   Incorrect. Disorganized schizophrenia involves inappropriate laughter and giggling, silliness, incoherent speech, infantile behavior, and strange behaviors.
b.   Incorrect. Catatonic schizophrenia involves disturbances of movement, sometimes a loss of all motion, sometimes with the opposite extreme of wild, violent movement.
c.   Incorrect. Paranoid schizophrenia is marked by delusions and hallucinations related to persecution or delusions of grandeur, loss of judgment, and unpredictable behavior.
*d.   Correct. Residual schizophrenia displays minor symptoms of schizophrenia after a stressful episode.

13. d   mod. 49 p. 556
a.   Incorrect. Learned helplessness is used to explain other problems (like depression) more than it is used to explain schizophrenia.
b.   Incorrect. The dopamine hypothesis relates schizophrenia to an excess of dopamine.
c.   Incorrect. The predisposition model suggests that a genetic predisposition exists for developing schizophrenia.
*d.   Correct. This attention to inappropriate social stimuli is the foundation of the learned-inattention theory.

14. c   mod. 49 p. 557
a.   Incorrect. This sounds like paranoia.
b.   Incorrect. Personality disorder is not considered a mix of schizophrenic symptoms.
*c.   Correct. Personality disorders are marked by inflexible, maladaptive personality traits, and these can take several forms.
d.   Incorrect. An extended sense of euphoria and elation is found in the manic state of bipolar disorder.

15. a   mod. 49 p. 557
*a.   Correct. Tanisha's apparent action without conscience and manipulation of the system are hallmarks of the antisocial or sociopathic personality disorder.
b.   Incorrect. This does not describe someone who is self-defeating.
c.   Incorrect. Because this is not cyclic behavior, it could not be considered premenstrual dysphoric disorder.
d.   Incorrect. While having multiple personalities is not ruled out, the condition is better described as sociopathic personality disorder.

16. a   mod. 49 p. 557
17. d   mod. 49 p. 557
18. c   mod. 49 p. 558
19. b   mod. 49 p. 557

20. medical   mod. 48 p. 534
21. anxiety   mod. 49 p. 541
22. agoraphobia   mod. 49 p. 542
23. repressed memories   mod. 49 p. 547
24. Aaron Beck   mod. 49 p. 550

25.
▪   Describe the major symptoms of schizophrenia.
▪   Distinguish process and reactive, and examine the list of types.
▪   Discuss the biological and psychological components.

511

Chapter 16: Treatment of Psychological Disorders

Module 51: Psychotherapy: Psychodynamic, Behavioral, and Cognitive Approaches to Treatment

Module 52: Psychotherapy: Humanistic, Interpersonal, and Group Approaches to Treatment

Module 53: Biomedical Therapy: Biological Approaches to Treatment

Overview

In this set of modules, the treatment of psychological disorders is discussed.

Module 51 presents the psychodynamic approach, which seeks to resolve unconscious conflicts. Also explained are the behavioral approaches, which suggest that the outward behavior must be changed, using behaviors such as aversive conditioning, systematic desensitization, observational learning, and contingency contracting. Dialectic behavior therapy, a new form of behavioral therapy, is also described. Cognitive approaches such as rational-emotive therapy and cognitive-behavioral therapy suggest that the goal of therapy should be to help a person restructure his or her belief system to reflect a more logical, realistic view of the world.

Module 52 offers a discussion of the humanistic approach, focusing on issues related to the person's taking responsibility for his or her own actions regarding the meaning of life. Interpersonal therapy focuses on the interpersonal relationships of the individual. Treatment involving both group and family therapy is presented. Finally, a discussion on the effectiveness of psychotherapy is presented.

Module 53 presents the biomedical therapy for the treatment of psychological disorders. Drug therapy has made psychotic patients calmer, alleviated depression, and calmed anxiety. Also, the controversy surrounding electroconvulsive therapy and psychosurgery, treatments of last resort, is presented. Finally, a discussion presents the issues that the community health movement now must cope with in providing care for deinstitutionalized patients. This movement has led to the development of such services as hotlines and campus crisis centers.

To further investigate the topics covered in this chapter, you can visit the related Web sites by visiting the following link: www.mhhe.com/feldmanup8.

Prologue: Conquering Schizophrenia
Looking Ahead

Psychodynamic Approaches to Therapy
Behavioral Approaches to Therapy
Cognitive Approaches to Therapy

- **What are the goals of psychologically and biologically based treatment approaches?**
- **What are the psychodynamic, behavioral, and cognitive approaches to treatment?**

Psychotherapy: Psychodynamic, Behavioral, and Cognitive Approaches to Treatment

The common goal of therapy is relief of the psychological disorder and enabling individuals to achieve richer, more meaningful lives. Psychologically based therapy is called

[a] _____, a process in which a patient (client) and a professional work together to deal with psychological difficulties. **[b]** _____ depends on drugs and other medical procedures. Many therapists today draw on the large number of therapies for the approach most suited to the client, and this is considered a(n) **[c]** _____ to therapy.

[d] _____ assumes that the primary causes of abnormal behavior are unresolved conflicts from the past and anxiety over unconscious impulses. The

[e] _____ that individuals use to guard against anxiety do not bury these anxieties completely, and they emerge in the form of *neurotic symptoms*. Freud said that the way to deal with unwanted desires and past conflicts was to confront them, to make them conscious.

The role of the **[f]** _____ is then to explore the unconscious conflicts and help

the patient understand them. Techniques such as **[g]** _____ and

[h] _____ are used. _____ **[i]**, or the transfer of feelings such as love or anger to a psychoanalyst, as well as its examination, also plays an important role in psychoanalysis.

The principles of reinforcement are central to **[j]** _____, which suggests that both abnormal and normal behavior is learned. To modify abnormal behavior, new behaviors must be learned. Behavioral psychologists are not interested in the past history of the individual, focusing instead on the current behavior.

Classical conditioning principles are applied to behaviors like alcoholism, smoking, and drug

abuse, with a technique known as **[k]** _____. In aversive conditioning, the unwanted behavior is linked with a stimulus that produces an unpleasant response, like a drug that produces vomiting when mixed with alcohol. The long-term effectiveness of the approach is questionable. The most successful classical conditioning technique is called [l] _____, in which a person is taught to relax and is then gradually exposed to an anxiety-provoking stimulus. It has been successful with phobias, anxiety disorders, and impotence.

[m] _____ is used in therapy by having the therapist or another person role model appropriate behaviors. People can be taught skills and ways of handling anxiety by observing a model cope with the same situation. Another technique used in behavioral therapy is

[n] _____, in which individuals are rewarded with tokens that can be exchanged for desired objects or opportunities. This technique is often used in group homes or other institutional settings. Behavior therapy works well for phobias and compulsions; however, it is not very effective for deep depression or personality disorders.

Cognitive approaches to therapy attempt to change faulty cognitions held by patients about themselves and the world. The therapies also typically involve the application of learning

principles and thus are often called [o] _____. [p] _____ is one of the best examples of the cognitive approach. The therapist attempts to restructure the person's belief system into a more realistic, rational, and logical set of views.

Evaluate

_____ 1. biomedical therapy

_____ 2. psychodynamic therapy

_____ 3. psychoanalysis

_____ 4. behavioral treatment approaches

_____ 5. cognitive approaches to therapy

a. Basic sources of abnormal behavior are unresolved past conflicts and anxiety.

b. People's faulty cognitions about themselves and the world are changed to more accurate ones.

c. Appropriate treatment consists of learning new behavior or unlearning maladaptive behavior.

d. A form of psychodynamic therapy that often lasts for many years.

e. Uses drugs and other medical procedures to improve psychological functioning.

Rethink

51-1   In what ways are psychoanalysis and cognitive therapy similar, and how do they differ?

51-2   *From the perspective of a child-care provider:* How might you use systematic desensitization to help children overcome their fears?

Spotlight on Terminology and Language—ESL Pointers

Page 556 "For weeks they had practiced dance steps, shopped for **formals**, **fretted** about hairstyles and what on earth to say to their partners."

Formals are dressy dresses or long gowns that are worn for important social events.

To **fret** about something is to worry about something.

Page 556 "Brandon Fitch, wearing a pinstripe suit and an ear-to-ear grin, **shimmied with a high-stepping blond**."

The **shimmy** was a popular jazz dance from the 1920's. When someone "**shimmies with a high-stepping blond**" they are dancing with someone with blonde colored hair.

Page 556 "Daphne Moss, sporting a floral dress and white **corsage**, delighted her dad by letting him cut in."

A **corsage** is a small bouquet worn on a dress or jacket during formal social events.

Page 556 "The usually quiet Kevin Buchberger leaped onto the dance floor and flat-out **boogied** for the first time in his life, while Kevin Namkoong grabbed an electric guitar and jammed with the band."

To **boogie** is to dance to fast music.

Page 556 "The prom at Case Western Reserve University had hit **full tilt**."

When you do something **"full tilt"** you are doing it fully and energenically.

Page 556 "The memories are too **bleak**, too fragmented to convey."

When something is **bleak** it is depressing or discouraging.

Page 556 "The dinner dance, organized with help from psychiatrists and counselors at Case Western Reserve's affiliated University Hospitals, in Cleveland, served as a **bittersweet** celebration of shared loss and regained hope. (Wallis & Willwerth, 1992, p. 53)."

Something that is **bittersweet** is both happy and sad at the same time.

Page 557 "**In light of** the variety of psychological approaches, it is not surprising that the people who provide therapy vary considerably in educational background and training (see Figure 1)."

The term **"in light of"** something means considering or taking something into account.

Page 557 "But therapy is also provided by people in fields **allied with** psychology, such as psychiatry and social work."

Allied with means related to. Can you identify any other field that might be associated with psychology?

Page 558 "How does one **rid oneself** of the anxiety produced by unconscious, unwanted impulses and drives?"

To **rid oneself** from something is to make you free of it.

Page 558 "To Freud, the answer was to **confront** the conflicts and impulses by bringing them out of the unconscious part of the mind and into the conscious part."

To **confront** is to face up to these impulses and conflicts.

Page 559 "They will then be able to 'work through' – understand and **rectify** – those difficulties.

To **rectify** is to correct, to cure.

Page 559 "Psychoanalysts tell patients to say aloud whatever comes to mind, regardless of its apparent **irrelevance** or senselessness, and the analysts attempt to recognize and label the connections between what a patient says and the patient's unconscious."

Irrelevance is insignificance or unimportance.

Page 559 "Because of the close, almost intimate interaction between patient and psychoanalyst, the relationship between the two often becomes **emotionally charged** and takes on a complexity unlike most other relationships."

Something that is **emotionally charged** is full of emotion or feelings.

Page 559 "Patients may eventually think of the analyst as a symbol of a **significant other** in their past, perhaps a parent or a lover, and apply some of their feelings for that person to the analyst—a phenomenon known as transference."

A **significant other** is a person who is important to you like a spouse or a lover.

Page 559 "It was my mother—**rest her soul**—who loved us, not our father."

When someone who says **"rest her soul"** they are asking that the soul or spirit of a dead person is allowed to rest peacefully.

Page 559 "You're just sitting there—**smirking**—making me feel like a bad person—thinking I'm wrong for being mad, that I have no right to be mad."

A **smirk** is a smile expressing feelings like self-satisfaction or superiority.

Page 560 "Moreover, no **conclusive** evidence shows that psychoanalysis, as originally conceived by Freud in the nineteenth century, works better than other, more recent versions of psychodynamic therapy."

No **conclusive** evidence means no definite, convincing, irrefutable evidence exists.

Page 560 "Furthermore, less **articulate** patients may not do as well as more verbal ones do."

Articulate persons are expressive and communicative. They speak clearly.

Page 560 "Determining effectiveness depends on reports from the therapist or the patients themselves, reports that are obviously **open to bias** and **subjective interpretation**."

A **bias** is an unfair preference or dislike for something.

Something that is **subjective** is based on someone's opinions and is not impartial.

An **interpretation** is an explanation or understanding. A **subjective interpretation** is an explanation that is based on someone's opinions and not on fact.

Page 560 "Critics have questioned the entire theoretical basis of psychodynamic theory, maintaining that **constructs** such as the unconscious have not been proved to exist."

A **construct** is an idea of theory that is the result of organized thought.

Page 560 "To proponents, it not only provides effective treatment in many cases of psychological disturbance but also permits the potential development of an unusual **degree of insight** into one's life (Barber & Lane, 1995; Clay, 2000; Ablon & Jones, 2005)."

The **"degree of insight"** refers to the amount self-awareness or ability to understand yourself and your won problems.

Page 561 "People who act abnormally either have failed to learn the skills they need to cope with the problems of everyday living or have **acquired faulty** skills and patterns that are being maintained through some form of reinforcement."

To **acquire** something is to obtain or get it.

Things that are **faulty** are out of order or have defects.

Page 561 "To modify abnormal behavior, then, behavioral approaches propose that people must learn new behavior to replace the faulty skills they have developed and unlearn their **maladaptive** behavior patterns (Bergin & Garfield, 1994; Agras & Berkowitz, 1996; Krijn, Emmelkamp, Olafsson, & Biemond, 2004)."

Things that are **maladaptive** are poorly adapted to a specific situation or purpose.

Page 561 "Behavioral psychologists do not need to **delve into** people's pasts or their psyches."

When you **delve into** something, you explore it further or verbally probe for more information.

Page 561 "Suppose you bite into your favorite candy bar and find that it is not only **infested** with ants but that you've swallowed a bunch of them?"

Infested with ants means it is bug-ridden, there are many ants here.

Page 561 "You immediately become sick to your stomach and **throw up**."

Throw-up is a slang word for vomit.

Page 561 "Also, important ethical concerns surround aversion techniques that employ such **potent** stimuli as electric shock, which therapists use only in the most extreme cases, such as patient **self-mutilation**."

Something that is **potent** is strong or powerful and produces a result.

Self-mutilation is the act of inducing injury to your self.

Page 562 "Systematic desensitization has proved to be an effective treatment for a number of problems, including phobias, anxiety disorders, and even **impotence** and fear of sexual contact."

Impotence is the inability to perform sexual intercourse in men.

Page 563 "Patients are taught that even if they experience unhappiness, or anger, or any other negative emotion, it doesn't need to **rule their behavior**."

When something "**rules your behavior**" it controls what you do.

Page 564 "If you assumed that illogical thoughts and beliefs lie at the heart of psychological disorders, wouldn't the most direct treatment route be to teach people new, more **adaptive modes of thinking**?"

A **mode** is a way of doing things.

An "**adaptive mode of thinking**" is a way of thinking that is usable in different conditions.

Page 564 "Such irrational beliefs **trigger** negative emotions, which in turn support the irrational beliefs, leading to a self-defeating cycle."

When something **triggers** something it starts it.

Page 565 "There are **nagging doubts** about what I should—"

Nagging doubts are uncertainties that repeatedly bother the person.

Module 52: Psychotherapy: Humanistic, Interpersonal, and Group Approaches to Treatment

Humanistic Therapy
Interpersonal Therapy
Group Therapy
Evaluating Psychotherapy: Does Therapy Work?

Applying Psychology in the 21st Century:
Virtual Reality Therapy: Facing the Images of Fear

Exploring Diversity: Racial and Ethnic Factors in
Treatment: Should Therapists Be Color-Blind?

- *What are the humanistic approaches to treatment?*
- *What is interpersonal therapy?*
- *How does group therapy differ from individual types of therapy?*
- *How effective is therapy, and which kind of therapy works best in a given situation?*

Psychotherapy: Humanistic, Interpersonal, and Group Approaches to Treatment

[a] _____ depends on the perspective of self-responsibility as the basis for treatment. The view is that we control our own behavior, make choices about how to live, and it is up to us to solve our problems. Humanistic therapists see themselves as guides or facilitators.

[b] _____ refers to approaches that do not offer interpretations or answers to problems. First practiced by Carl Rogers, [c] _____ was founded on the nondirective approach providing [d] _____. Rogers attempted to establish a warm and accepting environment in order to enable the client to make realistic and constructive choices about life.

[e] _____ has the goal of integrating the client's thoughts and feelings into a whole. The approach aims to help clients broaden their perspectives on a situation. He asked the client to go back and work on unfinished business, such as playing the part of the angry father and taking other roles in an unresolved conflict.

[f] _____ focuses on conducting therapy in the context of social relationships. It is typically more directive than other psychodynamic approaches, as well as shorter in duration. [g] _____ is a form of treatment that has several unrelated people meet with a therapist at the same time. Problems, usually one held in common with all group members, are discussed with the group, while members of the group provide social support.

[h] _____ is a specialized form of group therapy that involves two or more members of a family. Therapists focus on the entire family system rather than only on the family member with the problem, and each family member is expected to contribute to the solution. Family therapists assume that family members engage in set patterns of behavior, and the goal of therapy is to get the family to adopt more constructive behaviors.

Since Eysenck's famous study in 1952, a sizable body of research has been devoted to the question of whether psychotherapy works. Eysenck concluded that the majority of people recover without psychotherapeutic treatment, a phenomenon known as **[i]** _____. However, numerous studies since, using _meta analyses,_ experimental designs with control groups, as well as surveys, now make it clear that therapy works. Importantly, however, certain types of therapies are better for certain types of problems, and no single form of therapy works best for every problem or every person.

Evaluate

_____ 1. rational-emotive therapy

_____ 2. cognitive therapy

_____ 3. person-centered therapy

_____ 4. humanistic therapy

_____ 5. eclectic approach to therapy

a. Therapy in which a variety of techniques and perspectives is used to treat a client's problems.

b. The therapist reflects back the patient's statements in a way that helps the patient find solutions.

c. People have control of their behavior, can make choices about their lives, and are essentially responsible for solving their own problems.

d. Attempts to restructure one's belief into a more realistic, rational, and logical system.

e. People are taught to change illogical thoughts about themselves and the world.

Rethink

52-1 How can people be successfully treated in group therapy when individuals with the "same" problem arc so different? What advantages might group therapy offer over individual therapy?

52-2 _From the perspective of a social worker:_ How might the types of therapies you employ vary depending on a client's cultural and socioeconomic background?

Page 567 "As you know from your own experience, a student cannot **master the material** covered in a course without some hard work, no matter how good the teacher and the textbook are."

The phrase "**master the material**" means that a student has learned the subject that they have been studying.

Page 567 "The many types of therapy that fall into this category have a similar **rationale**: We have control of our own behavior, we can make choices about the kinds of lives we want to live, and it is up to us to solve the difficulties we encounter in our daily lives."

The therapies have a similar **rationale**; they have a similar underlying principle.

Page 567 "In this view, psychological disorders result from the inability to **find meaning in** life and feeling lonely and **unconnected** to others (Cain, 2002)."

To **find meaning in** something is to find significance or value in it.

When you are **unconnected** you are separate or not joined or linked together.

Page 567 "I somehow developed a sort of a **knack**, I guess, of—well—habit—of trying to make people feel at ease around me, or to make things go along smoothly . . ."

A **knack** is a skill or talent that is usually inborn and is difficult to teach.

Page 567 "Now the reason why I did it probably was—I mean, not that I was a good little **Samaritan** going around making other people happy, but that was probably the role that felt easiest for me to play . . ."

A **Samaritan** is someone who helps people in need.

Page 568 "By providing a **warm** and **accepting** environment, therapists hope to motivate clients **to air** their problems and feelings."

A **warm** environment is one that is friendly.

An **accepting** environment is a welcoming one.

To air something is to get it out in the open.

Page 568 "In turn, this enables clients to make realistic and **constructive** choices and decisions about the things that bother them in their current lives (Bozarth, Zimring, & Tausch, 2002)."

Constructive choices are those that are productive and useful.

Page 568 "**Furnishing** unconditional positive regard does not mean that therapists must approve of everything their clients say or do."

Furnishing unconditional positive regard means providing unconditional positive regard.

Page 568 "Person-centered therapy is rarely used today in its **purest** form."

When something is in its **purest** form it is free from contamination or impurities.

Page 568 "In gestalt therapy, people are led to examine their earlier experiences and complete any "unfinished business" from their past that may still affect and **color present-day** relationships."

To **color** something is to slant the way someone thinks about something.

Things that are **present-day** are current, or exist now.

Page 568 "However, humanistic treatments lack specificity, a problem that has **troubled** their critics."

Someone who is **troubled** is experiencing emotional conflicts or psychological difficulties.
Page 568 "Growing out of contemporary psychodynamic approaches, interpersonal therapy focuses more on **the here and now** with the goal of improving a client's current relationships."

The here and now is the present.

Page 569 "The other members of the group provide emotional support and **dispense** advice on ways in which they have coped effectively with similar problems (Yalom, 1997; Free, 2000; Alonso, Alonso, & Piper, 2003)."

When people **dispense** advice they are giving out advice.

Page 569 "But rather than focusing simply on the members of the family who present the initial problem, family therapists consider the family as a **unit**, to which each member contributes."

A unit is an organized group.

Page 569 "Many family therapists believe that family members fall into rigid roles or **set patterns** of behavior, with one person acting as the **scapegoat**, another as a **bully**, and so forth."

Set patterns are designs that are inflexible and unbending.

A **scapegoat** is a person that takes the blame for others.

A **bully** is an aggressive person who mistreats others.

Page 570 "He can't concentrate on his studies, has a lot of trouble getting to sleep, and—this is what really bothers him—has begun to think that people are **ganging up** on him, **talking about him behind his back**."

To **gang up** on someone is join together especially for the purpose of attacking them.

When someone **talks about another person behind their back** they say one thing when the person is present and then say the opposite when the person is not present.

Page 570 "He is fairly skeptical of psychologists, thinking that a lot of what they say is just **mumbo jumbo**, but he's willing to put his doubts aside and try anything to feel better."

Mumbo jumbo is unnecessarily involved and incomprehensible language, also known as gibberish.

Page 570 "In fact, identifying the single most appropriate form of treatment is a controversial, and still **unresolved**, task for psychologists specializing in psychological disorders."

When something is **unresolved** the issue remains unanswered and the resolution is unclear.

Page 570 "Although others quickly challenged Eysenck's conclusions, his review stimulated a continuing stream of better controlled, more carefully **crafted** studies on the effectiveness of psychotherapy, and today most psychologists agree: Therapy does work."

When we **craft** something we designed and make things by hand.

Page 570 "In most cases, then, the symptoms of abnormal behavior do not go away by themselves if left untreated—although the issue continues to be **hotly debated** (Bergin & Garfield, 1994; Seligman, 1996; Sohn, 1996)."

Things that are **hotly debated** are argued about with a lot of emotion.

Page 571 "Furthermore, a large-scale survey of 186,000 individuals found that although survey respondents felt they had benefited substantially from psychotherapy (see Figure 2), there was little difference in "**consumer satisfaction**" on the basis of the specific type of treatment they had received (CR, 1995; Seligman, 1995; Strupp, 1996; Nielsen et al., 2004)."

A **consumer** is a buyer of goods and services.

Satisfaction is happiness with something.

Consumer satisfaction occurs when buyers are happy with the goods or services they have purchased.

Page 572 "Jimmy does not pay attention, **daydreams** often, and frequently falls asleep during class."

When someone **daydreams** they experience a series of distracting and unusually pleasant thoughts while being awake.

Page 572 "There is a strong possibility that Jimmy is harboring repressed rage that needs to be **ventilated** and dealt with."

To **ventilate** is to publicly discuss grievances or opinions.

Page 572 "Clearly, therapists *cannot* be "**color-blind**."

A **color-blind** person is not able to determine the difference between various colors because of a defect in their vision.

Page 573 "For 20 years, the woman—**nicknamed Miss Muffet**—had suffered from an anxiety disorder in which she had profound spider phobia:"

A **nickname** is an invented or shortened name that is used affectionately or as a form of humor.

Little Miss Muffet is a children's storybook character who was afraid of spiders.

Page 573 "She routinely **fumigated** her car with smoke and pesticides to get rid of spiders."

To **fumigate** is to disinfect or sterilize something.

Page 573 "Every night she **sealed** all her bedroom windows with **duct tape** after scanning the room for spiders."

When we **seal** something we close it so tightly so that nothing else can enter the container.

Duct tape is a very strong wide type of tape that is designed to be used to make temporary repairs to pipes.

Page 573 "After washing her clothes, she immediately sealed them inside a **plastic bag** to make sure they remained free of spiders (Hoffman, 2004, p. 58)."

A **plastic bag** is a container made from plastic, a synthetic or artificial material.

Page 573 "What she found was a **novel** approach using virtual-reality therapy."

A **novel** approach is original or new and unique.

Page 573 "The display projects an image of anxiety-producing situation onto the inside of a **helmet visor**, and the image moves according to head or hand movements (Wiederhold & Wiederhold, 2005)."

A **helmet** is a hard protective head covering.

A **visor** is a transparent shade for the eyes that is attached to helmets

Page 573 "In this case, Miss Muffet saw a range of anxiety-producing images, beginning with a view of a realistic virtual tarantula in a **virtual** kitchen."

Something that is **virtual** is simulated; it is not real -- it is made by a computer.

Page 574 "Because no single type of psychotherapy is invariable effective, **eclectic** approaches to therapy have become increasingly popular."

An **eclectic** approach is an approach to therapy in which the psychotherapist combines techniques and ideas from many different schools of thought.

Drug Therapy
Electroconvulsive Therapy (ECT)
Psychosurgery
Biomedical Therapies in Perspective
Community Psychology: Focus on Prevention

Becoming an Informed Consumer of Psychology:
Choosing the Right Therapist

- ***How are drug, electroconvulsive, and psychosurgical techniques used today in the treatment of psychological disorders?***

Biomedical Therapy: Biological Approaches to Treatment

Biomedical treatments that treat brain chemical imbalances and other neurological factors directly are regularly used for some problems. In **[a]** _____, drugs are given that alleviate symptoms for several psychological disturbances. In the mid-1950s,

[b] _____ were introduced, causing a major change in the treatment of patients in mental hospitals. These drugs alleviate symptoms related to the patient's loss of touch with reality, agitation, and overactivity. **[c]** _____ are used to improve the moods of severely depressed patients. These drugs work by increasing the concentration of certain neurotransmitters. **[d]** _____, a form of simple mineral salt, has been used to treat bipolar disorders. It ends manic episodes 70 percent of the time, though its success with depression is not as good. **[e]** _____—Valium and Xanax—are among the drugs most prescribed by physicians. These drugs reduce the anxiety level experienced by reducing excitability. Long-term use can be problematic, however, because they can lead to drug dependence.

Physicians in the 1930s found a way to induce convulsions using electric shocks.

[f] _____ is administered by passing an electric current of 70 to 150 volts through the head of a patient. The patient is usually sedated and given muscle relaxants to prevent violent contractions. ECT is controversial because of its side effects, which include disorientation, confusion, and memory loss, but it continues to be used because it does help severely depressed patients when other treatments are ineffective. A new alternative to ECT is **[g]** _____, which involves directing a magnetic pulse to a specific area of the brain. It is still considered an experimental treatment, though results are promising.

[h] _____ is brain surgery used to alleviate psychological symptoms. An early procedure was **[i]** _____, in which parts of the frontal lobes are removed or destroyed. The patients are then less subject to emotional impulses.

[j] _____ is a form of psychology aimed at preventing or minimizing the incidence of psychological disorders. One issue community psychologists hoped to address was assisting in the process of **[k]** _____, in which patients are transferred from residence in institutions back into the community. Though many former mental institution patients still do not make this transition effectively, the community psychology movement has had a positive impact in other ways, such as developing "hot lines" and crisis centers.

Evaluate

_____ 1. antipsychotic drugs

_____ 2. antidepressant drugs

_____ 3. antianxiety drugs

_____ 4. chlorpromazine

_____ 5. lithium

a. Temporarily alleviate symptoms such as agitation and overactivity.

b. Used in the treatment of schizophrenia.

c. Improves a patient's mood and feeling of well-being.

d. Used in the treatment of bipolar disorders.

e. Alleviate stress and feelings of apprehension.

Rethink

53-1 One of the main criticisms of biological therapies is that they treat the symptoms of mental disorder without uncovering and treating the underlying problems from which people are suffering. Do you agree with this criticism or not? Why?

53-2 _From the perspective of a politician:_ How would you go about regulating the use of electroconvulsive therapy and psychosurgery? Would you restrict their use or make either one completely illegal? Why?

Spotlight on Terminology and Language—ESL Pointers

Page 576 "Probably no greater change has occurred in mental hospitals than the successful introduction in the mid-1950s of antipsychotic drugs—drugs used to reduce severe symptoms of disturbance, such as **loss of touch with reality** and agitation."

When some one has a **loss of touch with reality** they are not aware what is real and what it not real.

Page 576 "Previously, the typical mental hospital fulfilled all the stereotypes of the nineteenth-century insane asylum, giving mainly **custodial care** to screaming, moaning, **clawing** patients who displayed the most bizarre behaviors."

Custodial care involves mostly watching and protecting patients, rather than seeking to cure them.

To **claw** something is to scratch or dig at something or someone with claws or fingernails.

Page 576 "SSRIs target the neurotransmitter serotonin, permitting it to **linger** at the synapse. One of the latest antidepressants, Nefazodone (Serzone), blocks serotonin at some receptor sites but not others (see Figure 2; Berman, Krystal, & Charney, 1996; Williams et al., 2000; Anand, 2002; Lucki & O'Leary, 2004)."

To **linger** is to delay leaving or to wait around somewhere.

Page 576 "In particular, the antidepressant *Fluoxetine*, sold under the trade name *Prozac*, has been **highlighted** on magazine covers and has been the topic of **best-sellers**."

To **highlight** something is to emphasize or draw attention to it.

A **best–seller** is a book that sells a large number of copies in a short period of time.

Page 576 "Does Prozac deserve its **acclaim**?"

Acclaim is enthusiastic approval or praise.

Page 576 "Compared with other antidepressants, Prozac (along with its cousins Luvox, Paxil, Celexa, and Zoloft) has relatively few **side effects**."

A **side effect** is an effect of drug that is not wanted or liked.

Page 576 "However, like all drugs, Prozac does not **agree** with everyone."

To **agree** is to have the same opinion about something as someone else.

Page 577 "Often, people who have had episodes of bipolar disorder can take a daily dose of lithium that prevents a **recurrence** of their symptoms."

A **recurrence** occurs when something appears again after having gone away for some time. Lithium is used to prevent a reappearance or return of the symptoms.

Page 577 "But a more important issue concerns their use to **suppress** anxiety."

To **suppress** anxiety is to hold it back, to keep it in check or to block it out.

Page 578 "Thus, drugs that **mask** anxiety may simply be hiding other difficulties."

To **mask** something is to hide it.

Page 578 "But she **balked** when her therapist recommended electroconvulsive therapy, commonly known as "shock treatment."

To **balk** at something is to be unwilling to do it.

Page 578 "Despite her training and practice as a clinical psychologist, Manning immediately **flashed** to scenes from *One Flew Over the Cuckoo's Nest*, "with McMurphy and the Chief jolted with electroshock, their bodies **flailing** with each **jolt**" (Guttman, 1995, p. 16)."

When your thoughts **flash** to something you are experiencing a sudden and brief thought or emotion.

When your body **flails** you are tossing your body around violently or uncontrollably.

A **jolt** is a shock.

Page 578 "Although it did produce some memory loss and temporary headaches, the procedure also brought Manning back from the **brink of suicide**."

To be on the **brink** of something is to be on the verge or edge of doing it.

Suicide is the act of intentionally killing yourself.

The treatment brought her back from being **on the verge of killing herself**.

Page 578 "Usually health professionals **sedate** patients and give them muscle relaxants before administering the current, and this helps reduce the intensity of muscle contractions produced during ECT."

To be put under **sedation** is to anesthetize or to tranquilize.

Page 578 "Apart from the obvious **distastefulness** of a treatment that evokes images of electrocution, side effects occur frequently."

Things that are **distasteful** are unpleasant.

Page 578 "If ECT strikes you as a questionable procedure, the use of <u>psychosurgery</u>—brain surgery in which the object is to reduce symptoms of mental disorder—probably appears even more **dubious**."

Something that is **dubious** possibly of uncertain quality or approapriateness.

Page 578 "A technique used only rarely today, psychosurgery was introduced as a "**treatment of last resort**" in the 1930s."

A **treatment of last resort** is one that you would no choose unless there were no other choices left.

Page 579 "For example, in one common technique, a surgeon would **jab** an **ice pick** under a patient's eyeball and **swivel** it back and forth (Miller, 1994; El-Hai, 2005)."

To **jab** at someone is to punch sharply with short quick movements.

An **ice pick** is a long thin pick that is used to break ice into small sections.

To **swivel** is to spin or turn around.

Page 579 "Along with remission of the symptoms of the mental disorder, patients sometimes experienced personality changes, becoming **bland, colorless, and unemotional**."

Things that are **bland** are dull and featureless.

Things that are **colorless** have no color to them.

When someone is **unemotional** they are showing little or no feelings.

Page 579 "In some respects, no greater **revolution** has occurred in the field of mental health than biological approaches to treatment."

A **revolution** is a transformation or modernization in the field.

Page 579-580 "Research also makes it clear that no single treatment is effective **universally**, and that each type of treatment has both advantages and disadvantages (Brody et al., 2001; Hollon, Thase, & Markowitz, 2002; DeRubeis, Hollon, & Shelton, 2003)."

A treatment that is **universally** effective is on that is applicable to all situations.

Page 580 "In short, many people who need treatment do not get it, and in some cases care for people with psychological disorders has simply **shifted** from one type of treatment site to another (Kiesler & Simpkins, 1993; Torrey, 1997; Doyle, 2002; Lamb & Weinberger, 2005)."

To shift is to move to a different position.

Page 580 "Telephone **"hot lines"** are now common."

A **"telephone hot line"** is a phone number that people can call for advice or help.

Page 581 "If you decide to seek therapy, you're faced with a **daunting** task."

A **daunting** task is one that is overwhelming or discouraging.

Page 581 "It is not a **breach** of **etiquette** to put these matters **on the table** during an initial consultation."

A **breach** is a failure to obey or follow rules.

Etiquette refers to the rules of correct or polite behavior in social settings.

To put something **"on the table"** is to open it up for discussion.

Page 582 "The effort has the potential to **pay off handsomely**—as you experience a more positive, fulfilling, and meaningful life."

Things that **"pay off handsomely"** bring in an amount of money that is more than expected.

Test your knowledge of the modules by answering these questions. These questions have been placed in three Practice Tests. The first two tests consist of questions that will test your recall of factual knowledge. The third test contains questions that are challenging and primarily test for conceptual knowledge and your ability to apply that knowledge. Check your answers and review the feedback using the Answer Key in the following pages of the *Study Guide*.

PRACTICE TEST 1:

1. Clients requiring some form of medical treatment are typically treated by a:
   a. psychiatric nurse.
   b. counseling psychologist.
   c. psychiatrist.
   d. clinical psychologist.

2. Therapy in which change is brought about through discussions and interactions between client and professional is called:
   a. eclectic therapy.
   b. semantic therapy
   c. psychotherapy.
   d. interpersonal therapy.

3. Freud believed that in order to protect our egos from the unwanted entry of unacceptable unconscious thoughts and desires, we all use:
   a. transference.
   b. aversive conditioning.
   c. systematic desensitization.
   d. defense mechanisms.

4. Which alternative is **not** a term associated with psychodynamic therapy?
   a. Hierarchy of fears
   b. Neurotic symptoms
   c. Defense mechanisms
   d. Transference

5. Katrina wants to reduce her anxiety and eliminate her phobia of "confined spaces"; a technique that is based on classical conditioning is called:
   a. biofeedback.
   b. behavior modification.
   c. systematic desensitization.
   d. aversive conditioning.

6. Which of the following approaches to therapy would be **least** concerned with the underlying causes of abnormal behavior?
   a. Psychoanalytic
   b. Behavioral
   c. Eclectic
   d. Humanistic

7. The goal of rational-emotive therapy is to restructure one's beliefs about oneself and the world into:
   a. a view that focuses on problems that arise only when events fail to turn out as expected.
   b. a realization that it is necessary for one to love and be approved by each significant person in one's life.
   c. a rational, realistic, and logical system.
   d. an understanding of the role of emotion in behavior.

8. The best known of the humanistic therapies assumes at the outset that a person's troubles reflect unfulfilled potential. The approach is called:
   a. rational-emotive therapy.
   c. systematic desensitization.
   b. gestalt therapy.
   d. client-centered therapy.

9. Which therapies emphasize establishing inner rather than outer control of behavior?
   a. Psychodynamic and humanistic
   c. Rational-emotive and behavioral
   b. Psychodynamic and behavioral
   d. Behavioral and humanistic

10. The goal of person-centered therapy is to enable people to reach their potential for:
    a. getting in touch with reality.
    c. taking control of their thoughts.
    b. understanding the unconscious.
    d. self-actualization.

11. Dr. Johnson said that his client, Mr. Keane, was experiencing a spontaneous remission. This is:
    a. an attack, either verbal or physical, by the therapist against the client when provoked repeatedly.
    b. disappearance of psychological symptoms even without therapy.
    c. an emotional outburst by the client during the therapy session.
    d. behavior by a family member (especially one's spouse) that worsens one's psychological symptoms.

12. Mrs. Walleran was given antipsychotic drugs to alleviate psychotic symptoms by:
    a. increasing neurotransmitter function.
    b. blocking the production of dopamine.
    c. slowing down the autonomic nervous system.
    d. sedating her.

13. The most widely applied biological approach to treatment is:
    a. psychosurgery.
    c. genetic engineering.
    b. electroconvulsive therapy.
    d. drug therapy.

14. Which medication would most likely be given to someone experiencing a manic episode?
    a. Lithium
    c. Chlorpromazine
    b. Valium
    d. Librium

15. A procedure by which areas of the brain are removed or destroyed in order to control severe abnormal behaviors is called:
    a. psychosurgery.
    c. electroconvulsive therapy.
    b. shock therapy.
    d. personality therapy.

_____ 16. free association

_____ 17. manifest content

_____ 18. latent content

_____ 19. resistance

_____ 20. transference

a. A patient's transfer of certain strong feelings for others to the analyst.

b. The "true" message hidden within dreams.

c. The patient says everything that comes to mind, providing insights into the patient's unconscious.

d. An inability or unwillingness to discuss or reveal particular memories, thoughts, or motivations.

e. The surface description and interpretation of dreams.

21. Freudian therapy is called _____.

22. Systematic desensitization uses a(n) _____ of fears, where a patient is exposed to less threatening stimuli at first in order to treat phobias.

23. In Aaron Beck's _____, the therapist is less confrontive and more like a teacher.

24. Dr. Daly's training in psychotherapy gave him the skills to use a technique called _____, during which the patient will say anything that comes to mind.

25. _____ requires a written agreement between the therapist and the patient that specifies goals to be reached and consequences of reaching goals.

26. Describe the reasons why you think that psychotherapy works. Draw on the principles of psychology that have been discussed in previous chapters, such as learning principles, theories of development, and theories of personality, to explain why you think it is effective.

PRACTICE TEST 2:

1. Biomedical therapies:
    a. are the most common therapies used by clinical psychologists.
    b. are reserved for the less severe types of behavioral disorders.
    c. presume that many disorders result from improper nutrition, food additives, or exposure to toxic environmental chemicals.
    d. use drugs, shocks, or surgery to improve the client's functions.

2. With more and more information available, psychologists and psychiatrists often use an eclectic approach to therapy, which:
    a. first fragments the personality and then reconstructs it.
    b. is controversial because of its connection to the paranormal world of psychic phenomena.
    c. mixes techniques of various theoretical perspectives.
    d. is based on the teachings of Horatio Eclectic, a Danish therapist who promoted meditation as a therapeutic technique.

3. The basic premise of psychodynamic therapy is the notion that abnormal behavior is:
   a. repressing normal behaviors that need to be uncovered.
   b. the result of the ego repressing the superego.
   c. rooted in unresolved past conflicts, buried in the unconscious.
   d. the result of the ego failing to gain access to consciousness.

4. Psychoanalysts believe neurotic symptoms are caused by:
   a. defense mechanisms.
   b. anxiety.
   c. inappropriate choices.
   d. contingency contracting.

5. What technique is used in psychoanalysis to help the patient remember the experiences of a past relationship?
   a. Transcendence
   b. Transference
   c. Translation
   d. Transrotation

6. What happens to the reaction to alcohol following aversive conditioning for alcoholism?
   a. The reaction takes on that response associated with the aversion.
   b. There is no longer a craving for the alcohol.
   c. There is a fear of the alcohol.
   d. The alcohol becomes a source of anxiety.

7. Humanistic approaches to therapy emphasize:
   a. environmental control over actions.
   b. probing for unresolved hidden conflicts that arose long ago.
   c. discovering the unreasonableness of one's thoughts.
   d. personal choice and responsibility.

8. In rational-emotive therapy, the therapist challenges the client's:
   a. defensive views of the world.
   b. self-centered views of the world.
   c. paranoid views of the world.
   d. irrational views of the world.

9. Which of the following approaches to treatment takes the view that it is primarily the client's responsibility to make needed changes?
   a. Behavioral therapy
   b. Rational-emotive therapy
   c. Humanistic therapy
   d. Psychoanalytic therapy

10. In humanistic therapy, unconditional positive regard is provided to the client:
    a. as a reinforcement when goals have been met.
    b. as part of the contingency contract.
    c. no matter what the client says or does.
    d. to help resolve inner conflicts.

11. Which of the following therapies is most closely associated with the concepts of the "whole" and completing "unfinished business"?
    a. Behavioral therapy
    b. Rational-emotive therapy
    c. Humanistic therapy
    d. Gestalt therapy

12. As compared with individual therapy, group therapy gives the client:
    a. insight into his or her unconscious ideas.
    b. automatically performed fresh new habits.
    c. impressionistic feedback from others.
    d. logically correct thinking, free from delusions.

13. Chlorpromazine is most commonly used in the treatment of:
    a. mood disorders.   c. schizophrenia.
    b. anxiety disorders.   d. bipolar disorder.

14. Which drug is used to help prevent future occurrences of the behavioral disorder it is used to treat?
    a. Valium   c. Chlorpromazine
    b. Lithium   d. Librium

15. Antidepressant drugs improve the mood of depressed patients by:
    a. increasing the activity of the autonomic nervous system.
    b. suppressing the function of certain neurotransmitters.
    c. increasing the speed of neural transmission.
    d. increasing the concentration of certain neurotransmitters.

16. Which of the following types of treatment is rarely, if ever, still used?
    a. Electroconvulsive shock therapy   c. Psychotherapy
    b. Antipsychotic drugs   d. Psychosurgery

_____ 17.   aversive conditioning   a. A person is rewarded for performing desired behaviors.

_____ 18.   systematic desensitization b. Breaks unwanted habits by associating the habits with very unpleasant stimuli.

_____ 19.   token system

                                        c. Requires a written contract between a therapist and a
_____ 20.   contingency contracting   client that sets behavioral goals and rewards.

                                        d. A stimulus that evokes pleasant feelings is repeatedly
                                           paired with a stimulus that evokes anxiety.

21. In psychotherapy, the term _____ is used when a patient has the inability to discuss or reveal particular memories or thoughts.

22. _____ is a phenomenon in which the relationship between the analyst and the patient becomes emotionally charged and the analyst takes on the role of significant others in the patient's past.

23. An acceptance by the therapist of the individual, without conditions no matter what attitude is expressed by the client, is known as _____.

24. A method used by psychoanalysts of getting clues from the unconscious is _____.

25. Most therapists use a somewhat _____ to therapy, which provides several treatment techniques from which to select.

26. Describe the advantages and disadvantages of electroconvulsive therapy. Do you think that it should be banned from use? Explain your answer.

PRACTICE TEST 3: Conceptual, Applied, and Challenging Questions

1. If you were having trouble adjusting to the death of a friend, who would you be most likely to see?
   a. Psychiatrist
   b. Psychoanalyst
   c. Psychiatric social worker
   d. Counseling psychologist

2. Dr. Gaipo has clients explore their past by delving into the unconscious using dream interpretation and free association. Dr. Gaipo practices:
   a. gestalt therapy.
   b. cognitive therapy.
   c. behavioral therapy.
   d. psychodynamic therapy.

3. Professor Portis is the director of guidance at a student mental-health clinic. He holds a degree appropriate to his position, so he must hold a doctorate or master's degree in:
   a. psychiatric social work.
   b. counseling psychology.
   c. clinical psychology.
   d. educational psychology.

4. Which problem is **least** likely to be treated with aversive conditioning?
   a. Substance (drug) abuse
   b. Depression
   c. Smoking
   d. Alcoholism

5. _____ is the basis for behavioral approaches to therapy.
   a. Removing negative self-perception
   b. Emphasizing personal responsibilities
   c. Understanding the unconscious mind
   d. Training new habits

6. If a therapist asks you to act out some past conflict or difficulty in order to complete unfinished business, he or she most likely is using:
   a. behavior therapy.
   b. existential therapy.
   c. rational-emotive therapy.
   d. gestalt therapy.

7. Lane, a 17-year-old client of Dr. Griswald, explains, "I was uncomfortable and didn't interview well for a job I wanted and I made a perfect fool of myself." In response, Dr. Griswald says, "Is it important for you to be perfectly competent in every area of your life?" Dr. Griswald is using:
   a. behavioral therapy.
   b. rational-emotive therapy.
   c. humanistic therapy.
   d. gestalt therapy.

8. Betty is in therapy with a psychotherapist to work through her feelings about her recent broken engagement. She is telling her therapist that she really didn't love her fiancé and that she realized how different she and her fiancé are. Suddenly, her therapist says, "Betty, I heard the words that you just said, but they don't tell the same message that your facial expression and other nonverbal cues do. See if you can sense the differences." Betty's therapist is most likely a:
   a. gestalt therapist.
   b. psychoanalytic therapist.
   c. client-centered therapist.
   d. behavioral therapist.

9. Generalizing from the discussion in the text, both humanistic and psychoanalytic approaches to therapy are more appropriate for clients who are:
    a. highly verbal.
    b. severely disordered.
    c. experiencing sexually related disorders.
    d. reluctant to converse with someone else.

10. Which of the following types of treatment appears to actually *cure* the disorder, so that when the treatment is discontinued, the symptoms tend not to recur?
    a. Antipsychotic drugs
    b. Antidepressant drugs
    c. Antianxiety drugs
    d. Chlorpromazine

11. Melanie, after being assaulted, is nervous, overreacts to ordinary stimuli, and has trouble getting to sleep. Her psychiatrist prescribes a drug for her, which most likely is:
    a. an antianxiety drug.
    b. an antidepressant drug.
    c. an antipsychotic drug.
    d. an analgesic drug.

12. Electroconvulsive shock treatment (ECT) is usually reserved for severe cases of:
    a. mania.
    b. schizophrenia.
    c. depression.
    d. panic attack.

13. Electroconvulsive therapy (ECT):
    a. relieves the patient from severe depression.
    b. has been used since about 1910.
    c. is used in preference to drug therapy.
    d. can be administered by clinical psychologists.

14. Which of the following is **not** an accurate statement about the effectiveness of psychotherapy?
    a. For most people, psychotherapy is more effective than no therapy at all.
    b. Some people never show improvement with psychotherapy.
    c. Most survey respondents self-report that they have benefited from therapy.
    d. Certain types of therapy work for all of the disorders outlined in the chapter.

15. During a therapy session, Larry explores an image of his home that he had in a dream. The therapist asks him to say what the house feels, to express the unfinished business of the house. Larry's therapist is most likely:
    a. a psychoanalyst.
    b. a group therapist.
    c. a family therapist.
    d. a gestalt therapist.

16. Bethany has prepared a list of experiences that run from the most frightening to the least frightening. She has prepared a _____, and her therapist is probably a _____.
    a. systematic desensitization; behavioral therapist
    b. hierarchy of fears; behavioral therapist
    c. systematic desensitization; humanistic therapist
    d. hierarchy of fears; humanistic therapist

_____ 17. gestalt therapy

_____ 18. group therapy

_____ 19. family therapy

_____ 20. community psychology

a. People discuss problems with others who have similar problems.

b. Movement aimed at preventing psychological disorders.

c. Attempts to integrate a client's thoughts, feelings, and behavior into a whole.

d. Family as a unit to which each member contributes.

21. The _____ of dreams is the actual description of the dream itself.

22. In Eysenck's study on the effectiveness of psychotherapy, clients sometimes had symptoms go away without treatment; this was called _____.

23. The _____ of dreams is the message of the dream.

24. Former mental patients who return to the community in a process called _____ often do not get their needs met, and the goals of the program have not been met in most communities.

25. _____ have made the use of brain surgery to alleviate psychological symptoms nearly obsolete.

26. What are some things the patient has to keep in mind when selecting and working with a therapist? What are the patient's responsibilities in therapy?

Module 51:	Evaluate	Module 52:	Module 53:
[a] psychotherapy	1. e	[a] Humanistic therapy	[a] drug therapy
[b] Biomedical therapy	2. a	[b] Nondirective counseling	[b] antipsychotic drugs
[c] eclectic approach	3. d	[c] person-centered therapy	[c] Antidepressant drugs
[d] Psychodynamic therapy	4. c	[d] unconditional positive	[d] Lithium
[e] defense mechanisms	5. b	regard	[e] Antianxiety drugs
[f] psychoanalyst		[e] Gestalt therapy	[f] Electroconvulsive
[g] free association		[f] Interpersonal therapy	therapy (ECT)
[h] dream interpretation		(IPT)	[g] transcranial magnetic
[i] transference		[g] Group therapy	stimulation (TMS)
[j] behavioral treatment		[h] Family therapy	[h] Psychosurgery
approaches		[i] spontaneous remission	[i] prefrontal lobotomy
[k] aversive conditioning			[j] Community psychology
[l] systematic desensitization		Evaluate	[k] deinstitutionalization
[m] Observational learning			
[n] token system		1. d	
[o] cognitive-behavioral		2. e	Evaluate
approaches		3. b	
[p] Rational-emotive therapy		4. c	1. a
		5. a	2. c
			3. e
			4. b
			5. d

Selected Rethink Answers

52-1   Define group therapy. Because people are different and are dealing with similar issues, they may be able to provide a variety of coping mechanisms to one of the group members and to develop empathy for others with similar problems.

53-1   Biological therapies do treat symptoms. For some illnesses, the relief of the symptoms may be all that is required. Most successful therapies are a combination of the medical model with some type of therapy. When symptoms are somewhat relieved, a client may be better able to focus on the underlying problems associated with the illness.

Practice Test 1:

1.   c   mod. 51 p. 572
a.   Incorrect. A psychiatric nurse may provide some support in a nursing role, but the psychiatrist conducts the therapy in these cases.
b.   Incorrect. A counseling psychologist is not involved in medical treatment.
*c. Correct. A psychiatrist is a medical doctor who administers medical treatment for psychological disorders.
d.   Incorrect. A clinical psychologist does not administer medical treatments.

2.   c   mod. 51 p. 570
a.   Incorrect. Eclectic therapy may utilize approaches that do not involve discussions and interactions.
b.   Incorrect. There is not a major therapy called semantic therapy.

*c. Correct. Psychotherapy specifically involves this kind of direct interaction and discussion between the client and the psychotherapist.
d.   Incorrect. Also known as ITP, this approach does involve interaction, but psychotherapy is the larger category described by this item.

3.   d   mod. 51 p. 571
a.   Incorrect. Transference occurs in therapy, and it involves transferring emotional energy from other relationships into the therapy relationship.
b.   Incorrect. Aversive conditioning utilizes behavioral techniques.
c.   Incorrect. Systematic desensitization utilizes behavioral techniques.
*d. Correct. They are called defense mechanisms because they defend the ego from anxiety arising from unconscious conflicts.

4. a   mod. 51 p. 574
*a. Correct. A hierarchy of fears is used in the behavioral technique known as systematic desensitization.
b. Incorrect. Neurotic symptoms, defense mechanisms, and transference are all psychodynamic concepts.
c. Incorrect. See answer b.
d. Incorrect. See answer b.

5. c   mod. 51 p. 575
a. Incorrect. Biofeedback uses signals from the body to help the person control physiological functions and achieve states of relaxation.
b. Incorrect. Behavior modification includes classical and operant conditioning techniques to change undesirable behaviors.
*c. Correct. Systematic desensitization utilizes classical conditioning techniques by having the person imagine a hierarchy of fears and gradually becoming desensitized to the frightening stimuli.
d. Incorrect. Aversive conditioning uses both classical and operant principles to get the subject to avoid certain responses.

6. b   mod. 51 p. 574
a. Incorrect. The psychoanalytic approach is keyed to the problems caused by unconscious causes of abnormal behavior.
*b. Correct. The behavioral approach is only concerned with the observable causes of behavior, like the reinforcements or stimuli associated with learning.
c. Incorrect. An eclectic approach draws on the most appropriate technique for the problem being treated.
d. Incorrect. The humanistic approach is concerned with how the individual views him or herself, and this may include causes beyond the person's awareness.

7. c   mod. 51 p. 578
a. Incorrect. This may be a rational approach to problem solving, but it is not the approach of rational-emotive therapy.
b. Incorrect. Love and approval are not part of rational-emotive therapy.
*c. Correct. This is the goal of rational-emotive therapy.
d. Incorrect. This may be part of the theory behind rational-emotive therapy, but it is not the therapeutic goal.

8. d   mod. 52 p. 582

a. Incorrect. Rational-emotive therapy is a cognitive therapy, and thus it incorporates what the person thinks about him or herself.
b. Incorrect. Gestalt therapy is a humanistic approach that requires the person to accept parts of him or herself that he or she has denied or rejected.
c. Incorrect. Systematic desensitization utilizes classical conditioning techniques by having the person imagine a hierarchy of fears and gradually becoming desensitized to the frightening stimuli.
*d. Correct. Client-centered therapy assumes that the client has the potential to handle his or her own problems.

9. a   mod. 52 p. 571, 581
*a. Correct. The psychodynamic approach focuses on control of unconscious impulses and the humanistic approach focuses on self-control and responsibility.
b. Incorrect. The behavioral approach is entirely focused on outer forces.
c. Incorrect. See answer b.
d. Incorrect. See answer b.

10. d   mod. 52 p. 582
a. Incorrect. All therapies involve, in one way or another, helping the client get in touch with reality.
b. Incorrect. The psychoanalytic approach is focused on understanding the unconscious.
c. Incorrect. Cognitive therapies, like rational-emotive therapy, are focused on the person taking control of his or her thoughts.
*d. Correct. Humanistic therapy strives to help the client achieve some form of self-actualization, or at least move toward realizing his or her potential.

11. b   mod. 52 p. 584
a. Incorrect. This would be called unethical.
*b. Correct. Sometimes, simply allowing time to pass cures a psychological disorder.
c. Incorrect. This may be a spontaneous emission, but not a remission.
d. Incorrect. This is not remission.

12. b   mod. 53 p. 589
a. Incorrect. Antipsychotic drugs block the production of dopamine.
*b. Correct. Unfortunately, this is not a cure for the problem.
c. Incorrect. See answer a.
d. Incorrect. See answer a.

13. d   mod. 53 p. 589
a. Incorrect. Psychosurgery has always been a method of last resort.
b. Incorrect. ECT has become less common than it once was, but even in its heyday it was not the most common.
c. Incorrect. Genetic engineering has not yet been applied to direct treatment of psychological disorders.
*d. Correct. Even general practitioners will prescribe psychoactive drug therapies.

14. a   mod. 53 p. 591
*a. Correct. How this mineral salt works remains a mystery.
b. Incorrect. Valium is an antianxiety drug.
c. Incorrect. Chlorpromazine is an antipsychotic drug.
d. Incorrect. Librium is an antianxiety drug.

15. a   mod. 53 p. 593
*a. Correct. The original psychosurgery was the prefrontal lobotomy, where the frontal lobes are destroyed.
b. Incorrect. Electroconvulsive therapy, also known as shock therapy, does not destroy any tissue.
c. Incorrect. See answer b.
d. Incorrect. There is not a group of therapies or an approach to therapy known as "personality" therapy.

16. c   mod. 51 p. 572
17. e   mod. 51 p. 573
18. b   mod. 51 p. 573
19. d   mod. 51 p. 573
20. a   mod. 51 p. 573

21. psychoanalysis   mod. 51 p. 572
22. hierarchy   mod. 51 p. 576
23. cognitive therapy   mod. 51 p. 577
24. free association   mod. 51 p. 572
25. Contingency contracting mod. 51 p. 576

26.
- Identify the reasons you think psychotherapy works. These may include (1) psychotherapy offers a chance to reflect on life's problems in a safe environment; (2) it offers a sense of control over one's problems; and (3) it provides new ways of coping with and understanding stress.
- Select at least two of the previously discussed concepts and describe their roles in depth.
- Remember, Eysenck's early study that suggested that psychotherapy was no more effective than being on a waiting list.

Practice Test 2:
1. d   mod. 51 p. 570
a. Incorrect. Clinical psychologists cannot prescribe drugs.
b. Incorrect. Drug therapy is used for almost every disorder.
c. Incorrect. This may be part of the view, but the predominant view is that the disorders are medical in nature.
*d. Correct. Biomedical therapy uses medical interventions.

2. c   mod. 51 p. 585
a. Incorrect. That is not what eclectic means.
b. Incorrect. It is not connected to the paranormal.
*c. Correct. The therapist chooses the technique best matched to the client's needs.
d. Incorrect. It was actually his long-lost brother, Homer Simpson.

3. c   mod. 51 p. 571
a. Incorrect. In the psychoanalytic view, abnormal behaviors do not suppress normal behaviors.
b. Incorrect. The ego does not repress the superego.
*c. Correct. The focus in psychodynamic therapy is on past, unresolved conflicts, often going back to childhood.
d. Incorrect. The ego always has access to consciousness.

4. b   mod. 51 p. 571
a. Incorrect. Defense mechanisms may play a role when they fail to protect the ego from anxiety.
*b. Correct. Anxiety is the main cause of neurotic symptoms, and the anxiety arises because of undesirable motives or repressed conflicts.
c. Incorrect. Inappropriate choices would be the cause of symptoms, as viewed by humanistic theory.
d. Incorrect. Contingency contracting might be found in behavior therapy, but not as the cause for neurotic symptoms in Freud's view.

5. b   mod. 51 p. 573
a. Incorrect. See answer b.
*b. Correct. Transference brings the emotional energy of the past relationship into the current therapeutic relationship.
c. Incorrect. See answer b.
d. Incorrect. See answer b.

6.   a   mod. 51 p. 575
*a. Correct. The response to alcohol after successful aversion therapy is to avoid alcohol because it is linked to the aversive stimulus.
b.   Incorrect. The craving is probably still there.
c.   Incorrect. No fear of alcohol should develop.
d.   Incorrect. Properly undertaken, alcohol should not become a source of anxiety.

7.   d   mod. 52 p. 581
a.   Incorrect. This is the behavioral approach.
b.   Incorrect. This is the psychodynamic approach.
c.   Incorrect. This is the cognitive approach.
*d. Correct. Humanistic approaches focus on personal responsibility and self-healing.

8.   d   mod. 51 p. 578
a.   Incorrect. The views may be defensive, but those challenged are the irrational views held by the client.
b.   Incorrect. The views may be self-centered, but those challenged are the irrational views held by the client.
c.   Incorrect. The views may be paranoid, but those challenged are the irrational views held by the client.
*d. Correct. The therapist attempts to get the client to eliminate faulty ideas about the world and him or herself.

9.   c   mod. 52 p. 581
a.   Incorrect. The therapist is primarily responsible for establishing a program of stimuli or reinforcement that will retrain the client in behavioral therapy.
b.   Incorrect. The rational-emotive therapist attempts to get the client to eliminate faulty ideas about the world and him or herself.
*c. Correct. Humanistic therapy attempts to help the client gain insight into his or her responsibility for the need to make changes.
d.   Incorrect. The psychoanalytic approach seeks to understand the unconscious forces at work.

10. c   mod. 52 p. 582
a.   Incorrect. Reinforcement would be used in behavioral therapy, not humanistic therapy.
b.   Incorrect. A contingency contract is used in behavioral therapy, not humanistic therapy.
*c. Correct. Unconditional positive regard is the basis of any therapeutic relationship in the humanistic view.
d.   Incorrect. The psychoanalytic approach is aimed more at inner conflicts.

11. d   mod. 52 p. 581
a.   Incorrect. Behavioral therapy is not interested in these internal issues.
b.   Incorrect. Rational-emotive therapy is focused on changing the client's way of thinking about the world.
c.   Incorrect. Humanistic therapy is focused on helping the client take responsibility for his or her actions.
*d. Correct. This describes the goals of gestalt therapy.

12. c   mod. 52 p. 583
a.   Incorrect. Psychodynamic group therapy will focus on this aspect of the client.
b.   Incorrect. This is not possible in any kind of therapy.
*c. Correct. Others in the group have had similar experiences, and the client learns that he or she is not alone.
d.   Incorrect. Only in cognitive group therapy.

13. c   mod. 53 p. 590
a.   Incorrect. Antidepressant drugs are used for many mood disorders.
b.   Incorrect. Antianxiety drugs, like Valium and Xanax, are used for anxiety disorders.
*c. Correct. Chlorpromazine is an antipsychotic drug used to treat schizophrenia.
d.   Incorrect. Lithium is used to treat the mania of bipolar disorders.

14. b   mod. 53 p. 591
a.   Incorrect. Valium is an antianxiety drug without any preventive characteristics.
*b. Correct. Lithium is one of the few drugs that appears to provide a degree of cure.
c.   Incorrect. Chlorpromazine does not cure schizophrenia or any of the other disorders it is used to treat.
d.   Incorrect. Librium is an antianxiety drug without any preventive or curative characteristics.

15. d   mod. 53 p. 590
a.   Incorrect. Antidepressants do not increase the activity of the autonomic system.
b.   Incorrect. Antipsychotics decrease the production of dopamine, but antidepressants actually increase the concentrations of some neurotransmitters.
c.   Incorrect. Drugs do not increase the speed of neural transmission.
*d. Correct. Antidepressants, like Prozac and tricyclics, increase the concentration of neurotransmitters.

16. d   mod. 53 p. 593
a.   Incorrect. Electroconvulsive shock therapy is commonly used today.
b.   Incorrect. Antipsychotic drugs continue to be relied upon by the medical community.
c.   Incorrect. Psychotherapy is very common.
*d. Correct. The use of psychosurgery, especially the lobotomy, is used less and less for treatment of psychological disorders.

17. b   mod. 51 p. 575
18. d   mod. 51 p. 575
19. a   mod. 51 p. 576
20. c   mod. 51 p. 576

21. resistance   mod. 51 p. 573
22. Transference   mod. 51 p. 573
23. unconditional positive regard   mod. 52 p. 582
24. dream interpretation   mod. 51 p. 573
25. eclectic approach   mod. 52 p. 585

26.
- Describe your response to the idea of electrical shock being passed through your brain as a means of therapy. Would you want this to be done?
- What assumptions are made about the harm or benefit of using ECT? Do we assume that it must have some unseen long-term effect?

Practice Test 3:
1.   d   mod. 51 p. 572
a.   Incorrect. A psychiatrist would probably be inappropriate for this kind of short-term problem.
b.   Incorrect. A psychoanalyst would probably be inappropriate for this kind of short-term problem.
c.   Incorrect. A psychiatric social worker is trained to deal with other kinds of problems and would probably be inappropriate for this kind of short-term problem.
*d. Correct. A counseling psychologist is especially prepared for dealing with problems of adjustment such as this one.

2.   d   mod. 51 p. 571
a.   Incorrect. Some, but not all, gestalt therapists use psychodynamic techniques.
b.   Incorrect. Cognitive therapy would have the client explore conscious thoughts.
c.   Incorrect. Behavioral therapy would not have the client think much at all.
*d. Correct. Dream interpretation is a core technique for psychodynamic therapy.

3.   b   mod. 51 p. 572
a.   Incorrect. Someone with a degree in psychiatric social work would be more appropriately placed in a community health center.
*b. Correct. This is the most appropriate degree for this kind of position.
c.   Incorrect. A clinical psychologist could hold this position, but a counseling degree would be more suitable.
d.   Incorrect. An educational psychologist would not be suitable for this position.

4.   b   mod. 51 p. 575
a.   Incorrect. See answer b.
*b. Correct. Aversive conditioning works well with habits that are being broken, like drug habits, smoking, and alcoholism, but not with psychological problems like depression.
c.   Incorrect. See answer b.
d.   Incorrect. See answer b.

5.   d   mod. 51 p. 574
a.   Incorrect. Behaviorists are not that interested in self-perception.
b.   Incorrect. Humanistic approaches focus on personal responsibilities.
c.   Incorrect. Psychodynamic approaches focus on the unconscious mind.
*d. Correct. These new habits are meant to replace the old, malfunctioning ones.

6.   d   mod. 52 p. 582
a.   Incorrect. Behavior therapy does not ask clients to act out past conflicts.
b.   Incorrect. Existential therapy is much more focused on the meaning of life than on past conflicts.
c.   Incorrect. Rational-emotive therapy is focused more on the client's irrational ideas about the world.
*d. Correct. Gestalt therapy seeks to have clients integrate and "own" these conflicts to be able to resolve the issues for themselves.

7. b   mod. 51 p. 578
a. Incorrect. In behavior therapy, other avenues would be explored, like the reinforcements that were being sought.
*b. Correct. In rational-emotive therapy, this expectation of perfection would be viewed as irrational and thus in need of being altered.
c. Incorrect. In humanistic theory, the concern would be more about the issue of personal responsibility rather than thoughts about how others would view one.
d. Incorrect. In gestalt therapy, Dr. Griswald might have asked Lane to role play her past failures to see how they are connected to the current situation.

8. a   mod. 52 p. 582
*a. Correct. The gestalt therapist tries to integrate the nonverbal message with the verbal message and thus reduce Betty's conflict.
b. Incorrect. A psychoanalytic therapist might be interested in the nonverbal cues as efforts of the unconscious to get a message across.
c. Incorrect. A client-centered therapist would attempt to mirror Betty's concerns back to her so she could hear what she was saying.
d. Incorrect. A behavioral therapist might suggest that there is something reinforcing about Betty's breaking the engagement that she is failing to recognize.

9. a   mod. 52 p. 582
*a. Correct. These two approaches require much discussion and insight, so a verbal client will do well in these approaches.
b. Incorrect. Severely disordered patients should probably be treated with drugs and some psychotherapy.
c. Incorrect. People with sexual disorders would be best served if they sought a sex therapist.
d. Incorrect. People who are reluctant to converse with others would have difficulty talking to a psychoanalytic or humanistic therapist.

10. b   mod. 53 p. 590
a. Incorrect. Antipsychotic drugs only suppress the symptoms.
*b. Correct. After taking a regimen of antidepressant drugs, depression tends not to return.
c. Incorrect. Antianxiety drugs suppress the response, but they do not remove the cause.
d. Incorrect. Chlorpromazine is an antipsychotic drug and it suppresses psychotic symptoms, but they return if the drug is stopped.

11. a   mod. 53 p. 592
*a. Correct. These are symptoms of anxiety.
b. Incorrect. She is not depressed.
c. Incorrect. She is not psychotic.
d. Incorrect. She does not need an aspirin.

12. c   mod. 53 p. 592
a. Incorrect. See answer c.
b. Incorrect. See answer c.
*c. Correct. ECT is used for severe depression when other treatments do not work.
d. Incorrect. See answer c.

13. a   mod. 53 p. 592
*a. Correct. It does seem to relieve depression.
b. Incorrect. It was introduced in the 1930s.
c. Incorrect. Drug therapy is much preferred.
d. Incorrect. Clinical psychologists are not licensed to administer drugs or ECT.

14. d   mod. 52 p. 582
a. Incorrect. This is a true statement.
b. Incorrect. This is also true.
c. Incorrect. This is also true.
*d. Incorrect. Typically, patients show the best results when their problem, or disorder, is matched to a therapeutic technique or perspective that works best with it.

15. d   mod. 52 p. 582
a. Incorrect. A psychoanalyst would be interested in what the house symbolized for Larry, not the unfinished business it entails.
b. Incorrect. A group therapist would not likely be conducting individual dream therapy.
c. Incorrect. A family therapist who was also trained in psychoanalysis might be interested in what the dream represents.
*d. Correct. The gestalt therapist attempts to get Larry to recognize and integrate the unfinished business that his dream home represents.

16. b   mod. 51 p. 576
a. Incorrect. See answer b.
*b. Correct. This list is called a hierarchy of fears, and the behavioral approach is based on classical conditioning principles.
c. Incorrect. See answer b.
d. Incorrect. See answer b.

17. c   mod. 52 p. 581
18. a   mod. 52 p. 582
19. d   mod. 52 p. 583
20. b   mod. 53 p. 594

26. Patients should:
- Make sure therapists have appropriate training, credentials, and licensing.
- Feel comfortable with the therapist, not intimidated.
- Feel that they are making progress with the therapy.
- Be committed to making therapy work.
- Patients, not therapists, must do the work to resolve issues.

Chapter 17: Social Psychology

Module 54: Attitudes and Social Cognition
Module 55: Social Influence
Module 56: Prejudice and Discrimination
Module 57: Positive and Negative Social Behavior

Overview

This chapter illustrates how people's thoughts, feelings, and actions are affected by others. Both the nature and the causes of individual behavior in social situations are studied.

Module 54 explains how attitudes are composed of affective, behavioral, and cognitive components. People show consistency between their attitudes and behavior, and we form schemas to help us categorize people and events in the world around us. This helps us predict the actions of others. In addition, we also have a need to explain what causes others' behaviors, and use the process of attributions to do so.

Module 55 explores the effects that social influence has on an individual. These behaviors include behaviors that result from the actions of others, as found in conformity, compliance, and obedience.

Module 56 addresses the issue of prejudice as a consequence of stereotyping and how both of these create challenges for people living in a diverse society. How prejudice originates and its relationship to stereotyping and discrimination are discussed.

Module 57 presents a discussion on social behaviors. These behaviors include the study of liking and loving, the processes involved in creating aggression, and the behavior involved in helping others.

To further investigate the topics covered in this chapter, you can visit the related Web sites by visiting the following link: www.mhhe.com/feldmanup8.

Prologue: Everyday Heroes
Looking Ahead

Module 54: Attitudes and Social Cognition

Persuasion: Changing Attitudes
Social Cognition: Understanding Others

Exploring Diversity: Attributions in a Cultural Context: How Fundamental Is the Fundamental Attribution Error?

- *What are attitudes, and how are they formed, maintained, and changed?*
- *How do we form impressions of what others are like and of the causes of their behavior?*
- *What are the biases that influence the ways in which we view others' behavior?*

Attitudes and Social Cognition

[a] _____ is the study of how people's thoughts, feelings, and actions are affected by others. Attempts to persuade people to purchase specific products involve principles derived from the study of attitudes. [b]_____ are evaluations of a particular person, behavior, belief, or object, and can be negative or positive in nature.

Once formed, attitudes can be resistant to change. They are easier to change when the *attitude communicator* is attractive, and viewed as trustworthy and an expert. Generally, providing two-sided messages creates a situation where attitudes are more likely to change. Further, the *target* of the attitude changes matters. More intelligent people are more resistant to being persuaded to change an attitude. A small difference in persuadability exists between men and women, with women being slightly easier to persuade in public.

The means by which the information is processed also has an influence on the persuasion. [c] _____ occurs when the recipient gives considerable attention to the issues and arguments involved. [d] _____ occurs when the recipient uses factors extraneous to the issue, such as the source, length, or emotional appeal of the argument. Central route processing generally leads to stronger, longer-lasting attitude change. People who have a(n) [e] _____ are more likely to use central route processing.

Attitudes influence behavior, but the strength of the relationship varies. People do try to keep behavior and attitudes consistent. Sometimes, in order to maintain the consistency, behavior can influence attitudes. [f] _____ occurs when a person holds two *cognitions* (attitudes or thoughts) that are contradictory. In cases where dissonance is aroused, the prediction is that behavior or attitudes will change in order to reduce the dissonance.

The area of social psychology called **[g]** _____ refers to the processes that underlie our efforts to make sense of others and of ourselves. Individuals have highly developed **[h]** _____, or sets of cognitions, about people and experiences. Schemas are important because they organize how we recall, recognize, and categorize information about others. They also help us make predictions about others.

[i] _____ refers to the process by which an individual organizes information about another person, forming an overall impression of that person. Information given to people before meeting them can have dramatic effects on how the person is perceived. Research has focused on how people pay attention to unusually important traits, called **[j]** _____, as they form impressions of others.

Researchers in social cognition are also concerned with **[k]** _____, the theory that tries to explain how we decide what causes others' behavior. We generally focus on two main causes: **[l]** _____, in which we believe people's behavior is caused by something in their environment or circumstances, and **[m]** _____, in which we believe behavior is caused by the person's traits or personality characteristics.

People are not always logical in processing information, and biases creep into the attributions we make. One bias is the **[n]** _____, in which we infer uniformly positive characteristics to a person based on initially perceived positive characteristics. Another bias is the **[o]** _____, in which we tend to think of others as being similar to ourselves, despite never having met them before. A third bias is the **[p]** _____, in which we tend to attribute our own successes to personal factors, and failures to things outside ourselves. Finally, the **[q]** _____ makes us rely too heavily on personal factors to explain others' behavior, and ignore situational factors. This bias is more common in Western cultures.

Evaluate

_____ 1. attitudes

_____ 2. central-route processing

_____ 3. peripheral-route processing

a. Characterized by consideration of the source and related general information rather than of the message.

b. Characterized by thoughtful consideration of the issues.

c. Learned predispositions to respond in a favorable or unfavorable manner to a particular object.

Rethink

54-1 Joan sees Annette, a new coworker, act in a way that seems abrupt and curt. Joan concludes that Annette is unkind and unsociable. The next day, Joan sees Annette acting kindly to another worker. Is Joan likely to change her impression of Annette? Why or why not? Finally, Joan sees several friends of hers laughing and joking with Annette, treating her in a friendly fashion. Is Joan likely to change her impression of Annette? Why or why not?

54-2 *From the perspective of a marketing specialist:* Suppose you were assigned to develop a full advertising campaign for a product, including television, radio, and print ads. How might the theories in this chapter guide your strategy to suit the different media?

Spotlight on Terminology and Language—ESL Pointers

Page 586 "Kathleen Imel, 51, who was driving by, **screeched to a halt**."

To **screech to a halt** is to stop so suddenly that the car makes a high pitched sound.

Page 586 "**Leaping** from her van, Imel, the mother of two grown sons, **flung** herself on top of Joshua as the larger dog, a 60-pounder name Butch, bit into the child's left ear."

To **leap** is to move as if jumping across something.

When something is **flung** it has been thrown violently with a lot of force.

Page 586 "Releasing Joshua, Butch **chomped** into Imel's left eyebrow instead."

When a dog **chomps** at someone they are noisily chewing big bites.

Page 586 "As the dog **clamped** its jaws around her elbow, a neighbor, drawn by her screams, pulled Joshua to safety."

To **clamp** on to something is to hold on to it firmly.

Page 586 "Why do some people display so much violence, aggression, and **cruelty** toward others that people throughout the world live in fear of annihilation at their hands?"

Cruelty is the act of being cruel or unkind.

Page 587 "Each has appeared frequently in advertisements designed to **mold** or change our attitudes."

To **mold** something is to influence or guide the development of it.

Page 587 "Such commercials are part of the **barrage** of messages we receive each day from sources as varied as politicians, sales staff in stores, and celebrities, all of which are meant to influence us."
A **barrage** is a rapid attack that continues for a long time.

Page 587 "Moreover, the expertise and **trustworthiness** of a communicator are related to the impact of a message—except in situations in which the audience believes the communicator has an ulterior motive (Hovland, Janis, & Kelly, 1953; Ziegler, Diehl, & Ruther, 2002)."

Trustworthiness is the characteristic of being honest and dependable.

Page 587 "Generally, two-sided messages—which include both the communicator's position and the one he or she is arguing against—are more effective than one-sided messages, assuming the arguments for the other side can be effectively **refuted** and the audience is knowledgeable about the topic."

When something is **refuted** it is proven to be false.

Page 587 "In fact, the **magnitude** of the differences in resistance to persuasion between men and women is not large (Wood & Stagner, 1994; Wood, 2000; Guadagno & Cialdini, 2002)."

The **magnitude** of something is its importance or significance.

Page 588 "In central route processing, people are **swayed** in their judgments by the logic, merit, and strength of arguments."

To **sway** someone is to persuade or influence them to believe something.

Page 588 "Instead, factors that are irrelevant or **extraneous** to the issue, such as who is providing the message and how long the arguments are, influence them (Petty, Cacioppo, Strathman, & Priester, 1994; Petty, Wheeler, & Tormala, 2003)."

Extraneous is something that comes from the outside, and is not vital or essential. **Extraneous** to the issue would be off the point of the main issue.

Page 588 "However, if a person is uninvolved, unmotivated, bored, or distracted, the nature of the message becomes less important, and **peripheral** factors become more critical."

Peripheral factors are minor factors or secondary factors.

Page 589 "People who have a high need for cognition, a person's **habitual** level of thoughtfulness and cognitive activity, are more likely to employ central route processing."

Habitual is usual or customary.

Page 589 "You've just spent what you feel is the most boring hour of your life, turning **pegs** for a psychology experiment."

Pegs are a small piece of metal or wood used to secure or join parts together.

Page 589 "If you agree to help the experimenter, you may be **setting yourself up** for a state of psychological tension called **cognitive dissonance**."

To **set your self up** is to make something happen.

Dissonance implies conflict or a difference of opinion. **Cognitive dissonance** is the unpleasant psychological tension that motivates us to reduce our cognitive inconsistencies by making our beliefs more consistent with one another.

Page 590 "The reasoning behind this condition was that $20 was so much money that participants in this condition had a good reason to be **conveying** incorrect information; dissonance would not be aroused, and less attitude change would be expected.

Conveying is communicating.

Page 590 "**Hence,** a smoker may decide that he really doesn't smoke all that much or that he'll quit soon (modifying the cognition), that the evidence linking smoking to cancer is weak (changing the importance of a cognition), that the amount of exercise he gets compensates for the smoking (adding cognitions), or that there is no evidence linking smoking and cancer (denial)."

Hence means "because of, or as a result of this cause."

Page 591 "Regardless of Bill Clinton's personal **transgressions** and **impeachment** trial, many Americans genuinely liked him when he was president, and his popularity remained high throughout his term in office."

Transgressions suggest a lack of discretion, seen often in reckless behavior. A **transgression** is a behavior that goes beyond a boundary.

Impeachment is to charge a government official with a crime or serious misconduct while they are in office.

Page 591 "Our schema for 'teacher,' for instance, generally consists of a number of characteristics: knowledge of the subject matter he or she is teaching, a desire to **impart** that knowledge, and an awareness of the student's need to understand what is being said."

When you **impart** knowledge, you communicate it and make it known to others.

Page 591 "The simple substitution of "cold" for "warm" caused **drastic** differences in the way the students in each group perceived the lecturer, even though he gave the same talk in the same style in each condition."

Something that is **drastic** has a powerful negative effect.

Page 592 "In just a few seconds, using what have been called "thin slices of behavior," we are able to make judgments of people that are accurate and that match those of people who make judgments based on longer **snippets** of behavior (Hall & Bernieri, 2001; Choi, Gray, & Ambady, 2004)."

A **snippet** is a small piece of something such as information or music.

Page 592 "For instance, we may hold a "**gregarious person**" schema, made up of the traits of friendliness, aggressiveness, and openness."

A **gregarious** person is an outgoing, friendly and social person.

Page 592 "The other staff members looked on **resentfully**, trying to figure out why Barbara had worked night and day to finish the project not just on time but two weeks early."

To be **resentful** is to be annoyed or envious.

Page 592 "She must be an awfully **compulsive** person, they decided."

A **compulsive** person is one who is driven by an irresistible inner need to do something.

Page 592 "At one time or another, most of us have **puzzled** over the reasons behind someone's behavior."

To be **puzzled** is to be confused.

Page 592 "Perhaps it was in a situation similar to the one above, or it may have been in more formal circumstances, such as being a judge on a student **judiciary** board in a cheating case."

The **judiciary** refers to a country's court system.

Page 592 "After first noticing that something unusual has happened—for example, golf star Tiger Woods has played a terrible **round of golf**—we try to interpret the meaning of the event."

A "**round of golf**" refers to the length of one game. One **round** is made up of 18 individual challenges, or "holes."

Page 593 "For instance, someone who **knocks over** a quart of milk and then cleans it up probably does it not because he or she is necessarily a neat person but because the *situation* requires it."

To **knock something over** is to bump it and push it on to its side.

Page 594 "*The **halo** effect.*"

A **halo** is a ring or circle of light found around the head of a saint. The **halo effect** is a phenomenon in which an initial understanding that a person has positive traits.

Page 595 "When we view the behavior of another person in a particular setting, the most **conspicuous** information is the person's behavior."

Something that is **conspicuous** is easily seen.

Page 595 "For instance, a **tardy** person using English may say "I am late," suggesting a personal, dispositional cause ("I am a tardy person")."

A person that is **tardy** is late to arrive somewhere.

Module 55:
Social Influence

Conformity: Following What Others Do
Compliance: Submitting to Direct Social Pressure
Obedience: Following Direct Orders

- ***What are the major sources and tactics of social influence?***

Social Influence

The area called **[a]** _____ is concerned with how the actions of an individual affect the behavior of others. In uncertain situations, we tend to look to the behavior of others to guide our own behavior. **[b]** _____ is the change in behavior or attitudes that results from a desire to follow the beliefs or standards of other people. Conformity is more likely under certain conditions, including when the person in question feels he or she has low status, is required to respond publicly, is working on an ambiguous task, and when the group opinion is unanimous. **[c]** _____ is a type of thinking in which group members share strong motivation to achieve consensus, which leads them to lose the ability to critically evaluate alternatives. The group overrates its ability to solve problems and underrates contradictory information.

The behavior that occurs in response to direct, explicit pressure to endorse a particular view or to behave in a certain way is called **[d]** _____ . Several techniques are used by salespersons to get customers to comply with purchase requests. One is called the

[e] _____ technique, in which a person agrees to a small request and is then asked to comply with a bigger request. Compliance increases when the person first agrees to the smaller request. The **[f]** _____ technique is the opposite of the foot-in-the-door technique. The door-in-the-face technique follows a large request with a smaller one, making the second request appear more reasonable. The **[g]** _____ technique presents a deal at an inflated price, then a number of incentives are added. The

[h] _____ is another method that creates a psychic cost by giving "free" samples. These samples instigate a *norm of reciprocity*, leading people to buy as a matter of reciprocation. Employers may use these or similar techniques to bring about compliance among their employees. A field of psychology known as **[i]** _____ is concerned with employee activities and well-being, and studies issues such as worker motivation, satisfaction, and productivity.

Compliance follows a request, but obedience follows direct orders. **[j]** _____ is defined as a change in behavior resulting from the commands of others. Obedience occurs in situations involving a boss, teacher, parent, or someone who has power over us.

Evaluate

_____ 1.   cognitive dissonance

_____ 2.   foot-in-the-door technique

_____ 3.   door-in-the-face technique

_____ 4.   obedience

_____ 5.   compliance

a.   Behavior that occurs in response to direct social pressure.

b.   Going along with an important request is more likely if it follows compliance with a smaller previous request.

c.   A change in behavior resulting from the commands of others.

d.   A large request, refusal of which is expected, is followed by a smaller request.

e.   The conflict resulting from contrasting cognitions.

Rethink

55-1   Why do you think the Milgram experiment is so controversial? What sorts of effects might the experiment have had on participants? Do you think the experiment would have had similar results if it had been conducted not in a laboratory setting, but among members of a social group (such as a fraternity or sorority) with strong pressures to conform?

55-2   *From the perspective of a sales representative:* Imagine that you have been trained to use the various compliance techniques described in this section. Because these techniques are so powerful, should the use of such techniques be outlawed? Should consumers be taught defenses against such techniques? Is the use of such techniques ethically and morally defensible? Why?

55-3   *From the perspective of an educator:* Student obedience in the elementary and secondary classroom is a major issue for many teachers. How might you promote student obedience in the classroom? What are some of the potentially harmful ways that a teacher could use his or her social influence to elicit student obedience?

Spotlight on Terminology and Language—ESL Pointers

Page 597 "As you undoubtedly know from your own experience, pressures to **conform** can be painfully strong, and can bring about changes in behavior that otherwise never would have occurred."

Conformity is any behavior you perform because of group pressure, even though that pressure might not involve direct requests. The social pressure may be subtle or indirect. This pressure is to be in agreement or harmony with the group. What circumstances existed when you last felt the need to **conform**?

Page 597 "The task was seemingly **straightforward**: Each of the participants had to announce aloud which of the first three lines was identical in length to the 'standard' line on the second card."

Straightforward means uncomplicated. In this case the task appeared simple and clear-cut.

Page 597 "From the perspective of the participant in the group who answered last on each trial, all the answers of the first six participants seemed to be wrong—in fact, **unanimously** wrong.'

When something is decided **unanimously** it is agreed upon by everyone, no one disagrees.

Page 597 "The last participant faced the **dilemma** of whether to follow his or her own perceptions or follow the group by repeating the answer everyone else was giving."

A **dilemma** is problem in which a person must choose between one or more choices that are not acceptable.

Page 597 "As you might have guessed, this experiment was more **contrived** than it appeared."

When something is **contrived**, there's a scheme involved; the experiment here was not what it seemed.

Page 597 "The first six participants were actually confederates (paid employees of the experimenter) who had been instructed to give unanimously **erroneous** answers in many of the trials."

Erroneous is wrong; the confederates gave the incorrect answer on purpose.

Page 598 "Furthermore, a person's relative **status**, the social **rank** held within a group, is critical: The lower a person's status in the group, the greater the power of the group over that person's behavior."

The term **rank** is another term for status that is used to refer to the degree of importance of someone relative to others in a group.

Page 598 "Groups that unanimously support a position show the most **pronounced** conformity pressures."

Something that is **pronounced** is noticeable or distinct.

Page 598 "But what of the case in which people with dissenting views have an **ally** in the group, known as a social supporter, who agrees with them?"

An **ally** is someone who is a friend or supporter.

Page 598 "Furthermore, we understand that not adhering to group norms can result in **retaliation** from other group members, ranging from being ignored to being **overtly derided** or even being rejected or excluded by the group. "

When someone seeks **retaliation** they seek to get revenge.

An **overt** act is a very open and blatant act.

To **deride** is to ridicule.

Page 598 "Groupthink: **Caving** in to Conformity."

To "**cave in**" is to give in, or to allow something to happen without fighting it.

Page 598 "Despite the **misgivings** of some engineers, a consensus formed that the foam was not dangerous to the shuttle."
Misgivings are feelings of doubt or uncertainty about a decision or an action.

Page 598 "In **hindsight**, NASA's decision was clearly wrong."

Hindsight is to understand or judge an event in retrospect, or after it already happened.

Page 600 "A little later comes a larger request, which, because you have already agreed to the first one, you have a hard time **turning down**."

To **turn something down** is to refuse it.

Page 600 "The salesperson in this case is using a **tried-and-true** strategy that social psychologists call the foot-in-the-door technique."

Something that is **tried-and-true** is something that has been tested over and over and always occurs with the same outcome.

Page 600 "A **fundraiser** asks for a $500 contribution."

A **fundraiser** is a person who works by asking people for money with the goal to raise money for a non-profit or political organization.

Page 601 "The use of this technique is **widespread**."

Something that is **widespread** is common or well known.

Page 601 "You may have tried it at some point yourself, perhaps by asking your parents for a large increase in your **allowance** and later settling for less."

An **allowance** is money given on a regular basis to a child or member of a family so that that person is able to make their own purchases.

Page 601 "Similarly, television writers, by sometimes **sprinkling** their scripts with obscenities that they know will be cut out by network censors, hope to keep other key phrases intact (Cialdini & Sagarin, 2005)."

When we **sprinkle** something we scatter small amounts of it around.

Page 601 "But immediately after the initial offer, the salesperson offers an incentive, discount, or bonus to **clinch the deal**."

To **clinch a deal** is to resolve, or settle something that was uncertain.

Page 601 "Although they may not **couch** it in these terms, salespeople who provide samples to potential customers do so to instigate the norm of reciprocity."

To **couch** something is to phrase it in a certain way.

Page 601 "The test procedure requires only that you give learners a **shock** each time they make a mistake on the test."

A **shock** is an electrical jolt of varying intensity.

Page 602 "The participants, who were extensively interviewed after the experiment, said they obeyed primarily because they believed that the experimenter would be responsible for any potential ill effects that **befell** the learner."

When something **befalls** someone it means that something has unexpectedly happened to them.

Page 603 "Although most participants in the Milgram experiment said later that they felt the knowledge gained from the study **outweighed** the discomfort they may have felt, the experiment has been criticized for creating an extremely trying set of circumstances for the participants, thereby raising serious ethical concerns."

When something **outweighs** something else it means that it is more important than the other things.

Page 603 "For instance, after World War II, the major defense that Nazi officers gave to excuse their participation in **atrocities** during the war was that they were "only following orders.""

Atrocities are acts that are shockingly cruel.

Page 603 "Milgram's experiment, which was motivated in part by his desire to explain the behavior of everyday Germans during World War II, forces us to ask ourselves this question: Would we be able to **withstand** the intense power of authority?"

To **withstand** something is to be strong enough to stand up to someone under extreme pressure.

Module 56: Prejudice and Discrimination

Applying Psychology in the 21st Century: Fighting Stereotype Threat

Foundations of Prejudice
Reducing the Consequences of Prejudice and Discrimination

- *How do stereotypes, prejudice, and discrimination differ?*
- *How can we reduce prejudice and discrimination?*

Prejudice and Discrimination

[a] _____ are the beliefs and expectations about members of a group held simply because of their membership in the particular group. Stereotypes can lead to

[b] _____, the negative evaluation of group members that is based primarily on membership in the group rather than on the behavior of a particular individual. Even though people may appear to be unprejudiced, some still unconsciously hold prejudiced thoughts, as exemplified by experiments which demonstrate the existence of *modern racism.* When negative stereotypes lead to negative action against a group or group members, the behavior is called [c]

_____. Stereotypes can actually cause members of stereotyped groups to

behave according to the stereotype, a phenomenon known as [d] _____.
Expectations about a future event increase the likelihood that the event will occur. People are also primed to interpret behaviors according to stereotypes.

The [e] _____ say that people's feelings about various groups are shaped by the behavior of parents, other adults, and peers and the mass media. According to

[f] _____, we use membership in groups as a source of pride and self-worth. We then inflate the positive aspects of our own group (our *ingroup*) and devalue groups to which we do not belong (our *outgroups*).

Research indicates that prejudice can be reduced by increasing group contact, making values and norms against prejudice more apparent, providing education about positive characteristics held by the targets of stereotyping, and reducing *stereotype vulnerability.*

Evaluate

_____ 1.   self-fulfilling prophecy

_____ 2.   prejudice

_____ 3.   stereotype

_____ 4.   social identity theory

_____ 5.   discrimination

a. Negative behavior toward members of a particular group.

b. Negative or positive judgments of members of a group that are based on membership in the group.

c. The expectation of an event or behavior results in the event or behavior actually occurring.

d. Beliefs and expectations about members of a group are held simply on the basis of membership in that group.

e. The view that people use group membership as a source of pride and self-worth.

Rethink

56-1   Do you think women can be victims of stereotype vulnerability? In what topical areas might this occur? Can men be victims of stereotype vulnerability? Why?

56-2   *From the perspective of a corrections officer:* How might overt forms of prejudice and discrimination toward disadvantaged groups (such as African Americans) be reduced in state or federal prison?

Spotlight on Terminology and Language—ESL Pointers

Page 605 "**Stereotypes** can lead to **prejudice**, negative (or positive) evaluations of groups and their members."

Stereotypes are widely held beliefs that people have certain traits because they belong to a particular group.

Prejudice is an unfair, biased or intolerant attitude toward another group of people.

Page 605 "Over the years, various groups have been called "lazy" or "**shrewd**" or "cruel" with varying degrees of regularity by those who are not members of that group.

Someone who is **shrewd** is perceived to tend to interact with others in a dishonest way.

Page 605 "Even today, despite major progress toward reducing **legally sanctioned** forms of prejudice such as school segregation, stereotypes remain (Johnston, 1996; Madon et al., 2001)."

Legally sanctioned means permitted by law.

Page 605 "Even people who on the surface appear to be unprejudiced may **harbor** hidden prejudice."

Someone who **harbors** ideas keeps them in mind and continues to think about them privately.

Page 606 "He suggests that African American students who receive instruction from teachers who may doubt their abilities and set up special **remedial** programs to assist them may come to accept society's stereotypes and believe that they are **prone to fail** (Steele, 1992, 1997; Steele, Spencer, & Aronson, 2002)."

A **remedial** program is one designed to help correct or improve problem areas in learning.

Prone to fail is having a tendency or inclination toward failure.

Page 606 "Members of minority groups, convinced that they have the potential to be academically successful, may become immune to the potentially **treacherous** consequences of negative stereotypes."

Treacherous is unsafe, dangerous.

Page 606 "Eventually, they may **disidentify** with academic success by minimizing the importance of academic endeavors (Steele, 1997; Stone, 1999, 2002)."

To **disidentify** is to unidentify with something.

Page 606 "In short, the evidence from this study, as well as a growing body of research, **attests** to the reality of stereotype threat."

To **attest** to something is to confirm that something is true.

Page 606 "For instance, **bigoted** parents may commend their children for expressing prejudiced attitudes."

A **bigoted** person would be someone who is prejudiced, intolerant or narrow-minded.

Page 606 "Even today, some television shows and movies portray Italians as Mafia-like mobsters, Jews as greedy bankers, and African Americans as **promiscuous** or lazy."

A person that is **promiscuous** is someone that has many causal and careless sexual relationships.

Page 607 "Other explanations of prejudice and discrimination focus on how being a member of a particular group helps to **magnify** one's sense of self-esteem."

Your sense of self-esteem is expanded when it is **magnified**.

Page 607 "**Slogans** such as 'gay-pride' and 'black is beautiful' illustrate that the groups to which we belong **furnish** us with a sense of self-respect (Tajfel, 1982; Rowley et al., 1998)."

Slogans are a brief, attention-getting phrases.

The groups may **furnish** us, or provide us, with a sense of self-respect.

Page 607 "Consequently, we **inflate** the positive aspects of our ingroup – and, at the same time, **devalue** outgroups."

We **inflate**, or exaggerate and overstate aspects of our ingroup.

We may **devalue**, or diminish the value of outgroups.

Page 607 "For instance, some psychologists argue that prejudice results when there is perceived competition for **scarce** societal resources."

Things that are **scarce** are rare or in short supply.

Page 607 "Making values and norms against prejudice more **conspicuous**."

When you make something more **conspicuous**, you make it more noticeable or prominent."

Page 607 "Similarly, people who hear others making strong, **vehement** antiracist statements are subsequently more likely to strongly condemn racism (Blanchard, Lilly, & Vaughn, 1991; Dovidio, Kawakami, & Gaertner, 2000)."

Vehement arguments are intense and passionate arguments.

Module 57:
Positive and Negative Social Behavior

Liking and Loving: Interpersonal Attraction and the Development of Relationships
Aggression and Prosocial Behavior: Hurting and Helping Others

Becoming an Informed Consumer of Psychology: Dealing Effectively
with Anger

- *Why are we attracted to certain people, and what progression do
  social relationships follow?*
- *What factors underlie aggression and prosocial behavior?*

Positive and Negative Social Behavior

Another area of social influence is called **[a]** _____, which encompasses the
factors that lead to positive feelings about others. Research on liking has identified the following

factors as important in the development of attraction between people. **[b]** _____
refers to physical nearness or geographical closeness as a factor in development of friendship.

Proximity leads to liking. **[c]** _____ also leads to liking. The more often one is
exposed to any stimulus, the more the stimulus is liked. Familiarity with a stimulus can evoke

positive feelings. **[d]** _____ influences attraction because we assume that people
with similar backgrounds will evaluate us positively. We also experience a strong

[e] _____; in other words, we like those who like us. Greater

[f] _____ also leads to liking, and is a source of popularity. Physical
attractiveness may be the single most important factor in college dating.

Several kinds of love have been hypothesized, one being **[g]** _____ love,

which is an intense state of absorption in another person. Another is **[h]** _____ love,
which is strong affection that we have for someone with whom our lives are deeply involved.
Robert Sternberg has proposed that love is made of three components.

The **[i]** _____ component includes feelings of closeness and connectedness; the **[j]** _____ component is made of the motivational drives related to sex, physical closeness, and romance; and the **[k]** _____ component encompasses the initial cognition that one loves someone and the long-term feelings of commitment to maintain love.

Drive-by shootings, car-jackings, and abductions give a pessimistic impression of human behavior. The helping behavior of many people, however, counteracts this impression. Social psychology seeks to explain these extremes in human behavior.

[l] _____ occurs at societal and individual levels, and the basic questions concern whether aggression is inevitable or whether it results from particular circumstances. Aggression is defined as the intentional injury of or harm to another person.

Instinct theories explain aggression as the result of innate urges. Konrad Lorenz suggested that aggressive energy is built up through the instinct of aggression and that its release is necessary. The discharge of this energy is called **[m]** _____. Lorenz suggested that society should provide an acceptable means of achieving catharsis, like sports. There is no way to test this theory experimentally.

The frustration-aggression theory says that the frustration of a goal *always* leads to aggression. **[n]** _____ is defined as the thwarting of a goal-directed behavior. More recently, the theory has been modified to suggest that frustration creates a *readiness* to act aggressively.

The observational learning view suggests that we learn to act aggressively by observing others. Observational learning theory also suggests that the rewards and punishments received by a model are important in the learning of aggression. This formulation has wide support.

[o] _____ refers to helping behavior. The prosocial behavior studied most by psychologists is bystander intervention. When more than one person witnesses an emergency, **[p]** _____, the tendency for people to feel that responsibility is shared among those present, increases; consequently no single person is likely to take action. In some cases, people act altruistically. **[q]** _____ is helping behavior that is beneficial to others but may require self-sacrifice. People high in *empathy* may be more likely to respond than others. Situational factors and mood may also affect helping behavior.

Evaluate

_____ 1.   passionate (or romantic) love   a. The motivational drives relating to sex, physical closeness, and romance.

_____ 2.   compassionate love   b. Feelings of closeness and connectedness.

_____ 3.   intimacy component   c. The initial cognition that one loves someone, and the longer-term feelings of commitment.

_____ 4.   passion component

   d. The strong affection we have for those with whom our lives are deeply involved.

_____ 5.   decision/commitment component

   e. A state of intense absorption in someone that is characterized by physiological arousal, psychological interest, and caring for another's needs.

Rethink

57-1   Can love be studied scientifically? Is there an elusive quality to love that makes it at least partially unknowable? How would you define "falling in love"? How would you study it?

57-2   *From the perspective of a criminal justice worker:* How would the aggression of Eric Rudolph, who was convicted of exploding a bomb during the 1996 Summer Olympics in Atlanta and later attacking several women's clinics, be interpreted by the three main approaches to the study of aggression: instinct approaches, frustration-aggression approaches, and observational-learning approaches? Do you think any of these approaches fits the Rudolph case more closely than the others?

Spotlight on Terminology and Language—ESL Pointers

Page 609 "Like **philosophers** and theologians, social psychologists have pondered the basic nature of humanity."

A **philosopher** is a scholar who seeks wisdom and enlightenment.

Page 609 "By far the greatest amount of research has focused on liking, probably because it is easier for investigators conducting short-term experiments to produce states of liking in strangers who have just met than to **instigate** and observe loving relationships over long periods."

To **instigate** some behavior is to prompt or to set off this behavior.

Page 609 "*Proximity.* If you live in a dormitory or an apartment, consider the friends you made when you first moved in."

The term *proximity* refers to closeness in space or time.

Page 610 "Folk wisdom tells us that **birds of a feather flock together**."

The phrase **"birds of a feather flock together"** is used to imply that people that are alike will choose to be together.

Page 610 "Social psychologists have come up with a clear **verdict** regarding which of the two statements is correct: We tend to like those who are similar to us."

A **verdict** is a decision or judgment.

Page 610 "In a questionnaire answered by some 40,000 respondents, people identified the qualities most valued in a friend as the ability to keep confidences, loyalty, and warmth and affection, followed closely by supportiveness, **frankness**, and a sense of humor (Parlee, 1979)."

To be "**frank**" is to open and blunt; to be completely honest.
Page 611 "However, love is such a central issue in most people's lives that eventually social psychologists could not resist its **allure**."

Allure refers to a powerful, attractive quality that is often glamorous and sometimes dangerous.

Page 611 "As a first step, researchers tried to identify the characteristics that distinguish between mere liking and **full-blown** love."

Something that is **full-blown** is fully developed, or complete.

Page 611 "Psychologist Robert Sternberg makes an even **finer** differentiation between types of love."

A **finer** distinction is a more sensitive, or discriminating distinction.

Page 611 "Although **mutual attraction** and love are the two most important characteristics desired in a mate by men and women in the United States, men in China rated good health as most important, and women there rated emotional stability and maturity as most important."

Mutual attraction is attraction that is felt by all people involved.

Page 612 "**Drive-by shootings**, **carjackings**, and abductions are just a few examples of the violence that seems all too common today."

Drive-by shootings are shootings in which the person firing the gun is in a moving car when the gun is fired.

Carjackings are crimes that occur when some one steals a car by forcing the driver to drive somewhere against the drivers will.

Page 612 "The difficulty of answering such **knotty** questions becomes apparent as soon as we consider how best to define the term aggression."

A **knotty** question is a tough question; as you think about it the question becomes more complex and difficult to answer.

Page 613 "If you have ever **punched** an **adversary** in the nose, you may have experienced a certain satisfaction, despite your better judgment."

An **adversary** is an opponent or an enemy.

Page 613 "Konrad Lorenz, an ethologist (a scientist who studies animal behavior), expanded on Freud's notions by arguing that humans, along with members of other species, have a fighting instinct, which in earlier times ensured protection of food supplies and **weeded out** the weaker of the species (Lorenz, 1966, 1974)."

To **weed something out** is to exclude unwanted things from consideration.

Page 614 "In fact, some studies **flatly** contradict the notion of catharsis, leading psychologists to look to other explanations for aggression (Anderson & Bushman, 2001; Bushman, Baumeister, & Phillips, 2001; Bushman, 2002)."

Some studies **flatly** and completely contradict this notion.

Page 614 "Even though the clerk can see you gesturing and begging him to open the door, he refuses, **shrugging** his shoulders and pointing to a sign that indicates when the store will open the next day."

To **shrug your shoulders** is to raise and drop your shoulders to indicate that you do not know something.

Page 614 "At that moment, the feelings you experience toward the sales clerk probably place you on the **verge** of real aggression, and you are undoubtedly seething inside."

To be on the **verge** of something is to be on the edge, or at the point at which something is about to happen.

Page 614 "When first put forward, the theory said flatly that frustration *always* leads to aggression of some sort, and that aggression is *always* the result of some frustration, where *frustration* is defined as the **thwarting** or blocking of some ongoing, goal-directed behavior (Dollard et al., 1939)."
To **thwart** something is to block or prevent it from happening.

Page 614 "For example, in one experiment, angered participants behaved significantly more aggressively when in the presence of a **rifle** and a **revolver** than they did in a comparable situation in which no guns were present (Berkowitz & LePage, 1967)."

A **rifle** is a gun with a long barrel and is fired from the shoulder.

A **revolver** is a hand gun that holds multiple bullets in a circular chamber that revolves.

Page 615 "Whereas instinct theory would suggest that the aggression had been **pent up** and was now being discharged, and frustration-aggression theory would examine the girl's frustration at no longer being able to use her new toy, observational learning theory would look to previous situations in which the girl had viewed others being rewarded for their aggression."

Pent-up feelings are confined or repressed feelings.

Page 615 "For example, perhaps she had watched a friend get to play with a toy after he painfully **twisted** it out of the hand of another child."

Something that is **twisted** is distorted or bent.

Page 615 "**Diffusion** of responsibility is the tendency for people to feel that responsibility for acting is shared, or **diffused**, among those present."

When something is **diffused** it is spread or scattered throughout.

Page 615 "For instance, if people with training in medical aid or lifesaving techniques are present, untrained bystanders are less likely to **intervene** because they feel they have less expertise."

To **intervene** is to get involved in something, or to interfere

Page 616 "Piliavin (1972), who conducted a field experiment in which an individual seemed to collapse in a subway car with blood **trickling** out of the corner of his mouth.

When something **trickles**, it flows in a slow thin stream.

Page 616 "The results of the experiment showed that bystanders were less likely to help when a person (actually a confederate) who appeared to be a medical **intern** was present than when the "intern" was not present."

An **intern** is a doctor who is still in training.

Page 616 "Still, most social psychologists agree that no single set of **attributes** differentiates helpers from nonhelpers."

An **attribute** is an inherent characteristic, a trait or feature of that person.

Page 617 "However, don't spend too much time **brooding**: Fantasize, but then move on."

To **brood** is to think unpleasant, gloomy or dark thoughts.

Page 617 "People who always try to suppress their anger may experience a variety of consequences, such as **self-condemnation**, frustration, and even physical illness (Sharma, Ghosh, & Spielberger, 1995; Finney, Stoney, & Engebretson , 2002)."

Self-condemnation is to blame yourself or judge yourself as guilty of some wrong doing.

Test your knowledge of the modules by answering these questions. These questions have been placed in three Practice Tests. The first two tests consist of questions that will test your recall of factual knowledge. The third test contains questions that are challenging and primarily test for conceptual knowledge and your ability to apply that knowledge. Check your answers and review the feedback using the Answer Key in the following pages of the *Study Guide*.

PRACTICE TEST 1:

1. When advertisers hired Michael Jordan to sell men's underwear, their intent was to link a product they want consumers to buy to a:
   a. positive feeling or event.
   b. cognition.
   c. peripheral route.
   d. dissonant stimulus.

2. Sets of cognitions known as schemas serve as _____ for social cognitions.
   a. organizing frameworks
   b. defenses against stereotypes
   c. feeling-communicators
   d. insincerity whistle-blowers

3. People rely heavily on _____ when forming an impression of another person.
   a. central tendencies
   b. central traits
   c. primary traits
   d. schematic tendencies

4. The tendency for people to attribute others' behavior to dispositional causes and their own behavior to situational causes is known as:
   a. ingroup versus outgroup error.
   b. fundamental attribution error
   c. dispositional attribution error.
   d. stereotypic attribution error.

5. The classic demonstration of pressure to conform comes from a series of studies carried out in the 1950s by:
   a. B. F. Skinner.
   b. Solomon Asch.
   c. Philip Zimbardo.
   d. Stanley Milgram.

6. People working on tasks and questions that are ambiguous are more susceptible to:
   a. inoculation.
   b. obedience.
   c. forewarning.
   d. social pressure.

7. The classic experiment performed by _____ demonstrated the power of authority to produce obedience.
   a. Albert Bandura
   b. Solomon Asch
   c. Stanley Milgram
   d. B. F. Skinner

8. The idea that people may think they are not prejudiced, but nonetheless respond unconsciously with prejudice attitudes reflects:
   a. reverse discrimination.
   b. individualism.
   c. modern racism.
   d. deterrence.

9. Beliefs and expectations about group members held simply on the basis of their group membership are called:
   - a. self-fulfilling prophecies.
   - c. stereotypes.
   - b. culture.
   - d. contingencies.

10. Which of the following is **not** a strong influence on the formation of friendships?
    - a. Others who are like them
    - c. Others whom they see frequently
    - b. Others who live nearby
    - d. Others who know their families

11. Which of the following elements most distinguishes love from mere liking?
    - a. Proximity
    - c. Similarity
    - b. Complementarity
    - d. Physical arousal

12. Sternberg found that different types of love are made up of different quantities of:
    - a. liking, loving, and commitment.
    - c. emotion, motivation, and attraction.
    - b. passion, compassion, and attraction.
    - d. intimacy, passion, and commitment.

13. Tanya has been trying to quit smoking since her mother was diagnosed with lung cancer. Although she knows the risks, it is very difficult to refrain from smoking when she finds herself in situations where she normally would have a cigarette. Festinger calls this:
    - a. cathartic interference.
    - c. cognitive dissonance.
    - b. tension reduction.
    - d. frustration aggression.

14. Prosocial is a more formal way of describing behavior that is:
    - a. helping.
    - c. innate.
    - b. cathartic.
    - d. aggressive.

_____ 15. self-serving bias   a. Tendency to think of people as being similar to oneself.

_____ 16. central traits   b. Major traits considered in forming impressions of others.

_____ 17. fundamental attribution error   c. A tendency to attribute one's successes to dispositional causes, and one's failures to situational ones.

_____ 18. halo effect

    d. A tendency to overattribute others' behavior to dispositional causes but to underattribute one's own behavior to situational causes.

_____ 19. assumed-similarity bias

    e. An initial understanding that a person has positive traits is used to infer other uniformly positive characteristics.

20. Cognitive dissonance occurs when a person holds two _____ or thoughts that are contradictory.

21. _____ concerns how we decide what causes others' behavior.

22. An experiment by _____ demonstrated the power of the judgments of others on the perceptual judgments of an individual participant.

23. When people act on negative stereotypes, this _____ can lead to exclusion from jobs, neighborhoods, or educational opportunities.

24. Expectations that increase the likelihood that an event or behavior will occur are

_____.

25. Much has been made of attitudes and behavior and how they may or may not be consistent. Describe a situation in which your attitudes and behavior may not have been consistent, and then compare the cognitive-dissonance explanation and the self-perception explanation of the situation.

PRACTICE TEST 2:

1. Advertising executives are designing a new commercial to sell cellular phones. Which of the following advice would you give them?
   a. Use a supermodel as a spokesperson.
   b. Scare people into thinking they need a cell phone for emergencies.
   c. Use an "average guy" as a spokesperson.
   d. Make sure the audience knows the cell phone market is highly competitive.

2. The advertising industry draws on findings from _____ regarding persuasion.
   a. experimental psychology
   b. psychometrics
   c. abnormal psychology
   d. social psychology

3. Katrina is seriously training to earn a place on the Olympic swim team. When she sees a piece of cake, Katrina wants to eat it, but knows that she shouldn't. Festinger called this:
   a. cognitive dissonance.
   b. cathartic interference.
   c. tension reduction.
   d. frustration-aggression.

4. The processes that underlie our understanding of the social world are called:
   a. social cognitions.
   b. schemas.
   c. central traits.
   d. stereotypes.

5. The task of _____ is to explain how people understand the causes of behavior.
   a. discrimination theory
   b. social cognition
   c. attribution theory
   d. directive-behavior theory

6. Conformity is a change in behavior or attitude brought about by:
   a. an increase of knowledge.
   b. a desire to follow the beliefs or standards of others.
   c. intense pressure to be a distinct individual.
   d. an insecure self-image.

7. A change in behavior that results from direct, explicit social pressure to behave in a certain way is called:
   a. conformity.
   b. congruence.
   c. commission.
   d. compliance.

8. What is the correct term for the technique in which a large request is asked, followed by expected refusal and later a smaller request?
    a. Obedience
    b. Social compliance
    c. Door-in-the-face technique
    d. Foot-in-the-door technique

9. The negative behavior toward an individual because of his or her membership in a particular group is known as:
    a. stereotyping.
    b. discrimination.
    c. prejudice.
    d. self-fulfilling prophecy.

10. Proximity is defined as:
    a. nearness to another person.
    b. a tendency to like those who like us.
    c. a tendency of those whom we like to like us.
    d. distance from another.

11. _____ love is a state of intense absorption in someone, with bodily arousal, mental interest, and care for the other's needs.
    a. The intimacy component of
    b. The decision/commitment component of
    c. Compassionate
    d. Passionate (romantic)

12. Advertisers who design a fear-evoking advertising campaign know that messages are most effective when:
    a. they frighten people into buying the product.
    b. they reach a small and indifferent audience.
    c. viewers' cognitive defense mechanisms are activated.
    d. they include advice for steps to avoid the described danger.

13. When stereotypes are attributed to a particular group, they may induce members of that group to act in ways that confirm the stereotype. This is known as:
    a. the ingroup-outgroup bias.
    b. reverse discrimination.
    c. a self-fulfilling prophecy.
    d. the interdependent view of the self.

14. Being unable to read has led to a great deal of frustration for Manuel. This frustration is most likely to lead to aggression:
    a. in the presence of aggressive cues.
    b. immediately after being frustrated.
    c. during late adolescence.
    d. several hours after being frustrated.

_____ 15. proximity

_____ 16. reciprocity-of-liking effect

_____ 17. similarity

_____ 18. prosocial behavior

_____ 19. diffusion of responsibility

a. Any helping behavior.

b. The hypothesis that people are attracted to others who have common interests and lifestyles.

c. Nearness to another, one cause for liking.

d. The tendency to like those who like us.

e. The tendency for people to feel that responsibility for helping is shared among those present.

20. Research in social psychology has demonstrated that children as young as _____ years of age begin to show preferences for members of their own race.

21. Often, inaccurate portrayals are the primary source of information about a group, and they can lead to the maintenance of unfavorable _____.

22. People may come to think that their own group is better than others in an effort to maximize our own _____.

23. Some psychologists argue that _____ results when there is perceived competition for scarce resources.

24. Geographic closeness or _____ is one of the most important factors in establishing personal relationships.

25. What factors would be at work when prejudices erupt into violence against racial groups? Analyze the factors of conformity, obedience, and stereotyping, including ingroup and outgroup biases.

PRACTICE TEST 3: Conceptual, Applied, and Challenging Questions

1. A 12-year-old boy who overhears his father tell his mother that "girls can't play sports well" may grow up to believe this opinion and adopt it as a prejudice as a result of the process of:
   a. observational learning.
   b. central route learning.
   c. cognitive dissonance.
   d. persuasive communication.

2. If a target audience pays more attention to the celebrity doing the commercial than to the advertisement message, which processing route is being used the most by the audience?
   a. Central-route processing
   b. Circumference-route processing
   c. Peripheral-route processing
   d. The message is not being processed.

3. Many variables influence the effectiveness of a communication to create attitude change. In which of the following situations will the impact be the greatest?
   a. The recipient appraises the message with central-route processing.
   b. The recipient of the message is male.
   c. The recipient appraises the message with peripheral-route processing.
   d. The recipient is very intelligent.

4. According to Festinger's theory of cognitive dissonance, if a smoker holds the cognitions "I smoke" and "Smoking causes cancer," he or she should be motivated to do all of the following *except*:
   a. modify one or both cognitions.
   b. enter a stop-smoking program.
   c. make the attitudes consistent.
   d. change the importance of one cognition.

5. The best example of cognitive dissonance is:
   a. stating that women should earn less money than men for doing the same job.
   b. exaggerating the merits of a product in order to promote sales.
   c. knowing that cigarette smoking is harmful, but doing it anyway.
   d. believing that people who are disabled cannot hold good jobs and therefore not recommending them.

6.   Which one of the following statements is the best example of making a dispositional attribution?
      a.   John is being good because the teacher is watching.
      b.   Even though I am not feeling sociable, I will go to the party if you do.
      c.   I become very anxious when other people criticize me.
      d.   Sue is staying up all night to study because she is a conscientious student.

7.   Which of the following situations best describes a situational cause for the described behavior?
      a.   Tina straightens the guest room, which is normally a messy sewing room, because relatives will be staying at her house for a week.
      b.   Barbara helps an old lady across the street because she is always thoughtful.
      c.   Danny, who is normally grumpy, frowns about an exam as he walks down the hall.
      d.   Mary is a punctual person who is on time for school every morning.

8.   What measure may be most effective for reducing the tendency of people to conform in a group situation?
      a.   Make sure all members value the group highly.
      b.   Include lots of members in the group.
      c.   Use a show of hands when voting.
      d.   Use a secret ballot when voting.

9.   Stereotypes differ from prejudices in that:
      a.   stereotypes are beliefs that lead to prejudices, which are judgments.
      b.   stereotypes must involve action against a group.
      c.   prejudices must involve action against a group.
      d.   prejudices are beliefs that lead to stereotypes, which are judgments.

10.   Which of the following factors is **not** a predictor of whether two people will be initially attracted to each other?
      a.   Dissimilarity, because opposites attract   c.   Living nearby each other
      b.   Repeatedly "bumping into" each other   d.   Thinking the other is attractive

11.   Which of the following is **not** a component of Sternberg's theory of love?
      a.   Intimacy   c.   Decision/commitment
      b.   Passion   d.   Individuation/separation

12.   Instinct theorist Konrad Lorenz would argue that opportunities to exercise and play sports ought to be given to prisoners because they:
      a.   provide models of prosocial behavior.
      b.   present violent models to be seen and imitated by prisoners.
      c.   enable natural aggressive energy to be released harmlessly.
      d.   reduce the frustration that causes aggression.

13.   What measure may be most effective for reducing the tendency of people to conform in a group situation?
      a.   Use a secret ballot when voting.
      b.   Use a show of hands when voting.
      c.   Include lots of members in the group.
      d.   Make sure all of the members value the group highly.

14. Following the destruction of the Twin Towers in New York City, thousands of unpaid volunteers assisted at the site, thereby demonstrating:
   a. the fundamental attribution error.
   b. diffusion of responsibility.
   c. altruism.
   d. the halo effect.

_____ 15. rewards-costs approach

_____ 16. altruism

_____ 17. empathy

_____ 18. schemas

_____ 19. status

a. Helping behavior that is beneficial to others while requiring sacrifice on the part of the helper.

b. Sets of cognitions about people and social experiences.

c. One person's experiencing of another's emotions, in turn increasing the likelihood of responding to the other's needs.

d. The social rank held within a group.

e. The notion that, in a situation requiring help, a bystander's perceived rewards must outweigh the costs if helping is to occur.

20. While some might argue that opposites attract, other researchers believe we tend to like people who are _____ to us.

21. People who are _____ attractive are more popular than those who are not, other factors being equal.

22. Researchers believe that liking someone is qualitatively different than _____ someone.

23. _____ explains why some people helped complete strangers escape from the burning World Trade Center during the September 11, 2001 terrorist attacks.

24. _____ approaches propose that aggression is primarily the outcome of innate or inborn urges.

25. In the United States, the idea of arranged marriages often is seen with disdain. Our culture, for the most part, has always encouraged our freedom to select mates based on the notion of romantic love. Explain then the elements that may be present in arranged marriages that make them as successful as those partnerships we personally choose.

■ ANSWER KEY: MODULES 54, 55, 56, AND 57

Module 54:	Module 55:	Module 56:	Module 57:
[a] Social psychology	[a] social influence	[a] Stereotypes	[a] interpersonal attraction
[b] Attitudes	[b] Conformity	[b] prejudice	[b] Proximity
[c] Central-route processing	[c] Groupthink	[c] discrimination	[c] Mere exposure
[d] Peripheral-route processing	[d] compliance	[d] self-fulfilling prophecy	[d] Similarity
[e] need for cognition	[e] foot-in-the-door	[e] observational learning approaches	[e] reciprocity-of-liking effect
[f] Cognitive dissonance	[f] door-in-the-face	[f] social identity theory	[f] physical attractiveness
[g] social cognition	[g] that's-not-all		[g] passionate (or romantic)
[h] schemas	[h] not-so-free sample	Evaluate	[h] compassionate love
[i] Impression formation	[i] industrial-organizational psychology	1. c	[i] intimacy
[j] central traits	[j] Obedience	2. b	[j] passion
[k] attribution theory		3. d	[k] decision/commitment
[l] situational causes	Evaluate	4. e	[l] Aggression
[m] dispositional causes	1. e	5. a	[m] catharsis
[n] halo effect	2. b		[n] Frustration
[o] assumed similarity bias	3. d		[o] Prosocial behavior
[p] self-serving bias	4. c		[p] diffusion of responsibility
[q] fundamental attribution error	5. a		[q] Altruism
			Evaluate
Evaluate			1. e
1. c			2. d
2. d			3. b
3. a			4. a
			5. c

Selected Rethink Answers

54-1   Joan first experiences cognitive dissonance because her initial thoughts and attitudes about Annette were contradictory. Finally, with friends of Joan's treating Annette well, she was able to add positive cognitions, which enabled her to change her impression of Annette.

57-2   Define each approach to aggression. The frustration-aggression approach seems especially appropriate here. Rudolph may have been frustrated by not achieving his original goals in the Olympics bombing, so this led to more aggression and the bombing of the women's clinics.

Practice Test 1:

1.   a   mod. 54 p. 603
*a. Correct. Linking the product to a positive event originates with classical conditioning.
b. Incorrect. They seek to link the product to a pleasant stimuli, like a feeling or event.
c. Incorrect. The peripheral-route is one of the methods of communicating in persuasive communication.
d. Incorrect. A dissonant stimulus might be one that does not fit with the others or causes some kind of conflict.

2.   a   mod. 54 p. 607
*a. Correct. A schema is an organizing framework.
b. Incorrect. Schemas actually serve as the foundation for stereotypes.
c. Incorrect. Schemas are not communicators.
d. Incorrect. Schemers maybe, but not schemas.

3.   b   mod. 54 p. 607
a. Incorrect. Central tendencies are the measures like mean, median, and mode that are produced using statistics.
*b. Correct. Apparently we utilize major, evident traits that are central to the personality of the individual we are forming impressions about.
c. Incorrect. The term is central traits.

d.   Incorrect. The concept "schematic tendencies" is yet to be developed.

4.   b   mod. 54 p. 611
a.   Incorrect. The ingroup-outgroup bias (not error) may follow the fundamental attribution error, but its role is in determining the boundaries between groups and strengthening the sense of identity within the ingroup.
*b. Correct. The fundamental attribution error is common and may be understood in that we do tend to see the person's behavior more than the environment in which it occurs, and we see our own environment and not so much our own behavior.
c.   Incorrect. There is no dispositional attribution error.
d.   Incorrect. There is no stereotypic attribution error.

5.   b   mod. 54 p. 613
a.   Incorrect. Skinner did not conduct conformity experiments.
*b. Correct. Solomon Asch performed several experiments on conformity throughout the 1950s.
c.   Incorrect. Zimbardo conducted experiments on compliance and obedience.
d.   Incorrect. Milgram conducted a now-famous experiment on obedience.

6.   d   mod. 55 p. 614
a.   Incorrect. Inoculation occurs when the person is deliberately exposed to conformity pressures in order to be better at avoiding conformity.
b.   Incorrect. Obedience requires more direct pressure.
c.   Incorrect. Forewarning is a technique for developing the ability to resist pressures to conform.
*d. Correct. In ambiguous circumstances, social pressure is more likely to have an effect on conformity.

7.   c   mod. 55 p. 618
a.   Incorrect. Albert Bandura is known for his study of violence and the Bobo clown doll.
b.   Incorrect. Solomon Asch is known for his experiments on conformity.
*c. Correct. Stanley Milgram asked subjects to give an electric shock to other subjects, and he was able to get most to comply to the point of the highest shock level.
d.   Incorrect. Skinner did not perform any human conformity studies.
8.   c   mod. 55 p. 621

a.   Incorrect. This discrimination is not reverse.
b.   Incorrect. Individualism does not wholly explain these unconscious attitudes.
*c. Correct. This is the definition of modern racism.
d.   Incorrect. Deterrence is a concept that would prevent the actions of open group by threatening retaliation.

9.   c   mod. 55 p. 621
a.   Incorrect. These are stereotypes, and stereotypes can become self-fulfilling prophecies.
b.   Incorrect. Culture is the shared beliefs and practices of a group.
*c. Correct. This defines stereotypes.
d.   Incorrect. These are not called contingencies, they are called stereotypes.

10. d   mod. 56 p. 628
a.   Incorrect. See answer d.
b.   Incorrect. See answer d.
c.   Incorrect. See answer d.
*d. Correct. Living nearby, similarity, and frequent contact are the foundations of friendship, and knowing the family is not.

11. d   mod. 56 p. 629
a.   Incorrect. See answer d.
b.   Incorrect. See answer d.
c.   Incorrect. See answer d.
*d. Correct. To being nearby, sharing interests, and being similar, love adds the component of physical attraction and arousal.

12. d   mod. 56 p. 629
a.   Incorrect. See answer d.
b.   Incorrect. See answer d.
c.   Incorrect. See answer d.
*d. Correct. Sternberg's triarchic theory of love has three components—intimacy, passion, and commitment—which can be combined in different ways.

13. c   mod. 56 p. 606
a.   Incorrect. No such thing.
b.   Incorrect. If anything, it would heighten tension.
*c. Correct.
d.   Incorrect. It might lead to frustration, but not aggression.

14. a   mod. 56 p. 633
*a. Correct. Prosocial behavior is altruistic, helping behavior.
b.   Incorrect. Insofar as helping another is cathartic, this could be a good answer, but the term prosocial typically refers to helping behavior.
c.   Incorrect. Some biosociologists argue that prosocial behavior is innate because it promotes the survival of the species.
d.   Incorrect. Prosocial behavior is altruistic, helping behavior.

15. c   mod. 56 p. 607
16. b   mod. 56 p. 607
17. d   mod. 56 p. 611
18. e   mod. 56 p. 610
19. a   mod. 56 p. 610

20. cognitions   mod. 56 p. 606
21. Attribution theory   mod. 56 p. 610
22. Asch   mod. 56 p. 613
23. discrimination   mod. 56 p. 621
24. self-fulfilling prophecies   mod. 56 p. 621

25.
▪ Situations that might be relevant are those in which you did something, like go on a date with someone, that you really were not that interested in doing. The mismatch between the attitude (lack of interest) and behavior (going out), while not that great, does illustrate the problem.
▪ Describe how you felt after the specific incident or act and whether you changed your attitudes (she/he is actually pleasant to be with). Or perhaps, you wait until after the behavior to form your attitude (consistent with the self-perception theory).

Practice Test 2:
1. a   mod. 56 p. 621
*a. Correct. Attractive spokespeople are more persuasive.
b.   Incorrect. Scaring people should be used with caution, because if too much fear is evoked, people may ignore the message altogether.
c.   Incorrect. Unless the average guy is highly attractive, expert-sounding, and very trustworthy, he wouldn't make a great spokesperson.
d.   Incorrect. This would highlight the ulterior motive of the company—to sell product—which would not help in persuasion.

2.   d   mod. 56 p. 605
a.   Incorrect. See answer d.
b.   Incorrect. Psychometrics is an important technique that probably was used by social psychologists as they developed key ideas that are now being used in the advertising industry.
c.   Incorrect. Of all the branches of psychology, abnormal psychology has probably made the smallest contribution to the advertising industry.
*d. Correct. Social psychologists, some of whom are experimental psychologists as well, have made contributions that are useful to the advertising industry.

3.   a   mod. 56 p. 606
*a. Correct. The conflict between two cognitions becomes cognitive dissonance when this conflict is accompanied by an affective state.
b.   Incorrect. No such thing.
c.   Incorrect. If anything, it would heighten tension.
d.   Incorrect. It may lead to frustration, but probably not aggression.

4.   a   mod. 56 p. 607
*a. Correct. Social cognitions refer to the thoughts we have about other people and the causes of their behavior.
b.   Incorrect. Social cognitions are schemas, but schemas, the cognitive units of organization, refer to other cognitive categories as well.
c.   Incorrect. Central traits are the traits we choose to make early impressions about people, and they may be included in our social cognitions.
d.   Incorrect. Stereotypes are forms of social cognitions (but not all social cognitions are stereotypes).

5.   c   mod. 56 p. 608
a.   Incorrect. There is not "discrimination theory" that applies to this issue.
b.   Incorrect. In the broadest sense this is true, but another alternative is more specific and thus a better choice.
*c. Correct. Attribution theory involves the efforts people make to understand the causes of their and others' behavior.
d.   Incorrect. There is not a "directive-behavior" theory.

6.   b   mod. 56 p. 613
a.   Incorrect. More knowledge would not necessarily lead to conformity; it could just as well lead to nonconformity.
*b. Correct. Conformity is to the pressures of the group, and it is accomplished by accepting the attitudes and behaviors of the group.
c.   Incorrect. The intense pressure to be an individual would be counter to the pressure to conform.
d.   Incorrect. People with secure self-images may be highly conforming individuals.

7.   d   mod. 56 p. 616
a.   Incorrect. Conformity results from indirect social pressure and a desire to be part of the group.
b.   Incorrect. Congruence is a concept used in humanistic psychotherapy to describe different aspects of the self concept.
c.   Incorrect. A commission is an amount of money received for a specific task, like a sales commission.
*d. Correct. This is the definition of compliance.

8.   c   mod. 56 p. 616
a.   Incorrect. This is called the door-in-the-face technique; it is the opposite of the foot-in-the-door technique.
b.   Incorrect. But it is a form of social compliance.
*c. Correct. This technique is the opposite of the foot-in-the-door technique.
d.   Incorrect. It is the opposite of this, and called the door-in-the-face technique.

9.   b   mod. 56 p. 621
a.   Incorrect. Stereotyping applies to attitudes, not behaviors.
*b. Correct. Discrimination is the negative action toward another person based on group membership.
c.   Incorrect. Prejudice is positive or negative attitudes toward a group or member of a group.
d.   Incorrect. A self-fulfilling prophecy is an expectation that the occurrence of an event or behavior increases the likelihood that the event or behavior will occur.

10. a   mod. 56 p. 627
*a. Correct. Physical proximity is nearness to another person, and it is a major factor in both friendship and love relationships.
b.   Incorrect. This defines the effect of reciprocity on us.
c.   Incorrect. See answer b.
d.   Incorrect. Distance is the opposite of proximity.

11. d   mod. 56 p. 629
a.   Incorrect. This is from Sternberg's theory, and is separate from passion.
b.   Incorrect. See answer b.
c.   Incorrect. This type of love is seen in contrast to passionate love.
*d. Correct. Sounds like "romance."

12. d   mod. 56 p. 604
a.   Incorrect. This would be the measure of their effectiveness.
b.   Incorrect. Indifferent audiences are no more receptive to fear-based messages than any other audience.
c.   Incorrect. Defense mechanisms may make them ignore the warnings.
*d. Correct. Otherwise they are simply frightening.

13. c   mod. 56 p. 621
a.   Incorrect. In this bias, stereotypes are applied to help differentiate the two groups.
b.   Incorrect. Reverse discrimination occurs when one is making efforts to avoid the stereotype.
*c. Correct. Self-fulfilling prophecies are a danger to underprivileged groups because they sustain the circumstances.
d.   Incorrect. We are all interdependent.

14. a   mod. 56 p. 632
*a. Correct. Aggressive cues increase the likelihood of aggression (which initially creates a readiness to act).
b.   Incorrect. See answer a.
c.   Incorrect. See answer a.
d.   Incorrect. See answer a.

15. c   mod. 56 p. 627
16. d   mod. 56 p. 628
17. b   mod. 56 p. 628
18. a   mod. 56 p. 633
19. e   mod. 56 p. 633
20. 3   mod. 56 p. 623

21. stereotypes   mod. 56 p. 621
22. self-esteem   mod. 56 p. 623
23. prejudice   mod. 56 p. 621
24. Proximity   mod. 56 p. 627

25.
▪ Provide an example of recent violence against an ethnic group (or even an episode identified with a particular group).
▪ Gang violence is a clear application of the ingroup-outgroup bias. The riots in Los Angeles

suggest that many people have very strong stereotypes about the groups represented in the violence, including African American, Hispanic, and Asian.
- Describe how each of the factors of conformity, compliance, and obedience could work toward increasing prejudice and following group behavior.

Practice Test 3:
1.　a　mod. 56 p. 632
*a. Correct. This is an example of observational learning.
b. Incorrect. Central route learning would happen in a more direct way than this.
c. Incorrect. Cognitive dissonance involves contradictory thoughts or beliefs that then cause tension.
d. Incorrect. Persuasive communication usually involves a more direct message.

2.　c　mod. 56 p. 604
a. Incorrect. The approach known as peripheral-route processing is being used.
b. Incorrect. This applies only to well-rounded messages.
*c. Correct. The peripheral route avoids presenting much reasoning or detail about the product.
d. Incorrect. But it is!

3.　a　mod. 56 p. 604
*a. Correct. When the recipient puts effort into cognitively analyzing the message, as required in central-route processing, the change in attitude will be the greatest for the situations given here.
b. Incorrect. Being male does not make the message any more or less effective.
c. Incorrect. The recipient will do little work in appraising a message that is peripheral.
d. Incorrect. Intelligence does not affect attitude change.

4.　b　mod. 56 p. 606
a. Incorrect. See answer b.
*b. Correct. Cognitive dissonance would lead to modifying one of the cognitions, making them consistent, or revaluing them, but it is unlikely to make the person enter a program to stop smoking (this requires additional pressures).
c. Incorrect. See answer b.
d. Incorrect. See answer b.

5.　c　mod. 56 p. 606
a. Incorrect. This is simply a sexist position.
b. Incorrect. This is simply typical of salespersons.

*c. Correct. Here, two thoughts are opposed to each other and will certainly result in tension.
d. Incorrect. This is simply being prejudicial.

6.　d　mod. 56 p. 609
a. Incorrect. John's behavior is explained according to the situation.
b. Incorrect. The decision to attend the party comes from dispositional forces.
c. Incorrect. Anxiety is explained in terms of what others do (thus situational).
*d. Correct. The disposition of conscientiousness is used to account for staying up all night.

7.　a　mod. 56 p. 609
*a. Correct. Tina is engaging in a behavior because of the situation, not her disposition to keep the room messy.
b. Incorrect. Thoughtfulness is Barbara's disposition.
c. Incorrect. Grumpiness is Danny's disposition.
d. Incorrect. Punctuality is Mary's disposition.

8.　d　mod. 56 p. 614
a. Incorrect. The more the group members value the group, the stronger will be the pressures to conform.
b. Incorrect. The larger the group, the more likely conformity becomes.
c. Incorrect. Public statements increase the pressure to conform.
*d. Correct. Secret ballots remove pressure to conform because other members will be unaware of how the individual votes are cast.

9.　a　mod. 56 p. 621
*a. Correct. Stereotypes are applications of category knowledge and prejudices involve using stereotypes to make judgments about people.
b. Incorrect. Neither requires action.
c. Incorrect. Neither requires action.
d. Incorrect. This is reversed.

10.　a　mod. 56 p. 628
*a. Correct. Similarity, not dissimilarity, predicts attraction.
b. Incorrect. Mere exposure, as this is, does predict attraction.
c. Incorrect. Proximity also predicts attraction.
d. Incorrect. Physical attractiveness predicts attraction as well.

11. d   mod. 56 p. 629
a.   Incorrect. See answer d.
b.   Incorrect. See answer d.
c.   Incorrect. See answer d.
*d.   Correct. Sternberg's triarchic theory of love has three components—intimacy, passion, and commitment—which can be combined in different ways.

12. c   mod. 56 p. 632
a.   Incorrect. Sports are not considered prosocial.
b.   Incorrect. Lorenz was referring to civilized, game-oriented sports like football.
*c.   Correct. Because aggression arises from an instinct, in his view, it needs some form of release.
d.   Incorrect. This is from a different aspect of the frustration-aggression hypothesis.

13. a   mod. 56 p. 614
*a.   Correct. Secret ballots remove pressure to conform because other members will be unaware of how the individual votes are cast.
b.   Incorrect. Public statements increase the pressure to conform.
c.   Incorrect. The larger the group, the more likely conformity becomes.
d.   Incorrect. The more the group members value the group, the stronger will be the pressure to conform.

14. c   mod. 56 p. 634
a.   Incorrect. Fundamental attribution error accounts for attributing the bombers' acts to their own evil nature.
b.   Incorrect. Diffusion of responsibility would have left many people standing by and watching.
*c.   Correct. This prosocial behavior demonstrates that more must be involved than mere rewards.
d.   Incorrect. Only if they were angels.

15. e   mod. 56 p. 634
16. a   mod. 56 p. 634
17. c   mod. 56 p. 634
18. b   mod. 56 p. 607
19. d   mod. 56 p. 614

20. similar   mod. 56 p. 628
21. physically   mod. 56 p. 628
22. loving   mod. 56 p. 629
23. Altruism   mod. 56 p. 630
24. Biological   mod. 56 p. 631

25. Often partners are chosen because of their proximity to each other. Selections are often made based on similarities in terms of values, attitudes, and traits. Knowing someone has evaluated us positively has a reciprocity-of-liking effect. Once commitments are made, intimacy and passion often follow.

Appendix: Going By the Numbers: Statistics in Psychology

Module 58: Descriptive Statistics
Module 59: Measures of Variability
Module 60: Using Statistics to Answer Questions: Inferential Statistics and Correlation

Overview

Statistics is the branch of mathematics concerned with collecting, organizing, analyzing, and drawing conclusions from numerical data. In this set of modules, we consider the basic approaches to statistical measurement.

Module 58 offers a discussion on the approaches to summarizing data that allow one to describe sets of observations. Descriptive statistics, frequency distributions, and the measures of central tendency are presented.

Module 59 explains the techniques used for deciding how much scores in a set of data vary, or are different from, one another. The range and standard deviation are two measures of variability.

Module 60 demonstrates the approaches to measuring the relationship between two sets of scores. Inferential statistics—techniques that use data from samples to make predictions about larger populations—is examined in this module.

Prologue: Selma Vorwerk
Looking Ahead

Module 58:	
Descriptive Statistics	
Module 59:	
Measures of Variability	
Module 60: Using Statistics	
to Answer Questions: Inferential Statistics	
and Correlation	

Descriptive Statistics
The Mean: Finding the Average
The Median: Finding the Middle
The Mode: Finding What Is Most Frequent
Comparing the Three M's: Mean Versus Median Versus Mode

- ***What measures can we use to summarize sets of data?***

Measures of Variability
The Range: Highest Minus Lowest
The Standard Deviation: Differences from the Mean

- ***How can we assess the variability of a set of data?***

Using Statistics to Answer Questions
The Correlation Coefficient: Measuring Relationship

- ***How do we generalize from data?***
- ***How can we determine the nature of a relationship, and the significance of differences, between two sets of scores?***

Descriptive Statistics, Measures of Variability, and Using Statistics to Answer Questions

[a] _____ is the branch of mathematics concerned with collecting, organizing, analyzing, and drawing conclusions from numerical data. One branch of statistics is

[b] _____ statistics—the branch that provides a means of summarizing data and presenting it in a meaningful way. Scores on your psychology tests might be presented this way. If we look at the test scores of a class in psychology to find out the number of people who

obtained each score, one would produce a(n) [c] _____. This is an arrangement

of the scores that illustrates how often any score is present. A(n) [d] _____ is a way of presenting the scores that allows the researcher to visually inspect the data. Scores are ordered along one dimension of a graph, with the number of people obtaining each score on the other.

When precise ways of summarizing the data are desired, measures of **[e]** _____ are preferred. This measure is an index of the central location within the distribution of scores.

The three measures of central tendency are the **[f]** _____, the

[g] _____, and the **[h]** _____. The mean is the term used for the arithmetic average of all of the scores presented. The median is the point in the distribution that divides the distribution in half, and the mode is the most frequently occurring of the scores.

In large samples, the distribution of scores produces a bell-shaped curve in which the right half mirrors the left, referred to as the **[i]** _____. Most large distributions containing many scores produce a normal curve. This means that most scores would be near the center of the curve, with fewer scores at the extremes.

Another way to look at a set of data is to look at the spread, or dispersion, of the scores in a distribution. This is called the **[j]** _____. The simplest measure of variability is the

[k] _____, the difference between the lowest and the highest scores in the distribution. Range is a problem because it only focuses on extreme scores, and a single extreme score can distort the picture. The **[l]** _____ is the average deviation of a set of scores from their mean. This is the most frequently used method of characterizing the variability of a distribution of scores. In a normal distribution, 68 percent of the scores will fall within one standard deviation above or below the mean. Ninety-five percent will fall to either side of it, or two standard deviations away, and 99.7 percent of the scores will fall within three standard deviations.

[m] _____ is the branch of statistics that uses data from samples to make predictions about larger populations. Because in most situations it is not possible to collect data

on everyone you would like to study in a certain **[n]** _____, a(n)

[o] _____, or a subgroup of the population of interest, is selected to represent the larger group. Statistical procedures have been designed to determine if the difference between two samples is sufficient to say that the groups are different, or if, instead, the differences are attributable merely to chance.

Researchers in psychology are also interested in determining the extent to which two variables are related to one another. A(n) **[p]** _____ is the statistic used to describe the extent of the relationship. It ranges in value from +1.00 to -1.00. In a(n) **[q]** _____ high values of one variable are associated with high values in another variable. In a(n) **[r]** _____ high values in one variable are associated with low values in another variable.

Evaluate

_____ 1. normal distribution

_____ 2. mean

_____ 3. median

_____ 4. mode

_____ 5. histogram

a. Pictorial arrangement of scores that demonstrates the distribution of a set of scores.

b. The score that most students received on a test.

c. The average obtained by adding up the test scores and dividing by the number of tests.

d. When most of the scores on a test are located in the middle with only a few scores located in the extremes.

e. The exact middle score in a distribution of scores.

Rethink

58-1   Government statistics on family income are presented in a variety of ways. What would be the most useful way of providing a summary of family incomes across the country: the mean, the median, or the mode? Why might only providing the mean be misleading?

59-1   If you were interested in understanding the number of people living below the poverty line in the United States, why might the range and standard deviation provide you with a better understanding of the extent of poverty than measures of central tendency (the mean, median, and mode) alone?

60-1   For many years, cigarette manufacturers argued that because the data linking smoking and disease was correlational, one could not infer that there was a causal connection between them and therefore no reason not to smoke. Did the manufacturers have a valid argument? How could you refute their argument?

Spotlight on Terminology and Language—ESL Pointers

Module 58: Descriptive Statistics

Page A-2 "To supporters of that view, unless **drastic** measures were taken, it would not be too many years before Western civilization collapsed from a lack of intelligence."

Something that is **drastic** is extreme and has a powerful effect.

Page A-2 "Fortunately for immigrants such as Selma Vorwerk, observers in favor of immigration pointed out the **fallacy** of using data from a relatively small sample — when a considerably larger set of intelligence test data was available."

A **fallacy** is something that not true, but is believed to be true. It is a mistaken belief.

Page A-2 "This time, though, the debate is based more on analyses of social and economic statistics, with opponents of immigration suggesting that the social fabric of the country will be changed and that jobs are being taken away from longer-term residents because of the **influx** of immigrants."

An **influx** is a sudden arrival of a large number of something.

Page A-2 "A debate **reminiscent** of this one rages today, as some observers suggest that an unrestrained flow of immigrants—this time from Latin America and Asia—will seriously damage the United States."

Something that is **reminiscent** is suggestive, or similar to something of the past.

Page A-2 "Equally **vehement** proponents of immigration suggest that the relevant statistics are being misinterpreted, and that their analyses of the situation result in very different conclusion."

When someone expresses something **vehemently,** they are passionate or expressing their opinion with force.

Page A-3 You would probably start by using descriptive statistics, the branch of statistics that provides a means of summarizing data, presenting the data in a usable and **convenient** form.

When something is **convenient** it makes life easier or more useful.

Page A-3 "In that **histogram**, the number of people obtaining a given score is represented **pictorially**."

A **histogram** is a bar graph, used to represent a frequency distribution by means of rectangles whose widths represent class intervals and whose areas are proportional to the corresponding frequencies

Pictorially means these scores are represented in a graphic or symbolic fashion. The information is conveyed using a visual image – the bar graph.

Page A-3 "Central tendency is an index of the central location within a **distribution** of scores."

The **distribution** of scores refers to the frequency distribution, or dissemination of scores.

Page A-4 "Because of its sensitivity to **extreme scores**, then, the mean can sometimes present a deceptive picture of a set of scores, especially in cases where the mean is based on a relatively small number of scores."

Extreme scores would be scores found at the farthest possible point from the center.

Page A-4 "One feature of the median as a measure of central tendency is that it is **insensitive** to extreme scores."

The median is **insensitive**, or not responsive, to extreme scores.

Page A-4 "The median divides a set of scores in half, and the **magnitude** of the scores is of no consequence in this process."

Magnitude refers to greatness of size or importance.

Page A-5 "A normal distribution is a distribution of scores that produces a **symmetrical**, bell-shaped curve, such as the one displayed in Figure 3, in which the right half mirrors the left half, and in which the mean, median, and mode all have the same value."

Symmetrical means having corresponding points whose connecting lines are bisected by a given point or perpendicularly bisected by a given line or plane.

Page A-5 "There would be many scores **hovering** around the center of the distribution of scores, then, and only a few at the extremes – producing a normal distribution."

When things **hover** they are suspended or float in the air without moving very far from the same spot.

Module 59: Measure of Variability

Page A-7 "Variability is a term that refers to the spread, or **dispersion of scores** in a distribution."

Dispersion of scores refers to the scattering of the values.

Page A-7 "The fact that a range is simple to calculate is about its only **virtue**."

Virtue is a beneficial quality.

Page A-7 "The problem with this particular measure of variability is that it is based entirely on extreme scores, and a single score that is very different from the others in a distribution can **distort** the picture of the distribution as a whole."

Distort is to cause something to be seen inaccurately, as when someone **distorts** the facts by using the data to misrepresent the true meaning of the findings.

Page A-8 "The distribution on the left is widely **dispersed**, and on the average an individual score in the distribution can be thought of as deviating quite a bit from the center of the distribution."

Things that are **dispersed** are all over the place, they are spread over a wide area.

Page A-9 "In contrast, in the distribution on the right, the scores are closely **packed together** and there is little deviation of a typical score from the center of the distribution."

Packed together can be thought of as crowded together.

Module 60: Using Statistics to Answer Questions: Inferential Statistics and Correlation

Page A -11 "A sample, in formal statistical terms, is a subgroup of a population of interest that is intended to be **representative** of the larger population.

To be **representative** is to be typical, or just like something.

Page A -11 "Questions such as this –as well as whether the results found are due to chance or represent unexpected, non chance finding—revolve around how "**probable**" certain events are.

Something that is **probable** is likely to occur.

Page A-11 "Ninety heads in 100 flips, then, is an extremely improbably outcome; if ninety heads did appear, the odds would be that the coin or the flipping process was **rigged**."

Rig means to manipulate or control, usually in a deceptive fashion.

Page A-13 "The statistic that provides a **precise** mathematical index of the degree to which two variables are related is the correlation coefficient."

Precise means exact.

Page A-14 Although it may seem **plausible** to us, for example, that it is the mother's intelligence that causes higher intelligence in a daughter, it is just as possible that a daughter's intelligence affects how the mother performs on an IQ test."

When something is **plausible**, it is credible or probable.

Page A-15 The **crucial** point is that even if we find a perfect correlation between two sets of variable, we will not be able to say that the two variables are linked causally – only that they are strongly related to one another (Good, 2003)."

The **crucial** point is the critical point, the most important point.

Test your knowledge of the chapter material by answering these questions. These questions have been placed in a Practice Test. Check your answers and review the feedback using the Answer Key on the following pages of your *Study Guide*.

PRACTICE TEST:

1. The branch of mathematics that psychologists use to organize data is known as:
   a. quantum theory.
   b. statistics.
   c. calculus.
   d. algebra.

2. The tendency of measurements to cluster around some value near the middle is called:
   a. nominal tendency.
   b. norm.
   c. peripheral tendency.
   d. central tendency.

3. Measures of central tendency include all of the following **except**:
   a. mean.
   b. range.
   c. mode.
   d. median.

4. The mean of a set of numbers 15, 5, 25, 10, 15 is:
   a. 15.
   b. 10.
   c. 14.
   d. 16.

5. In correlation studies, the coefficients can range from:
   a. 34% to 68%
   b. 1% to 99%
   c. -6.0 to +6.0
   d. -1.0 to +1.0

6. The mean of a set of numbers is the:
   a. interval between the highest and lowest scores.
   b. point at which the largest number of scores occurs.
   c. arithmetical average calculated by dividing the sum of values by the total number of scores.
   d. point that divides a set of scores in half.

7. Margaret explained to her parents that she could predict from a student's score on one measure how he or she will do on another measure by using the:
   a. standard deviation.
   b. range.
   c. mode.
   d. correlation coefficient.

8. A shoe boutique owner wants to know which evening shoes should be stocked in the greatest quantity. She would be interested in the _____ of her customers' shoe choices.
   a. mean
   b. range
   c. mode
   d. median

9. Joseph explained to the class that on the first test, **most** of the students received an 87%. The most frequently occurring in a set of scores is called the:
   a. mean.
   b. range.
   c. mode.
   d. median.

10. The mode of this set of scores 21, 24, 23, 21, 34, 21 is:

a.   24.   c.   21.5.
b   21.   d.   23.

11. In Binghamton. most of the residents have reported incomes between $25,000 and $60,000. Which measure of central tendency would be most disturbed by an income of $300,000?
   a.   Mean   c.   Mode
   b   Range   d.   Median

12. The professor used a bar graph called a _____ to show the frequency distribution of test scores for the midterm.
   a.   histogram   c.   normal distribution
   b.   skewed distribution   d.   polygon

13. If variable A is closely and positively correlated with variable B, we know that:
   a.   variable A causes variable B.   c.   variable B prevents variable A.
   b.   variable B causes variable A.   d.   variable A and variable B are associated.

14. A statistical measure that measures the degree to which a college education is associated with higher earning power in the student's future years is called a:
   a.   standard deviation.   c.   correlation coefficient.
   b.   probability.   d.   normal curve.

15. A perfect negative correlation occurs when the dots on a scatterplot form a:
   a.   circle or random pattern.
   b.   straight line from upper left to lower right.
   c.   straight line from lower left to upper right.
   d.   curved line.

_____ 16 population   a.   Index of the central location of a score distribution.

_____ 17. significant outcome   b.   Calculated by finding the difference in the lowest and the highest scores.

_____ 18. central tendency
                                          c.   An index of the average deviation of a set of scores from the center of a distribution.
_____ 19. standard deviation

_____ 20. range   d.   When the results of a study were very unlikely to have occurred by chance.

                                          e.   All of the members of a group of interest.

21. Professor Gaipo added all of the scores on the first exam for the honors group and divided by the number of scores in order to record the group _____.

22. The point that divides a set of numbers in half is the _____.

23. A pattern of dots plotting two characteristics is called a(n) _____.

24. If the dots on a scatterplot form a circle or random pattern, there is _____ correlation.

25. When high values of X are associated with high values of Y, there is a(n) _____ relationship.

Modules 58, 59, 60	[h] mode	Evaluate
	[i] normal distribution	1. d
[a] Statistics	[j] measure of variability	2. c
[b] descriptive	[k] range	3. e
[c] frequency distribution	[l] standard deviation	4. b
[d] histogram	[m] Inferential statistics	5. a
[e] central tendency	[n] population	
[f] mean	[o] sample	
[g] median	[p] correlation coefficient	
	[q] positive relationship	
	[r] negative relationship	

Selected Rethink Answer

59-1. The *range* would show the highest and the lowest incomes reported by people living in the United States. The *standard deviation* would identify how far these incomes were from the mean or the average income. The *mean* would include the very high and also the very low scores, which would affect the average for everyone, although just a small minority of scores might fall into this "average" range. The *mode* would show how many people were in each income group. This would be the best for identifying the number who reported in certain income groups. The *median* would only identify the middle score in the group but would not help in identifying the number of people below the poverty line.

Practice Test:

1. b   mod. 58 p. A-2
a.   Incorrect. Quantum theory states that radiant energy is transmitted in the form of discrete units.
*b.   Correct.
c.   Incorrect. Calculus deals with limits and the differentiation and integration of functions of one or more variables.
d.   Incorrect. Algebra is a generalization of arithmetic in which symbols and letters represent numbers.

2. d   mod. 58 p. A-3
a.   Incorrect. Nominal tendency is small but insignificant.
b.   Incorrect. Norm is the mode or average.
c.   Incorrect. Peripheral tendency is located or pertaining to an outside boundary.
*d.   Correct.

3. b   mod. 58 p. A-3
a.   Incorrect. Measure of central tendency.
*b.   Correct.
c.   Incorrect. Measure of central tendency.
d.   Incorrect. Measure of central tendency.

4. c   mod. 58 p. A-3
a.   Incorrect.
b.   Incorrect.
*c.   Correct.
d.   Incorrect.

5. d   mod. 58 p. A-16
a.   Incorrect.
b.   Incorrect.
c.   Incorrect.
*d.   Correct.

6. c   mod. 58 p. A-4
a.   Incorrect. The range is the interval between the highest and the lowest scores.
b.   Incorrect. The mode is the point at which the largest number of scores occurs.
*c.   Correct.
d.   Incorrect. The median is the point that divides a set of scores in half.

7. d   mod. 58 p. A-16
a.   Incorrect. The standard deviation is the average deviation of a set of scores from the center of the distribution.
b.   Incorrect. The range is the interval between the highest and the lowest scores.

c. Incorrect. The mode is the point at which the largest number of scores appears.
*d. Correct.

8. d   mod. 58 p. A-5
a. Incorrect. The mean is the average, calculated by dividing the sum of the values by the number of scores.
b. Incorrect. The range is the interval between the highest and the lowest scores.
*c. Correct.
d. Incorrect. The median is the exact midpoint of a distribution.

9. c   mod. 58 p. A-5
a. Incorrect. The mean is the average, calculated by dividing the sum of the values by the number of scores.
b. Incorrect. The range is the interval between the highest and the lowest scores.
*c. Correct.
d. Incorrect. The median is the exact midpoint of a distribution.

10. b   mod. 58 p. A-5
a. Incorrect.
*b. Correct.
c. Incorrect.
d. Incorrect.

11. a   mod. 58 p. A-4
*a. Correct. The mean is the average, calculated by dividing the sum of the values by the number of scores.
b. Incorrect. The range is the interval between the highest and the lowest scores.
c. Incorrect. The mode is the most frequently occurring score.
d. Incorrect. The median is the exact midpoint of a distribution.

12. a   mod. 58 p. A-3
*a. Correct.
b. Incorrect. A skewed distribution indicates that most people had very low or very high scores.
c. Incorrect. A normal distribution occurs when the curve is symmetrical, the curve is a mirror image.
d. Incorrect. A polygon is a closed plane bounded by three or more lines.

13. d   mod. 58 p. A-16
a. Incorrect. Correlation never proves causation.
b. Incorrect. See answer a.
c. Incorrect. See answer a.
*d. Correct.

14. c   mod. 58 p. A-16
a. Incorrect. The standard deviation is the average deviation of a set of scores from the center of the distribution.
b. Incorrect. The probability is the estimate of an event's occurrence.
*c. Correct.
d. Incorrect. A normal curve is asymmetrical; one half of the curve mirrors the other.

15. b   mod. 58 p. A-15
a. Incorrect. Demonstrates little or no correlation.
*b. Correct.
c. Incorrect. Demonstrates a perfect positive correlation.
d. Incorrect. Demonstrates imperfect correlation.

16. e   mod. 58 p. A-13
17. d   mod. 58 p. A-9
18. a   mod. 58 p. A-3
19. c   mod. 58 p. A-11
20. b   mod. 58 p. A-9

21. mean   mod. 58 p.   A-4
22. median   mod. 58 p.   A-4
23. scatterplot mod. 58 p.   A-14
24. no   mod. 58 p.   A-15
25. Positive   mod. 58 p.   A-14